W9-BHB-489

Margaret Fuller, Wandering Pilgrim

Margaret Fuller

WANDERING PILGRIM

Meg McGavran Murray

WITHDRAWN

The University of Georgia Press

ATHENS AND LONDON

Frontispiece. Three-story stairwell with looking glass and candle, 71 Cherry Street, Cambridgeport, Massachusetts. Re-created in a pencil drawing by artist-architect Ron Murray.

© 2008 by the University of Georgia Press
Athens, Georgia 30602

Designed by Louise OFarrell

Set in 10/13 Adobe Minion by Graphic Composition, Inc.

Printed and bound by Maple-Vail

The paper in this book meets the guidelines for permanence and durability of the Committee on Production Guidelines for Book Longevity of the Council on Library Resources.

Printed in the United States of America

11 10 09 08 07 C 5 4 3 2 1

Library of Congress Cataloging-in-Publication Data

Murray, Meg McGavran.
    Margaret Fuller, wandering pilgrim / Meg McGavran Murray.
        p. cm.
    Includes bibliographical references and index.
    ISBN-13: 978-0-8203-2894-2 (hardcover : alk. paper)
    ISBN-10: 0-8203-2894-4 (hardcover : alk. paper)
    1. Fuller, Margaret, 1810–1850. 2. Authors, American—
19th century—Biography. 3. Feminists—United States—
Biography. I. Title.
    PS2506.M87 2008
    818'.309—dc22 [B]   2007016762

British Library Cataloging-in-Publication Data available

In loving memory
of my father
SAMUEL BROWN MCGAVRAN
&
of my friend
CHRISTOPHER LASCH
&
To my dear daughter
ALETHEA MURRAY SARGENT

. . . I wouldn't
take all Croesus'
kingdom with love
thrown in, for her

Sappho #17, about her daughter
translated by Mary Barnard

Father, they will not take me home,
To the poor child no heart is free;
    In sleet and snow all night I roam;
Father, — was this decreed by thee?

    I will not try another door,
To seek what I have never found;
    Now, till the very last is o'er,
Upon the earth I'll wander round.

from *Summer on the Lakes, in 1843*
by Margaret Fuller

Contents

        Contents

Acknowledgments

I wish first to express my gratitude to my thesis advisors many years ago at Cornell, Cushing Strout and Meyer Abrams. I am grateful as well to my former Cornell professor, Jonathan Bishop. Professors Bishop and Strout instilled in me a love of the American Transcendentalists, especially of Margaret Fuller. To Professor Abrams I owe most of what I know about the Romantics. To him I owe as well the underlying theme of this book, as I explain in the prologue. Another scholar to whom I am profoundly indebted is Joel Myerson. This book would not now exist had he not long ago expressed an interest in my scholarship on Fuller. Myerson, who had read my 1972 Cornell dissertation on Margaret Fuller and Mary Wollstonecraft, through the years sent me offprints of his articles on Fuller and other Transcendentalists and early on encouraged me to develop and publish my own research on Fuller. I am now doing that, thanks to the outstanding scholarship on Fuller not only of Myerson but also of Robert Hudspeth, Charles Capper, Joan von Mehren, Larry Reynolds, Bell Gale Chevigny, Jeffrey Steele, Paula Blanchard, and others. I am especially grateful to Joan von Mehren, who has been supportive and generous, even sending me the proofs of her latest publication so I could integrate her recent findings into my manuscript before my book went to press. Although I could not incorporate major information from Charles Capper's volume 2 of his Fuller biography into my book since it appeared while I was correcting my proofs, I do want to thank him for his gracious and prompt responses to my questions prior to his book's publication.

I also want to thank friends and fellow faculty at Mississippi State University. I am grateful first to history professor Pete Grill, whose spring 1996 lecture to my graduate seminar on the 1848 European Revolutions helped me to understand the complexities of those revolutions. Thanks as well to Jeff Mitchell, a visiting philosophy professor whose lecture on Plato's mysticism and theory of the Forms to my graduate students in another of my seminars made clear to me the powerful influence of Plato's idealism on Fuller. Thanks to MSU faculty Robert Wolverton and Richard Patteson. Dr. Wolverton offered valuable information about Greek and Roman mythology, and Professor Patteson alerted me to the meticulously researched and original scholarship of Victorian scholar James Kincaid. Not to be forgotten are the English Department graduate students who assisted me and offered insights that enriched my understanding of Fuller. These include Suzanne

Baga, Todd Bunnell, Tracy Carr, Lee Durrett, Andy Lowery, Staci McCormick, Amanda Myers, Bonnie Novak, Jennifer Southall, and Ann Taylor. I wish to give special thanks to my former MSU graduate student Sylwia Martin, who appeared in my 1996 seminar on the 1848 European Revolutions fresh from Poland. Sylwia proved a gold mine of information on Adam Mickiewicz and put me in touch with Grazyny Grochowiakowa at the Muzeum Literatury im. Adama Mickiewicza in Warsaw. Thanks to the museum and to Sylwia's serving as interpreter, I have been able to include in my book the 1898 drawing of Adam Mickiewicz by Kazimierz Mordasewicz after an 1839 daguerreotype by an unknown artist.

A special note of thanks to William McClung, who went to Mt. Auburn cemetery in Cambridge and took especially for this book the marvelous photograph of Timothy Fuller's tomb covered with snow. Thanks also to Jim Cawthorne of Camera 1 in Columbus, Georgia, who, along with Harvard's Imaging Services in Widener Library, reproduced quality images for me.

I am grateful, as well, to Willard P. Fuller Jr., who has generously given me permission to reproduce Fuller family photographs. Many thanks, also, to Constance Fuller Threinen for allowing me to reproduce a black-and-white image of Hicks's portrait of Fuller in Rome, which she owns.

To all the librarians at the various libraries who have aided me in my research I am indebted. Foremost among these are the many helpful librarians in the Houghton Library at Harvard University. The late Carolyn Jakeman of the Houghton was helpful to me in the early 1970s when I began my research on Fuller there. Librarians in the Houghton who in recent years have been helpful include Betty Falsey, Susan Halpert, Tom Ford, Emily Walhout, Jennie Rathbun, Peter Accardo, and Leslie Morris. I wish as well to thank librarians at the Boston Public Library, the University of Georgia Library (one of two in America to have a microfiche copy of the novel *Hesitation*), Widener Library at Harvard University, Mitchell Memorial Library at Mississippi State University, as well as at the Schwob Memorial Library at Columbus State University. Thanks to President Frank Brown for allowing me to borrow books from Schwob Memorial Library and to reference librarian Martha Ragan as well as librarians Brandy Epps and Shirley Hinckley for always being helpful. I am grateful, too, to Dalma Bogan, a CSU graduate student from Italy who generously translated letters from Italian for me. Thanks, also, to the following: Conrad Wright, Anne Bentley, Kim Nusco, Nancy Heywood, and Megan Milford of the Massachusetts Historical Society, who made available to me the second likeness of Timothy Fuller; Judy Fichtenbaum and Mary Lush of the Concord Museum, who provided me with valuable historical details; Constance Manoli-Skocay of the Concord Free Public Library, who secured the photograph of Emerson at midcareer for me; Stephen Loudren and Carolyn Dallas from the Margaret Fuller Neighborhood House, who each at different times toured me through 71 Cherry Street; Angelique Bamberg of the Cambridge Historical Commission, who gathered for me pertinent historical information on the original house at 71 Cherry Street; and Marty Saunders, who offered expert advice on nineteenth-century fashion.

I am of course very grateful to Mississippi State University for awarding me with a Humanities and Arts Research Program Grant. Funding from the HARP grant made possible my last visit to the Houghton Library at Harvard University and weeks of research there.

To my readers, I wish to express my gratitude. I thank first and foremost MSU French professor and feminist Kittye Robbins-Herring, who generously gave of her time in reading and editing both the scholarly papers that became the basis for this book and the book's early versions. Not only did she give invaluable editorial advice, she also offered numerous important insights, including the essential insight that appears in part 6 of this book that changed the way I thereafter viewed Margaret Fuller. I am likewise grateful to Tom D'Evelyn, who encouraged me back in 1984 when he was working as an editor at Harvard University Press to continue with my Fuller project and who for years thereafter graciously read and edited various versions. And, too, I am grateful to the late Joel Porte, who read drafts of parts 1 through 4 of this book and provided invaluable insights. Three anonymous readers generously offered several pages of specific suggestions for changes that have enabled me to transform a sprawling manuscript into a publishable book. To the historians among my readers I am indebted, for as historians they checked my English-professor tendency to wish to create embellished scenes from factual material. I am similarly grateful to my son-in-law, Daniel Sargent. Through our many long conversations as well as his review and editing of important parts of the last sections of this book, Daniel, who has a doctorate in history from Harvard and is now on a postdoctoral fellowship at Yale, likewise kept me on track as a historian committed to reporting facts. I am also deeply indebted to my cherished late friend Christopher Lasch. Kit read and commented on an early draft of this book. He told me that he wanted my book about Fuller to be one that would let him and other readers really *see* her. I promised Kit before he died that I would produce a book that would bring Fuller to life.

Thanks, too, to editors and staff at the University of Georgia Press who have been instrumental in getting this book into print. To Jane Kobres I am especially grateful for having encouraged me to send my manuscript to Georgia. I am similarly grateful to the press's director, Nicole Mitchell, who, prior to her arrival at Georgia, had written to express her continuing interest in my work on Fuller. For the editorial help of Georgia's assistant managing editor and my project editor Jon Davies and copyeditor Deborah Oliver I am, of course, most appreciative. If this book contains factual errors, it will not be the fault of Deborah, whose eagle eye hopefully caught most of them.

And, finally, there are those individuals without whose moral support I would never have been able to sustain the years of writing this biography. I am forever grateful to two people who are very special to me, former President and First Lady Jimmy and Rosalynn Carter, who have continued through the years to encourage me not only to keep working on my book about Fuller, but also, so to speak, to keep the faith.

To my dear father, long dead, I am forever indebted. Overburdened with caring for a son born barely a year before me, my mother gave me as a baby to my father to raise. No parent could have been more nurturing. And he was caring of me despite his own psychological depression brought on by the fact that, as a 1928 Harvard graduate who lost his job on Wall Street in 1930, he never thereafter found satisfying work. In a poem he penciled in the front of a book (Isaac Watts's *Improvement of the Mind*) that he left for me at his death in 1961, he asked that I give my life not to the pursuit of material wealth but to "the saving of the soul." I believe I have done that in having devoted so much of my life to trying to understand the complex person that was Margaret Fuller and in now sharing her story of courage and struggle with all those readers who are inspired and hence enriched in reading it.

Finally, I want to thank my artist-architect husband, Ron, who has patiently endured the many years I have commuted between Mississippi and Georgia with boxes of books in the trunk of my car, always tending to the welfare of both my daughter and my book. An example of his artwork appears as frontispiece to this book. I am, of course, most grateful to our daughter, Allie, who as a high school student translated Latin passages for me and whose vital, brilliant, caring self is for me and my husband a source of immeasurable pride and joy. That young women like Allie can now acquire undergraduate degrees at Harvard and then pursue doctorates at Yale University—or anywhere else—is a fact that should fill the spirit of Margaret Fuller with a certainty that her ardent protest in behalf of women's broader rights was not in vain.

✑ ✑ ✑

Manuscript material from the Fuller Family Papers is reprinted by permission of the Houghton Library, Harvard University, Cambridge, Massachusetts.

Acknowledgments

A Note to Readers

I refer to Margaret Fuller as Fuller throughout the text except when I mention other Fuller family members. Then, for the sake of clarity, I refer to Fuller as Margaret, as I also do when she is interacting in an intimate way with female friends like Cary Sturgis, who will marry and become a Tappen, and Anna Barker, who will marry and become a Ward. Moreover, to prevent readers from confusing Margaret with her mother, who is named Margarett, I refer to the latter by her maiden name, Margarett Crane.

Chronology

1809, May 28	Margarett Crane marries Timothy Fuller.
1810, May 23	Sarah Margarett Fuller is born in Cambridgeport, Mass.
1813, Oct. 5	Fourteen-month-old Julia Adelaide Fuller dies.
1813–16	Timothy serves in Massachusetts Senate.
1815	Eugene Fuller is born.
1817	Margaret meets Ellen Kilshaw, English lady whom she calls "first friend" in her "autobiographical romance." William Henry Fuller is born.
1817, Dec.–May	Timothy serves first of four terms as a U.S. Congressman.
1819	Margaret enters Cambridgeport Private Grammar School.
1820, Aug. 7	Ellen Kilshaw Fuller is born.
1821, April 2	Margaret attends Dr. Park's school, Boston.
1822, Aug. 10	Arthur Buckminster Fuller is born.
1824–25	Margaret attends Miss Prescott's Young Ladies Seminary in Groton.
1824, May 15	Richard Frederick Fuller is born, Margarett Crane's seventh child.
1825	Timothy returns home and is elected to the Massachusetts house.
1826	James Lloyd Fuller is born; he is mentally slow.
1826	Family moves to the Dana mansion near Harvard College.
1828, May 23	Edward Breck Fuller is born; dies sixteen months later.
1831, Nov.	Margaret undergoes mystical experience, Thanksgiving Day.
1832	Margaret meets teenager Cary Sturgis, whose family has undergone tragedy.
1833, April	Family moves to Groton, where John Todd is preaching.
1835, fall	Margaret plans to travel to Europe but falls ill and nearly dies. Timothy falls violently ill of Asiatic cholera; dies October 1.

1836, July–Aug.	Fuller visits the Concord home of Emerson, on his invitation; also meets Bronson Alcott there.
1836, fall	Fuller teaches at Alcott's Temple School, Boston.
1837	Joins Transcendental Club and begins eighteen months of teaching at Hiram Fuller's Greene Street School, Providence.
1838, summer	Becomes infatuated with Sam Ward. Emerson delivers his "Divinity School Address."
1839, Jan.	Back in Groton Fuller reads Plato, Plutarch, Sand, Ariosto, Ovid, etc., writing fifty letters her first week back (including mystical ones to Emerson). Translates Eckermann's *Conversations with Goethe*.
1839, April	The Groton farm now sold, Fuller moves with her mother, Ellen, Richard, and Lloyd to a home in Jamaica Plain. Continues letter writing to Emerson and Cary Sturgis.
1839, May	Publishes translation of Eckermann's *Conversations with Goethe*.
1839, summer	Undergoes crisis in her relationships with Sam Ward, Cary Sturgis, Ralph Waldo Emerson, and Anna Barker. In mid-June Fuller and Sturgis have a falling-out. In late summer she also has a crisis in her relationship with Sam Ward.
1839, Nov.	Opens her Conversation classes for women in Boston.
1840	Begins two-year editorship of the *Dial.* In the autumn undergoes a religious experience connected to marriage of Sam Ward and Anna Barker, October 3. Conversation classes continue. First issue of the *Dial* appears, July.
1841	In April publishes "Leila" in the *Dial,* in July, essay on Goethe.
1842, Jan.	In response to Emerson's essay "Friendship" publishes "Bettine Brentano and Her Friend Günderode," which becomes part of preface of *Correspondence of Fraulein Günderode with Bettine von Arnim.*
1842	Little Waldo dies of scarletina, January 27. Fuller visits the Emersons in Concord, autumn. That October Fuller moves with her mother from Jamaica Plain to rental house on Ellery Street in Cambridge.
1843	Publishes "The Great Lawsuit" in the *Dial,* July. Travels with Sarah Clarke and her younger brother William through Great Lakes region, May–September.

1844, April–June	Completes and publishes *Summer on the Lakes, in 1843*. Holds final Conversation class. Suffers depression when William Clarke rejects her offer of affection.
1844, summer	Fuller visits the Emersons and Hawthornes in Concord, July 9–August 3.
1844, Sept.–Nov.	Spends autumn with Cary Sturgis at Fishkill Landing, N.Y. Visits female convicts in Sing Sing and completes *Woman in the Nineteenth Century*.
1844, Dec.–Feb. 1845	Fuller moves to New York City, boarding with Horace and Mary Greeley, and works as literary editor and social critic for the *New-York Daily Tribune*. Falls in love with James Nathan. *Woman in the Nineteenth Century* published, February.
1845, Feb.–April	Fuller meets Nathan secretly; learns he has mistress.
1845, summer	Nathan and his mistress leave for Europe, June. Fuller's last visit to Concord, August.
1846	Fuller publishes *Papers on Literature and Art* and continues writing to Nathan.
1846, Aug. 1	Accepts jobs as tutor for son of Marcus and Rebecca Spring and as foreign correspondent for the *Tribune*; leaves for Europe.
1846	Tours England and Scotland. In London meets the Carlyles and Mazzini. In Paris that winter meets Adam Mickiewicz and George Sand.
1847, April	Fuller meets Ossoli in Rome. She parts with the Springs in late July. Returns to Rome alone and takes Ossoli as her lover; in December realizes she is pregnant.
1848, spring	Revolutions erupt all over Europe; Marx in February publishes *The Communist Manifesto*. Fuller in a dispatch asserts her faith in "the LABORING CLASSES," then retires early June to Aquila in the mountains fifty miles northeast of Rome.
1848, summer	Works on a narrative of current developments in Europe. In July moves to Rieti, forty-two miles from Rome.
1848, Sept. 5	Angelo Eugene Philip Ossoli is born, Rieti.
1848, early winter	Fuller returns to Rome, November; witnesses the attack on the Quirinal Palace; continues sending dispatches with news of the revolution in Italy. Christmas, Fuller travels to Rieti to find Nino recovering from illness.
1849, late winter	Fuller begins Roman Diary January 1. The Roman Republic proclaimed February 8.

1849, March–May	Fuller visits Nino in Rieti, March 27. Rome encircled by Catholic powers, April.
1849, April 30	Fuller named regolatrice in charge of the Hospital of the Fate Bene Fratelli on Tiber Island. The French begin their attack, which lasts for three days before they retreat.
1849, May	Fuller's May 27 dispatch celebrates the "struggle" now "commenced between the principle of Democracy and the old powers, no longer legitimate."
1849, June	The French launch a surprise attack on Rome, June 3. All-out assault begins on Rome, June 20; Fuller continues to serve at the hospitals. The French begin their final assault, June 22.
1849, July	French occupation forces enter Rome, July 3. Ossoli and Fuller flee Rome; arrive Rieti midmonth to find Nino near death.
1849, Sept.–Dec.	The three Ossolis seek sanctuary in Florence. Short of funds, Fuller begins to plan to travel to U.S.
1850, Jan. 6	Fuller writes last *Tribune* dispatch, published February 13.
1850, spring	Joseph Mozier helps arrange travel home on the *Elizabeth* for Fuller and her family. Fuller writes Costanza Arconati Visconti, saying she is "absurdly fearful about this voyage" and vowing that "in case of mishap" she will "perish" with her "husband and child," April 6. The Ossolis sail from Europe, May 17.
1850, June	With the *Elizabeth* under quarantine at Gibraltar, Captain Seth Hasty dies, June 2. The ship sets sail under the command of Acting Captain Henry Bangs, June 8. Nino contracts smallpox, June 10.
1850, July 19	The *Elizabeth* broadsides a sandbar off Fire Island (N.Y.) at 4 a.m.; breaks up over the next several hours. Fuller and her family are among the eight fatalities.
1852	Pressured by Horace Greeley to publish a biography of Fuller, Ralph Waldo Emerson, William Henry Channing, and James Freeman Clarke gather letters and recollections into two-volume *The Memoirs of Margaret Fuller Ossoli*.

Prologue

I have been a stranger here in my own land.
—Antigone, in Sophocles, *Antigone*

"Pain is very keen with me," Margaret Fuller wrote James Nathan, the German-born Jewish businessman she had fallen in love with while in New York. So it was. Though Fuller triumphed in public as author of *Woman in the Nineteenth Century* (1845), conversationalist, pioneering journalist, and political revolutionary, her private life was full of pain. Erotically attracted to women as well as men, including Nathan and her married mentor, Ralph Waldo Emerson, Fuller was repeatedly rejected in love. While working as a journalist in Rome she fell in love with a gentle young Italian, Giovanni Angelo Ossoli, from an old and noble family. Yet this relationship, too, became for her a source of pain when she discovered she was pregnant out of wedlock. Keeping this from her friend Cary Sturgis, Fuller nonetheless came close to revealing it when she wrote home to Cary: "I am a poor magnet with power to be wounded by the bodies I attract." In this case, however, the "body" she attracted, Ossoli, stayed. And when their baby was born on 5 September 1848 in Rieti, Italy, Ossoli was there. Though Fuller had long harbored doubts about the institution of marriage, one biographer has offered evidence that, before the baby's 6 November baptism, Fuller—America's first full-fledged intellectual woman—may nevertheless have married the kind but uneducated Ossoli. As a radical Romantic who defied nineteenth-century social conventions, a woman whose unorthodox thinking and actions led her to celebrity *and* "a premature grave," Fuller serves as inspiration and warning.[1]

Two months after her baby's birth, Fuller, who was sending reports home to the *New-York Tribune* about the republican fight to free Italy from the control of the pope, local kings and foreign invaders, wrote her mother about the stabbing death of Pope Pius IX's minister. In her letter she quotes words from a song sung by the pope's troops of the line as they marched that night alongside "the people": "Happy the hand which rids the world of a tyrant!" In this letter Fuller, whose recent motherhood has awakened in her a new appreciation of her own mother, tells her mother not to worry because "some higher power leads me through strange, dark, thorny paths" that are "broken at times by glades opening" into "prospects of sunny beauty." A less confident daughter, however, also confesses how "in the silence of the night" she has often recited to her mother the "most strange and romantic chapters in the story of my sad life." Ten years earlier in a letter to Sturgis, Fuller had similarly referred to her life as strange: "Yes, my life is 'strange' thine is strange.—We are, we shall be in this life mutilated beings."[2]

This biography recounts Fuller's journey along the "strange, dark, thorny path" that led sometimes to scenes "of sunny beauty," yet, finally, to a scene of tragedy. It examines the childhood circumstances that "mutilated" Fuller's soul and caused her thereafter to see herself as a "wandering pilgrim" destined, it seemed, to journey in search of answers to questions that, as a child, she had stopped herself on the stairs to ask: "How is it that I seem to be this Margaret Fuller. What does it mean? What shall I do about it?"—"it" here perhaps in part referring to her difficult childhood situation that had left her feeling psychologically conflicted.[3]

Fuller identified with the German Romantic writer Goethe, who similarly suffered from mental conflict. She saw his writings as a record of his life, a fact she stressed in her 1841 *Dial* essay on Goethe, which Perry Miller later called a "much too emotional exposition of Goethe's thought." Fuller also identified with Goethe's struggle to reconcile passion with intellect: "With the intellect I always . . . shall overcome, but that is not the half of the work. The life, . . . Oh my God! shall the life *never* be sweet!"[4]

Life for Fuller was not sweet. As a record of *her* life, her writings present us with a text through which we can get to know not just the overpowering public presence that was Margaret Fuller but also the sometimes strange but always passionate person behind the mask. *Margaret Fuller, Wandering Pilgrim* thus attempts, what Thomas Mitchell tells us Nathaniel Hawthorne did long ago, to "solve the riddle" that was Fuller. For it was far more than her formidable intellect (which Charles Capper highlights in his biography of Fuller, and Christina Zwarg argues was equal to Emerson's) that attracted people to Fuller. It was her passion, her very strangeness that intrigued friends like Emerson and Hawthorne.[5]

Henry James, who was seven when he heard of Fuller's death, later said in reference to the "underplot" of her "marriage" in Italy to Ossoli, that he could still feel Fuller's "haunting" presence. He imagines Fuller in Rome still walking "the old passages." James implies that Fuller's spirit still wanders not only because of the imaginative daring that enabled her to break the mold cast for "woman" in her day, but also because of the "lamentable" way she met her death aboard the sinking *Elizabeth* in sight of the New York coast in July 1850. Her death was made more poignant by the fact that her body was never found: the bodies of Fuller, her husband, and their friend Horace Sumner did not wash ashore with the others who had drowned. Fuller herself would have interpreted this lack of a proper burial as ominous. As an admirer of Greek tragedy—notably Sophocles' *Antigone*—she knew that the failure to bury a body, a fate the Greeks reserved for criminals, meant that the deceased's soul could not enter the next world but instead would continue to wander.[6]

Fuller's still wandering spirit continues to intrigue and "haunt" scholars and writers, one of whom, Barbara Novak, even titled her novel involving Fuller *The Margaret-Ghost.* Fuller's figure continues to disturb us in part because of the unsettling notions about human sexuality and gender she expressed not only in her public writings and in her unorthodox lifestyle, but also in her private letters and journals. Having painstakingly edited Fuller's letters, Robert N. Hudspeth warns readers of the "dangers of introspection." Yet Fuller's self-scrutiny gave her the insights into her complex intellectual and sexual makeup that she shared with the world in *Woman in the Nineteenth Century.* Certain self-revelations, however, she made only obliquely in pain-filled letters to friends as well as in autobiographical accounts that today seem too romanticized to contain any trace of truth. A close reading reveals that Fuller left in these documents hints, in her words, of "secret trials" she endured in her youth that she seems deliberately to have concealed from her friends as well as from the public. Yet if we read Fuller's words with care (especially those in her journals and personal letters), we can find clues that suggest the deeper causes of her lifelong psychic conflict. In one letter she says that she must follow her own law, "even if, like Oedipus, I should return a criminal, blind and outcast, to ask aid from the gods."[7]

Twice in her writings Fuller compared herself to the mythical Oedipus, who realized too late that he could not escape his fate, which was to murder his father and commit incest with his mother. Perhaps it is because it is human to resist the desire to delve into the darkness in one's heart that most critics have been unwilling to examine too closely one cause of the conflict that fueled Fuller's creative genius. It is a cause that seems to have been intuited by Hawthorne, who, in one of the works of fiction that grew out of his 1843–44 friendship with Fuller, links her to Beatrice Cenci, whose violent and cruel father developed an incestuous passion for her. Imagining Fuller in Rome, James, too, mentions Beatrice Cenci, and he does so on the same page he fondly talks of "Margaret." Hence when James says that Fuller's ghost continues to walk "the old passages," he perhaps had in mind not just Rome and the Cenci Palace, but also the corridors of the Fullers' Cherry Street house in Cambridgeport, Massachusetts, where, driven by dreams of detached eyes coming at her in the dark, Fuller as a child used to sleepwalk. Yet when she tried as a child to talk about "these things," she later wrote, "little notice was taken." Little notice is still "taken" of "these things" by biographers. Thus Fuller's troubled spirit still seems to wander, trying Cassandra-like to tell her story to whoever has ears to hear her.[8]

Fuller had a haunting recollection of the death of a younger sister when Fuller was three. The trauma was compounded for her when, after the baby died, her depressed young mother, according to her husband, "rather secluded" herself for several months, thus unintentionally depriving her living daughter of love. From her dim memory of the event Fuller as a child took a romanticized sense of "the beauty of death"—just one of many illusions in life she would use to protect herself from pain. As an adult, Fuller was haunted by the "image" of her domineering father, whose sudden death when she was twenty-five prevented her from making peace with this severe man who had bequeathed to her a "legacy," in the apt words of one historian, full of "lights and shadows." Margaret's father's relentless demands on her as her instructor in late-night studies overwhelmed her. They stirred in her a yearning (to borrow from Ernest Becker) "to drown" her "feelings of helplessness and inadequacy" in dreams of "some self-transcending source of sure power."[9]

His harsh tutoring also turned her into one of the best-educated American women of her era. Burdened after her father's death with guilt, rage, and feelings of inadequacy in relation to this paradoxical man she both loved and hated, Fuller imaginatively kept him alive in the figure of Waldo Emerson, through whose "pure" love she sought a kind of secular redemption. In her passionate friendships with Cary Sturgis and Anna Barker, Fuller likewise sought to acquire love. Through them she yearned to recover the love she felt she had lost when her sister died and her depressed young mother withdrew her love from her.[10]

This yearning in Fuller to recover love suggests that she harbored conflicted and unresolved feelings about her parents because of her mother's emotional withdrawal and her father's abrupt death. By failing to see her parents realistically, Fuller doomed herself to perceive the present through a lens distorted by feelings from the past. Through friends like Emerson she imagined she could acquire the love she felt she had been deprived of as a child.[11] Thus, imagining led to hope, and hope to belief and even creativity—though for Fuller it also led to obsession, to the fruitless pursuit of an illusion.

Much of Fuller's life was given to pursuing illusion, a fact Bell Gale Chevigny acknowledged when she selected as the epigraph to her fine anthology of Fuller's writings a plea Fuller penned in her 1844 diary: "In the chamber of death I prayed. . . . Give me truth[.] Cheat me on by no illusion." But Fuller, a Romantic, was time and again cheated by illusion. Of all the literature she read when she was young Fuller had most enjoyed the writings of the European and English Romantics, with whom she felt an affinity. Images and concepts from their poetry and prose became deeply imbedded in her mind and profoundly affected her life and writings.

Meyer Abrams once said that Fuller's "actual life enacted the paradigm" of the Romantic pilgrim's thinking. Abrams was referring to the circuitous journey of the Romantic pilgrim "through difficulties, sufferings, and recurrent disasters in quest of a goal" that ironically turns out to be "the place" the pilgrim "had left behind when it first set out," an "ancestral home" that Romantics depict "as a scene of recognition and reconciliation." This pattern of journeying out, of rebelling against the political establishment or sexual and social mores, then returning home to a forgiving parent, was one Fuller had internalized as a child while reading books like Sotheby's translation of the German Christoph Martin Wieland's *Oberon,* as well as while listening to her father read Bible stories to his family. The Christian knight's circuitous pilgrimage in *Oberon,* through hardship into manhood and his eventual return home, is based on the story of the prodigal son, which can be interpreted, says Abrams, "as the type of the journey of all mankind out of and back toward its original home." The internalized plot and pattern of such well-known Bible stories underlay and gave life to Fuller's lifelong quest for self-insight and love and thus helped give shape and meaning to her own personal pilgrimage—though in Fuller's story, as in so many Romantic variants of the traditional circuitous quest, the "yearning for fulfillment" is expressed as a desire for reunion with a female figure—in her case, the caring mother the wandering pilgrim had left behind.[12]

As a Romantic and heir of Puritans, Fuller early in life set out on such a pilgrimage. In this quest she saw herself at times as a queen destined for great love, at other times as Oedipus set on knowing "Truth at all cost." The price she paid for her pursuit of love and truth may well have been her life, which ended aboard the *Elizabeth* with an Antigone-like act of heroic sacrifice. Indeed, seeing herself as a mythical figure, a queenlike prodigal on a preordained journey, Fuller often asserted her belief in the Fates. Before setting sail, she wrote a friend that she had "a vague expectation of some crisis." She advised another to "look out for news of shipwreck" and said that she hoped Fate would not force her to be brave for the sake of her baby; yet, should she lose her "husband" and son at sea, she would not try to save herself but drown with them. Though she sailed from Leghorn knowing her mother in America waited to embrace her, she feared that, unlike the biblical prodigal, she would never make it home.[13]

That Fuller's story seems like that of a Greek figure whose tragedy has been preordained by Fate would not surprise this woman who, at age twenty-nine, had depicted herself as Oedipus, as a manly woman whose drive for self-knowledge had led her to a level of awareness about herself as a sexual and intellectual human being that made her behave in ways that seemed, in her own words, not just "strange" but "criminal" to most Americans. Although after her death her respectable Boston friends tried—as the ever-insightful Joel Myerson has said—to create a Margaret "more religiously orthodox and socially acceptable than they perceived the real Fuller to be," Fuller had seen herself as the outcast Oedipus destined, after wandering, to return home. Considered a pariah by many straight-laced New Englanders who condemned her not only as a sinner for her sexual relationship with Ossoli but also as a "Red" for her 1849 work in behalf of the Roman revolutionaries, Fuller chose to return to America with her unconventional family after the revolution's failure. She set out to do so knowing that, in the eyes of even her beloved mentor Emerson, her behavior made her seem "a stranger" in her "own land," a wayward pilgrim unworthy of love.[14]

In light of the defeat of the Roman republicans by the combined patriarchal powers of pope, king, and invading emperor in 1849, as well as of Puritan America's inhospitality to her, one could argue that Fuller did not fulfill the aim of her pilgrimage, which was to save her "soul" from the control of the tyrannical father. Yet to Americans who saw her soul as damned because she refused to repent her wayward behavior, a proud Fuller would have said, as she did of Antigone after seeing *The Antigone* performed in April 1845: "the question whether she could *repent* seem[s] strangest madness to her unfaltering soul." Considering "the blind madness of the tyrant," wrote Fuller, to have acted in a way other than she did "was impossible to her."[15]

Margaret Fuller, Wandering Pilgrim is hence a "story," *not* about the peace to be found in returning home after wandering but instead about the obstacles encountered by the bright, sensitive youth who has felt from the first, as did Antigone, like a "stranger" in her "own land." It is a tale told by a wounded soul whose very search for the meanings by which she lives, or might live, constitutes the meaning of her life and work.[16]

It is our quest as investigators to understand the forces that led Margaret Fuller to make this pilgrimage.

PART ONE

"No Natural Childhood"

She herself said she "had no natural childhood." Born into a family tradition of religious fervor, intellectual endeavor, physical restlessness, and Roman vigor, Margaret Fuller was the oldest child of Timothy Fuller, who was the great-great-grandson of "Lieutenant" Thomas Fuller, who in 1638 at age twenty had crossed the ocean from England to America. Touched by the soul-ravishing sermons of the Reverend Thomas Shepard and rumored to have been bewitched by the "black eyes of a certain Miss Richardson," Thomas Fuller settled in Cambridge. Though he finally married another woman and moved his family first to New Salem (later Middleton), then to Woburn, he remained through life a fervid Puritan, and at his death he left a poetic record of his religious experience. In it he told how Shepard's preaching had let him see not only his "woful" sinful state but also the "New Jerusalem." Believing in God's unpredictable ways, Fuller confessed that he had sometimes been "on mountains high, / Sometimes in valleys low." Still, though Satan "knew he had a friend ... within," Fuller had faith that "God [would] save [his] soul." Sounding very un-Calvinist he thus advised his "children dear" that, if through life "[you] fear the Lord," at death "your souls ... he'll save."[1]

The great-grandson of this self-assured man was the ill-tempered, coarse-mannered Rev. Timothy Fuller (1739–1805), one in a line of younger sons whose particular strength was intellectual, whose personality was brusque. As a student at Harvard he had been severely reprimanded for having thrown bricks and sticks into a classroom during a Hebrew recitation. When he returned to Harvard for a second degree, Timothy Sr. achieved it with a *Quaestio* defending the proposition that "not all dissimulation is untruthful." This thesis apparently appealed to his son Timothy, Margaret's father, who was to confess in the diary he kept at Harvard that he had avoided a Greek lesson by pretending he had been given the wrong assignment.[2]

As a Congregational minister in the frontier town of Princeton, Massachusetts, the elder Timothy did not endorse the American Revolution and was therefore dismissed from his pastorate in the spring of 1776. Timothy Sr. then took his family to the antiwar village of Chilmark on Martha's Vineyard, where he preached in the Congregational church. Stalwart and independent minded, he also brought a suit against the town of Princeton to recover his salary. Having lost his suit, Fuller proudly paid both court costs and legal fees, which "malignant" townspeople had predicted would crush him. On his return to Princeton, his former parishioners, who seemed to like him "better as a politician" than as a preacher, elected him to represent Princeton at the state convention called to ratify the U.S. Constitution. True to his contrary nature, however, Fuller refused to vote in favor of the document, arguing in part that he could not ratify a text that recognized slavery. At his home, located on seven hundred acres embracing Mount Wachusett, Timothy Sr. farmed; he also homeschooled all of his children—"the great object of his ambition" being, according to one of his grandsons, to prepare his five *sons* for Harvard.[3]

Margaret's father, Timothy (Timo), was the fourth of the fractious Rev. Fuller's ten surviving children, all of whom, like their father, were intellectually gifted, steel willed, and opinionated. The five sons became lawyers who were hardworking, ambitious, and politically active. They were also, according to Fuller family friend and biographer Thomas Wentworth Higginson, energetic and combative to the point of being overbearing and crass. Henry, the third son, was said during jury trials to have shot "shafts of raillery and sarcasm" that entertained jurors while riling and alienating his opponents. Self-assertive, public spirited, and proud, Henry's puritanically rigid eldest brother Timothy embodied eighteenth-century Enlightenment values. Determinedly self-reliant, he insisted that both he and his children exhibit moral righteousness and serve the community.[4]

Little did these abrasive but brilliant brothers imagine that one of them, Timothy, would father a daughter in whom many of their best as well as some of their less admirable traits—such as Henry's tendency toward sarcasm—would be concentrated, a daughter whose intellect and accomplishments would in time tower over their own.

1 ∽ Her Father's House

A strict Unitarian, Margaret's father routinely took his young family to church on Sunday and read aloud with them from the Bible in the parlor. A respected member of the political establishment, in his youth he had been rebellious. As stubborn and independent minded as his father and determined to obtain a level of material comfort denied him when young as the son of a poor country minister and farmer, the junior Timothy worked hard so that he could graduate from Harvard with highest honors. An inherited perversity of temperament, however, prevented this: while at Harvard, this fiercely competitive scholar and Phi Beta Kappa mem-

"NO NATURAL CHILDHOOD"

ber organized a student protest against new college regulations. For this the faculty denied him the right to graduate with first honors, giving him second-place honors instead, a demotion that "chagrined" him. Similarly, as a young adult set on social and business success in nineteenth-century Boston, Timothy stubbornly remained a Republican—"or, as men," according to Higginson, "were beginning to say, a Democrat"—amid Federalists and an ardent abolitionist (like his father) at a time when Massachusetts merchants favored trade with the South.[1]

The high-toned Timothy was an eccentric whose life was riddled with contradictions. Though stern and rigid, he passionately loved music and forced his tone-deaf daughter to learn to sing and play the piano. In letters he wrote his wife from Washington, he would say on one page how he "could not suppress" his "aversion to the things of the world" while elaborating on another on the loveliness of Mrs. Madison's or Mrs. Adams's dress. An advocate of human rights, he preached women's rights and wrote his wife in January 1820 that he was "so well pleased" with Mary Wollstonecraft's *Vindication of the Rights of Woman* that he intended to buy her a copy, a curious offer given he had written her just days earlier that Wollstonecraft's "conduct with [Gilbert] Imlay, of America, whom she loved so ardently & would not marry, but had a child by him . . . must completely discountenance her 'Rights of Woman,' which no woman dares to read, but she should be charged with libertinism." Likewise, though Timothy supported female education and independence of mind, he had a need to dominate the women he taught, which included not only the students at the academy where he was employed briefly after college but also his wife and daughter. Thus, though advocating greater freedom for women, he demanded that Margaret comply with his commands. Moreover, although he allowed no pets or any display by his children of frivolous behavior or emotion at home, he himself made a pet of a mouse that inhabited his Spartan, uncarpeted Court Street law office in downtown Boston.[2]

A sickly child and an adult of delicate health and short stature, Timothy apparently listened to the medical experts of his day who said that for a man to maintain his health (and hence his manliness), he must eat a lean diet and follow a strict fitness routine. For Timothy throughout his life and marriage that included bathing each morning in icy water, running barefoot through the snow, and sleeping with his window raised a few inches, even through frigid Massachusetts winters. Such routines were touted in Timothy's time as ways to douse the fire of "unnatural" sexual passion, which, for Puritan-minded New Englanders, meant any sign of sexual arousal apart from reproductive sex between a man and virginal woman who had been officially married in a church. Early-nineteenth-century hygienists encouraged men who found themselves aroused from sleep by a disturbing pulsation—or who found it difficult to resist what was thought to be the effeminizing effects of masturbation—to get plenty of exercise and to take icy baths. These morality experts preached that through such measures men could defeat the devil.[3]

And if ever the devil had a bit of a hold on any man, it was on the seemingly priggish Timothy Fuller. For despite his arduous efforts to curb his appetite ("especially," he wrote his wife from Washington, for "the *fair bosom*"), Timothy was always a would-be ladies' man with an appreciative eye for a pretty face, not only in his younger single years as a student and teacher but also later as a married U.S. congressman. Moreover, he unashamedly pursued pretty women while self-righteously preaching to them. His Harvard-era diary covers the brief period he taught at Leicester Academy (one of the few that accepted women) and reveals his "ample appetite" for the other sex.[4] In his Harvard diary, he confesses how, on a March 1800 visit to Boston, he had a "peep [from the street] at Margt Rogers; as she sat by Mr. Parkman's parlor fire." He tells of being "enraptured" by the musical talents of the young ladies he met at Hannah Woods's Princeton schoolhouse; by a girl who had given him a nosegay with a chrysanthemum in it and "promised to preserve its seed" for him; and by the "looks" he exchanged with a pretty lady on 13 July 1800, five days after he gave his summer exhibition oration titled "National Virtue." Later Timothy delights in having been selected by "several ladies" to walk and later talk with them at Judge Walker's house; he confesses how, amid a "world of sighs & k——s," he regretfully took leave of them.[5]

Entries in Timothy's diary as English preceptor at the Leicester Academy recount the "*delicious* hour[s]" he spent with his female students, as well as with other young women. Unable to decide at first which of the sweet flowers he, like a bee, ought to settle on in "my whole pasteur [sic]" (presumably his classroom), Timothy flits from expressing love for the "fairest," Lucretia Plimpton, to days later confessing how Isabelle Farish has become so "engaging" to him that he is "ashamed so soon to have forgotten Miss Plimpton." He rationalizes his simultaneously intense feelings for the two women in a 22 August 1801 entry, "But where is the crime to love them both? Or rather would it not be a crime *not* to love both?" But dancing at a ball with Miss Marcy Newell in September, he is "infect[ed]" (he says) with the "illness . . . L x x e!" And it is thus with "my beloved Marcy" that he soon passes an evening making "repeated contact of souls *through our lips!*" Yet even after having traveled on horseback to Marcy's Sturbridge home for a November evening of "palpitating pleasure," Timothy is eyeing other women whose honey (so to speak) he desires. One of whom, Miss Daniels, he says is "handsome, but . . . not immaculate in virtue." Because of Miss Daniels's rumored lack of virtue, he feels no guilt in seizing "a favorable opportunity to kiss" her while showing her the moon through a telescope at Christmas. In February 1802 Timothy again betrays Marcy, who has faithfully "indulge[d]" his "caresses," by spending an evening with "a servant girl, not yet fifteen," whose lips he "made free with" and "enjoyed her blushes." Timothy in his diary justifies his unmanageable sexual longings, noting he has "long since perceived" himself "capable *of* [a] *plurality of* loves." When the young women in his English class that spring protested the flirtatious behavior of

"NO NATURAL CHILDHOOD"

their self-righteous teacher, Timothy lectured on feminine morality, telling them how they ought to imitate the behavior of those "judicious, well informed, delicate, & amiable" ladies, "who attracted esteem and affection."[6]

Perhaps Timothy's short height fed his need to feel superior to women. One thing is for certain: his strong libido existed in tandem with a "hasty temper" from which he felt he would "never" be "free." Aware of his character flaws, the hot-tempered, short in stature yet charming Timothy took to the altar not a well-heeled lady but a nineteen-year-old Canton schoolteacher—a handsome, willowy, blue-eyed blonde who, as one biographer put it, was "worse than penniless" since "she was well endowed with poor relations."[7]

Margarett ("Peggy") Crane was the second of four children born to Peter Crane and Elizabeth Jones Weiser. Crane was a gunsmith and friend of Paul Revere; his pious wife spent much of her time reading the Bible and singing hymns. Comparatively poor and uneducated, Margarett Crane was inferior to Timothy in economic and social status. His urgent desire to unite with her conjugally is evident in a letter he wrote her two weeks before their 1809 wedding. In it he says that "potent, persuasive Love allures, and all my wishes impel me" to flee to her and yield to bliss even as "duty" demands that he not let "love" make him "unworthy of my Margarett." "Heaven forbid!" exclaims the self-censoring Timothy. "Forgive this conflict of duty & passion, & if the former prevail[, attribute it] to the reverence I feel for your virtue & your judgment."[8]

They made an oddly attractive couple—the tall, lean, picturesquely pretty, nineteen-year-old schoolteacher from Canton and the slight though suave, auburn-haired, up-and-coming thirty-one-year-old Boston lawyer. Margarett Crane's friends and family saw it as a fortunate match. Her parents were especially grateful for Timothy's solicitude through the years, even if they occasionally found Peggy's husband's habitual grimace a bit off-putting. For Timothy did not have an appealing personality. Although during the eight years (1817–25) he served as the U.S. Representative for Middlesex County, his letters from Washington to his wife abound with affected expressions of solicitous love for his wife and family, they are also larded with meticulous descriptions of the physical assets and social skills of the many pretty "ladies" he has met at Washington parties. Such descriptions read less as a desire to fulfill his wife's craving for the glittering details of Washington life than as a way to flaunt even to her his gleeful exploits. Given Timothy's acerbic personality—which several of his visiting siblings shared—the Fullers were not particularly popular in the Cambridgeport, Massachusetts, neighborhood (now Somerville) where they lived for almost seventeen years. Rather, they were viewed as gifted people who were tactless, opinionated, and pushy.[9]

Not that the Fullers' neighbors were themselves models of Victorian propriety and virtue. Cambridgeport, located on the Charles River a mile to the southeast of Cambridge, had been developed at the turn of the century by the town of Cambridge to serve as a port of entry. This new development failed to prosper, however, and property values plummeted after Timothy bought his house at 71 Cherry Street. With President Jefferson's embargo on British shipping, then the War of 1812, investors fled and Cambridgeport devolved into a wasteland of empty, unsold houses, decaying wharves, and dreary marshlands. Built to meet utilitarian needs, Timothy Fuller's three-story, wood-frame, Federal-style house was, as Fuller herself said, "ugly." Penny-pinchingly plain, it sat facing a soap factory. The surrounding undrained marshes, which occasionally flooded the Fullers' basement and kitchen, offered little relief from this dismal setting. Nor did the neighbors. Apart from the Fays, whose daughter Harriet was to become Margaret's playmate, there were the Raineys and the Allens, whose fates Margarett Crane would lament in a 25 January 1821 letter to her husband in Washington. "Many *dark surmises,*" she writes, "are whispered about the cause" of Mrs. Rainey's sudden death that morning. "Mrs. Allen . . . too," she continues, "has been unfortunate": "She fell into the fire on Sunday last & burnt her face & hands shockingly." Mrs. Fuller notes that both Mr. and Mrs. Allen are "very intemperate," and she "*accuses* him of pushing her into the fire."[10]

Margarett Crane may well have had firsthand knowledge of the kind of volatile man who might behave sadistically in relation to his wife. A romantic likeness of Timothy—wearing a Beau Brummell collar and tie and holding a pen and paper, the tools of his trade as lawyer and legislator—gives viewers a sense of the darkly attractive Byronic figure whom Margaret as a child so ardently adored and idealized. Yet another and more formal portrait, one he perhaps posed for as a U.S. congressman, hints at his nasty side. In both pictures his auburn hair twists in tendrils about his broad, fair forehead. But in the latter, his watchful light eyes seem to glare at the observer with disdain. His lips are pursed as if in a sneer, a look critics later said they often saw on the face of Timothy's elder daughter, who had a habit of lifting her upper lip whenever she readied herself to thrust a cutting remark at an adversary. Margaret's niece Edith Davenport Fuller would later concede that the subject of this latter painting "was not of an easy going lymphatic temperament." Indeed, when on 28 May 1809 the cocky yet adoring Timothy Fuller married the self-possessed and, in the fashion of *her* Puritan ancestry, pious Margarett Crane, who at twenty was taller by a head than her husband, he set out to engender children he intended to educate in a "severe though kind" way.[11]

His first child proved a perfect subject for his Spartan schooling. The first of Margarett Crane Fuller's nine children (two of whom were to die in infancy), Sarah Margarett burst like Athena onto earth on 23 May 1810 in the right front second-floor bedroom of Timothy's big, plain, blocklike corner house on Cherry Street in Cambridgeport.[12] Happy at his child's unusually alert mind, this rigidly principled, intellectually aloof yet occasionally passionate man decided when his daughter was three that he would tutor her himself, as his father had tutored him.

"NO NATURAL CHILDHOOD"

The young mother, too, played an active part in the early nurturing of her child. Biographer Charles Capper reports that Margarett breastfed her daughter well into her third year, hugging her and kissing her and making her feel as if she were the center of her mother's world. Fuller later recalled how special she felt as a toddler when her parents let her sit on a stool between them when they went out riding in their one-horse chaise. This focus of attention on the budding child was reinforced by Timothy, who wrote his wife when she and their four-month-old daughter were away in Canton, how he longed "to embrace my *pair* of M[argarett]s."[13] And he continued to dote on his wife and first daughter even after Julia Adelaide was born in August 1812. Already interested in the rearing of Sarah Margarett, Timothy had no trouble assuming control of her upbringing when his young and inexperienced wife found her energies consumed in caring for her newborn.

The father delighted in his elder daughter, who at age three was exhibiting less the characteristics of a sweet, petite, shy female than those of an aggressive—and hence, in her culture's terms, masculine—child prodigy. Interpreting the past through the views of child-rearing "expert" Amariah Brigham, who in 1832 saw mental precocity as "a symptom of disease" and hence urged parents not to overstimulate their female child's mind since such "unnatural" excitement might damage her brain, Fuller will later say that her father made the "great mistake" of forwarding her intellect while ignoring the effects on her developing emotions of his adult demands and passions. There was truth in this observation. For before she was three, Timothy began obsessing on his daughter's well-being, selecting the clothes she wore and setting conditions on the love he gave her. In March 1813 he sent Margarett Crane a note from Concord asserting that he will send "love & a kiss" to "Sarah Margarett" only "if [she] is a good girl." One year later he will inform his wife regarding "little Sarah Margarett," who is in Canton with her mother, that he will "love" his daughter "if she is a good girl & learns to read." This new condition he sets on his love he repeats in a July letter to his wife in which he adds yet another, daunting condition: "My dear love to my dear Sarah Margarett. She must be goodnatured & learn to read, & loving when desired."[14] Through her father's letters to his wife as well as his behavior toward her, Margaret thus came early to link her father's love with superior intellectual achievement and eager compliance with his desire.

And her father's love became ever more important to Margaret as her mother turned to grieving the death when Margaret was three years, five months old of the "lovely" thirteen-month-old Julia Adelaide. Though the mother tried not to "neglect" her elder daughter, the latter, who observed her mother's despair over her loss of Julia Adelaide, may have felt that her bad thoughts in relation to her mother's outpouring of love for the baby contributed to the death of this petted second daughter, whom even Timothy thought "unusually forward, pretty, & engaging." Fuller herself would later tell how the event traumatized her. Not only had the three-and-a-half-year-old Margaret lost a playmate to a force she was yet too young to understand, but she also felt abandoned by her grieving mother, who became self-absorbed and depressed as a result of the loss of her treasured second child.[15]

Preoccupied as a result of her loss, the mother seemed dead to her living daughter. Cut off thus from her mother by the birth, then death, of a sister, Margaret hungered thereafter for her mother's love. Margaret experienced her mother's emotional withdrawal, as French psychoanalyst André Green might put it, "as a catastrophe, as a narcissistic wound." As Green would have predicted, Margaret, given her mother's depression, instead of developing a feeling of close connection to her mother and hence to life felt a yawning emptiness within her, a distressing sense that the "'dead' object" was drawing her, in Green's words, "toward a 'deathly, deserted universe.'" To compensate for this empty feeling that will, according to Green, inform all later stages of development, such "victims" of what he calls the "dead mother complex" often turn to "intense intellectual activity," which is just what Margaret, encouraged by her father, did.[16] Early in life she was thus marked by death. Indeed, having been denied at this crucial time in her life the chance to grow close to her mother and hence resolve her ambivalent feelings, Margaret was thereafter to experience in life deeply divided feelings for the female figure.

In her autobiographical romance, written when she was thirty, Fuller vividly recalls the trauma caused her by her sister's death. She remembers their Cherry Street house still and dark, the nursery-maid's face streaming with tears, the mourners in "black . . . —the scent of the newly-made coffin," the sight of the spiritless form. She recalls, too, hearing "the clergyman,—the carriages," rolling to the grave. She did not remember, however, "insisting, with loud cries, that they not put the body in the ground." Whatever despair or feeling of terror drove the child to cry out against putting the body in the ground, the adult Fuller tells how the death of Julia Adelaide was indeed felt by her "as a catastrophe," as a rent in her heart now emptied of love. She had lost a "sweet playful" friend and felt "left" all "alone," save for the imaginary friends she found in her reading and conjured in fantasy as a way of escaping her father's commands, her bare and loveless landscape.[17]

After Julia Adelaide's death, Margaret began seeing herself as a "poor changeling" who had been "turned from the door of her adopted home," an "intellectually superior" "European princess" who had been "confided" to her parents' care. A sad reality underlay this fantasy. For rather than seeking compensation by lavishing love on her three-year-old daughter, Margarett Crane had not only "secluded" herself, as even her husband realized—she had also, when not visiting her parents in Canton or convalescing in her room, escaped her emotional distress and "disagreeable" household occupations by retreating to her backyard garden. There she found peace amid the flowers she nurtured and transplanted from one garden to another throughout her married life. Margarett Crane felt that flowers had the "power," she later wrote her daughter, "to soothe almost any irritation" and bring her "into harmony" with God. According to Higginson, Margarett Crane was so devoted to her flowers that her daughter quite "naturally" came to associate her mother with "some flower-like symbol."[18]

Distracted by pain for several months after Julia Adelaide's October 1813 death only to find herself then consumed with tending to the needs of baby Eugene, born in 1815 (the second of her seven children—two girls, five boys—to grow to maturity), Margarett Crane now found little time for her not-so-pretty yet precocious firstborn, whose education and general well-being fell to the father. Over the years the "impertinent" Sarah Margarett would increasingly become her father's child. Precociously setting herself apart from the other two women Timothy loved most—his wife and his mother—at nine she will tell her father not to call her Sarah, the name of Timothy's mother, but, instead, "Margaret alone," without a second "t." Meanwhile, the elder Margarett, who feared excessive reading would enfeeble her daughter's mind, saw her "opinionative" daughter as evidence of the correctness of experts' warnings about the adverse effects on healthy mental development of intellectual and sexual precocity in children.[19]

While Margaret's mother tended to her flowers as well as to her boys Eugene (b. 1815) and William Henry (b. 1817), Timothy taught his daughter as if it were still the eighteenth century and he were preparing a young son for Harvard. Her father's rigorous attention focused on her so early in her life had, as Fuller herself later said, a great influence on her. He demanded of her accuracy of speech and clarity of thought, insisting when she was only seven that she attend to her "studies with diligence," since he wished her to make "considerable progress in grammar, musick, history, chronology." Impatient with imperfection, Timothy, according to Margaret, expected her "to understand the mechanism of the language thoroughly, and in translating to give the thoughts in as few well-arranged words as possible, and without breaks or hesitation." And when she made mistakes, which she often did, Timothy expressed his great displeasure. He told her he would only be proud of her if she could "bear pain with courage," whether the cause of it was a broken tooth whose root had to be extracted, or his relentless criticisms. As an adult reflecting on her father's influence, Fuller says that his over-strict pedagogical methods were opposed to the "natural unfolding" of her character, which she describes as "fervent . . . and disposed to infatuation." Timothy taught her "to have reference to other minds" while forcing her to suppress what she believed were her "true" feelings. Thus "my natural bias," she notes, "was controlled."[20]

Fuller's thinking here reflects again that of Brigham, who argues that "undue excitement of the [child's] brain" by overzealous parents "is in opposition to the laws of nature." Brigham compares children's brains that are developed "unnaturally and prematurely" to "premature flowers, which are destined soon to wither away, without producing fruit." Both Fuller's and Brigham's views echo those of Romantics like Sampson Reed, who, in the 1821 "Oration on Genius" that he presented at Harvard, metaphorically described the infant's mind organically as unfolding from "within," "as the leaves and branches and fruit of a tree are said to exist in the seed from which it springs." Imbued with the views of the Romantics, Fuller in her 1840 autobiographical romance thus blamed the thwarting of her own "natural" development from a seedlinglike infant into a full-blossoming woman on her father's harsh teaching methods.[21]

On yet another level, Fuller's language suggests that Timothy may have had a more deleterious effect on her than she was willing to say. For when Romantics like Jean-Jacques Rousseau talked of the child's right to a natural unfolding, they had in mind an image of an innocent child unsoiled by precocious intellectual and sexual experience, someone who had not eaten of the fruit of Eden and hence had no knowledge of evil. Rousseau in *Émile* (1762), one of the first Romantic works Fuller read, contends that only a child who has had a chance to develop "naturally" would have the "'first seeds of humanity' sown in his heart" and thereby be able as an adult to establish a "natural" attachment (marriage).[22]

Rousseau here uses the masculine pronoun, for this man who defied Enlightenment thinking in his views on child rearing was in fact, himself, "freighted with [its] gendered assumptions." Hence the world for him in *Émile* is divided by sex and gender. According to Rousseau, males and females have essentially different natures. Born biologically presexed, male and female children are then socially, psychologically, and culturally programmed to reflect the gender biases prevalent when they are growing up. Through Sophie (an example of female education that influenced Brigham), Rousseau illustrates the way to raise a girl, whose aim in life should be to learn to govern her husband's household affairs, to tend to his garden and children, to protect his home and reputation, and to please him to the point of subjugating her own desires and obeying his every command.[23]

Rousseau was describing what it was like for men and women to be raised in accord with eighteenth-century demands that men exhibit rationality, self-control, and independence, the very qualities Timothy was inculcating in his daughter. From a Rousseauist perspective, Timothy was hence making, as Fuller herself later said, a great mistake, since, according to Rousseau, women by definition were expected to be passive, sensuous, private; and responsible for rearing children, managing home life, and maintaining family harmony. A "true" woman is tender, sweet, and concerned with the needs of others, whereas a woman in whom "man's qualities" have been cultivated is a man. A woman who has been given an education designed for males—like that Timothy gave his daughter—is hence not natural in Rousseau's view: she is both a man and woman, a "contradiction in terms."[24]

Because Timothy was himself a product of eighteenth-century thought, his attitude toward educating Margaret when she was a small child was more in line with the thinking of Enlightenment rationalists, in which a woman could still be viewed as a kind of "universal genius" responsible for public and private life, than it was with that of Rousseauist Romantics, who increasingly saw men and women as occupying separate spheres. He hence did not at first hesitate to educate Margaret as if she were a boy. Yet Margaret's father, whose thinking on childrearing was to change in accord with the thinking of the time and of the larger culture in which Margaret was growing up, would soon convey to her a different message. While it would affirm that physically she was a girl, from the perspective of intellect it would view her as a boy. For in culturally conservative 1830s New England, most people would come to believe that a woman's place was in the home and that her greatest virtue was her "purity," her ignorance of "dirty" things having to do with male desire, sexuality, and brutality. They would also come to believe that a woman was morally superior to a man, that a "true" woman exhibited those qualities that Margaret saw embodied in her mother and that she felt she would have acquired had Timothy's tutoring not nipped in the bud her "natural" female passions.[25]

To some extent Fuller was right. For when she was a child, Timothy imposed his vision of intellectual excellence on her. He did this by routinely assigning her challenging readings and making her recite for him late at night. His law firm work meant that it was often after ten when Timothy finally had time to review the lessons he had demanded his daughter prepare for him. In a note he wrote her when she was nine, he made his expectations clear: "To excel in all things should be your constant aim; mediocrity is obscurity."[26]

And excel she did, as her father desired. By age seven she was "reviewing" books like Richard Valpy's *Poetical Chronology of Ancient and English History,* she was writing her father about the warrior kings Charles XII of Sweden (1682–1718) and Philip II of Spain (1527–1598), and she was commenting in letters to him on the serious subject of slavery. She was being drilled in "the rules of Musick," in English and Latin grammar, as well as in math. And she was reading brief passages from Virgil. From these she retained a dim sense of the violent nature of Roman warriors, of men, it seemed, made of marble, whose lineaments gleamed strong in every light. With the Romans, she later wrote, "There is . . . —no divinity, no demon, no unfilled aim," just man "standing like the rock amid the sea." The Roman character spoke to Fuller of the "power of will." "Every Roman," she said, seemed "an emperor," as did her father, who imposed on her impressionable young mind reminders of *his* superior power.[27]

Fuller hints in her 1840 autobiographical romance that Timothy was a "tyrant in his home," an intrusive, controlling presence in his wife's and daughter's lives. The letters Timothy sent his wife from Washington between 1818 and 1820 reveal a man who was self-consciously writing, as he wrote his wife, for the "*publick*," yet who unwittingly was leaving to posterity a record of a picaro's (to use his wife's word) "piccadillos." These letters do offer historians a window on the times in which they were written, providing detailed accounts of house debates on such controversial topics as the extradition of fugitive slaves and the Missouri Compromise as well as of lavish parties held at the Monroe White House. They also, and more importantly for our purposes, reveal the personality of a sentimental yet sadistic man with a hot temper and a compulsive need to charm *and* control women. Even in the letters he wrote home during his first term in office (winter 1817–18)—some of which contain sentimental protestations of his conjugal love—Timothy reveals his inability to control his temper as well as his need to win the attention of women. On 15 February 1818 he tells his wife he loves her "*more romantically* now than when we were married." He goes on: "I looked this forenoon at a braid of your hair . . . [and] indulged a fine pleasing thought in seeing [it]."[28]

Such assurances of affection, however, are tainted by Timothy's compulsive need not only to remind his wife how often the "form & figure" of other women tempt him, but also to control this woman whose frequent failure to meet his expectations angers him. When in January 1818 Margarett Crane waited to write her husband until she had received a letter from him, which she thought the proper way for a lady to behave, Timothy exploded in rage and castigated her, writing her on January 18 that if he could be alone with her in "the chamber," he would teach her how to behave "in the manner of a *nice married wife*," a woman who *knows* her duty in life is to please her husband. Moreover, if she does not at once comply when he tells her to do something—like purchase a copy of Cicero for Sarah Margarett or have Andrew, their handyman, sell the sleigh or buy a cow—he suggests she is not a "good wife." He insists she must "be *agreeable, wise, handsome, & affectionate* now and always." When one of her letters was too short to suit him, he observes in his letter to her that Sarah Margarett has written most of it and that the latter's letter should be on a "separate piece of paper; unless," he snidely adds, "you had *nothing else to write*," which he "suspect[s]." When she spends too much money, Timothy writes sarcastically: "But mark me, extravagant girl,—I have placed my cash in all safety in negotiable notes payable [only] after my return. You cannot endorse them without a letter of Attorney *from me*, mark that? & restrain your passion for finery & nonsense." To humiliate her further, he notes: "O tempora, O mores! Sarah Margarett must interpret for you."[29]

In these letters wherein Timothy self-righteously demands that his wife resist finery, he describes the lavish dresses and hairstyles—even the color of eyes ("brilliant black") and eyebrows—of the beautiful women he (according to him) is charming at Washington parties. He has not been gone a month before he writes home about what his wife describes as "Mr. Brown's *fair wife*." Knowing how easily his wife becomes jealous, Timothy claims to allay her "floating fears" by assuring her that the "only entry to [Mrs. Brown's] parlor chamber is thro' the shop of stationary, where her husband constantly attends." That "is enough," he notes, "for your safety."[30]

During his second year in office (winter 1818–19), Timothy obsessively wrote his wife about his infatuation with a Mrs. Deforest. Since he commanded Margarett

Crane to preserve each of his letters and file them chronologically, we would expect the letters Timothy wrote to her during this period to be among his other letters preserved as part of the family collection. They are not, however: could Margarett Crane have destroyed them? The "fastidious" Timothy saved what appear to be all of his wife's pain-filled letters to him wherein she mentions her husband's obsession with Mrs. Deforest, which is how we know about her. In a December letter Timothy had apparently described Mrs. Deforest to his wife as being petite, "engaging handsome," a woman who "surpasses every other Lady in beauty at Mrs. Monroe's drawing room." In response to his "comparison between Ladies of *six* feet & the beautiful Mrs. Deforest," in her 30 December letter Margarett Crane says that she is so "vexed to find Mrs. Deforest the subject of so many letters"—letters her daughter is avidly reading!—"that I cannot forget her & cannot banish her from my imagination."[31]

Nor could she banish from her imagination the names and descriptions of the many other women whose wit and beauty Timothy praises in his letters. At first sweet and compliant, then hurt, and finally enraged by her husband's constant talk of women, Margarett Crane will write in response to a December 1818 letter wherein he tells his five-foot-ten-inch wife how women of "*low* stature" have an "elegance of beauty" lacking in women of "Herculean size," that maybe he is "*envious* at the superiority I have over you in size." "I have no inclination," she says, "to exhibit myself at Washington" where "comparisons [can be] drawn—to your disadvantage." When he responds by "condemning" what he considers "so censurable" in her "disposition," she retorts in January 1819 with a bull's-eye observation: unlike him, her "*conduct* & *principles* generally coincide."[32]

Timothy—at the same time he is flirting with the "Ladies"—makes it clear that Margarett Crane will pay a heavy price if she so much as looks at another man. From a remark he made in a letter regarding the behavior of the milkman Dix ("He is a man who requires being whipped and spurred"), it seems Timothy might, indeed, when they are alone in their chamber, "teach" Margarett Crane how to behave as "a good wife" should. In a disturbing letter dated 16 December 1819, Timothy tells Margarett Crane that he believes his dreams are warning him about her "wayward" behavior. In one, the two are coming "from home in a chaise & some young *chap*, . . . was with us—it had rained," he explains,

> & I invited him to ride in the chaise being as I thought [him] an invalid, while I walked, as I once *foolishly* did for Parson Waldo. We came to a place where I supposed he wanted to stop; but as he did not, I began to repent my condescension, & accordingly invited him to betake himself to his feet & I assumed my place by your side. I felt no jealousy, or *very little*, at the time, as I had you in my eye constantly; but on reflexion *since* . . . I cannot but consider it as an admonition to me to warn you to keep away from light & frivolous *chaps* who sometimes are honored with your courtesy. And what I say to you, I say to all—watch.

Her Father's House

That night he had another dream. In it Eugene was asleep on a bed with no mattress and almost no bedclothes. Timothy asks his "dear Margarett" if this dream, too, is "admonitory": "Are our little ones neglected because you are listening to the flatteries & fooleries of fine fellows?" "Take care," he cautions her, "to explain in your answer to this all your wayward movements." "Be frank," he says, "& tell the whole," "let not even a whisper or a smile be forgotten": "If any thing is suppressed, I shall certainly know it."[33]

Timothy Fuller's pattern of conduct with women seems to have been to demand that they comply with his commands—which were not always honorable—and then to lecture and threaten them if they defied him. When Margarett Crane objected to his obsessive talk of women, he predictably lectured her about how he wished her to be an agreeable, dutiful wife. And "*dutiful*" is precisely what, in her letters to him, she insists she is—even as she also makes clear that she wishes she might, "like the 'recording Angel[,]' drop a tear and blot out every every thing unkind from you forever."[34]

He was equally intrusive and controlling in relation to his daughter. In letter after letter he insists his wife tell him how Sarah Margarett progresses in her studies, how her time is employed, what hour she retires. To Timothy's immense satisfaction, his daughter, unlike his wife, enacted *his* script almost perfectly, according to Margarett Crane. The daughter eagerly awaited his letters from Washington and according to her mother felt "exceedingly disappointed" when he failed to mention her in them or when she found at "the P.O." only a letter containing a congressional quarterly. When in January 1818 Timothy included an "affectionate notice" of "little Sarah Margarett" amid his talk of congressional debates and the loveliness of "the ladies" in Washington, his wife noted that "S. M.['s] eyes sparkled with pleasure." Just as her eyes sparkled with pleasure that same January when he sent through a letter to his wife "this kiss & this kiss . . . for my girl," Sarah Margarett. In December 1818, Margarett Crane wrote her husband: "S. M. sends love & says she *will* do every thing you wish to have her."[35]

Fuller's later rebellion makes sense when we realize from Margarett Crane's letters that as a child Margaret was reading each of her father's letters "several times." In these letters addressed to his wife he did on occasion send a kiss for Sarah Margarett, but more often than not he was unkind not only to his wife but also to his daughter, who "could scarcely avoid a few contortions of her face & a few tears" whenever she found neither an affectionate reference to her in a letter he had written his wife nor a letter to her from him at the post office. When she did find a reference to her in a letter to his wife or, better, a letter just for her, it was invariably fraught with Timothy's relentless criticism of her "habit of *shutting* [her eyes] *partly* when she enters a room," her "defective habits of holding [her] hands & fingers" when playing the piano, her "mistakes" too numerous for him to delineate in her translation of the Lord's Prayer into Latin she was so proud of, and,

"NO NATURAL CHILDHOOD"

above all, her general "slovenliness" in writing and hygiene. In the letters he wrote Margaret from Washington (1817–24), he harps on her need to correct her "faults" and "defects," insisting she "be as near perfection as possible" in all she endeavors to do.[36]

Hungry for love and intent on pleasing, the daughter imbibed each word her father wrote. By age ten she was thus imitating Timothy's stilted rhetorical style, as is evident in a November 1820 letter to her grandmother, Timothy's morally righteous mother, Sarah: "The great entertainment and instruction I have recieved [sic] from your letters to my father and mother has induced me also to request that I may be favoured with a correspondence with my grandmother."[37]

Margaret mimicked this father who aroused in her strong feelings, some of which were no doubt erotic in the polymorphous way a child experiences sexual desire as a generalized craving that can be excited and gratified in a number of ways. Craving her father's "approbation" in "every thing" she did, Margaret strained to please him, though the late-night recitations stretched her nerves to a point she felt she might, as she later wrote, "go mad."[38]

In her autobiographical romance, Fuller tells how she would be roused from deep sleep and brought before her father, who was probably waiting for her in the cozy, fire-lit front parlor. We can almost see her: a joyful child with light flowing locks and sparkling eyes, anxiously reciting for her father with the hope she might win from him a rare word of approval. She would recite by candlelight the day's assignment, which was usually, as she says and as the historical record confirms, far above her intellectual and emotional level. When she was only nine years old, he wrote her he expected her to be "*profoundly* into" the *Aeneid*—"*into*" that blood-soaked text wherein enemies are "miserably cut down," the "quick hoofs" of horses "splash[ing] their way through gory spray," and where enemies' heads are severed from their bodies so the victors can hold them high in pride on pikes![39]

Fuller recalls her dread of going to bed after these intense late-night sessions, a dread that increased dramatically when, to satisfy the command of her severe father, she did in fact, at age nine, read the entire *Aeneid* in Latin. After she had recited and with her mind "over-excited," she was led—presumably by Betsy, the maid, since Timothy insisted his wife retire early—up the two-run staircase that dominates the cramped front hall. The climb by candlelight to the second floor would have been scary; for, rising high above her was yet another winding flight of stairs that led to the servants' quarters on the third floor. It may have seemed to the terrified child that the winding staircase led not to sleep and heaven but to Hades, a place black as pitch. To a visitor even today, that staircase still seems formidably steep and scary.[40]

It might well have been around that time that Margaret began to be tormented with night terrors, with ghoulish visions she thought at the time real but which she later decided were "spectral illusions." Her visiting aunts and uncles could not understand why she "was never willing to go to bed." Yet, once the lamp had been taken away and she lay alone in the dark, it seemed that huge shapes—usually colossal faces with dilating eyes—would come at her from the corners of the room and press down upon her, shapes that grew larger and larger until she thought they would crush her. Terrified, she thought she saw giant saucer eyes approach her through the dark, eyes that at times, she said, "would detach themselves from the faces and come upon me," like the eye of the blood-thirsty Cyclops Polyphemus in the *Aeneid,* or perhaps like the eye of her powerful father that was always, as he said, "watching." Haunted by these specters, the child would drift into a troubled sleep, only to be awakened again, this time by nightmares of horses trampling her body or of trees dripping blood into pools that threatened to drown her. Both these latter horrific dreams are like those experienced by people who have survived severe trauma. As an adult Margaret would recall how in one such dream she waded through a sea of blood and caught at twigs and rocks "to save myself: they all streamed blood on me."[41]

The Fullers attributed their daughter's dreams to her "incessant reading of Virgil," whose *Aeneid* does indeed contain horrific images that may have powerfully impacted Fuller's imagination. Perhaps her terrible dreams, as her parents said, did in fact replay themes and images familiar to her from the *Aeneid*—such as Turnus's thirst for war in book 12, or the Sibyl's oracle in book 6 wherein the prophetess foresees "the Tiber foaming with much blood," or the scene in book 9 wherein the vengeful Latins "uplifted pikes" on which they had skewered, for Aeneas and all the Trojans to see, the heads of Nisus and Euryalus, "impaled, held high, / . . . heads that drip black gore." Or maybe some images came from the scene in book 3 wherein a myrtle tree spurts blood on Aeneas.[42]

Yet images of water becoming blood could also have come from the Bible, from Revelation, when at the end of time the rivers and seas turn into blood in which guilty sinners drown. Twigs and trees dripping blood could likewise have come from the *Metamorphoses* by Ovid, whose exotic tales Fuller came to love for they gave her a way as a child, she later said, "to creep from amid the Roman pikes to lie beneath this great [Greek] vine." An image of blood gushing from a tree could have come from Ovid's tale of Mestra's father, Erysichthon, who was so cruel that he kept axing into an oak in a grove sacred to Ceres, although blood gushed from the wound and the tree pleaded with him to stop—for she was not a tree but a nymph loved by Ceres. In retaliation for Erysichthon cutting down the tree, Ceres sent Famine to make him feel hunger, no matter how much food he ate.[43]

When the adult Fuller sat down to write about her childhood nightmares and terrors, she had in mind not just vivid images from Virgil's *Aeneid* and Ovid's *Metamorphoses* but also ideas then current about the dangers of promoting intellectual precocity in children. Perhaps Ovid's sad story of Mestra surfaced at this time. Certainly Mestra's story was relevant to Fuller's life, despite her parents' tendency to idealize their family's functioning and avoid any talk that acknowledged pathology. Erysichthon, like Timothy, held a tyrannical power over his daughter. After going through his fortune in trying to satiate his hunger, Erysichthon sold his daughter as a slave. Mestra, whom Ovid thought "worthy of a better father," at first resisted her father's attempt to sell her into slavery. She ran to the sea and begged her lover, Neptune, to save her, crying out, "Oh, you, . . . Who have deprived me of virginity, / Deliver me from such a master's power!" Neptune transformed her into a "fisher-man," a gender-switch disguise that let Mestra escape her abusive father, for in the form of a man Mestra knew her father would not recognize her and thus could not hurt her.[44]

To a thirty-year-old woman trying to reconstruct what it felt like to have been controlled by a tyrannical father, stories like Mestra's and others by Ovid provided themes and images as well as a frame into which Fuller could fit together dimly remembered scenes from her difficult past so as to make of them a coherent story. Placed within this frame, disturbing memories were lifted by the child out of their ordinary context and instilled with mythical meaning. Thus literature gave Fuller as a child a way to deal with a distressing reality, just as it also enabled her as an adult to interpret the past. It gave her images and ideas to express her pain.[45]

Images in a recurring dream of following "to the grave the body of her mother" derived from Fuller's memory of her sister's funeral. This dream captures two of Fuller's emotional concerns: her sister's death and her fear as a child that she might likewise lose her mother, who already in a way seemed dead to her. Such bad dreams upset the child, as did a need to be relieved of a sleep-disrupting tension that was caused in part by the unspoken strain in her parents' relationship but also by Timothy's routine at night of entering the room where his children slept "and pressing a kiss upon their unconscious lips." Stimulated by this intense expression of fatherly affection, Margaret walked in her sleep. Fuller tells how once when she sleepwalked and her parents "heard her, and came and waked her," and she told them about her dreams, her father offered her no comfort. Instead he "sharply bid her 'leave off thinking of such nonsense, or she would be crazy,'—never knowing," says Fuller, "that he was himself the cause of all these horrors of the night."[46]

2 ∞ Hungry for Love

In her autobiographical romance, Fuller depicts her father as a man whose tyrannical control she, like Mestra, tried unsuccessfully to evade. Her mother she paints as a passive person with a delicate, flowerlike nature, a shadowy figure who played only a small part in helping to shape her firstborn's life. Time and fantasy have, to some extent, colored Fuller's memory. For during her first two years Fuller was, indeed, as scholars say, "surrounded with love and affection," and her mother probably was not as "self-effacing" as Fuller and also Higginson later recalled her as being. If Margarett Crane subordinated herself to her husband, it was not because she lacked spunk, but rather because, like her husband, she was raised in a world that accepted as Truth the Law as outlined in Blackstone's *Commentaries on the Laws of England* (1765), which presumes that a wife must obey her husband. While teaching at Leicester Academy, Timothy had read Blackstone, who says that "husband and wife are one person in law": that the wife is to her husband like a piece of property subject to a power "that ceaseth onely in Death." Unquestioningly accepting this view, Margarett Crane wrote Timothy in March 1818, that this is "as it should be."[1]

Though Blackstone here misrepresented the actual letter of the law of equity, Timothy—who, as his father had before him, argued the need for education for women but was himself in fact frighteningly dictatorial with women—behaved in a way he felt was in accord with "the law." The letters he and his wife exchanged when he was in Washington reveal that a willful Margarett Crane dutifully submitted to her husband's command, whether it be to write him a daily letter or yield control of their eldest child to him. As we have seen, when she had at first hesitated in writing him, Timothy got angry. He wrote her that should she be alone in his "chamber" with him, "I would shake your faith a little." Whatever Timothy meant by this, his wife got the message. Seldom thereafter did a day go by that she did not send a letter discussing household matters (the outhouse's progress, the plentitude of quilts, firewood, money, etc.), the children's behavior, and the appearance of family members as she read his letters to them by the dim light of a lamp on the table in the parlor by the looking glass.[2]

These letters reveal a woman who, despite her pain, chose with quiet dignity to submit to her sometimes cruel, always controlling, authoritarian husband. Early in the exchange when Margarett Crane tried to shield her son from the scorch of her husband's temper—asking him on 13 January 1818 not to "whip [Eugene] for any (thing) [sic]" and attempting unsuccessfully two years later to "efface" a "blot" the boy had made on her writing paper—Timothy wrote her regarding the latter that he was "resolved to overlook every thing in hopes of soon finding you penitent for your fault." When he thought she was not sufficiently penitent or forthright with him ("your absent *Lord*," he says, who "holds the purse strings"), he tended to write something condescendingly saccharine to his "pretty little wife," then to threaten his "disobedient spouse," as he does in April 1820: "I wish I was near enough to *enforce* respect for my just command." One week later, he cautions her: "Always tell the truth, my girl.—Never deceive nor *attempt* to deceive your husband. It is useless, for he will discover all at last."[3]

If Fuller's story distorts, it is not, then, because it paints her mother as less involved in her daughter's upbringing than she in fact was, or her father as more dictatorial than he actually was, but rather because it does not convey how profoundly as a child she craved both her parents' love. And when it ceased to be forthcoming from her depressed young mother, she sought it with an unnatural intensity from her father. We have already seen how eagerly she awaited her father's letter—trekking alone at age seven to the "P.O." in the snow with the hope she might find there a letter addressed to her, or at least one to her mother with "mention [of] her particularly." Both her own and her mother's letters reveal that as a small child she hungered for the love of this man who controlled her heart, her mind, her very soul. She craved his praise, his touch, his nighttime kiss.[4]

Through these letters we also get a glimpse at how Margaret, early on, in a childlike way began fancying herself her father's lover. When she was not yet nine, she would inquire of her mother whether she "thought the violets would blossom before" her father came home from Washington, "as she wishe[d] to dress an *arbour* to entertain" him in after his "return." In this letter it seems Margaret aspires to be "a *lady*" and entertain her father in the way he says ladies in Washington entertain him in the letters he is writing his wife, this woman who continued to bear his babies. Resentful yet smitten, Margaret would be like the mythical Mestra, who escaped her father's control only to return to let him sell her again and again for money to buy food to satisfy his insatiable hunger. Fuller's adult pattern will be, then, like Mestra's: to return time and again to the father figure who both loves and misuses her, until at last, through her participation in a bloody revolution against the combined powers of pope and kings, she takes a stand against him. But that will come only later, after Fuller has had time as an adult to reflect on her "sad" past.[5]

As a child her desperate need for love and attention shows through her dreams, even in the one where her mother is dead. If a dream captures in a central image a dreamer's major emotional concern, then that one conveys Fuller's fear that her mother might die, or that she is already dead to her daughter. It may also, however, relay a wish that her mother were dead, a wish motivated by her anger at this inattentive woman who was, as a still angry Fuller would later put it, "much absorbed in the care of her younger children." Another of Fuller's dreams appears in a December 1818 letter she wrote at age eight right after Timothy left to begin his second session as a U.S. congressman. In it she dreamed that her father was sick and his life "despaired of." This dream, like that of her mother in a coffin, had a basis in fact: Timothy's stagecoach had overturned on its way to Washington. Though his face was badly bruised, he wrote home that he was otherwise unhurt. Fuller's dream hence conceptualizes her fear that Timothy might die and leave her alone with her mother, who, "not withstanding [her husband's] devotion to the ladies" and the "*pain*" his wandering eye is causing her, still considered him "dearer" to her "than any thing" and remained *his* "affectionate *dutiful* wife." Determined to win her father's attention, Margaret ends this letter about her dream of his impending death with a jealous reminder to her "Dear Papa" that she is as worthy as her mother to receive his love; though he may think "a relation of [his] pain would be uninterresting to any but an affectionate wife," he must "not forget that I [Sarah M Fuller] am Your afectionate Daughter."[6]

✧ ✧ ✧

Fuller felt an intense mix of love and rage in relation to this father who drove her to excel yet rarely showed her affection commensurate with his demands, whose expression of tenderness was always tense, whose kiss, while yearned for, troubling. To compensate for the lack of an appropriate touch from either parent, Fuller escaped to fantasy, transforming herself Mestra-like into a changeling or a boy, but also, in mimicry of her mother, to the garden. In the voice of a child who has defensively assumed a grandiose sense of self for survival, the adult Fuller later wrote of her mother's flowers, "my mother's hand had planted them, and they bloomed for me."[7]

As a child Fuller liked nothing about their massive, flat-faced, corner Cambridgeport house except the elms her father had planted in the small front yard in honor of her birth, and the "little garden behind." The back door of their house opened onto a high flight of stairs that descended to a narrow plot of grass beyond which lay her mother's garden, a view Fuller thought "injured" by the sight of the pump and toolhouse. At the back of the garden, a wooden gate in a high, unpainted board wall opened into the fields beyond. The wall was "embowered in the clematis creeper," a "protecting vine" whose beautiful flowers reminded her of her mother. Standing in the gate's black frame and gazing at the sunset sky, Fuller as a child had felt "at home."[8]

James Freeman Clarke, son of a Boston doctor and druggist who became Fuller's close friend, recollected meeting Margaret when they were both about age five. He remembers her as a joyful child with light hair and bright face who "led me by the hand down the back-steps of her house into the garden." Going into the garden was for Fuller like entering a wondrous fairyland where her "thoughts" were "not called to fly . . . before the time." Within the garden's confines she felt safe and alive. There she spent the best hours of her lonely childhood gathering the violets, pinks, lilies, and roses. Playing amid her mother's roses, she petted the breastlike underside of the petals; she smelled the perfumed sweetness of their female fragrance; she felt no threat from the outside world. She loved her mother's roses: "I looked at them on every side. I kissed them, I pressed them to my bosom with passionate emotions, such as I have never dared express to any human being." She vowed someday "to be as beautiful, as perfect as they." It is a "vow," she confesses, "I have not kept."[9]

Margaret had trouble identifying with her mother, who acted perfectly the part of a nineteenth-century woman; she was dutiful, caring, managerially efficient, pretty. And she was wondrously good at nursing her children when they became sick. At five foot ten, Margarett Crane seemed like a Greek goddess to her daughter, who, at age ten, stood "five feet two inches high." But she was awkward and heavy, unlike her mother, who was slender and had an air of refinement that her robust daughter was never to acquire. Her mother's self-possession, her beauty, her unusually smooth, milky white complexion, all helped to make her overweight, aggressive, plain-looking daughter feel self-conscious about her own noticeably unfeminine looks and behavior. Margaret was so self-conscious about the way she looked at age ten that she was "unwilling," according to her mother, "to expose herself"—even, apparently, to her mother.[10]

Though her mother was physically present to her during most of her childhood, it felt to the child as if she did not care for her. In a letter in which Margarett Crane tells her husband how "clums[il]y" Margaret walks in the snow, she also notes how surprised her seven-year-old daughter seemed that she had "taken the trouble to go out and meet her" as Margaret came home alone from the post office. The mother's inattention can be explained to a great extent by the fact that she was too busy tending to her domestic chores and the needs of her other children to pay much attention to her firstborn child. Like many firstborn children, Margaret was expected to perform routine household chores as well as to attend to the needs of her younger siblings. Her parents counted on her to be reliable, conscientious, the standard bearer, in effect, for the whole family. And they did so to such an extent that she would later lament that she had been "called on for wisdom and dignity long before [her] leading strings were off."[11]

But it was not just that Margaret was the oldest and the mother was preoccupied with her other children that created the distance that existed between mother and daughter. Rather, her aggressive behavior and odd looks no doubt did make her seem, even as a child, strange to her traditionally feminine mother. In contrast, Margarett Crane would openly adore her "little darling" daughter Ellen (b. 7 August 1820), whose pretty face she would constantly kiss and whom, in a January 1821 letter to her husband, she would defiantly call "my pet." Timothy's "indiference" to this second girl while remaining unnaturally attached to his elder daughter—whose sharp mind and feisty style reminded him of himself—did not help endear Margaret to her mother.[12]

Fuller's flawed relationship with her mother would lead her later to feel a special connection to the Romantics, in whose writing the figure of the woman—whether as "ideal goddess," evil seductress, deserted woman, or maternal Nature—is central. One critic notes of the English Romantics that the "relationship with the woman which [their] poetry either expresses or implies is rooted psychologically in the relationship with the first woman of all our lives, the mother." For several nineteenth-century American Romantics—including Thoreau, Hawthorne, and Poe—the relationship with the mother was the central factor in their emotional and mental development. Of course, no parent is perfect. Hence every infant sees its mother ambivalently as good when it satisfies its need for warmth, food, and attention, bad when this would-be nurturer deprives it of nourishment, protection, and affection. Psychologists and psychoanalysts agree that when the mother offers a secure place from which the infant can explore the world, that is, when she confirms the child's existence by mirroring back affirming looks of recognition and affection, this fundamental ambivalence all children feel toward the mothering figure may be resolved. The child is able to take in a coherent self-image that is consistent with the way others in the actual world perceive it. It builds its "ego"— that is, the mental-emotional centering power that enables a person to navigate through life and impose a *"framework of meaning"* on experience—to the point that it is able to see itself as an entity distinct from things in the external world. The infant has thus developed "within" a sense of a core self (however "phantasmic" that "self" might actually be) capable of feeling concern for the wellbeing of people outside itself. Its centering "self"—its "ego" or, as Plato would say, "soul"—is secure enough to control its libido, its strong primal feelings of love and hate for the mothering figure.[13]

A problem, however, arises when the mother fails to provide a secure base upon which the child might depend. This is what happened when Margarett Crane turned her concentrated attention from her still-nursing two-year-old daughter after Julia Adelaide was born in August 1812 and then abruptly deprived Margaret of love when she "secluded" herself from her husband and daughter after the baby's death in October 1813. In a case like this, the love-hungry child compensates for the mother's sudden absence by detaching its libido from real objects in the world and attaching them, instead, as Margaret did, to larger-than-life fictions, idealized images of itself, as well as of all-powerful parents from whom it thereafter seeks love and attention. In such a way the developing child gets "hung up" on its image. It compensates for this narcissistic wound, for its feelings of emptiness within, in a number of ways *including,* as noted, "turning to intense intellectual activity." It develops a superficial self that fulfills an ideal image of itself in an effort to win the love and approval of the real parent (or parents) or of people it misperceives to be ideal embodiments of the absent, inattentive, or abusive parent (or parents). Such a child sometimes develops, as did Fuller, an incoherent or divided sense of self: there is the "good child" that does what the difficult parent demands, and the "true" self that lies buried deep "within" and can be retrieved "only" (as Fuller would later say of herself) by "the experienced diver." The child, whose "true" self is sealed within a superficial shell, projects his or her fantasy image of what a good parent ought to be onto parents or parent surrogates.[14]

The child thereafter seeks itself in the outside world in much the same way as did Narcissus in the myth by Ovid that Margaret had read. As she knew, Narcissus was the son of the blue-eyed Liriopë. Spoiled by his lovely nymph mother, Narcissus spurned the love of the nymph Echo (who was "then a body not a Voice"), boasting, "Better death than such a one / Should e'er caress me!" Responding to the appeal of a youth who had been spurned by Narcissus, Nemesis granted Narcissus the fate for which he unwittingly yearned when, after spying his own image in a spring, Narcissus mistook the "mirrored image" for a "thing of life to love," thereby condemning himself to seek love from a phantom, a search that will lead to his death. "Fatally" in love with the "peerless boy" on whom he gazed in the water, Narcissus thus fell in love with his own image and, "tortured by a strange desire," died a victim of his inability to feel real love for the living creatures in the world around him.[15]

In blurring the boundaries between self and reality, the "me" that seems so "mountainous" in this narcissistically inclined personality is, at its core, insecure, unstable, and small. It is, as the late Christopher Lasch wrote, "a minimal self." Lacking an ego strong enough to integrate its primal feelings of love and hate into a coherent sense of self, the growing child feels increasingly empty and vulnerable. It feels empty even as it develops a theatrical personality it presents to the world, a magnetic persona that draws people to it. Concealed behind their theatrical masks, these flawed individuals tend to misperceive themselves as well as people and things in the exterior world for their fictional renderings of them. Such an individual is, as Fuller will later say of herself, "egotized."[16]

Placed in a nineteenth-century context, he or she would be inclined to identify with the figure of the wandering, homeless Romantic, with, say, the impulse-driven poet in Shelley's *Alastor*, who is forever yearning to merge his being with that of the ideal woman he has seen in a dream. The wish underlying this "narcissistic" drive is to recover the love that was missed by the child when the mother, for whatever reason, deprived it of nurturing love, and when the father (or other caretaker) did not provide appropriate compensatory affection. In the absence of such adequate nurturing, an absence that generates a feeling of emptiness within, the child tends to accept the image that the nonnurturing parent imposes upon it. Timothy, himself, confessed in a 12 January 1820 letter to his wife that he hoped to form Sarah Margarett into a girl who could live up to his ideal image of what a daughter ought to be: an "easy and agreeable" learned young "lady" who is worthy "to merit our love and esteem."[17]

There was in Fuller's heart, as Higginson said, a "void" that "under ordinary circumstances, the mother's influence comes in to fill." Fuller's mother, however, had trouble accepting her strange child, and her father, who, as Higginson put it, "control[led] the daughter's whole existence," kept her "feelings on the stretch" until late into the night while at the same time depriving her of nurturing love. As a friend of the Fuller family, Higginson wrote that even as a young lady of twenty, Margaret was not "intimate" with her mother, a woman who remained "fiercely loyal" to her husband.[18]

Timothy expected from his daughter a similar submission: Margarett Crane herself later said that her husband's "habit" had always been "implicit obedience to parents and in all essentials he required this of [Margaret]." Hence in his letters from Washington he demands that Margaret excel in all she endeavors to do—whether it be to commit to memory passages from Gombach's Greek Testament or to learn to play like a "lady" the piano he bought expressly for her to learn to play. While on the one hand it seemed to Margaret that Timothy wanted her to be feminine like the ladies he was meeting in Washington, on the other it seemed he wanted her to excel as a masculine intellectual like himself, an accomplishment that would make her his equal. This latter prospect appealed to Margaret's fancy. For it was becoming increasingly clear to her that the way to become her father's companion *and* to win the hearts of pretty women like her mother was to be a man like her father: witty, charming, *and* full of the kind of power he had as a U.S. congressman. In an undated fragment about her sister's death, Fuller envisions herself as a boy who seeks to comfort his mother after her daughter's death. The mother pines her life away after the infant dies. Her death leaves her surviving child, her *boy*, with a "feeling of infinite loss." Had the mother lived, says Fuller of her male self, "there was enough in me corresponding with her unconscious wants to have roused her intellect and occupied her affections."[19]

3 ∽ "Gate of Paradise"

In light of the child's hunger for love, it is easy then to see how Margaret, age seven, attached herself passionately to Ellen Kilshaw, the lovely daughter of a wealthy Liverpool merchant who met the Fullers in the summer of 1817 during her visit with her sister and brother-in-law in Boston. Timothy thought Ellen, who was about the same age as his wife, pretty, and initiated a friendship with her. In her autobiographical romance, which she wrote during her 1839–41 spiritual and gender identity crisis, Fuller wrote of her love for Ellen that this was "my first real interest in my kind." The minute in church Margaret first saw Ellen—"her dress, her hazel eyes, and clustering locks"—"my thoughts," she recalls, "were fixed on her."[1]

Timothy invited Ellen to their Cambridgeport home. In a letter she wrote the Fullers after her return to Liverpool in November 1817, Ellen recalled how the seven-year-old child had stood at the window and "flushed" excitedly as she approached, how she had opened the door for her, then "ran, and concealed herself" behind a chair. Flattered, Ellen invited Margaret to her place. Twenty-three years later, Fuller would depict Ellen, who painted in oils and played the harp, as the embodiment of female perfection. When they walked hand in hand in the fields behind Ellen's house, Margaret was in heaven: Ellen's "presence" was to her "a gate of Paradise" in the same way that the gate at the back of her mother's garden had both opened out into the fields, and sealed her safe within a womblike fairyland, a place apart from the real world of human cruelty, coercion, pain.[2]

In Ellen the child found an ideal female with whom she could enact a mother-daughter relationship in which the mother would be more loving. Ellen would love the lonely child and not let her father interrupt the love they shared in their private garden. To some extent, Kilshaw filled the part. She "was not cold" but turned on the girl looks "of full-eyed sweetness" as she guided her through paradisiacal fields where every bird and tree "greeted" the duo and said, recalled Fuller, "what I felt, 'She is the first angel of your life.'"[3]

Ellen was Margaret's angel in much the same way Margarett Crane had been an "Angel" to Timothy. In loving Ellen, Margaret thus played the role, not only of a child searching for a mother to love her, but also of a man able to satisfy his wife's—as Fuller put it in the fragment about her sister's death wherein she envisions herself a boy capable of satisfying her mother's emotional needs—"unconscious wants." In an unsent letter she wrote Ellen in November 1819, two years after the latter's return to England, Margaret tells Ellen how she likes writing her, since, "while I am writing to you I think I am with you." She boasts she is "so tall some persons think I am thirteen," that she remembers "just how you [Ellen] looked," and that surely thirteen is old enough for a person to marry.[4]

Fuller recalls how, during a visit with Ellen, the latter, who had gone to greet visitors, left her alone with a novel they had been reading together, Scott's *Guy Mannering*. Fuller recalls that she opened the book where Ellen's "mark lay, and read merely with the feeling of continuing our mutual existence." The scene was that of rocks on the seacoast. She was "the little Harry Bertram, and had lost her,—all I had to lose,—and sought her vainly in long dark caves that had no end, plashing through the water." Meanwhile, "the crags" that "beetled above" threatened "to fall and crush the poor child." "Absorbed" in this "painful vision," tears "rolled down my cheeks." Upon returning, Ellen noted the girl's distress and "fixed" on the lonely child "inquiring looks of beautiful love." "I laid my head against her shoulder and wept," says Fuller, "dimly feeling that I must lose her and all,— . . . that the cold wave must rush over me." She remembers "little else of this time, . . . except the state of feeling in which I lived. For I *lived*."[5]

These memories tell as much about Margaret Fuller's gender/sex identity crisis in 1839–41 as they do about her feelings as a child. Still, Fuller's feelings for the woman depicted in the romance are real. They suggest the depth of her yearning, age seven, for the tender love of her mother, whom Kilshaw resembled. It also suggests how easily Fuller identified with the male figure. The enduring power of her love for Ellen is evident in a letter she wrote Timothy when she was almost ten. "*Deep rooted*," she wrote, "is my affection for [Ellen.] May it flourish an *ever* blooming flower till our kindred spirits . . . mount together to those blissful regions where never again we shall be seperated." "I love Ellen," she adds, "better than my life."[6]

In this romantic idyll, we can see Fuller's inchoate sense of herself as a sexual being. Fuller reveals in it not only how profoundly as a child she craved the love of an attentive mother, but also how at times she lived imaginatively as a boy. The child associates her love for Ellen with a flower, symbol to her of her mother. Fuller's asserted wish to merge with Ellen thus reveals a complicated contradictory desire. On the one hand she wishes to take on the identity of a feminine woman and be the object of her father's desire. On the other, she sees herself, in effect, *as* a man and hence as a replacement for her father as the aggressive male lover of a beautiful woman. To be the aggressor meant she did not have to see her father as the one in control, someone who might in fact be hurting her; it also could mean that she identifies with her father and is hence free to love a woman with the same intensity of passion that Timothy felt for pretty women.[7]

That Fuller wrote Ellen more than two years after she returned to England tells how indelible was the mark this lovely lady left on her impressionable young mind and how hungry she was for love. It also tells of her unconscious wish to defy her father by loving a woman whom he adores and competing with him for power and position. Yet even as she extols Ellen as the one person who can "fulfil my wishes," she also exclaims to her father how grateful she is to be "possessed of the greatest blessing of life a good and kind father. Oh I can never repay you for all the love you have shown me But I will do all I can."[8]

The phrase "possessed of" occurs often in *Hesitation; or, To Marry, or Not to Marry?*, a novel Fuller was reading at the age of nine. In the novel, however, the word "possess" is meant literally as "to have as one's own"; yet here, in light of Margaret's feelings for her father and Ellen, her assertion that she is "possessed of" a good father carries with it a suggestion of demonic possession. Lacking a mother's attentive love and with it a secure sense of self within, Fuller felt inhabited by a supernatural power in the shape of a larger-than-life father who spent half each year in the celebrity world of Washington, an exalted being she worshipped and dreaded.[9]

"Possessed of" her father, Margaret felt controlled by a mysterious power which monitored her every thought and move—as Timothy in effect did through his continuing relentless demands in letters that included translating Bible passages as well as Oliver Goldsmith's *Deserted Village* into Latin. Possessed by him, Margaret's soul was a slave to the will of a man who exacted absolute obedience from this daughter whom he aimed "to make," he wrote her when she was nine, "a good scholar & a good girl." When she was bad, as her mother wrote him she often was, Timothy in letters made her feel his wrath, as he did when he threatened to send her to work in a factory if she did not mind her mother. Eager to comply with her father's commands, Margaret in her letters to him began exhibiting an anxious need to please him as early as December 1818. On December 16 she tells him she is attending Latin lessons twice a week and has been doing her arithmetic with her

Aunt Elizabeth, one of Timothy's two unmarried older sisters who visited when Timo was away, as did Aunt Abigail ("Abba") Crane, who was loving. Margaret disliked Elizabeth because she reported the children's bad behavior to Timothy. In this 16 December letter to a father who seems hauntingly present even in absence, Margaret confesses: "If you have spies [her aunts and mother] they will certainly inform you that we are not very dissipated."[10]

This possession by the father's spirit—this sense his "watching eyes" are everywhere—made Margaret exceedingly self-conscious even as it contributed to her exaggerated sense of herself. It was as if Timothy were not only watching her activities but living in her as a part of her self. The resulting egotism is evident in her boastful November 1819 letter to Ellen: "I as you well know am a queen." Elsewhere she calls herself "prince-like." Her father fostered her inflated sense of self. Seeing her one day in the garden, Timothy, she recalls, said, "*Incedit Regina.*"[11]

But this feeling of regality was not a constant in Fuller's life. Her letters and recollections reveal a pervasive sense of insecurity and concomitant psychic depression that inevitably dissipated her ego-inflating dreams. In the letter to Ellen where she says she is a queen, Margaret is uncertain about her writing ability, confessing that she cannot write "as easy as some persons who seem to have so much to say." This underlying sense of insecurity had deepened when Ellen sailed to Liverpool in November 1817. According to Fuller, Ellen's failure to stay and play the role of perfect parent that Margaret had scripted for her caused the child to fall "into a profound depression," the kind of soul-devastating sense of disappointment with the ideal object that psychologists say accompanies the collapse of such an ego-inflating, merged, idealized state.[12]

Even if she exaggerates, Fuller had reason to be depressed. Not only had Ellen failed to rescue her from her emotional wasteland, but also, in December, one month after Ellen had sailed to England, Timothy had departed for Washington. Fuller recalls how she withdrew into fantasy and became cold and uncommunicative. She avoided the dinner table, took long walks, and lay hours on the floor of her room, behavior Fuller will later see as being "out of the . . . natural course." Such "joy," she says, as there might have been in her father's Cambridgeport house, "seemed to have departed with [Ellen], and the emptiness of our house stood revealed."[13]

4 ∾ The World of Books

With Ellen gone, Margaret became more dependent than ever for affection on her father, who had made it a condition for his love that she excel intellectually. Intent on fulfilling his high expectations, she was soon doing just as he asked: reciting not just Latin but Greek twice a week for her uncle Elisha, the youngest and most genial of the Fuller brothers, who was then a student at Harvard Divinity School. At her father's insistence she was learning to play the piano and also taking singing lessons (which she hated), as well as attending classes at the "Cambridge Port Private Grammar School." The Port School, as it was commonly called, was the school of choice for parents who did not want to send their sons into the city to attend Boston Latin, the traditional school for preparing boys for Harvard. Unlike Boston Latin, the Port School admitted girls. It had a rigorous curriculum, and when Fuller attended it she became more proficient at translating and reciting passages from Virgil and Cicero, as well as at translating English texts into Latin. She also learned to write English compositions, one of which she enclosed in a letter to Timothy, noting that she had "made *almost* as many corrections [on it] as your critical self would were you at home."[1]

For Margaret knew that Timothy's "corrections" were inevitable. On the cold, windy Christmas Day of 1819 she hence defensively confessed in a letter to him that her translation of Goldsmith's *Deserted Village* into Latin "goes on slowly." As if to deflect his attention from the fact that she has "only translated a page and a half," she tells him about a book she is reading, Mrs. Ross's recently published *Hesitation; or, To Marry, or Not to Marry?* This "moral-novel," as Margaret refers to it, tells in 532 pages how the principal characters, both of whom are well educated and wary of marriage, eventually do marry. Margaret hopes Timothy will read this novel that mocks politicians and the political life while cautioning women not to rush into marriage, a "connexion, which death alone can dissolve." Eager to please, she includes in her letter character sketches of the heroine, Miss Argyle, who "has not such superhuman wit beauty and sense as to make her an improbable character," and of her reluctant lover, "Fitsroy earl of Montague," whom she describes as "a sensible well informed man posessing a superior genius and deeply versed in the human character but improbably delicate in his ideas of love."[2]

That a nine-year-old child would choose to read such a socially dense English novel focusing on the difficulty of marriage indicates an emotional maturity far beyond her years. Margaret's precocious intelligence is evident in the provocative analysis of the novel's major characters that she included in her letter with the hope it would entice her father into wanting to read the novel "to see," as she wrote him on 16 January, "if [the characters] were rightly delineated." She sent him her analysis even though she knew that her father thought most novels were "*trash*" and that through even immoderate "indulgence" in reading fiction, "*often*," he wrote her on 25 January, "we are betrayed into vice and crime."[3] Hence, even as Margaret attempts in this letter to impress her father with her insight into character, she is at the same time slyly defying his commands by opening herself, as he sees it, to a life of vice and crime, a notion he ironically may have implanted in Margaret's mind. Whatever the case, the nine-year-old Margaret cleverly jockeys to both please her father and defy him and thereby win his undivided attention.

Margaret read several literary works when she was about nine that had a powerful impact on her life. Her letters reveal that images and thematic patterns from

Hesitation, Sotheby's *Oberon,* and the *Aeneid*—the only one of the three Timothy approved of—left indelible imprints in her mind. The enduring impact of *Hesitation* on Fuller is evident both in the language she uses and in her views about human nature and male-female relationships. Some form of the word "possess"—a word Mrs. Ross seems obsessed with—now appears in Fuller's letters. Later, moreover, in Italy, Fuller will call her "connexion" (and she, too, will use the British spelling) with her young Italian lover, Giovanni Angelo Ossoli, "unfit," which is precisely the way Mrs. Ross describes what she sees to be a socially inappropriate or sexually "unnatural" relationship.[4]

Hesitation's Lord Montague, through whose eyes readers view the novel's action, equates (as did Timothy) society's moral laws with "the laws" of nature. "*Delicacy,*" a moral attribute Montague believes that spiritually superior females exhibit, is "founded on the basis of feelings and principles implanted by nature." These laws, he says, are necessary for both society's well-being and man's individual happiness, their "necessity" having been "occasioned by the departure from natural feelings in our first parents, who violated a natural principle, when they disobeyed the commands of their Creator." As Montague sees things, Adam and Eve swerved from the straight path of "natural morality" when they engaged in God forbidden "impure"—presumably sensual—relations. Thus it was Adam and Eve's "unnatural" sex that "brought 'death into the world,'" an idea that remained locked in Fuller's mind and helped determine the way in the future she would behave in relation to certain friends, both men and women, to whom she felt erotically drawn.[5]

As did the notion that it is difficult for a man and woman to form a lasting "connexion" in marriage. Only after careful consideration and a gradual revelation of their mutual feelings do Montague, who has vowed never to marry, and Isadora Argyle, whom Montague thinks "will engage only with hesitation," agree to marry. And then they do so only after Montague has rescued Isadora from drowning in a river and pursued her to Paris, where, through a series of letters, he convinces this "cold and haughty" woman of the sincerity of his love.[6]

The novel ends with Montague and Isadora in a state of transcendent marital bliss in which no sign of sensual desire has "sullied" the "purity" of their love or "shadowed it with the dross of this world," in the words of the narrator. Ideas like these from a turn-of-the-century English novel that advised women to stay sexually pure until marriage became a part of Fuller's rigid moral mindscape—deflecting, resisting, and twisting her later yearnings for sensual pleasure. As heir of Puritans, Fuller did not question these moral terms. After all, in Isadora Argyle she saw the kind of "modest," feminine woman with a superior mind Timothy admired.[7]

But Fuller as a child did not feel feminine. Even as she attempted to conceal her robust figure beneath a tightly laced corset and praised Miss Argyle's character in her letters to her father, her heart rebelled, just as she had defied her father in reading the novel in the first place. Indeed, in this disapproved novel, Margaret met the free-spirited Comtesse de Pologne, a woman who, in Montague's words, has the "power to disengage herself from the shackles of custom, without losing one attribute of modesty." She is "a sun," he says, "whose splendour irradiates the lesser planets that revolve around her." Emerson would later use similar language to describe Fuller's magnetic power over her "brilliant circle" of friends, noting how she "quite reduced them to satellites." Another of the Comtesse's characteristics that may have lingered in Fuller's mind is that—though the narrator gives her age as past forty—her spirited behavior made her appear "no unfit companion for the youngest and gayest." Indeed, "it seemed, as if youth, delighted with the Eden" she offered him.[8]

In the Comtesse de Pologne Fuller would have found a woman of independent mind and means who leads others with her wit and conversation and even forms relationships with younger men. She does this "without incurring the charge of eccentricity," "volatility," or "imprudence," the price Montague's friend, the bishop, says women pay for defying social conventions. Bold but controlled, the comtesse might well have served as Fuller's first role model, an intellectual woman whom she probably found more appealing than Isadora, who accepted "the fetters" custom places on women.[9]

Though enthralled with the novel, Margaret had the good sense to know that the way to win Timothy's praise, and maybe money, was not to read "frivolous" fiction but to do the homework he had assigned her. On 16 January 1820 she thus writes to ask if he will give her a dollar when she finishes translating *The Deserted Village*. She wants to give it to "a poor woman of the name of Wentworth in Boston." She has seen her "wandering in all the snow without food or shelter" and needs money to help this "*wretched*" woman survive the effects of the terrible snowstorm that had blanketed Boston that very morning. This image of a homeless woman forced to wander alone in the snow will find a reflection years later in bitter lines Fuller will write with her father in mind: "Father, they will not take me home, / To the poor child no heart is free; / In sleet and snow all night I roam; / Father,—was this decreed by thee? / I will not try another door, / To seek what I have never found; / Now, till the very last is o'er, / Upon the earth I'll wander round."[10]

The particular images and ideas Fuller's imaginative mind was absorbing at this time suggest she was developing into a singular human being with a will of her own. Unlike the typical middle-class girl of her time who learned the social graces so she could win a good-provider husband, Fuller was striving to become the feminine, intellectual woman her father wanted her to be. Yet she was also increasingly seeing herself in the role of a woman like the Comtesse de Pologne, whose keen mind and financial independence let her play a malelike part in society, leading conversations at her hotel at which she enchanted young admirers.

Another strong woman Fuller was attracted to was Dido from the *Aeneid*, the epic poem Fuller consumed over a four-month period prior to her tenth birthday.

"NO NATURAL CHILDHOOD"

Her earlier readings from the epic made translating it for her amiable Uncle Elisha easy. On 3 February 1820 she wrote her father that she has gotten "half through the fifth book of Virgil" and boasts: "In my last lesson I got the whole of the fourth book and Uncle Elisha said I got it extremely well." Indeed she did. For fifteen years later in a letter she quotes from memory the three lines from book 4 that follow Virgil's account of Dido's passion for Aeneas, a mad passion that led to an impulsive sexual union with him in a cave during a thunderstorm. Though conspired by the gods, this lust-driven coupling was for Dido, according to Virgil, "the cause first of death, and first / Of misfortunes." For even though Dido knows that the "marriage" is spurious, she no longer speaks of "secret love" but shamelessly, says Virgil, "calls herself wife. With this name, / she cloaks the fault."[11]

It was Dido's "fault," indeed. Or, so Virgil thought, as Fuller found out in reading the *Aeneid*. The lines in Latin Fuller years later quotes in a letter tell how, after Dido's fall, Fama, or Rumor (as the lines translate literally from Fuller's misremembered Latin), "gains strength by going. At first / small because of fear; Soon she lifts herself into the skies, / And establishes her head in the clouds." To add to the pain for Dido of Rumor pummeling her reputation, Aeneas abandons the passionate queen, who has thrown away her life for a man who justifies leaving her by saying: "I neither hoped to hide this flight / with stealth (Do not imagine this), / Nor did I ever hold out the bridal torches, / Or come into these agreements of marriage."[12]

In her 3 February letter to her father, Margaret did not mention Dido's passion, an illicit passion that "extinguished" the "honor and fame" by which "alone" Dido felt she "was approaching the stars" and that hence *was* "the cause first" of her suicide. Margaret, nonetheless, must have been acutely aware of Dido's "madness" at the time she wrote this February letter to her revered father, one she ends with her translation of the Lord's Prayer into Latin. By including this prayer, she may have been attempting not only to please her father but also to ask his forgiveness for her "sins," since the Latin words she actually wrote, "da veniam nobis nostra peccata," literally translated mean "Give us pardon with respect to our sins." Innocently, she added, "PS Correct it for me papa will you?" In his response, Timothy was merciless; he cites "several passages" to give her a sense of the "many . . . mistakes" she has made—mistakes "occasioned," no doubt, "by inattention"—then adds: "it would be ludicrous to correct this whole in a short letter." Timothy's harsh criticism of Margaret's imperfect yet still impressive translation echoes Virgil's damning of Dido for her careless behavior. For in his letter he says he hopes the severity of his criticism will not discourage her, even as he cruelly chastises her, asserting that her single worst "*fault*" is her "carelessness."[13]

৵ ৵ ৵

When she was only eight, Margaret had sent Timothy a letter with a blot of ink on it and the disclaimer, "it is not my fault." The fault lay with Eugene, who had "laid the point of a penknife . . . on it and in taking it up he made a blot." She would not have tattled on her brother, she says, "but I was afraid you would think me careless." Margaret had plenty of reason to fear that her father might think her careless; for it seemed no matter how hard she tried, in the eye of her father she kept making mistakes. Despite Margaret's efforts to earn her father's praise, Timothy still addressed his most ardent letters to his wife, noting, for instance, in his 10 February 1820 letter that he has spent half an hour gazing at her letter "like a miser at his treasures, or rather like a lover at his mistress."[14]

A none-too-subtle competition with her mother for Timothy's affection would intensify over time. This competition is evident in a December 1821 letter Margaret sent her mother from Boston, where she was attending school and living with her father's youngest sister, Martha, and her husband, Simeon Whittier. In it the eleven-year-old Margaret tells her mother what she thinks is wrong with her father's plan of making her mother his secretary in Washington: "I fancy you will be too engaged besides you do not write half so fast as he can, and are not sufficiently fond of letter writing; do tell my father that I expect some letters from him." The intense nature of her love is particularly evident in a letter she will write Timothy in December 1823. Then thirteen, she addresses her father as if he were her lover: "I hope you do not miss me the thousandth part as much as I do you. . . . I feel your absence more . . . every day."[15]

A precocious yet conflicted sexuality is expressed in Fuller's childhood letters. She makes jealous demands on an absent father who has stirred in her intense feelings yet who continues to write long letters to his wife, a woman who embodies the female "*beauty* & *shape*" he finds "always pleasing" and who is continually bearing his children. In addition to Eugene and William Henry, by the time Margaret turns thirteen there will be Ellen (b. 1820 and named in honor of Ellen Kilshaw) and Arthur (b. 1822). Arthur, who will later graduate from Harvard Divinity School and serve as a chaplain in the Civil War, considered his mother "one of the fairest ornaments of existence."[16]

At age ten, Margaret was five foot two inches tall and looked thirteen. Even then she tended toward robustness, and she had honey-brown hair, sharp features, and small, blue-gray nearsighted eyes through which she often squinted since eyeglasses were not yet commonly used.[17] Such an awkward child with a tall, lean, lovely mother would have had trouble looking in a mirror and liking what she saw there—unless, of course, the mother could have accepted and loved the child for the person she was, something Margaret's mother apparently could not do.

Driven by loneliness, Fuller found a haven in that ugly house she hated. It was by a closet in the second floor back room that was, presumably, her "father's room." Full of books, this closet seemed an oratory full of sacred texts that provided the child with the fantastic scripts upon which she patterned her life. But it also held books that conveyed social customs and mores that confined women to a life in the home and that carried the force of law. By the closet at a back window that looked out over distant fields, Fuller liked to sit, read, and dream. And in her dreams she was free of society's fetters. Hidden in the back room by the closet, she attained a kind of regal calm. Thus the studies once exacted of her by her father became linked in her mind—as her father feared they would—with pleasure; reading became for her "a habit and a passion."[18]

One of the writers Fuller had loved early on was Ovid. In his poetry she found a path out of her lonely life and had taken it. Ovid's *Metamorphoses* provided her with a pagan counterpart of the Bible. Like the Bible it begins with stories of creation and flood, but then proceeds to luxurious tales of erotic seduction, of betrayal and metamorphosis. Many of these involve man's alienation from nature, but the focus in Ovid is on regeneration within the cycle of nature's seasons, not on spiritual redemption. In reading Ovid, the child imaginatively removed herself from her harsh Puritan past and "the mailed clang of Roman speech" in order to enter a wondrous fairyland consisting of "shifting shows of nature, [of] Gods and Nymphs born of the sunbeam, the wave, the shadows on the hill." Later Fuller will observe that men suckled by the Roman wolf gain a different complexion from those fed on Greek honey. Curled in a chair by her father's book closet—with Timothy safely away in Washington—Margaret got a taste of the honey she now hungered for. She "lived in those Greek forms," just as she felt she had "*lived*" in her relationship with Ellen, "the true faith of a refined and intense childhood."[19]

In her fantasies Fuller found a happiness not available in the real world of rules, regulations, and hard work she faced daily in the Fuller household. In her autobiographical romance she recalls one cold Sunday afternoon that her father was home and entertaining company in the parlor. Timothy had told her she could read a book, as long as it was neither a novel or play. But Margaret, who had discovered Shakespeare, felt so warm a glow on that dark wintry day in reading *Romeo and Juliet* that she disobeyed him when he told her to put the book up and get another. She instead only pretended to get another. Playing the part of dutiful daughter, she returned to her seat by the parlor fire and kept on reading. Noticing her niece's willful disobedience, one of her aunts (probably Elizabeth, whom Margaret thought tattled on family members to Timothy) who was sitting with them in the parlor noticed that Margaret was still reading *Romeo and Juliet*. "What is that child about," she inquired, "that she don't hear a word that's said to her?" Timothy angrily ordered her directly to bed, where her "fancies," recalls Fuller, "swarmed like bees." For into her room "no care of his anger followed me": "Alone, in the dark, I thought only of the scene placed by the poet before my eye, where the free flow of life . . . seen in the broad lustre of [Shakespeare's] imagination, gave just what I wanted, and brought home the life I seemed born to live."[20]

The child needed no playwright's script to keep the drama alive in her mind. She took pleasure in the sense of power she gained as her mind created and commanded imaginary beings who lived in a world "just" as *she* "wanted," one not run by a father's rules. In her imagination Margaret became the hero or heroine she read about, whether it was a Don Quixote, a Hamlet, or an abandoned orphan discovered to be a European princess in disguise. Margaret especially liked Hamlet, who, like herself, had been forced to assume the burden of a father's existence, a burden that denied his own. The child frequently identified more with male characters than female. Men's lives, after all, were more exciting than women's, not to mention the fact that when boys grew up they had more power than did girls. Fed on "meat instead of milk," Fuller thus increasingly came to see herself as "princelike," a youth who would "bend only to 'the king, my father.'"[21]

She saw herself as princelike when reading in March 1820 the third book that had a profound effect on her as a child: William Sotheby's translation of the German Wieland's *Oberon,* which she had taken from her father's book closet without asking his permission. For while reading this 1798 English version of a tale about sexual transgression, forgiveness, and redemption, Fuller identified more with the Christian knight Huon than she did with his lover, the pagan princess Rezia. Carried away on a tide of their mutual passion, Huon and Rezia defy the decree of the fairy king Oberon, who has ordered them not to give in to their sexual passion prior to their church-sanctioned marriage. As soon as she finished reading this tale, the nine-year-old Margaret wrote her father that she had "never read any thing that delighted me so much as that book." "My father," she pleaded, "When I get the card that has *Best* upon it at school may I read it again?"[22]

His letters to Margarett Crane before their marriage reveal that Timothy had likely read *Oberon.* Given the novel's many lascivious scenes of erotic love and sexual seduction, and the obviously powerful impact of the book on his daughter's impressionable mind, it is surprising that Timothy granted her permission to reread *Oberon.* According to a letter he wrote his wife in March 1820, his reluctance to allow Margaret the book was primarily his fear that "she is only in pursuit of the story without regarding the poetry—the stile & imagery." Indeed. For this story of forbidden lust and premarital sex, a tale so compelling that an austere young John Quincy Adams would gain pleasure in translating it in 1800, must have seemed titillating to such a love-starved child.[23]

Certainly the plot would have intrigued her. For this fairy tale involving heroic feats follows the parallel stories of two father figures—the French emperor Charlemagne and the fairy king Oberon—and how they teach a wayward pilgrim to obey their stern commands. In penance to Charlemagne, whose son he has killed in a duel, Huon—a Christian knight whose faith was strong but "knowledge weak"—sets out on a journey that takes him from Paris to Babylon.[24] There he is to complete tasks assigned him by Charlemagne. He must kill whoever sits to the left of Babylon's caliph, seize four of the latter's teeth, grab a handful of hair from his beard, and then demand the caliph's daughter's (Rezia's) hand in marriage. Huon accomplishes these feats with the help of the forest fairy, Oberon, a magical and powerful father figure who keeps a watchful eye on him and cautions him not to indulge in illicit sex. No model of perfect behavior, Oberon is at the time of the story feuding with his fairy queen wife, Titania, from whom he has vowed to stay separated until a young couple is willing to accept death rather than be untrue to each other.

Seated at her window, a nearsighted Margaret lost herself in the pages of this tale about Huon, whose pilgrim virtue is perfect until in a dream at his journey's beginning he sees the beautiful Rézia and thereafter is compelled to find her. Contrary to Timothy's fears, Margaret absorbed not just the story but also *Oberon's* "imagery." For the imagery is all too clear: The lovely maid quickens Huon's erotic pulse and generates in him a soul-consuming sense of love's "sweet control." Huon, "'mid floods of joy," seeks relief from his anguish by touching his dream maid's "ivory breast." His pleasure, however, turns to despair when the maid's "angel form" is torn from him by "the destin'd storm" and "hurl'd" out "amid the howling waves!"[25] This is indeed astonishing reading for a nine-year-old.

In the tale, Huon tries to save his dream maid from drowning in the cold waves, only to find—as happens in dreams—that he is unable to act to save her. Huon watches helplessly as this ideal feminine figure bobs in the waves and, in "life's last struggle" (says Sotheby), prays. Fuller, who later recorded a dream containing similar images of her own death by drowning in the "cold wave," internalized this disturbing scene as well as a discussion between Huon and his late father's squire about the power of dreams to prophesy the future. The squire contends that dreams are "forgeries . . . of the brain!" He tells Huon about a dream in which a phantom lolled out a long tongue and pointed at him a cold skinny finger of a wrinkled hand (another image that would appear in one of Fuller's dreams), then felt his ribs. Such dreams are products of a "heated brain," says the squire Sherasmin; they have no power as prophecy: "A dream is but a dream."[26]

Many images that appeared in Fuller's dreams—both in her childhood and later life—were products of her own "over-excited mind" reacting to the potent images in the adult-level books she was reading, such as the *Aeneid* and *Oberon*. She had "never read any thing," she said, that made her so happy as this tale about the Christian knight Huon, who kept his pledge to Charlemagne by decapitating the knight seated next to the Babylonian emperor, although the image of the dead heathen's head as it flies off "and o'er the caliph" and "spirts . . . boiling blood" on the banquet table apparently made quite an impression on her; for, such cut-off heads would inhabit her dreams. The child no doubt nonetheless thrilled when Huon first kissed Rezia, the caliph's daughter, as well as made the caliph's men spin in "giddy" waves by blowing an ivory horn given him by Oberon to summon the fairy king to help him.[27]

Vital images like these from *Oberon* became a permanent part of Fuller's mental landscape, as did Oberon's cautionary command to Huon to "grave it [deep] in [his] brain!" to remain chaste in his relationship with Rezia as brother is to sister until a priest in Rome can bless their union. "Taste not," says he, "the fruit forbidden" of sexual pleasure before that time, or, "in vengeance of the crime," he will abandon them "on life's wide desert, lost, alone!"[28] The fatherly Oberon's expectation of sexual purity prior to marriage would have seemed right at that time to the child, since it accorded with the ethic of her Puritan upbringing.

But in *Oberon* the lovers do not stay chaste until marriage. Aboard the boat to Rome, Rezia, now baptized Amanda and "rob'd in light," appears by Huon's bed and tempts the Christian knight, who impulsively pulls her to him. His touch stirs in her "strange anguish." "Impetuous passion," in him, "streams thro' every throbbing vein." Though his passion flows freely here, according to Wieland, Huon is not free. Conscious of his sinful state, the Christian knight struggles with his desire. "He ... / Tears from her touch—her kiss, her throbbing breast, / Would fly—remains—returns, all fear at rest," then rushes "on death" in the "enfolding arms" of Amanda, who gives "like a stream of fire." She "yields"; he "defies the god—his arms the maid enchain" as Huon's "glowing lip, embath'd in bliss, / Sucks nectar-dew in each inebriate kiss." The text then depicts in graphic detail how the knight's "mouth the never-sated draught renews, / And from her lip in sweet voluptuous dews," Huon "drinks deep" and dreams "foreboded woes!" Desire mounts with each hungry kiss, and Eros, in Sotheby's words, "ere Hymen crowns, their secret union views!"[29]

This uncensored depiction of sensual love would have been exciting to a nine-year-old girl even if it was not entirely understandable. She would understand that the lovers must pay for defying the decree of "stern Oberon." For their "sole offence," they are "lost for evermore!"[30] Enraged, Oberon conjures a storm at sea and threatens to wreck their ship unless Huon agrees to sacrifice his life. Huon and Amanda jump together into the sea.

Miraculously, in this cautionary fairy tale the errant lovers do not die. Instead, the raging sea calms, and the couple floats to an island. They are saved by the inherent virtue in a magic ring that Huon had earlier taken from a giant and given to Rezia as a pledge of connubial love, a "ring of gold" eventually proven to be the one Titania once gave Oberon. After months of penitence and a meager existence on the island, Amanda, who is pregnant out of wedlock, gives birth to a boy, and Huon learns humility. As adults they accept responsibility for their rash act. They triumph by gaining, as the Christian Wieland sees it, self-control.[31]

Weiland's tale does not end there. For the lovers are still not officially married, though they view their union as sacred and honor it when they are soon faced with temptation. Amanda, kidnapped by pirates, is forced to leave her three-year-old boy (Huonet) on the island, where (unbeknownst to Amanda) Oberon's queen cares for him. Saved and mysteriously spirited by Titania to the court of the

King of Tunis, Amanda, who has been followed by Huon, rejects the king's sexual advances, just as Huon, disguised as a gardener, similarly resists those of Tunis's queen. Amanda, her face hidden behind a silvery veil symbolizing her purity, tells the king that she is the gardener's "wife," despite the fact that her union with Huon has not yet been sanctioned by the church. "Indissoluble bands," she tells the king, of a kind "Not form'd on earth" do "bind me forever to this much-lov'd youth." She says she is caught in a "web" woven by "heavenly hands" and will die before she will desert her "husband" Huon. As a reward for their fidelity, Huon and Amanda regain the respect of the powerful father figure Oberon, who, now reconciled with Titania, transports the faithful lovers to France. Once "home return'd," Huon is recognized by Charlemagne as a hero, and Amanda, the silvery veil falling from her face, looks like an angel when she is linked to Huon in "holy"—that is, church-sanctioned—matrimony.[32]

In the autobiographical romance she wrote at age thirty, Fuller says that reading such stories raised in her expectations and desires "after which I must long toil before they can be realized." In the case of *Oberon*, this was so; for so powerful was the impact on Fuller's impressionable mind of this story about a love transcending conventional vows that central images and themes from it stayed alive in her mind until her death. Thus images and themes from *Oberon* were to influence the choices she made and thereby play a part in determining the person she later became. She never forgot the hypocritical monks and nuns whom Oberon, by blowing his horn, made dance in dervishlike whirls as punishment for their sensual sins. A similar image of wild dancing would appear in Fuller's 1843 depiction of her life as a child at a boarding school when her fictional self, Mariana, like "the spinning dervishes of the East," spun "until all around her were giddy." Nor did Fuller forget the passionate love of Huon and Rezia, a love so great they consummated it before they received a priest's blessing in Rome.[33]

This favorite story read in her childhood remained present in the depths of Fuller's mind and may indeed have influenced her later seeming impulsive act in Europe when, rather than traveling from Florence to Germany with her Quaker friends, the Springs, she took the path that twisted back to Rome, to illicit sex and forbidden passion. It may also have influenced her decision when she is pregnant out of wedlock not to marry until she is sure of her lover's loyalty and has learned humility during a period of isolation and (so to speak) penitence spent in a small town outside of Rome.

Fuller's childhood letters reflect the glow of her imaginary world in which she lived at times as the unconventional Comtesse, at other times as the impulsive Huon. Three months before she read *Oberon*, Margaret had tried to assure her father that, despite her love of "trifling" novels, she has been "a very good girl." Still, her unabated eagerness to read such popular works as *Oberon* and *Hesitation* upset Timothy. Away in Washington, he felt he was losing control of her. In his chilly 25 January 1820 letter in which he warns that such pleasurable reading often leads to "vice & crime," a stern Timothy commands her to "acquire a taste for books of higher order, than tales & novels." Graved deep in the child's brain were the harsh words of her father as they linked with those of the "stern Oberon," who forbade any expression of sexual pleasure outside marriage. At the same time, vivid images of illicit passion from books like the *Aeneid* and *Oberon* stayed alive in her and would later fuel a need to satiate an "unnaturally stimulated" childhood sex drive.[34]

PART TWO

The Transition Years

In her autobiographical romance Fuller says that the "peculiarity" of her early education deprived her of her childhood. Though seldom allowed to play with the neighborhood children in the marshland surrounding her house, she occasionally joined them in their games, but even then, she recollects, she preferred "violent bodily exercise" to their less-demanding play. The girls "did not hate me," Fuller recalls, "but neither did they . . . wish me to have them with me." She tells how her father decided "I needed change of scene." He blamed himself for keeping her at home because in teaching her he gained, Margaret recollects he said, "such pleasure." Thus began Margaret's more formal schooling away from home: first at a school in downtown Boston and then at a finishing school in Groton. No sooner, however, had Timothy learned that in either case the school had not successfully, as he had hoped, "feminized" his daughter, than he called her home.[1]

Upon returning from school in Groton, Margaret in these transition years between adolescence and adulthood pursued a self-imposed plan of study of languages and literature, a fact that pleased Timothy, who nonetheless continued to insist that his daughter excel not only in her studies, a pursuit then seen by society as masculine, but also in her feminine deportment. But what mattered most to Margaret was always the life of the mind. Her studies suddenly came alive for her when in the summer of 1826 she found herself living in close proximity to the brilliant young men studying at Harvard and bringing home from their European travels the radical ideas of the German Romantics, for Timothy that summer moved his family from the Cambridgeport house to a mansion that had been built by the late Chief Justice Francis Dana. Perched atop a hill (called Dana Hill), it was located about a quarter mile from the college. During this period of relative prosperity for Timothy Fuller, his daughter—with the help of her Cambridge friends—metamorphosed from an odd aggressive girl lacking social skills into a brilliant young woman, a captivating and powerful presence. As ever full of contradictions, Timothy unrelentingly demanded that his daughter excel in her studies—

not so she could attend Harvard (where in the pattern of his father he intended to send his sons), but so she could help him homeschool her younger siblings, in particular her brothers.

This demand broadened the breach between father and daughter that opened after Timothy moved his family yet again, this time from the heart of Cambridge's scintillating society to a farm in Groton in 1833. The bitterness that hung in the air between Margaret and her father—especially after the latter insisted that for added income she tutor not only her little brothers and sister but also three neighborhood children—was to leave Margaret, upon her father's abrupt death in October 1835, burdened with intense unresolved feelings of guilt and rage in relation to this difficult man whose contradictory demands had turned her into an intellectually gifted but emotionally conflicted woman, as we shall see in this part of the text titled "The Transition Years."[2]

5 ✑ Boston Schooling

On the subject of the effect on her of the early education forced on her by her father, Fuller notes in her autobiographical romance how her too-intense focus on books as a child had "given a cold aloofness" to her outward expression while the intensity of her inward life, as was evident in the "profound depression" she experienced when Ellen Kilshaw sailed home to England, "was out of the gradual and natural course." Like the violent games Fuller played with neighborhood children, the letters she wrote her father when she was ten reveal her unusually intense feelings, in this case for her father, whose speeches before Congress made him seem to his daughter like a god and who was at last beginning to notice her antisocial nature. In late November 1820 she wrote him how, though he has not asked her to write him, she thinks he "would like to have me do it." She hopes, however, he "will not criticise" her "writing very severely." Mimicking Timothy's stiffly arrogant tone, she asks him to send her his speeches to read since speeches by anyone else (excepting the famous orator John Randolph) she reads only "to laugh at." Defensively she adds, "notwithstanding the very mean opinion you have of my understanding, I should value one of my dear fathers [sic] speeches more than a thousand lighter works," more than the novels he tells her she is "foolish" for reading and is even "angry" at her "for being so." "I know well," she tells her father, "you think me, light, frivolous, and foolish," "but—I am yet capable of affection to one to whom I stand so highly indebted as to you."[1]

In this same defensively presumptuous tone, Margaret in January 1821 wrote her father that she expects him to bring her home from Washington "a complete case of jewels," or at least "a gold ring plain or twisted." Perhaps she had in mind a gold ring like that Huon had given Rezia as a pledge of their connubial love. She is "sorry" he writes her "so seldom" and fears his "affection" for her has "decreased."

She acknowledges she has often "pained" him, though she says it remains her hope that "you still love me," then adds that she "should be most happy" to study with Dr. Park in Boston: "I will endeavor to gratify all your wishes." Two weeks later she writes to assure him that she is keeping up with her studies and will soon be taught at home by a divinity school student whom the family has asked to come twice weekly to hear her recite "in Caesars Commentaries and the Greek Grammar." In late January, she observes that although she has received only one letter from him that winter, she is nonetheless counting the days until he returns. She needs his affection more than ever in the absence of Miss Kilshaw, whose letters she fears have been lost at sea on a boat that "must be either wrecked or blown southward."[2]

Concerned that his daughter was not growing into a well-mannered lady who preferred high-minded literature and writes tidy letters, Timothy had reluctantly come to the conclusion that going to a school with girls her age would improve her "manner and disposition." So he had enrolled Margaret in Dr. Park's Lyceum for Young Ladies in Boston, which she attended from April 1821 until December 1822. At first she had lived at home and walked three miles to and from school every day. But in the winter of 1821–22 when both her parents were in Washington, she boarded with her Aunt Martha Whittier. There, the trundle bed Margaret slept in was only two-thirds her length. Her aunt failed to keep a fire burning in the evenings in the room where Margaret studied, so at night Margaret sat in the parlor, where her rowdy female cousins played cards and ignored their studies, a domestic situation that distressed Margaret's mother. It also upset her that Timothy's sister was constantly reading "trash[y]" novels. In the same period, Margaret's vision was worsening, but she still had no glasses. And near the end of the winter term she had to share her cold room with her terminally ill grandmother, Sarah Williams Fuller, who would die in April 1822, shortly after Margaret returned for spring term. Her grandmother's funeral upset her so much that she had to be removed from it when she almost fainted.[3]

In Boston it became increasingly hard for Margaret to know how to gratify her father, since in his letters he never offered her a word of praise or kindness. The harder she studied, the more Timothy stepped up his demand that she "improve in *ease & grace*," while expecting her to excel academically, which she did with aplomb. The first word Elizabeth Peabody in Boston heard of Margaret Fuller was of this "wonderful child at Dr. Park's school, talking pure mathematics with her father, at 12 years," though it seemed to those who knew her that she "had no religion."[4]

By December 1821 Margaret through hard work was at the head of her class, having avoided, she wrote her mother in Washington, even "one mistake" in composition. Two days before Christmas she noted to her mother that she is "happy" at school and hopes her father will let her stay. She loves "the Dr" and is having fun at the cotillion parties held at Dana Parks's dancing school she is attending. At one ball she attended with her Aunt Martha and Uncle Simeon and their daughters she had danced thirteen times, though twelve of her partners, the eleven-year-old confesses, "were grown up gentlemen." "One good partner," she boasts, "was one of the scholars." Trained to recite for her father, she felt more at ease talking with the grown-up scholar than she did with the boys her age. Aware, nonetheless, that she is writing her mother, Margaret echoes in her letter her mother's censorious attitude toward "the ladies." She reports on the indecent dress of some of the women who "could not be content without shewing their bosoms and shoulders completely, there was one lady with her sash brought up so as to come over a part of her bosom and nothing more." Though her Uncle Simeon had laughed out loud and said how "he hoped she would dance her gown completely off," Margaret assures her mother that she herself was most "ashamed for her," especially since she was "in the decline of life and her neck none of the whitest."[5]

In this letter Margaret tells how the school's four oldest scholars had shed an "abundance of tears" at their December term-end party, and how the girls had then taken to throwing their arms about one another and "kissing us all around [as] they went." Margaret feels that "we are all sisters," but the girls apparently did not feel the same. According to the sisters of Henry Hedge (later Fuller's friend), who were also at Dr. Park's school with her, Fuller had intimidated her classmates with her formidable wit and intelligence. Hedge reports that at about this time she was "so precocious in her mental and physical developments, that she passed for eighteen or twenty." All these traits—Margaret's physical maturity, squinting, awkward manners, extravagant tendencies of thought, and pedantic talking style made her a butt to be made fun of by her classmates.[6]

Disturbed by reports he received in Washington regarding his daughter's continuing "deficiencies" in "female *propriety*, & disposition," Timothy wrote her an emphatic reproach on 22 January 1822: "Nothing Nothing can be nearer my heart than to see you fast improving in your manner & disposition—in your habits of neatness & regularity, no less than in your acquirements of literature." No sooner, however, had the eleven-year-old Margaret improved in etiquette than Timothy wrote to note coolly that the letter he had demanded she write him *in French* was "several weeks" overdue. He would be "very unhappy," he informs her, should he find her lagging in her lessons. At least on this point he thinks she will not "disappoint" him, as she constantly has, he implies, in female propriety. He then insists she practice piano "one or two hours every day" and "take care to keep" her "person & dress neat & *spotless*—since without these [attributes] no lady can be respectable or even tolerable."[7]

However, apparently Margaret failed to improve her appearance. For while Mrs. Fuller worried that her daughter was growing too thin in Boston, Hedge recalls that at age twelve she was in fact "very corpulent, and greatly disgusted at it, and began to lace [herself] very tightly." Once when she was a guest at the

Hedges' house, young Henry's mother was forced to call a stout Irishwoman from the kitchen to help Margaret refasten her dress, which had come undone in the back, as it had been laced too tightly. Hedge recollects that his sisters and other school friends giggled "criticisms not inaudible, nor meant to be inaudible to their subject."[8]

When Timothy learned of his daughter's continuing eccentricities, he withdrew her from Dr. Park's school. In December 1822 an unhappy Margaret headed home. There she progressed slowly in her studies and not at all in social poise, though she worked to make herself pretty. She attended Latin classes at the Port School, where her brother Eugene was enrolled, though she more or less studied it on her own, as she did French, and Greek. And she went to parties for which she spent hours dressing. In preparation for one party, Margaret apparently kept her abundant light-brown hair, which she usually piled atop her head in a crown of heavy braids, tied up all morning "in unsightly curl-papers" in an attempt to have fluffy curls like those of her pretty neighbor, Harriet Fay, daughter of Timothy's colleague Judge Samuel Fay. The result of such attempts, according to Higginson, was often ludicrous.[9]

Yet Margaret let nothing deter her in her attempt to impress her father, a need to please that had by now become, in Capper's apt words, "almost an obsession." On 15 January 1823 Fuller gave a party to which she invited ninety people, though by 12 January only nine had replied. Margaret's aim in inviting so many people to her party seems to have been to mingle her Boston friends with Cambridge friends like Harriet Fay. However, her lack of tact, as well as a tendency toward sarcasm that was becoming an annoying trait, offended her guests. Her piercing eyes and fast talk frightened her shy young guests, who stayed away from her.[10]

Margaret worked hard to improve her piano playing and to be popular like Harriet Fay, if that would satisfy Timothy. She was so intent on pleasing him that in describing her party to him she misrepresented it to him as "exceedingly agreeable," and in other letters to him she brags of her success at the cotillion parties she has attended. In a letter she lists the boys she has danced with as well as the girls who have accompanied her on "the flute and flageolet" while on the piano she has played "Mary list awake" and "Oh this is the spot." Responding no doubt to the report of his sister Elizabeth, who often stayed with the family when he was in Washington and kept a watchful eye on the children, Timothy was still in his absence always ready with censure, even scolding her in a letter for her "defective" way of "holding [her] hands & fingers" when she played, criticism she nevertheless expected. For in December 1821 she had written her mother that her Uncle Abraham had said he would "as lieve [sic] see Mr Whittiers children take a cane and ride around the room as hear me play on the piano." Still, at parties, Margaret bore forward, determined to win Timothy's approbation.[11]

Toward that aim, in a January 1823 letter she tells how she had gone with her

---

Aunts Sarah ("Sally") and Martha to attend a reception honoring one of Timothy's newly married cousins. It was cold, so Margaret had made a point of dressing warmly. Her aunts had derided her choice of outer apparel, saying they would be forever "disgraced" by having to appear with their niece "in so improper a habit, as a merino mantle, dark blue cloth coat, and chinchilli cap." Before they left the house on that bitter cold January day, her Aunt Sarah had pinned four shawls about her shoulders. Aunt Martha "tossed a veil upon her head, and put a white shawl on over a thin black silk gown, and away we went," reports Margaret in a letter, who "could not help smiling" when she saw that at the reception not a woman was without her bonnet and coat, and that "even the waiting maid perceived that I was the only one that was properly drest."[12]

But all Margaret's efforts to convince her father that she has been gaining in social grace failed. Whether through letters from her Fuller aunts and uncles—the criticism coming now from her Aunt Sally, who, like Elizabeth, visited for months at a time when their brother was out of town, and Margaret's ill-tempered Uncle Abraham—or from Mr. Fay, their neighbor, word again got to Timothy in Washington that his daughter's manners were still outré. Rather than practicing needlepoint, Margaret was perfecting her Greek, a fact that began to trouble Timothy, who knew that Greek mastery was of no use whatsoever to a homely young lady who would need a husband.

Margaret's Fuller aunts and uncles, who, according to Margarett Crane, had started questioning their niece's "*habits* & education . . . freely, & frequently," thus advised their brother to send his odd eldest child to a finishing school where she might yet be made into a lady. Timothy was now determined to correct his daughter's "faults," as he frequently notes in letters to Margaret. In letters in December 1823 and the spring of 1824, Timothy informs her that he has decided to send her to a Groton academy run by "a judicious country lady." He tells her in his December letter that he thinks she is badly "in need of some of the instruction & feminine discipline which Miss P. is said to excel in." Acknowledging that Margaret "might be discouraged" were he "to name some of [her] deficiencies," which he has already "so often mentioned" in his letters, Timothy nonetheless persists in criticizing her. He reminds her of her unladylike manners, of the "intolerable" quality of her penmanship, of her flawed complexion, and of her numerous "defects" in dress and hygiene. On 3 April Timothy writes his "dear" daughter that her parents' "*pride* and *satisfaction*" depend upon her "acquiring a discreet, modest, unassuming deportment," which he sees as "indispensable to endear any one, especially a young lady to her friends, & to obtain 'the world's good word.'" He closes with an offer of conditional love: "Depend upon my undiminished affection, as long as you continue dutiful."[13]

Indeed, the "slovenliness" of her writing seems to Timothy to be, as he had written her earlier, emblematic of her total "carelessness," the "fountain" of all her "faults." Timothy was constantly signaling to Margaret that what he wanted foremost from her was intellectual precision, a quality in her culture deemed masculine. William C. Todd later recorded his impression of the father's interaction with his daughter, who was, he thought, about fourteen when he visited the Fullers in their Cambridgeport home. Margaret, he recalls, "sat apart . . . with a book open on her knee. At some moment, Mr. Fuller said[,] 'Margaret what have you to say about this?'" Margaret "lifted her eyes for a moment and gave him an answer, good, full of common sense, but such as many people might have given. 'Is that the best that you can say?' returned her father." The child "started," recollects Todd, "laid down her book, and instantly recast her thought, giving the same idea but a most eloquent statement!" Thus Timothy Fuller insisted his daughter be, in his words, "as near perfection as possible."[14]

The daughter did her best to comply with her father's contradictory demands: that she be docile and feminine and have good penmanship but also exhibit in writing and speaking a masculine sense of precision and self-control. Only rarely did she defy him, as she did in January 1824 when she asserted her wish to attend the school run by Boston's leading progressive schoolmaster, George B. Emerson, rather than go to Groton. After all, she coyly argues like a mistress to a prospective lover, were she to be boarded in Groton, "I must be compelled to give up seeing you at all."[15]

Having asserted her wish to go "to Mr. Emerson's on every account," Margaret nevertheless quickly promised her father that "I will do all that is in my power to manifest my gratitude for the indulgence and kindness you have ever shown in endeavoring to gratify even my slightest wishes." For, "there never was so kind and affectionate a father as you and I am most profoundly and ardently sensible of it." Though her own "wishes[,] feelings and judgement," she insists in a letter the next month, "are decidedly on Mr Emerson's," Fuller will nonetheless comply with her father's desire. Margaret pledges to do as her father dictates, "as it is the first and dearest wish of my heart to conform *to your* wishes in every thing."[16]

Shaping herself to conform to her father's wishes meant she became yet more eccentric, theatrically acting the part of a "queen" fit to marry a king, as she saw her father. Clothed in the images of heroes and heroines drawn from books and from her imaginings of others' expectations for her behavior, Fuller spoke and acted in others' words and terms. As a result, she lacked, as Emerson later said, self-possession; or, as Gamaliel Bradford, a Boston biographer (b. 1863), put it: "Margaret had so many selves you could peel her like an onion."[17]

6 ∞ Boarding School at Groton

In May 1824 Margaret traveled by stagecoach with her high-spirited, sociable Uncle Elisha thirty-five miles northwest of Boston to Massachusetts apple country and Miss Susan Prescott's Young Ladies Seminary in Groton run by Susan Prescott, the twenty-seven-year-old eldest daughter of Judge James Prescott. There, Fuller's egotistical need to play center stage was initially tolerated by her mostly Unitarian, upper-middle-class schoolmates, who saw her as a prodigy. In the evening she entertained them by declaiming verses or acting out parts with seeming mystical power that made her "hearer" convulse "with laughter, sometimes to melt [her] to tears."[1]

At least that is how Fuller recalls her Groton experiences in an 1843 story titled "Mariana" in *Summer on the Lakes* about a gifted child named Mariana (a fictional alter ego for Fuller) who had been sent to a girls' school whose narrow social routines and rigid rules frustrated her "non-conformist" ways. As Fuller tells it, Mariana at first enchanted her companions with her exotic theatrics and odd costumes. Having found "a vent" for her "too early stimulated nature" in the school's theatricals, Mariana "ruled, like a queen." But when unresolved childhood conflicts spoke through Mariana/Margaret in fits of sleepwalking and dervishlike dancing—like that she had read about in *Oberon*—her classmates shunned her.[2]

The students found a way to mock one of Mariana's "singular habits": putting carmine blush on her cheeks even on days when there were no plays. "This irritated the girls," observes Fuller, "as all eccentricity does the world in general, more than vice or malignity." Put off by their classmate's bizarre looks and behavior, the girls banded together and all appeared one night at dinner "deeply rouged, with a bright glaring spot, perfectly round, in either cheek . . . a suppressed smile distorting every countenance." Even the teachers enjoyed the joke. As did the servants, whose failure to arrest their laughter humiliated and angered Mariana.[3]

After that, according to Fuller, Mariana became a "genius of discord amongst" the girls, sewing seeds of envy, jealousy, and dissension among them, until at last they reported her "calumny and falsehood" to the principal. In this fantasy retrospective of her Groton experience, Fuller tells how the principal asked Mariana to account for her behavior, whereupon she threw herself on the iron hearth so she deliberately hit her head. By hurting herself, Mariana/Margaret meant to make the girls regret their cruelty. Instead, says Fuller, it was this painful experience that made her aware of how stained and sad her soul was. The thirty-three-year-old Fuller tells that she would have died in this "sin-defiled" state had there not been a teacher (based on Susan Prescott) who rescued Mariana/Margaret by offering her a mother's comforting love. Summoned home not long after that, Mariana, says Fuller about her repentant alter ego, felt less like a queen than she did a "returning prodigal."[4]

Though the story is surely largely fictional, in it Fuller highlights themes that were important to her as a child and that replay through her life: her early passion for theatrics, her self-conscious sense of her eccentricity, and her lust for power over others. A significant new theme appears in her self-inflicted suffering to win pity and attention while she also further develops her conflicted fantasy of herself as both queen and returning prodigal. There is, moreover, for Fuller, the unforgettable memory of being laughed at as a teenager, and needing a mother's love. Five years after her return from Groton, Fuller confessed in a letter to Prescott that her memory of that humiliating evening at school "subdues every proud, passionate impulse." Yet Prescott's "image" still "shines as fair to [her] mind's eye"—even now she is twenty—"as it did in 1825, when I left you with my heart overflowing with gratitude for your singular and judicious tenderness."[5]

As a fifteen-year-old at Groton, Fuller had poured onto Susan Prescott, a nurturing woman in a position of malelike authority, the same exaggerated affection she had felt for Ellen Kilshaw. She said in a letter to her father she sent shortly after she arrived in Groton that she "really" loved and admired Miss Prescott. That September she even wrote her Uncle Abraham, her father's younger brother, that in life she was sure of two things: "that my father has not written to me for a week, and that I adore Miss Prescott," who is "gold without alloy."[6]

When Prescott fell ill, Margaret made much of her sickness to Timothy, declaring how she would like "to be her sister," since then she "should have an undeniable right to attend on her." Still, she asks Timothy, "are not the privileges of a daughter superior to those of a sister?" This question will recur in Fuller's life, taking on ever deeper meaning, though here Fuller's meaning is still ambiguous. Is she asking Timothy whether the privilege of being a daughter to him (the authoritative father) and Margarett Crane (the feminine mother) shouldn't be superior to the delight that would come from winning an exclusive right to care for Miss Prescott as a "sister"? Or is she wondering about what it would be like to be Miss Prescott's daughter, the female child of a nurturing yet authoritative woman, a stand-in for Timothy as teacher and mentor? Fuller's final answers to these questions will have a great deal to do with her eventual sense of herself as a woman. In the life of a daughter of an overbearing man like Timothy—of a girl who has no clear sexual identity—the answers can also play a key part in determining whom she prefers as her domestic partner.[7]

But thoughts like these regarding her self-consciousness of herself as a gendered human being come only later. At this point, Margaret was still very much a needy child and hence was happy that Miss Prescott let her see herself as her "adopted daughter"—especially since, writes the child in words heavy with hurt and yearning, maybe her own mother is sick. This is the explanation by which Margaret rationalizes receiving only one letter from her mother in the months Margaret has been in Groton.[8]

Fuller's exaggerated adolescent expression of affection for the female figure—whether embodied in Ellen Kilshaw or Susan Prescott—implies her continuing search to find the maternal love she felt her mother had not given her and seemed even less likely to give her as time passed on. Indeed, at home in Cambridgeport, Margaret's mother had other things on her mind. She had not yet recovered fully from the stresses of having had surgery to remove a tumor from her breast and of having given birth to her seventh child, Richard, just four days after Margaret left for school in May 1824. Preoccupied and exhausted, she was not eager to have back home their eldest child, whom she thought too hotheaded, opinionated, even, she had complained to her husband, on occasion "repulsive" when interacting with others in public. Convinced of her daughter's "*deficiencies*," Mrs. Fuller believed that she and her husband had "*erred*" in their "system of educating" Margaret. "Ambitious" of her father's praise in all she did, said Margarett Crane, their daughter ignored her own mother's more "*practical* views" on how to make it in "*real*" life.[9] These spiteful remarks reveal the depth of Margarett Crane's displeasure with her daughter, her husband's brilliant protégée, Timo's "special" darling.

Alas for Margarett Crane, Susan Prescott's attempts to turn Margaret into a "lady" were for naught. For when Margaret returned to Cambridgeport to find her overtired mother even more distant, she became more impertinent. She was too young to understand that her overworked mother, again pregnant, was exhausted from constantly attending to the needs of her four sons—Eugene, William Henry, Arthur, and baby Richard—as well as of her younger daughter, the kind-hearted Ellen, whom everyone thought pretty.

And the less her mother showed her love, the more Margaret identified with Timothy and sought compensatory affection from women. In July 1825 she boasted to Susan Prescott in a letter that the teacher's former "pleasure-loving pupil" has managed to get out of having to accompany her "honored father" to church, which will allow her to devote her time, instead, to Prescott. This devotion, Fuller is careful to note, comes despite the fact that lying on her writing desk and waiting to be read are tempting books by Helvetius and Ariosto. Surely Prescott did not miss her former student's reference to *Orlando Furioso,* Ariosto's sixteenth-century Italian romantic epic. One tale told by Ariosto in this lighthearted epic is the well-known account of the adolescent Fiordespina's "strange" same-sex crush on Bradamant, the Amazon.[10]

For defying Timothy's wish that she accompany him to church, Margaret felt great guilt; she felt guilty also because it expressed her failure to live up to his demand that she be domestic and feminine, and because it set up, at least in her mind, a rivalry between her father and Miss Prescott for her affection. These conflicted feelings of inadequacy and guilt appear in a letter Margaret had earlier sent Timothy from Groton. In a stiff prose style mimicking his, she acknowledges she has received *seven* letters from him in two months and confesses that, though she has "*endeavored* to comply with [his] wishes," she has been unable to send him some notes about music he had requested because she "cannot copy music." It is for her, however, "a subject of extreme regret" when her father expresses "the slightest wish" that she "cannot fulfil." Still, insists Margaret, "it is not in my power to comply with your desire on this head."[11]

Nor did it seem within her power to fulfill the wish of her critical father that she write him tidy letters (she confessed that her letter of 5 January had "blots" on it), or be the clever, pretty lady her father expected. It was hard for her to be pretty when her face erupted in a feverish red rash (likely adolescent acne) that "destroyed," she said, her complexion. Aware that she could never be pretty enough to please her "papa," that she would not be content, at any rate, with securing merely the "*succes de societe*," Fuller vowed in her July 1825 letter to Prescott to attain "distinction" by means of her intellect. She aimed to be, as she put it bluntly elsewhere, "bright & ugly."[12]

7 ∽ Metamorphosis in Her Young Adulthood

There was nothing about Margarett Crane's ambitious, irreverent daughter that would have fit a conventional nineteenth-century American mother's expectations of what a lady should be. Nor did Margaret seem to indicate any desire or aptitude to be remade into a lady. On the contrary, after returning to Cambridgeport in the spring of 1825, Margaret worked hard to achieve the goal of intellectual perfection that her father had set out for her. More obstinate than ever, she strove to turn herself into an intellectual person worthy of a place at her father's side as an equal, rather than try to meet the contrary expectations of both her parents that she be an enlightened feminine lady.

To achieve intellectual perfection, Fuller on a typical summer day in her fifteenth year got up before five, walked for an hour, then practiced piano until the family breakfasted at seven. Next, as she wrote Prescott in July 1825, she read French "till eight, then two or three lectures in Brown's philosophy." At half-past nine she was off to "Mr. Perkins's school," where she studied "Greek till twelve," after which she recited, went home, and practiced piano "again till dinner, at two." After dinner, if the conversation suited her, she lingered over her dessert for "half an hour." Then, when possible, she spent two hours reading Italian. At six she went out for a walk or drive, after which she yet again practiced piano, or sang. At eleven she retired to her room, writing in her diary before going to bed.[1]

Students at the Port School where Yale graduate George Perkins now taught and Fuller took a class in Greek recitation reported that she would strut into the classroom like a queen. Squinting through half-shut eyes, she carried her head and long neck in a "peculiar" swanlike way ("ophidian," said her enemies), "which," as Hedge recalls, "all who knew her" remembered "as the most characteristic trait in her personal appearance." But many schoolmates, especially younger girls, now treated her with respect. Still given to dramatically acting, the teenage Fuller now flaunted her intellectual prowess, and she walked with a saucy sprightliness that enchanted some but repelled others and made them shun her. In one of the village shops was a library she routinely visited. Taking off her cloak, Fuller would fill its hood with books, then swing it over her shoulder and carry it home. One young female admirer said, "We all wished that our mothers would let us have hooded cloaks, that we might carry our books in the same way."[2]

While young girls admired her, many of the boys, even the smartest, were intimidated by her intelligence. One former Port School classmate, the writer Oliver Wendell Holmes, later described in a recollection cited by Higginson in his Fuller biography "the awe with which he regarded the opening sentence of one of her school compositions: 'It is a trite remark.'" Holmes later confessed that he had no idea at the time what "trite" meant.[3]

A friend of Higginson recalled Fuller's appearance in her home at a party for children. Fuller, who was then fifteen, had in hand a fashionably large handkerchief. Rolling her handkerchief into a baton, she assumed direction of the games, guiding the children like a born leader. This tall girl's presumptuous style amused Higginson's friend's mother and older sisters, who were nonetheless glad to be relieved of having to entertain the children. The younger sister told Higginson, however, that she liked the "peculiar swaying grace" in Fuller's motion as the latter led the children, and that she had felt "drawn" that day to this spirited stranger.[4]

Whatever reservations Timothy had regarding his daughter's "faults" faded as he came increasingly to view his gifted daughter with pride. Timothy, who became speaker of the Massachusetts House of Representatives after retiring from the U.S. Congress in 1825, now enjoyed Margaret's companionship in his own studies, an historical fact about their interaction that "tells the whole story," according to Higginson. For though Timothy's "companionship" might have been "stimulating, even flattering" to his daughter, "tender, wise, considerate" it was not. In a damning assessment of Timothy's part in his daughter's life drama, Higginson said he thought his earlier "candle-light" tutoring sessions with her were "evil."[5]

Thus there remained in Margaret's heart a "void," as Higginson put it, that a mother's love usually "comes in to fill." It was not, then, just that Timothy's wife was so absorbed in her (by then six) younger children that she had no time for Margaret, but that (according to Higginson) the father deliberately claimed his right "to control [his] daughter's whole existence." If Margaret received an invitation, it was Timothy who decided whether she should accept it, and it was he who suggested what she should wear. When Margaret wished to receive friends at home, Timothy decided who should come; and when the evening came, he received the guests along with Margaret. During such visits Margarett Crane only occasionally, and then quite casually, appeared—a "dignified figure" in the background. Her letters to Timothy suggest she preferred to play the part of "perfect recluse."[6]

That the father had thus selected his eldest daughter as his protégée suggests how close an affinity with her he felt, even as he himself—stiff, dictatorial, fastidious, proud—failed to demonstrate what others would recognize as filial love. For even as Timothy at this time made clear to Margaret his high expectations for her intellectual achievement, he sustained in his relationship with her a perversely intense emotional distance, which made it hard for her to know if she had pleased him. Thus just when most girls were beginning to let up in their studies in order to develop domestic attributes that would win for them good-provider husbands, Margaret, in trying to fulfill her father's desire, was perfecting the part in life that it seemed that destiny meant her to play: that of female prodigy. Though younger girls may indeed have envied Fuller's obvious intellectual superiority and seeming self-confidence, and though Fuller at times sensed within herself and exhibited a queenly pride, a later memory of her childhood suggests how lonely she felt in her father's house. She recalls how, in their home on Cherry Street, she "used to long and pine for beautiful places such as I read of" while she knitted a stocking or rocked the cradle of one of her younger siblings. Only when she walked over the red wooden bridge that took her from Cambridge to Boston did she sense that somewhere, beyond her vision, lay a place where her heart might finally feel at home. "I liked that very much," she said: "the river, and the city glittering in [the] sunset."[7]

Fuller's yearning for a beautiful home was briefly satisfied when, in the summer of 1826, Timothy, who had just completed his term as speaker of the Massachusetts House, bought the late Chief Justice Francis Dana's mansion in Old Cambridge. Built in 1785, it sat off the main road to Boston, about a quarter mile east of Harvard. A large, wood-framed, two-story Georgian building, it stood back on a hill facing the Charles River and distant hills of Brookline and Brighton. The estate with its ample stables was surrounded by several acres of undeveloped land. Guests approached by carriage down a flower-lined lane that cut through a landscaped yard. Fuller later recalled how she loved to sit for hours at her window and look out to the view in the distance of "the river so slow and mild, the gentle hills, the sunset over Mt. Auburn."[8]

Beneath the seeming quiet of this still-countrified setting of Cambridge, the population of which was then about five thousand, an intellectual revolution was brewing. With its colleges and libraries funded by civic-minded capitalists striving to make New England a vital cultural center, the Cambridge-Boston area was fast becoming the country's leading literary destination. In that electric setting, Fuller's conflicted energies soon found a creative outlet in the revolutionary literary and philosophic theories circulating through Cambridge's intellectual circles.

These radical ideas had been brought home to conservative Cambridge by Harvard scholars who had studied at the University of Göttingen, Germany's leading university.

In the years after the Fullers moved into the Dana mansion, from 1826 to 1829, Fuller ached to be a part of this vital intellectual circuit. To win entrée, she at first read works by diverse writers like Epictetus, Milton, Racine, Locke, Byron, and, most importantly, Rousseau. Rousseau's ideas on men and women as biologically different, socially constructed entities had already influenced her view of herself as a gendered human being. Now, at sixteen, she felt drawn to the dark vision in *The Confessions* where Rousseau says that Tasso had written a line in his epic poem *La Gerusalemme liberata* that "predicted" his "misfortunes." She wrote that she understood this "remote seeking for the decrees of fate, this feeling of a destiny, casting its shadows from the very morning of thought." She agreed with Rousseau that a person's existence is not only determined by biology, but also "moulded" by the "deep thoughts" we absorb early in life from both society and literature. She had a dark foreboding about her fate as an educated woman in a world where women were denied a sphere of action. At this time she was most moved, she later said, by these fatalistic thoughts of Rousseau.[9]

No longer a student at the Port School, Fuller was reading books she borrowed from friends and the local athenaeum. Denied the right to attend Harvard because of her gender, on her own she familiarized herself with some of the great works of British and European literature and found she gained most pleasure from reading, not just Rousseau but Shelley and all the Romantics, an affinity she shared with male scholars attending Harvard in the 1820s. Thus even before she had become friends with Harvard men like Henry Hedge and James Clarke, Fuller was being influenced by writers who reflected the revolutionary spirit of the age and who were defying in word and deed the limits set for them by traditional patterns of human behavior. One of these was the Rousseauist novelist Anne Louise Germaine, Baronne de Staël-Holstein, whose life became a model for Fuller in her youth.[10]

Fuller fashioned herself in her transitional adolescent years after the "brilliant De Stael," as she refers to Germaine de Staël in a May 1826 letter. Like a sponge she absorbed all she read about this passionate French author and conversationalist whose salon was frequented by the crème de la crème of French society. Fuller's affinity for de Staël makes sense. Both in their youth had been overly attached to public-spirited, powerful fathers. We recall that the pattern underlying Fuller's life and identity was an obsessive paternal presence linked with a sense of missed maternal love—of too much love of a wrong kind from her father, of not enough tender nurturing from her mother. Such a potentially negative double (what some critics call) "identity theme" in a girl's life could be played out in relatively positive ways if she were able to find—whether in her immediate culture or in the pages of literature or history—a strong woman with a similar pattern of early parental interaction in her life with whom she could identify.[11]

Such was Madame de Staël, a real-life Comtesse de Pologne, with whom Fuller identified so closely that, before he became her friend, William Henry Channing "suspected her of affecting the part of a Yankee Corinna." Channing refers here both to the tragic heroine of de Staël's famous work, *Corinne*, and to de Staël herself, whom readers fondly called Corinne, a woman torn between her need to be her own unorthodox self and her wish to be loved as the kind of feminine woman traditionally valued by men.[12]

Born Anne-Louise Germaine Necker in April 1766, de Staël was the only child of Jacques Necker, a wealthy Swiss banker and finance minister to Louis XVI. Twice dismissed by Louis XVI—first for his exposé of the king's squandering of public funds and mismanagement of the nation's prisons and charity institutions, and second for his failed attempt at economic reform—Necker was nonetheless revered by the French people for his efforts. Germaine was in her twenties when, on 30 July 1789, her father made a triumphant return to Paris; and she later commemorated the event as "the last of pure happiness in my life." As Necker neared the Hôtel de Ville, "the square was filled with a multitude . . . pressing forward to receive a single man, and that man," says de Staël, "was my father."[13]

This powerful father and daughter bond grew out of Germaine's deep-seated anger at and rivalry with a Calvinist mother who reigned like a queen in her salon and seemed to care more for the adults who surrounded her there than for the bright daughter who sat beside her. The image of Germaine Necker at age eleven, entertaining men with her wit and charm while her mother behaved coolly toward her, appealed to the sixteen-year-old Margaret, whose mother was admired in Washington for her conversational skills and beauty even as she remained emotionally remote from her bright daughter.[14]

The women's lives didn't parallel each other exactly, however. Germaine's mother, not father, insisted on the girl's education. It was the mother who decided to raise her daughter, she would write, "not like Sophie, but like Émile," referring to the work by Rousseau, and so she kept her daughter close to her while offering little love. Germaine, moreover, had the money and charm to realize her dream of replacing her mother at the center of Europe's most celebrated salon, as well as in her father's heart. After Necker's death in 1804, de Staël, age thirty-eight, expressed her love in words that merged her father's image with God's: "Oh my God! Forgive your weak creatures if their hearts which have loved so much can imagine in heaven only the smile of a father who will receive them into your heavenly courts."[15] Germaine's yearning for the unequivocal love of a mortal father imaginatively made heavenly will find an echo in Fuller's later letters to Emerson, onto whom she would project an ideal image of her dead father.

De Staël offered Fuller a model of the kind of proud and defiant female genius she might become. At home in her salon where her witty repartee dominated political discussions, de Staël in the first days of the French Revolution fearlessly defended her liberal aristocratic friends when they were imprisoned by the French Tribunal. She was incensed by the tribunal's display of irrational tyrannical power, as she was by that of Napoleon, who exiled her from Paris for criticizing him. And wherever she went—Germany, Switzerland, Italy—friends and lovers went, too, including the French writer Benjamin Constant, the twenty-three-year-old wounded hussar John Rocca (whom she met when she was forty-five), and her close friend, Madame Récamier.[16]

Since she was living like a princess in the grand Dana mansion as she read Isabel Hill's translation of *Corinne; or, Italy* (as many middle-class girls of her era did), Margaret easily saw herself as the passionate Italian "improvisatrice" Corinne. Attracted in Rome to Corinne, the Scotsman Lord Nevil finally marries Corinne's proper English half-sister, Lucy, leaving the exotic Corinne to despair and premature death. While reading *Corinne,* Fuller imagined herself both the character and her creator, and she began envisioning herself an American Germaine de Staël, someone destined for romance in Italy. In Jacques Necker she saw her own father, who, like Necker, was a man of some political consequence, having served four terms as a U.S. representative. Like Necker, Timothy was certainly idolized by his daughter, who, like the young Germaine, was beginning to enthrall her friends with her charm, intelligence, and wit. Margaret was also, of course, imitating Timothy, who had even convinced his wife (or so she critically once wrote him) of the necessity of his humoring "the ladies" in Washington through a studied display of wit and charm.[17]

Margaret may have even felt that she had metamorphosed into Germaine Necker when the Fullers, in September 1826, gave a dinner and ball in the Dana mansion in honor of President John Quincy Adams, from whom Timothy hoped to win a diplomatic "mission to Europe" for his work for Adams during the campaign. But Adams did not stay for the after-dinner ball. Perhaps it was just as well. Cambridge gossips later told how an overweight, nearsighted Margaret appeared at the ball gaudily dressed in a badly cut, muslin-covered, pink silk gown. In her tight-laced, low-necked dress and with her "hair curled all over her head" and eyes half shut from squinting, she looked, reported guests, ridiculous, especially when she danced quadrilles. Still, like de Staël, she swelled with pride at being the daughter of the Honorable Timothy Fuller. Thus she held her head high, spoke well, and gestured so dramatically with her smooth white hands that Cambridge ladies charged Margaret with making too much of her one point of beauty, the same criticism that had been leveled at Germaine de Staël.[18]

Fuller reveled in the comparison. And whenever she now appeared in public she made a point of putting to use her early training in elocution. To her delight she found that, like Madame de Staël, her charismatic conversation drew people to her. Though some young people thought her haughty, those she wished to impress she treated with a studied gentleness and respect. This engagingly fluent yet subtly manipulative style made each person she conversed with feel as if he or she had been singled out for some extraordinary interaction. Her words made the commonplace transform into something wondrous. Her rude self blossomed like a rose in winter sun.

With her theatrics Fuller drew to her a select few to take part in the colorful drama she made of everyday life: Almira Penniman, a beautiful woman who married but later divorced the 1824 Harvard class poet and Unitarian minister David Barlow; Elizabeth Randall, whose physician father had tutored his daughter as rigorously as Timo had Margaret; and Amelia Greenwood, who married a Harvard-educated physician and was the only one of the three to adapt to the traditional role of wife and mother. Newer friends included the writer Lydia Maria Francis (later Lydia Maria Child) and Ellen Sturgis, daughter of a wealthy Boston merchant and sister of Cary Sturgis, who would soon become Fuller's closest friend.[19]

Patterning her behavior after that of de Staël, the fictional Corinne, and the Comtesse de Pologne, Fuller began in the early 1830s to cultivate the friendship also of young Harvard men, along with their women consorts and sponsors. Cambridge ladies began to note Fuller's odd habit of passionately attaching herself to older women. Higginson's elder sister remembered her as being in her young adulthood a "studious, self-conscious, overgrown girl ... sitting at my mother's feet, covering her hands with kisses." Another woman Margaret adored was the Azores-born Mrs. J. W. Webster. Described by Higginson as a woman of "tropic softness and sweetness," she was married to a man whose "countenance" had "not pleased" Margarett Crane, who had observed to Timothy in 1820 that the man's "expression is storm, and nothing amiable. . . . I know he is not *happy*." Though a stranger to her sight, his type, she wrote, is "familiar to my *imagination*." Indeed. Webster, a Harvard chemistry professor, twenty-nine years later would murder his colleague George Parkman. Perhaps Margaret saw in Mrs. Webster a woman like her mother, a lovely woman married to a domineering, hot-tempered man. Perhaps this similarity between the women is what magnetically attracted Margaret to her.[20]

One of these older women to whom she was drawn saw potential in this "odd and sometimes inconvenient adorer." The tall and portly yet proper Eliza Rotch Farrar, the English-born wife of a Harvard math professor, decided to try to improve the girl's appearance and manners. A crusader against tight lacing and hoops and an advocate of cold baths as a cure-all for women's ills, Farrar was writing a book on female etiquette, *The Young Lady's Friend*, during the years she helped transform Fuller from homely protégée into a vital public presence. Aided by her wealthy and exotically beautiful New Orleans–born cousin Anna Barker, who boarded in her home, Farrar taught Fuller to make the most of her looks by losing weight, parting her abundant light-brown hair in the middle and wearing it pulled back, braided, in a bun, and concentrating, in Fuller's words, "on the niceties of a Lady's dress," a lesson Fuller (who was later to spend literally hours preparing to appear in public) took to heart.[21] Still, what mattered most to Fuller was the life of the mind. She was eager to meet men who could talk to her about the exciting new ideas afloat in Cambridge, who had studied abroad and absorbed the writings of the European Romantics.

8 ∞ The Influence of the Harvard Romantics

Out of French revolutionary hopes, the German idealism of Kant and his disciples, and English literary Romanticism, Harvard men like Waldo Emerson (class of 1821), Frederic Henry Hedge (class of 1825), and James Freeman Clarke and William Henry Channing (both class of 1829) generated a philosophy that God was not a Newtonian mechanical principle but instead a spirit that dwelled "within." The philosophy embraced the idea that, just as God had created the universe, so the human mind, drawing on the power of this spirit within, could by means of the imagination reshape the world to suit human desire. Their hope of attaining a literal heaven after death undercut by Newtonian physics, these young New England idealists now located the source of creative power deep in the mind's internal heaven. Raised in the Unitarian Church by Harvard men whose radicalism had cooled into a formal style, conservative politics, and a commonsense view of the world while not completely losing their liberal faith in man's capacity for rational action, these younger scholars fell upon the warmer, wilder writings of Coleridge, Wordsworth, Goethe, and Carlyle with, as Emerson later said, "pleasure and sympathy."[1]

Both English and American Romantics relied on the thinking of Coleridge, who attributed to the mind a power greater than had John Locke, who had described it as a machine. Countering Locke, Coleridge argued that during the creative process, the energy fueling mental activity partakes of the power of a greater creative energy that Romantics like Fuller tended to refer to as spirit, power, or "the One." In partaking of this power, the mind, like God's light as described in the Bible, sends forth its rays to penetrate objects in an otherwise fixed and dead world, setting them, as Coleridge had said, "now all *a-glow*, with colors not their own." In rendering the mind "intuitive of the *spiritual* in man," Coleridge fell back on terms from the Bible: "Never flag in zeal, be aglow with Spirit, serve the Lord" (Rom. 12:11).[2]

Romantic writers like Wordsworth and Emerson fused the language of biblical vision with the terms of natural philosophy and proclaimed the immanence of God in nature, a divine presence they sensed in the breath of a summer breeze whose freshness they felt could redeem, so to speak, a fallen soul. Though experience may have left its imprint on you like a leaf in a rock from long ago, Romantics believed that the germ of who you are is "within," and "it,"—that spark of who you are—is divine. Moreover, just as the seed sprouts into a plant whose leaves reach outward and upward to the light, so each individual soul moves through stages of existence on its journey through life to death and perfection, its final home in heaven, "the light," so to speak, "of setting suns."[3]

One need not fear death because, in the mind's capacity to transcend the bodily "Me" and encounter what Emerson would sometimes call the "Oversoul," at other times the "unconscious," the individual could bridge the split Romantics believed to exist between conscious and unconscious self, body and soul. Indeed, the main point of Emerson's 1836 essay *Nature* will be to teach men to love mother nature without mediator or veil, as well as without having to deal with the authority of the church fathers. In *Nature* and "Circles," Emerson tells readers about his own "divine moments" in nature when it seemed as if "waves of God" had flowed into him and he had become "part or particle of God." Both Emerson and Wordsworth *believed* that in these, so to speak, "Transcendental" moments, a man by means of his imagination could achieve, as one Emerson scholar has said, "an integrity of being consonant with the integrity of the universe (God)."[4]

In their attempt to keep alive the idea of the spirit in an increasingly materialistic world, many American Romantics appropriated the findings of science— including such dubious ones as animal magnetism and animal electricity—to reinforce their faith not only in the authority of the soul's intuitive insight into the divine ground of being, the unifying reality behind experienced data, but also in the superiority of their own speculative organicism over Newtonian physics. Thus theirs was a philosophy of self-reliance, *not* of Christ-reliance, as a defiant Emerson was soon to affirm. Heirs of men who thought and talked in biblical terms yet who also believed that man with his reason could improve the human condition, most American Romantics looked less than had their rationalistic fathers to political revolutions for solutions to social problems than they did to psychological interpretations of the self and its relation to reality.[5] Keenly aware of man's spiritual need to make peace with his impulsive animal nature, Romantics sought redemption primarily not in church but in the wild.

So entirely did Emerson and the other young men attending the Harvard Divinity School identify with the Romantic faith in the individual's capacity for self-reformation and redemption that, during the years Fuller lived in the Dana mansion (1826–33), they came to be seen as "infidels" by the staid divinity school faculty. Though the men on the faculty taught the unity of God, they still believed in Christ as their mediator, as Christians' "*only* master." Most of them, moreover, were socially conservative and economically prosperous, and they preached to congregations more interested in property rights and material well-being than in a search for individual salvation, the incentive that drove young men like Emerson to rebel against them.[6]

In contrast to these professors' sedate outlook on life, Emerson's vision of self-reliance grew out of a Spartan-like determination to overcome adversity, a determination evident in "Circles" when he says, "Valor consists in the power of self-recovery." Of course, when Emerson and his fellow scholars talked about self-reliance, they meant it as a male virtue. Such a masculine perspective did not particularly bother Fuller at this time, since she was frequently mentally seeing herself as male and was, like her male counterparts, eagerly absorbing what, in 1826, she called the "liberalizing, regenerating principles" of the Romantics.[7]

Fuller, who already had doubts about the power of the human will to overcome difficult circumstances, was drawn to those Romantic writers who understood the struggle of the inner man with the outer, of human passion with social stricture. She felt an affinity with thinkers who praised the imagination and its capacity to connect the individual soul with what seemed to be a higher, self-consuming power whose existence transcended gender lines. Indeed, by the time she was twenty, Margaret Fuller wholeheartedly embraced the imaginative life. Had she not, after all, as a child, one who had disobeyed her father's command not to continue reading *Romeo and Juliet* on Sunday, escaped his anger when sent to her room by imagining people taking parts in scenes that she, not he, controlled? Had she not also discovered the pleasure of ruling her classmates in Groton "like a queen" by means of theatrical scenes that "wove figures from the scenes of her . . . childhood," and the dignitaries she saw, "with fantasies unknown to life"?[8] Moreover, had she not found in de Staël a real female Romantic who commanded by the power of her personality a coterie of women and men who existed, in effect, to do her bidding?

Fuller's sense that she could become a Romantic radical was thus fostered by her love of reading and of acting out fantasies in such a way that she was able to counter a troubling reality that otherwise might have crushed an odd girl like her. Among the Harvard men who were reading the Romantics, Fuller at this time befriended men who shared her passions: Frederic Henry Hedge, who had studied at the University of Göttingen and at Harvard College before enrolling in Harvard Divinity School, as well as William Henry Channing, the nephew of Dr. William Ellery Channing (chief spokesman for New England Unitarianism). But her closest friend in these formative years was James Freeman Clarke, who was to graduate from the divinity school in 1833. Though Clarke had met Fuller when both were about age five, it was not until 1829 that they became close friends. From that year until Fuller moved to Groton in 1833, they saw each other or communicated by letter almost daily. Clarke, son of an unsuccessful Cambridge inventor-druggist, was the grandson of America's first avowed Unitarian preacher, Dr. James Freeman, who raised him. A liberal-minded Unitarian clergyman and scholar, the elderly Dr. Freeman had been kind to his grandson, but his secluded lifestyle had had a negative effect on the boy's developing personality. As a result of his reclusive upbringing, the dark-eyed, unkempt Clarke became so neurotically intellectual and self-conscious that he had difficulty fitting into Cambridge social life.[9]

As intellectual eccentrics, Clarke and Fuller understood each other. Not only were both bookish, each also felt an affinity with the Romantics. Clarke loved the Romantics' emphasis on the power of the individual imagination to create its own personal paradise on earth apart from the ordinary happenings of a shared social reality. Later he would credit Coleridge with showing him "from Kant, that though knowledge begins *with* experience it does not come *from* experience." Through studying the Romantics, Clarke became convinced that there exists in each individual a divine spark that is the person's essence. His positive outlook provided the confidence he needed to succeed in life. Clarke especially liked Fuller because she reinforced his faith that he could lift himself above the limits placed on him by his environment; she poeticized, he said, his life.[10]

These three young men—Frederic Henry Hedge, William Henry Channing, and James Freeman Clarke—were soon to play an important part in promoting New England Transcendentalism as well as in insuring Fuller's presence in the mid-1830s as a participant at meetings of the Hedge Club, the name the Transcendentalists gave their discussion group, since it met each time Hedge returned to Boston from his pastorate in Bangor, Maine. Hedge became known as the sole American who had actually read Immanuel Kant in the original German; and Clarke was soon to become editor of the *Western Messenger*. In this Cincinnati-based journal Clarke boldly broke with Boston's Unitarian Church fathers (among whom was his grandfather) by preaching Transcendental doctrine. Whether from a radical or conservative perspective, such men as Clarke and Hedge, like the European Romantics whose ideas provided the frame for their own thoughts, placed prime importance in their lives on "the flowering of the individual personality."[11]

Encouraged by Clarke, Fuller now began to read the more introspective Romantic writers Coleridge and Wordsworth, and she soon discovered Goethe. Like the honey-tongued Greeks she had loved as a child, these writers hinted at a wonderful wildness lurking behind the polite words she heard uttered in the Dana mansion's parlor, where her father had forced her one "livelong" spring evening to play "auditor" to a judge whose "jokes and anecdotes" were "pleasant enough," she wrote Amelia Greenwood, but not soul-inspiring.[12]

In this March 1830 letter, Fuller tells her friend how bored she had been the previous night while sitting silent in the parlor for "three hours in boarding-school attitude hemming a ruffle," in contrast to how "*happy*" she had been earlier that same day when she had run out into the fields behind the house "and passed the morn[in]g reading Moores Byron and inspiring delight in every breath." Returning to the house, she had sat where the west wind could blow on her cheek and she could continue reading. Reading about Byron's life in Thomas Moore's just-published *Life, Letters, and Journals of Lord Byron* sent her into "a kind of delireum [*sic*]" during which she "read senselessly and dreamed consciously at the same time." Her heart seemed to float "in luxury of realized bliss No! not *bliss* [but] *felicity*," exclaims Margaret. She says she lacks words to explain her feeling, except that—"My whole being is Byronized at this moment c'est a dire my whole mind is possessed with one desire—to comprehend Byron once for all."[13]

Two years later Fuller would feel similarly ecstatic in reading the German Romantics, whose deliciously addictive writings she had tasted at age ten with Wieland's *Oberon* and now rediscovered through Carlyle's articles, then appearing in the old *Foreign Review* and the *Edinburgh Review*. Inspired by Carlyle, Fuller would eventually read Lessing, Schiller, Richter, Tieck, Korner, and Novalis— "and, above all," as Emerson later noted, "GOETHE." And as she read him she felt so "overwhelmed" by the "immense superiority" of Goethe's mind that she could not think of anything to say, "except 'It is so.'" In a 7 August 1832 letter, she confessed to Clarke how she feels as if when reading him that he "comprehends every feeling I ever had so perfectly" that "when I shut the book, it seems as if I had lost my personal identity."[14]

Maybe she did. For these letters written by Fuller in her early twenties show how in these transition years she imaginatively metamorphosed into the characters in the fiction works she was reading or identified with Romantic writers, as she does here with Goethe. If her letters from these years of private searching give any indication of the actual life Fuller was living, then it appears she had so "lost" her "personal identity" into the literary characters she was reading about in her books that she herself had no (as even her mother said) "*real*" life at all, that her "true" self lay, as she will later put it, buried "deep within." It seemed even to Fuller that in the context of her nineteenth-century Cambridge culture she lived a divided life. In November 1832 she wrote Clarke that it was as if "I had two souls and they seem to roll over one another in the most incomprehensible way." By alluding here to Goethe's *Faust*, Fuller seems to mean one soul that is clinging to the world and one that seeks to transcend it. There was, on the one hand, the sentimental, well-mannered lady that Mrs. Farrar had worked to create. This side of herself, so like her father, had a cold heart, delighted in witticisms, and enjoyed shallow flirtations.[15]

This superficial part of Fuller became enchanted when she was twenty with her ambitious cousin George Davis, a Harvard graduate who, like her father, was a lawyer and would later be a U.S. representative. In the role of witty society lady, Fuller flirted with Davis, whose intellect and wit made her think he would make her a perfect mate—as did no doubt the fact that he reminded her of her father. Though she confided to Clarke that Davis was "the only friend to whom I was all truth and frankness," the affected style of her letters to him suggests otherwise. With a head full of Rousseau and chivalric ballads, she had become infatuated with Davis, a calculating young man whom she idealizes in her letters. In the end, he did not reciprocate the affection. Like Fuller's father, Davis preferred a witty, pretty *lady*, something Fuller would never be, despite her efforts at this time to enact the traditional feminine role expected of her by friends and family members.[16]

In trying to comply with feminine conventions, Fuller grew increasingly adept at part-playing. But she paid a price for her self-conscious attempt to narrow her questing mind. While part of her enjoyed the theatrical social repartee, another part, she wrote Clarke in March 1830, sensed that there were "within" her "many voices" of her "soul" that are "necessarily repressed" once she has ascertained the expectations of the men and women around her.[17]

Still, there was for her a certain allure in speaking words that seemed scripted and not hers. It gave her, she knew, a "peculiar power" over others. In November a self-described "egotized" Fuller wrote her recently married "bluestocking" friend, Almira Barlow, that she has "imposed" herself "on the world" in such a way that she has exhibited her "own rich invention and the credulous ignorance of [her] auditors." "In short," says she, "so well have I played my part, that in the self-same night I was styled by two several persons 'a sprightly young lady', and 'a Syren!!'"[18]

It was the patent insincerity of such exaggerated emotion that made people turn from Fuller. Put off by her "pedantic," sneering ways, they called her "'Supercilious', 'satirical', 'affected.'" "Cross-mouthed," even kindly old Dr. Freeman had called her, and told his daughter that he hoped his grandson would not fall in love with her, predicting that if "Poor James!" did "go and marry that woman," he would "be miserable all the days of his life."[19]

Clarke, however, was infatuated not with Fuller but with Elizabeth Randall, whom Fuller fondly calls "Elschen" or "Lizzy" in letters. Lizzy, James, and the few who truly knew Margaret saw beneath this off-putting egotistical facade to the warmer, softer, vulnerable "me" of Margaret that raised the fake front to protect her "true" self from pain. The social persona Fuller projected to the world sneered in the same way her father did, and it similarly hurt others with its cutting wit and derisive intellect. But in her interactions with Elizabeth and James, Margaret to a certain extent took off this mask of supercilious lady. In late October 1830 Margaret wrote "my dear James" to tell about her visit with "Elschen" to Marblehead. "T'was perfectly droll," she said, "to see [Elizabeth] stand gazing . . . on the waves as they broke on the shore; her eyes fixed in rapt enthusiasm on the overwhelming dash, break, boom &c while with both hands she held her red-cloak tight over her mouth lest that insidious East should seize the time to invade the soul's frail dwelling." The image of a red-cloaked Elizabeth scrambling over the rocks beside, in Fuller's words, "my no *less hapless* self," while the "lynx eyed" seagulls laughed and exhorted "us to jump and run . . . into the very arms of the vasty deep," seems, indeed, to have invaded her "soul's frail dwelling." It is a striking image that Fuller seems never to have forgotten. For, years later it will find a reflection, as we shall see, in a haunting dream about the drowning at sea of her intimate friend Cary Sturgis.[20]

9 ∽ The Search for Self

Fuller's fluctuating sense of self—her feeling of being at one moment elated and full of power and then, at the next, guilt ridden, conflicted, and vulnerable—fits the pattern of other Romantics. And Fuller at this point was certainly a Romantic. Having immersed herself in their literature, she was now acquiring from Romantic writers attitudes and a vocabulary by which she could express her emotional and intellectual experiences. In so doing she became one Romantic whose self-exploration helped establish subjectivity as we now know it, though from a feminized perspective.[1]

During her Cambridge years, Fuller thus began self-consciously to question her identity as a woman in this world whose guiding concepts and power structures were conceived and controlled by men. Her quest for identity took place within the frame of ideas provided by the Romantics, in which nature replaced the Bible as the ultimate source of moral truth. Moreover, the traditional scheme of Eden, fall, and redemption from sin through Christ merged with a new consciousness of subject-object separation coupled with a psychologically based faith in the imagination as a means to self-cohesion and grace.[2]

As a direct descendant of Puritans, Fuller had long been concerned with questions regarding man's potential for salvation. She saw herself as a pilgrim in search of truth. Though she believed in the immortality of the soul, and also in its redemption, she had no clear sense of *how* a person arrives at salvation. When Mrs. Farrar, as Farrar later recalled the episode to James Clarke, "was suffering" at this time "from a severe trial," Fuller had attempted to comfort her only to find that Farrar was a woman of deep religious conviction whereas the then twenty-year-old Fuller had never undergone an experience like that which Farrar described to her of "surrender[ing] self-will to God's will, . . . till at last His great mercy" brought "infinite peace" to one's "soul." Eager for a similar immediate experience of God's power, Fuller only knew that the Unitarian Church she grew up in offered no satisfying answers to her spiritual questions and yearnings. During the services that Timothy insisted the family attend each Sunday, she escaped the sermon by daydreaming because she "heard nothing" there "that had any connection" with her "inward life." Despite her expressed faith "in the paternal government of a Deity," Fuller felt dissatisfied with the paternal government of her father's rationalistic religion. Hence when on Thanksgiving Day 1831, her father compelled her to attend church with him, the twenty-one-year-old Margaret, who sat at Timothy's side, felt in marked disharmony with the preacher and congregation.[3]

Reflecting on the experience a decade later, Fuller also noted that she had felt that day like an orphan. Though she did not know what it meant to have God's mercy fill her soul the way it did her older friend, Fuller still felt more in harmony with Mrs. Farrar's spiritual experience than she did with the religious experience of the people attending the Unitarian service in 1831. For their faith was based on reason and their behavior on social convention.[4]

"Wearied out with mental conflicts," Fuller that Thanksgiving Day had "envied all the little children," whom she thought had parents to protect them. She felt that they could never know the "strange anguish" experienced by a "lonely" girl like herself. She felt within her great power, generosity, and tenderness, but these feelings "were all unrecognized." At that age she was not yet aware, Fuller said, "that I was not the selected Oedipus." Ridden with anxiety, Fuller fled after the service to nature. Recalling her experience through the filter of her readings in the Romantics, Fuller reports that she walked many hours "till the anguish was wearied out." She felt isolated, as if she "could never return to a world in which [she] had no place."[5]

By a silent pool of water, Fuller found momentary peace. Withered leaves blew about her. Then "the sun shone out," as it suddenly sometimes shows itself on a cold autumn day. She felt an almost Hindu sense of the loss of self into God. She saw "there was no self; that selfishness was" entirely the "result of circumstance"; that she "suffered" only because she "thought self real."[6]

But such uplifting moments for Fuller were rare. Her confidence in God and in her own powers changed, it seems, with the weather. On luxurious spring or fall days when the beauties of nature awakened in her a faith in "Eternal Progression," "God," "Beauty and Perfection," she felt, instead of Christian uplift, a Shelleyan sense of consecration, of having been touched, as Shelley felt, "by some unseen Power." Yet even these "halcyon hours" of spiritual lightness were invariably followed by a mood of despondency "unworthy," she said in a letter, "of a Christian" or of "any one who believes in the immortality of the soul."[7]

This pattern of having her lightest moods suddenly clouded by doubt and uncertainty—as when on "a cold rainy day" pleasure "departs with the sun"—Fuller came in time to accept as a condition of her fluctuating emotional life. When Mrs. Farrar later spoke with her about "God's light in the soul" and asked: "Margaret! has that light dawned on *your* soul?" Fuller, alluding presumably to her 1831 Thanksgiving Day epiphany, said she thought it had. "But, oh!" she exclaimed, "I dare not speak of it, lest it should be gone."[8]

While Fuller in her twenty-first year rejected what Emerson was to call "the corpse-cold Unitarianism" of the Boston merchants and Brattle Street Brahmans, she was also unable to embrace conventional Christianity, and she openly acknowledged to a friend her "ignorance of the Christian Revelation." As an intellectual young woman seeking to understand complicated truths about herself and the natural world around her, Fuller found the ritual of traditional Christianity—with its determinedly male, antinature, supernatural bias—oppressive. For a religion at this point to have had real meaning to her, it would have had to teach her, she wrote a friend, how "to know and feel my pain, to investigate its nature and its source."[9]

This investigative exploration of self in search of the source of one's individual divinity and pain was typical of Romantics who believed that God is "deep within" and cannot be found in traditional Christian rituals. Fuller now exhibited, as we know, psychological characteristics typical of other narcissistically inclined Romantic writers of the period, where the child compensates for its lack of satisfactory nurturing and subsequent feelings of emptiness by fixating on the splitting process, attaching its libido to larger-than-life fictions both of itself and of all-powerful imaginary parent figures from whom it thereafter seeks love and attention.[10]

It has been argued that such theatrical fictions were consciously created by Romantics like Fuller and Emerson to conceal their anxieties pertaining to sexual desire, that they deliberately wove over their emotional insecurities "a myth of transcendental power." As we have seen, this was true for Fuller, whose sense of self was always shifting and whose theatrics magnetically attracted others to play along with her in her ongoing psychodrama. So given was Fuller to theatrics that Emerson would later say that she "looked upon herself as a living statue, which should always stand on a polished pedestal . . . and under the most fitting lights." This self-consciously "superficial," idealized self served Fuller as a cover for her deep, real sense of deprivation, uncertainty, insecurity, and rage, just as idealized images of her parents compensated for the depriving real parents.[11]

Whether on stage or at home, Fuller was always in search of herself. In late October 1830, she wrote Clarke about a "horrid dream" she had that suggests her awareness of certain anxieties about her own identity. In response to the claim that "the soul lives most in sleep" and that dreams link us to the divine, Fuller confesses that dreams do indeed reveal "strange secrets." They are secrets, however, she says, that are as likely to be linked to our meanest jealousies and suspicions as they are to higher truth. Her night dreams tend to reveal to her "detached scenes, sometimes ludicrous, sometimes distorted and terrible." In her dream, Fuller was in a room with a person she sensed she loved but whose face she could not see. "I believe I urged or tempted this person," she confesses to Clarke, "to look up a chimney." Then she heard "two loud reports quick one after the other." The person she had tempted to look up the chimney "exclaimed 'God almighty' in a voice of the utmost anguish and horror, and seemed about to fall back into my arms," when she awoke.[12]

Nightmares such as these intrigued her; they suggested a dark layer to her being over which her consciousness had no control, one that existed apart from society's assumption about the "self" as gendered. Though neither the gender nor age of the figure Fuller tempts in her dream to "look up" the chimney is clear, the loud quick reports of a pistol suggest male orgasm or the firing of her father's gun. Whatever the case, the price the figure pays for yielding to Fuller's Eve-like seduction is a terror so great that he or she faints. After her dream of following to the grave her mother's body, Fuller similarly awoke terrified, in that case at the thought of losing her mother, whom she believed had failed to love and protect her. Maybe Fuller dreaded confronting the emotional concerns her night dreams suggested: her deep need for her mother's love and the perverse intensity of her feeling for her father.[13]

Fuller's appreciation of psychic conflict in writers like Goethe and Byron taught her to see that such anxiety can cause an "ache" that "is like a bodily wound, whose pain haunts even when it is not attended to, and disturbs the dreams of the patient who has fallen asleep from exhaustion." Unfortunately for Fuller, such inner conflict tended to act as a "curse," a "palsy" over her "affections." Instead of inspiring, as it did for Romantic male artists like Byron and Goethe, it paralyzed her capacity to create. Later, in a November 1843 fantasy-laden letter addressed to Beethoven, Fuller will ask if her psychic paralysis has something to do with the fact that she is a woman: "Is it because as a woman I am bound by a physical law which prevents the soul from manifesting itself[?]" "Sometimes," she ponders, "the moon seems mockingly to say so."[14]

10 ∾ The Farm in Groton

Had Fuller stayed in Cambridge, she might have found a way to deal with the problems caused by her inner conflict about her parents. As an intellectual female, she would have received support from her Cambridge friends, who were arguing for radical reforms, including rights for women. Maybe she could have found a way to reconcile what one critic calls the "'real me' (the sense of self distinct from [the] dramatization)" with "'the alien me,'" the public persona.[1]

Maybe. But her father's decision to leave Cambridge deprived her of the chance to try. Timothy's hope that John Quincy Adams might reward him with a diplomatic assignment to Europe for his campaign work in the president's behalf disappeared when Adams first "forgot," as Richard tells it, "to reward" Timothy with a position in 1825, and then lost his 1828 bid for president against Andrew Jackson. That disappointment, along with Timothy's failure to win the race for Massachusetts's lieutenant governor, meant he had to either reopen his Boston law practice or find another way to support his family. Facing a financial strain, Timothy moved his family from the Dana mansion to the pre-Revolutionary house near Harvard Yard built by Colonel Brattle and owned by his wealthy brother Abraham. Instead of returning to law, Timothy now decided to follow in his father's footsteps by trying his hand at farming.[2]

For over a year Timothy's family lived in the Brattle Street house. On the grounds of her uncle's grand house with their formal gardens, ponds, bridges, and springhouses, Margaret wandered and pondered the instability of her situation. On 7 August 1832 she confided to Clarke that she feels "quite lost; it is so long since I have talked myself—To see so many acquaintances, to talk so many words and never tell my mind completely on any subject . . . makes me feel strangely *vague* and *move-able.*" In September she depicts herself in a letter to him as a "seeking soul, lost in an unspeakable labyrinth of doubts fears and conjectures." To Clarke's suggestion that she needs some "all-comprehending" system "to cling to" during this unstable time of transition, Fuller in jest talks about the ever-shifting nature of the self. She cites a passage from Novalis's *Die Lehringe zu Sais,* which translated means, according to Ralph Manheim: "Anxiously, the novice listened to the criss-crossing voices. Each seemed to him right, and a strange confusion overcame his spirit."[3]

Fuller confesses in this letter her feelings of confusion about the future and her hope that she find an intellectually superior person to talk to. She is seeking someone she can count on more than she feels she can her father, whose failure at law and politics has condemned them to exile in Groton. Just "the sight of a being so confident of his ground as to be unwilling" to yield his individuality to try-ing circumstances might entice her, she says, to become his "voluntary disciple." Needing such a companion in her studies, she concedes, is her habit and suggests "a second-rate mind."[4]

She assures Clarke that she is also seeking a new philosophic system. She wants a system, she says, "in whose applications I shall have faith—I do not wish to *reflect* always, if reflecting must be always about one's identity, whether '*ich*' [I] am the true *ich* &c." She wants "to arrive at that point where I can trust myself and leave off saying 'It seems to me' and boldly feel it *is* so *to me.*" "This," she affirms, "is the philosophy *I* want—." Until then, however, she will flow with the "stream of events."[5]

That stream of events took the Fuller family in April 1833 to Groton and a farm that Timothy had bought from Judge Samuel Dana, a former state senate colleague and father of one of Margaret's Prescott classmates. The large, white frame house was located thirty-five miles northwest of Boston in the same quiet town where, nine years earlier, Margaret had attended boarding school. Timothy hoped on his farm to imitate Thomas Jefferson by becoming a farmer-scholar and writing a his-tory of the United States. This stalwart little man also aimed to subject his sons to the "same hardening process" he had endured as a boy on a farm where his stern minister father had raised and educated him and his siblings. The setting seemed ideal. The imposing house with ten spacious rooms stood on the crest of a hill. Its side piazza looked into an orchard, and it was surrounded by forty acres of mowing and tillage, ten acres of pasturage, and, at the outskirts of the estate, a thick forest of tall pines. Timothy hoped that with corn, potatoes, beans, milk from his cows, and hay from the acres of land he was to cultivate with the help of hired hands, a team of oxen, and his sons, the farm would be self-sufficient. In his attempt to make his dream real, he sometimes worked so hard loading grain in the heat of summer that, as Richard recalls it, he was "obliged to lie down for hours."[6]

Hard farm life not only prostrated Timothy, it proved disastrous for the entire family. During the first summer, Margaret overcame her isolation with visits from friends like James Clarke and Lizzy Randall. She voraciously read the periodicals, books, and letters such Cambridge friends sent her by coach, and she wrote them back. Such an exchange of books and letters with friends in other cities was soon to become her way of staying connected to the world. It was a pattern of behavior she had acquired as a child, when writing letters had been her way to connect to her powerful father when he was in Washington. In her first letters from Groton, Fuller wrote romantically about nature as a paradise. In early May 1833 she praises her new house, saying she never feels a prisoner in it—as she will later say she had felt in their Cherry Street house. She tells Clarke how on "every sunny noon" she takes her copy of Goethe's *Faust* and goes out "to a wood about a quarter of a mile from the house" where "the birds and wind rustling . . . do their best to make me feel at home." And when at night she is not writing letters or translating Goethe's *Tasso*, she goes down to the river's edge to watch the radiant sun set over the water.[7]

On a peaceful mid-June evening, she and her houseguests Lizzy and Belinda Randall paddled out on the river. "The girls [were] singing sweet songs," she wrote Clarke, "and when night came on . . . the reflection of the shrubs and the thinly veiled stars convey[ed] [a] feeling of purity and fixedness." Although Timothy was sure the girls would drown if they went out at night on the river, Margaret had no such fear. Rather, as they floated in their boat, she thought of Shelley and how much more she liked his writing than she did that of the Puritan-minded Milton.[8]

Fuller at first felt "wild and free" in nature. Feeding her fantasy was the idealism of the German Romantics she was reading—Goethe, Ludwig Tieck, Friedrich von Schlegel, and Novalis. Fuller thought Novalis a good example of the central concept of the Romantic school in that his writings focused on "the secret principles of the individual mind." She valued Novalis for his psychological insights and disagreed with those who criticized him for his tendency to mysticism. She sympathized with this German mystic's *yearning:* his wish to merge his being with that of an almighty mysterious Spirit whose gender-neutral power seemed to transcend that of the petty, dictatorial father. She appreciated the notion of the existence of such a mystic-romantic entity—whether it appeared in the shape of Nature, a vehicular Energy, or a great Creative Spirit, what Germans saw as a Primordial I (the *Ur-Ich* of Friedrich von Schlegel).[9]

Like the German mystics, Fuller yearned to experience such a moment of transcendence during which—as Novalis's friend Friedrich Schleiermacher, the leading Romantic theologian of the period, put it—"the whole soul is dissolved in the immediate feeling of the Infinite and Eternal." At the end of one beautiful June day, Fuller wrote Clarke that she had never felt "any-thing like" the joy she felt that "divine" day, except during her Thanksgiving Day 1831 mystical experience alongside the pool of water. For Fuller, then, it seems, mysticism was a means to Dionysian connection to godlike power.[10]

Later, in Italy, when she became a mother and an active player in the Roman Revolution, Fuller merged this exalted view of mysticism with revolutionary activism. Now, however, she read Germans like Schlegel for enjoyment. She confessed to not understanding Johann Gottlieb Fichte, who Schlegel said had "solved" the metaphysical problem of dualism with his philosophy positing: "Everything which is for the I is by means of the I," that is, by means of the *Ur-Ich* (the Primordial I), which is, in Schlegel's view, "the grounding principle of philosophy because it is the ground of reality."[11]

Alone in Groton, Fuller's restless mind kept turning over ideas like these in its search for an all-embracing idea that could answer all her questions and satisfy her hunger—not just for intelligent conversation but also for love. Even Clarke was soon to tell her that he liked her as a friend of the mind, not as a lover. Unattached to a man, as it were, Fuller sought to find a center in herself that she could rely on. Her search led to the Romantics' ancient ancestor, Plato, whose mystical idealism she found as alluring as the Germans' and Shelley's. On 3 June to Clarke, who had graduated from Harvard Divinity School and accepted a pulpit in Louisville, Kentucky, Fuller wrote how the idealism of Plato's dialogues, of Socrates' insistence therein that within each interlocutor lay a truth to be uncovered, corresponded with her own current outlook on life. Yet as much as she liked what she read in the "Apology" and "Crito," she found Plato's argument for the soul's immortality in "Phaedo" inadequate. She thought he did not "clearly show . . . what the soul is, whether eternal *as* the Deity, created *by* the Deity, or how."[12]

This last distinction was important to Fuller. In the religion of her Puritan forebears, God was the original creator, the giver of life and light. Man himself is not the light but exists to bear witness of that light, which is viewed as the true light, the Father's Word made flesh in Christ. Redemption thus depended upon a person's acceptance of Christ as savior, and those who accepted Christ into their lives served as conduits through which God's light shines. Such a passive part, this position of servitude to God as Father, was unacceptable to Fuller, who, like her fellow Transcendentalists, wanted the Father's power *in* her "*as* the Deity." Only then would she have the creative power to remake the world to suit her.[13]

Though earlier she had joked to Clarke about her ever-fluctuating sense of self, now in Groton she began to feel uneasy about being so unanchored, as if, she wrote Clarke in the autumn, she must be "as painfully seeking for the centre of my orbit as I was formerly to 'wander into the vague.'" After all, while on the one hand German idealism gave her a way to expand her sense of self, on the other it left her feeling like a wanderer with no center, no real home. She felt that way especially in Groton, where she had nothing to say to the local folk, and tension between her and her father was mounting. With the fall air full of cascading leaves and the cicadas chanting "melancholy bodings," it became increasingly clear to her that unless she could find a way to earn enough money to leave Groton, she might have to live there the rest of her life. Depressed by that fact, as well as by the thought of some "painful domestick circumstances" she had apparently witnessed in the Boston home of her Uncle Henry, with whom she was staying after a ten-day visit with the Farrars in Cambridge, she wrote Clarke a dark letter on 7 October. In it she notes how, "in many respects," she is "less happy" than he. "O pray for me," she tells her minister friend in this cryptic letter: "Hard as has been the part I have had to act, far more so than you ever knew; it is like to become much more difficult." She is less happy in part because he can "speak freely" to her about "all" his "circumstances and feelings," whereas: "It is not possible for me to be so profoundly frank with any earthly friend. Thus my heart has no proper home."[14]

Such talk of the want of a "real home" was typical of the German Romantics' sense that they were wanderers on earth without actual fathers and hence without homes. All Fuller knew, however, was that she felt she had no "proper home" in Groton and was hence searching literature for a better way for her to exist in a world where circumstances dictated against her. Thus she buried herself in books, particularly those of Goethe. In August she had read Goethe's "second residence in Rome" with "an earnest desire to live as he did—always to have some engrossing object of pursuit." It was hard, however, to do that, when a heavy load of domestic chores deprived her even of the time it took to exchange letters with friends, the "all of freedom that has fallen to my lot," she had written Hedge on 4 July, "the anniversary of our independence." "Free?" she had cynically asked Clarke on 30 August. "Vain thought!"[15]

Fuller was growing increasingly skeptical about the individual's capacity to control his or her fate. On her first Christmas Eve in Groton, she pondered the subject in a letter to Clarke, who was discouraged at having failed to convince Christian evangelicals in Louisville to convert to Unitarianism. Fuller tells Clarke that she admires his "faith in the power of the human will." She herself, however, feels that no one should underestimate "the incalculable power which outward circumstances have over character," her own having "been formed amid . . . secret trials and petty conflicts" which make her "memory" of her "transition state [apparently from childhood to adolescence] so hateful" to her.[16]

The Fullers' living conditions in Groton might suggest the kind of "secret trials" to which Fuller refers. For at the farm, circumstances *were* grim. Fuller's overworked mother was "subject to violent illnesses." Her grandmother Crane, a pious moderate Calvinist who stayed with them during the winter of 1833–34, was also frequently ill. By March 1834 Fuller was writing Amelia Greenwood that "circumstances" had forced her to promise her father that she would teach her younger siblings five days a week for five to eight hours a day. That duty, along with needlework and the absence of adequate help (at one point they had only one servant to help with the farm work), left her no time to read or "*think.*" In the meantime, Fuller observed that Timothy was growing embittered over "the cares" of his "narrowed income" as well as over his two rebellious elder sons, Eugene and William Henry, whom he had battled with and who had thus fled from home.[17]

Maybe, among other things, they did not like the bizarre routines that Timothy subjected himself and his sons to in his perverse effort to teach them Spartan endurance and the value of hard work. Richard says his father persisted in his youthful habit of "immediately on rising in the morning . . . plung[ing] into cold water—breaking the ice for the purpose in winter." And his granddaughter Edith Davenport Fuller, the daughter of Arthur, tells how he insisted on using "rough towels" to dry after bathing in ice-cold water. These trials of endurance he forced on his sons. According to Edith, "on winter nights he would rush with his boys barefooted for a run through the snow." Other severe teaching techniques included demanding that Richard and Arthur arise the minute he called them to work at dawn and beating their bare backs with a riding-stick when they misbehaved.[18]

Richard, who was eight when they moved to Groton, remembers his father as a "very affectionate" man with a "delicate constitution" who "hum[med] to himself some gentle strain" when he was "engaged with his papers." The combined recollections of others indicate, however, that Timothy Fuller in the country was essentially the same man he had been in Cambridge: fastidious, sadistic, intrusive, and controlling. Perhaps in "the *icy* seclusion of Groton," he hoped he could retake command of events and his family. Though Richard depicts his father as having mellowed, almost everything Timothy did was still full of contradictions. For instance, though he let each son make a pet of a chicken, he reserved the right to repossess it when he wanted to eat it. And he demanded Margaret perform an impossible load of domestic duties even as he urged her to read the letters of Jefferson with him. Doing the latter was the only time in Groton she felt in harmony with this man who kept an eye on his daughter, whose "strong" nature, according to Richard, was beginning to aggravate him.[19]

In the silence of that isolated farmhouse, a palpable tension had developed between father and daughter. The fastidious Timothy was a man who insisted on order and control in every area of his life, whether it be in the precise way he numbered letters from his wife and laid them in a row on his desk in Washington, or in the perfection he had demanded from his daughter as a child in translating the Lord's Prayer into Latin. Unresolved, emotion-laden issues caused bitter feelings now to surface in Margaret as her father watched to see if his daughter was performing to perfection those domestic duties thrust upon her.

In fact Timothy was always watching for signs of errant behavior on the part of his wife, his children, as well as himself, this man who had confided to his wife in a February 1820 letter that at night in his room in Washington he daydreamed about testing his daughter's memory and confessed: "It is rather an effeminate &

idle life I lead when in my room alone in the evening." How in Groton was Timothy to control not only his boys' bad behavior but what he here hints are his own errant urges, since as Timothy knew from the Apostle Paul, neither fornicators "nor effeminate . . . abusers of themselves" would "inherit the kingdom of God." Timothy's carnal urges would have been even more circumscribed by the frequent illness of his wife, an overworked woman who had borne nine children. Perhaps his solution to this problem can be found in the peculiar routines he forced upon his family.[20]

We recall that hygienists in Timothy's day were touting cold baths—preferably in "icy water"—"followed by a brisk friction of the skin" with a rough towel as effective means of quelling "unnatural" sexual impulses in adults as well as in children. They advised "violent exercise and physical discomfort" as the two most effective preventives against the eruption of such dangerous urges. "The shock of cold water falling on the organs" they thought "most beneficial." Such experts' advice on how to control sexual arousal is remarkably like the regimen the self-policing Puritanical Timothy now imposed on himself and his children. One expert suggested that the way to curb a precocious daughter's sinful energies was to have her "lead a quiet life" in the country and engage in regular "out-of-door exercise." And, in addition to a cold bath every second day, she should be made to "avoid anything calculated to arouse the passions, such as going into gay company, reading exciting works of fiction, etc." Living in Groton certainly kept Timothy's elder daughter out of "gay company." It also kept her from becoming too absorbed in books not directly related to the tutoring of her siblings, which occupied her time when she wasn't mending clothes. Timothy's routines may especially have been meant to control the errant energies of Margaret's youngest sibling, Lloyd. Though only seven when the family moved to Groton, Lloyd was surely already exhibiting signs of the intrinsic hostility and mental instability that were to become manifest later not only in his wild claims that the food was poisoned at home and that he was hearing "voices in the air," but also in his, of all things, compulsive masturbating.[21]

The appeal of the Romantics for Fuller may have been, then, at this time, not so much because of their faith in the imagination's constructive power to transform reality into paradise, but because of their darker premonition that the conscious ego may at best be, as Northrop Frye put it, like a drunken boat that "struggles to keep afloat on a sea of libidinous impulse." Fuller fought to keep afloat, to maintain her sanity amid circumstances that, as she said in a January 1834 letter, had "appalling power." In light of the harsh routines Timothy imposed on his family at the farm, Fuller's February 1835 assertion in a letter to Hedge that she has "no confidence in God as a Father" makes sense. She tells him she wishes she "could believe in Revelation and consequently in an over-ruling Providence," for then "many things which seem dark and hateful to me now would be made clear or I could wait." But, as of now, "it . . . seems to me that we are ruled by an iron destiny."[22]

Under Timothy's dictate at the farm, it must have seemed that way to Margaret. Despite Richard's rosy recollections, Timothy remained for the most part a powerful force that his elder sons collided with in a battle "which would not," Margaret later wrote Richard, "have ended" at the farm. Not only, then, had family life at the farm *not* provided Margarett Crane and her children with what Timothy had hoped it would, a (to borrow from the late Christopher Lasch) "haven in a heartless world" wherein a U.S. president had "forgot[ten]" to award him for his loyalty with an embassy post abroad and Massachusetts voters had overwhelmingly rejected him in his run for Massachusetts's lieutenant governor; not only did it *not* provide a quiet place where he could write his U.S. history, it had been in fact outright dangerous to their mental and physical health. Looking back on those days, Margaret would later remember spending her first weeks there in a darkened room nursing ten-year-old Arthur, whom a servant had almost blinded by hitting him in the eye with a piece of wood. In another disturbing incident, Timothy perhaps unconsciously acknowledged to his children that Margaret's strong will—the "struggle of chaotic elements" in her—was on a collision course with his: One day while demonstrating pistol safety at the fireside in the parlor, Timothy noted the importance of handling even unloaded pistols with care. "Now children," Richard recalls his father saying, "I know perfectly well that these pistols are not loaded; yet, in showing you the operation of the lock, I shall not point the pistol at the head of some one, as a boy might do, for bravado." "For instance," he continued, "I shall not point it at your sister Margaret," whereupon he pointed his pistol at the wall near the floor and pulled the trigger. The bullet hit with such force—for indeed the gun *was* loaded—that it pierced clear through the wall and floor, into the cellar.[23]

Timothy had encouraged her to pursue her studies in Groton, but reading Jefferson's later letters had merely increased Margaret's religious skepticism. In November 1834 she confessed to Hedge that she often meets with "Infidels," deists, and the rationality of their arguments has been "haunting" her. She recognized in Jefferson's later religious views her own "distressing skeptical notions" about God and Christianity. She mused in her journal about Jefferson's radical religion whether "self-respect without the love of God" can keep man "upright" in "modern times?"[24]

Though she admired Jefferson as an intellectual man of action, a statesman who gave her an idea "of what a genuine citizen of this republic might become," she remained angry at her father for having gotten the family exiled to Groton. She had tried for a while to play "Margaret Good child" for him, but it was not a role she was able to sustain. For, despite her need to please her father, the "dust and weariness and burden of [their] state of seclusion" got to her. Hard farm life—especially after she complied with her father's command that she tutor, in addition to her siblings, three local children for added income—made her irritable and anxious.

As signs of her father's satisfaction with her grew scant and work accumulated, she felt less and less confidence in her abilities.[25]

Fuller felt this anger at her father at a time when Timothy, who, as Richard later put it, "had not always well comprehended nor adequately sympathized with" his daughter's strong nature, needed her more than ever. Not only did he need her to look after the children and help with those demanding household chores that his wife was barely able to complete even when she was well, but his calling on her to read Jefferson with him may also have been his way of acknowledging that through her intellect and actions his political work might live on. Though his descendents would indeed later remember the Honorable Timothy Fuller as "an ardent advocate for freedom and the rights of man," his inability to meet the challenge he had set for himself to emulate the brilliant Thomas Jefferson as a scholar-farmer made him feel his life was a failure.[26]

Adding to his distress was the fact that George Bancroft had recently published the first volume of his *History of the United States* before Timothy had been able to find the time even to begin writing his own (a major reason for his having moved to the country). Timothy urged Margaret to write an article in response to one Bancroft had published in the October 1834 issue of the *North American Review* about slavery in ancient Rome. In it the populist Bancroft blamed Rome's decline on an aristocracy that had nurtured slavery. His article's aim was to bolster the theme of his *History* that Americans ought to follow the path of popular democracy to social enlightenment and reform. Margaret did as her father dictated. Her reply, which appeared in the 27 November edition of the *Boston Daily Advertiser,* argues that it is unwise to "be too hasty in questioning what is established." In taking on her father's republican perspective, Margaret reveals how Timothy had instilled himself in her and how she now dutifully assumed the burden of his existence.[27]

She also wrote three long review articles that Clarke published in the *Western Messenger,* the monthly magazine he would edit from 1836 to 1839 and through which he and his Harvard friends hoped to bring culture and Unitarian liberalism to conservative Cincinnati and Louisville. In an article on the Classical and Romantic that appeared in the December 1835 issue, Fuller acknowledges her affinity with the Romantics, agreeing with them that we are not merely "like mirrors": "The mind has a light of its own." Still, regarding her earthly pilgrimage, she says she hopes to move through Romantic delirium and conflict to a higher spiritual plane.[28]

Fuller in her article asserts her preference for Classical calm to Romantic "*abandon*" and contrasts what she sees at this time as the "lowness of Lord Byron's standard of character" with the purity of Goethe's vision of the pagan Iphigenia. Through her comments on *Iphigenia,* Fuller hints how bad things were for her at

Groton. She notes how important it is to the play's progress that the *mind* of Iphigenia, Agamemnon's virgin eldest child whom he sacrifices to save Greece, "be kept unsullied" so "that she may be a fit intercessor to the gods in behalf of her *polluted* family" (emphasis added), as if to hint that her own family has sunk to an unspeakable low.[29]

Before the December 1835 publication of her article, there were to be tense and even tragic failures of communication between father and daughter. When Margaret, who had been visiting the Farrars in Cambridge, wrote her parents on 2 June 1835 asking for permission and money to travel with the Farrars to Trenton Falls in July, Timothy sent her money, apparently also letting her know of his reluctance to do so. In that 2 June letter, Margaret had commented on her father's coolness to her, saying, "I have felt as if you thought of me less than I wished you should." Seeking his approbation by proving her mettle, she lists her activities in Cambridge, including the fact she heartily rode "twenty two miles on horseback" during a single day's outing. Perhaps as a subtle dig at her father she also gives news about her brothers: William Henry is pleasing people in Boston, where he is working for their Uncle Henry, and she has heard that Eugene is doing fine as a schoolteacher in Culpeper County, Virginia. She tells Timothy of "the positive extacy" she will feel if he will give her fifty-seven dollars for the trip. She ends this epistle with a manipulative twist: "*Will* you not write to me immediately and say you love me and are very glad I am to be so happy???"—happy, that is, provided Timothy gives her both love and money.[30]

In this letter, as well as the last she wrote her father (dated 13 August 1835 from Cambridge), Margaret appeals to Timothy for money and love but offers no words of concern about his own well-being. Having long wanted to meet the much-talked-about Emerson, she ends her remarks to her father in her 2 June letter saying it was "unkind" of their Groton minister, Mr. Robinson, "to have Mr [Waldo] Emerson [preach] during my absence." She tells her father she is thinking about leaving the liberal Robinson's Unitarian church, which she attends with him, and joining Richard and Arthur at the evangelical Union Congregational Church. Margaret's threat to leave her father's church seems meant to hurt Timothy, who as a student at Harvard had abandoned the Calvinism of his father to become a Unitarian. He did this in part to escape the Calvinist emphasis on predestination as well as the fire-and-brimstone sermons by ministers like John Todd, who, until early autumn 1833, had been the preacher at Groton's Union Congregational Church.[31]

Upon returning to Groton from Cambridge, Margaret was looking forward to traveling with the Farrars to Europe the following summer. Accompanying them would be Anna Barker and the wealthy, handsome eighteen-year-old Sam Ward. But plans fell through when, that September, she became deathly ill, which Capper thinks may have been partly caused by psychological stress.[32]

It may be true as Capper contends that public reaction to a story by Margaret titled "Lost and Won: A Tale of Modern Days and Good Society" that was published in the *New England Galaxy* on 8 August 1835 featuring "a sneering and calculating womanizer" (a character apparently based on a well-known Cambridge ladies' man) contributed to her despair. Certainly the anger people expressed after seeing themselves parodied in print by Fuller would have upset her, but that was just one factor contributing to her depression. What made her "vaguely suicidal" was her overall situation: the inescapable circumstance of being stuck in the country with her father, who, when he thought she might die, "hung over her couch . . . tenderly," as Richard tells it, for nine days and nights. As Margaret recollects the scene (which may confuse wished-for-words with what her father really said), Timothy stood by her bed and, perhaps motivated by an awareness of his past relentless criticism of her "faults," said: "My dear, I have been thinking of you in the night, and I cannot remember that you have any *faults*. You have defects, of course, as all mortals have, but I do not know that you have a single fault." And when her fever after nine days had broken he said to his wife: "I have no room for a painful thought now that our daughter is restored."[33]

Before Margaret had recovered enough to be able to tell her father how grateful she was for his "extravagant expression of regard," Timothy fell ill with Asiatic cholera, possibly caused by contaminated water, and died. The days before his death, he had spent draining some lowlands on the farm. On 30 September for dinner he ate his usual rice and milk. That afternoon, while still in the house, he suddenly started vomiting, then sank to the floor. For twenty hours he experienced alternate spasms and chills until "there was a lull, preparatory to the final onset, which was to . . . liberate the tried spirit," recalls Richard, echoing Revelation 21:4, "to know no more pain, no more sorrow, no more death."[34]

Timothy died on the morning of 1 October 1835. Aged twenty-five, Margaret stood by his bed and closed his eyes. With no more chance to set things right with her father, her memory of him was colored by guilt; she had never even visited the "little wood" he had fondly called "Margaret's Grove," where he had recently constructed a seat for her to read. Stunned and numb, Margaret, who moved into the power vacuum left by her father's death, called the younger children to her and bade them kneel with her around his bed. She prayed to God in heaven and pledged, as Higginson was later to record the story her mother often told, "that if she had ever been ungrateful or unfilial to her father, she would atone for it by fidelity to her brothers and sisters."[35]

Margaret grieved. But lingering feelings of sadness, anger, hurt, and guilt complicated her mourning the death of this father whose "image," she said in her journal, "follows me constantly." "Whenever I am in my room, he seems to open the door, and to look on me with a complacent, tender smile. . . . The saddest feeling is the remembrance of little things, in which I have fallen short of love and duty." Thus the intrusive Timothy, though dead, seems to have continued to impose himself upon his daughter—even to have, as Capper has said, "uncannily reincarnated" himself in her memory.[36]

Beneath Margaret's guilt was a barely repressed sense of rage that her father had wronged her by dying. Later both she and Richard would suggest that their father's death was perhaps inevitable. For shortly before Timothy died he had expressed "a presentiment" to Arthur "that his departure from earth was near at hand." And in an 1842 letter to Richard, Fuller will conclude that their father's death was for the best since his fortunes would have only continued to decline, with failure inevitable. Both seem to suggest there was something suicidal about his death. At the time of his death, however, Margaret was primarily aware that Timothy had left her and her mother with a terrific financial burden. On 3 November she wrote how much she now regretted "being of the softer sex." If she were the "eldest son," she could be her siblings' guardian; she could "administer the estate, and really become the head of [her] family." But as a woman with no business skills, what was she to do? Her father, she recalls in her 1842 letter to Richard, had died intestate, bequeathing his wife a "heavy burden of care" and his daughter seemingly irresolvable "conflicts" of mind, "as I doubted whether to give up all which my heart desired"—that is, a yearlong tour of Europe with the Farrars—"for a path for which I had no skill, and no call, except that *some one* must tread it."[37]

Taking charge of the estate, Timothy's brother Abraham eventually managed to secure on a first distribution of assets $1,333.34 for each of Timothy's seven children; on a second distribution in 1844 each child received $252.88. But that happened only later and involved the sale of noninterest accruing bank stocks and notes as well as some depreciated houses—including the Cambridgeport house and a couple small farms Timothy had managed to lose money on. According to Capper, for several years the total net income per year was less than four hundred dollars, enough only to allow the family minimal maintenance on the farm. Faced with their dire financial situation, Margarett Crane and the siblings nonetheless urged Margaret to use her meager immediate inheritance to go to Europe as planned. Margaret struggled over several months in deciding whether she should go to Europe or stay home to assume the role of provider for the fatherless Fuller family. The decision, notes Capper, was made for her in May when her Uncle Abraham pointed out that her share of the estate would cover expenses for only half the projected year she planned to travel with the Farrars. Moreover, she felt that for the sake of her mother and younger siblings she had to stay in the United States and find a way to earn money—and that meant teaching, the only socially acceptable way for a middle-class woman like herself to earn money.[38]

Six months later she bitterly wrote that her heart had been broken "by sorrow and disappointment." To have "looked upon Death very near," only to have awakened to find herself fatherless, was a shock she would not easily get over. The shock was greater since she had never had a chance to make amends with this obsessively critical man who had taxed her young life, yet who had also given her an extraordinary education. The yearning she had felt since early childhood—"to pour out my soul to some person of superior calmness and strength"—surfaced in this time of stress. Before Timothy's death she had expressed hope that maybe the English writer Harriet Martineau, whom she had met at the Farrars, might be such a guide, but the English Unitarian Martineau, who had (according to Capper) not "a particle of faith in Christ's divinity," had left Fuller with doubts about her spiritual life. And when Martineau sailed home to England, Fuller was left still wishing "some friend" still might "do,—what none has ever yet done,—comprehend me wholly, mentally, and morally, and enable me better to comprehend myself." Feeling overwhelmed by adult responsibility in Groton, she wanted a friend like Goethe who could show her "how to rule circumstances, instead of being ruled by them."[39] The person from whom she would seek intellectual support and guidance would be Ralph Waldo Emerson.

PART THREE

Emerson, Epistolary Friend and Guide

After her father's death, Fuller wanted a friend more than ever to help her find a "centre" within "the ceaseless fluctuation of [her] mind." She had begun to see Emerson as this wished-for friend long before she actually met him. She had heard much about him from James Clarke and Henry Hedge and in letters to friends was already being playfully "familiar" in referring to him. To Almira Barlow she relays gossip about "Waldo Emerson *dining in boots*" at the home of a wealthy dry-goods dealer during his 1832–33 tour of England, and adds, "absolument a faire mourir!" (it would absolutely make you die laughing). On 6 October she again wrote Barlow, who was in Brooklyn with her husband, how at the Farrars the month before she had heard Emerson's cousin Orville Dewey speak "with due admiration of the Rev W. Emerson, that only clergyman of all possible clergymen who eludes my acquaintance." "Mais n'importe!" (but not important!), she exclaims, "I keep his image bright in my mind."[1]

And as she did, she increasingly linked Emerson's image with that of her father. Thus when Hedge the next month reported that Emerson was reading her Tasso translation, Fuller replied that it "gratified" her to feel "that a mind which had affected mine so powerfully should be dwelling on something of mine." She would, she wrote him, "very much" like "his corrections." To be corrected by a father figure was, after all, her "habit." She cannot even "think alone," she had written Clarke, "without imagining some companion."[2]

Ten months after Timothy's death, Fuller's wish to meet Emerson was fulfilled. Both Martineau and Hedge had praised her to Emerson. Hedge spoke of Fuller's work as a German scholar and loaned Emerson her manuscript translation of Goethe's *Tasso*. Impressed with Fuller's German aptitude, Emerson in July 1836 invited her to spend three weeks as a guest in his Concord home. The invitation lifted her spirit. For, with Timothy gone, Margaret, we recall, had decided not to travel with the Farrars to Europe that summer but to stay in Groton to help her mother and siblings with the farm. In the absence of the two older boys, who had fought with Timothy and fled the farm before their father's death, Arthur, now thirteen, was the oldest of the remaining sons able to help with hard farm work. Nonetheless, Margarett Crane and her remaining children planted corn, beans, and pumpkins, milked the cows, and got the cooking, cleaning, and mending done. Mrs. Fuller even managed to keep her garden in order. And Margaret that winter continued homeschooling her siblings "at a time," she later confessed to Arthur, when her "mind was much excited by many painful feelings."[3]

Emerson himself was well acquainted with "the house of pain." In addition to the February 1831 death from tuberculosis of his lovely young wife, Ellen, his brilliant brother, Edward, who in 1828 had suffered a mental collapse, had died of tuberculosis in Puerto Rico in October 1834. And, most recently, in early May 1836, his greatly admired and beloved brother Charles, who had made him laugh more than anyone, had caught a cold. Already sick with tuberculosis, he had gone to stay with their eldest brother, William, in New York when, on 9 May, he collapsed and died before Elizabeth Hoar (his fiancée) and Waldo could reach his bedside.[4]

Though the way people grieve is as varied as their fingerprints, Ralph Waldo Emerson and Margaret Fuller were individually responding to the deaths of their loved ones in a similar way. Grief lingered long after their loved ones had passed, and they each sought in others the loved ones they had lost. Their searches to find surrogates—brothers, in particular, for Emerson and a father for Fuller—were especially intense because the deaths had been so sudden. Neither Emerson nor Fuller had an opportunity to say good-bye or to resolve outstanding issues in their individual relationships.[5]

Timothy's unexpected death stirred in his daughter a strong desire to seek a personal relationship with Emerson as the ideal companion she had been seeking. Emerson, in turn, would seek to find in Fuller a replacement for the loquacious Charles, as well as for his bold, self-educated, Calvinistic spinster aunt, Mary Moody Emerson, who in his youth had been his intellectual guide yet who did not now approve of the radical direction of his religious inquiry. Thus death, as critic Christina Zwarg argues, frames the narrative of the letters between Fuller and Emerson, which tended to replay the epistolary relationship a younger Fuller had with her father when Timothy was away in Washington. According to Zwarg, viewed from Emerson's perspective the correspondence took place from the time shortly after the May 1836 death of Charles up to right before Margaret's July 1850 death. From Fuller's perspective, however, the exchange took place from the time shortly after her father's death in October 1835 up to the symbolic death of her friendship with Emerson. That happened when Emerson at first did not respond to Fuller's last letters from Italy, and then only to write his despairing friend—who, having just witnessed the 10 June 1849 bombardment of Rome, had written him pleading to him for love and understanding—that she should not come home.[6]

11 ∽ The Search for a Guide

In 1836, the year he published *Nature,* Emerson's psychological state was marked by a need to generate a life-sustaining philosophy from his lingering grief over the loss of his wife, Ellen Tucker, and his cherished brothers, Charles and Edward, a philosophy more satisfying to him than was either "an effete, superannuated Christianity" or the reason-based beliefs of New England Unitarianism. Self-reliant fortitude was imperative to him in light of his haunting memory that both of his brothers, before their deaths from tuberculosis, had exhibited signs of mental instability—Edward's mind having "collapsed" to such an extent that Emerson had to have him committed to McLean's Asylum in June 1828. If ever there was for Emerson an outward sign of the terrible uncertainty of the inner life, it was his brilliant brother's mental instability and fatal illness.[1]

Still, for all his foreboding about this "gloomy epoch," Emerson had reason to feel good about life. In September 1835 he had married the earthy and effusive, punctilious and intense Lydia Jackson, whom he called "Lidian" and describes in a letter as having "a noble heart & an ingenious mind" but no "brilliant genius for Economy." Despite her apparent inability to stay within a budget, Lidian would prove to be managerially efficient when it came to raising their children, tending to her mother-in-law, and entertaining a constant flow of Waldo's houseguests. Cheering Emerson immensely was the fact that Lidian, in October 1836, would bear their first child, Waldo. Moreover, Emerson was able to eke out a decent living as a public lecturer, a kind of lay preaching he enjoyed, a profession made possible in part due to the inheritance bequeathed him by Ellen, whose father had been a well-to-do merchant. And, too, as Joel Porte has said, his life was brightened when 1836 brought into his "orbit" Margaret Fuller.[2]

From the first, the "superabundant" Fuller unsettled the usually reserved Emerson. Emerson had always been reticent in expressing affection for others, half suspecting that "the presence of real emotion" in relation to a loved one "is a sign" (as he had just written in *Nature*) that he or she will be "withdrawn from our sight in a short time." Emerson had learned this lesson in loving Ellen. He had loved her tenderly, yet death had stolen her just sixteen months after they married. Even the mere thought of loving again made him anxious.[3]

Such anxiety in relation to a "real" human touch does suggest, as some critics say, not only how profoundly he had been wounded by death but also how insecure Emerson felt. His was a fundamental insecurity grounded in feelings of uncertainty about his mental as well as his physical (including, presumably, sexual) prowess. Critics have long noted that the dominant mood of Emerson's early journals is a sense of impotence, an awareness of a "defect of character" that made him uneasy "in the company of most men and women." After all, of all the Emerson sons, he had been the "silly one," having graduated thirtieth in a class of fifty-nine from Harvard, whereas Edward and Charles had both been at the top of their class. That he fell so deeply in love with the poetically talented but tubercular Ellen suggests that he may have found it easier to love a traditional albeit witty, bright female than a brilliant, bold, unconventional woman, just as it was easier for him to idealize the dead Ellen than it ever was for him to write a passionate love letter to his second wife, who had "a gift" (according to Emerson) "to curse and swear," and who shared his bed for forty-seven years. As he himself later wrote Lidian, who frequently lamented her husband's lack of passion for her, he could not easily change from a "photometer" to a "stove."[4]

Biographers note that Emerson's mother, Ruth, a calm and deeply religious woman, believed discipline should be stressed over affection and hence rarely showed her sons signs of her love. The aim of her child-rearing practices, they say, was to instill in her children "the kernel of Calvinism in its most fundamental, pre-verbal form." Emerson nevertheless kept her close to him until her death in 1853. Mary Moody Emerson, whom Emerson fondly called Father Mum, also had a profound effect on his development. After the death when he was eight of his father, William, a conforming Unitarian minister who was "severe" toward his children, the unmarried Aunt Mary lived with them and helped her sister-in-law raise him. The indefatigable, death-infatuated Mary, who slept in a bed shaped like a coffin and wore her burial shroud whenever she traveled, tried to instill in her nephews the tenets of Calvinism, especially those of the New Lights evangelical branch that clung to the Westminster Catechism. This kind of neo-Calvinism stressed not only original sin, human depravity, and salvation by election, but also the mystical nature of the Trinity and God's overwhelming power. Despite her adherence to this dark vision of human potential, the bold-spirited, four-foot-three Mary Moody gave Waldo a model of fiery intellectual power from which he would draw much of his will to survive illness and despair.[5]

He also drew strength from the example of his widowed mother, a solid woman who made ends meet by running a rented boardinghouse and borrowing money. Sometimes, however, her frugality proved embarrassing to her reserved middle son. Forced to sleep in their Hancock Street boardinghouse basement with its dismal view of broken furniture and gravestones, Emerson as a boy felt "imprisoned in streets." Once he even had to share an overcoat with Edward and thus endure the mean "taunts of vulgar-minded school-fellows inquiring: 'Whose turn is it to wear the coat to-day?'"[6] Such teasing taunts from male classmates may only have added to his psychological insecurity.

All too aware of life's uncertainty, Emerson sensed that his strength might lie not so much in politely adhering to social mores as in obeying what he was later to call the "sentiment of virtue." For Emerson, the sentiment of virtue is a "reverence and delight in the presence of certain divine laws" that become apparent to us through a transparent nature when we are living true to the divinity "within" us. Later, in his momentous 1838 "Divinity School Address," Emerson will describe these "higher laws" as "the perfection of the laws of the soul," as a transcendent vision of God's will that cannot be written on paper or spoken. Yet even as a student he intuited that by exhibiting "virtue" in his daily life he could maintain his sense of dignity. And he could do this despite the teasing taunts of his more confidently masculine classmates, or the fervid crushes he developed in college on young women and, in one instance, a young man, named Martin Gay.[7]

He took this vision of virtue from Socrates, whom he read at Harvard as an undergraduate. It was an ethic respected by the philosophers of the Scottish Common-Sense School, who were responding to the skepticism of David Hume, who showed that a cause cannot be completely proved and that belief in a cause is a conditioned reflex. For Hume, then, belief in the external world, as well as in personal identity and God, is the result of conditioning. Responding to Hume, as well as to Locke who argued that morality is not something we innately possess, these Scottish philosophers insisted that the ability to prefer good choices to bad is *not* conditioned behavior but an innate function of the mind, that moral perceptions are an essential part of the human constitution. In tune with their spiritual father, John Calvin, whose ideas Aunt Mary had instilled in her nephew, these Scottish Common-Sense philosophers concluded that men and women have rooted in them a *natural* capacity to distinguish between good and evil, right and wrong.[8]

Like Montague in the novel *Hesitation* that Fuller had read as a child, these philosophers argued that the moral capacity is "natural" because the physical universe operates in accord with laws that in their daily working illustrate the harmony and unity God conferred on the universe when He (God) created it. Virtue—or overall moral excellence, which includes qualities such as courage, justice, and sexual self-control—was thus for Emerson adherence to the course of nature and the laws implanted in humanity by nature's creator, God. He would soon find this idea reinforced by Samson Reed in his *Observations on the Growth of the Mind*. In it Reed argued that we should "account every moment of the existence of the universe as a new creation, and all as a revelation proceeding . . . from the divinity to the mind of the observer."[9]

Natural laws, then, were spiritual, and Emerson early on began to see vice as a violation of the way nature intended a man to behave in his relationships with others. In *Nature* Emerson will note how men throughout history have acknowledged this analogy between the natural world and the spiritual by their use of natural facts as signs of the supernatural. "*Right*," he will note, "means *straight; wrong* means *twisted. Spirit* primarily means *wind; transgression,* the crossing of a *line.*" Since to be natural for Emerson meant to walk the straight and narrow path—that is, to behave in an upright, self-controlled way—to be perverse meant for him the converse, as it had, also, for John Calvin. It was deliberately to take the twisted way, to pursue the path of carnal desire and hence to transgress the laws of God whose ultimate power made possible the universe as well as the capacity for moral judgment in man. In short, to be perverse was to defy God's plan for man, one's divine personal destiny as dictated by the god "within."[10]

So important was the concept of virtue to Emerson that in his first sermon, "Pray without Ceasing," he defined "virtue" as habitual uprightness of character. To live rigidly by the ethic of virtue, as Emerson did, left little room in his life for expressions of pity, fear, despair, sensual love, or sexual desire. This does not mean that Emerson would not later ponder intellectual questions on the complexity of gender. That he would, indeed, do that is evident in a June 1842 journal entry in which he notes: "A highly endowed man with good intellect and good conscience is a Man-woman and does not so much need the complement of woman to his being as another." But pondering questions about gender did not threaten his essential sense of who he felt he was; questions pertaining to his sexuality did. They cut to the quick of Emerson's sense of himself—a self he felt might always be slipping on a sliding earth. Thus throughout his long life, in the style of a conventional Calvinist, Emerson persistently insisted on "uprightness" of character, a term that encompasses sexual self-control.[11]

Indeed, to act on one's virtue meant, according to Emerson, to channel one's sexual energies into deeds that revealed one's homage to the higher laws that shine through nature when a person is being true to his or her better self. Whatever the "terrible freedom" Emerson felt when he broke with the Unitarian Church in 1832, that "freedom" was not consciously thought by him—in any way whatsoever—to be sexual. Emerson never intended to equate spiritual freedom with sexual license, but rather "to *demonstrate*," as he did in his radical 1838 "Divinity School Address," that, as Porte says, "religious truth and human pleasure must coexist." To align human pleasure with religious truth was, for Emerson, not to lower mankind's vision of truth but to lift our idea of sensuous pleasure up from its lowly association with sex to a prayerful contemplation of night's "almost spiritual rays."[12]

On the subject of male sexuality, Emerson, along with most intellectuals of his generation, was strongly influenced by the notions about the organization and appropriate use of vital energies apparent in almost all nineteenth-century writings—whether by men or women, blacks or whites. Social historians have long noted that popular theories in Emerson's day discussed male sexuality in economic terms. Certain celebrated "spermatorrhoeic quacks" had circulated the widely accepted theory that the price a man pays for the ejaculation of sperm is the loss of an invaluable flow of energy that would otherwise be available for intellectual or creative endeavors. Summing up the thinking of his age, the phrenologist Orson S. Fowler (who in November 1837 would examine Fuller's head) observed that "every intellectual genius . . . evinces every sign of powerful manhood, while the ideas of the poorly sexed are tame, insipid, emasculated."[13]

The tendency to see the whole man, psychological and physiological, in economic terms, to link the rationing of one's genital activity with the soul, had an effect on Emerson, whose childhood had taught him to connect masculinity with money, and in particular to equate economic dispossession with impotence and powerlessness. During the years of Emerson's friendship with Fuller, churchgoers regularly heard from pulpits disturbing notions about sexual overindulgence and masturbation. A key minister responsible for spreading anxiety about these matters was John Todd. Todd, we recall, was preaching at the evangelical Union Congregational Church in Groton in 1833, the year the Fullers moved there. Since the Fullers had moved to Groton in early April and Todd was not replaced until October, it is reasonable to assume that both Timothy and Margaret, though members of Robinson's liberal Unitarian church, had at least heard about this flamboyant man and his well-publicized determination to inspire boys to cease their "self-abuse." Indeed, at the time of Timothy's death, both Richard and Arthur were attending the Union Congregational Church.[14]

The fiery Todd taught the necessity of disciplining the sexual energies. Todd believed that semen flows from the mind through the veins to the sexual organ, and that any release of sperm, other than for procreation, wasted male creative energy. Thus he saw masturbation, as well as profligate male or female sexual activity, as both a sin and a threat to a man's masculinity. We know that Emerson had assimilated this language because of his insistence that books be "vital and spermatic" and that a man spend his energy thriftily by pouring it forth on a page in "spermatic, prophesying, man-making words."[15]

For a man of low energy like Emerson, the presence of an aggressively sexual, smart female like Fuller, a woman whose mind excited him, unsettled his carefully monitored scheme of creative-sexual energies. Emerson was from the start "enormously troubled," as Zwarg has said, "by the seductive energy released through his intellectual conversation with Fuller." Her stimulating presence seems to have stirred in him a fear that his "manly" cloak of prophetic words might cover not a powerful man but, instead, as Henry James Sr. later suggested, a "maidenly" man. His fear was perhaps exaggerated by his awareness that his life as a self-reliant male writer had been made possible, in part, by money left him by a woman: Ellen.[16]

When Fuller entered Emerson's "orbit" on 21 July 1836 to stay as a guest in his comfortable Concord home, she was eager to shine brightly as Emerson's satellite, to take in and reflect on the "man-making words" he poured forth to her during her three-week visit. Before setting out by coach from Groton, she had no doubt spent her usual hour and a half "*fixing*" her hair and dress. For Emerson recalls that Fuller, who was under average height but athletic in frame, appeared "carefully and becomingly dressed"; according to him she had fashioned herself that day into a woman "of ladylike self-possession."[17]

Fuller that day had styled her "muscular" outer self and corralled her "super-abundant animal" energies so she might give the best performance of her life, since her aim was, as Emerson himself later acknowledged, to please this man she had admired for so long from afar. Taught by Mrs. Farrar how to conceal her physical imperfections, she had slipped a horsehair shoulder pad under one side of her dress to disguise the appearance that one shoulder was slightly higher than the other. And she no doubt would have arranged her abundant light brown hair so as to soften what a later admirer, Caroline Dall, called "sharp features": her thin mouth, Roman nose, high forehead, eyes "small & grey"—squinting eyes that seemed nevertheless electric when she talked or when she burst out, as she so often did, in exuberant, almost childlike laughter.[18]

What Fuller failed to understand was that in Emerson she had chosen a man who could be only at best a reluctant actor in her scripted play. For Emerson, as we have seen, in his attitude toward strong women was admiring yet cautious. In a lecture, "Woman," he would give after her death, he went so far as to say that "Man is the will, and woman the sentiment." On "this ship of humanity, will is the rudder, and sentiment the sail. When woman affects to steer," says Emerson, "the rudder" becomes "a masked sail." And few things were so unsettling to Emerson as the thought of a feminine skirtlike sail masking—or emasculating—his masculine rudder. Thus Fuller, a woman with, as Emerson himself put it, "a strong temperament," had set out on a quest to win the heart and mind of a man who, though profoundly impressed by her mind, would, as historian Ann Douglas said, eventually abandon and hence damn her.[19]

Emerson recalls in the *Memoirs* how, during their first half hour of conversation, Fuller's "extreme plainness,—a trick of incessantly opening and shutting her eyelids,—the nasal tone of her voice,—all repelled" and made him say to himself, "we shall never get far." But Fuller on that hot summer day was "in the finest vein of humor"; and despite his efforts to resist her repartee she roused in him, he later said, "a strange, painful excitement" that kept him for several fun-packed hours on a rollicking ride "between laughing and crying." "She made me," he confesses, "laugh more than I liked"—more, perhaps, than he had laughed since the death of Charles, who, before Margaret entered his life, had made him laugh more than anyone.[20]

Emerson recalls that she made no attempt to "conceal the good opinion of me she brought with her, nor her wish to please." Her talk was "a comedy in which dramatic justice was done to everybody's foibles." Later that night when Emerson went to his study, he merrily thought "of the crackling of thorns under a pot." Soon enough, as the days bounced by, "the eyes," wrote Emerson, "which were so plain at first, soon swam with fun and drolleries, and the very tides of joy and super-abundant life."[21]

In the presence of an attentive Emerson, Fuller relaxed. She saw Emerson's cool blue eyes grow warm with laughter as she magnetically drew him near to her with her "perpetual brilliant sallies." Increasingly at ease, Fuller wrote her sister Ellen, who had written Margaret from Groton complaining about her own worn-out dresses, how at the Emersons' she had worn "a 'faded calico frock,'" which did not, found Margaret, "prevent my exciting respect and interest." And sometime in the course of this first visit, while sitting and talking with Emerson in his study (her childhood pattern with her father and increasingly her "habit" with Emerson), he read to her a draft version of his "little book called 'Nature.'" In late June he had drafted what was to become the final paragraph of the book in a section titled "Prospects" that he would finish the day after Fuller left, 11 August. Despite the lack of a polished final section, Emerson, on 20 July, the day before Fuller arrived, wrote Hedge he had the manuscript in "solid prose."[22]

Emerson's study is in the northwest corner of his large New England farmhouse. This cozy book-lined room had in it a sturdy rocking chair, a velvet-upholstered wood-frame lounge chair, a round writing table piled with books and papers, a Persian throw rug on top of an ingrain carpeted hardwood floor, and hanging over the mantel, the copy of a painting Emerson had brought back from his 1833 European travels of the Moirai, or Fates—those three female figures from classical mythology who twine, measure, and cut life's yarn, and whose laws even Zeus could not defy.[23]

Having spent the morning sequestered in his study while Fuller read undisturbed in her room, Emerson would appear at one or two to enjoy dinner with Margaret and his wife. Afternoons were spent in visiting, walking, or reading aloud, as Emerson read *Nature* aloud to Fuller sometime during her extended late summer visit, this essay that taxes the minds of its readers. One unfriendly critic, a contemporary of Emerson, was soon to mock Emerson's dialectical essay as a piece of "obscure" prose containing "a vein of mysticism" that makes a reader feel "as in a disturbed dream." Little wonder, for in *Nature* Emerson asks readers to rethink the way they see the world; he attempts to come to terms with the problem of Cartesian dualism, with our awareness of ourselves as both immortal souls and bodies that will die. For, as Emerson darkly notes in his chapter "Discipline": the painful lesson nature teaches is that when "God sends a real person to outgo our ideal" such that "we cannot choose but love them," then "it is a sign to us that his [her] office is closing." He or she "is withdrawn from our sight in a short time." The essay thus aims to answer the vexing question "to what end is nature," this *not me* that ends in death. It is to affirm that the soul outlasts nature, "the knell of this coughing body." Unfortunately, studying the essay can make even the sanest readers feel as if they are conversing "with disembodied spirits." It seems to have had such an effect on Fuller. For she later confessed to Emerson that on that summer day when he had "originally" read *Nature* to her, she understood less of it than she would have liked to. Shortly after returning home she wrote him, "I hear much conversation about [*Nature*] that amuses me."[24]

It seems that Fuller did connect that day with a few of the essay's more memorable ideas and images. Such as Emerson's initial charge that, to enjoy an original relationship with God, we must lie for a season "embosomed" in nature and allow her "floods of life" to "stream around and through us." With this striking image of streaming fluids, Emerson no doubt did hold Fuller's attention when he thereafter contended that, scientifically speaking, "all phenomena" can be explained, even those that are "thought not only unexplained but inexplicable," such as "language, sleep, dreams, beasts, sex." Fuller, a reader of the Romantics who was fascinated by dreams and sex yet who felt divided within and sought redemption for her sins, thus would have agreed with Emerson's reminder that, philosophically speaking, the universe is divided into nature and soul. And surely this woman who was overseeing a farm was intrigued and amused by Emerson's assertion that to rediscover God and redeem the soul, we must go out into nature and "look at the stars." For in "the presence of nature," according to Emerson, who gently here alludes to his personal heartache, "a wild delight runs through the man, in spite of real sorrows." "Crossing a bare common, in snow puddles, at twilight," and "under a clouded sky," he had himself, he affirms, "enjoyed a perfect exhilaration."[25]

The essay's most memorable and wittily comic passage seems also to have had an effect on Fuller, for in it Emerson tells how, in a mystical moment, he was able to transcend his own sense of inner division by becoming one with God: "Standing on the bare ground,—my head bathed by the blithe air, and uplifted into infinite space,—all mean egotism vanishes. I become a transparent eye-ball. I am nothing. I see all. The currents of the Universal Being circulate through me; I am part or particle of God."[26]

Though the poet Christopher Cranch, who would eventually become a Unitarian minister and Fuller's friend, was soon to make a "droll" cartoon figure—a large eyeball in top hat with a tuxedoed small round body and spindly long legs—of the passage, Fuller seems to have been touched by it. We know this because her own account of a mystical moment in the woods, one involving a similar loss of ego into God that she experienced that Thanksgiving Day in 1831 but recorded only much later, seems to have been interpreted through the frame provided her by Emerson's vision. We know that Fuller felt so powerfully drawn that evening to this soft-spoken yet eloquent man that, as she wrote him four years later, she had deliberately not read the "little book" through on her own because she "missed the voice." Perhaps, however, she did notice the man's daring comparison of nature to Jesus when he said how nature "stands" like "the figure of Jesus . . . with bended head, and hands folded upon the breast," "pointing always" beyond her to "the absolute." Yet this "Spirit," affirmed Emerson in organic terms, which is "the Supreme Being, does not build up nature around us, but puts it forth through us, as the life of the tree puts forth new branches and leaves through the pores of the old." "As a plant upon the earth," he continued, invoking Romantic metaphors, "so a man rests upon the bosom of God; he is nourished by unfailing fountains, and draws, at his need, inexhaustible power." Thus man draws the breath of God and, in so doing, becomes god.[27]

Surely Emerson shared with Fuller his draft version of *Nature*'s final chapter, "Prospects." Perhaps the "unsettling force" of her strong presence even inspired him to revise it a final time using such "*suggestive*" organic terms. For in it Emerson observes that "Man" was once "permeated and dissolved by spirit." Now, "the dwarf of himself," he no longer "fill[s] nature with his overflowing currents." Once, according to Emerson, man had godlike powers: "Out from him sprang the sun and moon; from man, the sun; from woman, the moon." Yet "having made for himself this huge shell, his waters retired; he no longer fills the veins" but "is shrunk to a drop." A Freudian interpretation might conjure an image as ludicrous as Cranch's walking eyeball. To Fuller, however, who was deeply self-conscious about her own sense of inner division, that is, her lack of spiritual redemption, Emerson's concluding paragraph, even in rough draft form, would surely have had real meaning: "the world lacks unity . . . because man is disunited with himself." And did he perhaps read to her this? "Deep calls unto deep. But in actual life, the marriage is not celebrated." Or, did Fuller's electric presence, as muse and conversationalist, inspire him to add that thought after she had left on 11 August? If he read it aloud to her, she could not have helped but note its implication. Nor could she have missed his warning: "What we are, that only can we see." And, too, she would not have missed his charge to his reader at the essay's end that the way to restore "perfect sight" and hence beauty to a world rendered dead by Newtonian physics is "by the redemption of the soul," a redemption that will come through the loving embrace of a "fluid" nature.[28]

12 ∽ A Fluid Friendship

That Emerson's flow of words filled Fuller's "soul" is evident in her essay, "Modern British Poets," which appeared in two parts in the September and October issues of the *American Monthly*. For in it she focused on writers' psychic conflict as a sign of the times, arguing that, as society has become increasingly mechanistic, so the creative soul that expresses its "individuality" is "brought into a state of conflict" with it. She cites Byron as a poet in conflict with society. Though in her essay she castigates Byron—whose licentious life was the opposite of Emerson's of sexual self-control—for his "moral perversion," she also concedes that in complicated men like Byron, the soul must sometimes struggle hard "with its horrors" before it can acquire peace of mind.[1]

Fuller contends that such periods of psychic "conflict" in poets mark "a transition-state"—a period of "gradual revolution"—during which bold men like Byron "try all things." "Dissatisfied and represt," they enjoy their struggle, for at least in struggling "they feel themselves . . . free." Fuller, however, believes that the vision of men like Wordsworth and Southey who can see the "eternal in man's nature" is superior to the poetry that grows out of the struggle of the bold but "diseased" individual with society. Unlike Byron, such men do not "drift across the waves in the hope of finding *somewhere* . . . a home." Rather, they see with a clear eye "the blue sky" above them. Men like Wordsworth—and surely here she was also thinking of Emerson—"study Nature and *feel* God's presence." They "see the great in the little," and trace through "the petty operations of Nature . . . her most sublime principles." Thus Fuller had already appropriated one of Emerson's precepts: "to see the miraculous in the common."[2]

The echoes of Emerson in this early essay suggest that Fuller, in listening to Emerson, had begun taking in his ideas and attitudes, becoming as if "pregnant" with his "spermatic" words. These words she then poured into her own writing, though not without first altering his ideas to fit her needs as a woman. Thus this new fluid friendship with Emerson had already begun to enhance her intellectual life and her writing, just as she in turn became for him an essential sounding board and source for new material for his own writing.[3]

Here in Emerson was the intellectual guide Fuller had been seeking, an ideal man through whose teachings she could grow and learn as she had in her early relationship with her father, who had been dead not yet a year. In Emerson's presence she felt a familiar need to recite to perfection and hence please this man who stirred to life in her not just pleasurable but also painful sensations she associated with her father, whose "image" followed her "constantly." She had confided to Hedge before she met Emerson that she did not expect to be "disappointed in him" as she had been "in others to whom" she had "hoped to look up."[4]

But at that early point she was not sure what she wanted from Emerson. She knew she wanted an intellectual companion. But she was uncertain whether that person should be male or female because she had no firm-set sexual identity, no sense of herself as a specifically gendered being. She knew, of course, that she was female. But her sense of herself as an intellectual and hence, in her culture, masculine, had been enhanced, as we know, while her father was alive by her strong identification with him. And after his death his image stayed alive in her when she failed to resolve outstanding emotional issues that complicated her mourning. In this guise of the father, whose "image" she had said had "possessed" her in childhood, she did indeed seem to friends like Emerson, "burly" and "masculine."[5]

Like an oyster's shell, this "strong ego" protected what Fuller (who "never forgot," wrote Emerson, "that her name, Margarita, signified a pearl") felt was her gemlike self, buried deep in her center. It also concealed her anxieties about who, in fact, she might really be. In an essay on James MacIntosh that she wrote shortly after her father's death, she noted that the Scottish writer's too-bookish upbringing had deprived him of the centered sense of self a writer needs. Here Fuller had herself in mind, she who always seemed to be wandering in search of a center. The "real me" that she believed lay buried "deep within" still yearned for the loving touch of a mother, the uncritical love and approval her father had failed to give her. This childlike part of Fuller's "self" would seek through Emerson to win her father's approbation.[6]

Yet even on those hot summer nights as the self-consciously intellectual Fuller entertained Emerson in a seductively naive way, the woman in her was not altogether blind to the sexual implications of her discourse. After all, this woman whom Emerson would later call "the queen of discourse" had earlier confessed to Clarke that she was "not a nun." She had even been an early champion of Goethe's *Die Wahlverwandtschaften, ein Roman* (*Elective Affinities*), a novel considered scandalous by many New England readers who disapproved of its unconventional attitude toward marital infidelity.[7]

Fuller, moreover, knew that moralists like the evangelist Todd at that time equated certain sexual practices with sin. Todd had explicitly discussed the debilitating effects of masturbation in his 1835 book, *The Student's Manual,* which went through seven editions in two years. Having been charged with the raising of her four brothers, the youngest of whom, the slow-witted Lloyd, was guilty of the "sin" Todd railed about, Fuller was perhaps aware of the manual's controversial contents. After all, this best-selling book was drawing young men from all over America to the Reverend Todd to say, "Sir, I owe most or all of what I am to your pen."[8]

The language of the day associating male genitalia with the soul certainly would not have embarrassed Fuller. Nor, having commented in an 1835 letter to Hedge on the odd choice of "Mr Emerson" for a second wife (so "entirely unlike [his] first"), would she have been naive about the possibility of a romantic intrigue between herself and Emerson. In April 1836, just three months before her visit with Emerson, she had asked Clarke to tell her all he knew about Goethe, especially information about the German writer's life with his mistress, Christiane Vulpius, suggesting that the subject does not embarrass her. Aware there are "subjects on which men and women usually talk a great deal, but apart from one another," Fuller confides to her close friend James Clarke that she herself is "destitute of what is commonly *called* modesty." When the "blush does not come naturally to my face, I do not drop a veil to make people think it is there." She ends: "All this may be very unlovely, but it is *I*."[9]

Still, Fuller did not consciously at first think of Emerson in sexual terms; it was only through her increasingly intense interaction with him that she would even begin to develop a "sexual vocabulary" adequate to express thoughts about feelings that she and her soon-to-be fellow Transcendentalists still lacked and that Perry Miller long ago summed up as "the one really dangerous theme." That is, sex. Rather, Fuller's professed goal was to develop an intellectual-spiritual relationship with this man she had long admired. She hoped to feel the soothing effect of his presence as a person "fortunate in more accurate knowledge." The guestroom (called "the Pilgrim's Chamber") where she stayed was across the hall from Emerson's study on the ground floor.[10] There in that cozy study the two would sit late at night talking. Perhaps those talks reminded Fuller of the nights her father would have her recite for him in the parlor. What Fuller felt for Emerson at this point was principally the innocent love of an adoring daughter for her father or of a female supplicant for a spiritual father.

In her essay on modern British poets, much of which she wrote in Concord, Fuller excoriated Byron for having yielded to what she calls his "sickly" feverish feelings, his "perverse" impulses. She saw his poetry as a record "of that strange malady, that sickness of the soul, which has, in our day, cankered so visibly the rose of youth." In light of such assertions, it is likely that whenever forbidden (and at this point unconscious) sexual urges surfaced in Fuller, as they might have during her visit with Emerson, her Puritan conscience repressed them. These generated in her the "anxiety" she confessed to him she felt about an anticipated second visit with him in September, which never materialized.[11]

Indeed, as we shall see, her relationship with Emerson mobilized in time virtually every level of her psychosexual being: from her earliest yearnings for motherly love, to the daughter's desire to please and possess the critical father and be recognized by him for her intellectual acumen, to the woman's wish to be loved by a man, to the converse desire in her, as a manlike woman, to caress and control a man whose passivity in the face of her "assault" made him seem (even to him) vulnerable and feminine.[12]

Because Fuller merged the memory of Timothy with her mental representation of Emerson and hence projected onto him her conflicted feelings for her father, she increasingly came to experience Emerson as an extension of herself. This experience made her feel, at times, as if he were actually within her—as if, with his flow of words, he had pierced to the quick of her being. Moreover, because it felt to her as if Emerson had touched her "true" self, it also seemed to her that he could, like Christ, with a touch of his hand heal "the sickness of [her] wounded heart." Such intense and conflicted energies, turned full force on Emerson, had a profoundly unsettling effect on a man self-consciously set on channeling his energies into self-reliant virtue.[13]

These abundant yet conflicted psychosexual energies gave Fuller a magnetic aura as they sparkled through the raucous laughter and chatter of her self-consciously created public persona, a fictional persona that protected her sensitive, "secluded" self from pain. This was the laughter that struck Emerson as the "crackling of thorns under a pot." But in private, especially in her relationship with Emerson or when she was under stress, such defensive theatrics did not shield her from hurt. Although Emerson in the *Memoirs* criticizes Fuller, saying that "persons were her game" and she had a "dangerous reputation for satire," he also concedes he sensed, even during this first visit, that something was amiss beneath this seemingly "haughty" personality. He "felt her to be a foreigner,—that, with her, one would always be sensible of some barrier. . . . She had a strong constitution, and . . . its reactions were strong"—which is why he thought she had "so much to say of her *fate*." Emerson tells how she would be "in jubilant spirits in the morning," yet end the day "with nervous headache, whose spasms, my wife told me, produced total prostration." He thought she lived at a rate so fast that he "foreboded . . . painful crises, . . . which no friendship could avert or console." "She seemed," he sums up in the *Memoirs*, "vulnerable," while in his private journal he calls her "hysterical."[14]

When Emerson made this observation while reviewing after Fuller's death her papers for the *Memoirs*, he was distressed at having found in them a frank statement of her desire for a passionate sexual experience, for "a godlike embrace from some sufficient love." Shortly after she left his home on 11 August he wrote in his journal that, while he found Fuller to be "a very accomplished & very intelligent person," he also considered "how rarely can a female mind be impersonal." Noting how "wonderfully free from egotism of place & time & blood" is Sarah Alden Ripley, wife of his half-uncle Samuel Ripley, Emerson portends: "'M[argaret]. F[uller].' by no means so free with all her superiority. What shall I say of MME [Mary Moody Emerson]."[15]

Emerson's intuition that Fuller was not "so free" was prescient, just as were his later observations that in her need for love she seemed "hysterical" and "vulnerable." Though the term *hysteria* is largely discredited today, certain observations about that late-nineteenth-century personality type made by Stuart Schneiderman in 1981 are relevant to a discussion of Fuller. In *Jacques Lacan*, Schneiderman describes "the classic hysteric" as a sexually repressed person who has no clear sense of sexual identity. He also says that, while it is true that hysterics are sexually repressed, they are nevertheless intensely curious about sexual matters and make "love" a central focus of their lives. Schneiderman, moreover, notes a connection between the onset of a patient's hysteria and the death of an oppressive parent who had previously been much involved in that patient's life. The patient desperately wants to keep "the dead alive"; his or her hysteria derives, then, from "a failed attempt to stay in touch with the dead."[16]

Fuller's story in the past has been interpreted as a classic case of hysteria. Though Fuller did exhibit these personality characteristics (she had an unclear sense of sexual identity, set love as a major theme of her life, and harbored unresolved feelings for her dead father), to cast her as a "classic hysteric" is insulting to Fuller and unhelpful in understanding her. Though in response to a particular situation, Fuller, as we shall see, did experience the panic and pain that twentieth-century psychiatrists associated with "hysteria," for us to interpret her story strictly in those terms does not let us bring to light the complicated set of circumstances she endured as a child that made her later express her pain in a way that made people—even Emerson—label her as hysterical. And though we do not yet know enough about Fuller to be able to speculate on the deeper cause of her lifelong anguish, as we will later in this book, we do know that Emerson was right when he said she seemed "vulnerable." Fuller was, after all, a Romantic, and Romantics tend to display stronger narcissistic characteristics and a more vulnerable and exposed ego than do writers from earlier literary periods. We also know that Romantics self-consciously assume idealized images of self—"fictions," if you will—to compensate for and cover deep and often repressed feelings of anxiety, uncertainty, deprivation, and depression. Because the narcissistically inclined personality has trouble recognizing boundaries between its self and reality—as Fuller sometimes did—it tends to relate to objects as if they were extensions of the self or as they can be used in the service of the self and of the maintenance of its instinctual investment.[17]

Yet Emerson did not need such psychological insights to have an idea of what he was dealing with in the powerful personality of Fuller. For at that point their situations and ambitions were similar. Both had been raised by harsh Unitarian fathers, now dead. Both were caring for reserved, dignified, deeply religious mothers they loved—mothers who were not demonstrative in returning their love. Both had younger brothers who were mentally slow (for Emerson it was Robert Bulkeley, and for Margaret it was Lloyd). Both, moreover, were seeking replacements for beloved others who had recently died—as well as, in Emerson's case, to a divergence in points of view. For Aunt Mary did not now approve of her nephew's religious views. And both, in their fashion, were seeking to affirm—despite personal doubts, anxieties, and uncertainties—a stable sense of self by attending to the still voice of God within. Thus Emerson's response to Fuller was empathic; he sensed that her unsettled inner life seemed to mirror, in a disturbing way, his own.

Sensing an underlying identity with this nervous, laughing, talkative woman while maintaining a glacial outward calm, Emerson listened attentively to the provocative thoughts of this scintillatingly bright, self-described "patient," whose "pain," she said, disturbed even her dreams. As with his Aunt Mary, he internalized many of the words she poured out to him in her letters, as well as in their conversations in his parlor and study, ideas and words that reappeared in his writings. Emerson could not help but to fall, as the late Joel Porte speculated, a little "in love" with this woman who understood the deeper meaning of his discourse. And he fell a little in love with her even as he felt that his mental and emotional health—in effect his sanity—depended on his ability to resist Fuller's seductive wiles, just as she, too, came in time to see that, to gain her center as a writer and hence "self" control, she had to resist his power over her.[18]

Though we have no record of their conversations, we do have Fuller's voluminous notes and letters, which in James Clarke's opinion "contain more of her mind" than "her published writings." These private writings show how, during 1836–42, Fuller moved from a position of worshipful reverence for Emerson as an idealized father figure, through a sense of trust in him as a limited man who could not satisfy her deepest needs and desire, to a place where she was able to make some of his most vital ideas her own. She did this even as the exchange helped her also to see that he and she had significantly different points of view and powers. These personal writings reveal that Emerson was so effective in teaching Fuller to believe in her own unique *power* that, even though he initially enjoyed being swept up in the wave of her conversation, he came increasingly to fear that his "solitary river" was in danger of being depleted by her siphoning sea. When the wave became tidal, he abruptly withdrew, as we shall see, into an embarrassed silence.[19]

13 ∽ A "Forlorn" Boston Winter

After her death Emerson observed of Fuller that, as "a woman, an orphan, without beauty, without money," she had to overcome a lot of "negatives" in order to succeed as a teacher and writer. Fuller's poverty was significant. Forced, in her words, to "get money," in the fall of 1836 she moved to Boston to teach at the innovative Temple School of Human Culture run by the affable but impractical Bronson Alcott.[1]

Located in the Masonic Temple on Tremont Street, the school when it opened in 1834 had been heralded by Boston liberals as a welcome alternative to traditional schools where children learned by a recite-by-rote method. Countering Locke's notion that we are born blank slates, Alcott believed that babies are born, as Wordsworth said, "trailing clouds of glory . . . from God" and that a teacher's job was to stoke into flame each innocent child's still-smoldering spark of divinity. He also thought that children should be taught to speak spontaneously. His Socratic pedagogical method was to lead on and bring out the minds of pupils rather than impose his views on them. Classes were taught by a conversational style in a pleasant environment in which no topic was seen as too profane to discuss, including ones concerning circumcision, conception, and birth.[2]

Fuller liked this approach to teaching. But Elizabeth Peabody, Alcott's assistant since 1834, had been so distressed by gossip about the blasphemous nature of what students at Alcott's school were learning that she had quit her job in July. On 2 August 1836, at the Emersons' home, Alcott met Fuller. And before he had left Emerson's house that day, Alcott, who instantly liked Fuller, offered her the vacated position as teacher of languages and recorder of his conversations with children. Fuller saw the offer as an opportunity to get to Boston, close to friends with whom she could communicate on an intellectual level, as she could not with the country people of Groton. It would also enable her to see more often her new friend, Ralph Waldo Emerson.

Since her visit to Concord, Fuller's drive to win Emerson's friendship had included a couple of comical missed encounters between two people destined, it would seem, to travel in different directions. A 21 September letter to Emerson suggests that she had received an invitation from Mrs. Emerson to visit in Concord too late to make the proposed trip. From Boston, where she was visiting Anna Barker, Fuller expressed her exasperation that her minister, Mr. Robinson, had invited Emerson to exchange pulpits with him on the next Sunday when she would again be away. He had extended this invitation despite her having egotistically begged him *not* to invite Emerson to preach in Groton without first ascertaining if she would be there. "I *detest* Mr Robinson at this moment," she wrote Emerson. Not only had she missed a visit with him in Concord and must also now miss him in Groton, still more disappointing was her discovery that she and Emerson had both attended an event in Boston but because of her nearsightedness she had not recognized his slim imperial figure among the blurred forms before her.[3]

In her September letter, Fuller confesses to her "great ... disappointment" in having to miss him in Groton, yet concedes it is "a great gain to be able to address" him "directly instead of intriguing," as she had the year before. She asks him to take "seriously" her "anxiety" at the thought of seeing him again, brought on in part by her fear that Emerson might reject her open affection. She acknowledges to him that when they were together during her summer visit he "very justly corrected me for using too strong expressions on some subjects." In the voice of a daughter fearful she will displease a powerful father figure, she says: "—If you were to see me just now, dear Sir, you would not like me at all for I am very far from calm." She ends by telling him the address at which his letter can reach her if he thinks "this ebullition worthy an answer." In her need for paternal regard, Fuller here is enacting with Emerson her earlier pattern, when she replied to her father's fault finding and scant love with gratitude.[4]

After moving to Boston, Fuller saw Emerson often. Along with her teaching, which included private classes for "Ladies in German, Italian, and French Literature" that she taught in rooms at No. 2 Avon Place next door to her Uncle Henry's, one night a week she translated Wette and Herder from the German for Dr. William Ellery Channing. Channing, whom everyone respectfully called Dr. Channing, was the revered minister of the Federal Street Church and chief spokesman of New England Unitarianism. He was also the uncle of the future socialist and Transcendentalist William Henry Channing, whom Fuller had met in Cambridge along with Hedge. Though not a follower of Locke, Dr. Channing was also no

Transcendentalist. While believing that "the elements of the Divinity" exist in man, Dr. Channing saw God's relation to man as being that "of a parent to a child." Moreover, he firmly believed that "Jesus Christ" is Christians' "only master."[5]

A shy, socially remote yet eloquent man who was unwilling to cut his ties to eighteenth-century rationalism, Dr. Channing was nonetheless the American spokesman for the only theme that would unite the disparate Transcendentalists. That is, that revelation of the divine is to be attained not so much through dogma as nature, and that such a revelation comes through individual insight and intuition, not systematized theology. Some of Dr. Channing's ardent admirers would drop in to talk with him in his Boston flat where Fuller sat in the background, translating Wette.[6]

One such visitor was Emerson, in town to give a series of lectures, "The Philosophy of History." Another was the outgoing Alcott, who looked like the saint he aspired to be. His skin was extremely fair, and he wore his long flaxen hair brushed away from his angelic face. He had a high, domed forehead and shaggy brows that protruded out over deep-set, sky-blue eyes. A self-absorbed intellectual, Alcott talked nonstop during his visits, boring Fuller, who otherwise loved her translation job. Among other pluses, it gave her a chance to renew her friendships with Elizabeth Peabody and Lydia Maria Child. The latter was married and already a successful writer and well-known abolitionist. In Channing's busy Boston flat, Fuller also met the radical minister George Ripley, as well as another of Dr. Channing's nephews, the handsome, mercurial, irresponsible poet William Ellery Channing, who was soon to win the heart of her pretty but frail sister, Ellen, who was at that time still living in Groton, where she was being taught by a local schoolmaster.

Talking with these forward-looking intellects in Dr. Channing's flat and attending lectures like Emerson's were two of the more pleasant parts of Fuller's life in downtown Boston. Five days and two or three nights a week she taught classes at the Temple School of Human Culture. She began each day at nine giving lessons in Latin and language arts to thirty-seven boys and girls in room 7 of the Masonic Temple, the building that housed not only Alcott's Temple School but also the large lecture hall where Emerson gave his talks on philosophy, reform, and human culture to ever-growing audiences. In this large, carpeted, white, wainscoted room with its tall, arched windows, Fuller read first from *Pilgrim's Progress* or the Bible to the children seated in a semicircle around her. Afternoons she recorded Alcott's talks with his students, one volume of which, *Record of Conversations on the Gospels Held in Mr. Alcott's School,* was published that December.[7]

In the meantime, Fuller was glad for a steady salary and even sought extra pay by teaching in the late afternoon and evening her classes for adolescent girls and young women—most of whom (like Cary Sturgis) were from wealthy and highly literate families—in German literature (Schiller, Tieck, Goethe, Lessing, and Richter) and Italian (Tasso, Petrarch, Ariosto, and Dante). These classes met in rooms she had rented from her Uncle Henry, at whose house at No. 1 Avon Place she boarded. She also privately tutored other students, including Jane Tuckerman. She loved instructing young women like Tuckerman, who became her friend, as did Cary Sturgis; but she found teaching children at the Temple exhausting. Hence days faded into nights and weeks of incessant toil that left her with little time to reflect and re-center, let alone to do research on the life of Goethe she hoped to write. Fuller had imagined for herself a life like de Staël's, but without her wealth and social position, reality fell far short of her dream. Always aiming at perfection, Fuller in Boston, by her own confession, took on more than she "was able to bear." The result, she said, was constant illness—headache, backache, and general malaise.[8]

In early April 1837, she confessed to Hedge that she had "been very unwell all winter" and "must prepare either to leave this scene or become '. . . a confirmed invalid.'" To Emerson she explained how she felt she "sh[ou]ld never recover" from teaching children. To another she described her Boston "winter" as "forlorn": "I was always ill; and often thought I might not live." She suffered, she said, the usual disappointments—not getting aid from those from whom she expected it, while those "who aided did not understand" her aims. She could not get a "proper point of view" nor "keep a healthful state of mind." "Mysteriously a gulf seemed to have opened" between herself and her "most intimate friends," and, "for the first time for many years," she felt "entirely, absolutely, alone."[9]

Fuller, in fact, was not alone, She was surrounded by people: inquisitive children, men and women friends, and culturally and intellectually sophisticated adults. As a witty improvisator, she performed to perfection for many, it seems, but not herself. Her problem was that she *was* performing. Her "true" self, she felt, was not present to her students or social acquaintances. This put-on air of superiority, disconnected from any real feeling for the topics on which she talked, made Fuller feel vague and empty.[10] Mentally and emotionally stretched, Fuller seemed split in two. There was the public self that performed to perfection in her work, and the private self that yearned, as she had as a child, for words of kindness and affection from a powerful, fantasized father figure who was away in Washington or Concord.

❧ ❧ ❧

That same April Fuller received a note from Alcott telling her the school was bankrupt and he could no longer pay her salary. It seems that after the second volume of his controversial *Conversations with Children on the Gospels* appeared early in 1837, reviews exposing their "indecent and obscene" contents moved parents to withdraw their children from the school. To Emerson on 11 April she wrote that she was looking in dream "to Concord as my Lethe and Eunoi after this purgatory of distracting, petty tasks." About an anticipated May visit to Concord she said: "I am sure you will purify and strengthen me to enter the Paradise of thought once more."[11]

Fuller's visit, however, had the opposite effect on her. On 2 May 1837 from Concord, where she was giving Emerson lessons in German pronunciation, Fuller wrote Jane Tuckerman how she had at first felt anxious about the visit. But her "drive here with Mr Emerson" had been "delightful," as had been Sunday's ride "to Watertown with the Author of 'Nature.'" Though the "trees were still bare," she said, the "little birds" seemed not to care. Like a young woman in love, Fuller waxed lyrical in telling Tuckerman how the birds "revel, and carol, and wildly tell their hopes, while the gentle, 'voluble' South wind plays with the dry leaves, and the pine-trees sigh with their soul-like sounds for June."[12]

During those "beauteous" rides with "Mr E," as she fondly called him, "care and routine" momentarily "fled." Back in Concord, however, and alone again with this "gentle" though "voluble" man in his study, wild "hopes" arose in Fuller's heart. Such hopes arose even though she had told her "heart not to expect too much when I came here"—especially in light of the fact that Emerson was married and had recently fathered a "beautiful," blue-eyed baby, Waldo, who at six months was beginning to look like his father. In Concord Fuller thus found an ebullient Emerson in rare conversational form whose warm laughter and flow of talk so powerfully stimulated her mind that she found she could not sleep at night. So intense were her feelings for Emerson that she had trouble, she later confessed, controlling them. Like the birds in the leafless trees, her unruly emotions reveled. Yet the final effect was not pleasure but pain. She confided to Jane that, while she was "passing happy" at the Emersons, she was "not well," and in fact felt "so unwell that I fear I must go home." "The excitement of conversation prevents my sleeping."[13]

Fuller left Concord in early May 1837 feeling strangely agitated—disappointed that her expectations had not been met and afraid that—even worse—she had not met Emerson's. She had felt the same way after she had tried to please her father by reciting her lessons, producing an excitement that had likewise prevented sleep. As if intending to leave with Emerson a symbol of her feeling for him, Fuller left behind a neck chain, along with some of her books. Earlier she had confided to Clarke regarding her need of Clarke's "intimate" friendship that she despised that "impulse" in her that had shown her to be "a slave . . . —a child— . . . still." But to the "Revd and dear" Mr. Emerson, her heart, it seems, was now, slavelike, enthralled.[14]

From Concord she traveled by stagecoach to Groton, hoping that her "good" mother's "sunny kindness" might calm her. It was mid-May and all the birds were singing and clusters of white flowers had burst out on the apple trees. Yet at the farm Fuller still felt anxious. To her former student and new friend, the gypsylike Cary Sturgis, she confessed in a 14 May letter that only at Concord had she been "happy." "Nothing is *satisfying*," she said, "in this wale of tears," alluding presumably to her mother's unhappiness while simultaneously mocking the local folks' accent.[15]

Tomb of Timothy Fuller in Mount Auburn Cemetery, Cambridge, Massachusetts. Photo by William McClung.

Timothy Fuller. Oil portrait by an unknown artist, 1820s. Courtesy of Willard P. Fuller Jr.

Timothy Fuller. Portrait by an unidentified artist of the American school, ca. 1825–30. Photo courtesy of Robert N. Hudspeth. Original painting at the Massachusetts Historical Society.

Margarett Crane Fuller, early 1840s. Courtesy of Willard P. Fuller Jr.

The house at 71 Cherry Street in Cambridgeport, where Margaret lived from 1810 to 1826. The 1890 photograph was taken after the porches were added as well as the two-story ell in 1827. FFP: HM (MS Am 1086). By permission of the Houghton Library, Harvard University.

Margaret Fuller. Pencil sketch by James Freeman Clarke, ca. 1830–32. FFP: HM (MS Am 1086). By permission of the Houghton Library, Harvard University.

Small portrait of Margaret Fuller. FFP: HM (MS Am 1086). By permission of the Houghton Library, Harvard University.

Landscape, with the Story of Narcissus. From the original picture by Claude Lorraine. Print in Fuller's papers depicting the mythical Narcissus of Ovid's story. FFP: HM (MS Am 1086). By permission of the Houghton Library, Harvard University.

Portrait of a Distinguished Authoress. Caricature by Boston artist Samuel E. Brown accompanying a lampoon of Fuller by Edgar Allan Poe published in the *Broadway Journal* (8 March 1845) and reprinted by Burton R. Pollin in *Women and Literature* 5 (spring 1977).

Margaret Fuller, head in hand. Daguerreotype, 1846. FFP: HM (MS Am 1086).
By permission of the Houghton Library, Harvard University.

Emerson at midcareer.
Courtesy of the Concord
Free Public Library.

James Nathan. From a
photograph accompanying
a 1903 review of *The Love
Letters of Margaret Fuller*
in *Literary Digest*.

Adam Mickiewicz. Drawing by Kazimierz Mordasewicz, 1898, after daguerreotype by unknown artist from 1839. Courtesy of Muzeum Literatury im. Adama Mickiewicza, Warsaw.

The Fuller Family: Arthur Fuller, Eugene Fuller, Ellen Fuller Channing, Margarett Crane Fuller, and Richard Fuller. Daguerreotype, circa 1853–55. Courtesy of Willard P. Fuller Jr.

Giovanni Angelo Ossoli. Daguerreotype, late 1840s. FFP:HM (MS Am 1086).
By permission of the Houghton Library, Harvard University.

Margaret Fuller in Italy, 1848. Photo of Thomas Hicks's painting showing Fuller in Venetian scene with a courting couple to the left, a nosegay of flowers at Fuller's feet, and a statue of Eros behind her. Courtesy of Constance Fuller Threinen.

14 ∽ Providence, Pain, and Escape into Illusion

The excitement Fuller had felt in Emerson's presence, a wild exhilaration followed by a prostrating anxiety, increased when in early June 1837, just a few weeks after her return, she left Groton to teach at Hiram Fuller's (no relation) new Greene Street School in Providence, Rhode Island. The experience was at first uplifting, especially when Emerson appeared to give the school's dedicatory address. But teaching was again to prove perplexing. The stress of dealing with recalcitrant students made Fuller's head ache. For relief she turned to the medical pseudosciences of her day—phrenology, mesmerism, and animal magnetism—which were all the rage but failed to cure her migraines. In her distressed state she turned for reassurance and support to the fatherly Emerson as well as to her former student Cary Sturgis. And she turned, as she so often did, to fantasy. Her feelings of attraction for Emerson as an intellectual mentor became enmeshed with her frustrated sexual needs producing an anxious state of mind from which at this time she found no constructive outlet.

Fuller had accepted the Providence job because it gave her a financial security she badly needed. In Groton she had not been able to do productive research on a biography of Goethe that George Ripley had invited her "to prepare," she thought, "on very advantageous terms." Uncertain about her talent and short of time, she had turned down the offer and instead signed a contract to translate Goethe's conversations with his secretary, Johann Peter Eckermann. Eager for the independence a sure income of a thousand dollars a year would give her, a salary roughly equal to that of a Harvard professor, she had then accepted a job teaching young women in their late teens and early twenties at the school in Providence, which was to open in June. She had been told that it would require only four hours of classroom instruction a day and that she would be able to choose her own classes and arrange her own courses.[1]

Fuller's first experience of the school was positive. Her working environment was pleasant. The new schoolhouse—a one-story Greek revival building with portico and columns and white interior walls trimmed in pink—was lovely. She applied the Socratic pedagogical method she had learned from Alcott, also encouraging the girls she taught to speak freely in class and express their views. One female student saw the aim of "Miss Fuller" as being "to arouse our dormant faculties and break up the film over our mind in order that the rays of the sun might shine upon it." In early July she wrote Emerson that her wish was to teach students to aspire to "activity of mind, accuracy in process, constant looking for principles, and [to] search after the good and beautiful."[2]

All thus went well at first. Though already suffering from a headache and a touch of homesickness, Fuller had nonetheless experienced one of her "halcyon moments" when Emerson on 10 June 1837 gave the school's dedicatory address in place of Alcott, whose February 1837 publication of volume two of his *Conversations with Children* had, as we have seen, cast a shadow over his character. Asked to speak after Alcott had wisely declined the invitation, Emerson reluctantly accepted. According to Capper it was a "Transcendental jeremiad" that Emerson delivered to an overflow audience in the Westminster Unitarian Church. In his talk he had said that "a desperate conservatism clings . . . to every dead form in the schools, in the state, in the church." Instead of a truly religious people, there is now in America, he warned, a political, tithe-paying, churchgoing crowd that is afraid of thought and afraid of change. Scholars and educators must learn, observed Emerson, that "the capital secret of their profession" is to convert life into truth by guiding their students to see "the symbolic character of life." They must teach that the key to overcoming apathy in a materialistic age is "self-trust."[3]

Many in the audience were baffled by the talk, including a reporter from the *Providence Daily Journal,* who confessed, "There was much of what he said that I could not possibly understand." Fuller, however, wrote Alcott later that month how "Mr Emerson's 'good words'" had "cheered and instructed" her. Even if for others in the audience Emerson's Christlike seed of wisdom fell "on stony soil" and failed "to fertilize the spot for which it was intended," Fuller felt sure "the fowl of the air" might "carry it away to some more propitious clime." His seminal words had fertilized *her* soil; his seed had taken root in *her* soul. With Emerson near, she wrote a friend, she felt no "want of animal spirits." Reflecting the thinking of the popular phrenologist Orson Fowler, who that November would be in Providence to lecture on mesmerism and animal magnetism, she added, "Animal Spirits are not to be despised." For "unless the blood can dance at proper times, the lighter passages of life lose all their refreshment and suggestion."[4]

Fuller's buoyant animal spirits fast deflated when, instead of, as she was promised, being able to teach classes of her choice to refined "maidens," she ended up teaching sixty students whose minds she described, after a half year on the job, as sieves that "retained only the bad." Given her heavy load, Margaret found that the job of teaching not only mature young women but preadolescents, including raucous boys who squirmed and giggled, taxed her energy to such an extent that she had none left at the day's end to undertake creative endeavors. The task of teaching sixty (she said) "absolutely torpid" students four hours each morning in subjects ranging from composition, reading, English poetry, and history to Latin, natural philosophy, and ethics was daunting. After eight months of teaching she was increasingly missing classes due to illness (mostly migraines)."[5]

Fuller's migraine pain was so great that at the end of September 1837 she went with James Clarke, who was in town preaching, to see a female "mesmeric subject." The woman supposedly located the place in Fuller's head where her portion of animal magnetism—the universal fluid that mesmerists said linked every orderly process in nature—was out of balance and hence causing her pain. Though Fuller never quit believing in the power of animal magnetism, especially in the magnetic effect one person can have on another, she complained in a letter to Cary that "the blind girl . . . is good for nothing" since she could not relieve the pain in her head. By mid-October she felt so unwell that she had had to be bled. Always seeking a cure for her migraines, in November she let both the phrenologist Orson Fowler and the Yankee novelist John Neal examine her head.[6]

In Providence Fuller became fascinated with Fowler's views on phrenology, the new "mental science" that held that examining the skull and understanding the topography of a person's brain could let a subject know which personality traits to develop or suppress to improve his or her well-being. The most successful of the phrenologists were upstate New Yorkers Orson and Lorenzo Fowler, who toured the country with their measuring tapes and plaster casts, examining heads and making character analyses. This kind of quack science intrigued Fuller, who believed in demons as well as in an invisible universal fluid called animal magnetism by mesmerists, who had chosen Providence as their base of activity. Mesmerists believed that this invisible fluid either drew people magnetically together or drove them apart. Fuller, who had just read the French mesmerist Joseph Philippe François Deleuze, was so fascinated with the blue-eyed, charismatic, twenty-eight-year-old Fowler, who advocated cold water as a cure for most ills and also argued against corsets and tight lacing, that she invited him to speak in November at the Greene Street School. She even undid the blue chenille cord from her abundant brown hair so that he might read her skull with the tips of his fingers.[7]

But even such an attempt by a charismatic mesmerist to relieve her migraines failed. Stress from a taxing and unfulfilling job, as well as "animal" energies aroused by the visits of exciting men like Emerson and Fowler, left her tense. To escape pain, Fuller, as was increasingly to become her pattern, withdrew her "true life" deep within and projected in public a charming though, as she herself had so often acknowledged, "superficial" self that tended to "smile brightly and talk wisely all the time."[8]

In this divided state, Fuller again felt depressed and alone. Her head hurt constantly even as she attended political meetings, parties, and lectures, even those she arranged at the school by the Shakespearean Henry Dana and the Portland, Maine, editor John Neal. The latter talked to her "girls on the destiny and vocation of Woman" in America. At a party at the school held just one week after Fowler had lectured there, Margaret let Neal, a charming Byron-like poet with an interest in phrenology, do a reading with "his sentient fingers" of "her haughty head," and when he walked her home in the evening after his lecture she told him she knew only three or four men whom she liked better. And none of them, she said, "was so truly a *man*." Though she felt magnetically drawn to the man's "genius," she failed to pick up on his suggestion that if women were given an education equal to men's without also being given the right to vote and hence access to power

(Fuller thought women were not ready), their frustration with their lot would only increase.[9]

Though an experienced educator from her years teaching not just Alcott's students but her brothers and sister as well, she also failed to pick up on hints that her Greene Street students were having problems with her severity. During her first days as a teacher, she was so distressed at "the great ignorance" of the girls that she "did little else but show them their ignorance." Her severe criticisms forced the girls to work hard, learn much, and admire but fear her. One wrote home how Fuller "is very critical, and sometimes cuts us to bits." It seems she was almost as demanding of the girls in her classes as Timothy had been in demanding from her precision in writing and reciting. And just as Timothy had denigrated his daughter's intellectual efforts, noting her "numerous mistakes" and charging her with "carelessness" and "inattention," so Fuller at the start of the term told the girls that she wanted them to become aware of their "great deficiencies" before she made an effort to educate them. She returned student Anna Gale's paraphrase, noting, in Gale's words to her journal, that "it was wrote without lines—and she did not like to take the trouble to read anything so crooked, and likewise there was some mistakes in spelling." When Fuller noted that such writing was the result of "carelessness" and lack of "attention," Gale complained sardonically in her journal, "It is indeed a great fault, . . . I suppose." Not all had Gale's gall. In her Latin recitation requirement, Fuller was so strict that girls fled the room in tears. One girl literally "had a hysterical fit" when she could not satisfy Fuller's high expectations. Thus Timothy's cruelly "critical self" continued to live in the guise of his strict schoolmistress daughter.[10]

Fortunately, the older girls in the class interceded before things worsened. Having read their complaints presented in a round-robin letter, Fuller responded by blaming her insensitivity on poor health and a too heavy work load and by promising them that in the future she would attend to their personal complaints and needs. Fuller's honesty won the young women's respect. Biographers note that some grew to appreciate and love from afar their formidable teacher, though they never fully overcame their fear of her.[11]

Overwhelmed by her workload and frustrated with her students, Fuller nonetheless fulfilled her "duties," as she would write Emerson on 1 March 1838, "except to myself." The schedule she had set for herself was rigorous. She arose no later than five so she could put in at least an hour on her own work before breakfasting at half past eight, and then taught nonstop for four hours. Though she was supposed to remain at school until one, she frequently stayed until past two. By the time she returned to her rooms on the second floor of a "*dingy*" boardinghouse owned by the mother of a fellow teacher, she felt uninspired and empty.[12]

Some essential connection was missing that she needed for solace and inspiration. Her head and back constantly ached. Unhappy, unsatisfied, lonely and in pain, Fuller retreated to fantasy and to dreams of Concord, imagining the pleasure she might experience there with Emerson.

Fuller's habit and pattern seem increasingly to have been, when under stress, to retreat to fantasy. There, her adoration for Emerson became colored by an old craving for gratification. Soothing her pain with opium, she longed for what she fancied would be his calming presence. Having been in Providence for only a week, yet already afflicted with a migraine, she curiously misquotes Hamlet in noting to Emerson how "every day" she had "mentally addressed Concord, dear Concord, haven of repose where headach—vertigo—other *sins* that flesh is heir to cannot long pursue" (original emphasis). "I willingly seize," she says, "this excuse for writing to you, although it is too true that I have nothing to say which can be said in such a way." "How I rejoice," she had excitedly exclaimed regarding his June visit to give the school's dedicatory address. She looked forward to his presence "as the weary traveller does to the Diamond of the Desert—Flowers will, I trust, spring up." She asked him to bring with him the chain that she had left at his house and ended her epistle urging, "do come to see me, if possible, as soon as you arrive."[13]

Fuller here tells Emerson that her "flesh" has inherited from her ancestors not Shakespeare's "natural shocks" but "*sins*." Though not a traditional Christian, she was still the product of a Puritan ancestry and, despite her earlier pronouncements that she was neither "a nun" nor a "Calvinist," admitted being touched by her mother's and grandmother's religious piety. Moreover she was—or at least she tried to be—as her mother would later say of her, "a good girl," a woman dutiful to the point of martyrdom in her actions toward others.[14]

To what sins, then, might Fuller have been hinting she was "heir to"? She neither drank alcohol nor smoked. And it is unlikely that she had ever kissed either of the young men she imagined she loved: George Davis, her Harvard-bred lawyer cousin whom she had adored in her late teens, or Sam Ward, the artist-banker seven years her junior who had traveled with her and the Farrars to Trenton and whom she fancied she might marry.

Alone in her rooms in Providence, depressed and anxious and seeking relief from migraine and stress with opium and fantasy, the lonely twenty-seven-year-old Fuller felt the pain of her unsatisfied yearnings. Viewed in the context of her nineteenth-century cultural setting in which mesmerists were lecturing on animal energies and ministers were obsessing on the sin of self-pollution, it would not have been inconceivable that Fuller—a highly imaginative yet sexually frustrated adult woman who felt herself powerfully attracted to a married man like Emerson and a "*manly*" man like Neal—indulged in a fantasy of sensual pleasure and hence experienced a lust in her heart that her inherited Puritan conscience would have policed and punished as "sin."[15]

For no matter how naive Fuller may have been about some aspects of sexuality or how self-righteously she responded to friends on the subject of sex, she was nonetheless drawn, as Capper has said, to "the darkly irrational side of human consciousness," especially—in the fashion of her father who had made her "heir of all he knew"—in her pursuit of intimate relationships. She continued, for instance, to be fascinated with the sexual side of Goethe's life, an interest she had conveyed in 1836 to Clarke, who had then warned her that Goethe's "moral code was not of the strictest kind." Writing to Hedge on 12 July 1837, just a month after Emerson's visit to Providence, Fuller pleads: "Will you, Henry, can you tell me all the scandal about Goethe—about his marriage and so forth?" She says she has "asked Mr Emerson and others" for information about Goethe's "liaisons"—especially "about his living so many years with the person he afterwards married—"; but the "little" they tell her, she tells Hedge, "only puzzles and disturbs" her.[16]

Although Fuller liked to imagine flowers like those in her mother's garden "spring[ing] up" with Emerson's appearance in Providence, the pleasure she felt in fantasizing a "*man*" like Neal—recalling, she confided to her journal, his "every look and gesture"—or even the saintly Emerson, was accompanied with a sense of "vertigo," anxiety brought on by guilt, as well as by daunting thoughts about her duties. Her schizoid sense that "a gulf" exists between her and "most intimate friends" is evident in her 14 August 1837 letter to Emerson wherein she confesses she has been, of late, "in an irreligious state of mind, a little misanthropic and sceptical about the existence of any real communication between human beings." She informs Emerson of her August vacation plans, noting she hopes he might find a way for her to see him. She tells him she is coming to Cambridge on 31 August to hear him give Harvard's Phi Beta Kappa Address, and suggests, "Perhaps you will take me back with you [to Concord], but do not trouble yourself in any way to do this." She also tells him, "I only should like to be with you that I might see you more." Unlike "the Gods," she confesses, she needs "illusions" to keep her "in action."[17]

Even as she declared her intention "to dispense" with "illusions" forever, Fuller was aware that she needed illusions to protect her from pain. Increasingly she turned to an idealized and absent Emerson in her search for emotional soothing as well as for intellectual recognition. In these retreats to illusion she was repeating her childhood pattern of retreating to her father's book closet where she read, dreamed, and prayed to an idealized absent Timothy in her drive to excel and thus win from him the ever-elusive recognition she craved, as well as to get a reprieve from his relentless criticism. And as Fuller now dreamed, her feelings for a deified "Mr E" fused even more fast to those she still felt for her father. Hence it seemed as if Emerson were somehow in her, even as, at her very center, she felt (as Higginson in his biography astutely observes) a "void" where a sense of an active "I" ought to be. In this state of what Heinz Kohut in the twentieth century called narcissistic vulnerability, Fuller became, in effect, if only briefly, an eager receptacle for what Emerson himself called his "spermatic words," a symbolic impregnation of a female figure that made him feel secure as both a teacher and a man.[18]

In their conversations, Emerson promoted and enhanced her intellectual efforts and offered her insights. She was pleased by the power of his mind over hers, and she felt it strengthened and sweetened her life to take in his flow of manly virtue. She had already been soothed by his "beautiful" voice as he read to her his "little book called 'Nature,'" had heard him recite from it that to see the universal father he must pierce through "my beautiful mother," and that the "happiest man is he who learns from nature the lesson of worship." She had felt the "contradictory desire" he had talked of, both to translate "upward" her untoward energies and to yield to the "downward" pull of the flesh to lie "embosomed for a season in nature." She had listened attentively in June as he read his "noble" address at Providence, and on 31 August she was in the audience at noon in the small church across from Harvard Yard to hear the "seminal thought" he professed in "The American Scholar."[19]

In this radical declaration of the dignity of the individual, Fuller, who had won from Emerson the invitation to travel by coach with him and Lidian afterward to Concord, heard her adored "divine" proclaim that the "one thing in the world, of value, is the active soul," that the true scholar "defer[s] never to the popular cry." "Man Thinking," said Emerson, is a person who knows from experience that "the deeper he dives into his privatest, secretest presentiment," the more "he finds" that "thought" that has passed "from the unconscious to the conscious" is a form of action "universally true." "Not he is great," augured Emerson, "who can alter matter, but he who can alter my state of mind." And how badly, said he, the "mind of this country" now needs altering. It is time for a scholar to come and teach that the "world is nothing, the man is all." It is time, declared Emerson, to renew our country's "confidence" in the "might of man" because the spirit of the American freeman is imitative and tame. Yet if each man were to "plant himself indomitably on his instincts," then he would see that "the huge world will come round to him." Then would exist a "nation of men . . . because each believes himself inspired by the Divine Soul which also inspires all men."[20]

As Fuller sat that August afternoon among that proper Cambridge crowd with her friends Jane Tuckerman and Cary Sturgis beside her, she heard Emerson's call for the American scholar to attain "self-trust," to be "free and brave," to believe in "his instincts," "to know all," and "dare all." But what did she make of words that may have seemed an admonition meant especially for her—that "help must come from the bosom alone"—since at that time she still feared she lacked the confidence, the "self-possession" necessary, for self-reliant action?[21]

As for Emerson, once he got over his "shock" at Fuller's "familiar" style, he felt flattered and then admiring of, what he called, her "noble traits & powers." But the latter came not without first cautioning her, as he did in his reply to her earlier letter wherein she talked of Concord as a haven from sin: "Power and Aim, the two halves of felicity seldomest meet. A strong mind with a great object finds good times . . . but wit without object and not quite sufficient to make its own,—turns all nature upside down & . . . Byron-izes ever." In his 17 August letter inviting her to visit, he addresses her as a woman whose presence he thinks might "gentilize" the "meeting of Mr Hedges Club" to be held at his home "on the day after Φ. Beta." Regarding her need for illusions, which she had confessed to in her mid-August letter, Emerson responded positively, suggesting she might use her power of mind and imagination to "mould" the men attending the Hedge Club into something altogether new, a challenge she would soon rise to meet. After her death, however, he was less generous in his assessment, observing that "the omelet and turtle" often got in the eyes of "our noble Margaret" and that in her correspondence she was frequently "self-deceived by her own phantasms." "She made numerous mistakes," he said, unwittingly echoing Timothy's accusation in a letter he had written his ten-year-old daughter that there were so many "mistakes" in her translation of the Lord's Prayer into Latin that it was not worth his time to correct it.[22]

⌒ ⌒ ⌒

In August 1837, at the same time that she had been writing Emerson how much she hoped she might soon see him, she was urging her young friend Cary Sturgis to come room with her in Providence. Cary was a daughter of William Sturgis, a wealthy and powerful maritime merchant whose family had made money in the China trade, and Elizabeth M. Davis, whose father was a judge of the U.S. Court for the District of Massachusetts. After the drowning death several years earlier of the Sturgises' only son, a distraught Mrs. Sturgis had abandoned her husband and daughters. During her absence, the twelve-year-old Cary had met Fuller and seems to have sought in Margaret, who was nine years older than herself, a kind of surrogate mother. Perhaps Fuller in turn found in the free-spirited Cary the little sister who had died when Margaret was three. At least in loving Cary, Margaret was able to compensate for the love she had lost when Julia Adelaide died as well as for the love she felt her own mother had denied her. Cary, too, remained as if without a mother, for even after returning home Mrs. Sturgis continued to suffer bouts of depression. The mother's precarious mental state made Fuller feel an acute concern about the mental health of Cary, whose relation to her family has been described as one of "affectionate strife." Because of family tension, Cary seldom stayed home long. When Fuller moved to Providence, she hence understandably thought Cary might want to flee her family to share with her the private rooms she was renting in Mrs. Aborn's boardinghouse. On 16 August Margaret wrote Cary saying that no matter how depressed she was, "you must not die, my Cary," but bear up "nobly" and "come here and live with me in November."[23]

Cary, however, did not reply. A worried Fuller wrote again, only to get from the girl several letters in which she evaded the subject of coming to Providence. When Fuller pressed for an explanation, Cary explained that her father had forbidden her to live with Margaret. He feared, she said, that too close an association with

Fuller, whom he linked with "Transcendentalism" and "liberal" views on sex and religion, might mentally unbalance his daughter.[24]

The news that it was Cary's father who had forbidden his daughter to stay with her in Providence distressed Fuller. Here was a father who openly disapproved of her in what Fuller believed to be a withdrawal of permission granted earlier. Repeatedly in letters to Cary, Fuller replays her recollection of her conversation with Captain Sturgis when she had visited the Sturgises' Brookline home; his words of approval were, in fact, "impressed on [her] memory" in such a way that she could not accept that she might be mistaken. She was shaken by her awareness that Cary's father disapproved of her so vehemently that he was prohibiting his daughter from even visiting her in Providence. Because of Cary's father's negative view of her, Margaret wrote Cary that she "might cease *to visit*" her friend ever again in Brookline. As for Cary's father's view of "transcendentalism and the non-sense which is talked by so many about it," Fuller asserts, "if it is meant that I have an active mind frequently busy with large topics I hope it is so—. If it is meant that I am honored by the friendship of such men as Mr Emerson, Mr Ripley, or Mr Alcott, I hope it is so." "*But*," she angrily added, "if it is meant that I cherish any opinions," as Cary's father seemed to imply, that "interfere with domestic duties, cheerful courage and judgement in the practical affairs of life," then "I challenge any or all in the little world which knows me to prove such deficiency from any acts of mine since I came to woman's estate." At her letter's end, Fuller tells Cary that if Cary has merely "dallied" with her, she knows it is not *Cary's* "fault."[25]

Perhaps hoping to make Cary regret not having come to Providence, Fuller wrote her young friend on 3 January that she felt "a happy glow" about her teaching, since five or six young women from eighteen to twenty (Cary's age) had registered to study with her that term. All of them, she noted to Cary, seemed eager to be "wakened to . . . the life of thought," as did members of the German literature night class Margaret had taken on as an overload in January to help earn money. (In particular the money went to enroll her sister Ellen—who in November had moved into her boardinghouse rooms with her—in a school in Boston since her Uncle Abraham had denied her mother money from the estate to put toward Ellen's education.) Fuller's night class consisted of ten adults, six of whom were men. One was an assistant professor of rhetoric and English at Brown University, and another was William Hague, a popular young Baptist minister she had met at a meeting of the Coliseum Club, a literary club of mostly well-to-do professionals—lawyers, ministers, professors, schoolmistresses, and female writers. Still smarting over Mr. Sturgis's comment, Fuller sarcastically says she feels "a little afraid of so many grown men" but assumes that when it comes time to appear in the classroom, she will not "*seem* abashed at lecturing to so many of our natural lords and masters!!!"[26]

Fuller's defensive sarcasm suggests how badly her confidence had been shaken by Captain Sturgis's negative assessment of her. As does the tone and content of a

1 March 1838 letter Fuller wrote Emerson, wherein she says she has not written to him because "I have not felt worthy to address you." In an effort to control what felt to her like the dissolution of her personality, a sudden lack of self-confidence prompted by a father's asserted disapproval of her, Fuller in fantasy turned Emerson into an ideal paternal being, a trusted companion who understands and approves his daughter's views. In this achingly sweet 1 March letter she appeals to a deified Emerson: "—I want to see you and still more to hear you. I must kindle my torch again." In the tone of a daughter whose father has been away all winter and not written, she asks him, "Why have I not heard you this winter?" And confesses, "I feel very humble just now yet I dare to say that being lives not who would have received from your lectures as much as I should." She notes that she has "noble books but one wants the breath of life sometimes." In Providence she sees "no divine person" and believes that "I myself am more divine than any I see—." She knows Dr. Wayland, president of Brown University, but thinks, "He would never understand me"; and, even "if I met him, it must be by those means of suppression and accommodation which I at present hate to my heart's core. I hate every-thing that is reasonable just now," including Emerson's "'wise limitations' and all." In fact, says Margaret, "I have behaved much too well for sometime past." Alluding to a Bible verse she knows Emerson will know (Matt. 6:24), she teasingly asserts, "I cannot serve two masters"—that is, God and Mammon (though here she clearly also means Dr. Wayland and Emerson)—then provocatively adds: "But why do I write thus to you who like nothing but what is good . . .? It is partly because yours is an image of my oratory[,] . . . and if I do not jest when I write to you I must *pray*."[27]

In the "oratory" of her mind, Fuller here prays to an idealized Emerson as a father confessor who will finally not find her unworthy of love, as she felt Cary's father had. Intuitively she felt that to control her seemingly uncontrollable inward tendency toward psychological dissolution, she had to hold onto her image of an idealized Emerson, to attach her "divine," pure self to it. By clinging to this ideal image, she could stay afloat. Yet in Emerson she had intuitively chosen a man who, in the fashion of Timothy Fuller, would never give her the unconditional love and recognition she craved. After all, this faithfully married, spiritual man repeatedly stressed to Fuller the need to channel such "subterranean" energies as were then swelling in her heart upward and into what she had heard him call "the Divine Soul" in his Phi Beta Kappa Address.[28]

During that dismal winter of 1837–38, Fuller knew she was in danger of all-out psychological disintegration. By March she felt severely stressed and depressed. Her head ached now, it seemed, all of the time. And, too, though Fuller had satisfactorily handled her students' complaint, their criticism of her harsh teaching had hurt her. So, too, did rumors she heard that a group of Calvinists and other concerned conservative citizens was building a school in Providence to teach views countering "the heretical doctrines" taught at Greene Street.[29]

Not until 4 May did Emerson respond to Fuller's 1 March letter. In his letter he explains the delay by bluntly saying that unless his "belief in immortality is at the moment very strong" and "indulges" him "in a free use of time," he finds letter writing "an ugly bracket in one's afternoon." A remark in an April letter from Cary to Margaret suggests that friends other than Emerson thought her to be a bit unbalanced that spring. Despite her distress over Captain Sturgis's view of her, Fuller had nonetheless visited Cary in the Sturgises' Brookline home shortly after she wrote Emerson in March. Instead of writing how glad she was that Margaret had come to visit, Cary tells her older friend that she has "'repaired' from her," and then accuses Margaret of leading "a strange life." To this woman who confessed in her 17 April reply to Cary, "Yes, my life is 'strange' thine is strange.—We are, we shall be in this life mutilated beings," Emerson said in his 4 May letter: "I dreamed even of being the Auricular confessor you spake of in Boston to whom every day's fancies & results were to be dotted down & transmitted."[30]

In this teasingly intimate statement, Emerson reveals his ambivalent feelings for Fuller, an "ambivalence" highlighted by the fact that he has waited so long to "kindle [her] torch again." Emerson's ambivalence is evident in most of the letters he wrote Fuller while she was in Providence. In his letter of 28 June 1838 he informs her that he is at heart a "hermit" and asks her to "live with moderation," while in September he notes with no self-conscious irony that he lacks the "organs which others have" that make "the stimulus of society" satisfying. On 12 October he cautions her "that almost all people *descend* somewhat into society," an idea he will incorporate into his essay "Friendship." To this already chilly admonition he adds: "What a perpetual disappointment is actual society even of the virtuous & gifted." Yet two paragraphs later he warms this cool tone with a hint of a wish for intimacy, saying how happy he is "that you are getting a vulgar [robust] health Nothing is so divine. And when the school is done you are coming to spend a year in Concord, Are you not?" "Will you commission me to find you a boudoir," he wistfully asks her, "or, much better, will you defy my awkwardness & come & sit down in our castle . . . & find an abode at your leisure?"[31]

Here Emerson is self-consciously addressing the Fuller he knew she saw as a queen, even as with his solicitous humble tone he turns into lighthearted verbal play the part of divine, authoritarian king, the role her father had enacted in relating to her as a child. In an earlier letter Emerson went so far as to refer to himself as her "audience." By refusing to enact the part in the preconceived script Fuller subconsciously wished him to play (father figure become almighty king–savior– lover), he chipped away at her illusory image of him. By pointing out the discrepancy between himself as a mortal man lacking the "organs" and energy necessary to satisfy her desire and her projection-ridden image of him as an omnipotent power, Emerson won her trust as a friend who would not take advantage of her ready openness to be taught and guided by him, no matter how urgent her unstated wish that he might seduce her. By winning her trust, Emerson briefly aligned himself on Fuller's healthy side in her struggle to uncover what she felt was the "real" Margaret buried beneath the masks of her multiple "dramatized selves."[32]

Emerson, who argued the importance of "self possession" and criticized the theatricality of Fuller's superficial public persona, often cautioned Fuller about the danger of losing herself into her dramatized parts. Lacking a solid center, Fuller, however, needed the admiration of the "thousand-eyed" public to confirm her wavering sense of herself as, so she wrote to Cary in April, "a queen." Yet queen was just one of Fuller's myriad selves. Another self, as noted, was that of her harsh, authoritarian father who confessed to gaining personal "pleasure" from having "immediate and invariable power over the minds of [her] pupils." Like a skilled politician, Fuller gained immense pleasure from her ability to mobilize her friends into the enactment of her fantasies. Emerson's attempt not only to chip away at Fuller's image of him as a divinity, but also to teach her to channel her "animal spirits" into constructive creative effort and a stable system of spiritual values, was hence ironically experienced by Fuller, whose "soul" (she said) was "intent on this life," as an ecstatic awakening of her "self" (so to speak) to her deepest psychosexual needs.[33]

The result of her frustrated effort to win from Emerson recognition and love would be to throw her ever deeper into the well of herself where she sought to re-create in fantasy the type of relationships that satisfied her most primitive needs. This hunger for a love to satisfy her desire for "a godlike embrace from some sufficient love" and make her feel "worthy" of the regard of an imaginary parent would lead her increasingly to tinge with erotic overtones her feelings for friends, both male and female.[34] Thus the empowering of self that Emerson encouraged, when placed in the context of his ongoing conversations with Fuller on the fluid nature of gender, would ironically unleash in Fuller—much to Emerson's dismay—a yearning for erotic gratification.

Moreover, whereas Emerson thought that the "mental changes" Fuller underwent in these months that came to a climax in the summer of 1840 were unhealthy and even perverse, Fuller, in contrast, felt empowered by this "plunge" into "the deepest privacy" of her self. She began, she said, "to be myself." And as her new self "unfolded," it felt to Fuller as if she had been reborn, as if many of Emerson's manly ideals had become her own. She had often felt she had "Power"; her encounter with Emerson gave her "Aim."[35] And with this new sense of self-confidence she will be able to aim her energies into her writing, her most significant work being about self-reliance, but from a woman's point of view.

15 ∾ "Drawn" by Fuller's Siren Song

By the end of the fall teaching term in late November 1838, Fuller was prostrated by pain. Earlier, in August 1838, she had noted in her journal that she was "in a state of sickly unresisting sensitiveness such as I do not remember in myself ever before." By late autumn of that year, she was so stressed that she had trouble meeting her classes and resorted to asking Ellen, who was still sharing rooms with her on the second floor of Mrs. Aborn's house, to cover her elementary-level sections in history and natural science for her.[1] In December Fuller gave up teaching in Providence and moved home to live with her mother in snowbound Groton.

Back in Groton, Fuller retired to her room. Dressed in loose-fitting gowns, she spent most of her time reading in bed; when not in bed reading, she sat at a table and wrote. By the end of January 1839 she had written more than fifty letters. Sick from fatigue from writing letters, after catching up with her correspondence she nonetheless turned to working on her four-hundred-page translation, *Conversations with Goethe in the Last Years of His Life*.[2]

Isolated from society, Fuller retreated again into reverie, and her feelings for her absent friends, both male and female, became increasingly eroticized. Emerson, flattered by her adulation, fed her fantasy by writing her warmly encouraging letters and by lending her books and essays, including Jones Very's essay on *Hamlet*. Like Fuller, Very was an Emerson protégé. As a poet and Greek tutor at Harvard, Very in the autumn of 1838 had experienced a religious hallucination, believing himself to be a resurrected spirit sent by God to deliver a message. As a result, in September he had been committed to McLean's Insane Asylum in Charlestown, the same place that Emerson had taken his brother Edward ten years earlier.[3]

In November 1838 Emerson reported to Fuller that Very, just released from the asylum, had visited Concord and confounded "us all with the question—whether he was insane?" "At first sight & speech," said Emerson, "you would certainly pronounce him so." "Talk with him a few hours," he added, "and you will think all insane but he." By the following March, however, Emerson had changed his mind. He wrote Fuller that Very is "becoming hopelessly mad."[4]

Aware of his own ever-unsteady mental state, Emerson was finding increasingly unsettling his interaction with not only Very, who was verifiably mad, but also Fuller, whose taste for gems, ciphers, talismans, and omens, he later wrote, as well as her tendency to catch at straws of coincidence and to fuse man with maid, sea with sky, and heaven with earth he interpreted as either "the luxury of nearsightedness" or an indication of her own incipient insanity. Whichever it was, both friends were on Emerson's mind as he wrote his lecture on "Demonology," which he read in the large lecture hall of the Masonic Temple in Boston on 20 February 1839.[5]

In this, the last of a series of lectures in the Human Life course he was giving in downtown Boston, a "course" of lectures he arranged through local contacts and was being paid for handsomely, Emerson seems almost to be talking to Fuller. For in it he cautioned his audience about placing faith in ephemeral phenomena that—though he did not say Fuller's name he clearly had her in mind here—were being widely talked about: "Dreams, Omens, Coincidences, Luck, Sortilege, Magic," and other so-called "facts" like those, he noted, of "Animal Magnetism." Believers in dreams, omens, and amulets, said Emerson, who knew that Margaret always put on a carbuncle or other (in his words) "selected gem, to write letters to certain friends," think that when they are about to die, ghosts announce "the fact to the kinsman in foreign parts." Such people (including presumably Fuller, whom he will excoriate in the *Memoirs* for having been "attracted" to "Demonology") who believe in these "moanings" from the spirit world do, indeed, he conceded, experience an exhilarating sense of dislocation between the self and reality. Yet when faced with "the storm at sea," they are unable, he warned his audience, to steer their "rudder true."[6]

In this lecture, a psychologically prescient Emerson notes how astonishing it is that in our dreams we so fearlessly allow ourselves to "become the theatre of delirious shows." According to Emerson, dreams remind us that we are two people: the person who works earnestly all day in accord with the principles of reason, and the being who at night drops into this dislocating "dusthole of thought" in which noble persons behave in the most "pitiful and insane" ways. Dreams bring no messages from the gods. Instead, said Emerson in this public lecture-essay that Fuller would soon read, they are "our own evil affections embodied in frightful physiognomies," a thought that surely made Fuller pause when she read it, since one of her recurring dreams was that her mother was dead. In Emerson's view, the "ghosts" we pursue in dreams are reflections of our dead.[7]

In "Demonology" Emerson also discusses Goethe's notion of the kind of "guardian genius" he knew Fuller believed in, observing that it is commonly believed that this "Daemon" appears in the form of a shining star. If it is attached to the head of an evil or vicious person—like the pale star Margaret will soon tell Cary she saw shining one night in Groton outside the window of a girl she had visited who was dying (according to Fuller) because she had "profaned her maiden state" by having indulged in out-of-wedlock sex—then, says Emerson, "the Daemon [was] so immersed in his body that the light became dim as of a quenched star." However, if it is attached to the head "of a wise and divine person" (so people like Fuller believed), then "the star was a pure splendor floating free over him and illumining the way before him." Rarely seen by the eye, this "Daemon," says Emerson, was supposedly heard "as a voice" by "divine and extraordinary men," as it purportedly was by Socrates.[8]

Dismissing this notion, Emerson concluded by telling his audience on that cold February day that a significant proportion of these (so-called) demonological "facts" are "merely physiological" phenomena that have nothing to do with religion or metaphysics. Rather, they are something seductive that call to us from a realm apart from human virtue. Thus Walter Scott, whom Emerson calls "Doctor of Demonology," made the White Lady reply to the Monk's inquiry, "who and what she is?" with "That which is neither ill nor well, / That which belongs not to Heaven nor to hell / . . . A form that men spy / With the half shut eye / In the beams of the setting sun am I."[9]

Presumably alluding to that kind of magnetic power Fuller exhibited in her interactions with others, Emerson then cautioned his audience—and perhaps himself as well—to be wary of the seductive power of people possessing this gypsy power. For this force, he augured, is "without virtue," and when it centers in one person, it is most "fearful." Such a person "extends" his or her "foolish individuality" into "the domain of the infinite and universal." "A force goes out from them," said Emerson, no doubt thinking of Fuller, that "draws all men and events into their favor."[10]

Emerson calls this magnetic aura "Mother power," a kind of power that Fuller, deliberately countering Emerson, will highlight as positive in *Woman in the Nineteenth Century.* It is a force he sees present in the facts of animal magnetism, or mesmerism, the popular pseudoscience that had indeed intrigued Fuller in Providence. Emerson, however, sees the force behind animal magnetism as "so fuliginous, nocturnal, and typhoid" that its presence indicates "the phenomena of Disease." Linking demonology with the occult, Emerson, who was sick with bronchitis, ended by asking his audience: "Why," when the "voice of divination resounds everywhere," "look so wistfully in a corner?" "Why run after a ghost or a dream?"[11]

At the very time Emerson was talking to his Boston audience (and indirectly to Fuller, too) about the danger of cults and Demonology, Fuller was beginning to run after her own ghosts and demons. In December he had lent her not only Very's *Hamlet* essay, but also a volume of Plutarch's *Morals* as well as Plato's *Phaedrus* and *The Symposium.* She read these works as a break from her translation project, *Conversations with Goethe,* which she finished at February's end. She then threw herself into organizing her father's forty years' worth of papers. Sifting through them, she thought fondly of Emerson and hence increasingly fused her feelings for her father with her reveries of Emerson. As Fuller worked alone in her room in her family's snowbound farmhouse, she gave her imagination free rein, and it took off like a sleigh on ice.[12]

Not that she was unaware that she was thinking a little crazy. In a 4 March 1839 letter to Emerson she confesses that her "pen inclines to the Hiero, glyphic style." She tells him she intends to drop an "olive branch" at the door to his home on her way to her "future Ark," the house she was scheduled to move into on 1 April. She will "not salute any body," she says in this cryptic letter, "for my last benediction still lingers on your roof tree; no kind wind having yet blown it back to me." Preoccupied with the birth on 24 February of a baby he named Ellen for his first wife and still battling bronchitis, Emerson was taken aback by the esoteric tone of his friend's letter, especially in light of his growing suspicion that Jones Very was indeed crazy. Deliberately echoing the inquiry of Scott's monk he had cited in his talk on "Demonology," a "modest" Emerson hence asks Fuller in his reply: "That is what we really would [like to] know—What you are?"[13]

In April Fuller moved with her sister, mother, and whichever brothers were home into a comfortable large rental house called Willow Brook, perched on a hill in the rural suburb of Jamaica Plain. Located south of Boston, Jamaica Plain was within walking distance of the city, a fact that delighted Fuller. Her 20 March stopover at the Emersons' home on her way by coach to Jamaica Plain from Groton had only increased her desire for him. She had found Emerson in Concord almost cured of his illness but still upset over the furious reaction of Andrews Norton and other theologians to his mid-July 1838 "Divinity School Address" in which he had chastised Unitarians for worshiping a "Cultus" (his word) of Christ rather than having Jesus' faith "in the infinitude of man." "Faith makes us, and not we it," Emerson had admonished his audience of divinity school students and faculty. It is faith in the soul that makes for "the dignity of spiritual being," and individual dignity, he said, has to do with "a certain solidity of merit" within us "that has nothing to do with [public] opinion." The "remedy" to the "deformity" in the systems and forms that already exist, advised a bold Emerson, is, hence, "first, soul, and second, soul, and evermore, soul."[14]

Emerson's iconoclasm had cost him the respect of the Harvard faculty and had resulted in a ban on his speaking at Harvard that was to last almost thirty years. But his courage in speaking his mind had made him all the more dear to Fuller, who agreed with the thesis of his address that Jesus alone knew "that God incarnates himself in man," that "churches are not built on his principles, but on his tropes," and that each of us must hence have the courage "to refuse the good models, even those which are sacred in the imagination of men, and dare to love God without mediator or veil." Admiring the man more than ever, Fuller welcomed the encouraging words he sent her in May 1839 about her ability to write a biography of Goethe. In his letter he says that he knows she cannot possibly "write a bad book[,] a dull page" if she bestows the same concentrated effort in formulating her "thoughts on Goethe" as now flows into her conversation and journal entries, which are "rich gay perceptive & never dull."[15]

Aglow with warm praise of a kind her father had never sent her, Fuller on 3 June from Jamaica Plain wrote Emerson a letter rife with desire that he satisfy all the layers of her being. To her "dearest friend" Emerson, who had loaned her a copy of his "Demonology" talk, she teases in the voice of a lady enthralled by an ideal father-lover, of the child who had once, according to Margarett Crane, "dress[ed]" an "arbour" with violets for her father in eager anticipation of his "return" from Washington: "I am just at present . . . walking through Creation in a way you would nowise approve. The flowers peep, the Stars wink, the books gaze, the men and women bow and curtsey to me, but nothing nor nobody speaks to me, nor do I speak. Yet I seem to receive a great deal though I cannot . . . utter it forth again unless . . . by 'lyrical glances.'" Fuller seems to be saying that people are speaking, but not "to me," nor do "I" speak from beneath the masks of my dramatized selves. She interacts with people who do not "see" her "true" being, even as she receives Emerson through the memory of his lyrical glance.[16]

As Fuller wrote her letters to an absent Emerson, her words spun her back in time to when, as a child, as we've already seen, she had by day in the garden caressed her mother's roses and at night recited for her father, hoping to win his recognition and love. Evoking the language of the past, Fuller thus wrote the constitutionally cool Emerson who had recently cautioned his audience about the danger of projecting one's personal demons onto others: "Since you have deigned to be pleased with former letters of mine I heartily thank you for your encouraging word about my work and I pray you always to encourage me whenever you can." Her words are like those long ago she wrote her father, thanking him for finding her careless "hand improved." Responding to Emerson's implied criticism of her in his 20 February talk, "Demonology," Fuller concedes that the "Ghosts [speak] very lifelike to me who understand the language of Hades," the underworld where Persephone reigned after having been taken there and raped by Hades, her uncle. With "the shades" of her past now speaking through her, Fuller twines around her "philosopher" friend metaphors of eroticized affection. "Will you not come to see me," she asks. "If you will come this week I will crown you with something prettier than willow, or any sallow. Wild geranium stars all the banks and rock clefts, the hawthorn every hedge. You can have a garland of what fashion you will Do but come."[17]

The language of the day may have been lavish, but this, with its reminiscence of traditional love lyrics, surely exceeded decorum. The daughter-protégée pleads here with an idealized Emerson to satisfy what she imagines to be their mutual sexual urgings. One notes the imagery of lush vegetation, the missing period, the hurried "Do but come"—and suspects that Fuller, even if subconsciously, is suggesting she would like to "crown" her king with something more sensually pleasing than a wreath of sweet-smelling flowers.

Emerson replied 7 June with praise of her Eckermann translation (published 27 May), saying it shows "the breadth" of Goethe's "common sense." He says he is "sorry" she has moved to Jamaica Plain, which is "so inaccessible" to him, urging her to therefore be "the more generous" in writing him. He urges her also to "speed the pen" in beginning her biography of Goethe. A month later, after having attended an exhibit at the Allston Gallery with Fuller, he wrote cautioning her that impetuous women like "Bettina" (Elizabeth Brentano, who as a girl had corresponded with Goethe) who are "without any reserve" in expressing their affection, "offend our cold Saxon constitution." Perhaps he meant by this to deflect what was beginning to feel to him like an outright sexual assault on Fuller's part. As if to divert her attention to her work, he asks her in his 31 July 1839 letter to report on her "resolution" to write her Goethe biography.[18]

What Emerson could not have known when he wrote his June letter to Fuller was that, during the same period she was writing lyrical letters to him, her passionate appeals for love to both Sam Ward and Cary Sturgis were being rejected. From Ward she sought an expression of romantic love, from Cary of soulful communion. When Ward had returned from Europe in the summer of 1838, he had brought with him hundreds of engravings, which he had shared with Fuller. In late fall and early winter 1838, she had met him at the Boston Athenaeum during her trips into the city. Her archaic erotic energies now awakened by Emerson, Fuller had found herself powerfully attracted to Ward, who was seven years her junior, and she had increasingly pressured him to return the love. With her emotions overflowing, as they were that June when she wrote to Emerson, Fuller had also felt "strange" feelings for her friend Cary Sturgis. Attached to her deepest archaic urges and needs, this "strange" yearning for love was fed, as we will see, by her readings in the Romantics and her own vivid imagination. Its expression in an outburst of emotion directed full force at Cary unsettled the younger woman when it surfaced during a mid-June 1839 trip the two took together to Nahant, a beach resort north of Boston. Not only did Fuller's relationship with Ward disintegrate that summer, but Cary had been so shaken by Fuller's behavior that she had recoiled in "passive repulsion." Fuller, in defense, had declared to Cary afterward that it was doubtful the two could continue to be "*intimate*" friends.[19]

In the next months Fuller focused her feelings more intensely than ever on the fatherly Emerson, a shift in attention that relieved Cary, who loved her older friend, though not as much as Fuller wished. And the more Fuller poured her feelings into her letters to Emerson while exchanging books and ideas with him on the fluid nature and complexity of gender, the more he found himself enchanted by the alluring power of her eloquent words, despite his admonition in his February lecture about the danger of such a sirenlike seduction. He also greatly enjoyed at this time hearing from Cary, whose loving letters flattered without being sexually threatening to him. Almost against his will, however, Emerson felt himself "drawn" by Fuller's siren song "into" the quagmire of her decentered sexualized self. However, in yielding to her power he ran the risk of letting himself fall psychologically under her spell, and, as a consequence, of losing touch with what he felt was solid and safe in their relationship. Thus he was to write her on 27 November 1839 how he had "plunge[d] with eagerness into this pleasant element of [her] affection with its haps & harms." In it he seems to "float all the time." In an attempt to understand her, he cautiously says that he will yet come "to know the world through your eyes," rather than through this "quarantine of temperament wherefrom I deal courteously with all comers, but through cold water."[20] Even if Emerson hints here of a wish to escape the confines of his cold temperament, the intensity of feeling Fuller now unleashed onto him, as we shall see, would increasingly tax his patience, cooling his desire to do so.

16 ⮡ Retreat from Her Siphoning Sea

Complicating Fuller's life the winter of 1839–40 were two new projects she undertook that, though rewarding, were physically and emotionally draining. She accepted editorship of the Transcendentalists' new literary journal, the *Dial,* in the fall of 1839. Larry Reynolds contends that this journal was largely Fuller's inspiration because it grew out of the propensity of Fuller and her friends to exchange among themselves "pacquets" or "portfolios" of letters, prints, books, journal entries, critical essays, and poems, many items of which Fuller later included in the *Dial.* The journal was in effect an outgrowth of Fuller's love of letter writing, of her way of staying connected to the world. Fuller's habit of making the exchange of letters the hallmark of true friendship began when Timothy moved the family to Groton in 1833. It was a way of interacting she had been trained to practice as a child by her congressman father, who expected to receive from her finely written letters while he was in Washington. Fuller continued this practice in her interaction with Emerson, who grew to know and love her through her warm and informative letters. Just as Emerson liked getting letters from Fuller, so he liked the idea of a Transcendental journal and credited "her radiant genius & fiery heart" as being "perhaps the real centre that drew so many & so various individuals" to agree to write for it. In a letter soliciting poems from Ellery Channing, Emerson early on said he thought the *Dial* was "of better promise than any [journal] we have had or have in America." He wrote Ellery how he had promised Margaret that he would offer her his "assistance to write & to collect for her."[1]

Apparently he did not have much success doing the latter. For, though all members of the Transcendental Club thought the journal a good idea, few had the time to write for it. Thus Fuller from the first had trouble finding contributors for it. James Clarke, still in Cincinnati, was now married and involved in a half-dozen other projects, including trying to keep the *Western Messenger* afloat. Dr. Channing's Unitarian socialist nephew, William Henry Channing, who had been eager to see the *Dial* started, now had no time to write for it since he had recently agreed to take over the *Western Messenger* for Clarke, who wanted to bring his pregnant wife back east. Even Henry Hedge, who had been one of the first people to argue the need for a Transcendentalist magazine, had changed his mind. He was upset that people were increasingly linking New England Transcendentalism with atheism and the denial of the supernatural in religion. And they were doing so even though the *Dial*'s May 1840 prospectus had plainly stated that its writers were united in their love of freedom, hope for social progress, and faith "in Divine Providence, rather than in human prescription."[2]

The aims of the *Dial* as initially stated were so vague that its "united" writers were constantly clashing. Alcott complained that it was too worldly for his "Orphic Sayings" (apothegms extracted from his journals). The social agitator Theodore Parker argued that it lacked substance. Another critic, the Unitarian scholar and charter member of the Transcendental Club, George Ripley, thought the *Dial* "not *prononcé* enough," while Carlyle from across the Atlantic complained that it had "a very good soul, only no body." Still, the journal might have been a success had Fuller been able to get the more professionally trained writers to submit their articles on time, or even, despite promises, to write them at all.[3]

As a result, during the two years of her editorship, Fuller often used unpolished materials sent her by friends in personal portfolios or, and increasingly, in her second year, her own writing, as she did in the spring of 1841. She wrote "in every gap of time," sometimes by candlelight in her chilly Jamaica Plain bedroom. When pressed for material, she scrambled through her copious notebooks for passages to pad the blank pages. Fuller's own writings comprised more than half the October 1841 issue; her essays on Philip Bailey's *Festus* and her "Lives of the Great Composers" took up eighty-five pages. Yet for all her work, Fuller again earned no real income from the *Dial*. Since the circulation remained small, the promised salary of two hundred dollars a year never materialized.[4]

It was her second project that proved for Fuller to be not only more fulfilling but also more physically draining. On Wednesday, 6 November 1839, she began her "Conversations," a class for adult women that initially met Wednesday mornings (later sometimes Thursdays) for two hours a meeting—first, says Megan Marshall, in a room rented by Mary Peabody and then, after August 1840, in Elizabeth Peabody's bookstore at 13 West Street in Boston. These classes were to continue for two series a year (winter and spring) for five years, each series consisting of thirteen meetings. Fuller's aim in her Conversations—which were attended the first year primarily by the wives and daughters of wealthy merchants and professional men, almost all of whom had ties to various social reform movements—was to teach women to systematize their thinking and speak intelligently and precisely in public. The core of the group consisted of, among others, Cary and her sister Ellen, Anna Barker, Jane Tuckerman, Almira Barlow, Eliza Farrar, James Clarke's artist sister Sarah, and the Peabody sisters Elizabeth and Sophia (the last was engaged to marry the elusive, darkly handsome Nathaniel Hawthorne). Twenty-five women paid ten dollars each to participate in each series; over the five years Fuller held them about a hundred women took part in them. Not coincidentally, this second project like the first, drew on a skill instilled in her by her father, who had drilled her in the art of speaking perfectly before him. Confident of her own public speaking, she also knew that most members of her sex were "deficient" in that skill. She therefore hoped to enable women to achieve in the private confines of her classes the same kind of vital intellectual activity men in her day were traditionally expected to exhibit in the public sphere.[5]

Conversation was the right medium for Fuller to reach the women in her classes. Trained from childhood to speak precisely, she had honed her conversational skills to perfection, as an impressed Emerson had discovered. Certainly she was not the first to turn talk into a kind of art. Many of the Romantics were great talkers; for Carlyle, Coleridge, de Staël, and Goethe, their talk in effect became their art. In the poetic form perfected by Coleridge, the greater Romantic lyric ("conversation poems," Coleridge called them), the poet sustains a colloquy, sometimes with himself or the outer scene, but more often with a silent human auditor (present or absent), as Wordsworth addresses Coleridge in the *Prelude* and as Fuller, in the conversational letters she sent Emerson, communes in fluid prose with her absent, silent friend. In the greater Romantic lyric, a scene from an exterior landscape spurs the narrator to recall a similar scene from his past. This turns his thoughts inward, evoking a memory that frees slumbering childhood feelings, archaic emotions that fuse with his mature adult feelings. The point of the speaker's meditation is to achieve an insight, to come to a moral decision, to resolve an emotional crisis, to face up to a tragic loss.[6]

Fuller's conversation with Emerson—which began in a setting, a study, similar to one from her childhood—had similarly evoked childhood feelings, a process that as a student of the Romantics she would have viewed as positive. For it freed spontaneous emotions to flow not only into her writing, but also into her public presentations before the women in her Conversation classes. Like the Romantics who in their lyrics sought to find in "simple childhood" the base on which man's "greatness stands," Fuller hoped to guide each woman attending a session to probe her mind through a process of spontaneous association until she, too, could free slumbering feelings and hopefully attain an authentic insight.[7] Through the seeming spontaneity of her fluid yet rigidly trained speech, Fuller inspired the women attending the Conversations to emulate her, and they thereby gained confidence in their own speaking powers. By all accounts Fuller was now an effective group leader. Participants, so many of whom were friends, said she seemed to fill the room with her electric presence, sparking confidence in women as lightning ignites dry timber. In the role of improvisator, Fuller excited her audience and made the women feel for awhile as if they existed on a higher plane of being.

For Fuller, however, her weekly Conversation classes with the admiring women who attended them were, as she herself said, "theatre." Yet if eyewitness accounts are accurate, the conversations were "well-performed," so much so that Elizabeth Peabody confessed some people came primarily "to be entertained." Peabody also noted that "the [members of the] class, by their apprehension of Margaret," did not do "justice to the scope and depth" of her mind. And Emerson continued to express his regret that his friend should let "this flowing river of [her] speech . . . sweep away" the "fine castle" of her writing, "whose pinnacle is waited for by the States and by the nations."[8]

Emerson feared—and he had a valid point—that Fuller was wasting her creative energy by channeling it into what seemed to him to be "the game of conversation." While these theatrical sessions no doubt did help build Fuller's self-esteem as her audience applauded and approved her performance, just as they helped enhance the confidence of the women who attended them, still, her high-toned two-hour (on occasion) "monologues" were often followed by "a long attack of nervous headache," no doubt a migraine. The headache that came on after her first lesson on 6 November 1839 took three weeks to run its course, indicating the seriousness of her condition. Calling her energies to the fore, Fuller poured herself out to her audience with the skill and intensity of a maestro conducting a symphony orchestra.[9]

Standing before some twenty-five to thirty attendants seated on various chairs and sofas, with a bouquet of bright flowers on a table beside her and her lorgnette in hand, Fuller would begin each session around eleven in the morning. Attired in a black bombazine or modest alpaca dress with pointed waist and full pleated skirt, a brightly colored shawl thrown over her shoulders and her brown hair braided, and pulled into a knot at the back of her head, with ringlets on either side, Fuller would start by looking directly at her audience and outlining the subject for discussion that day (say, beauty). She would ask the women to give their definitions of the term. Imitating the style of Socrates (and Timothy), she encouraged the women to see how much less they knew about the subject than they thought they did. She next taught them how to turn vague definitions into clear thoughts by having each rephrase her definition into a coherent statement supported with concrete examples. After that she entertained questions and criticisms.[10]

No doubt Fuller led these discussions in much the same way as she led conversations with men at Transcendental Club meetings. Her dear friend the socialist minister William Channing later said how Fuller with eyeglass in hand would at first "unfold her own view." In so doing, she was always articulate, poised, "affluent in historic illustration and literary allusion"; she "knew how to concentrate into racy phrases the essential truth gathered from wide research." Though one eyewitness said Fuller could behave "imperiously," others thought she exhibited "bright wit, . . . shrewd discernment, promptitude, and presence of mind." "She blended in closest union," notes Channing, "feminine receptiveness with masculine energy."[11]

For many of the women who attended a Fuller performance, the effect was exhilarating and seductive. "Encountering her glance," said Sarah Clarke, who had taught with Margaret in Boston, "something like an electric shock was felt": "Her eye pierced through your disguises. Your outworks fell before her first assault, and you were at her mercy."[12]

In the all-female world of her Conversation classes, where the doors were at first closed to men, Fuller's piercing eye and flowing emotions penetrated these women, making them feel that she saw the pearl buried deep beneath their decorous outer shell. Like a powerful tragic actress, Fuller with a penetrating look peeled back the facade of culture that bound the women (they thought) in "foolish social customs" and exposed (they felt) the "soul" within. She was the prince whose kiss awakened each woman to new life. Though many at first feared "her too powerful dominion" over them, they came in time to appreciate her demand they do their best. It was a "most powerful stimulus," said Sarah. "It was like the sun shining upon plants and causing buds to open into flowers. This was her gift, and she could no more help exercising it than the sun can help shining." Most of the women who attended her sessions came all aglow; they came away commenting on, among other things, "her beautiful looks."[13]

In these sessions, Fuller intellectually and physically "rouse[d]" not only the women in her audience but also herself. "No woman ever had more true lovers among those of her own sex," wrote Sarah. Conscious of her power "over the minds of [her] pupils," Fuller saw that the women were all "in a glow" over her, that they were, in her own words, "quite as receptive as I wish" to the flow of her spirit, her sensuous, sexual being, just as she had been open to Emerson. She was the Emerson to their Margarets, the father to his daughters. Yet when the Conversation classes were over, the women who had been so attentive to her words went home to tend to the needs of their husbands, families, or male suitors. The sudden letdown after each stunning performance left Fuller alone to fight a migraine.[14]

Although Emerson did not attend her early Conversation classes, he perceived a "glow" about her at this time. Two days before Christmas 1839, he found himself wishing "heartily" that Fuller were with him in Concord and wrote her he wanted "to live a little while with people who love & hate." And while in his letter he continues to stress the importance of their staying "clean & permeable channels" for high thoughts, he also says: "I should indeed be happy tonight to be excited by your eloquence & sympathy up to the point of vision."[15]

Sidestepping the question of his sexual attraction to her, Emerson nonetheless reveals here that he has been magnetically drawn into the magic of Fuller's circle; he has let himself be seduced by what he will later call "her honeyed tongue." In this play of power between two equally eloquent parties, for a brief time the terms shifted and Emerson felt himself spellbound by Fuller. He became, for her, as he said, an "audience," a man eager to hear what she had to say to him. In February 1840 he wrote her a lyrical letter telling of "magical" spring winds, of blue birds come back to their box on the barn, and of "days of passion when the air is full of cupids & devils." Watching his boy Waldo observe the melting snow and speculate on the probability of early grass for his horse, Emerson gave thanks, he said, for "that omnipresent Animation whereof & whereto his world is made." Though he is no longer young, Emerson has "not yet forgot the enchantment" of "dead leaves & wizards that peep & mutter": "Let us surrender ourselves for fifteen minutes to . . . these nymphs or imps of wood & flood of pasture & roadside, and we shall quickly find out what an ignorant pretending old Dummy is Literature who has quite omitted all that we care to know—all that we have not said ourselves." For the moment Emerson felt "not self commanding." In March he wrote another similarly lovely letter to Fuller from Staten Island, exclaiming how happy he was to get her letter since, he says, "I left behind me at home all excitability" and have been but "a poor Animal ever since."[16]

In light of such a letter it is little wonder Fuller's love for Emerson crescendoed, especially in these months when her strenuous work on the *Dial* threw her into regular and tantalizing epistolary contact with him.[17] When Fuller grew depressed, Emerson spurred her on. Though the major duties in preparing the *Dial* fell to her, Emerson did come through by helping with the editing. He also aided by using his contacts to help her find people who could contribute to the journal, like his protégé Henry Thoreau. And when Emerson in turn asked her to publish a piece, Fuller usually agreed.

As for her writing, however, Fuller still lacked confidence. In April 1840 she wrote Emerson that when she looked at her own papers she felt as if she "never had a thought that was worthy the attention" of anyone but herself. She told another friend that when she met people in person she could easily "adapt" herself to them, but when she came to write, it was "into another world," and "not a better one." She felt she was not an "original genius." In her diary she complains that she thinks she has "too much feeling." "What a vulgarity there seems in this writing for the multitude," she despaired during that spring of 1840: "We . . . have not made ourselves known to a single soul, and shall we address those still more unknown? Shall we multiply our connections, and thus make them more superficial?"[18]

A discouraged Fuller felt vulnerable. She was preparing the *Dial* with little assistance, still filling out its pages with her own writing when unpaid contributors failed to come through with promised articles. To make matters worse, reviewers were cruel from the first. They made fun of the journal's inflated aims. A New York monthly derided Emerson's opening essay as a "literary euphemism," while the Philadelphia *Gazette* called those editing it "zanies," "Bedlamites," and "considerably madder than the Mormons." Worse, the public, as noted, did not buy enough subscriptions to the journal for Fuller to be paid for her work. On 17 April 1840 Fuller wrote in her diary, "every body finds fault with me just now . . . with regard to this new journal." The public "had nursed its fancy with promises of what these works should be and is very angry that they do not realize its hopes." "These gentlemen" who criticize wonder why "I write no better, because I talk so well."[19]

Thus both projects were lightning rods for Fuller's anxiety and with it the distance she always felt to exist between her "true" self and others. Her confident public self continued to function effectively in the world while her private self, fed by fantasies about Sam Ward as well as by the unspoken erotic promises of Emerson's teasingly sweet letters, yielded to illusion. She had already confessed to Emerson early in 1840 how she no longer tried to "domineer" herself. On 23 February, she had compared herself to a "poor traveller of the desert" who toiled a long day to reach a "distant palm" (Emerson) which, when "he reached it, alas! It had grown too high to shade the weary man at its foot." That Fuller in her phallic parable sees herself as a man and her love object as a tree is interesting, even comical.[20]

Fuller's letters to Emerson continued in this vein, with fancy fed by frustration and growing anger at Emerson's reluctance to be more forthcoming in expressing affection. On 25 April she embodied herself in her letter as "a Queen" with the power and privilege of conferring bouquets to "every person of distinguished merit." But Emerson, she says, will only receive "sweet pea or lavender because you are merely a philosopher and a farmer, not a hero, nor a sentimentalist." On 31 May she teasingly objected to his confession that "weeding onions" was more important to him than "read[ing] twenty pages in any volume," suspecting he was alluding to her long letters to him. He did her "wrong," she said, in not coming to see her "all the beautiful, solitary summer," adding, "I will try not to wish to see you." In his next letter Emerson offered ironic thanks for her "kindness" toward him. Two weeks later, perhaps as a "defensive strategy," he sang praises to her of Anna Barker: "A woman in every part beautiful is a *practical poet*, is she not? awakening tenderness & hope & poetry in all whom she approaches." "Write me," he thoughtlessly urges the noticeably not beautiful Fuller, "all you can of Anna."[21]

In mid-July 1840, at about the same time she learned that the same Sam Ward she adored intended to marry the "beautiful" Anna, Fuller took to bed with "a violent attack of headach" and wrote Emerson that she was "in no state for [his] criticism." Her head hurt so badly, she said, that she was "not fit" for writing "any thing good." Feeling not "fitted to be loved," and pained by "close dealings with those [like Emerson and Ward] who do not love [me], to whom my feelings are 'strange,'" she ended her letter with a childlike plea to an imaginary father whose touch can heal the hurt "within": "Be good to me, [and] by and by I will be good so as to deserve it."[22]

But Emerson could not be "good enough" to her, nor could Fuller be quite good enough "to deserve" his love, just as when she was a child she could never be quite good enough to win her cold father's uncritical love. Thus in August, just when Emerson (as he recalls it in the *Memoirs*) was congratulating himself "on the solid good understanding that subsisted between" them, Fuller angrily turned on him and accused him of counting and weighing but not loving his friends. Looking back, he recalls that she taxed him with "superficiality." She accused him, he wrote

Sturgis, for whom he also had tender feelings, of standing "apart critical, & after many interviews [of being] still a stranger." Emerson defended himself, confessing "to the fact of cold & imperfect intercourse, but . . . not to the deficiency of my affection." It was not for him to speak openly of his affections. He felt it better, he said, that words of "love . . . remain a secret from the lips to soften only the behaviour."[23]

But Fuller, whose once dammed up "rivers of life" were now, she said, flowing, continued to push for what Emerson felt to be an erotic response. At August's end he thus wrote this "friend" "whose heart," he said, "unceasingly demands all, & is a sea that hates an ebb," that, while he is "happy" to be her "debtor," "my solitary river is not solitary enough." Emerson is here withdrawing his creative energy from any further psychologically consuming "conversation" with her; he is withdrawing the flow of his "river" from her siphoning "sea." Emerson felt his friendship with Fuller had become too intimate. As he candidly told her in his 13 September 1840 letter, he felt as if this burly woman were sucking him "dry," whereas it was he who—as he put it to Fuller in this same letter in reference specifically to their friendship— ought to be able "by the help of heaven to suck this orange dry—no that cannot be—the expression is profane."[24]

In their relationship Fuller was increasingly the aggressor and threatened, with her high tide, to rob Emerson's river of its waters, "to suck," as he said, his "orange dry." Both he and Fuller, given the language of the day, would have recognized that, on one level, his "solitary river" referred to the necessity for a prudent man to "concentrate" his "energies," to control the flow of his emotions, as he controlled the flow of his semen. Emerson himself would refer in his journal obliquely to— what men like John Todd in his day proclaimed and he had "observed" to be—"the effeminating effects of sexual indulgence." He believed in the need for a man to economize by not spending his semen in uncreative ways; though he had "organs" and "delight[ed] in pleasure," he saw such pleasure as "the bait of a trap."[25]

Despite Emerson's obvious reluctance thus to carry on with their conversation, Fuller still yearned to merge her being with this imaginary "divine," to recover the love she felt he had for her. And so she wrote a letter, now missing, to which Emerson on 25 September replied: "You must always awaken my wonder: our understanding is never perfect: . . . And yet there is progress." Emerson had begun to sense that it was a matter of decisive importance—not just for Fuller's psychological health but for the sake of his own mental balance and his marriage—that he make clear to her that his thoughts and feelings for her were significantly different from hers for him. Thus he wrote her: "Now in your last letter, you, O divine mermaid or fisher of men . . . do say, . . . that I am yours & yours shall be, let me dally how long soever in this or that other temporary relation. I on the contrary do constantly aver that you & I are not inhabitants of one thought of the Divine Mind, but of two thoughts, that we meet & treat like foreign states, one maritine, one island, whose trade & laws are essentially unlike."[26]

His journal entry the next day reveals just how profoundly he was shaken. "You would have me love you," he wrote. "What shall I love? Your body? The supposition disgusts you. What you have thought & said? Well, whilst you were thinking & saying them, but not now. I see no possibility of loving any thing but what now is, & is becoming; your courage, your enterprize, your budding affection, your opening thought, your prayer, I can love,—but what else?"[27]

Scarcely able to tolerate the flow of chaotic emotions that he through his teasingly suggestive words had freed in Fuller, Emerson recoiled when he received yet another immoderate letter from her on 29 September, one that touched him where he was most vulnerable. "I have felt the impossibility of meeting far more than you; so much," she wrote, "that, if you ever know me well, you will feel that the fact of my abiding by you thus far, affords a strong proof that we are to be much to one another." "How often," she said, "have I left you despairing and forlorn. How often have I said, this light will never understand my fire; . . . this simple force will never interpret my need of manifold being." Thus she continued, revealing a well of need and desire far deeper and more complicated than anything Emerson could ever give her. "In me," she said, "I did not think you saw the purity, the singleness, into which, I have faith that all this darting motion, and restless flame shall yet be attempered and subdued. I felt that you did not for me the highest office of friendship, by offering me the clue of the labyrinth of my own being." "Then indeed," she wrote in words that reveal the depth of her need, "when my soul, in its childish agony of prayer, stretched out its arms to you as a father, did you not see what was meant by this crying for the moon . . . ? Did you then say 'I know not what this means; perhaps this will trouble me; the time will come when I shall hide my eyes from this mood;'—then you are not the friend I seek." While she may seem to Emerson to be, says Fuller, echoing words from his essay "Friendship" that grew out of his interaction with her and Cary, a "large formidable nature," she sadly acknowledges she knows she is not, in his eyes, "a beautiful foe."[28]

"My life," she confesses, "is now prayer. Through me sweetest harmonies are momently breathing. Shall they not make me beautiful,—Nay, beauty!" "Shall not," she asks Emerson, "all vehemence, all eccentricity, be purged" by his "streams of divine light?" In self-consciously androgynous terms, she added: "Again I shall cease to melt and flow; again I shall seek and pierce and rend asunder." When she is in harmony with him and "the central power," she confesses she feels "at home." Yet should she lose his love, she knows "not how again to wander and grope, seeking my place in another Soul." "I need," she cries out to Emerson, "to be recognized."[29]

Fuller in this letter is asking the limited Emerson to give her the "clue" to "the labyrinth" of her "being": an insight into her self that would free her from the bonds of eccentricity. She yearns to receive from him a love that will satisfy all levels of her "manifold being," an uncritical recognition of her beautiful existence. The child in her thus cries to the obsessively critical father for natural love and recognition. The woman in her wishes to be as lovely as was her mother so that Emerson might feel tender toward her as he does toward Anna Barker ("I have no coldness no commonness," he had recently written Fuller, when "thoughts of the fair Anna come"). But neither of these appeals unbalanced Emerson as did that of the aggressive manly Fuller who, as Sarah Clarke put it, "broke her lance upon your shield," and who, in her own terms, sought to "pierce and rend asunder." This latter Fuller touched the untouchable in Emerson, his fear, as Fuller would later say in a review of his essays, that "beneath the veil of [Emerson's] words" lies, yes, "the still small voice of conscience," but it is a still small voice that appears—not as the fire of "God's lightning striking Sinai"—but as, in the words of Eric Cheyfitz quoting Fuller, a "'vestal fire[. . .],' the domestic fire of Woman."[30]

Thus Fuller sought through Emerson to find the love not just of the dead father but also of the mother. "Did you not see," exclaims Fuller, "what was meant by this crying for the moon?" Surely Emerson guessed at what she meant. For in his crucial 25 September 1840 letter to her he had already mentioned Isis, the fierce moon goddess—she who was ravished by Zeus in the form of a bull, and who, in bird form, in turn ravishes her dead husband, Osiris, having provided him first with a wooden phallus to replace the penis she could not find after Osiris's enemy, Typhon, dismembered him.[31]

Emerson was especially sensitive on the subject of Osiris's entombment by Typhon (the god associated in Plutarch's *Morals* with irrationality) and of his "final dismemberment." On 2 January 1833 he had jotted in his journal thoughts that had crossed his mind while the boat he was on tossed and rolled and passengers got sick during a violent storm. Regarding his dread of sinking to the ocean's floor and becoming scraps for "harpy feeding" he noted: "I remembered up nearly the whole of Lycidas, clause by clause, here a verse & there a word, as Isis in the fable the broken body of Osiris." Here Emerson equates the fragmented lines of Lycidas with the broken up, dismembered body of Osiris, revealing in the process his own dark fear of bodily dissolution and castration.[32]

Fuller's demand that Emerson recognize what she meant by "crying" to him "for the moon," emblem of Isis, the goddess he had mentioned to her but four days before, could only have aroused in the writer anxiety, a fact that Fuller, on some level, knew. Two years later she will write about herself that she has "a great share of Typhon to the brise's wild rush and leap, blind force for the sake of force." That Emerson apparently changed "brise" to "Osiris" when he placed this passage in the *Memoirs* suggests the depth of lingering sexual anxiety he still felt in relation to Fuller, who depicts herself in it as the monstrous Typhon. Thus Fuller's "wild" enticement at this time may indeed have seemed to Emerson, as Typhon's allurement of Osiris to his tomb, "the bait of a trap."[33]

An agitated Emerson seven days later excoriates Fuller in his letter for "this wild element in woman . . . which when perverted & outraged flashes up into a

EMERSON, FRIEND AND GUIDE

volcano jet, & outdares, outwits, & outworks man." A manly Fuller had demanded that this—to borrow the adjective the elder Henry James used to describe the tone of Emerson's letters—"maidenly" man love her. In interpreting her needs as "perverted," that is, as sexually rousing the woman in him, Emerson in turn retreated from further participation in these unsettling conversations with Fuller, inherently believing that the man who lets the woman in him prevail is not a true man but an effeminized being who has been outwitted and outworked by a manly woman.[34]

With this demand Fuller touched Emerson's deep-set fear that he might be, not a morally upright and active man who "stands in the erect position" and "keep[s] things under his feet," but an impotent and hence passive feminine being who "commands" not "his limbs," his life. In making this demand, Fuller lost forever Emerson as a lover. In his immediate response to her appeal Emerson had jotted a note on 1 October saying, "Today I think I shall not reply to your seven chords of melody which came to me last night." On 20 October he asks, "what would another day have done to reconcile our wide sights?" But Fuller refused to accept what he meant and wrote a letter that Emerson destroyed, the contents of which we can, however, surmise from another letter she wrote, this one to Cary Sturgis on 22 October. In that "hysterical" letter, Fuller speaks of her emotional "crisis" as if she were experiencing a kind of religious "second birth." Lost in language that confusedly fuses sex with religion, she sees herself to be mystically pregnant "like the holy Mother": "Does a star point out the spot. The gifts I must receive, yet for my child, not me. I have no words, wait till he is of age, then hear *him*."[35]

In response to similar outbursts to him, these indeed "perverse" yearnings to become pregnant without sex yet *with* a man whom she perceives to be "beneath the veil" a vestal virgin, Emerson on 24 October 1840 commanded Fuller to cease, forever, with her demands. "I have your frank & noble & affecting letter, and yet I think I could wish it unwritten. I ought never to have suffered you to lead me into any conversation or writing on our relation, a topic from which with all persons my Genius ever sternly warns me away." "Touch it not—speak not of it," he writes in anger. "It may do for others but it is not for me to bring the relation to speech." Perplexed, he continues: "Up to this hour our relation has been progressive. I have never regarded you with so much kindness as now." Yet, "there is a difference in our constitution. We use a different rhetoric." It seems to him as if they "had been born & bred in different nations." He then says he sees "very dimly in writing on this topic." "Do not," he coldly concludes, "expect it of me again for a very long time."[36]

Feeling that no man or woman—let alone a being of such low energy as himself—could ever finally satisfy his passionate friend's desire, Emerson had acted to end her fantasies about him. When he thought the crisis had passed, he reestablished their friendship on a safer level, writing Fuller in a friendly but patronizing way, saying he remembers her always "with joy & hope." To Cary Sturgis, whom he perceives to be "a prudent cautious Sister," he wrote: "Margaret's wonderful talent her stream of eloquent speech I always recognize: her native nobleness, I see also—her capacity for virtue[.] And now I see with joy a certain progress out of her complex into a simpler life & some of the gorgeous palaces in which she has dwelt are losing their lustre for her[.] Let us behold with love & hope." Still, he grieves over her ill health: "She is too costly a life to be prodigally spent." He wants her sane and well, for "she is of the greatest importance to me."[37]

Safe in his "citadel," having recemented his "outer wall" that had crumbled under Fuller's assault, Emerson, though in his own defensively superior way, had nonetheless done a service for Fuller, just as she had been of service to him. It was and would continue to be, once this crisis had passed, as Zwarg has said, a "mutually empowering and interactive" friendship. In their early conversations, Fuller had played Coleridge to Emerson's Wordsworth, though later, via the fluid prose of her letters to him, Emerson had become *her* Coleridge. She had helped steer his thoughts and poetic energies into writing on topics of interest to a truly broad audience, like "Love" and "Friendship," just as he had helped her direct her energies into the creative action of writing. Indeed, in the midst of their heated exchange, Emerson would produce, as we know, his essay "Friendship." As Fuller's guide, Emerson in turn had enabled her to rethink her way of being in the world, had helped her to open her "self" to taking in, as one scholar said, "a new model for interpreting the self, a new set of interpretive strategies for construing the psyche." Not only Emerson's words, but—as we will see in part 4 of this book—the words and images of women writers and friends, as well as the images of powerful mythical female figures that were central to her Conversation classes: these all blended in her being into a vision of self-reliance for herself and for other women.[38]

There would be moments in the future of flirtatious play. During her May–June 1841 visit to Emerson's home, she sent a note to him via little Waldo: "I wanted this afternoon as soon as you were really out of the house to run after you and call as little children do kiss and be friends; that would not be decorous *really* for two Editors, but it shall be so in thought shall it not?" Aware by now, however, of her sexualized feelings for him, she self-consciously signed this note, "Your affectionate ~~Margaret~~ Magdalen," making clear that, if in the past she wished to prostitute herself to him, she is now, as it were, a repentant sinner.[39]

As Emerson's audience and friend, Fuller had consumed and incorporated certain aspects of the orator and his teachings. Yet another result of Emerson's conversation with her was that, just as he had hoped and anticipated, she had learned to listen to, and to respond to, the powers in her own mind. Thus when Emerson early in 1841 attended one of Fuller's Conversations on Greek mythology, Elizabeth Peabody noted: "Mr. E. only served to display her powers. With his . . . uncompromising idealism, his absolute denial of the fact of human nature, he gave her opportunity and excitement to . . . illustrate her realism and acceptance of conditions." Fuller, in fact, may not have accepted the social and psychological conditions for women in her day, but at least she was trying to confront them in a positive way. Comparing Fuller to Emerson, James Clarke wrote his sister Sarah that "S.M.F. has less theoretical respect for humanity than R.W.E.—but more natural affinity with the mass." A prescient Clarke predicts regarding Fuller that "when she gets her principles & feelings in harmony she will do something."[40]

PART FOUR

The Seductive Lure of Nature

From January 1839 to late summer 1841—during the time of her intense friendship with Emerson—Fuller experienced an emotional crisis that for her constituted a religious conversion. In these "crisis" months, Fuller moved from a self-imposed solitude in nature, through dramatic encounters with friends to whom she wrote fantasy-filled letters, to a resolution in self-discovery that made her think, as William Henry Channing later said, that she was "of the Elect." In an important 1840 letter to Channing, a Unitarian minister, Fuller speaks of life in terms commonly used by ministers preaching about the Christian journey from sin to salvation. In it she depicts life as a "pilgrimage," an effort to overcome "worldliness." Echoing the prophets and preachers, she notes: "Men go an undulating course,—sometimes on the hill, sometimes in the valley. But he only is in the right who . . . knows in darkness that the sun will rise again."[1]

Like Christian in *Pilgrim's Progress,* Fuller knew that she, too, was on "an undulating course," one that had led her and would lead her again through sloughs of despond and the shadow of death. Despite the agony accompanying these detours into life's dark side, Fuller refused to be, as she thought Emerson was, "content with the blue sky alone."[2]

In these psychologically unsettling years, Fuller was looking for a way to balance her exalted feelings of power, when, as she wrote, we "mount the heights of our being," with the ensuing feelings of inertia, emptiness, and desertion when we "look down into darker colder chasms." Her search took shape as an exploration of the "vast powers" she felt that she had inherited as a woman. In her exploration of these dangerous passageways, Fuller faced her own dark demons. In touch with the forces within her that might have crippled her psyche, Fuller in this period of self-scrutiny not only confronted her darkest fears and desires but also attempted to make intellectual sense of her mental conflicts.[3]

Her life up to her crisis, which began upon her return to Groton in January 1839, had been, we recall, unusually stressful. She had hoped at the farm to find the peace she needed to alleviate anxiety. But once she was there, she had worked hard to earn money for her financially strapped family, quickly finishing her Eckermann translation. She had also read the volumes of Plato and Plutarch that Emerson had lent her, and, too, as we have seen, had entertained romantic fantasies about this treasured friend. It was only after the family had sold the farm, auctioned off their household effects, and moved in April to a pleasant, leased house south of Boston in Jamaica Plain that she found peace. There, in Willow Brook, the front parlor of which looked out over orchards and meadows to the wooded hills and western sky, Fuller finally found the leisure she longed for in a season during which she intended to "do nothing but think and feel."[4]

It was during this season of leisure—before she began her Conversation sessions in November 1839 or agreed to edit the *Dial* (the first issue of which was to appear in the summer of 1840)—that Fuller penned some of her most tenderly lyrical letters to Emerson. She did so, however, as we have seen, without receiving from him the recognition she craved. Moreover, in that same summer of 1839 Sam Ward rejected her offer of love. And at Nahant in June she suffered a traumatic falling-out with Cary Sturgis, the nature of which would move her to declare in letters to Cary a need to "redeem" their "friendship" from "the search after Eros." She would seek this redemption by channeling her unruly psychosexual energies into a quasi-mystical religious experience, as we see in this part of the book.[5]

In the summer of 1839, Fuller let herself be led by the lure of nature, a lure that drew her to an exploration not only of the dangerous passageways of sexual desire but also of all aspects of the female self in her effort to answer questions like those Emerson had asked in *Nature*: "to what end is Nature?" How do we explain "inexplicable" phenomena such as "language, sleep, dreams, beasts, sex"? "What is woman?" Unlike Emerson, however, Fuller did not attempt to "put nature under foot." She instead took literally her mentor's call for "us" to lie "embosomed for a season in nature." Whether in walks through "Bussey's wood" near her home in Jamaica Plain or along the shore at Nahant or Cohasset, Fuller sought to find in the sensuous embrace of "mother" nature relief from stress and pain. She sought peace and harmony in relating to nature as well as to friends, both male and female. However, as she continued her readings in the ancients and the European Romantics, she began increasingly to feel—instead of a harmonic calm—an unsettling "irregular" affection for various friends, male and female.[6]

A thoughtful look at this luxurious season in Fuller's life will let us see how one Transcendentalist's indulgence in innocent religious "excitement" and Romantic dreams did indeed lead her, as Karl Keller and others would have predicted, to the dangerous subject of sex. On this topic New England Transcendentalists lacked even an adequate vocabulary. Thus Fuller, in exploring what it meant to be a woman, unintentionally became a revolutionary on the subject of sex and a forebear of a modern age.[7]

This "Seductive Lure of Nature" section of the book thus necessarily begins with a reminder to readers as to why the idea of spiritual rebirth was so congenial to Fuller. It also reviews the texts she was reading (especially Plato and Plutarch) during her icy isolation in Groton in January 1839, texts that provided the intellectual and literary frame through which Fuller looked as she undertook her psychologically unsettling self-analysis. It then turns to look at Fuller's exploration of external nature, after which it investigates not only the Eros-tinted nature of Fuller's friendships (chapters 21 through 24 focus closely on this aspect of her life), but also her imaginative merging with powerful figures from both myth and European history in this crisis period when her sense of self was in flux. In this section I stress Fuller's imaginary identification with passionate female figures who undergo magical transformations of being, as Fuller was to feel that she had undergone a mystical metamorphosis upon emerging from her crisis.

As we travel with Fuller in her letters and journals along the "stream of thought" as it flowed through her mind during these years 1839–41, we occasionally depart from a strictly chronological perspective. For, as in the exquisite pattern of a fine Persian carpet, the thematic threads of Fuller's life are intricately tied and woven. From this nonlinear analysis of these brief years in Fuller's life, we gain a clearer sense of what it was about her that both drew friends to her and drove them away. Such an analysis reveals how a crisis of identity that threatens one's self-possession by seemingly drawing one down to the primal life "within" can likewise stir the imaginative mind to convert its knowledge into a work of creative genius. Fuller's letters and journals reveal how the words and images she gleaned not only from her Puritan past, Emerson, Christian evangelicals, and the ancients, but also from her outings in nature, her friendships with women, her readings in Romantic literature, and her nighttime dreams all interwove in her fecund imagination into a vision of self-reliance for women.[8]

17 ∞ Religious Crisis

Both by temperament and by the influence of her Puritan past, Fuller as an adult felt at ease with the idea of religious rebirth. As late as August 1844 she was still attending family devotionals, like one she took part in with her mother and Richard during which she read Charles Wesley's hymn, "Jesus, My Strength, My Hope."[1] Still, like Emerson, Fuller had trouble accepting conventional religious dogma, whether it appeared in the literal terms of the fundamentalists or the rational precepts of liberal Unitarians.

Craving a religion of the heart, part of Fuller responded to the more passionate vision of her Puritan ancestors for whom temptation, sin, and redemption were live ideas that helped determine their everyday actions. As a young woman she had hence rebelled against the religion of her father, a Unitarian who disliked not just Calvin's dark view of humanity as depraved and of God as an almighty power that predetermines man's destiny, but also the evangelical's easy access to redemption through instantaneous conversion.

Drawn to the religious vision of the Baptist and Methodist that gave hope of redemption through an intense emotional experience, Timothy's daughter in Providence had responded positively to Baptist minister William Hague. Fuller admired the way Hague, a student in her German seminar, combined in his oratorical manner an active intellect with generous emotion. Though short, as was her father, Hague, she thought, nonetheless achieved in his preaching style the "perfect *abandon*" of his whole being that she sought to attain for herself. With his sparkling hazel blue eyes and sweet pleading tones "he throws himself," she said, "into the hearts of his hearers," as he apparently threw himself into hers. For on a July Sunday in 1838, she had partaken, she confessed, "for the first time, of the Lord's Supper." "Feeling strongly that God is love," the Reverend Hague, she said, "speaks direct from the conviction of his spirit," and "his mind has not been fettered by dogmas, and the worship of beauty finds a place there."[2]

In light of her preference for Hague's heated preaching, it is easy to understand Fuller's fascination with the feverish preaching of the religious enthusiasts whose evangelical ultraism peaked in New England between 1825 and 1836, when Fuller was maturing. Looking back, Emerson in the *Memoirs* wrote, though in noticeably negative terms, that Fuller was familiar with the "literature of asceticism and rapturous piety," as well as with the "conversation of certain mystics, who had appeared in Boston" around 1839–41. As we've already seen, in the summer of 1840 he thought she began exhibiting "mental changes" that seemed to Emerson not "quite healthy." Her letters of this time, he said, "are tainted" with "mysticism."[3]

Two ultraevangelists whose language and charisma seem to have influenced Fuller were Charles Grandison Finney and the Reverend John Todd. She was only twenty-one and living in the Dana mansion in Cambridge when the Billy Graham of his day, Charles Finney—a lean, athletic, strikingly handsome man with a rich strong voice and piercing blue eyes—first came to Boston to preach from August 1831 to April 1832. It is perhaps no coincidence that on Thanksgiving Day 1831 Fuller had her first conversion experience. Finney, who was to preach again in Boston in 1841, near the end of Fuller's second conversion experience, upset his staid Presbyterian brethren when he asserted in his 1835 *Lectures on Revivals of Religion* that sinners "never will give up their false shame . . . till they are so excited that they cannot contain themselves any longer." In terms like those Fuller later used to describe her own crisis, Finney contended that God "found it necessary . . . to produce powerful excitements among [men]," such that when they prayed they became "wet with perspiration." At such revivals, "extreme fervor" apparently ran "over into experiments in sex relations" evident, according to Whitney Cross, in "indiscriminate kissing" and "licentious advances." Despite these signs that spirituality was flowing into sexual fervor, Finney continued to argue for "an ingenuous breaking down" of constraints and "a pouring out of the heart" till "the flood-gates will soon burst open, and salvation will flow over the place." Though Finney was obviously not advocating free love, the connection between religious enthusiasm and erotic excitement is nonetheless clear.[4]

Todd, Groton's fiery fundamentalist preacher when the Fullers moved there in April 1833, used the liquid metaphor in a different way. Todd's popular *Student's Manual* had, as we have seen, linked male genitalia with the soul. Todd accepted as fact the then widely held notion that semen flows through the blood from the brain to the genitals. Hence he was, we recall, urging young men to abstain from masturbation, since the release of sperm by this "evil" practice, to use Todd's word, depleted a man of the energy necessary for creative effort. Fuller's reference in an 1835 letter to Clarke to the flood of words she would "pour forth" to him if only he would visit her in Groton, as well as her talk in her crisis of "tides of feeling," of the "life that flows in upon me," the "dews of night," and "seas surg[ing] between me and you," thus reflects to some extent her internalization of terms commonly used by evangelists like Finney and Todd. But it also reflects her absorption of terms frequently used by the European Romantics, for whom surging seas connote, among other things, sexual excitement and orgasm.[5]

Water imagery floods Fuller's letters to Emerson; in letters to friends during this period of personal probing, Fuller tends to summon up images—like those of flowing fluids—that suggest that, during the winter months of 1839–40, she was undergoing not only a spiritual renewal but also, as an uneasy Emerson suspected, a sexual awakening. This baptism was fed by her immersion in the exotic writings of the European Romantics and ancient Greeks, as well as in the electric flow of luxurious nature.[6]

18 ∞ A Divine Madness

After she had come home to Groton in January 1839, Fuller focused her attention on the writings of Plato that had enchanted her in 1833. She borrowed again Emerson's volume of Plato, but this time she limited her reading to two dialogues: *Phaedrus* and the *Symposium*. In the latter, which Fuller called "The Banquet," Socrates explores the meaning of love, and in the *Phaedrus* he argues that love is a form of "divine madness." Socrates was always interested in eros, particularly of a homoerotic kind, but only in these two late dialogues did Plato's teacher attempt to anchor eros in a metaphysical search for a transcendent vision of Beauty. In the *Symposium,* where Socrates reportedly fell into mystical fits of abstraction, his vision is spoken through the wise woman Diotima, who says that people more creative in their souls than in their bodies conceive wisdom and virtue, instead of babies. He goes further in the *Phaedrus,* saying that although the poet whose "organs" enable him to see beauty may seem demented to others, such a person is really divinely possessed, "and when he that loves beauty is touched by such madness he is called a lover." Such love, says Socrates, is above bodies fusing; it is the restoration of the soul's wings, the regaining of purity through the contemplation of the ideal form of beauty. Though poets and artists who see a perfected form of beauty in a mortal may seem "strange" to others, they are in truth suffering from the "fever" that comes when a person perceives divine being behind the ordinary objects of everyday life.[1]

In these dialogues, Plato turns to Orphism for its mystic vision, making Diotima its advocate. Orphism was a mystical strand that came by route of Pythagoras, who had refined the doctrines of Orphism, just as Orphic ritual had been an intellectual upgrade of Bacchic orgiastic rites. This religion was born of the fertility rites honoring the Thracian Bacchus. God of the vine, Bacchus was imprisoned in winter and released in spring, and his reformer, Orpheus, had the power through his music to charm trees and animals and even persuaded the rulers of the dead with his music to let him attempt to retrieve his wife, Eurydice, from the underworld. The women who worshipped Bacchus (or Dionysus) celebrated the god's death and resurrection with wild dancing, drinking, and the shredding of a sacrificial animal, which was eaten raw. Eating an animal raw was apparently a primitive form of communion, a symbolic taking in of the flesh and blood of their god.[2]

This form of worship was at odds with Plato's upper-class and predominantly masculine ethic of prudent self-control, the kind of cool vision Emerson advocated. It fostered instead a respect for violent emotion, as well as for women, and it was associated with a frenzied all-body expression of the spiritual self. The original female followers of Bacchus were called Maenads, or Bacchantes. In contrast to violent Bacchaen rites, the Orphics' aim was figurative, not literal, intoxication, the wish being to become united imaginatively with Orpheus by means of ecstatic wild dancing. Through this act of frenetic dancing, the body—considered by Orphics the prison of the soul—was purportedly cleansed of impurities and pain.[3]

Fuller's 1839–41 mystical experience was anchored in these ancient rituals she knew about through her reading of classical literature. As a passionate person, Fuller was attracted to this sort of ecstatic release, a frenzied form of religious madness that appears also in *The Bacchae* by Euripides, whose *Iphigenia in Aulis* was one of Fuller's favorite plays. A form of the wild religious ritual described in *The Bacchae* was apparently practiced in ancient times by women who sought through it to gain relief from the pain of their hard lives.[4]

In contrast to the ethic Plato advocates in *The Republic* of rational prudence and self-control, Orphism's emotionalism appealed to oppressed people, including women, who felt they had little control over their lives. Such an emotional religion offered hope to people who believed their views did not count in matters pertaining to the state. Through such frenzied dancing, women Orphics were able to gain a momentary sense of freedom from their oppressive conditions, since when they danced they felt as if they were in direct contact with the mysterious power they saw as God. To a passionate woman like Fuller, the self-restraint urged on her by Emerson seemed like a cage from which, in the fashion of women Orphics, she yearned to fly free.[5]

Fuller felt she understood not just women Orphics but Socrates, who with his snub nose and considerable paunch was said by Xenophon to be "uglier than all the Silenuses in the Satyric drama" and whose "queerness" was frequently commented on by all who knew him. Knowing that even his followers thought Socrates "strange" may have made remarks Cary had made about Fuller's own strangeness less painful to her.[6]

Yet neither Orphic mysticism nor evangelical Christianity finally fulfilled Fuller's needs. She wanted a religion that would satisfy the longings of her body as well as of her soul. She had already discovered the naturalistic ideas on the soul that appeared in the writings of Shelley, Goethe, and Wordsworth, the last of whom in his poetry combines pagan passions with Christian wisdom. That Fuller's approach to religion had a Wordsworthian cast is not surprising, since she noted in a letter she wrote pertaining to her father's death that she had dealt with her loss by reading from both Wordsworth and the Bible.[7]

By divesting the terms of the religious enthusiasts of their literal theological significance and sectarian trappings and by translating them, as Romantic writers characteristically did, into epistemological and psychological terms ("symbolically," said Fuller), Fuller was able to make conceptual sense of her complex emotional and spiritual needs.[8]

Fuller's assumption of new self-knowledge was made possible in part, as we have seen, by Emerson, who sustained her during her crisis much as the imagined presence of Coleridge sustained Wordsworth on his pilgrimage through the *Prelude*. Risking the psychic dangers of intense introspection, Fuller metaphorically "plunge[d]" into the sea of her tumultuous emotions. The aim of her daring exploration of the "mysterious grottoes" of her being, of what William Channing called her "unchartered impulses," was to reconcile her divided inner self, to return, in her words, her "self" to herself.[9] However, when she sought, as Romantics often do, a loving reunion with the feminine figure, her desire was either rebuffed or misunderstood, as it was at first by Cary. This failure to heal the narcissistic wound "within" can result in the kind of idealization of self and others evident in Fuller's letters to Emerson. Her letters to him do yield the impression she is talking in vain to someone who could never be the one she really desired. Such a failure to comprehend what it is one really desires can also lead to a psychologically destabilizing desire for re-fusion with the mother.[10]

Though psychologically destabilizing, Fuller's self-exploration would also prove rewarding, bringing her the pain that came with her unsettling new self-insights but also the pleasure that she attained, as she herself said, from the sense of an inward life "rich and deep, and of more calm and musical flow than ever before." The danger for Fuller of relinquishing "self" possession in her drive to find truth was that, once touched and unloosed, her instinctual energies might push her to pursue, not truth, but an *ignis fatuus* to destruction. For the lure cast by nature is "especially deceptive." It offers the tempting promise of achieving a final release from pain—a whole soul-body climax that frees one, through death, from anxiety, the tragic agony of life.[11]

19 ∞ The Siren Song of Nature

In her quest to affirm her female self, Fuller looked to find in literature a writer who could point the way to her "spiritual" awakening. So when the family moved to the house in Jamaica Plain, she continued her readings in the classics and the Romantics. She found Wordsworth's faith in a sublime "presence" whose "dwelling is the light of setting suns" more spiritually uplifting at this time than what one preacher she admired called "the Idolatry of Jesus." During the spring and summer of 1839, Fuller thus relaxed and let her emotions be drawn not just up to heaven but down to "that immortal sea" within whose "undulatory motions" she thought, like the stirring of a pool of water, "of all earthly things most lovely," "the heaving of the bosom."[1]

Like Indiana in George Sand's 1832 novel who had always been "drawn to the banks of rivers" where she naively dreamed how "sweet" it would be "to die" by drowning, Fuller found the sight of a body of water so lovely that she felt she understood why "gazers on a riverside" might be tempted to drown themselves. Frustrated with men's inability or unwillingness to give her the love she sought, Fuller turned in her search for reassurance and comfort away from male icons to Mother Nature. In letters she talks at this time of lying down by "gay little brooks" and of giving herself "up as much as possible to enjoyment of the fine weather." The earth seems to her as "delicate as a bride." On 10 June Fuller will write the poet Sarah Helen Whitman how "blest" she feels "now in living at harmony with myself which I never did in [Providence]," where Whitman had been in her graduate seminar. She says she believes she has earned "this beautiful episode" in her "Crusade" in which "my desires dilate with my horizon."[2]

Though Fuller in her 10 June letter to Whitman says that her mind "flows on its natural current," she was, nevertheless, under great stress. She knew that these leisure months were but a respite and that she must soon return to work to earn money to support the family. Moreover, her fantasy romance with Sam Ward was disintegrating. And Emerson continued to deflect her love.[3]

Fuller that summer went again to the seashore where she sought soothing in the sound of the surf, the embrace of the breeze. The sea breeze is healing, she tells

Elizabeth Hoar; "it soothes my brain, and new strings every sense." She thinks Elizabeth, too, will be happy if only she will go to the seashore and be "embraced" by the "arms of nature."[4]

While on one level Fuller's talk is quintessentially Romantic, on another level something else is happening here in the way she views both nature and women. William Channing, in describing how Fuller appeared to him in 1839–40, wrote that, in temperament, she seemed to him a Bacchante. After writing it, he realized that this was how Fuller had described George Sand. Though he thought about striking the passage after realizing this coincidence, he decided, on second thought, to keep it, "as indicating an actual resemblance between these two grand women."[5]

Channing here is perceptive. For Fuller was finding in Sand a woman who felt as passionate as did she about nature and the "problem" of "being a woman." Fuller, who had known about Sand since 1832 when her novels *Indiana* and *Valentine* were published, by 1839 had surely heard about Sand's 1833 succès de scandale, *Lélia,* an essaylike novel about the overwhelming force of female sexuality. After all, during the years 1832–33 she had consumed "romantic articles" in the "old *Foreign Review,*" the *Edinburgh Review,* and the *Foreign Quarterly.*[6]

Women writers who were less inquisitive than Fuller about sexual matters had read *Lélia.* In 1844, before she met Robert Browning, Elizabeth Barrett wrote that what is "dangerous" in George Sand is "the irresistible power she attributes to human passion": "Love, . . . guilty love, . . . cannot be resisted by the . . . most virtuous individuality." Barrett declared that Sand had a "disgusting tendency" to present "the passion of love under its physical aspect." *Lélia* was so shocking, she said, that she could not read the book, even though the title character is "capable of noble elevations both intellectual and moral." Her tune, however, changed once she met Browning. Then she confessed that, when she "was a prisoner," it was "Balzac, George Sand" and the like who "kept the colour in my life," though in "discreet England," she dared not "confess to such reading."[7]

Julia Ward Howe, who would attend Fuller's 1842 Conversation classes, likewise read Sand's novels in secret as a girl. She recalls how parents would not let their daughters read Sand. But "at stolen hours," and "in a dreary, wintry room, with a flickering candle warning us of late hours . . . the atmosphere grew warm and glorious about us," for "a living sympathy crept near us." Sand "had given us a real gift; no criticism could take it away. The hands might be sinful, but the box they broke contained an exceeding precious ointment."[8]

These women writers knew better than to confess to reading Sand. Sand wrote the soul-searching *Lélia* when she was twenty-nine. In Fuller's twenty-ninth year—in that crucial summer of 1839—she experienced a gender identity crisis that can best be understood when viewed in the light of the literature she was reading as well as of the way she was thinking during this period of imaginative exploration.

That spring and summer, in preparation for writing a review of modern French literature, Fuller was reading Sand and other writers in the original French, including Alfred de Vigny and Pierre de Béranger. She was sharing Sand's writings with Emerson, and, at the summer's end, sent him her essay on "la jeune France."[9]

From this essay we know that by the fall of 1839 Fuller had in fact read and been impressed by, among other works by Sand, *Indiana, André, Leone Leoni, Jacques, Spiridion, Mauprat, Lettres d'un voyageur,* and *Les sept cordes de la lyre,* the last of which she read in *La revue des deux mondes,* the journal Sand had been publishing regularly in since 1832. It's doubtful that Fuller would not have also come in contact with Sand's *Lélia,* if not read it in its entirety. We know, too, that by July 1840 Fuller had read Balzac's *Le livre mystique.*[10]

We know, then, that until July 1840 Fuller was attentively examining the tangled sexual relations depicted in the brazen romances of Sand and Balzac. In a later review of "French Novelists of the Day," Fuller would criticize Balzac for his tendency to transform poetic "joy" into merely "the thrilling of the blood in the rapture of sense." But in her twenty-ninth year, in *Le livre mystique,* according to Emerson, Fuller "found something of true portraiture" in that in it "an equivocal figure exerts alternately a masculine and a feminine influence" on the plot's characters. Though Emerson found the novel "disagreeable," Fuller was intrigued by it.[11]

In an unpublished note she wrote in 1835, Fuller identifies with the fecund French writer's divided sense of herself as half female, half male. But it was not until the summer of 1839 that the image of a defiant Sand who dared to dress in men's clothes, a taboo in Fuller's time, captured Fuller's imagination. In a highly susceptible frame of mind, Fuller was open to being easily influenced by others. Fuller's evolving "self," like a flower unfolding its petals to receive the beams of the sun, thus took in that summer not just Emerson's ideas and affects, but also, and of equal import, alternative images for women.[12]

20 ∞ The Seductive Sand

In the seductive George Sand, who boldly broke with traditional thought and behavior by dressing as a man, taking lovers like a man, and writing about love between women, Fuller found a powerful woman who would point the way to her awakening as a woman. She loved Sand's multifaceted personality and her analyses of the psychological complexity of women and men, this woman who, as the younger Henry James said, "put a premium on all passion, on all pain, on all experience."[1]

Sand voiced opinions close to Fuller's own on the obstacles intellectual women encounter in a culture that saw passivity and passionlessness in women as signs of piety and virtue. A good woman neither discussed nor participated in any sexual act, unless it was in marriage for procreation or for her husband's pleasure.

When "good" women loved, they did so supposedly free from the heat of what men and women alike deemed "the demon, sexuality." Fuller was hence elated to read in Sand's preface to *Indiana* that the title character is a type of "woman, the weak creature who represents repressed passions, or rather, passions suppressed by the law."[2]

Recasting the French writer's views on suppressed passions into apocalyptic terms closer to her own, Fuller in her unpublished 1839 essay "La jeune France" wrote: "So materialistic is the course of common life, that we *ask daily* new Messiahs from literature and art, to turn us from the Pharisaic observance of law, to the baptism of spirit." In Sand, Fuller found the literary messiah she sought, a woman who could lead her from her social bondage as a female to the spiritual rebirth she sought. Yet to follow Sand was to seek to be cleansed of one's sins not by water but by "fire," as Fuller acknowledges in her 1839 essay.[3]

In *Indiana,* the young Creole heroine, whose mother is English, in an attempt to escape an abusive marriage to a colonel loyal to his Napoleonic heritage, risks death by sailing on a ship manned by dangerous sailors in pursuit of a Frenchman named Raymon, who does not love her. Though Indiana risks being raped and then thrown into the sea by the sailors, the fiery pain that accompanies her fruitless quest cleanses her, in effect, of her sensual sins and paves the way for the happiness she at last attains in her mature relationship with her cousin Ralph. *Mauprat,* in a similar vein, tells about a man, as Fuller puts it, "raised by the workings of love, from the depths of savage sensualism, to a moral and intellectual life." Impressed by *Mauprat,* Fuller that autumn encouraged Emerson to read it.[4]

Whereas friends had understood her early identification with de Staël, they thought Fuller's absorption of images and ideas from Sand and other notorious nineteenth-century French writers, to use Channing's words, "wild in its daring." Indeed, if morally self-righteous New Englanders thought, as Higginson observes in his biography of Fuller, that the "mere perusal" of books by Goethe and other Germans to be "dangerous," then they must have seen Fuller's reading of Sand and writing about her as radically subversive.[5] Even Fuller saw Sand as quite different from her. In light of the differences in their backgrounds, breeding, religion, and social class, it is surprising that Fuller identified with Sand to the extent that she did.

No daughter of frugal Puritans obsessed with sin and saving souls, Sand was an example par excellence of the "Mother power" that Emerson condemned in "Demonology." Self-consciously maternal and sensual, Sand accepted female sexuality as a natural part of life. About the "Holy Virgin," whose image Fuller treasured, Sand said, she "resembles me not in the slightest."[6]

George Sand, born Aurore Dupin, was a child of old wealth and privilege; she was brought up by people who, as her grandmother Dupin said, "enjoyed life and when the time came" knew how "to leave it." Aurore was proud of her dual heritage: on her father Maurice's side she was descended from a Saxon king; on her mother Sophie's, from a French bird seller. Sophie was, in Sand's words, "bad and at the same time good." Little Aurore, too, was bad but good. And she grew up exhibiting the kind of self-possession and confidence that is the bequest of heirs of the aristocracy. This bold daughter of a mismatched couple was the flesh and blood changeling that Fuller as a child had imagined herself to be, a European princess of high birth and pagan passions.[7]

Though Sand sprang from aristocrats and adventurers who bent social rules to suit personal desires, whereas Fuller came from sexually repressed Puritan stock, the women shared enough traits that Fuller could see in Sand a side of herself that she "necessarily repressed" in New England. Like Fuller, Sand had been an imaginative child who loved fairy tales and Greek myths. Sand remembered her father, who had died in a riding accident when she was four, as being "all heart, all impulse, courage and trust," entirely unlike Timothy. Also unlike Fuller, the adult Sand saw herself as mother, not daughter, of her father. In her relationship with Sophie, however, Sand came to see herself—as did Fuller in relation to Margarett Crane—as her mother's protector.[8]

There are other similarities. Both at age fourteen were sent to finishing schools by parental figures concerned about their rebellious behavior, Margaret to a boarding school in Groton, Aurore to the Convent of English Augustinians. At their respective schools, each entertained her classmates with theatrics and formed, as girls their age typically did, schoolgirl crushes. But instead of attaching herself to a pretty teacher, as Fuller did, Sand cared for a ten-year-old girl "as if," she later said, "she were my daughter." And at the convent Sand underwent what seemed to her a religious conversion during which she felt she was in direct communication with God in much the same way Fuller experienced a loss of self into God in her mystical experience on Thanksgiving Day at the age of twenty-one.[9]

But whereas the twenty-one-year-old Fuller at the time interpreted her Romantic experience of egoistic piety as an authentic religious conversion, when Aurore, who was only fourteen, told her confessor, the Abbé de Prémord, about her conversion, to her surprise she was given a lecture on the good of worldly common sense. Thus Sand passed through this period of egoistic self-expansion and was soon back doing theatrics and interacting in a realistic way with her classmates, who respected her as a friend and leader.

Except for this brief teen foray into mysticism, Sand was a down-to-earth person who sought pleasure from life. Once she had inherited her grandmother's estate, Aurore at eighteen hastily married Casimir Dudevant. No sooner did she discover that the marriage would not work than she began to seek her freedom through writing. She chose this mode of making money because she knew she was a talented storyteller and letter writer. To succeed as a writer, Aurore dressed as a man. In Paris she became friends with writers Theophile Gautier, Honoré de

Balzac, and Jules Sandeau, the last of whom she took as a lover and collaborator on a novel, *Rose et Blanche,* which they published under the androgynous pen name J. Sand. *Indiana,* which was published in April 1832 under the pen name George Sand, was written only by her.

The patrician Sand did not much care if her libertine behavior shocked her contemporaries. Besides, the trim, black-haired, bright-eyed, olive-skinned Sand had, as Balzac said of her, "an awesome clarity about herself." If people were offended by Sand's lax attitude toward marital sexual fidelity, it was because she was so direct about her behavior. Unlike Fuller, Sand did not feel divided, as if her masculine need for self-assertion conflicted with her feminine need for love, nor did her desire for sensual pleasure trigger, as it did in Fuller, the punishing response of anything like a zealous Puritan conscience. Sand instead freely expressed both the male and female aspects of her vital personality. The bold, strong woman the writer Alfred de Musset thought "very beautiful" was also a woman who was, when with a man she loved, passionate and tender. Musset, one of her lovers, said of Sand after she had left him, "she is . . . the most womanly woman I have ever known."[10]

Unlike Fuller, Sand did not flee frustration by seeking love in fantasy. Sand knew passion, as Fuller herself later said, "at a *white* heat."[11] She had been loved by men and borne them children. If she had a deep need it was to mother men, and in the tubercular, fair-haired Frédéric Chopin, six years her junior, she found a frail male to mother.

In Sand Fuller thus found a woman who dared to think, speak, and act her passion, a woman committed to a Utopian vision of Christian communism. Here was a woman who, in October 1836 when Fuller was idealizing Emerson, sent a frank letter to her lawyer lover Michel de Bourges telling him how she had suffered "exhausting dreams" during a trip she took to Switzerland without him: "The blood has rushed to my head a hundred times. In the midst of the mountains when the sun was high and I listened to the song of the birds . . . I often sat apart from my companions— . . . , my knees trembling with voluptuous desire."[12]

In her 1839 essay on French writers, Fuller ironically condemned Sand for "bewailing her loneliness, bewailing her mistakes, writing for money!" In *André* and in *Jacques,* says a self-righteous Fuller, "the sophistry of passion . . . disgusted" her. Yet despite this Puritan display of disgust, Fuller subconsciously let Sand's bold images lead to her own liberation as a woman. After all, here was a woman who aggressively courted her men and declared that she was not "reconciled to society." In *Jacques* Sand scorns marriage as a barbarous institution that must "be abolished" if "the human species" is to make "progress towards justice and reason." She asserts that "a more human and no less sacred bond will replace it, assuring the existence of children who will be born of a man and a woman without forever enchaining the freedom of the one and the other."[13]

Sand's defiant figure became a living presence in Fuller, despite the attempt by her Puritan conscience to suppress it. It was present in her when she wrote her exotic letters to Emerson and Sturgis during her 1839–41—what might be described as—psychosexual-spiritual crisis. And it was vitally alive when she took a job as a journalist in New York, and also, later, when in Italy she became both a political radical and the lover of Giovanni Angelo Ossoli, ten years her junior.

Yet Fuller felt deep ambivalence about these French aesthete-decadent writers, whose bold aim was, as the French would say, "*épater le bourgeois*" (astonish the middle class). On one level she shared the aesthetes' antipathy to philistine middle-class morality, even though her own moral perceptions were grounded in bourgeois virtue and she professed to be disgusted with their passions. Writers like Henri de Latouche, Gautier, and Balzac flaunted in their poetry and prose exotic images of erotic encounters between women as well as between men and women. Latouche's *Fragoletta,* published in 1829, tells of a woman disguised as a man who seduces another woman. This was followed in 1835 by Gautier's *Mademoiselle de Maupin,* in which the heroine has heterosexual sex and minutes later homosexual sex. In *The Girl with the Golden Eyes,* Balzac that same year dazzled readers with ornate descriptions of the luxuriously sensual relationship of the blue-eyed, black-haired, "natural son" of Lord Dudley, Henri de Marsay, and the plush Paquita Valdes, a beautiful girl with golden eyes with whom Henri becomes obsessed after seeing her one spring morning in the Tuileries. This young Adonis, who "believed in neither . . . God nor the Devil," allows the mysterious girl, whose mother has sold her as a slave to some unnamed person, to have him transported to an exotic chamber where she urges Henri to indulge her wildest fantasies. To please Paquita, who wears "orange blossoms in her black hair" (Fuller herself will take to wearing a fresh flower every day), he dons a red velvet dress, woman's hat, and shawl before making love to her. Paquita turns out to be a sexual slave of the Marquise de St. Real, who, in a jealous rage, stabs Paquita to death for betraying her. "Stimulated by the struggle," the panting marquise does not at first note that she is being watched by Henri. When their eyes meet, a "ghastly surprise chilled the blood in both their veins." "Indeed," says Balzac, "twins could not have been more alike." For both were children of Lord Dudley.[14]

In researching "La jeune France," Fuller may have come upon subtle references to Sand's passionate attachment to the actress Marie Dorval, with whom she had a brief romantic fling. After all, Dorval was the mistress of the romantic writer Count Alfred de Vigny, whose ability to turn his life into art Fuller praises in her 1839 essay. In her 1845 review, "French Novelists of the Day," Fuller will again praise Vigny, saying that he has "touched some of the most delicate springs of human action." In his journal, which Fuller mentions in her 1839 essay, Vigny calls Dorval, "My Sappho," an allusion to Dorval's intense attachment to Sand in Paris, where they were known as "the inseparables."[15]

Sand wrote *La Marquise* as well as her third novel, *Lélia,* with Dorval in mind. In *La Marquise,* the male actor, Lélio, is loved by a woman who resembles Sand and who has been "rendered frigid" by her late husband. Disguised as a man she goes to the theater. After the lovers have met, confessed their love, and kissed, "Lélio wept," says Sand, "like a woman." In *Lélia* the eponymous heroine is a female version of Lélio. When the coolly intellectual Lélia is reunited with her sensualist sister, Pulchérie, who was inspired by Dorval, Pulchérie tells Lélia that watching her as she slept gave her "my first lesson in love, my first sensation of desire."[16]

Fuller, Emerson, and their friends knew of the sexual perturbations underlying Sand's writings, just as they were aware of the decadent depiction of passionate female love in the novels of Balzac, Gautier, and Latouche. Emerson found himself repelled by Sand, pointedly noting in a November 1839 letter to Fuller that, while he likes Sand's sometimes "authentic revelations of what passes in man & in woman," he objects to Sand herself, contending that she is "sick with the sickness of the French intellect." Hawthorne, in *The Blithedale Romance,* depicts Zenobia, a fictional rendering of Fuller, as a reader of "George Sand's romances"—Zenobia, the "queenly," the "exotic," the women's rights advocate and "sister of the Veiled Lady." The Veiled Lady turns out to be the gypsylike, orphaned Priscilla, a girl who resembles Cary Sturgis and who, as in the novel *Lélia,* is powerfully attracted to her imperial and passionate, intellectual half-sister, Zenobia.[17]

In the electrically alive Zenobia, Hawthorne successfully captured the magnetic power of Margaret Fuller's emotive force. And when Hawthorne labels the hothouse flower in Zenobia's dark hair "exotic," he—with his sixth sense regarding perverse or passionate sexual desire—seems to associate the flower and its bearer with an overpowering female sexuality, for which the word "exotic" both evokes the primordial erotic urge and denies its full expression. Fuller with her daily fresh flower would be figuratively qualified by Emerson in an 1846 letter that Hawthorne surely read, as "an exotic in New England, a foreigner from some more sultry and expansive clime."[18]

21 ∞ Demonic Desires

Fuller's complex response to her female friends during her 1839–41 crisis was thus shaped to a great extent by the literature she was reading at the time, as is evident in a letter she wrote Sturgis on a Sunday evening from Groton in January 1839 shortly after her return from Providence. While reading the volume of Plato that Emerson had lent her containing Plato's *Phaedrus* and *Symposium* ("The Banquet") the evening before, Fuller had let her imagination run riot over the unchartered terrain of unorthodox ideas she was ingesting from Plato's dialogues on love. She was especially impressed by Aristophanes' theory in the *Symposium* that once there were three sexes: male, female, and a third having equal male and female attributes—though "nothing is left" of this complex sexual being, says he, but the "name" Hermaphrodite, now "used in reproach."[1]

Here is an image that appealed to Fuller, one that Emerson, presumably reflecting the views of Fuller and her friends, would in 1843 equate with "the symbol of the finished soul," someone who marries the two sexes in his person. But even by January 1839 Fuller was already familiar with such unorthodox images of gender arrangements and relations. In addition to being well read in Ovid and Plato, she had recently taught Ariosto's romantic epic *Orlando Furioso* to the older girls in her Italian class in Providence. Daydreaming in snowy Groton, she may have recalled Ariosto's playful tale of gender shifting when Fiordispina falls in love with Bradamant, an Amazon warrior destined to marry Rogero. In the first rush of passion, Fiordispina mistakes Bradamant for a man and finds a way to spend a night beside him (really her), only to find that her sleep is "troubled" by "strange dreames and fancies." Frustrated that Bradamant cannot satisfy her physical desire, Fiordispina's "passion" grows "stronger." Bradamant, aware of the "great danger" she is in, tells her brother about Fiordispina's "strange" passion. The brother, dressed in his sister's clothes, then woos in the form of a woman the passion-possessed princess, convincing Fiordispina that a nymph has given her (actually him) the physical apparatus she needs to relieve her lover's distress. Fiordispina, who "now did see, and feele, and touch, / That which she long had longed for in vaine," is suddenly filled with a rapturous happiness. And "that same bed," explains the mischievous Ariosto, which "the night before" were full "Of teares, . . . anguish and annoyes," thence has in it, "smilings, sports" and "joyes."[2]

A tale that ventured into the dangerous territory of unconventional sex thus concludes in a way that would have pleased even conservative nineteenth-century New Englanders: the crush of one girl on another ends happily in heterosexual love. With images like these from Ariosto as well as Plato's *Symposium* in mind, Fuller in her letter to Sturgis notes whimsically how, "last night," when she "banqueted" with Plato, she found herself wishing for Cary's "accompaniment" to the flageolet, bugle, or harp. For, confesses Fuller, "I have many feelings in reading Plato, perhaps not orthodox."[3]

Fuller's wishing Sturgis were with her is understandable. They had been friends since 1832 when, we recall, the twelve-year-old Cary's mother had undergone a religious crisis during which she had abandoned her family. After her mother's breakdown, the high-strung, artistic Cary saw herself as an orphan, though she never lost her Christian faith despite the trauma introduced into her life by her mother's religious crisis and lifelong depression.[4]

Nine years younger than Fuller, Sturgis had turned to the authoritative Fuller for maternal love and guidance. Fuller's 1839–41 psychological crisis may, in turn, have seemed to Sturgis like a repeat of her mother's, though in this one she may have felt she could play a constructive part in a way she could not with her mother.

For Fuller it seems that Cary, on some level, even if only subconsciously, replaced, as earlier noted, the sister she had lost when Julia Adelaide had died. That she was so much older than Sturgis enabled her also to enjoy playing the part of father-tutor in relating to Cary.[5]

A mutual dependency developed between these two intelligent, talented women, neither of whom was noted for her looks and hence was not the ideal kind of woman a conventional nineteenth-century man would romanticize, as even Emerson did, for instance, the beautiful Anna Barker. One scholar has observed that their letters display at times "a fervor tinged with erotic overtones and, at other times, a coolness brought on by wounded pride or fancied rejection": "Their spats . . . resembled lovers' quarrels."[6]

Viewed in the context of the nineteenth-century cult of friendship, where lavish expressions of love between women was the norm, there is nothing unusual about Sturgis's hyperbolic talk in her letters to Fuller of God and Jesus, of lessons "learnt . . . from rocks, & waves, & bare hills," and of her desire, "oh!" to have "a child to love." In Fuller's New England culture, an intimate friendship with an older girl was considered almost necessary to prepare a girl to move from maidenhood to marriage. No matter how intimate—from today's perspective seeming sometimes homoerotic—the relationship became, it was usually perceived by all as spiritual. For in the minds of most women living in a pre-Freudian world, this emotional and physical closeness never carried with it any hint of the "demon of sex." Christian women saw themselves as asexual human beings, as did Cary, whom Emerson praises in letters as "Angel," "sister," pious "child," "my saint," even as he also refers to her in an October 1840 letter as "a Sappho," by which he presumably meant a poet. One older woman said in a letter regarding her lifelong love for her deceased female friend: "Love is spiritual, only passion is sexual." Only passion—not love—was taboo, a view accepted by the free-spirited yet religiously pious Cary.[7]

But Fuller did not fit comfortably within the limits of this female sphere. Try as she did to take care of her mother and fulfill her domestic duties, men like Captain Sturgis remained suspicious of her. Worse, she was considered "masculine" even by the men who admired her within her narrow New England culture wherein women were supposed to be, indeed, not passionate but passive and accept their "place" within the home. Hence, while Sturgis admired Fuller and felt a real affection for her, Fuller's feelings for Cary and other friends were moving into a sphere where familiar Victorian definitions and conventions regarding female behavior fell short.[8]

In a nineteenth-century society with rigid gender-role division—where men were supposed to be active, autonomous, intellectual, and hence masculine, and women passive, family oriented, sentimental, and hence feminine—the aggressively intellectual Fuller was seen by others and hence was forced to see herself as a "masculine woman." Finding she fit neatly into neither of the above categories, she summed up her dilemma thus: "One should be either private or public. I love best to be a woman; but womanhood is at present too straitly-bounded to give me scope." That she wished to be recognized as a being who was both intellectual and womanly meant she was going to have to envision a new way for women to be in the world, one that would allow them to be active and nurturing, intellectual and feminine. But such bold envisioning on Fuller's part would come only after she had struggled in her crisis with her personal demons and learned to control, as Plato advises in the *Phaedrus* and she believed, the unruly steed of her physical passion, the "evil" winged horse of erotic desire.[9]

This would not be an easy thing to do in light of the excited state of her psyche with its unrelieved narcissistic tensions, as she quickly absorbed the highly suggestive and stimulating images from the romantic literature she was reading. It is likely that on that lonely January night in 1839 as Fuller sat in bed and read Plato's *Symposium*, she thought of Sappho, the famous Greek lyricist whom Fuller had compared herself to and whose unrequited love for the ferryman, Phaon, Ovid chronicles in *Heroides*. Though Sappho is said to have been short, dark, and ugly, Plato calls her "fair" in *Phaedrus*, which we know Fuller was also reading that winter weekend. Because she later alludes to it in *Woman in the Nineteenth Century*, we know as well that Fuller knew Ovid's tale about Sappho's impossible quest for love. She could not help but be intrigued by it, prone as she was to pursuing impossible objects. At that very time she was fantasizing about Sam Ward as a lover, and she was also still a little "in love" with Emerson—if to be "in love" is, in the Romantic sense, looking to find in another person a love that is not there.[10]

As she read about Sappho, Fuller surely realized that, like Sappho, she had been given "genius" instead of "beauty" and that she, too, loved nature. In Fuller's letters, as in Sappho's lyrics where horses "graze knee/deep in flowers" and "breezes blow . . . honey sweet," one finds a similar love of the loveliness of nature. Moreover, orphaned at age six, Sappho missed her mother's love and also grieved for her politically active father, "dead before his time." And both women were to teach classes for women, Fuller opening her Conversations in November of that year.[11]

Given their many similarities and the drift of Fuller's thinking in 1839, Fuller may have seen a bit of herself in Sappho, even if she did not entirely approve of her as a person. Though Fuller did not read Greek, she still knew through several sources, including Byron and Plutarch, that Sappho of Lesbos loved not just men but also women. Even Sappho's eighteenth-century translator, Francis Fawkes, concedes in the preface to his "Odes of Sappho," which appeared in an 1810 volume of English verse available to Fuller, that after her husband's death Sappho was unable "to confine" her "passion to one person," or "even to one sex." In his translation of "An Hymn to Venus," Fawkes, however, is careful to attribute Sappho's appeal to Venus for a female beloved to relieve her of her agony to the fact that her passion for "young Phaon" was unrequited.[12]

Channing in the *Memoirs* later observes that Fuller's immersion that year (1839) in romantic literature spanning from ancient to modern times exalted "her passions" and fed her fermenting imagination. He contends that it was in "the world of imagination" that she then "discharged the stormful energy" that tormented her life. Certainly her immersion in such romantic literature colored her response to Sturgis in the letters she wrote her from January to June of that year. Those letters reveal an increasing intensity of feeling such that—given Fuller's fluid sexual identity and continuing disappointments with men, coupled with her ability to envision for women new, more expansive roles in both the private and public spheres than members of polite Victorian society permitted—she might understandably have pressed Cary to share a whole soul kind of communion that was simply beyond Cary's capacity to deal with. In looking back on Fuller's friendships with women, Emerson depicts her at this time as overflowing with emotion. He says in reference to her expressions of feeling for her female friends that they "were not unmingled with passion," and had about them "passages of romantic sacrifice and of ecstatic fusion."[13]

In this period of imaginative exploration and expansion, when Fuller had unwittingly formed in relation to Emerson what today we might see as a narcissistic transference, it makes sense that the mystical-minded Fuller would seek some sort of "ecstatic fusion" with a beloved female friend. Her attachment to Emerson had stirred her deep need for love and recognition, what she felt she had been deprived of by her parents. The danger here for Cary, as well as for Margaret, is that the latter might sexualize the feelings accompanying the surfacing of these powerful archaic needs. Indeed, echoing Plato on the joy of erotic love in *Phaedrus*, Fuller said of the flood of emotion flowing through her at the time that it made her "feel so beautiful just now in my soul."[14]

In January 1839, when Fuller was immersed in Socrates' dialogues, so many of her thoughts were focused on the nature of love that it is hard to imagine that she was *not* feeling erotically drawn—not only to Ward and Emerson but to Sturgis and other friends as well. In her 10 January letter to Sturgis Fuller says she was "pained" by Cary's "want of affection" for her when the two were together recently in Boston but thinks there is no "danger" that Cary will cease "to love" her. On 27 January she tells her young friend that feasting on Greek intellectual life is like banqueting with "the Gods." For "Socrates does not soar, he does not look up, he sees all around him, the light wells out from him, every object round assumes its proper hue." "He is a man, not an angel," she writes. Regarding Emerson as idealist, she adds: "For my part I should be ashamed to be an angel before I have been truly [a] man."[15]

In this long 27 January letter, Fuller tells Cary how "these Greeks no more merged the human in the divine, than the divine in the human, the wise charioteer managed both his steeds." As for herself, she attests, "I love the stern Titanic part . . . the Drachenfels of life—I love its roaring sea that dashes against the crag." She wonders who "can know these" and "the horror" and "majesty of earth," yet be satisfied with "the blue sky alone." "Not I," she notes, "for one."[16]

Fuller goes on to complain to Sturgis that, while Sturgis in etchings she had sent Fuller captures a sense of the "sacred" in her feminine figures, still, "the fleshly undulations" that might make them human "are wanting." Though in February Fuller suggests to Cary that "it is best to receive me principally through the intellect," she nevertheless commands her to "love me as much as you can."[17] Shortly after writing this Fuller had moved to Jamaica Plain where, as we have seen, she lost herself not only in nature but also in exotic fantasies connecting her with Emerson and other friends.

It was thus in mid-June 1839, in the throes of this fertile period of aroused erotic energies and aggressive romantic fantasizing, that Fuller had vacationed with Sturgis at Nahant. Though Fuller said in a late June letter to Jane Tuckerman that, despite a headache, she had enjoyed her three days at the beach, what happened between her and Sturgis there had greatly upset her. And it tested to the outer limits Cary's tolerance for her "strange" friend.[18]

In her important June 1839 letter to Tuckerman, Fuller conveys a sense of the tension between Fuller, then twenty-nine, and Sturgis, nineteen, while at Nahant. The first night it had stormed. At six the next morning Fuller had taken a walk by herself on the beach before breakfast in bright clear air and then gone for another one afterward; these walks exhilarated her yet sent her home with a "frenzied headache." After a midday dinner she had walked yet again, this time, she tells Jane, with Cary, who, on some high rocks, "perched close to the fissure, far above me, and in a pale green dress she looked like the nymph of the place. I lay down on a rock low in the water, where I could hear the twin harmonies of the sucking of the water into the spout and the washing of the surge on the foot of the rock." Fuller says she "never passed a more delightful afternoon."[19]

Fuller's letter depicts their activities of the next two days in language that conveys a disarming sense of psychic undertow: of the lure of nature's "sensuous radiance," of her deceptive promise that the way to paradise lay through immersion in the feminine wet element, the womblike water of the ocean. Fuller tells how in the afternoon "I was out alone and had an admirable place, a cleft between two vast towers of rock with turret-shaped tops." There, on a ledge at their foot, "I could lie and let the waves wash up round me, and look up at the proud turrets." "This evening," she continues, "was very fine; all the sky covered with crowding clouds, profound but not sullen of mood, the moon wading, the stars peeping, the wind sighing very softly." About Cary she writes: "We lay on the high rocks and listened to the plashing of the waves." Fuller ends her lyrical letter, presumably about her interaction with Sturgis, telling Tuckerman, "I wish you could come to me now." Her appeal to Jane to "come to me now" seems even more urgent in light of the fact that, after that idyllic moment at Nahant, there had been a terrible falling out between Fuller and Sturgis.[20]

✧ ✧ ✧

It seems that Sturgis at the beach had felt put-upon by Fuller's emotional intensity, an apparent appeal for love that, according to Fuller herself, had not been fully purged of the element of Eros. To complicate matters, it seems that Cary had recoiled, manifesting passive repulsion toward what went on between them. Emerson, who could identify with Cary's situation, expresses sympathy for Sturgis in the *Memoirs* when he notes about the outcome of this traumatic encounter: "There were, also, the ebbs and recoils from the other party [Cary],—the mortal unequal to converse with an immortal," and what seemed "ingratitude" on Cary's part was "more truly," he says, "incapacity, the collapse of overstrained affections and powers."[21]

Fuller, however, did not at first see it that way. Indeed, on 25 June, and again three days later, an upset Fuller wrote Sturgis that she is not sure that "we can continue *intimate*." On 11 July, at the same time that she was writing Sam Ward about the "bitterness of checked affections, the sickness of hope deferred"—alluding presumably to Sam's *and* Cary's rejection of her expansive love—a wounded Fuller declared to Sturgis: "If Fate has in store for my Caroline a friend . . . of more equal age and fortunes . . . more beautiful and pure, I should accept." Fuller's distraught emotional state is apparent in her uncharacteristically broken and cryptic prose. "Your letters," she wrote Cary, "move m [hole in text] unspeakably and, if I wrote wha[t] I feel from one, my words would flow as balmy soft as tears. But I feel it is best to drop the heart for the present. I might—no matter what now. Let it be so.—"[22]

That Fuller knew the nature of the "fever" that was causing her "agitation" and coloring her love for Emerson, Ward, and Sturgis, we know from a letter she wrote Tuckerman in August 1839. In it she mentions "these diseases of the mind" that she knows her "will cannot conquer." On one level Fuller is referring to the pain of a migraine. On another level, however, her sense that a "disease"—like that Emerson had described in "Demonology"—has corrupted her mind, that with the "boding sky" has come a "gloom, black as Hades," suggests she is suffering from guilt and depression. That she describes her state of mind in terms once used by her Puritan ancestors—as being enthralled by a "demon," afflicted with a moral "sickness" that has infected her "immortal soul"—reveals her spiritual and sexual confusion.[23]

In this August 1839 letter, Fuller entreats Tuckerman to believe in "the immutable essence that cannot be tarnished; . . . to live as far as possible by its light," despite Fuller's own awareness that the "mode of our existence is not in our own power." She recommends to Tuckerman a lifestyle that prevents a slide into obeisance to the dark powers that too often have "mastery" over Fuller's own "soul." She implores Jane not to look for guidance from a woman like herself who struggles with unruly passions but to go to Concord and stay with Elizabeth Hoar, idealized in her letter as "the spirit of Love, as well as of Intellect."[24]

For all her agony, Fuller's experiences and explorations were helping her to see that women, like men, should not be condemned for their "strong passions." And this new awareness would lend life and energy to the writing of her feminist tract, *Woman in the Nineteenth Century*. It is hence no coincidence that in her July 1839 letter to Sam Ward in which she mentions "the sickness of hope deferred," she quotes lines from Byron's "Stanzas to Augusta," the half-sister Byron incestuously loved, noting that, like Byron, she wants a friend who will not forsake her.[25]

Fuller's reference in this letter to "the sickness" that accompanies "checked affections" is to the damaging effect on both her mind and body of not just Sam's but also Cary's unwillingness or inability to reciprocate the intensity of her love. And what better writer to allude to here in her letter to Ward than Byron, whose bisexual escapades in Greece and Turkey had caused such scandalous rumors to fly throughout England that he was forced to flee his homeland.[26]

In 1830 Thomas Moore, in publishing extracts from Byron's letters and journals, deleted passages revealing Byron's homoeroticism. Despite these starred deletions, Fuller, who was twenty when she read Moore's edition, understood the erotic nature of Byron's schoolboy yearnings, though she no doubt thought they were all, in fact, "violent, though *pure*," assertions of "love and passion." In an 1821 journal entry that Fuller read, Byron, looking back, confesses that though he knows his "thoughts" are "strange," still, his teenage passion for a Trinity College choirboy named Edleston and another Trinity boy represented "the most romantic" period of his life. In a letter to a friend in July 1807—written when he was nineteen—he noted how, with "*tears*" in his eyes, he intended "to devote the hours of the *Sabbath* to friendship," since he must soon part with Edleston.[27]

It is a strange and curious coincidence that Fuller in her 1825 letter to Susan Prescott wrote that she has chosen to "devote . . . the hours" of the Sabbath to friendship, preferring to stay home to write her teacher than to attend church with her father. Yet it is certainly not a coincidence that she and Byron thought along similar lines and that both spread their erotic energies out over many people, male and female. Though Fuller would not have known this, Byron, like Fuller, as a child had been subjected to an intense late-night experience that had, so to speak, "unnaturally stimulated" him. His nurse May Gray, a strict Presbyterian by day, at night for three years had molested him, starting when he was nine.[28]

When Fuller, age nineteen, had first felt a desire to "comprehend Byron once for all," it had been in March 1830 after having spent a day sitting primly in the parlor of the Fuller's Dana Hill mansion and playing auditor to an important friend of her father, all the while hemming a ruffle. Like the little girl who on a Sunday had read *Romeo and Juliet* in defiance of her father's decree that she ought not read Shakespeare on the Sabbath, Margaret, who had sat silently for three hours in compliance with her father's wish that her "presence" might give "a finish to the scene," had "absconded at last to read in solitude" the writings of the rebellious Lord Byron—her heart beating hard as she did, she exclaimed, "in luxury of realized bliss!"[29]

After her father's death, however, Fuller had found the adventuresome Byron too bold even for her. In her 1836 review, "Modern British Poets," she had moralized about this Byronic "sickliness of feeling," this "moral malaria," whose influence is "impalpable till we feel its results within ourselves." When she was twenty and "intent on this life," Fuller had been eager to experience all the pleasure and pain it had to offer. But in 1836, still oppressed by her sense of duty toward the fatherless Fuller family and under the moral influence of Emerson, Fuller saw Byron's "dissonance, cynicism, irritability, and . . . uncharitableness" as the "natural fruits" of his sexual self-indulgence. Yet just three years later, after having faced the "results" in herself of her own demonic "diseases of the mind," one part of herself felt deep empathy with Byron, this man who had, she said, "passed through this process" of the soul "struggling with its horrors."[30]

22 ∽ "The Daemon Works His Will"

In her crisis years 1839–41, Fuller struggled with her own demonic desires, even as she was aware that authentic creative activity often involves such soul-endangering confrontations. Unlike Emerson, who decried the demonic as a force "without virtue" and equated it with "Animal Magnetism" and "Disease," Fuller was fascinated by the idea of demonic forces, of an instinctive power "within" us that is deeper than reason can fathom. After all, without being told its location, the blind somnambulist in Providence, through hypnosis, had put her hand on Fuller's head where the pain originated. Though the woman failed to relieve her headaches, Fuller remained intrigued with the thinking of the phrenologists and mesmerists. The latter posited the existence of an invisible energy, or fluid, which they called animal magnetism and believed to be the ethereal medium through which sensations of every kind—light, heat, magnetism, electricity—pass from one physical object to another.[1]

Like the mesmerists, Fuller believed that if this cosmic essence is evenly distributed throughout a person's body, then he or she will have good health and live in harmonious relation to the earth and other people. She also thought that when this electrical essence was out of balance, one or more of the body's organs would be deprived of sufficient energy and hence begin to falter, as her head began to ache when she was under stress. Since out-of-balance energy was considered by believers in animal magnetism to be the cause of illness, the secret to a healthy life was to restore equilibrium to the body's supply of this invisible magnetic fluid. At least in a metaphoric way, Fuller accepted the mesmerists' views; for it seemed to her that when her body was most fluid and electrically alive, as it was during her Boston Conversations, then it was indeed like a magnet that attracted people to it. To Clarke she boasted of her "magnetic power over young women."[2]

In positing the magnetic effect that one personality can have on another, Fuller, like the mesmerists, was quite by accident uncovering a depth to human experience that would soon lead Freud to his theory of the unconscious and instinctual drives (aggression and libido), as well as to his realization of the power in the transference situation of the therapist over his patient. Fuller understood the power of this uncanny kind of attraction, for she had felt it in relation to Emerson, whom she idealized as a father confessor and healer. It intrigued her to see the interaction between the mesmerized subject and his or her healer, particularly how the healer slowly gained a kind of hypnotic control over the will or soul of his or her subject. In her wish to probe this mysterious region of human behavior, Fuller was unlike Emerson, who called talk of a universal fluid uniting all people "gibbering nonsense" and instructed Fuller to channel her "subterranean" energies and "animal" fluids upward into spiritual vision. Emerson advised this, perhaps suspecting that for Fuller, as for some of the European Romantics she had read, the thrill of her body becoming suddenly fluid had more to do with sexual excitement than it did with spiritual awakening.[3]

Fuller's frequent use of the liquid metaphor, as well as her fascination with "the darkly irrational side of human consciousness," is like that of the more passionate Romantics she admired, who refused to turn from the lure of the "subterraneous" in nature but insisted, instead, on facing its seductions. In exploring this enchanted ground, Fuller hoped to find a way to gain control of her often unmanageable instincts, to reconcile her downward drive toward physical pleasure with her enormous mental need for spiritual uplift. For Fuller this was a dangerous venture. Her own demons, she believed, were ambiguous: they were "*instinctive*" energies that partook equally of creative and destructive impulses. According to Emerson she defined "the *daimonische*"—that deep force that Socrates thought "divine" and Goethe aligned with the "instinctive"—as "Energy for energy's sake." She recognized this energy as the essence of artistic inspiration, even as she knew, as did Sappho and Ariosto, that its presence indicates "danger."[4]

In the summer of 1839, Fuller had taken literally Emerson's advice and "embosomed" herself "in nature"—in the splash of the waves at Nahant, in the smell of perfumed roses in her mother's garden, and in the brush of the breeze as it rustled leaves in Bussey's wood, her favorite retreat. And as nature embraced her it felt to her as if there really did flow in and through all nature an electrical current, a "power," she wrote in her journal, that "moves only to seize its prey." In nature this "unconscious," "daemoniac" agent is present, says Fuller, "in all volcanic work-ings, . . . in whispers of the wind, . . . in deceitful invitations of the water, . . . and in the shapes of all those beings who go about seeking what they may devour." It is in the eye of "beings who lurk, glide, fascinate, mysteriously control." "For it is occult," she says, "by nature": "We speak of a mystery, a dread; we shudder, but we approach still nearer, and a part of our nature listens, sometimes answers to this influence."[5]

In contrast to Emerson, who strove to put nature underfoot and railed against any mesmerist's "attempt to put me asleep by the concentration of his will without my leave," Fuller gained pleasure in attaining an egoless state of mind in which it seemed she communed with the Daemon in nature, whose magnetic power over her she acknowledges. Whereas Emerson stiffly resisted the urge to succumb to the pleasures nature proffers, Fuller felt the pull of pleasure to be irresistible. Drawn by nature's lure, Fuller that summer self-consciously acknowledged that she was "in danger" of giving herself "up to experiences . . . in the rich present." She knew that part of her was listening to the siren song of nature. She did not regret this experi-ence, nor deny that within her was an answering "*daemon*," a "gnome-like" power that was "busy" confusing and limiting her life. "With me," she will confess in 1843, "for weeks and months, the daemon works his will."[6]

As a power that dwells deep in the "unconscious," this "daemon," Fuller believes, reveals its meaning in dreams. Around the time she was penning her long August 1839 letter to Tuckerman, Fuller recorded a dream, part of which she interpreted. In it an Egyptian attempts to lure a giant, crimson-winged butterfly to alight on her "skinny finger." Instead, it "settled on the *left* side" of Fuller's forehead and "plunged his feet, bristling with feelers, deeper and deeper into my forehead till my pain rose to agony." Fuller here projects the pain of a migraine into images familiar to her from literature. The "skinny finger" may have come from *Oberon*, the fairy tale she had excitedly read as a child. In one of the old squire's nightmares, a long "skinny finger" had appeared that had sent a chill down his back when it touched him. From literature Fuller also knew that the butterfly symbolizes the soul's per-fection, Psyche, whose drive to know casts light on sleeping Love, causing him to wake and leave her. But Fuller's butterfly is a male, one that "plunged *his* feet, bris-tling with feelers," deep into her forehead.[7]

Although Fuller did not interpret this segment of her dream, a reader might imagine that for her it had a double meaning. She may have seen herself as the butterfly, as Psyche, whose malelike intellect had prevented Sam Ward from lov-ing her. But she may also have equated the pain of the butterfly's feelers digging into her brain with her father and her chronic headaches. In her autobiographi-cal romance, which she will write in 1840, she accuses her father of irritating her nerves by keeping her up "several hours too late" to recite. The result of his ruthless tutoring, says Fuller, was a habitual tendency throughout her life to bring "to every thought and every feeling" an "undue force" of energy that "re-acted on the brain" and caused "continual headache, weakness and nervous affections, of all kinds."[8]

Though the butterfly's intrusion in her brain (apt emblem of her father's power over her mind) awakened her momentarily, Fuller fell again into a fitful sleep. She then dreamed she was ill and in a room of a hotel with a bed upon which was a pink bedspread. It was like one, she says, in a bedroom where she had suffered "many weeks of nervous headache." In her dream she wandered through strange rooms. Exhausted, says Fuller, she settled in an entryway. "I thought I must die in this forlorn condition." But "a sweet female form approached" and, sitting at her side, held Fuller's head to her breast as she "wept." "Wrapt in a long robe" and lying in a doorway, Fuller in dream was as if reborn to a motherly woman who comforted her.[9]

In her journal Fuller wrote what this dream meant to her: "As I have masculine traits, I am naturally often relieved by the women in my imaginary distresses." She added that the dream seemed "very illustrative of the influence of the body on the mind when will and understanding are not on the alert to check it. Let those who undervalue the moral powers of will analyze their dreams and see what they become without it."[10] Without it, pain in Fuller's dream is seen as male intrusion, love as a nurturing female embrace.

Thus Fuller was relieved when she received a letter in early October from Cary, with whom in June she had had that terrible falling-out at Nahant. Still smarting from the wound and perhaps fearful that Cary had misinterpreted her "mental raptures" and felt she was "exacting too much" from Cary, Fuller replied on 7 October 1839. In her letter she defensively tells Cary how Anna's recent visit to her Jamaica Plain home had made it impossible for her to consider her "relation" with Cary, "so filled was I so intoxicated, so uplifted by that eldest and divinest love." Fuller reveals how deeply Cary had hurt her when she provocatively insists in her letter on the electric effect of Anna on her. The minute Anna left, says Fuller in the overwrought prose of nineteenth-century female friendship, she was "obliged" to take to her bed. For the "nights of talk and days of agitation, the tides of feeling which have been poured upon and from my soul" have so taxed "my . . . body [and] mind" that, "Even yet I cannot think of you, my Caroline."[11]

She tells Cary—whom she now formally calls "Caroline"—that she had once "loved" her "with truth and nobleness" and "counted to love" her "much more." However, that "hope" had "turned sickly" and she had felt that it (her hope) could never "recover from its wound." Yet "blessed the Great Spirit," she continues, that "only for a moment did I cease to love you. . . . I would have given all but self-respect to save you. I said, Worldwise, at least I can always be her friend in the spirit realm I will wait for her."[12]

Linked with Emerson by her skewed view of him as a divine protector, Fuller at this time indeed *was* vulnerable; her emotional life *was* open. As Emerson had hinted in his February 1839 talk, "Demonology," it was, indeed, as if she had spread her "self" out over others. Regarding, for instance, the near end of her friendship with Cary, Fuller narcissistically said to Cary, "I wept at the loss you were to sustain *in me*." Thus we can see how, once the lid was off, as in the myth of Pandora's box, Fuller's psyche had released its enormous need for love and recognition. So powerful and primitive was this narcissistic need that it probably did feel to Fuller as if "eros"—seen as erotic energy and not as a Greek god—was drawing her in search of an object, someone who could love her and relieve her of her terrible need. For a while the search had led her to Cary, then to Sam Ward, whom she had mistakenly believed might marry her, yet who had rejected her shortly before Anna came to visit her in Jamaica Plain. Thus Fuller's frustration in relation to these friends now was depriving her of the sanctuary of imaginary love. Such a love was, in the absence of any sustained reciprocal tenderness from another person, really nothing but an extension of her ego, what Shelley called a "soul out of my soul." Minus this shield of illusory love, the unstable ego—especially an unstable ego under great stress—can itself become "what the id wanted sexually."[13]

In turning to the erotic love of the feminine figure, Fuller, then, had indeed taken on the identity of her father, but she was also unconsciously searching for a way to love her female self. George Sand, whom she was reading that autumn, gives insight into this process in *Lélia*. Pulchérie, gazing at herself in a mirror, wants "to embrace that reflection in the glass," an image which "inspired me," she says, "with a senseless love." But then she finds Lélia and learns to love both her sister and herself.[14]

Repeatedly in her letters to Emerson and Sturgis, with whom, in the autumn and winter of 1839–40 she was discussing Sand's romances, Fuller pleaded for confirmation of her existence. This "wish," in her words, "to be seen as I am," and to "lose all rather than soften away anything," is most evident in a December 1840 letter she wrote Emerson, who had refused to respond to what seemed to him, in Fuller, a not "quite healthy" craving. Surely, says Fuller, some day, "there will be no more negations. . . . Then our actions will not be hieroglyphics any more but perfect symbols. Then parting and meeting will be equally beautiful, for both will be in faith. Then there will be . . . perfect communion with full-eyed love." This wish for a look of "full-eyed" love is on one level a primitive wish to see the gleam in the mother's eye that reflects to her baby, before language, her unconditional love and approval. It is also a wish to find in a relationship with another human being a love that transcends both language and troubling bodily pulsations. Unlike the fully physical Sand, the Puritan-minded Fuller hoped to find on *earth* an angel-like love that would free her from what now seemed to her to be the sinful hunger of her flesh for pleasure.[15]

THE SEDUCTIVE LURE OF NATURE

23 ∞ Redeeming Her Friendships from "Eros"

In 1839, the year Fuller experienced the worst of her psychosexual-spiritual crisis, her lifelong friend James Clarke married Anna Huidekoper of Meadville, Pennsylvania. Then, Sam Ward and Anna Barker early in 1840 announced their intention to marry. This was just a few months after Fuller had imagined that Sam actually loved *her* enough to want to marry her. Once it had become clear he did not, she had written him in September 1839 despairing that he loves her "no more."[1]

In the *Memoirs*, William Channing tells about visiting Fuller at her house in Jamaica Plain on his return from the west in the summer of 1840. Channing was standing in the parlor when Fuller entered carrying a large vase full of flowers she had been gathering from the garden. After lunch, the two went for a walk through Bussey's wood. According to Channing, Fuller talked that day about the flowers, about the engravings hanging in her parlor (of Beatrice and Dante, the Madonna del Pesce, and Raphael), about gems, medallions, and seals, about Greece and the Greeks, whose mythology she had been reviewing for her Conversations in Boston. Yet streaming through all was the message Fuller seemed eager to share with him: news "of the betrothal of two of her best-loved friends," Sam and Anna.[2]

Hoping to understand why no man in New England had sought her hand in marriage, Channing, who had been married since 1836, listened intently to this woman not yet "recognized" for "the rare beauty of her spirit." It occurred to him that Fuller, this relentless seeker after truth, was suited by intellect and strength of character to mingle with the brightest minds in Europe but had been forced by circumstances to pass her "early womanhood" amid the "decent, yet drudging, descendents of the prim Puritans." To Channing it seemed that in Protestant New England there were no men capable of appreciating Fuller's "peculiar power." Seeing her loneliness, Channing attributed her "Egoism," "unchartered impulses," her "morbid subjectivity" and mysticism in the years 1839–40, to her obsessive reading of "the romantic literature of ancient and modern times," as well as to "the morbid influence of affections pent up to prey upon themselves." The resulting tension triggered headaches and other ailments, "the sickness," in her words, "of hope deferred."[3]

Despite frustrated love, Fuller, as we know, did not at this time give in to depression. Rather, she channeled her potent emotions into teaching innovative classes for women in Boston. Perhaps, as noted, she found a model in the school for women run by Sappho, where the famous Greek lyricist placed herself at the center of a circle of admiring women. Though Fuller would later distance herself from Sappho ("as a woman," she would say, "she is repulsive"), Fuller family friend and biographer, Thomas Wentworth Higginson, saw a parallel between Sappho's classes and Fuller's. In an 1891 biographical sketch of Sappho, Higginson, in fact, attempted to redeem the reputation of Sappho as a "corrupt woman" by comparing her school at Lesbos (seen by his contemporaries as "a nursery of sins") to Fuller's Conversation classes, noting approvingly how, in the latter, expressions of love were spiritual in nature.[4]

Certainly the women who attended her classes had strong feelings for Fuller. At her class's second session, which met on 13 November, the women discussed the high position of beauty (parent of love) among Plato's forms. About the success of the class, Fuller wrote Emerson regretting that she could not make the "ladies . . . ascend to principles," for they "kept clinging to details."[5]

Fuller wanted the women in her classes to reach through their socially constructed outer shells to the vital "I" she believed was "within" them. She wanted them to identify with the gods and goddesses that had vitalized Greek life before the men of their own Judeo-Christian culture embodied God as an all-powerful patriarch that limited women's potential. She wanted the women to be like the Bacchantes, those otherwise-respectable matrons who roamed the mountains and shared in the passion of the Greek god Bacchus through frenzied chanting and dancing. In letters she wrote in late 1839 and early 1840, Fuller compares Apollo as "Genius" with Bacchus as "Geniality," rhapsodizing on the passionate self-surrender experienced by women possessed by Bacchus. Bacchus's "whole life," she told her class, "was triumph." "Born from fire; a divine frenzy; the answer of the earth to the sun,—of the warmth of joy to the light of genius," Bacchus, she said, "is beautiful, also; not severe in youthful beauty, like Apollo; but exuberant,—and liable to excess," as she knew she was too.[6]

Fuller hoped to ignite in these proper Boston women the same Bacchante passion she now felt flowing in her. In late November she assured a friend that "there is more Greek than Bostonian spoken at the meetings, and we may have pure honey of Hymettus to give you yet." All the attendees seemed as "receptive" as she wished.[7]

These women thirstily drank of the draughts Fuller felt she was drawing from some fluid higher power. She then poured what she believed to be her animal energy into the women sitting near her—especially into Anna, whose perfect beauty at this time especially delighted her. As Plato depicts love's progress in *Phaedrus,* which Fuller had read in January 1839 and would reread in December, the mere sight of such a divine love had the power to free in her a flow of spiritual feeling such that she felt that she gained a brief "respite" from her "sufferings."[8]

In the company of these educated women, Fuller became the confident woman she wished she could be all the time. In a jubilant January 1840 letter to Sarah Helen Whitman about her class, she affirmed: "You joke about my Gods and Goddesses but really my class in Boston is very pleasant. There I have real society . . . We have time, patience, mutual reverence and fearlessness eno' to get at one another's thoughts."[9]

The class's charged exchanges took tremendous energy to conduct even as they also tapped her deepest instinctual need for love. Fuller's awareness at this time of the "irregular pulses" of the human heart and her need to suppress them are both present in a letter she wrote Sturgis on Christmas Eve 1839. In it she included a poem by Ellery Channing, "The Bible Is a Book Worthy to Read," in which he warns that one should not be "afraid to utter what thou art / Tis no disgrace to keep an open heart." "Better live unknown," he advises, than "From thyself to flee: . . . Better be forgotten / Than lose equipoise!"[10]

Though Fuller did not much like the poem, she agreed with its premise that it is best to be true to the person one feels one is than to "lose equipoise," that harmonious state of physical being wherein one's supply of animal energy is in balance throughout one's body. Confessing she is feeling "discomposed," Fuller then hints at "thoughts" that she, having devoured that day "nearly a volume of Plato," is "dreading." Feeling guilty over the drift of her thinking, two days later she wrote the fatherly Emerson and confessed to him as if to a "holy" man: "If you could look into my mind just now, you would send far from you those who love and hate." She says she is "on the Drachenfels"—that is, letting herself be devoured by unmanageable instincts—"and cannot get off; it is one of my naughtiest moods."[11]

Though Sturgis will continue to be baffled by her friend's strange thoughts and feelings, Fuller tells Cary in an early 1840 letter that she has faith that, just as "W.[aldo] also at times resists or leaves me, . . . he always returns, and so I think will you." She tries to assure Cary that she (Fuller) can now control her "mental raptures." She reminds Cary in another letter she wrote at about the same time that "thought" alone cannot "save" Cary "from the grand mistake of sometime fancying" she loves "a mortal." "I write hastily," adds Fuller, not knowing "what daemon hurries my pen."[12]

In these two cryptic letters written early in 1840, Fuller alludes again to Sturgis's attitude of "passive repulsion" toward her at Nahant where it appears that Cary was put off by the sheer intensity of Fuller's feelings. It seems that Fuller's passionate expression to Cary of a desire for a full soul communion exceeded Cary's estimate of what was permissible between female friends in nineteenth-century New England. Emerson later politely said of Fuller's exaggerated expressions of affection for her female friends that he had "heard with his ear what he could not trust his pen to report." Fuller's letters of 1840 record an awareness of her barely manageable instinctual urgings, unruly emotions she spread out over her friends, male *and* female. They show her willful struggle as a child of Puritans and Plato to redeem her friendships, as she carefully phrased it in these two significant letters to Sturgis, "from the search after Eros."[13]

24 ✑ Mystic Cleansing

In a letter about a ten-day visit Anna paid her in August 1840, Margaret tells Cary that the two had been "even happier together" than they were in 1839—before she knew of Sam's engagement to Anna. In another letter three weeks later to Cary, she exclaims: "Rivers of life flow, seas surge between me and you I cannot look back, nor remember how I passed them."[1]

In an 1842 reflection on whether "a woman may be in love with a woman, and a man with a man," Fuller focuses not on Cary but on her less-complicated relationship with Anna. Echoing Socrates' argument in the *Symposium* "that the desiring desires what it lacks," Fuller affirms that the law of such love "is the desire of the spirit to realize a whole." "How natural," she says, "is the love . . . of Me de Stael for de Recamier, mine for Anna Barker." Such love "is regulated by the same law as that of love between persons of different sexes, only it is purely intellectual and spiritual, unprofaned by any mixture of lower instincts." About Anna she adds: "I loved Anna for a time I think with as much passion as I was then strong enough to feel." This love "for me," she explains, "was the carbuncle (emblematic gem) which cast light into many of the darkest caverns of human nature."[2]

In an October 1840 letter to Sturgis, Fuller elaborates on the value of the carbuncle she associates with the very feminine Anna, saying that she (Fuller) has gone to the "heart of the untrodden mountain where the carbuncle has lit the way to veins of . . . diamond." In using an image of a carbuncle to represent a light by which she explores the "untrodden" depths of nature's caverns and mountains, Fuller affirms her ability to use feminine instincts and intuitions to burrow to the unexplored unconscious core of power and break through the masculine barriers that restrict her activity as a woman in the social and physical world.[3]

In light of Fuller's new knowledge of her psychosexual complexity and power, her search to find a religion into which she could channel her strong erotic energies makes sense. It was during this period of psychological struggle, after her friends had hurt her and when she was trying to define herself sexually and spiritually, that William Henry Channing had visited her in Jamaica Plain. On that summer 1840 day she had shown an "unflagging spiritual energy," which had caused a throbbing headache. Fuller tried, says Channing, to justify her pain, contending that "we are born to be mutilated; and the blood must flow till in every vein its place is supplied by the Divine ichor." Identifying with Persephone—the daughter of Demeter and Zeus who was abducted by Hades, her uncle, and forced to live half each year in the underworld—she said: "It is only when Persephone returns from lower earth that she weds Dyonysos [sic], and passes from central sadness into glowing joy."[4]

Fuller's talk at this time of her need to replace her human blood with "the Divine ichor," as well as her mention of Dionysus, shows her continuing interest in the Orphic cults. Fuller, we recall, was drawn to these ancient mystery cults (as to the cult of Isis) because women were actively involved in the worship, and also because they were forerunners of the Christian idea of spiritual rebirth. In the mythical accounts of this god of the vine and the wet element, Dionysus was known as the twice-born god because Zeus had plucked him from the womb of his dying mortal mother and sewn him into his thigh; Dionysus emerged from Zeus's thigh at term and perfectly formed. The women who worshipped this god, we recall, were sometimes called Bacchantes or Maenads (mad women), since while worshipping him they experienced fits of mystical ecstasy during which they felt possessed by Bacchus (Dionysus). Women similarly seemed to go insane when they worshipped Orpheus, who myth says was torn to shreds by the Maenads. Because his head kept singing after his death, Orpheus became the center for this mystery cult that helped women endure the cold of winter and promised them life after death. Whether a person's soul in the hereafter was rewarded with bliss or suffered torment Orphics thought depended on the purity of a person's life on earth.[5]

Fuller knew about the Orphics from her omnivorous reading, as well as from Alcott's "Orphic Sayings," which she included in the July 1840 issue of the *Dial*. Unlike *Dial* readers, Fuller appreciated Orphic doctrine, which preached the fallen nature of humanity and the necessity of purity as the way to revelation, spiritual rebirth, and ecstatic union with God. In light of her enthusiasm for Orphic doctrine, her cryptic pronouncement to Cary in her 8 September 1840 letter—one that fuses classical and biblical images—becomes understandable: "There can be no 'stern holding back' but all the pure in heart must be seeing God." So, too, does her strange exclamation, as if in a mystic trance, in a letter she wrote Cary two weeks later: "All has been revealed, all foreshown. . . . Experiment has given place to certainty, pride to obedience, thought to love, and truth is lost in beauty 'I am no more below'—."[6]

In accord with Orphic doctrine, Fuller believed that part of man is Titanic, low and mortal; another part is divine. In her 10 January 1839 letter to Cary, she had warned of the dangers of the flesh, noting that the Titans "never entered Olympus." As earth's rulers before Zeus came to Olympus, the Titans killed and ate the boy, Zagreus, whom Zeus had fathered incestuously with his daughter, Persephone, goddess of the House of Hades and a figure, as we have seen, with whom Fuller identified. After eating the boy, the Titans took his preserved heart to Zeus, who retaliated by chaining them under a volcano. Humans, says the myth, sprang from the Titans' ashes. However, because they had eaten the child-god Zagreus, mortal men, who are partly evil, also have in them a spark of divinity. According to myth, if a person wishes to cleanse his or her soul of crude matter and evil, he or she must burn it out by passing into a trancelike state that others see as madness. In light of this, we can understand Fuller's comment in her journal at this time that there was "much rude matter" in her "that needed to be spiritualized," and when in letters she talks of her "raptures" and exclaims, as she does on 22 October 1840 to Cary, "Oh . . . My Caroline, I am not yet purified. Let the lonely Vestal [virgin] watch the fire till it draws her to itself and consumes the mortal part."[7]

In these "mystical" visions she also identified, as Fuller biographers note, with the Virgin Mary and "vestal virgins watching over holy fires," just as she was interested in the virgin goddesses Isis and Diana, who are associated with the moon and female creativity. Perhaps her devotion to Isis began when, as a child, she read in Ovid's *Metamorphoses* the story of Iphis, a character with whom she would have identified.[8]

In Ovid's account, Iphis's father, Ligdus, wants his first child by his wife, Telethusa, to be a boy and orders her to kill it if it is female. Isis in a vision appears to Telethusa and tells her to rear her child, whatever its sex. Telethusa thus pretends her baby girl is a boy. Lidgus, ignorant of the deceit, names the baby Iphis, a gender-neutral name, and raises Iphis as a boy. This reverse-gender upbringing makes Iphis feel as if she were a boy, though she knows she is a girl. Soon she falls "madly in love with another girl." "Oh, what will be the end of me," cries out Iphis, "whom a love possesses that no one ever heard of, a strange and monstrous love?" The distressed mother prays to Isis, whereupon Isis's altar seems to move, the doors of the temple shake, and from the goddess's moon-shaped horns shoot gleams of light while her sistrum rattles loudly. Isis then bestows on Iphis those attributes that make her, "in fact, . . . now a boy!" According to Ovid, a "natural" union of the two is now possible.[9]

Fuller valued so highly the myth of Isis that, according to Emerson, she chose as her own symbol "the *Sistrum*," emblem of the power of Isis, goddess of the moon, and in the *Memoirs* he cites lines from her poem, "To the Moon": "But if I steadfast gaze upon thy face, / A human secret, like my own, I trace; / For, through the woman's smile looks the male eye." In devoting herself thus to the moon goddess Isis, Fuller seems to have been seeking a way to combine the masculine (intellectual) and feminine (emotional) sides of herself in a way that would let her feel natural, and also give her the power to break through the constraints imposed on her by society. One of those was that she could not be both intellectual and a woman. Yet Fuller "love[d] best," as she herself said in the early 1840s, "to be a woman." Apart from the adoration heaped on her by women, like them she wanted, as a woman, to be loved by a man. Moreover, in accord with both Ovid and the Bible, Fuller felt that for her *as a man* to love a woman with passion was not only unnatural but also a sin. Confused and conflicted, Fuller in the autumn of 1840 thus committed herself to a "nun like dedication." She yearned, she said, "to be virgin," to burn up all the "evil" in her, which to this descendant of Puritans meant to purge her heart of lust. She felt that only when she was free of sin could she attain, as Plato promised, "inward peace." A firm believer at this point in Platonic love, Fuller increasingly came to see any surfacing in her of sexual desire as a defilement of her maiden-

THE SEDUCTIVE LURE OF NATURE

hood. It made her feel stained, as if she had committed a "crime," one that might yet cause her to be cast in what she saw as an "abyss" reserved for the "lowest in humanity," that is, those who seek sex "for the sake of sensual pleasure."[10]

Yet even as she struggled to purge her soul of sin, Fuller continued to feel guilty over her own—what Emerson had angrily labeled—"perverted" yearnings. Her agony in her effort to control her instincts is evident in her 22 October letter to Cary, the one in which she stresses her need for purification. Spilling her emotions onto the page, Fuller croons a last vexed hope that she might yet be saved by a loving and protective Emerson from succumbing to her demonic desires: "Oh child who would'st deem thee mine canst thou read what I cannot write." But no, she wrote, Cary could not, for there is "only one soul . . . that can lead me up to womanhood and baptize me to gentlest May. Is it not ready? I have strength to wait as a smooth bare tree forever, but ask no more my friends for leaves and flowers or a bird haunted bower." Fuller felt as if her erotic yearnings had caused her, like Eve, to be cast out of Eden. In the process thus of writing this anxiety-ridden letter, she veered with one stroke of the pen from talk of the "great sea" in her that "burst against all rocks," that "sobbed and wailed over my endless motion," to self-righteous condemnation of a poor girl whose "sin" of sexual lasciviousness, she tells Cary, had caused her to become sick with consumption and die.[11]

It is in this important October 1840 letter to Cary that Fuller tells about her encounter with the dying girl in the cottage in Groton. Rumor was that the girl had ruined her health by having given in to the "sin" of out-of-wedlock sex. Her "stain" had "placed her on this bed of death." Seeing in the girl's "macerated body" a reflection of the "sickness" of her own "low" self, Fuller recalls to Cary how it seemed to her as if the girl's "room was full of . . . base thoughts." In terms more severe than any she was to use against Byron or Balzac, she recorded her horror at the abyss she sensed to exist in herself. Feeling oppressed by the memory of the girl's dark image, Fuller "comprehended the meaning of," the necessity of, *for herself,* she says, "an ascetic life." She ends with a prayerful song celebrating the coming of winter, rejoicing, she says, "in her bareness, her pure shroud, her judgment-announcing winds": "These will help me to dedicate myself, all these Winter spirits will cradle my childhood with strange and mystic song."[12]

The "mystic song" Fuller sang that autumn made her seem "strange" even to friends, who now labeled her a "sibyl," or a girl with the gift of prophecy who speaks in delirious ravings. Yet Fuller's song was not really that strange. She was like the women of old who sought solace from sorrow and suffering by ritually chanting and dancing, attempting thence to find peace through union with their god. Fuller's mystical rapture, coupled with her sexual continence, derived from her understanding of the Orphic vision of love described in Plato's *Phaedrus,* the dialogue Fuller had read in January and again in December of that crucial year, 1839. In *Phaedrus,* Socrates tells of the strange shuddering that comes upon one at the sight of a godlike beloved, and of the warmth that flows through one's veins and fosters the growth of the wings by which one's soul will eventually fly to heaven—if only one can abstain from indulging in physical passion.[13]

Fuller yearned to grow wings, to purge her soul of the alloy of passion. For the purist moral vision of her Puritan ancestors was as integral a part of her person as the earthy woman who hungered for physical love. She hence believed at this time what Socrates taught, that the highest love is that which resists the urge to link sexually. In *Phaedrus*, we recall, Plato tells of a struggle between the good and bad horses of one's soul, which the charioteer of one's "higher elements of mind" controls. So even when lovers "lie side by side" and "the wanton horse of the lover's soul" demands guerdon for his trouble, the good steed sides with the driver in resisting "the power of evil" in him, that is, the desire to engage in an act of sexual passion. Thus sublimated sex in Plato became the basis for religious vision.[14]

And thus Fuller, "a poor wandering pilgrim," found in Orphic vision, especially as it came to her through Plato, a way to deal with what she herself saw as these "strange arrangements" of her "mortal lot." It enabled her to transmute her erotic yearnings into religious vision and art, to reframe the born-again belief of the Christian evangelicals into a vision of spiritual redemption more in tune with the needs of her "soul." Believing God's "plan is All," Fuller that fall came to see her suffering as a necessary part of a providential plan inducing her "to embody in beautiful forms all that lay in my mind." Though she was wary of human schemes like the one then being proposed for a utopian community at Brook Farm nine miles southwest of Boston in West Roxbury, Massachusetts, her newfound faith inspired her to explore and create new ways for men and women to relate to each other in both the private and public spheres.[15]

25 ∽ Paradise Regained

Sometime in 1840 Fuller wrote William Channing the letter in which she depicts life as a "pilgrimage," an ongoing effort to overcome "worldliness." In it she tells how her new self-insight has helped her to understand the men who are part of the "Transcendental party" and the ways she "differ[s] from most of them on important points." While sympathizing with their wish to awaken in people an awareness of a "standard transcending sense and time," she nonetheless feels that these men do not sufficiently consider the role of emotions in our lives. If ever she finds time to think "deeply" on these "subjects," she will put what she means "in print." She will write, she says, from her "position as a woman."[1]

As Fuller gained confidence as a woman, she began to see the depth of "the gulf" that separated her way of thinking from that of men like Emerson. Her attempt to explain to him the "mighty changes in [her] spiritual life" when she visited him in Concord in October 1840 was met, she told Cary, "by a sneer." When she had looked "with great love" at Emerson, who had just received a letter about Margaret and magnetism from Cary, both letter and loving look "seemed to have puzzled and disconcerted him."[2]

It was finally Sturgis who gave Fuller the affirmation she felt she needed. In the anguished 22 October 1840 letter she sent Sturgis a month after she wrote the two climactic letters of her crisis—that of 29 September to Emerson demanding he recognize her needs, and that of 26 September to Cary declaring she is "no more below"—Fuller blessed her friend for her "recognition," presumably Cary's validation of Fuller's thoughts and needs.[3]

In this 22 October letter, Fuller sees herself as a flowering plant. She tells Cary that, though she has never been what she is now, "it is only transformation, not alteration": "The leaf became a stem, a bud, is now in flower." Now that winter approaches, however, the "winds of heaven" and "dews of night" will convert the "flower" of her being "into dead-seeming seed." Yet as surely as Persephone emerged each spring from the underworld, so, too, will she emerge in spring after this winter of pain "far fairer" than before. This season of suffering had, indeed, made Fuller feel alive. "For months," she later said, "I was all radiant with faith, and love, and life. I began to be myself"—the "natural" female human being she felt her father had suppressed.[4]

In a late October 1840 letter she asks Channing in his role as Unitarian minister why the religion of her nature is so hidden from her peers. She tells him how she felt she had been "cheated" out of her Sunday by having gone to hear Orville Dewey, Emerson's cousin and a popular Unitarian minister visiting from New York. She was glad when he read from Isaiah and "the fourth of John's Epistle," but she also recalled Dewey denying "mysteries," "the second birth," and "the sovereign gift of insight, for . . . what he deemed a 'rational' exercise of will." Though she could understand Dewey's reservations regarding the old religionists who "talk about 'grace, conversion,' and the like, technically," but do not strive "to enter into the idea," Fuller thinks the time has come to preach "the Holy Ghost as zealously" as the Unitarians have been "preaching Man, and faith instead of the understanding and mysticism instead &c." Like Charles Finney who argued that "groans" evince the presence "within" of "the Holy Ghost," she says, "Give me tears and groans," even if they include "physical excitement and bigotry." Fuller then urges Channing to preach a religion of nature: "Speak thunder and lightning and dew and rustling leaves." Confessing to being a "wandering pilgrim, yet no saint," she affirms her faith in the God she believes will not condemn her—"the God of the human heart."[5]

Almost exactly a year after her first Conversation session, on 8 November 1840 Fuller met again with the women in her Boston conversation class and told them of "the great changes" in her mind. Her presentation "kindled" Anna, who sat beside her "glowing" and, the moment Fuller finished, "began to speak." Fuller saw herself as "kindling the same fire in all their souls"—the fire she felt necessary to purge their souls of sin. Here in this circle of women, Fuller felt she had been reborn; their recognition seemed to breathe new life into her soul. How rapturous "this swoon," she wrote Sturgis on a Sunday evening in late January 1841, "as the soul was ready to be born."[6]

However rapturous her purported rebirth, Fuller was aware that not only nature's but also her own demons consisted of both creative and destructive energies. In "Leila," an essay she published in the *Dial*'s April 1841 issue, Fuller embodied nature's power in a figure she called Leila, a godlike being that exists in the bowels of the earth and appears only at night. When she had first read the name Leila—whether in Goethe or Byron—Fuller had said that she thought it was hers because "it meant *Night*."[7] "At night," says the speaker (presumably an alter ego for Fuller), she looks "into the Lake for Leila," who, as the form of "all the elemental powers of nature," "rises and walks on its depth." She tells how the "electricity accumulates many days" before Leila appears. Yet when she does at last appear, "at her touch," the "rivers of bliss flow" and "the shadow of sin falls," notes the speaker, who has no fear of being absorbed into what she believes lies beyond "sense, time, and thought." For in that transcendent realm, "prison walls"—barriers erected by men—grow "into Edens," the kind of paradise Fuller felt she had found in her closed world of women, the undefiled garden that had existed prior to the father's intrusive entry into it.[8]

The defiant speaker then pledges her allegiance to the "Angel Leila," saying, "I will be thy fellow pilgrim." "From slavery," she affirms, will come "freedom, from parricide piety, from death . . . birth."[9]

It may well have been Goethe's Leila, who was loved by the androgynous incest-child Mignon, or Leila of Byron's *The Giaour*, who was slain by a Turk and buried at sea, from whom Fuller took the name Leila. The name is also close to George Sand's fictional Lélia, whom English critics had labeled "a monster, a Byronic woman." Whatever the source, Fuller's "Angel Leila" is a wandering phantom, a "mighty sea" that at night "swells up" and "rushes over you till you plunge on its waves, affrighted," but that by day retreats "into the secret veins of earth." As such, Leila is apparently meant to represent the feminine source of life itself, but Fuller realizes this force will drown the seeker if it is not restrained by the polite conventions of daylight life.[10]

ೂ ೂ ೂ

In her letters and writings of 1841–42, Fuller expresses her awareness of both the curative and destructive powers of nature. In an August 1841 retreat she took with Sturgis to Sachuset Beach, about a mile and a half from Newport, Rhode Island, Fuller celebrated nature's healing power. The first two weeks they stayed in a white farmhouse on a slope a quarter mile above the sea. Called Paradise Farm, the little house, Fuller noted, was appropriately flanked by an old apple orchard. With two beaches nearby, Fuller thought the beach that lay a quarter mile below the house was the more beautiful because it seemed "in its curve to clasp the ocean to its breast." "Every thing seems sweet here," she wrote Channing on 6 August: "The never ceasing break of the surf is a continual symphony calming the spirits." At night she sat atop a high rock at Paradise Farm. From there she could see Cary in her long dress "wandering, and the horsemen careening on the beach, so spectrally passing into nature" that it felt as if she might be dead and "in the *land of souls!*"[11]

Here, in harmonious reciprocity with nature and her friend, Fuller felt happy. Though the cool evenings required her to pull a shawl about her shoulders as she and Sturgis walked along the beach, mornings were warm enough to bathe in the sea. Thanks to the bathing and fresh sea air, after only five days there she felt strong. She wrote Channing that being in nature had made her feel so good that she wished he would build his church "on this gentle shore" and learn "to worship," as had she, "the declining Sun" and "holy uprise of the stars." At the end of the beach, she says, "is a very tall rock, one of those natural pulpits." She thinks he might preach a sermon there in tune with the "voice" of Mother Nature.[12]

By the power of her mind and imagination, Fuller had at least momentarily created for herself a kind of paradise on earth. She had done so both at Paradise Farm with Cary and behind the closed doors of her Boston conversations where admiring women looked to her for education and guidance. Except for the sessions in 1841 when a few men were invited to attend, it was a world for women only, a place apart from the male-run world of business, hard work, and coercion. This private place had two shortcomings, however. It sealed her off from the public sphere of action, and it did not really free her from the "Law of the Father," that is, from the "world of rules" that necessarily guided the behavior of, as Fuller put it in a letter to Channing, "subscriber[s] to the social contract," rules that continued to dictate her behavior as conscience, no matter how great was her wish to create a counter-order for women.[13]

26 ∽ The Law of the Father and the Embrace of Mother Nature

If it is true, as Harold Bloom has suggested, that we are mature to the extent we relinquish our wish for a "godlike embrace" from "some sufficient love" in a place set apart from the social world, then Fuller's retreat during her crisis to the embrace of Mother Nature must be seen as a step backward in her journey to wisdom. Yet it can also be seen as Fuller herself saw it: as a step forward. For it offered her, as Romantics promised, psychic healing: a way to explore and affirm her female self, a process she would advocate in her female empowerment writing. Certainly for a person undergoing such intense self-scrutiny as was Fuller, a wish to retreat to the world of the mother is not really, as she thought, so "strange." After all, the original object of desire for both men and women is the mother, a truth the mythical Oedipus discovered. Indeed, not to wander off the path to wisdom requires, says Plato, "self-mastery," mental control over physical passion. Though Fuller in the midst of her crisis said she sought "the divine rather in Love than law," the law still lived in her and she lived in its dictum, in particular as her conscience condemned women who took pleasure in sex outside of wedlock.[1]

Fuller was never free from the rigid moral dictums of her Puritan fathers. As a child she had internalized the stern paternal decrees prescribed for her not only by the Bible and her high-minded ancestors, but also by the unforgiving father figures that appeared in European literature—such as Wieland's fairy-father Oberon, who cautions the Christian knight Huon regarding the "woes without end" that "oft spring from transient lust," and Milton's archangel Raphael, who warns Adam and Eve of the evil that will befall them if they eat of the tree of knowledge in paradise. This message of divine vengeance for sexual waywardness had hence been engraved deep, indeed, in the developing brain of Fuller, who, as a teenager, had kept "Paradise lost" close at hand. Milton's words, like Wieland's, lived in her and influenced her actions: "In loving thou dost well, in passion not"; "heav'nly Love" leads up to God, not down to "carnal pleasure." Certainly Milton, whom she calls "the purity of Puritanism," was as integral a part of Fuller's mental landscape as were the wild Maenads singing songs to Bacchus; or the "gifted" but "ill-fated" Shelley, who died by sailing into a storm; or the sensual Sand, whom Fuller would applaud in February 1845 for "systematically assail[ing] the present institution of marriage and the social bonds which are connected to it."[2]

But it was not just the retribution of the law of the father that troubled Margaret Fuller; so, too, she dreaded nature's retaliatory rage for what still seemed to her to be her "unnatural" passionate yearnings. Her dread of the destructive power of nature is evident in the 6 August 1841 letter she wrote Channing from Paradise Farm near Newport, Rhode Island. Fuller tells Channing about watching Cary wander at night on the beach, noting also that she is aware that "the sea is not always" so "lovely and bounteous." One night she stayed late with Cary "out on the far rocks." The moon was red, as if "angry," and "the damp, cold wind came sobbing, and the waves began sobbing and wailing, too." "I was seized," said Fuller, "with a sort of terrible feeling such as I never had before. . . . The moon seemed sternly to give me up to the demons of the rock, and the waves coldly to mourn, a tragic chorus, and I felt a cold grasp. . . . It seemed to me we should never get home without some fatal catastrophe." Suddenly the moon "shone forth" and the waves put on a "silvery gleam, and looked most soft and regretful." Was the mournful, raging sea, or the softly regretful sound of the waves, she wonders, the "real voice from Nature; what did it say?"[3]

Fuller's ambivalence about nature and her own human nature appears in the contrast between her published 1842 translation of Bettina Brentano's *Günderode* and her private nighttime dreams. She used the series of fictionalized letters exchanged between the as-yet-unmarried Brentano von Arnim, a peripheral figure in Goethe's literary circle from 1807 to 1811, and the beautiful Canoness Caroline von Günderode, a poetess about ten years older than Brentano, to affirm her friendship with Sturgis. These letters immortalized the kind of intimate yet Platonic friendship between women that Fuller hoped to find for herself. For in the letters, an impulsive Brentano is seen throwing her arms in a childlike way about the coolly intellectual Günderode, holding the woman's hand on walks, and dreaming in letters to her older friend of the "rattling of the branches covered with snow; . . . the little fire blazing up," and Bettina "playing with thy fingers" as the women lay by one another in bed and talked. In her preface to the translation, Fuller wrote: "We feel of these two that they were enough to one another to be led to indicate their best thoughts . . . and therefore theirs was a true friendship." She mocks Emerson by replaying words from his recently published essay "Friendship": "They needed not 'descend to meet.'"[4]

Thus Fuller criticized Emerson, who, she wrote Channing in August 1842, had "disappointed" her in their friendship. She thought he "met men, not as a brother, but as a critic." She would know; for Emerson's life had, indeed, as she confided to Channing, gradually stolen into hers. His criticisms had become a part of her conscience. It might then have been Emerson who appeared in a dream Fuller had in autumn 1842 in the prophetic shape of judgmental "friends" who deem Fuller not worth saving from drowning.[5]

Fuller's dread of both society's and Nature's condemnation of her Romantic yearnings, as well as her hurt over her friends' rejections of her impassioned appeals for love, bleeds into this dream she had that October while visiting Anna when her husband Sam Ward was away. Instead of the innocent pleasure felt by Bettina in sharing a bed with her cherished female friend, Fuller felt the kind of anxiety that found symbolic representation in her terrifying dream. With Ward away, Fuller was pained by the realization that she did not relate to the lovely Anna as she had before Anna's marriage to him. Conscious of this fact, she confesses in her October 1842 journal how she nonetheless "took pleasure in sleeping on Sam's pillow," where her "eyes solicited . . . visions like his [of the fair Anna]." But the price Fuller paid for her self-conscious solicitation of pleasure was pain: "I had a frightful dream of being imprisoned in a ship at sea, the waves all dashing round, and knowing that the crew had resolved to throw me in." Finally, friends came on board: "At first they seemed delighted to see me & wished to talk but when I let them know my danger, & intimated a hope that they might save me," they turned and "with cold courtliness glided way."[6]

For the "pleasure" she felt in sharing a bed with Anna—then a common sleeping arrangement between female friends—it seems her conscience punished her. She had a nightmare of her death at sea by drowning after having been spurned by her judgmental friends. Certainly she had plenty of relevant memories and literary images to inspire her dream: of the high rocks and "plashing of the waves" at Nahant where Sturgis had been put off by Fuller's intensity; of the scene in *Oberon* where Rezia nearly drowns in "the howling waves"; as well as of Fuller's recent visit with Cary to Paradise Farm at Sachuset Beach where at night from atop a high rock she had watched Cary in her long dress wander on the shore. Commenting on the source of her dream images, Fuller herself had said in her journal that she could "analyze" them and "find," more often than not, such images "to be made up from what she had seen."[7]

In this instance, the oppressive mix of guilt and hurt and anguish she had felt about Cary, Anna, and Sam—each of whom had, in a fashion, rejected her—found its imagistic representation in dream in a "cold wave" that threatens to drown her, the same icy wave that Huon in a dream had foreseen his visionary princess drowning, the tragic price destiny made her pay for disobeying the harsh father, Oberon. The images in Fuller's dream of drowning are likewise fraught with pain: the psychological pain that comes with the rejection of us by those we love; the physical pain that accompanies stirred yet unsatiated sensual yearnings. Such might engender feelings of suffocation, of drowning, of being overcome by a "love" that can find no outlet in mutual satisfaction. For although asexual "Divine" love may indeed "save" us, "love also," as Freud has said, "makes things wet." The overpowering wish to immerse herself in the "rivers of bliss" that "flow" when she is with those she passionately loves, both male and female, is countered here by the pain awakened in Fuller by the expression of "cold courtliness" on the faces of the friends who scorn her when she says she is in "danger" and asks for help. "Oh it was horrible," Fuller wrote about this nightmare—"these averted faces and well dressed figures turning from me, from captive, with the cold wave washing up into which I was to be thrown."[8]

But such dreams of drowning did not always have a negative connotation for Fuller. One dream, recorded in 1842, occurred four times. "In C. S."—"C. S." surely being Cary Sturgis—Fuller notes, "I . . . distinctly recognize[d] the figure of the early vision whom I found after I had left Amelia, who led me on the bridge towards the city glittering in sunset, but midway the bridge went under water." This dream, unlike the other, suggests a sensuously satisfying, spiritual experience: a feminine figure leads her to the celestial city in the sky, her yearned for baptismal purging by water, instead of fire.[9]

This latter dream merges images from her Cambridgeport childhood—"the bridge, . . . the river, and the city glittering in sunset"—with the memory of a more recent, similarly sensuous experience. For in October 1842, when Fuller had recorded her nightmare about drowning, she had also noted in her journal: "Anna walked over the bridge with me: it was a mellow pensive sunset, I like this bridge as much as ever, sights from it have been to me the parents of infinite suggestion and still the distant line seems worthy to engirdle a little world of love and thought and goodness."[10] Here the land embraces a lake, like a "little world," Mother Nature's "wet" element, source of life, the womb.

Whatever the source or meaning of her dream images, Fuller did not hide from the insights about herself that she felt were revealed to her in dreams. Part of her greatness lies in her ability to acknowledge the contradictions within her: the civilized sexual morality demanded of her by her conscience, as well as the insatiable hunger for love underlying it.

PART FIVE

The "Fine Castle" of Her Writing

One of Fuller's favorite dialogues of Plato was the *Symposium* ("The Banquet"). In it Plato records a conversation that Socrates had with Diotima of Mantinea in which the prophetess says to Socrates: "Those who are pregnant in body only betake themselves to women and beget children.— . . . But souls which are pregnant—for there certainly are men who are more creative in their souls than in their bodies—conceive that which is proper for the soul to conceive or contain . . . —wisdom and virtue in general. And such creators are poets and all artists who are deserving of the name inventor." These words were in Fuller's mind when she wrote George Davis in December 1842 that she felt "that the darkest hue" on her lot was that she had "neither children," nor was yet "the parent of beautiful works by which the thought of [her] life might be represented to another generation."[1]

That she confided this thought to George Davis is curious, for Davis had been one of the young men whom she had thought she might marry who had rejected her. All the men she imagined she might marry and society might have thought right for her had chosen to marry more conventional women, as had Sam Ward and her long-time friend James Clarke. Indeed, any man society might see as right for her as a husband might be disconcerted by Fuller's sauciness, intelligence, and intensity, or by her unconventional looks: her "cross mouth" (according to Clarke's Grandfather Freeman), her squinting blue-gray eyes, her small head (according to Caroline Dall) "thrown almost wholly in front of the ears." But it was far more than merely her looks or saucy style that repelled men: anyone who got to know Fuller through conversation or letters would have been aware that what she really wanted from a man was well beyond the conventional; she wanted a partnership of intellectual and emotional equals. Such a demand would have scared off most nineteenth-century American men.[2]

When she visited the Emersons in the late summer of 1842, she and Waldo had often talked on the subject of marriage. Fuller recalls in the journal she kept during her monthlong stay how Emerson had speculated that if Fuller had the chance, she "would do no better" than other wives: she would say that her "aim" was "to further the genius of her husband" while claiming "a devotion" that would be "injurious to him" were he to yield. Fuller "made no reply." Indeed she did not. For during her stay she had thought of the troubled married lives of so many of the women she knew—including those of both Lidian and her own sister, Ellen. And she wrote in her journal at this time how even Lidian, who was wife to a man she saw as a saint and "mother of that child [little Waldo] that is gone," had called her "the most privileged of women." At first Fuller had thought it "a little too insult-ing." "And yet," she confesses, women like Lidian "are not altogether wrong."[3]

That winter Fuller began to see just how fortunate she was not to have to live obeisant to a man in marriage, an imperfect institution wherein a woman's identity as a thinking and caring human was subsumed within that of her husband. For each man from whom Fuller had sought love and recognition had fallen short in his ability to see her as a whole human being, a woman who combined in her per-son intellect and emotion in equal portion. During her psycho-sexual crisis, even Emerson had failed to acknowledge her deepest emotional needs. He could not see the latter because "his life," Fuller wrote on 2 September 1842, "is [in] the intellect not the affections." She was still angry, moreover, over the earlier misogynist behav-ior of Uncle Abraham, who, as lawyer for the family estate, had insulted Margarett Crane by refusing her request for money to send the younger boys and Ellen away to school, suggesting in a "vulgar" letter to Margaret's mother that a local Groton school was good enough for the boys and that for Ellen, a girl, no further educa-tion was necessary. This refusal of funding by her father's brother, who lorded over the family finances and had even threatened to take guardianship of the younger children away from Mrs. Fuller, had forced Margaret, we recall, to take on an over-load to earn extra money for Ellen during Fuller's brief career as a teacher in Provi-dence. Motivated by her awareness of how greatly marriage limited women's lives, by her anger at men for lording over women and her wish that women might have the right to an education equal to men's, as well as by her ambition, Fuller felt at this time, she confessed in her December letter to Davis, "emboldened to an immortal hope" that she might yet be "the parent of beautiful works."[4]

And indeed, between the years 1843 and 1845—in a burst of great and sus-tained creative energy—Fuller parented three significant works. Beginning with her forty-seven-page *Dial* essay, "The Great Lawsuit. Man versus Men, Woman versus Women," which was printed in the July 1843 issue, to her memoir of her travels in the Great Lakes region, *Summer on the Lakes, in 1843*, which came out in June 1844, and ending with her two-hundred-page history-making feminist tract, *Woman in the Nineteenth Century*, which appeared in bookstores in mid-

February 1845, Fuller focused on her writing with the confidence that, as Emerson had advised, if only she would take up her "work . . . proudly," she could not "write a bad book." She might even write a great one, as happened in the case of *Woman in the Nineteenth Century,* in which, as we shall see, she discussed the problems confronting nineteenth-century women and how each woman might gain control of her life and emerge a person, as Fuller put it in her book, "born for Truth *and* Love in their universal energy."[5]

27 ∞ A Time to Write

In "Self-Reliance" Emerson observes "what a blindman's-buff" is "this game of conformity." It loses your time and "scatters your force." "But do your work," he says, "and I shall know you. Do your work, and you shall reinforce yourself." Fuller took this message to heart, especially after little Waldo's death in January 1842 when Emerson, numb with pain, cut himself off emotionally from others. "Well, souls never touch their objects," he says in "Experience": "An innavigable sea washes with silent waves between us and the things we aim at and converse with. Grief too will make us idealists."[1]

In loving his son, Emerson had opened a place for a wound and fate had found it. Although in "Experience" he will attest that the death of "my son, now more than two years ago, . . . does not touch me," the boy's death hung heavy in the air during Fuller's late summer 1842 visit with the Emersons. On a dark, rainy September evening, as Fuller sat by her fire and read in "the red room"—the "Pilgrim's Chamber"—which was hers again during her long visit, Emerson had walked in with lines from "Saadi" in hand. While wiping her eyes, Fuller had listened as Emerson read from his poem how the Muse told Saadi not to follow falsehood but "to scale the sky" and be true to a vision that transcends human scorn, conflict, and pain. When he finished reading, Emerson, laying aside his manuscript, had asked Fuller how on earth she had got herself such a bad cold. The question made her laugh, she said, "to see that grief was the *last* thing Saadi [Emerson] ever thought of," whereupon she explained to her emotionally distant friend that Lidian, in talking about little Waldo, had made her cry. To this reminder of his recent loss, Emerson, as if distracted, murmured, "What, my boy?"[2]

Fuller had felt that night an "unspeakable tenderness" for her tall lean friend as he read his poem by the light of her small flickering fire, its gentle flames casting "a beautiful light upon him" and softening the deep lines pain had carved in his face. Yet she was not prepared at this juncture in her life's journey to understand the depth of the crevice in the heart of this man who had suffered so much sorrow, the last and greatest hurt being the sudden death of little Waldo in January from scarlet fever—"Dear Boy," he had keened in his grief, "too precious and unique a creation to be huddled aside into the waste and prodigality of things!" Nor was she yet able to comprehend entirely Lidian's love for her lost child. In her 1842 journal Fuller tells how she had walked with this severe silent woman through tall wet grass to the cemetery on a night "of moon struggling with clouds." Shrouded in black from head to toe, Lidian had "knelt & leaned her forehead on the tomb." As Lidian prayed, the moon had burst forth from behind the clouds and cast its cold light upon her. To Fuller, the praying woman's grief seemed only the ghost of a mother's joys. Lidian never felt the reality of Waldo's death, wrote Fuller, a remark that seems ironic, coming as it does from a woman who earlier had confessed to Emerson she needed "illusions" to keep her "in action."[3]

After the boy's death, Fuller had confided to William Henry Channing, "He was the only child I ever saw, that I sometimes wished I could have called mine." Yet a child is not a "sometimes" item. Fuller knew this and was beginning to suspect that her life was not so hard after all. "I have no child," she noted in her journal; "but now, as I look on these lovely children of a human birth, what low and neutralizing cares they bring with them to the mother! The children of the muse come quicker, and have not on them the taint of earthly corruption."[4]

In her crisis Fuller had preferred Socrates' Orphic-influenced mystical vision as in the *Symposium* and *Phaedrus* to the image of Jesus the Jew on the cross. Much as many women Orphics saw sex and death as pollutants, so sex and death were increasingly seeming now to Fuller like dross to the pure gold of her soul. In a June 1842 letter, Fuller had observed to William Channing how happy his prayers had made her during a Sunday Unitarian service, especially those that "touched the inmost heart." She wonders, however, if it is a "defect" of her "spiritual experience," that, while she needs the sting of keen insight to satisfy her genius, "the undertone of . . . a deeper knowledge" does not "please" her. When listening to Handel's *Messiah,* "the strain, 'Was ever sorrow like to his sorrow' is not for me, as I have been, as I am."[5]

In a letter to Richard Margaret says she has recently been reading plays by the Greek Euripides, as well as writings by the Athenian soldier-historian-biographer Xenophon, who knew Socrates and portrayed him as an unoriginal moralist. To Channing Fuller reports that she prefers Plato's view of Socrates because it depicts "the growth of the rational mind" and illustrates "keen truth by received forms." By this she means that the latter Socrates gave life to moral ideas that he believed existed prior to the universe by conceiving of each as an ideal form in relation to which all earthly examples are imperfect instances. Fuller thought this was Socrates' "right way" to teach, since "his influence was, naturally, private, for individuals." It seemed to her that inquisitive individuals who were pursuing the path to self-knowledge could "respond to the teachings of [Socrates'] 'demon,'" that "voice" that Plato's Socrates credits with directing him in his quest for ultimate knowledge of being. Socrates saw such ultimate knowledge as the sum of all the disparate forms in which the form of the supreme good is manifested.[6]

In this 17 June 1842 letter to Channing, Fuller notes that it did not matter to Socrates that the multitude would not understand him, whereas "it was the other way that Jesus took, preaching in the field . . . on the Sabbath day." But then, Jesus was a missionary of religion, she says, unlike Socrates, who was a sage. Because of this (to her) limiting aspect of the Christian religion, Fuller was surprised, she says, to have heard Channing speak in his sermon "as if the extent of the Christian triumph proved its superiority," since "that of other faiths is numerically greater; and their hold as strong in the nations they rule."[7]

Having recently undergone a spiritual crisis, Fuller in 1842 appreciated Socrates' pedagogical style. Fuller found more appealing Socrates' admonition to each person to acquire self-understanding by exploring his or her singular self than the telling of parables by Christ, whom in "The Great Lawsuit" she will see as the "type of [human] excellence." She liked Socrates' teaching style, since what mattered to him was not that a person conform to any particular moral vision or religious sect, but rather that he live a virtuous life in accord with the form of the good that he feels is right for him. Thus the good to which he aspires might be to excel as a sports hero, a judge, a political leader, or a teacher. According to Socrates, so long as courage, moderation, piety, justice and wisdom are present in a man's life, he is virtuous.[8]

In Socrates' dialectics Fuller felt she had found a philosophy that offered a broader scope for her restless intellect than did the Judeo-Christian ethical vision of her ancestors and friends. She liked how Socrates challenged each of his interlocutors to find the path in life right for *him*, the path of *his* desire, *his* destiny. Of course, Socrates was not much concerned with the plight of women. Although he may have meant for his dialectical method to apply to all people regardless of social status or sex, his teachings were aimed at an aristocratic cadre of men who believed, as did he, that virtue by itself is sufficient proof of goodness. In the cool world of Socratic vision, where chance dictates individual fortune and God is the highest form of the good, there was little room for pity. In the *Apology*, which Fuller had read, Socrates contends that pity is an emotion unworthy of free men. Especially the sorrows and sufferings of women and slaves were not important to these men who believed that their prudence, piety, and, as Plato said, "self-mastery," proved their superiority as moral human beings.[9]

In *Woman in the Nineteenth Century* Fuller will note the limits of Plato's vision, in particular how in *The Republic* he treats women as property. But at the time she wrote "The Great Lawsuit" she was still enchanted with "Plato's marvellous Dialogues," especially the two from Socrates' middle period, the *Symposium* and *Phaedrus*, where his religious vision is mystical. As a friend of Emerson she was naturally impressed with Plato's notion of "self-mastery," with his definition in *Phaedrus* of the soul as "self-mover." Her respect for this masculine concept bolstered her own growing confidence that she had the will and capacity to maintain

THE "FINE CASTLE" OF HER WRITING

the self-discipline she needed to write and thus pursue the path destiny intended for her to take.[10]

Cast in the light of her thinking at this time, Fuller's distant response to Lidian's and other friends' suffering can be understood, as can her sense that destiny is leading her to take a path that diverges from the one most women of her class and culture are traveling. In light of her adherence to Plato's thinking, we can understand her remark in a letter to William Henry Channing about the despairing cry of Emerson, who had said in a letter he wrote her the day after Waldo's death, "Farewell and Farewell. O my Boy!" whose "wonderful beauty could not save him." About the boy's beauty, Fuller had noted to Channing: "But it is all gone, and is another of the lessons brought by each year, that we are to expect suggestions only, and not fulfilments, from each form of beauty."[11]

We can understand as well her "wary" reaction to Alcott, who with his lean face and figure, his gray worn temples, and his mild radiant eyes had personally appealed to her in March for understanding and mercy. Weeping in front of her a "shower of gracious tears," Alcott, she wrote Emerson, had confessed that he had sought sympathy "in the society of crude reformers" but had found them to be as "limited as the men they opposed" and that he had learned to know his own limitations.[12]

We also now have context for her comment in her 1842 journal that nothing made her so "anti-Christian, & so anti-marriage" as her talks in Concord with Lidian, who "lays such undue stress on the office of Jesus, & the demands of the heart," and had twice burst into tears in front of her. It apparently did not occur to her that perhaps Lidian feared that her husband enjoyed the company of this brilliant conversationalist more than he did his wife's.[13]

Fuller dismissed Lidian's outburst of tears "as a mere sick moment of L's." After all, her "expectations" in relation to Waldo, she said, "are moderate now." Though in some ways Fuller never felt closer to him, and even spent hours at night talking to him in either Emerson's study or her room, what may have appeared to others as intimate talks were in truth, as Fuller knew, just the same old conversations wherein Emerson declared his god was truth while Fuller said hers was love. Still, having stayed more than a month in his home, Fuller confessed she was not yet ready to live too near him because she still felt "*intoxicated*" with his mind when she was too often left alone with him. She even felt "faint" when too near him, as if she were not in full possession of her mind. In October she wrote Emerson that she felt "a conviction that I shall be worthy of this friendship," telling him not to "screw up your lip" at hearing these "words of frank affection" or be so "terrified at this prophecy" that "[you] look about for the keys of your cell."[14]

That Emerson had reason to feel uneasy over the hypnotic effect his presence still had on her is evident in words she jotted in her journal about their interaction, words that convey a potent undercurrent of need still to please her father. "My time to go to him," she wrote, "is late in the evening." In a part of her heart, Fuller wanted "always" to live in the red room "& Waldo be stimulated / By the fine days / to write poems & come the rainy days to read them to me." The erotic pull she felt when alone with him continued thus to be strong, perhaps, she knew, even stronger than ever, for her love for him was now real. In her journal Fuller confesses how pleasant it is to sit at night in the great red chair from which she can open the window and look up at the sharp white stars shimmering in the sky and also out at Waldo walking beneath them preparing his head, she says, "for his pillow," knowing he has just been stimulated by her talk.[15]

No matter how pleasant her situation or how powerful the erotic pull, Fuller also knew that to do her work she must move on. For she was throwing away her creative energies in caring for Emerson. According to her, the man himself had said he felt "shut up in a crystal cell" from which only "a great love or a great task" could free him. And when he talked of a "great love," Fuller knew he did not mean her. Their understanding, after all, would always be imperfect. Whereas Emerson "had faith in the Universal," he had none "in the Individual Man," in man "as a brother." Nonetheless, in a last, even if unintended way of conveying her feelings in relation to Emerson, she had left behind in her room, she wrote him upon returning to Jamaica Plain, her penknife and key, items she saw as "touching symbols" of their relationship. Lidian promptly returned them. Though Fuller does not say what door the key opened or what she used the penknife for, both items have symbolic meaning. Lidian certainly knew that Fuller enjoyed holding the "key" that unlocked the door to her husband's inner sanctum, though she may not have seen the knife as a symbol of Fuller's masculine power. Indeed, she probably did not know how sweet it was for Fuller to gain a sense of command over the man, since being in control made Fuller feel manly and strong. Fuller gained a similar pleasure in interacting with the women in her classes. While it had been sweet indeed to unlock the door into Emerson's "cell," it had been equally sweet for her to see adoration in the eyes of the intelligent women who attended her Conversations. Their regard was an elixir to her; and like clay in the hands of a potter, an idea began taking shape in her mind: how better to prove she was "worthy" of Emerson's "friendship" than to produce a literary work that responded to Emerson's views on manly self-reliance from a woman's point of view?[16]

Fuller had long thought about writing an essay on women and their special genius. Not until now, however, did she feel she had the self-control to write it. With her mind now calm and sweet, she felt destiny urging her to commit to print her ideas on women. Writing in December 1842 from the comfortable Cambridge house that she and her mother had recently moved into, she tells George Davis about the past as well as about her dream of reaching the stars through her writing. Her current small house, she says, sits in the shade of trees she had once looked out on from her upstairs bedroom in the Dana mansion, which had been destroyed by fire in 1839. The view is the same: "the river so slow and mild, the gentle hills, the sunset over Mt. Auburn." And though it still gives her pleasure, what Fuller says she remembers most about life back then was how often her father had tried to check her "pride" by painting for her "a picture of the ills" that would attend her if she could not learn humility. She never did, she tells Davis, and the predicted sickness, poverty, and failure of ties and plans have followed. It nonetheless seemed to Fuller that none of these misfortunes had hardened her heart. No, boasts Fuller, "I feel the same heart within my breast, I prize the same objects," and they, in turn, she believes, prize her. She feels "for all of them," as well as for herself, "an immortal hope" that, though she has no child, she might yet give birth to "beautiful works" through which she might convey her thoughts to future generations.[17]

This, then, thought Fuller, was the path fate meant for her to take: it was not to bear babies but books. She would gain immortality by responding to Emerson (and Timothy, whose eye even in death seemed to be watching her) with a *Dial* essay in which she would argue woman's right as an immortal soul to lead an independent life of thought and action. It *was* absurd, she wrote a friend on 16 January 1843, for her to fritter away her time commenting on such a subject in letters and conversation. Besides, for the first time in her life she felt healthy and centered enough to write with clarity. In late January she noted in another letter that she had been healthier in the previous three weeks than she had been during any winter for the last seven years. It had been, after all, a good winter. Safe with her mother in the well-lighted chambers of her snug Cambridge home, with the wind outside howling and driving snowflakes thick against her windows, she felt warm and secure and reflected on what a good year 1842 had been. Her translation of *Günderode* had come out in March, and her Conversation classes continued to be enormously pleasant and successful. The mere sight of her beautiful friends surrounding her in her Conversation sessions had spurred to growth the wings by which she felt she could fly to immortal heights, just as Plato in the *Phaedrus* had predicted about the influence of beauty on genius.[18]

Still, Fuller knew that through talking, just as through letter writing, she would never merit a place among the stars of recorded history, the pages of which sparkled with the exciting tales of men and their heroic deeds. That her Conversations, moreover, were viewed by some friends to be merely a game, as Emerson had cautioned, became apparent to her during an October 1842 visit to Brook Farm, the Transcendentalists' Fourierist commune in rural West Roxbury where, she wrote Emerson, she "gave *conversations* on alternate evenings with the husking parties." Perhaps she recalled at this time how Emerson had earlier urged her not to let this "flowing river" of her speech "sweep away" the "fine castle" of her writing "whose pinnacle is waited for by the States and by the nations." "So let us say," he had admonished her, "self possession is all; our author, our hero, shall follow as he may." Fuller now felt within herself the power to be "our author, our hero," to transmute the fleeting thoughts of her actual conversations with Emerson and the women who attended her classes into printed words with which she could converse, as it were, with the world. In short, it was time for her "proudly," as Emerson had advised, to take up her real work, her writing.[19]

28 ∽ Millennial Fever

During a blustering May—with the odious east winds beating against her windowpanes—Fuller, who in April had handed over *Dial* editorship to Emerson, sat down at her desk and wrote as much as the foul weather—and a hurting head—would let her. The result was "The Great Lawsuit. Man versus Men. Woman versus Women." The title of this *Dial* essay, which she would later expand into *Woman in the Nineteenth Century*, points to how far she thought men and women have fallen from the Greek ideal (form) of what each might have been as man and woman.

The essay is both a defense of Fuller as an unmarried, intellectual woman and an argument in behalf of women's rights. As such it intertwines a theme of personal exploration and rebirth with a vision of an out-of-kilter earth soon to be restored to harmony by self-reliant women who have been given the freedom to seek self-knowledge and develop fully as men's equal. In creating her vision of equality, Fuller mixed ideas and images she had gleaned through the years from sources including Romantic literature, utopian views on marriage and women, Emerson's thoughts on self-reliance, mesmerists' ideas on animal magnetism, as well as talk in her culture of the impending millennium.

For beneath the text's Orphic-influenced Platonism and infusing it with energy is not only Fuller's belief in a universal electrical fluid called animal magnetism that influences both human behavior and planets' motions, but also the spirit of millennial expectation permeating the air in that spring of 1843. Five years earlier, in 1837, the Northeast had suffered an economic depression, during which time people there increasingly turned to the word of God as preached by itinerant religious ultraists—Adventists, Baptists, and Wesleyan Methodists—who were seeing signs in the heavens of the Second Coming of Christ and who believed the end of time was near. Such men believed that when Christ came again he would cast the wicked into hell while ushering in a thousand-year period of heaven on earth for all who had led a genuinely "Christian" life.[1]

Chief among the millennial visionaries was William Miller (b. 1782), who in his youth had declared himself a deist, and whose followers became known as Millerites. During a Baptist revival in 1816, however, he had been converted and thereafter embraced the teachings of Baptists. Driven by his belief that Bible stories are factually accurate, Miller became obsessed with a notion shared by many of his contemporaries, that historic events and astrological signs indicated that

Christ would appear on earth sometime around 1843, the year Fuller wrote "The Great Lawsuit."[2]

Millennial thinking like Miller's had been known before in northeastern New York, Vermont, and western Massachusetts, but only after reaching Boston in 1839 did it spread like wildfire. Orphism, to which Fuller had been attracted since 1839, similarly promised a person relief from stress through an apocalyptic fusion with God. And two years before that, we recall, she had been impressed by the preaching of William Hague, the Baptist minister who had been in her seminar in Providence, the city to which renegade mystics and Baptists in seventeenth-century New England had fled to escape persecution by the Puritans. Like the mystics of seventeenth-century Puritan Boston, Baptists like Hague believed that a person can be born again through a sudden and permanent change in the way he or she relates to the world, and that his or her life thereafter will be transfigured and lightened by that person's faith in Christ.[3]

When Fuller wrote her essay she believed she had experienced a genuine spiritual rebirth, a permanent change in psychological outlook that dated, she said, "from the era of illumination in my mental life." Hers, however, was not a rebirth based on an acceptance of Christ as her savior. She instead believed that the divine spirit had passed directly into her. The renegade nature of her faith was evident back in Providence when she took Communion for the first time from the Baptist Hague since he was "willing," she said, "to admit me on my own terms." By insisting on translating Communion into terms that suited her, Fuller revealed her sympathy with the heretical message of Emerson's "Divinity School Address": that Jesus was a prophet who taught that God lives in every man and that each must hence live in accord with the "shining laws" within him.[4]

Believing God to be within her, Fuller, in preparing her essay on female regeneration and self-reliance for publication in the *Dial*, was simultaneously following Emerson's lead and breaking with his masculine moral vision. For Emerson never meant his attack on church ritual and call for a "new Teacher" in the "Divinity School Address" to be interpreted as directives for people to turn their backs on the patriarchal vision as relayed to them by both Plato and the prophets and preachers of the Old and New Testaments. On the contrary, in the harsh manner of a Calvin without Christ, Emerson, in daring his audience to love God without mediator or veil, meant that we are free only to be, as his Puritan precursor John Winthrop had declared, "good, just, and honest." According to Winthrop and Emerson, people sacrifice their souls when they advocate pagan rituals like those enacted by rapturous women in ancient Greece instead of revering the "real higher law," the "law of laws" that "man in all ages," as Emerson had said in *Nature*, "embodies . . . in his language, as the FATHER."[5]

Yet that is just what Fuller did in "The Great Lawsuit," whose title suggests the legal battle she intends to wage against all men in all ages and cultures who have limited women's lives with their laws, customs, and moral codes, and their built-in bias that men are superior to women. As a result of her 1839–40 religious experience, one rooted as much in pagan mystery rituals and the quasi-mystical machinations of mesmerism as in the Judeo-Christian tradition, Fuller felt that she had been born again as a woman in touch with the mystical energies in her soul. What she felt was her "soul" hence now seemed full with the electrical flow of a creative power greater than her own, what she and other Romantics preferred to call, not God the father, but the great creative spirit. Awake with this intense yet highly personal religiosity, a religious *sense* that was in fact greatly at odds with Emerson's, Fuller no doubt knew about the Adventist journal edited by Miller in Boston, *Signs of the Times,* which was also the title of Carlyle's famous 1829 essay on the Romantics. Nor could she have missed excited talk in the wider community about how the Reverend Miller expected the end of time to take place between 21 March 1843 and 21 March 1844.[6]

29 ∞ Fuller's Apocalypse

Within the electric context of religious enthusiasts awaiting the Second Coming, Margaret Fuller wrote "The Great Lawsuit" in which she forwarded her case against every man—including her lawyer-congressman father—who wishes, in her words, "to be lord" in his "little world." As men in the past had felt called by God to offer mankind a celestial vision, so Fuller, extending Emerson's call for soul liberty to include women, felt called by God to give birth to a vision of a New Jerusalem in which the relationship between the sexes had been righted and music restored to the spheres. In generating this vision of "celestial harmony," Fuller mingled ideas and images familiar to her from ancient myth and history with images from two popular cultural movements. In writing the essay she thus fused Plato's notion of the Forms with nineteenth-century millennialists' hopes for Christ's imminent Second Coming and mesmerists' ideas about animal magnetism, transmuting all into "psychotheistic" terms that transferred the theater of apocalyptic events from the heavens and earth to the site of the individual female soul. In so doing she shifted the task of redeeming humanity from man to woman. And she did this even as she introduced an ideal female figure named Miranda, whose "dignified sense of self-dependence" she attributes ironically to a father who held "a firm belief in the equality of the sexes" and respectfully addressed her as "a living mind." To Fuller, Miranda's excellence as a woman is just one of the "signs of the times" indicating that this new era in America was fast approaching, one in which man would relate to woman *not* as father but as brother, and marriage would be an ideal union of man and woman traveling side by side as pilgrims to heaven.[1]

Fuller thus begins her essay by noting how far men have fallen from the Platonic ideal of man, from what men might have been had they heeded the vision preached by Jesus that "all created beings are brothers." Lifted by Jesus, men lived for awhile in harmony with the law of the "universe-spirit."[2] But Jesus was crucified and mankind now needed, wrote Fuller, another leader: a being of "purer blood" who could, in the words of an eighteenth-century French mystic, "purge the terrestrial atmosphere from the poisons that infect it." Because even Jesus failed to provide humanity with the answer to evil, man is "still a pleader, still a pilgrim."[3]

Though "The Great Lawsuit" is permeated with the language of the anticipated impending millennium when Christ would come again and save believers' souls, Fuller was no traditional Christian, but a Romantic. As such she gave broad play to the power of human imagination and agency to re-create paradise on earth. Fuller thus says she has "no doubt" that a "new manifestation is at hand, a new hour in the day of man," when humans will act to turn earth into heaven. Then, the promise of the Declaration of Independence will be fulfilled, slavery will end, and women and men will be filled with conviction that God is within all people equally. She believes that people will recognize this truth after a divinely inspired teacher has taught them to see it.[4]

According to Fuller this new manifestation will be less like the vindictive Christ of the Millerites than like the idea of man depicted in the form of the ancient lawgiver Orpheus, who saw "nature as seen in the mind of God" and understood the meaning of love. Seeking his lost love, Eurydice, Orpheus feared neither death nor hell, nor "could any presence daunt his faith in the power of the celestial harmony that filled his soul." Fuller's language here reflects the influence not only of Orphic vision but also of the mesmerists. For the celestial harmony to which she alludes is the sense of emotional and mental well-being that mesmerists believed filled one's "soul" when in a state of "equipoise." According to Fuller, this was when the flow of "animal magnetism"—the etheric medium through which (in Franz Anton Mesmer's terms) sensations of every kind passed—was in balance throughout one's body. Fuller believed that a person with a surplus of this "electrical fluid" exudes a "magnetic" power that attracts or repels people. To Fuller, who believed in animal magnetism, it thus seemed as if waves of magnetic electrical energy were flowing through her as she poured her vision onto the page. In it she affirms that, since no male savior has succeeded in redeeming fallen men, it is now up to "the daughters" to reform—not the fathers but—"the sons," to teach them to be like Orpheus, who descended into hell to seek what he loved. For, only in experiencing the agony of hell, in suffering as did Orpheus (and Jesus), can a person, says Fuller, "to second life arise."[5]

In the forms of Jesus and Orpheus, men were thus given "type[s] of excellence" to imitate; but in Fuller's opinion they failed to live up to either ideal. Yet still, she says, fallen men declaim "on moral and religious subjects," and never so much "as now." She implores these "word-Catos, word-Christs, to beware of cant above all things; to remember that hypocrisy is . . . the meanest of crimes, and that those must surely be polluted by it, who do not keep a little of all this morality and religion for private use." Perhaps as she wrote these words, Margaret had in mind an observation her mother had made in a January 1819 letter to her husband regarding his self-righteous moralizing: at least "my *conduct* & *principles* generally coincide."[6]

Though one might want to keep in mind Margarett Crane's observation for when we later examine the reasons behind Fuller's virulent attack on male hypocrisy, it is worth noting now that Margaret's words echo those of Robert Collyer, an English mesmerist who lectured in Boston in 1837. In his pamphlet Collyer notes how dumbfounded he had been in his travels by the street-corner evangelism of rival religious sects. He cynically observes that in America "any unlettered biped who has sufficient cant and hypocrisy may become a minister of the Gospels." "Daily," he says, "some poor unfortunate falls a victim to these murderous quacks," an idea Fuller replays in her essay when she says that women are the "easy victims of priestcraft, or self-delusion." According to Fuller, women would not fall prey to priestcraft if they were allowed to develop intellectually. In her discussion of Fuller's use of the word "cant," Christina Zwarg notes that "cant" is the chant of beggars in Western culture, "the song of the cultural outcasts," whose ranks might "include women."[7]

Women are cultural outcasts, contends Fuller, because men have prevented them from attaining maturity of thought and feeling by defining the ideal woman as a being of bridelike beauty and childlike innocence and by marking with "precision the limits of woman's sphere, and woman's mission." Yet, she says, in fighting slavery women are now beginning to understand the real meaning of servitude and hence they are seeking broader outward freedoms for women. But outward freedoms for Fuller are not enough; she wants for women inward freedoms, too. She wants women to break down the barriers of cultural and social restrictions that for centuries have kept them out of public positions and hence made them outcasts from the public sphere of action.[8]

According to Fuller, men have indoctrinated women into believing that mankind's "happiness" was "forfeited through the fault of woman" and that "Mosaical law" binds her to men "like a serf." Thus male heirs of the Judeo-Christian religious tradition have limited what women might be. Playing on the notion of women as "cant," Fuller says that men from early childhood are taught that "girls cant do that, girls cant play ball." Yet, says she, *if* a man's "thought and feeling" were elevated to the point he could see himself not as a woman's "lord and tutor" but as her "brother and friend," then harmony in the spheres would ensue. For what woman wants and needs, she contends, is what she felt her father had deprived her of as a child: the right to grow naturally and freely into an independent being. In the fictional Miranda with her "strong electric nature" and "good father," Fuller thus offered readers an ideal alter ego. Miranda was taught "self-dependence," she says, which is "deprecated as a fault in most women." Most are "taught to learn" their "rule from without, not to unfold it from within." Stressing the word "fault," a term both Virgil and the Bible link with woman, Fuller boldly says through Miranda, "This is the fault of man."[9]

To illustrate the kind of female Messiah she believes will point the way to men's salvation, Fuller reached back to pre-Christian pagan times when women, though shut out from the marketplace and not allowed at civic forums, were nonetheless free to take equal part in religious festivities. To make her point Fuller hence relied again on the Platonic concept of the forms by which the Greeks lent substance to abstract ideas—as the Greeks and Romans embodied the idea of sensuous love in Aphrodite and Venus, and the Egyptians embodied the idea of "divine wisdom" in Isis.[10]

Two female forms important to Fuller, as well as to women initiated into the mystery rites of ancient Greece, were the goddesses of Eleusis: Ceres and Proserpina. In Greek myth, the Roman goddess Proserpina was identified with Persephone, who was abducted by her uncle, Hades, god of the Underworld, who then forced her to live half each year with him in hell. From Plutarch as well as *Faust,* part 2, wherein Faust makes his initiatory descent into the mysterious realm of the mothers, Fuller knew that those to be initiated into the Eleusian mysteries descended into the underworld, as did Orpheus. There, according to myth, they saw a vision of the suffering Persephone, a revelation of female (*not* male) divinity that purportedly redeemed their souls.[11]

Other "forms" of woman Fuller tells readers she finds inspiring are Diana, Vesta, and Minerva. None needed a man to complete her being. The form of Minerva, the Roman goddess identified with the Greek Pallas Athena, presided over intellectual (especially academic) activity, and it contrasted sharply with that of Cassandra, who represented electrical, mystical, prophetic female power.[12]

In this ancient world where women in fact occupied "a very subordinate position," Fuller applauds the poets who produced images of strong women in Iphigenia, Antigone, Macaria. A "zodiac of the busts of gods and goddesses" reveals the kind of "heavenly order" Fuller longs for, where each "male head is that of a brother and a king, each female of a sister and a queen." Could the idea "be lived out," says Fuller, "nothing more" would "be desired." But it cannot be, she says, in a Western culture that promotes the myth of "rude man" in Adam, who said his fall was woman's "fault."[13]

Fuller concedes that few nineteenth-century women had sufficient education to convert fallen men. She nonetheless believes that times were changing and that women would soon have that capacity. Like a Millerite, Fuller heralds these changes as one of many "signs of the times" indicating that "an era approaches which shall" more nearly "approximate" a "state of perfect freedom" and "pure love" than any that has yet existed on earth. Though strong women such as England's Elizabeth have existed in history, for most women, says Fuller, "a gulf of Death" lies between the idea of self-sufficiency embodied in Minerva and the reality of their mundane lives.[14]

And nowhere, according to Fuller, is the gulf broader between the ideal and the actual life for women than in marriage, a topic on the mind of the unmarried, thirty-three-year-old Fuller. Though in Europe the institution of marriage was in what Fourier termed "a transition state," in New England, notes Fuller, traditional marriage is so expected of women that any woman who does not marry is contemptuously called "old maid."[15]

On the subject of marriage, Fuller differed radically with Emerson, who did not accept the bourgeois romance of marriage that a man and a woman in love can marry and be happy ever after. He believed, instead, in the Hebraic idea that marriage is an institution meant for the perpetuation of the family and society. "In these twilights of the gods," he wrote in his journal, "[we need] all the conventions of the most regulated life," and he predicted that the "least departure from the usage of Marriage would bring too strong a tide . . . for so weak a reed as modern love to withstand."[16]

Fuller, however, wanted an apocalypse on earth of perfect communion between two free people who desired to be together in a "holy" union. She argued this view in her essay even as in May 1843, at the time she was writing it, she knew how far short the reality of marriage fell from her ideal of it. Her sister, Ellen, had shocked both her and her mother by marrying the poet Ellery Channing, whom Margaret thought unstable, shortly after announcing her engagement to him in early September 1841. Predictably, within a year the marriage was in trouble. Even in the more seasoned Emerson marriage there were signs of tension. Fuller had spent enough time with the couple to know that Lidian held onto "a lurking hope" that someday her husband would "be capable of an intimate union." However, Fuller's 1842 visit had "convinced" her that it would "never be more perfect between them two"—any more than it would be more perfect between her sister and Ellery, or between ever so many husbands and their wives. The latter seemed always to be despairing of their husbands' failure to care for them adequately.[17]

Fuller argues that if woman was given broader scope for her talents and intelligence, if she was allowed to become a "thinking" being, then she would not be "perverted" into believing "that she must marry," if "only to find a protector, and a home of her own." Woman seen as a soul that needs to be "brought out towards perfection" would be, she says, man's "fellow pilgrim."[18]

Four kinds of marriage embody Fuller's idea of equality, the highest being a "religious" union, where woman is not "led" by her husband "as a father"—a point she stresses—but looked on as a "sister and friend." Unlike in Bunyan's *Pilgrim's*

Progress, where Christian with "a great burden upon his back" sets out on his journey to the Celestial City leaving his wife and children behind, in Fuller's ideal "religious" marriage, a man and woman take a "pilgrimage" together "towards a common shrine." In alluding to Bunyan's Christian allegory, Fuller, however, seems to have ignored that in the context of a patriarchal nineteenth-century New England culture, a church-sanctioned Christian marriage was not seen as a union of equals. In such a marriage a wife was seen as an extension of her husband and was expected to obey him as the Bible dictates, just as men still ran the churches and synagogues and believed that their power derived ultimately from God, the father. Indeed, few people in Fuller's predominantly Christian culture questioned the role of the husband as his wife's "lord" and master. Thus even as Fuller envisioned marriage as a union of legally equal people, by depicting it as a "religious pilgrimage" she ironically pointed women back on life's path to a position of subordination not only in marriage to their husbands but also in their religion to their priests, pastors, rabbis—the latter having been invested by the state with the power and authority to create the civil bond even as they solemnized the sacred one.[19]

Though Fuller sees the ideal marriage as a religious pilgrimage undertaken by a woman and man who are equal, she nonetheless acknowledges the need for a couple to form a "household partnership," since "these pilgrims must . . . assist one another to carry their burdens." Here again, however, Fuller reveals her indebtedness to Judeo-Christian religious concepts and patterns of thinking, for her words echo those appearing in *Pilgrim's Progress* and also in Psalms 38:4, "as an heavy burden [mine iniquities] are too heavy for me."[20]

Her conflicted response to cultural mores and religion owes something, as we know, to her father. At age nine, we recall, she had read letters to her mother from Timothy in which he had both praised Mary Wollstonecraft for having written *A Vindication of the Rights of Woman* and damned her for her out-of-wedlock sex with Gilbert Imlay, a man she refused to marry after bearing a child by him. In her *Dial* essay Margaret shared his disapproval, calling Wollstonecraft's personal past "repulsive." Sounding eerily like her father, Margaret on this subject was adamant: women who wish to reform the world must be models of morally righteous behavior; "their lives must be unstained by passionate error; they must be severe lawgivers to themselves." When women like Wollstonecraft fall, says Margaret, unwittingly damning herself like Oedipus, "society is in the right to outlaw them."[21]

Unlike her father, however, Fuller praises William Godwin's courage in loving—and marrying—a woman whose personal past was so sullied. She sees this "good fact" as a "sign of a new era." Just as she does the fact that even the scandalous Sand in her novel "*La Roche Mauprat*" depicts a man "raised" by love for a "pure object" from "the depths of savage sensualism to a moral and intellectual life." Despite both women's sullied pasts, Fuller feels she can praise these defiant female writers who did not "steer straight" in life but instead took the path that society sees as crooked and hence will never, she says, remove "the brand it has set upon them."[22]

The fact that women like Wollstonecraft and Sand were able to gain a public platform Fuller sees as another sign foretelling the "future heaven" she believes that men and women will soon create together on earth. One problem she foresees for women, however, is how they are to go about getting and then keeping such a platform. Wollstonecraft was lucky to have had Godwin, a man who supported her not as a father but "like a brother"—a distinction Fuller frequently repeats.[23] Fuller sees a better way for women to gain a public platform than by relying on men: by becoming educated. They should be taught, however, not by a male teacher, who would merely perpetuate the myth of women's inferiority to men, but by a woman. Preferably this teacher should be an unmarried "thinking" woman, since, like the saints and sibyls, an unattached "thinking" woman can maintain "a closer communion with the One" and act as an "intellectual interpreter" of her times, the role Fuller sees herself as now playing.[24]

Indeed, just as Fuller felt she had communed with "the One" during her mystical rebirth, so she believed the great spirit had "visited" Mother Anne Lee, founder of the Shaker sect in the United States; Joanna Southcote, a Devonshire servant who believed she was pregnant with the second Messiah and inspired a cult of working women; and the Seeress of Prevorst. Fuller calls the last "the best observed subject of magnetism in our times, and who, like her ancestresses at Delphos, was roused to ecstacy or phrenzy by the touch of the laurel." Fuller herself felt ecstatic when writing, as if there was flowing through her the kind of electrical energies praised by the prophets of "Magnetism, or Mesmerism"—"occult" energies Emerson had mocked as "merely physiological" in his 1839 "Demonology" lecture.[25]

In that lecture Emerson had defined "the demoniacal" as a force "without virtue" that can be found in "popular religious creeds" and political movements. Yet it was precisely mesmerism's tendency to imbue "psychological ideas with an aura of ultimacy" that drew American spiritual seekers like Fuller to it and made them feel they had found a way to make "nonphysical communication" with the "One." Passionate women like Fuller—women given to falling into mysterious trancelike states when responding to the "physical gestures" of a "dominating male"—were drawn to phenomena like mesmerism. Fuller notes that "the trance of the Ecstatica purports to be produced by the agency of one human being on another, instead of . . . direct from the spirit." Worldlings "sneer," she says, at women's talk of "magnetic states," as had Emerson, who had decried this force as "Mother power."[26]

Fuller thus in "The Great Lawsuit" seems deliberately to have been responding to Emerson when she wrote that woman's power lies in her ability to come in touch with this flowing magnetic force, a psychospiritual energy she saw as unique to women. Ironically, European mesmerists—men like Collyer, whose Boston lectures in 1837 were the talk of the town, and the Frenchman Charles Poyen, who had lectured in New England the year before—never thought of this magnetic energy as supernatural. Not until they were in the States did they comprehend the depth of Americans' spiritualist yearnings, a need Collyer satirizes in his 1838 pamphlet *Lights and Shadows of American Life*.[27]

Of course, near the century's end, as we have noted, this seeming substratum of psychic energy would provide a field of study for scientifically oriented psychologists and psychiatrists. This enigmatic energy, and with it the power one individual seems mysteriously to exert over another, would lead men like Jean-Martin Charcot, Josef Breuer, Pierre Janet, and finally Freud to the foundations of dynamic psychiatry and to their articulation of a view quite at odds with Fuller's belief: that at the deepest levels of man's (and woman's) subjective lives lie, not the energies of the "Most High," but, as Emerson suspected, primal cravings that predate our social conditioning. Aware of how little she really knows on the subject, Fuller says merely that the "electrical, the magnetic element in woman, has not been fairly developed at any period." Yet, everything, she believes, "might be expected from it; she has far more of it than man."[28]

Fuller suggests that it is precisely because women are more directly connected to Mother Earth and hence to the core of this kinetic energy that they have the power to heal the rift that exists between mankind and nature. Their closeness to this seat of power gives them the power to reestablish in the now-discordant spheres that celestial harmony about which Mesmer had written. Yet it is not women in general, says Fuller, who will make this new world happen, but rather *American* women. For they are not as tied to social and cultural traditions as are women who live in older cultures.

Moreover, not all American women have the capacity to make this new era happen. That Fuller sees herself as the "new teacher" who will guide women to self-insight, self-impulse, and self-reliance is evident in that she thinks this "Ideal" woman should be able, if the male parent dies, to serve as "father to the children," as Margaret had served her younger siblings after Timothy died. Moreover, says Fuller, the new teacher must be a virgin, since a married female in Puritan America legally belongs to her husband, instead of "forming a whole with him."[29]

Assuming the role of that being of "purer blood" whom she had called for at the essay's outset to redeem fallen men, Fuller then instructs women about their special genius, the complexity of gender, and the process of self-reformation they must undergo if they wish to be reborn as pure souls capable of redeeming men. Drawing again from the mesmerists, Fuller describes the "especial genius of woman" as being "electrical in movement, intuitive in function, spiritual in tendency." Like the flowing universal substance mesmerists called animal magnetism, that which is feminine, she proclaims, "pervades like air and water all this seeming solid globe," renewing it and—as Christ did in his time—"purifying its life."[30]

Fuller then makes an assertion about gender that may have unsettled her con-

---

servative readers but that was common in literature she had read from Plato to Sand and familiar to her from her own life: gender is not rigidly set but fluid. For while male and female, she says, represent the "two sides of the great radical dualism," these two sides are "perpetually passing into one another": "Fluid hardens to solid, solid rushes to fluid. There is no wholly masculine man, no purely feminine woman."[31]

As Fuller sees it, it ought not to matter in what form the soul appears on earth. For each soul should equally have the right to acquire a sense of "religious self-dependence." And how does a woman free herself from dependence on men and the patriarchal religious establishment? Fuller here advocates "celibacy" as the way for women to gain control over their bodies and hence spiritual independence. Like an Orphic from ancient times who sought through sexual purity to attain union with God, Fuller wants women not only to refrain from having sex with men but also to strip themselves of all limiting definitions of the feminine that have been imposed on them by men. To accomplish the latter she advocates that American women, like the pagans who took part in ancient mystery rites, explore what Fuller calls "the groundwork of being" until they have attained a "religious" vision like the one Fuller experienced in her great religious crisis when it seemed to her that nothing and no one—not Christ, not Moses, not even the saintly Emerson—stood between her and the Almighty.[32]

The crux of Fuller's argument in "The Great Lawsuit" is thus this: If women were allowed by men to investigate that "misunderstood" region from which emanates the power that propels the soul, that region in myth over which Persephone reigns, then they could use their newly acquired self-insight and wisdom to help men see that the right relation between the sexes is not that of father over daughter. Indeed, though she concedes that fathers, when they are "leading a little girl by the hand," *seem* "refined to the eye," this relationship, she says, is invariably distorted by the "perverted mind." The kind of relationship she hopes will prevail between men and women in the new heaven on earth is that of brother to sister.[33]

At her essay's end Fuller affirms a position that was, in the context of her nineteenth-century New England culture, far more radical than that forwarded by Emerson, who wrote and spoke in behalf only of men's soul liberty. Fuller contends that: *only* when a woman can establish a sense of "religious self-dependence"— that is, *only* when she can free herself from the restrictions of the father-oriented Judeo-Christian religious tradition—will she be able to live in harmonious relation to the genderless central soul and hence be truly free.[34]

And what, then, of marriage, of her vision of husbands and wives as "fellow pilgrims"? Until women have attained religious self-dependence, she argues, they should not marry. Playing on Virgil's damning of Dido in the *Aeneid* for calling her out-of-wedlock sexual connection with Aeneas "marriage," Fuller contends that it "is the very fault of marriage"—not, as the Hebrews claimed, "the fault of a woman"—that women are so dependent on men and let love define their "whole existence": "It is a vulgar error that love, *a* love to woman is her whole existence; she also is born for Truth and Love in their universal energy."[35]

Only after women have explored the groundwork of being, only after they have tapped this gender-free core of power and converted their "material" energies into spiritual vision will women, according to Fuller, be able to turn their soul's "dross"—debris from the storms of earthly passion—"to gold." Only then, she believes, will women be able to redeem men and bring peace to a world now in chaos and disarray.[36]

Merging the biblical vision of a Second Coming with Mesmer's of the "harmony" to be "established between the astral plane and the human plane" once animal magnetism's "two-fold stream" flows unimpeded, Fuller asserts near her essay's end that "the divine" on earth "shall reappear" and that this time it will be in the female form of the "Muse, or Ceres, the all-kindly, patient Earth-Spirit." "Then," prophesies Fuller, a woman's "sweet singing shall not be from passionate impulse," as she felt hers had too often been, but from "the lyrical overflow of a divine rapture, and a new music shall be elucidated from this many-chorded world."[37]

30 ∞ Contradictory Wishes and Dreams

As Fuller was finishing "The Great Lawsuit," she wrote Emerson telling him about a "really good book" on her desk: Andreas Justinus Kerner's account of the case of the mystic Friederike Hauffe. In her letter she scolds Emerson for having said in his 29 April letter to her about the birth of the Wards' baby girl, "though no son, yet a sacred event": "Why is not the advent of a daughter as 'sacred' a fact as that of a son. I do believe, O Waldo, most unteachable of men, that you are a sinner on this point."[1]

A good-natured Emerson in July replied: "'The Great Lawsuit' is felt by all to be a piece of life." He notes that it had even pleased Thoreau, who had called it "a noble piece, . . . talking with pen in hand."[2] Despite Emerson's praise, in his journal at this time he recorded his thoughts on the danger to the stability of American society of altering an iota the conventional structure of marriage, where wives were viewed as subsidiaries to their husbands and as keepers of the cradle.

But Emerson was not the only one full of contradictions. In her essay Fuller had argued that if all humans—black and white, man and woman—are souls appareled in flesh, then all are accountable "to one master only." In this assertion wherein Fuller extends to women and blacks the human rights attributed to "all men" in the Declaration of Independence, Fuller reveals the paradox of her position.[3]

In it Fuller both demands freedom as a woman independent of man and concedes dependence on a being she calls "master." Here she means Jesus, the reference being to Matthew 6:24: "No one can serve two masters." However, in a

March 1838 letter to Emerson from Providence, she had alluded to the same verse when, in comparing Emerson as her "master" to the president of Brown University, she had said: "I cannot serve two masters." In yet another letter, one she will write on 25 November 1843 to a fantasized Beethoven, she calls the dead composer her "blessed Master" and then confesses to him that she has "not been true" to her destiny and hence has "suffered" "the pangs of despised love." Not the sweet Jesus, not golden Plato, not even Shakespeare, she says, compares with Beethoven, this apparent fantasy stand-in for the man she perceives as her real master, her father, whom she feels now ready she says, in words resonant with submission, to "receive . . . wholly." Then adds: "Oh, if thou wouldst take me wholly to thyself."[4]

This letter represents a fantasy self-surrender to an omnipotent father figure that sadly annihilates Fuller's "I" as the independent, active agent she had argued in "The Great Lawsuit" is woman's "right" to be. Fuller boasts in this fantasy letter that it is *her* "triumph" that she "can understand." But she also begs Beethoven's forgiveness for loving "them who cannot love me" and says she knows it is not her "fault" that conflict in her does not always induce creativity. Despite these flaws, asserts Fuller to this ideal father, "I am worthy audience for thee."[5]

Two years earlier in a note Fuller had written Emerson, she confessed how much she likes to be in his library when he is not. In her note she depicts Emerson's library as a chapel where she can go to pray in the same way that her father's book closet had seemed an oratory to her as a child. She says she had gone that night to his library so she might feel Emerson's "life come to me" and thus feel "worthy to sleep." Here she seeks his blessing in the way that the disciples let Jesus' "peace" descend upon a person they deemed "worthy" of their master's blessing, or as the father blessed his prodigal son who had proved himself "worthy" of his father's love. Fuller's language here, as well as in other letters where she asserts her aim to be "worthy" of Emerson's friendship, reflects the imprint of biblical vision on her: it reveals her acculturated sense that women by nature are inferior to men. This acquired view is evident in the contrast between her conscious chiding of Emerson for not seeing a daughter's birth as equal to that of a son and her praying to a fantasy Beethoven that this worshipped icon might "give me a son of mine own."[6]

No matter how ardently Fuller had argued the equality of men and women, she still harbored doubts about her worthiness in the eyes not only of Emerson but also of her dead father, who still always seemed to be watching. This conflict between her desire as a woman to be free of her "lord and tutor" father and her contradictory wish as a child to please him appears in "The Great Lawsuit" as the conversation between herself as narrator and Miranda, in whose figure Fuller says she "proudly painted" her ideal self. Miranda attributes her "faith and self-respect" to her father, who believed in the "equality of the sexes" and who, insofar "as he possessed the keys to the wonders of this universe," allowed Miranda free use of them. Thanks to her father's high expectations, Miranda, who lacked feminine charm, was able to take "her place" in "the world of [the] mind." To her "good father's early trust," Fuller-Miranda hence attributes her sense of self-dependence.[7]

To this ideal image of her father, to him whose "image" lived in her, Fuller paid homage in words that reveal her continuing bondage to a haunting, godlike man, her reluctance to see the dead father as flawed. In so doing she exposes her unconscious subjugation to the same social, religious, and legal laws that she questions in both her essay and later feminist tract, *Woman in the Nineteenth Century*. In Miranda, Fuller thus created a paper self free of inner conflict and troubling sexual urges, just as in the father she created a one-dimensional figure who, totally unlike Timothy, "cherished no sentimental reverence for woman," a glorified parent entirely happy with his unattractive, intellectual daughter. In offering her reader as models these figures purged of their humanity and pain, Fuller evaded confronting the cause of her anxiety, her contradictory wish to be both man's sister and equal *and* his dutiful yet desirable daughter, an obedient child whom the seeming "good" father leads lovingly "by the hand."[8]

In both essay and tract, Fuller avoids discussing the emotional turmoil and social pressures actually experienced by women like Wollstonecraft and Sand when she implies that both irreparably stained their lives by failing to control their sexual impulses. In these works, Fuller will go so far as to argue that the lives of revolutionary leaders who would "reform the world" must be "unstained by passionate error," and that those who break the laws should be deemed outlaws. She argues this even as she acknowledges that the laws must be altered so that "beings as these" will not "find themselves by birth in a place so narrow, that in breaking bonds they become outlaws." In conceding that the laws must be altered to be more tolerant of women whom society has deemed to be sexually wayward, Fuller revealed her own underlying uneasiness about her millennialist vision that the world can in fact be "redeemed" by celibate, educated women. Regardless of the strength of her utopian longings, a realistic side of herself had doubts about the capacity of imperfect people—whatever their race, religion, or gender—to carry out idealistic revolutionary programs.[9]

31 ∽ Pilgrims and Prodigals

Like her Christian ancestors, Fuller saw her life as a pilgrimage from innocence, through the valley of sin and death, to the "hill-prospect," where, by way of "wise" self-control, she would be able, as she had written William Henry Channing in 1840, to "bring the lowest act" of her life "into sympathy" with her "highest thought." Yet Fuller's life journey, as James Clarke said, was only "almost Christian." Impatient with the image of a suffering Jesus on the cross, Fuller thought religion should make her more aware, not of suffering, which she felt she knew too well, but of "unceasing revelation," of a never-ending sense of harmony between herself and the celestial spheres. She felt especially frustrated with Christianity's failure to put women "on a par" with men, to see them as men's fellow pilgrims.[1]

For images of powerful female divinities, Fuller had turned to the mythical figures of Minerva and Isis, of Ceres and Proserpina, as well as of other forms in which the ancients embodied their idea of the divine in woman. One mythical figure she found appealing but did not mention in her essay was that of the human Psyche. To the dismay of the clergymen who attended her 1841 Conversations, she had interpreted Psyche's journey from hardship to divinity as "the pilgrimage of a soul," a "story of redemption."[2]

In *The Golden Ass,* which Fuller had read, Apuleius tells how Psyche's beauty is so radiant that no man will marry her. Despite the machinations and interventions of her parents and various gods, someone does indeed fall in love with her: Cupid (Eros). Cupid rescues her after her parents, obeying the oracle's command, abandon her on a mountaintop where she is to await her future husband, whom she fears is death (Thanatos). Psyche and he then become lovers, but their love seems doomed. Having failed to respect Cupid's request to love him nightly without trying to see him, she loses Cupid whereupon she throws herself into a river, whose waters carry her to shore. Only after many obstacles are surmounted, and Psyche appeals to Venus for help, does the myth end happily with Psyche and Cupid married. This story of how mortal intellect and divine love persevere through disunion and hardship until they are united gave Fuller one model for marriage as a "pilgrimage towards a common shrine" that she praises in "The Great Lawsuit." It also gave her a memorable way to describe, as she had put it in her 1841 "Goethe" essay, "the progress of a soul through the various forms of existence." In the pattern of Romantics, who tend to figure the spirit in maternal terms, Goethe, says Fuller in her essay, "always represents the highest principle in the feminine form," as he does in *Wilhelm Meister.* In discussing Wilhelm Meister's "Wandering Years" in *Woman in the Nineteenth Century* and in her essay "Goethe," Fuller will develop her theme about how the soul on its life journey progresses upwards. She will note how Wilhelm, as he "advances" on his "upward path," becomes acquainted with "better forms of woman." The highest of these, she says in her essay, is Macaria, form of divine Philosophy, who crowns "the faithful Seeker at last with the privilege to possess his own soul."[3]

In *Woman* Fuller will celebrate Macaria as "the centre of all relations," as "a pure and perfected intelligence," indeed as the kind of woman Fuller aspired to be. Goethe, she says, called this highest feminine principle Macaria because this daughter of Hercules had "offered herself as a victim for the good of her country" and was worshipped by the Greeks "as the Goddess of true Felicity." In Macaria, Goethe "embodied this Felicity as the Serenity that arises from Wisdom."[4]

In her own pilgrimage, Fuller imaginatively merged the pattern in the writings of Romantics like Wieland, Wordsworth, and Goethe with her female quest as a modern-day Psyche in search of love, truth, and wisdom. Like Wordsworth Fuller saw herself as a traveler whose tale was of herself. Thus even though Fuller identified with feminine forms like Psyche and Minerva, in her quest she tended to follow the circuitous route traveled by male Romantic protagonists. This pattern was so deeply ingrained in her that her desire to follow it was, to some extent, beyond her conscious intent or control. It had been ingrained in her as a child when her family each Sunday read together from the Bible: Old Testament stories about exiled wanderers, or that in the New Testament about the prodigal son, who took his inheritance and journeyed to a far country, where he squandered his property in loose living and then, "when he came to himself," returned home. There, he humbled himself before his father, saying he was no longer "worthy" to be the son of his father, who nonetheless joyously received him and thanked the Lord for the return of this boy who "was dead, and is alive again," who "was lost, and is found."[5]

Throughout her life Fuller repeatedly alluded to the story of the prodigal son. We notice it in a letter to Arthur where she had referred to their difficult younger brother Lloyd as "our prodigal son." It appears on page one of *Woman in the Nineteenth Century* and elsewhere throughout her writings, the most poignant mention of it being in a December 1843 letter to Anna Barker wherein she compares the tragic exodus from home of her mother's beloved only brother to that of a prodigal who was lost and never returned. From this parable many Romantic writers derived their own psychologically oriented account of "the fall" of man from an original sense of unity with nature, into self-conscious awareness of the self as a subject separate from the world, to redemption through harmonious reconciliation with the feminine figure (as nature, wife, or loving mother), a redemption made possible (so Romantics like Wordsworth believed) by the active imagination.[6]

For Fuller, however, the story presented problems. For one thing, in the case of her mother's brother, Peter, this (as Fuller refers to him) "wandering son" who left one day from the family farm, reality did not live up to fiction: the son did not come home. For another thing, the biblical prodigal is male, as it similarly is in Romantic appropriations of the wayward soul motif. Such include works that meant a lot to Fuller—Wieland's *Oberon,* Goethe's *Wilhelm Meister,* and even *The Prelude,* where Wordsworth tells of his return after years of questing to the hill country he had loved as a child. There he lives in harmony—not with his father and brothers—but with nature, wife, and sister. In the Judeo-Christian tradition Fuller was heir to, this journey was not meant to have been undertaken by a female, and the figure who awaits the wanderer's return is the father. However, in the case of Fuller's Uncle Peter, as in Romantic renderings of this familiar story, it was Margaret's loving grandmother who awaited the return of her prodigal son.

Still, the wandering son was the role with which Fuller most closely identified through life. As an emotional woman playing a malelike part in public, she had encountered failures and misunderstandings in her attempt to win love and recognition from others, as her offer of "pure" love had been "sneered" at by Emerson, who saw her religion as "tainted" with "mysticism."[7]

On the subject of mysticism, Emerson and Fuller continued to differ. Fuller felt that in writing "The Great Lawsuit"—wherein she praises magnetism, mesmerism, and mysticism—she had effectively demonstrated her ability to convert her "mystical" energies into creative effort. As she wrote she felt alive with an electric-like energy, "the presence" in her of special "unseen powers." These powers she continued to associate with the occult: with her gems, her stones, her flowers, as well as with the animal magnetism that seemed to flow from her whenever she wrote. She felt these powers to exist in her as she packed to set out in late May 1843 for the Great Lakes region with James Freeman Clarke; his sister, Sarah; and their mother, Rebecca Hull Clarke. James was to escort the women to Buffalo. In Chicago, Sarah and Margaret were then to meet Sarah's brother, William. To her delight, Fuller discovered that William shared her interest in mysticism.[8]

Fuller's dawning knowledge of her power, of a magnetic energy she felt forced to repress in the Northeast, generated an anxiety she hoped to overcome by leaving New England and finding a place where society's laws were more tolerant of passionate women like herself. With Uncle Peter's blood in her veins, Fuller had felt a need to see if elsewhere in America she might find a place where she could be, as she put it, "truly human."[9]

∽ ∽ ∽

Fuller's trip began with a late May visit to Niagara Falls, which she first glimpsed on a bitter cold day "under lowering skies with few fitful gleams of light." As planned, in Buffalo James parted ways with Sarah and Margaret, as did Mrs. Clarke. The two young women boarded a steamer that wended its way through the Great Lakes region to Chicago, where they were joined by William, who made Margaret's "pilgrimage in Illinois" some of the happiest hours of her life. The three traveled together in a covered, horse-drawn lumber wagon that left them free to wander. William was able to take the team off the path into fields and woods, where they idled while Sarah and Margaret gathered flowers. As he maneuvered the wagon through mud holes and creeks, William charmed Margaret by noting "the habits of all the fowl, and fish, and growing things, and all the warlike legends of the country."[10]

Once back in Chicago, Sarah and Margaret set out again, this time in a carriage with a "regular coachman" to spend a fortnight in the territory of Wisconsin. As they toured, Fuller was touched by the sight of wandering Indian tribes that had been forced to abandon their native lands east of the Mississippi as a result of the Indian Removal Policy inaugurated by the U.S. government in 1830. She had wanted to help the displaced Indians she had seen camping along Silver Lake, the remnant of a tribe that had returned to the fertile lakes region from which the white man had driven them. She felt for these homeless natives, just as she did for the Scandinavian immigrants she had seen near Milwaukee: people all "seeking a home." The latter group, she said, had come to America with "golden dreams" of riches but had found instead backbreaking labor, penury, and the deaths of children. One young Swedish mother with an injured husband had buried her first child with her own hands.[11]

Having witnessed the hardships of the wandering Indians and immigrants, Fuller recorded some of the memorable and evocative encounters from her trip. During an August visit to the campsite of a fragmented tribe, a violent thunderstorm had come up. Crouched at the mouth of a tent belonging to a family group of this "extremely destitute" Potawatomi tribe was a beautiful, "wild-eyed boy" who was "perfectly naked" except for the large gold bracelet he wore on his arm. From the mouth of the tent in which she had sought shelter, Fuller could see out through the sheets of rain to where the Indians' horses, excited by the claps of thunder, were wildly careening among the trees. She saw an old Indian out in the pouring rain, his arms folded and eyes uplifted to the storm-blackened sky. As rain slashed the earth in sheets and lightning flashed above him, he stood unfazed, gazing upward, the hard rain pelting his weathered face and unprotected body.[12]

Fuller also told of a farmer's tale of an Indian he had seen standing on the brow of a hill, "with folded arms, surveying the old home, over whose soil the tent poles [were] still scattered." The speaker, the new owner of the land, confessed to her that he had been "*somewhat* moved by the melancholy" of the Indian's look, which disappeared the instant he sensed the farmer was watching him. The Indian "started, snorted out an angry *hui*, turned on his heel, and stalked away." Fuller understood the Indian's anger as he surveyed a land he could no longer call home. Writing about it later in *Summer on the Lakes*, she wondered how he could "forbear to shoot the white man where he stands."[13]

Fuller had been disappointed with Chicago, where all the men, it seemed, worked for money, and the women, she had written Emerson in June, "belong to the men." "I am silenced by these people," she wrote him again from Chicago in August; "they are so all life and no thought" that "Truly there is no place for me to live." She liked neither "the petty intellectualities, cant, and bloodless theory" of the Harvard crowd in Cambridge, nor the "merely instinctive existence" of the rough men she had met in her travels. She had not "reached forth" her "hand" to them, nor had any been extended to her. To Channing now she sadly said, "My friend, I am deeply homesick, yet where is that home?"[14]

32 ∞ Discordant Energies

On her way home from Chicago, Fuller stopped to visit William Channing in New York, where he was a minister and leading social activist. Channing introduced her to his friends, including Horace Greeley, the progressive editor of the *New-York Daily Tribune*. Back in Cambridge by September, Fuller, between migraines, prepared for her fifth round of Conversation classes; the first of twenty-four sessions was to meet at eleven on the morning of November 16 at Elizabeth Peabody's place in downtown Boston. She also gathered materials for a Washington Irving–like sketchbook, her memoir of her "summer's wanderings," *Summer on the Lakes, in 1843*. Along with sketches of places she had visited, she hoped to capture in writing those moments in nature when, as Wordsworth put it, "the light of sense / Goes out, but with a flash that has revealed / The invisible world."[1]

Yet as she wrote, Fuller found herself focusing less on divine moments in nature than on scenes conveying the discord she experienced in trying to relate to the raw, new world around her. She had meant, for instance, to experience a moment of transcendence at Niagara Falls but was filled instead with a sense of dread, of uncanny fear that "naked savages" were creeping up on her "with uplifted tomahawks," so she kept starting and looking behind her. She had felt the same fear as a child at night when the light had been taken away and she was left alone with visions of detached heads coming at her through the dark. Her current fear may have been fed by tomahawk marks she had seen on felled trees in Illinois. Perhaps Fuller's fear of being scalped stemmed in part from her ability to identify with the rage of these displaced people who had been driven from their home by invading white men. These white men, wrote Fuller, had grown to loathe the Indian on whom they had encroached, "the aversion of the injurer for him he has degraded."[2]

Like the displaced Indians, Fuller felt a stranger in her native land, captive in a culture that prevented her from singing freely and also imprisoned her soul, it seemed, in collarets, corsets, and cumbersome crinolines. Eager to merge with Mother Nature, Fuller at Niagara Falls had seated herself on Table Rock, close to the great fall. Dressed perhaps in her cambric-lined and corseted black mousseline dress—her folding eyeglass pressed to her nearsighted eyes—Fuller says she was still hoping to lose all consciousness of herself in the spectacular sights and sounds of the cascading falls when she was interrupted by a tourist. He had come, he told her, "to take his first look," then, "spat into it."[3]

As Fuller sat at her writing desk and looked out to the river, it occurred to her that, though she had meant to imitate Irving, her story was in fact not at all like his. No gentleman of leisure, Fuller was a comparatively poor female intellect, though one gaining respect in New England as a writer. She had even been given permission—the first woman ever—to use Harvard's library for research.[4] Still, try as she did to write like Irving, Fuller's pen would not comply.

The style and content of *Summer on the Lakes* reveal how out of sync she felt with the literary conventions of her time. For instance, she had not been moved by the sight of the great falls but had instead felt most alive when she crossed the frail bridge to Goat Island. From the middle of the river she could see about a quarter mile of tumbling, rushing rapids and hear the roar of the waters sweeping beneath her feet. It occurred to Fuller then how often she had felt "most moved in the wrong place." Early in *Summer on the Lakes* she mentions such a moment of disjunction when she tells about a chained eagle with a broken wing she had seen in the Niagara area. Unlike Wordsworth, who had visited childhood scenes to arouse slumbering feelings of wonder, Fuller had recalled how sad she had felt as a child when she saw a similar eagle "chained in the balcony of a museum" and people poking sticks at it. It had occurred to her even then that this "monarch-bird" ought to have been riding a "panoply of sunset"—like the wild eagle she reports she had recently seen striding the streaked evening sky high above the "White Mountains."[5]

The chained eagle at Niagara had stirred in her memories—not of a happy past—but instead of how she had been mocked by her Groton classmates, girls who could not see that, beneath her blighted exterior, wings were budding by which her soul would someday fly to heaven. So susceptible was Fuller to the symbolic meaning of wings that when she found a dead bird beneath her window that June of 1844, after she had finished writing *Summer on the Lakes,* she grieved for it, then cut off its wings to keep them. Fuller saw herself in the chained yet majestic eagle.[6]

The yearning to break free of her chains and to fly like an eagle above the fray was constantly in Fuller's heart. She had felt this yearning in seeing the eagle flying high above the mountains and in staring at a body of water. She feared that the water's "undulatory motions"—"of all earthly things most lovely"—might yet seduce her, she had earlier said, "from humanity."[7]

This wish to break free and to bury her troubles in the "*winning gentleness*" of feminine waters was present in Fuller as she worked on her book. She was conscious of this undercurrent of yearning in her, a longing that always brought to mind an image of a loved one. Sometimes it was Sam. At others it was Anna, or Emerson, and, now, in the spring of 1844, she was thinking frequently about William Clarke, whose friendship she had enjoyed in Illinois and with whom she had hoped to form a love relationship. But her relationship with this younger man, who, like her, enjoyed attaining trancelike states, had come to nothing, a fact she lamented in a 1 May journal entry. She had gone with Sarah and William to greet the Emersons in Concord, after which she had accompanied them to a late afternoon tea at the Concord home of Ellen and Ellery. During these visits William had ignored her. His indifference had heightened her sense of alienation from her friends, especially that night as they rode home in a carriage. Her hurt highlighted with clarity "the white horses shimmering in the moonlight" as they galloped through the darkening woods. The night wind lifted loosened strands of her hair and the pale moon waded in thin clouds while Fuller, her face hidden in the shadows, "wept and sobbed most of the way."[8]

With the intellect she knew she could always overcome but that is not, she thought, but half of the work. "The life, the life Oh my God!" she wrote in her journal at this time, "shall the life *never* be sweet!"[9]

Though such moments of depression still came, Fuller nonetheless sensed that this was an important era in her life. She wrote in her journal on her birthday in May 1844 that she would publish *Summer on the Lakes* and then deal with the critics, who would, she knew, "abuse it." Reflecting on her childhood, a week later she noted that since there was no real way to make peace with "the Past," she would do her best to deal with the present.[10]

And so as she wrote that spring, Fuller surrounded herself with outward emblems of her inward struggle. Anchoring her to the earth, she kept on her desk a bouquet of fresh-cut flowers, and she tuned her ear to the wistful song of a yellow bird that had perched in an apple tree outside her window. Opposite her she had hung a color drawing of Del Sarto's *Madonna,* reminding her of how important it was for her to maintain her virgin purity. As a reminder of her penchant for errant passion, she had placed behind her a framed picture of Silenus holding the infant Pan, the satyr god of shepherds and flocks. Father of the satyrs, Silenus was a nature demon whose upper torso was that of a man and whose bottom half that of a goat or horse. The beast had a long thick tail and a large male organ, emblematic of its bestial nature. Like his lecherous progeny, Silenus served Dionysus, the god he had raised and whom the Maenads worshipped in wild dances that made them feel they had been purged of their carnal cravings.[11]

Images suggesting a feminine cleansing of the body's physical cravings appear in the journal Fuller kept when in Cambridge, where she was content, she said, with her pen, her bouquet, her yellow birds, and Cary. The latter had kept Margaret company for a fortnight in June when Mrs. Fuller went to Concord to help Ellen with her new baby, Margaret Fuller Channing, who had been born on 23 May, Margaret's birthday. Fuller's journal suggests that she and Cary have made their peace. She tells how Cary had come to her room on a calm June night while she lay resting on her bed in the twilight. Cary "came and lay there with her head on my bosom." "We talked till one," she says. Then Cary went to her room, and Fuller sat alone at her window. Fuller confesses that at that moment she felt stronger "for the future: clearness seemed dawning on my mind." "O God," she prays, "ground me more deeply in reality."[12]

33 ⌘ Mesmerism and Romantic Yearning in *Summer on the Lakes*

In *Summer on the Lakes, in 1843,* Fuller included the stories of two women who sought to escape an intolerable reality: the nineteenth-century German mystic Friederike Hauffe, Seeress of Prevorst, and the fictional Mariana, the rebellious boarding-school student whom Fuller modeled on herself. Into the narcissistic Mariana, Fuller projected the "me" that desired "a godlike embrace from some sufficient love," a remark that appears in her July 1844 journal. In a June letter to Channing she confesses that though her friends could see her as Miranda in "The Great Lawsuit," none dreamed that Mariana was also "like me." In this sentimental tale of romantic yearning, Mariana, whom Fuller calls "the returning prodigal," returns home from school and marries Sylvain, a name that Fuller took from an Austrian dancer, yet that suggests an ancient divinity of the woods, Silvanus. The Romans identified him with Pan, who had been endowed with so much sexual energy that he pursued boys and nymphs with equal ardor. We recall that Fuller kept near her as she wrote a drawing of the infant Pan in Silenus's arms.[1]

In the story Mariana worships Sylvain, who does not share her intellectual interests. Mariana yearns for a more soulful communion with this man who sees his home as a place for "indolent repose" after having enjoyed "affairs of pleasure" in society. His desire for peace at home clashes with Mariana's consuming desire to find a soul mate; it drives him to prefer society's "careless . . . dames" to his wife, whose Cassandra-like passion, says the narrator, "overpowered" him. From the narrator's perspective, Mariana's "repression" of her "powers" destroyed her health; for want of love, she died.[2]

In this story wherein Fuller embodies herself in the love-hungry, self-destructive Mariana, she includes her poem "Disappointment." In it Fuller depicts Mariana as one of the "sad outcasts" from the "prize" of life awarded those who have been "wholly loved" as infants. Unlike the blest "Babe" of Wordsworth's *Prelude,* who "Drinks in the feelings of his Mother's eye!," those like Mariana who have been deprived of love in childhood are doomed as adults to wander homeless until they die. Such women, says Fuller, "By father's love were ne'er caressed, / Nor in a mother's eye saw heaven." "Father," cries the speaker, "they will not take me home, / To the poor child no heart is free; / In sleet and snow all night I roam; / Father,—was this decreed by thee?"[3]

Fuller's poetic rendering of a female Ishmael thus has no happy ending: "I will not try another door, / To seek what I have never found; / Now, till the very last is o'er, / Upon the earth I'll wander round." This account of a female prodigal ends with an assertion of suicidal yearning: hers is a "thirst, that none can still, / Save those unfounden waters free" that "soothe me to Eternity!" Personifying Death as a woman who brings peace, the speaker in "Disappointment" croons: "Death, /

Opens her sweet white arms, and whispers Peace; / Come, say thy sorrows in this bosom!" This haunting image of feminine comfort—the white arms beckoning out in "the whelming wave"—ironically portends the tragic end Fuller would eventually find at sea.[4]

In the Seeress of Prevorst, Fuller offers her reader another female who fails to reconcile with reality. She introduces this section with a dialogue between four Platonic forms, each representing a different worldview. The first, Good Sense, urges people to heed the lessons of daily living. The second, Old Church, argues the necessity of maintaining the rituals and customs that link peoples' lives in a shared symbolic system. Old Church believes that God intended to confine human knowledge within set limits lest by "wild speculation . . . we violate his will and incur" perhaps "fatal, consequences." As a counter to Old Church, Fuller playfully parodies Emerson in Self-Poise, who argues for an "upright" life of "sublime prudence" free of "nonsense."[5]

Fuller speaks her own view through the fourth form, Free Hope, who, with the heretical fervor of Anne Hutchinson, acknowledges "no limit, set up by man's opinion." Like a Hutchinson influenced by mesmerists, Free Hope asserts the right of each person to tap "the hidden springs of life" for the source of power, the "dynamic of our mental mechanics, [the] human phase of electricity." She wants to attain what she calls the "aromal state," such as is felt by a person in the presence of someone to whom he or she feels drawn by "animal magnetism," that mysterious electric fluid that mesmerists believed linked "human consciousness to some transpersonal psychic reality."[6]

Free Hope thus seeks truth by means of magnetism in the realm of the supernatural, in the divinity she believes is revealed in those "breaks in habitual existence caused by the aspect of death, the touch of love, the flood of music," when a person feels "freed from [the] body" and purged of impurities. Fuller's thinking here blends Fourier's on "aromal state" with that of American seekers who imbued magnetism with spiritual meaning. It seems also to reflect the vision depicted in wall paintings in the Villa of the Mysteries on the outskirts of Pompeii. These ancient murals show women being initiated into the cult surrounding the mysteries of Dionysus. While the women bend to listen to the gross Silenus play his lyre, a female Pan offers her breast to an initiate (in the form of a kid). These initiates believed (as did Fuller) that music and a divine touch could purge their souls of impurities and prepare them to be reborn.[7]

Through Free Hope Fuller thus reveals her continuing fascination with Dionysian mysticism as well as mesmerism, then popular in the Northeast. One pamphlet on the subject reported that, by 1843, some twenty to thirty mesmerists were lecturing in New England, and in Boston alone more than two hundred "magnetizers" were practicing. Fuller, as we know, was particularly fascinated with animal magnetism, especially with how the magnetizer tapped into those "*instinctive*," demonic energies in the depths of the subconscious mind, energies Emerson had mocked in his "Demonology" lecture. Fuller through Free Hope mocks back. She attests to not finding in Self-Poise's Puritan resolve "room enough" for "the mysterious whispers of life"—those "whispers of the wind" and "deceitful invitations of the water" that, as Fuller had earlier said of the demonical, make us "shudder" though we are drawn to them. Fuller believes it is better to abandon self-possession, to be infatuated and follow those beings who "mysteriously control," "than always," like Emerson, "to walk in armor."[8]

Fuller through Free Hope seems intrigued with the idea of yielding her self-possession to a person possessing demonical power. She can see how people with such power are able to exert a mysterious "control" over others, for the knowledge they possess, she says in her unpublished piece on "the Daemonical," is "occult." Fuller believed such people to be in possession of old and venerable secrets like those revealed to women initiated into ancient mystery religions. In the murals in the Villa of the Mysteries, pagan women are shown being initiated into the mysteries of Dionysus in much the same way that disciples of Mesmer in France centuries later were initiated into the Society of Harmony. Initiates into the latter not only swore an oath of fealty to Anton Mesmer and the society, but they also learned "secrets pertaining to the technical application" of his theories. Initiates into the technique of putting others into a trancelike state were given secret knowledge about how to control their subjects (women) by drawing them "magnetically" into their circle, as Fuller drew women into hers. Fuller, who had read the writings of Joseph Philippe François Deleuze, whose *Instruction pratique sur le magnétisme animal* had been recently translated into English, saw herself as possessing such a magnetizing power. In her comments on the demonical, Fuller says that what distinguishes magnetic people is that "Power tempts them."[9]

According to Fuller, people who have the capacity to enchant and control others "draw their skills from the dead, because their being is coeval with that of matter, and matter is the mother of death." It seems that Fuller is saying that these "not immortal" people have a feeling of emptiness or deadness within them that drives them to "seize" and "devour" their "prey."[10] Their vital power over others hence paradoxically comes from the presence in them of the dead, of a silence that cannot speak, a specter where a vital "I" ought to be.

Fuller is insightful here: in nineteenth-century terms she is speculating about a psychological state of mind like that described in the late twentieth century by the French psychoanalyst André Green as "the dead mother complex." Earlier we noted how adults who suffer from this complex feel empty within. Green theorizes that as children they had been emotionally severed from their mothers when the latter became self-absorbed and depressed as the result of a loss. Children then develop, says Green, "negative primary narcissism" that is compensated for in a number of ways, including engaging in intense intellectual and creative activities.

Green maintains, however, that the "dead mother" is, in fact, not dead enough but "remains in the child's psyche as a 'cold core,' a 'black' void associated with mourning." Thus, in contrast to positive primary narcissism that tends "toward unity and identity," negative primary narcissism is connected "with feelings of emptiness" that the child as an adult attempts to fill through winning others' admiration. Such people have "a natural desire to be at the center of attention," or, as Fuller describes Macaria in her tract, to be at "the centre of all relations." Fuller sees Macaria as a "perfected intelligence," the kind of woman she aspires to be.[11]

In Christian theology, the ability to draw others magnetically to one—charisma—is considered a divine gift. Fuller observes, however, that when charisma is "*self*-asserting" and "unwilling to acknowledge love for its superior," this seemingly mysterious power over others is "the devil." She thus attributes the legend of Lucifer, "the star that would not own its centre," to the human hunger to acquire this kind of self-serving power. Put in Fuller's terms, such Lucifer-like beings, lacking a solid "I," acquire their identity and energy by feeding off the adoration of others, by "possessing," so to speak, their followers' souls—if the "soul" is, as Plato said, a "self-mover," the principle of initiative in life, mind, and morals. An individual "in possession" of his or her "soul"—what Fuller saw as the end of a pilgrim's journey—has the capacity to initiate action, to resist the seductive appeal of such a mysterious, powerful being. Thus, though Fuller did "sometimes" enjoy "answer[ing]" the "deceitful" call of such an enticing, powerful person, such a *self*-surrender nullified her "I" as an active agent, which is what was to happen happen when she became enthralled by the charming businessman, James Nathan. Indeed, the capacity to act responsibly is lost when a person surrenders his or her "soul" to a seductive charmer.[12]

Many a nineteenth-century woman fell prey to a magnetizer, a man who put his subject in a trancelike state for the purpose, he said, of curing her "soul." Such was the power of the magnetizer that he could gain control over the will of his female subject by placing her in what Charles Poyen, a "self-proclaimed Professor of Animal Magnetism" who had lectured in New England in 1836, called a somnambulistic state. This was a kind of telepathic bond between male magnetizer and female subject that one magnetizer candidly confessed had definite sexual overtones to it. Once the magnetizer had mesmerized his subject, he would relay to her nonverbal commands through the supposed invisible liquid medium of animal magnetism. Because Fuller believed in the curative power of mesmerism (in New York she would see a mesmerist) and saw the German clairvoyant Friederike Hauffe, the Seeress of Prevorst, as "the best observed subject of magnetism in our times," she shared her story as recorded by the spiritualist Andreas Justinus Kerner with her readers.[13]

In telling Kerner's story of this Christian mystic born in the hamlet of Prevorst in 1801, Fuller stresses her "peculiar inner life," a visionary possession that eventually consumed her. Whereas in Mariana Fuller depicted a woman whose passion "overpowered" the man she loved, in the Seeress of Prevorst she discovered a woman whose mystical trances drew crowds to her. Fuller's focus, however, is not so much on Hauffe's religious faith as it is on the relief from suffering she gained from her withdrawal from society into apparent somnambulistic trances during which she seemed to be in touch with "unseen" forces, or, as Fuller sees it, the dead. Fuller felt that she, too, was at times in touch with such mysterious forces, the spirits of the dead. There were other similarities. Hauffe, like Fuller, had been an excitable child who suffered waking dreams wherein she "saw ghosts." Also like Fuller, as a teenager she was more intellectual than other girls and had poor eyesight. Perhaps due to squinting, both had a "penetrating" look. And both gained "a sense of concentrated life" from contact with "precious stones."[14]

While Hauffe was still very young, her parents "let her go," presumably for schooling—first to her grandfather, who raised her until she was seventeen, and then to a man in an arranged marriage when she was only nineteen. Coincidentally, on the day she was married she accompanied to the grave the "dear remains" of an older man who had been her mentor, the preacher "T." That day, in Fuller's words, "began the period, not . . . yet of sickness, but of her peculiar inward life."[15]

A critic today might say that Hauffe's peculiar inward life—her "hysteria," so to speak—dated to the scene at the churchyard when she stood beside the casket of her dead father figure. "Suddenly relieved," notes Fuller, Hauffe became thereafter "indifferent" to the "concerns of this world," concerns that included sex with a man the young woman did not love. Though Kerner tells his readers that Hauffe tried nobly to fulfill her wifely duties, he notes that her "body sank beneath the attempt."[16]

For those who missed the sexual implications, the next image Fuller gives avoids any chance of a misreading by modern or nineteenth-century readers. She reports that Friederike took refuge in a dream that the dead body of the fatherly Preacher T. lay at her side. When physicians tried to help her, Hauffe cried out that her "dead friend would help her; she needed no physician."[17] Fixated on the scene at the father's grave, Hauffe, possessed by the dead, entered a five-year period of frenzied existence consisting of alternating periods of intense physical suffering and mental exaltation.

At this point a physician called for Kerner, who first attempted to treat her physical ills and, when that failed, tried, at her request, a magnetic cure of this woman who was hemorrhaging and experiencing night sweats and spasms and whose teeth had fallen out. So repulsed was Hauffe, says Kerner, by the touch of the actual world that she did all she could to sever herself from life. She abstained periodically from food and was bled by doctors whose well-intended efforts made her sink, notes Fuller, "into a fear of all men." In her illness, Hauffe thought that she could see "the electric fluid." She believed that if only Kerner could return the animal magnetism in her to a state of "equipoise," of harmony, she could be cured. She also believed that her lapses into a comalike state were "magnetic trances" and that in her "out of the body" states she was in contact with spirits. This fluctuation in her mental and physical state continued the last seven years of her life, observes Fuller, who published this account of Hauffe's illness and death almost exactly seven years before her own death.[18]

As someone who believed in mysterious magnetic forces, Fuller felt sympathy with this woman who already "belonged," as Fuller said, to the dead—not only to her preacher mentor but also to her father. She was reported to have had a "presentiment of her father's death" and to have felt a special "connexion with him in the last moments" of his life.[19]

Like Fuller's, Hauffe's life was hence a paradox. She was obsessed with the dead father whom she lived to please even as she fought in life to free herself from the iron cage of laws and customs her fathers had created for her, a woman, to live in. Fuller tells us that Hauffe went so far as to generate her own language, a kind of gibberish that was "no gift from without, but a growth from her own mind." While Fuller seems to see Hauffe's language as a "strategy to escape the strict patriarchal forces of her culture," a prison in which Hauffe was given in marriage to a man she did not love, the consequence for Hauffe was that such a liberation led her to death. For in relying in her gibberish on the dead father to help her, that is, in keeping his image alive in her head, she severed herself from life. She let the dead determine her actions and control, in effect, her "soul."[20]

Like Hauffe, Fuller wanted to escape the system of signs and symbols that tied her, she felt, like a slave to men, the Judeo-Christian vision that had driven her Puritan forefathers across the ocean in their attempt to establish a New Jerusalem in America, a noble vision that nonetheless kept women in a social and psychological prison. In seeking to escape this prison, Fuller, however, like Hauffe, faced a problem. For though Fuller's retreat to pagan vision may have filled her with a sense of power and hence of freedom from a Puritan society too narrow to appreciate a brilliant woman like her, just as her identification with the Seeress may have bolstered her sense of her self-worth as a Sibyl, in the end it was a negative identity. For it made her finally seem, as even her friend Cary Sturgis had said, "strange" to ordinary people in a biblically based culture, most all of whom unquestioningly accepted the patriarchal basis of the Judeo-Christian belief system.

Fuller may have momentarily escaped reality through imaginatively identifying with the figures of Mariana and the Seeress of Prevorst, each of whom pursued a private vision at the expense of her health. But in the end Fuller would have to return to reality and either deal with life as it was offered her by her country—however difficult that life might be—or flee it. For whether she identified with Friederike Hauffe, Mariana, the broken-winged eagle, or even the displaced Indians, each of those identifications led her to death.[21]

THE "FINE CASTLE" OF HER WRITING

Like each of them, Fuller was destined to defeat, unless by the power of her will and imagination she could bend the lens of American social and cultural reality to fit her vision of America as a country in which women—as well as Indians, blacks, and other powerless people—were recognized, and accepted, as the equal of white men. That is, she could survive and even thrive in her own country if she could find a way to broaden the base of the American power structure to include women. One way to achieve her aim, as she knew, was to reach a broad audience with her writing. Through her persuasive use of rhetoric, a skill drilled into her by her father, she needed to alter people's attitudes toward women by changing their perception of women's attributes and abilities. She needed to convince them that women, like men, possess minds and spirits as well as bodies.

To do this Fuller felt she needed first to lead women to the source of their power and hence to dependence not on men but, as she saw it, on God. "This power is good for nothing," Fuller concedes in *Summer on the Lakes,* "unless the woman be wise to use it aright."[22]

Even if used "aright," however, "it" was still her personal will to power she was pitting against that of the fathers whose puritanical male vision had made America possible and that continued to live in her as conscience. To realize this new vision for women, Fuller had to cross not merely the fathers but also her deepest sense of herself as her father's dutiful daughter. The subsequent mental conflict could lead her, as it had led Macaria—Hercules's daughter who slew her father's killer and embodies Goethe's highest form of the feminine principle—into a classic tragic dilemma from which there is no out but death. Like Macaria, whose "perfected intelligence" Fuller admired, she might have to pay for her vision, in the end, with her life should her Puritan fathers demand it of her. Conscience is, as Ernest Becker has said, humanity's fate.[23] Defy it and we descend into chaos, like a riven ship in a raging sea.

To accomplish her task, Fuller needed to speak words that ordinary women could hear and take to heart, and then be moved to work together to make the system more just in its valuation of women. To do this—to fly free like an eagle—she had to cease pursuing illusions and keep doing what her fatherly mentor, Emerson, had told her to do: write. She decided first to revise "The Great Lawsuit" to reach a wide audience. After that she intended to write for the *New-York Daily Tribune,* whose editor, Horace Greeley, had encouraged her not only to expand her *Dial* piece into a book but also to accept a job as his literary editor.

34 ∾ Mother Power, Beastly Men, and *Woman in the Nineteenth Century*

The complexity of human sexuality and gender was on Fuller's mind as she revised "The Great Lawsuit" while vacationing with Cary from mid-October through November 1844 at Fishkill Landing (now Beacon, New York), a resort community on the Hudson River. In the quiet of her rented boardinghouse room, Fuller felt better situated than she had the previous summer during her restless journey through the West, where she had spent too many nights in noisy hotels to concentrate on her writing. Her evenings now were spent in the company of Cary, singing birds and katydids. From her window she could see over the tops of trees to the Hudson and the Catskills' purple heights beyond.[1]

A letter she had written Sturgis two months earlier reveals that as she had packed for the mountains she was thinking about the complexity of gender as well as about her father, female friendships, and redemption. In that 4 August letter she wrote after visiting her father's grave, Fuller addresses her dead father in an apostrophe. Recalling her experience with him as her tutor she says, "Father, thou hast taught me to prostrate myself in the dust, even with my brow in the dust and *ask to be taught.*" Though in October she will profess to being at peace, Fuller's conflict here is clear. For even if her father had in fact forced her to prostrate herself before him, she nevertheless in her letter begs him to teach her. Fuller then suggests to Sturgis that, as a "pure" Christian, Cary may be "worthier to aid souls to a pure and enduring service" than is she.[2]

In this long August letter, Fuller expresses a wish that the next time she and Cary meet they might "redeem the hours" by making their time together "joyful and like the hour of Elizabeth and Mary." She hopes that in meeting Cary she might be, as was Elizabeth in meeting the Virgin Mary, "filled with the Holy Ghost."[3] Fuller also alludes in her letter to the second Homeric "Hymn to Demeter," whose mythical story was in her mind as she rewrote and expanded "The Great Lawsuit" into *Woman in the Nineteenth Century.* In the "Hymn" Persephone (Proserpina) is seen playing with her girlfriends in a field of violets, roses, irises, and crocuses. As she picks the narcissus, Hades appears, rapes her, and takes her to the underworld. While there, she eats the sacred pomegranate offered her by Hades, an act that binds her to spend three months each year in hell with him, where she is "consumed within herself by desire for her mother." Fuller thus implies that if she and Cary cannot meet in peace, then, she writes Cary, she will be like Persephone's forlorn mother Ceres (in Greek Demeter), who knows what it means "to wander."[4]

In both this letter and one from September to Sarah Shaw, whose husband was a translator of George Sand's writings, Fuller sees herself a virgin or virginal mother. She tells Sarah, who is Roman Catholic, that she feels like "a Mother" to her. Noting that the "Virgin was made worthy to be the mother of Jesus by her purity," Fuller hopes that she, too, might be pure so as to be "worthy" of Sarah's affection.[5]

In contrast to her relationship with Sarah, Fuller had good reason to doubt herself worthy to be Cary's friend: just three weeks after she wrote Sarah, Fuller had dreamed Cary was dead on the seashore, an image that suggests Fuller's lingering ambivalence about her friend. In her dream, the waves kept "wash[ing] up [Cary's] dead body on the hard strand & then draw[ing] it back again," while Fuller "seemed rooted to one spot," her red silk cloak falling off each time she reached out to grab her dead friend.[6]

Despite her still obviously conflicted feelings for Cary, once she was sequestered in nature Fuller said she never felt in better health, perhaps, in her life. Close to "the sources of the streams, where the voice of hidden torrents is heard by night, and the eagle soars," she felt in tune, she said, with the flow of Being, a substratum of seeming liquid energy that, on her last day of writing, kept the tract "spinning out beneath [her] hand."[7]

༄ ༄ ༄

Thus into the pages she added to "The Great Lawsuit"—the only ones we consider in this chapter—she poured her thoughts on why nineteenth-century women needed broader rights. Fuller writes frankly about sex and marriage, and she stresses mysticism's mother power as the way for women to acquire religious self-dependence and with it the power to redeem men. In a departure from her more abstract essay, Fuller discusses the problems nineteenth-century American women confronted when it came to sex, marriage, and acculturation into a society that said women were to be seen and not heard, kept ignorant on the subject of sex, and obedient even to abusive husbands. In the persona of Virgin Mother–teacher, Fuller then, near her tract's end, instructs women on how to go about acquiring the self-knowledge necessary for them to be reborn mentally and emotionally as whole human beings.

Fuller begins *Woman in the Nineteenth Century* by reaffirming women's right to soul-liberty. She asserts her belief that Man's (meaning all of humanity's) "destiny" in the course of the ages is to "ascertain and fulfil the law of his being, so that his life shall be seen, as a whole." Although "prejudices and passions" have always obstructed men's attempts "to make the earth a part of heaven," a daughter, she argues, not less than the "prodigal son," has a right to the same "conditions of life and freedom" as the father has given him. The daughter should be allowed the same freedom to wander in search of an Eldorado and, like the son, to be joyfully greeted upon her return home. With millennial fervor Fuller affirms that "the time is come" for "Woman . . . to take her turn in the full pulsation" of civilization. For "improvement in the daughters" is "the best aid in the reformation of the sons."[8]

As Fuller sees it, male heirs of the biblical myth of Eve who consider woman the cause of man's fall have not only failed to acknowledge that women are "possessors of and possessed by immortal souls," but they have forbidden women the right to develop intellectually and sexually. She accuses men of denying women the freedom to learn to know themselves as thinking beings, as well as of keeping women "ignorant" of their sexual rights and needs. Men accomplished this by having instilled in women "for centuries" the belief "that men have not only stronger passions than [women], but of a sort that it would be shameful for them to share or even understand," and that wives must therefore "submit implicitly to their [husband's] will."[9]

And, according to Fuller, "there is no way that men sin more . . . than in their conduct towards their wives." Thinking of her mother's plight, Fuller argues the need for laws to "secure married women rights" over both "their own property" and their bodies. A married woman, she says, needs "legal protection" against a dissolute husband who seeks the "shelter of men's laws to steal" his children from their mother who has left him and hence "deprived" him of what "they [men] call" "the rights of a husband." A few bold women have been able to defy their culture's traditions and laws, including, as Fuller had noted in "The Great Lawsuit," Mary Wollstonecraft and George Sand. Fuller, however, now adds a caveat regarding the unorthodox behavior of such women: "Their liberty must be the liberty of law and knowledge"—not of unlicensed passion.[10]

Fuller offers, in contrast, examples of "virtuous" women from history and literature who either on their own defied social conventions or in married life behaved heroically. She mentions "the heroine of the last revolution of Poland," the Countess Emily Plater, who fought alongside men "in favor of liberty." She notes Eloisa, and also Sappho, whose names and deeds "were not more suitably met in their own time" than was that of the Countess "on her first joining the army," despite their "vast superiority." Of the stories she added to her essay when writing *Woman in the Nineteenth Century,* Fuller thought "the most exquisitely told history of married love" to be that of Xenophon's Panthea, who stabbed herself out of love for her dead warrior husband whom she had "urged" on to fight in the battle he died in. She calls theirs a "true marriage."[11]

Yet Fuller's aim now is not to argue the need for laws extending particular rights to women, nor is it merely to celebrate the lives of brave women who have successfully defied their culture's limits. It is, instead, she says, "to go to the root" of the problems encountered daily by ordinary women and to teach them how to acquire self-knowledge and with it self-dependence. Give a woman "legitimate hopes, and a standard within herself," then "marriage," she contends, "and all other relations [will] by degrees be harmonized with these."[12]

To gain a standard within themselves, Fuller suggests that women must break free altogether from the prison of father-oriented traditional church worship and turn for spiritual guidance to mysticism—to, in her words, the cult of "the mothers"—which she calls "the brooding soul of the world" and believes "cannot fail of its oracular promise as to woman." To uncover the secret of their power, women must separate from men and delve "within" themselves. Here Fuller accepts as a given American society's rigid gender-role differentiation. For she asserts that masculine intellect is cold, whereas feminine emotion is warm and "rushes towards mother earth." In accord with the mesmerists, Fuller argues that "the magnetic element," this "mysterious fluid" that is conveyed by a woman's "depth of eye and powerful motion," has never at any period been sufficiently revealed. Yet it is precisely this "Mother power"—the very power Emerson in his "Demonology" talk had said was evil—that Fuller sees as the means to man's redemption.[13]

Fuller repeats her earlier recommendation of mesmerism and mysticism as means by which women might attain their fluid female power. Before they can tap into and use such power effectively, however, according to Fuller women must come not only to see how men have prevented them from developing their powers but also to comprehend the dire consequences for them of their continuing to repress their energies. Women themselves must thus come to understand the negative effects on them of social conditioning and sexual repression, of oppressive sex in marriage, and of prostitution and excited passions. In the persona of teacher, Fuller alerts American women to the damage done to them by their social and sexual oppression and then gives them direction as to what they might do to improve their condition.

Fuller thus teaches her female readers how men with their laws, language, and social customs have prevented women from acquiring power by forbidding them "to explore" and become "acquainted with regions" in their being that could give them a power equal to men's in terms of intellect and passion. Forbidden by men "knowledge" of self as well as "reflection," a woman, says Fuller, "conceals, represses, without succeeding in smothering" emotions too complex for her, in her ignorance, to understand.[14]

Because they must repress their creative energies, Fuller says that many women, especially women of genius, are "unhappy at present." They see reality too clearly to be able "to act in conformity with those around them." According to Fuller, such women who are in tune with the magnetic fluid at the core of being appear electrically "*over*-flowed," thereby "frighten[ing] those around them." They are "overladen," she explains, "with electricity" (defined by one American mesmerist as "the power of an invisible agent to produce actual effects in a material world"). Fuller thinks that female geniuses are more likely to be thus overcharged since, while seeing more deeply than most people, they are allowed at the same time few outlets for their energy. She contends that this suppressed energy causes physical or mental "sickness." Rather than turning their agony into art or using it as fuel for action, these women "are, indeed," she says, echoing mesmerist Robert Collyer, "the easy victims both of priest-craft and self-delusion." Such women, according to Fuller, seldom marry, and when they do, as in the case of the Seeress of Prevorst, their "remarkable powers" are "broken and jarred into disease" by the unsuitability of the relation.[15]

Influenced by Fourier as well as by Sand, who used Fourier's ideas to support her radical views on marriage, Fuller then writes bluntly about problems nineteenth-century women confront when they discover the reality of sex in marriage. Fuller believes that all women suffer under the current terms of marriage, where most women marry because it is expected of them, while others do so because they have been "given in" marriage by their fathers to men who will be, for their daughters, good providers. Kept ignorant on matters pertaining to sex by men who believe women's ignorance benefits them, most women enter a lifelong union unprepared for the real-life sex demands and domestic drudgery expected of them by their mates, who Fuller charges are too often brutish. Taught not to complain, a woman lets her body be used for her husband's pleasure in exchange for the provisions he gives her, and she suffers long years in silence.[16]

Fuller notes that in many other cultures—pagan, Asian, American Indian—this was not the case. In these cultures men were permitted multiple wives and hence the burden of satisfying a husband's domestic and sexual demands did not fall on one woman. An Indian chief, for instance, had many wives. Though they were "but servants," says Fuller, "still they enjoyed the respect of others and their own."[17]

Aware she is writing in a Christian culture, Fuller now points out, as she had not in "The Great Lawsuit," the problem presented to women by a church-sanctioned union, "where marriage is between one and one" and a "Christian rule" offers men and women "a standard to appeal to." Given the unequal status of, so to speak, "man and *wife*" in Christian marriage, this standard exhausts the woman who, implies Fuller (surely with her mother in mind), must do housework, bear and raise babies, as well as be there for her husband's pleasure. Not forewarned by their mothers about "woman's lot" but taught, instead, that marriage is the aim of their existence, excited girls use their sex appeal to win the affection of men who gaze at them not with love but lust. Lavishly dressed girls then link with these men in marriages where they expect to be touched with love, only too soon to recoil in horror at their husband's animallike aggressive behavior and their own repeated pregnancies. They begin viewing men, in general, as "a kind of wild beasts [sic]."[18]

Still, taught as they are that men are anatomically "so constituted" that they "must indulge [their] passions or die," the daughters obey. "It may be," observes Fuller, quoting from a passage by a female writer on female affairs, "that a young woman," respecting her family's interest or fearing "suffering celibacy," marries a man for whom she feels no "inclination." Should she show the least sign of "*repugnance*" in response to her husband's sexual advances, men label it "*an affair of the imagination.*" Fuller notes that such "antipathy" felt by a woman for her husband was recently treated by, in her own words now, "an eminent physician as sufficient proof of insanity." "If he had said sufficient cause for it," she wryly adds, "he would have been nearer right."[19]

Fuller continues her assault on the institution of marriage, noting that if a wife denies her mate his conjugal "rights," then he takes his unrelieved needs to a prostitute, who willingly lets herself fall "prey" to the "brute passions of man." Fuller had been so interested in the plight of prostitutes that, while she was at Fishkill Landing and revising her essay into *Woman in the Nineteenth Century*, she had visited Sing Sing, the prison located thirty miles north of the city on the banks of the Hudson River. There she had interviewed women inmates. The imprisoned prostitutes were frank in answering her questions. Fuller told them that she "was writing about Woman" and wanted information from women like them "who had been tempted to pollution and sorrow." She reports that when she asked a group of such women "stamped by society as among the most degraded of their sex" how they had come to be in prison, they said, "love of dress, love of flattery, love of excitement." For "excitement," then, observes Fuller, these women had thus "drowned the voice of conscience." She seems here to see little difference between prostitutes and fashion-conscious "American *ladies*," except that prostitutes harbor no illusions about men's sexual needs, and in order to dress like their rich sisters they are willing to profane "their persons."[20]

To show her readers how these women had fallen so low that they equated their value with their sex appeal to men, Fuller turned to Plato's myth of an original "One Man" and also the mesmerists. The latter believed that a female subject (somnambule) when in a clairvoyant trance experienced visions in which her "soul" (seen by some mesmerists as spirit combined with etheric fluid) separated from her animal nature to dwell on a higher plane of being. Drawing images and ideas from both the mesmerists and Plato gave Fuller a way to talk in quasi-psychological terms about complicated matters pertaining to sex and gender while affirming the existence within each individual of a fluid spiritual essence—the soul. In Plato's myth, the first Man is depicted as a "circle" or "sphere," a being of equal male and female parts. This sphere, says Fuller in accord with the mesmerists, is a "being of two-fold relations," beholden "to nature beneath, and intelligences above him."[21]

To cultivate his higher nature, "Man," says Fuller, must value his soul, the growth of which is itself both masculine and feminine, though no individual, she reminds her readers, is ever entirely masculine or feminine. In a moment of insight, Fuller here stresses the constructed nature of gender. She notes how at birth an infant is assigned a role in life it is expected to play. For, unlike an animal, as it emerges into social life it acquires a language wherein it is designated, if male, as "masculine," which Fuller defines as energy, power, and intellect; if female, as "feminine," defined by her as love, harmony, and beauty. According to Fuller, had these two sides developed in "perfect harmony," then they would have corresponded to one another "like hemispheres, or the tenor and bass in music"[22]

As Fuller sees it, a woman, unlike a man, is twice penalized for her existence. Not only is she born to expect, as are we all, "a happiness that cannot exist on earth," but she is also acculturated thereafter to see herself in language, myth, and history as inferior to man. This degradation of woman happened, says Fuller, because men abused their power. Rather then respecting women as men's equal, they treated women as slaves and underlings, an attitude toward women they show when they say, "Tell that to women and children." This "contemptuous phrase," she observes, contains in it an assumption that "the infinite soul" works through women "in already ascertained limits; that the gift of reason, man's highest prerogative, is allotted to them in much lower degree." Most women, then, "are so overloaded with [denigrating] precepts" "that their minds are impeded by doubts" about their abilities and they accede without question to society's limits. Each wife unquestionably obeys her husband, whether he is a bully who beats her, a drunkard who demeans her, or an adulterer who betrays her.[23]

Feeling her power, a furious Fuller in *Woman* depicts men primarily as brutes and hypocrites, as wild beasts whose eyes are "clouded by secret sin." She hence advises women to beware and avoid "the froth and scum" of whirlwind social life as well as men for whom "manliness" means "lawlessness" and lewdness. Fuller imagines an innocent young girl, "child of an unprofaned wedlock," who sees a "fair woman carried in the waltz" by a man "who appeared to her a Satyr." Though shocked at first, the girl may learn, suggests Fuller, to live with the situation and may even acquire "a taste for satyr-society, like some of the Nymphs, and all the Bacchanals of old." Thus a Puritan-minded Fuller criticizes the once-innocent girl who becomes sexually active every bit as harshly as she does the lecherous man.[24]

Not all men, she concedes, are lechers; some, she acknowledges, have recently "been awakened" to "the stains of celibacy, and the profanations of marriage." These men have begun to lecture and write "about it," "it" presumably being, not only abusive sex within marriage, but also other sexual practices her culture deemed perverse, such as masturbation and adultery. Concerned lecturers and ministers "endeavor," she says, "to help the erring by showing them the physical law," by which she means the procreative aim of sex. Possibly thinking of Timothy and his winter ice baths and barefoot runs through the snow, Fuller declares that "cold bathing and exercise" alone will not "keep a life pure, without an inward baptism and noble and exhilarating employment for the thoughts and the passions."[25]

Like men, women, she contends, must also be permitted a life of thought and action if they are to be prevented from expending their energies in degrading ways. Women, she argues, have the same God-given right as men to "an inward baptism" and "exhilarating" work. But men, she knows, are not ready to grant women this right. Hence a woman who now becomes aware of her power must face, as did Fuller, "a crisis" in her life wherein she must choose either to stay in the bonds of girlhood with "its blind pupilage and restless seeking," or to break through into "self-possessed" womanhood.[26]

Fuller offers her readers suggestions about how a woman might prepare herself to be reborn as a person in possession of her soul. A woman must first stop seeing her body as an object of male sexual desire and see it instead as an "organ of the soul." Like women Orphics, she must free her body of impurities resulting from "voluptuous indulgence," from dependence on opium, as well as from unhealthy habits of hygiene. In tune with the views of the fitness experts whose advice her father had obsessively heeded, she advocates daily bathing. She urges women to pay attention to their "personal neatness"; she also recommends that they wear comfortable dresses—without corsets—as well as clean "under-clothes." For, only "in a strong and clean body," says Fuller, "can the soul do its message fitly."[27]

In advocating spiritual purity, Fuller did not mean that women were to stay ignorant on sexual matters. On the contrary, the route to spiritual rebirth that Fuller offers women in *Woman in the Nineteenth Century* is, as we have seen, similar to that practiced by women being "initiated to [the] mysteries" of Ceres and Proserpina in the first century BCE as depicted in Pompeian wall paintings. Though little is known about the actual experience of initiates into the Eleusinian mysteries, in the mystery rites of Dionysus as reflected in the wall paintings, the women—like Persephone, who ate the pomegranate seeds, and Eve, the apple—yield to temptation. Unlike in the biblical myth of Adam and Eve, however, the women who have become aware of their "grosser" sexual side are not cast out of Eden. Instead, they are purified of their lewd desires through a ritual cleansing and the comforting friendship of other women. As part of the ritual they abandon their fine clothes and expose their backs to the rod. This self-denial and flagellation bring them to a ritual death, and, eventually, with penitence and the compassion shown them by other women, to resurrection as pure souls whose reward is revelation of the divinity.[28]

Fuller thus argues in *Woman in the Nineteenth Century* that for women to be reborn as spiritual beings they must first become aware of their propensity to sin and then suffer humiliation. They must next purify their lives by renouncing "all artificial means of distortion"—whether it be frivolous dress, excessive food, or addictive drugs. Fuller believed, moreover, that for women to recover their integrity, like the Bacchantes in the Pompeian wall painting, they must retreat from men and help one another. It is her hope that after a period of retreat and introspective questing, women will be able to "come forth again, renovated and baptized," "freed" of their "weakening habit of dependence on others." Then, rhapsodizes Fuller, when women's "intellect and affections are in harmony," the woman who advances "With rapturous, lyrical glances, / Singing the song of the earth, singing / Its hymn to the Gods," will not be, as Fuller felt she had been, "shrunk from as unnatural."²⁹

In this poem, Fuller refers indirectly to both herself and Sand, from whom she borrowed the phrase "lyrical glances." Her deliberate reference to intense and even potentially "unnatural" passions—what Emerson referred to as "perverted" erotic "flashes"—hence cannot be overlooked here. Still, Fuller makes it clear throughout her text that she does not want to be a man or even "a manly woman." She contends that the only reason women appropriate any of men's "masculine" qualities is that they are not allowed to develop their feminine faculties fully.³⁰

Were women, however, allowed to develop their full strength as women, then an intellectual woman like herself might be "fit" to run for the Senate. Fuller asserts her belief that a Senate made up of women could "affect the morals of the civilized world," could even redeem it since, says she, reflecting a common view, if women have power at all, "it is a moral power."³¹

In the voice of a romantic millennialist who wishes to remake earth into heaven, Fuller ends the pamphlet by declaring: "the time has come when a clearer vision and better action are possible. When man and woman may regard one another"—not as "lord and tutor" over woman as "blind" pupil—but as "brother and sister, the pillars of one porch, the priests of one worship." Until that day, however, Fuller knows that she, as "a daughter"—nay, more, as a daughter of Timothy Fuller—must "live through the life of man."³²

35 ∞ "What Is the Lady Driving At?"

As Fuller in mid-November was finishing *Woman in the Nineteenth Century* at Fishkill Landing, she wrote her friend William Channing that she felt as if she had left her "foot-print" on the earth.¹ When the pamphlet came out early the next year, it would lift Fuller into the ranks of the immortals who have helped to shape our shared world with their vision. She had shaken readers into an awareness of the complex nature of sexual identity, as well as of the many unacknowledged problems that women then had to face daily having to do with sex, work, and marriage, intractable problems brought on by Americans' inculcated sense that women are inferior to men. In a Bible-based society, for a woman to challenge the hierarchical structure of Christian marriage, to dare call men hypocrites and beasts and even urge women to separate from men to seek religious self-dependence, was, indeed, bold.

In arguing women's right to religious self-dependence and power, Fuller challenged the biblical view propounding that man's position over woman as guide, protector, and provider is God given. American men who were raised on the Bible believed what Paul in his letters to Timothy (1 Tim. 2:12) and the Ephesians (5:22–24) taught: that women should neither "teach" nor "have authority over men." They should "keep silent" and as wives "be subject in everything to their husbands" since "the husband is the head of the wife," a perception that had been reinforced in the United States by the writings of John Locke and Sir William Blackstone.

Locke, whose vision of human rights underlay the affirmation of equality in the Declaration of Independence, had also concluded that women in some sense belong to men, their protectors and providers. For he believed that between husbands and wives there existed a difference of understandings and wills such that authority in a family must "naturally" fall "to the man's share, as the abler and the stronger." Supporting Locke's seventeenth-century view on the descending staircase relation of men to women in marriage was Blackstone's *Commentaries on the Laws of England,* which fixed in Americans' minds the biblical view of women as chattel. Relying on tradition, Blackstone in 1765 wrote that "the husband and wife are one person in law; that is, the very being or legal existence of the woman is suspended during marriage, or at least is incorporated and consolidated into that of the husband; under whose wing, protection, and *cover,* she performs every thing." According to Blackstone's *Commentaries,* which Thomas Jefferson said were to Americans "what the Alcoran is to the Mahometans" and an ambitious Timothy had read while studying to become a lawyer, a woman in marriage becomes an object, a piece of property subject to a power "that ceaseth onely in Death."[2]

Though Blackstone's statement misrepresented the actual letter of the law of equity, which was meant to protect and safeguard married women's separate property rights, facts lack the compelling power of images, and Blackstone's image of woman as subject to the will of her husband in marriage, backed by Scripture, was engraved deep in the minds of most Christian men and women in Fuller's Bible-based New England culture, noted historian Mary Beard six decades ago. These unquestioning people accepted as fact Blackstone's misconception of the husband's legal possession of his wife, a point driven home for Fuller when her father died intestate and her mother, as a dependent wife with no written will, could not handle the estate. Nor could the unmarried Margaret, who greatly regretted "being of the softer sex." Not only had she no legal right to control family finances, she was also ignorant "of the management and value of property" and was hence forced to call on her tyrannical Uncle Abraham for help, a move that proved humiliating. In 1845, at the very time that Fuller was writing *Woman in the Nineteenth Century* and just three years before the first "woman's rights" convention in Seneca Falls, New York, Edward Mansfield's *The Legal Rights, Liabilities and Duties of Women* appeared. In it Mansfield reinforced Blackstone's view of women as chattel by quoting from the Bible that "the person of the wife belongs to the husband." According to Mansfield, the first "great principle of Scripture" is that husband and wife are, "*in law, one person*" (original emphasis): "This great principle has, therefore, all the authority of human and divine law."[3]

Given the shared perception in nineteenth-century American society regarding a wife's divinely appointed place as a piece of property belonging to her husband, Fuller's pamphlet with its radical view of marriage as a union of equals, of a husband and wife traveling through life as, in Fuller's words, "fellow pilgrims," was bound to stir controversy. In this expanded version of "The Great Lawsuit" Fuller had wanted to make her meaning clear regarding what she felt the relation between men and women ought to be, not only on the high plane of spirit but also on the "lower" one of sex.[4] However, in highlighting men's hypocrisy and the brutal ways they sometimes treated their wives in marriage, Fuller brought into the open a topic that heretofore had been taboo. It was her shift to this latter perspective that helped win for her the broader audience she sought. It transformed the earlier *Dial* essay from a nonthreatening philosophical meditation on the relation between the sexes into a classic feminist polemic on the special problems confronted by women who seek not only freedom and equality with men but also a balance in their lives between their spiritual yearnings and sexual desires.

Certainly Fuller's main argument here—that women as well as men have a right to soul liberty and hence human dignity—today is not considered debatable. What was and still is debatable is whether the end result of a Romantic vision that posits the fulfillment of individual desire as of foremost importance actually leads to human improvement and better relations between the sexes or instead, as some might claim, to the end of Western society as we know it. We recall that Emerson himself had earlier wondered whether the traditional institution of marriage could survive the demands placed on it, not just of idealized modern love, but also of each person's placing the pursuit of self-development and pleasure ahead of a commitment, as Emerson preferred, to a shared traditional marriage vow.[5]

Soon enough Fuller herself would have to deal with this difficult question. Regardless of the answer, however, one thing about *Woman in the Nineteenth Century* was certain. Though the document itself looked benign—it was (including the index) a 201-page, light blue-green, plain-looking, paperbound pamphlet with a mandala as its frontispiece—with its theme of female religious self-sovereignty and frank talk of women's marital sexual happiness, it instantly became the focus of hot critical debate when it was published in February 1845 by Greeley & McElrath—ironically in their Cheerful Books for People series.[6]

A sample of responses from the many reviews shows that critics' attitudes toward the book reflected their liberal or conservative perspective, though most praised the accomplishments of Fuller as an author and agreed that the book's publication was a good thing. The *New-York Daily Tribune* elaborated on Fuller's plea for equality in sexual relations and suggested it should be read by people "interested in the advancement of humanity." In a review in the *Broadway Journal*, Fuller's friend Lydia Maria Child wrote that portions of the book were bold. She confesses it contains passages that some readers will find offensive in that "they allude to subjects which men do not wish to have discussed, and which women dare not approach." She notes, for instance, Fuller's emphasis on the degrading nature of passion when divorced from higher sentiment. Despite these reservations, Child applauds Fuller for raising questions that she believes can no longer be ignored, such as, "Is love a mockery, and marriage a sham?" She ends her review by praising the book's thesis that woman should be "the real partner of man in all his pursuits" rather than an ornament or a "servant of his senses," and by noting that the human heart in women that makes these observations regarding men's low opinion of them "cannot be silenced." In Boston, Elizabeth Palmer Peabody Sr. wrote her daughter Sophia, "Fuller's book has made a breeze."[7]

Unsympathetic male reviewers were understandably less positive. For in *Woman in the Nineteenth Century* Fuller especially attacks the hypocrisy of men while passionately arguing the right of women to speak and act in public life, in effect, to control their own lives and share power with men. Thus even as they acknowledge that problems can grow out of male-female inequality, these male reviewers were critical of Fuller's radical affirmation of woman's right to possess her own soul. An anonymous reviewer for the *Ladies' National Magazine* wrote: "We are willing to grant that many abuses toward woman exist in the social system, . . . [but] we are yet to be convinced that the whole system should, therefore, be overthrown." Convinced of the divine rightness of Blackstone's depiction of wives as chattel meant to serve their lords, this reviewer concluded that it is God's will that woman be "the guardian angel of man," that she make him happy "with the light of her smiles."[8]

Male reviewers with little sympathy for Transcendentalism criticized Fuller for being incoherent, talking bluntly about sex and pagan religious practices, tampering with the terms of traditional marriage, and imagining humans can re-create paradise on earth. The *Spectator* accused Fuller of imitating "to exaggeration" Emerson's "peculiarities of style and manner" but having done so "without reaching the searching depth of thought he occasionally exhibits." Former Transcendentalist Orestes Brownson, who had objected to Fuller's feminist views in "The Great Lawsuit," complained in the April 1845 issue of his *Quarterly Review* that *Woman in the Nineteenth Century* "has neither beginning, middle, nor end, and may be read backwards as well as forwards, and from the centre outwards each way, without affecting the continuity of the thought or the succession of ideas." It seemed to him that it had been thrown together by a feverish woman "who turns from one side of the bed to the other, but finds no relief." In his view the tract had less to do with nineteenth-century women than with heathen deities, obscene rites, frightful orgies, and the writer's "gnawing" sexual needs. Reading it made Brownson wonder: "What is the lady driving at? What does she want?" As a way of relieving women's anxiety, does she really want to "reproduce the wild Bacchantes with loosened tresses and loosened robes, and lascivious satyrs?"[9]

A former Presbyterian and recent Roman Catholic convert who believed that God blundered when he made man and woman, that "Nature cannot be trusted,"

---

and that paradise cannot be re-created on earth, Brownson thought Fuller's Romantic views to be not merely "sick" but "evil." Known for his own mental instability, Brownson believed all reformers were mistaken—"from him who undertook in the Garden to reform God's commandment to our first parents, down to the author of the 'Orphic Sayings.'"[10]

One of the most ruthlessly critical reviews was that of Charles F. Briggs, who in his three-part March review expressed views he claimed many Americans shared. He accuses Fuller of "wasting the time of her readers," noting that she seems "offended that women should esteem it a compliment to be called masculine, while men consider it a reproach to be called feminine." As Briggs sees it, this is just one of many "radical errors" in Fuller's reasoning, and she would not have made them if she had conceded the truth, as Blackstone recorded it: "It is the law that woman shall reverence her husband, and that he shall be her head. We may love those whom we protect, but we can never wish ourselves in their place, although we naturally wish to be like those from whom we receive protection." "If there is anything clear in revealed and natural law," wrote Briggs, "it is that man is the head of the woman."[11]

Briggs notes the book's admirable passages, like those concerning how to make the body a fit temple for the soul. But he does not share Fuller's belief that abstaining from opium, abandoning corsets, and having women work independent of men will result in a general upsurge in women's mental health, any more than he thinks isolating women from men or baring their backs like pagans for a ritual beating will have a positive effect on women's spiritual well-being. If ancient Greek women actually believed that they were obeying God's will by "lacerating the form" God gave them as a punishment for their sins, then, says Briggs, they were victims of an illusion.[12]

Briggs argues that whether "the Mosaic cause of the fall [of man]" be interpreted as fact or embodiment of truth, "the lesson which it teaches is the same": "It was a violence done to his own body that brought suffering upon man and caused his expulsion from Eden." The only way for man to recover anything like paradise on earth, he believes, is to obey the Word of God as recorded in the Bible and to abstain from eating "the forbidden fruit which destroys [the body]." Since, as the Bible says, it was woman's eating fruit from the tree of knowledge that "brought death into the world," it is best that we all do as Paul preaches and live righteous lives. "The true position of woman," he says, "is not a disputable point; the universal sentiment of mankind has determined it; God himself has said 'her desire shall be unto her husband, and he shall rule over her.'"[13]

Briggs' attack highlighted the paradox of Fuller's position: she sought for a woman the right to be both the father's innocent, dutiful daughter and a sexually knowledgeable and hence "fallen," independent woman. Fuller had argued woman's right to explore previously forbidden regions of her being, even as she also

THE "FINE CASTLE" OF HER WRITING

contended that women are strong to the extent they are pure—as if once having been "reborn" a woman is "cleansed" forever of her desire to "sin." From the perspective of her contemporary male critics, this thinking is flawed. For it seemed to them that Fuller's entire argument is based on her erroneous belief that a woman can, like Orpheus, explore dangerous regions without being lured to destruction by the Sirens' song because there is "in woman as woman . . . a Greek moderation" that prevents her from committing "excesses."[14] Men like Briggs and Brownson believed that, precisely because women find it as difficult to resist sin as do men, it is best to keep women ignorant.

Fuller half laughed off the reaction of Briggs and other male critics to *Woman in the Nineteenth Century.* Whereas her fellow Transcendentalists spoke to an elite crowd of intellects and academics, Fuller felt now the need "to aid in the great work of popular education," something she thought she could do through writing for a newspaper.[15] Such mature happiness as Margaret Fuller was eventually to find would come only after a Psyche-like quest through grueling life experiences as a newspaper reporter in New York and Rome.

PART SIX

Professional Woman, Private Passion

When Fuller in November 1844 went to New York City to work as a literary critic and social commentator for Horace Greeley's *New-York Daily Tribune,* she meant to focus on her public career and less on personal relations. Though some friends thought journalism beneath her, Fuller hoped that in writing for a newspaper she might "soar and sing" in a way she had not before. Like the character Wilhelm Meister, who moves in Goethe's novel from the pursuit of theatrical illusion and pleasure to maturity of vision, Fuller, at the age of thirty-four, intended to cease pursuing the childish illusions of a girl with a "head full" of Hamlet and Rousseau and become a keen observer of the New York world.[1]

As a writer, Fuller did mature. Her writing style sharpened as she witnessed disturbing urban scenes of human poverty and suffering.[2] Yet even as she began to channel her tumultuous energies into writing newspaper columns about actresses and theater productions, reforms needed to improve hospital and prison conditions, as well as Fourierist solutions to the problems of poverty and inequality, her hunger for love gradually undercut her asserted resolve not to yield to illusion. Though in public Fuller functioned as a social activist and celebrity, in private she continued to escape her demons by retreating to dreams, this time to an unfortunate fantasy obsession, one we examine in the eleven chapters in this section of the book.

36 ∽ A Divided Life

Determined to live the chaste, productive life she had recommended for women in *Woman in the Nineteenth Century,* Fuller now in New York City cultivated the image of an independent professional woman. As such she made, as Greeley said, "a good appearance before the world." During her twenty-month stay in New York—where she lived first with the Greeleys in their ramshackle house on the East River in Manhattan and then in two different boardinghouses and in various friends' homes—Fuller published *Woman in the Nineteenth Century* (February 1845), a collection of her essays titled *Papers on Literature and Art* (1846), and approximately 250 reviews, essays, and translations from foreign papers in the *New-York Daily Tribune*. These articles, which were bylined with a star, inspired contemporaries to joke, as did Greeley in a letter: "The * of the *Tribune* is Miss S. Margaret Fuller." Indeed she was. Taking into account the unsigned and unstarred essays of a literary nature that appeared in the front-page literary section of the paper, one critic thinks it is likely Fuller wrote far more than the three essays she had been hired to write each week. Moreover, Fuller's writing, as Emerson put it, was "never dull," and hence it brought in readers.[1]

In her reviews Fuller offered provocative analyses of American and European literature and literati. She dismissed, for instance, Henry Wadsworth Longfellow as a poet of "moderate powers" and found James Russell Lowell "absolutely wanting" in the "spirit and tone of poesy." In reviewing in December Emerson's *Essays: Second Series,* some of which he had read to her during her July 1844 visit to Concord and which was published that October, she tried to establish a tone of critical distance. While praising Emerson as "a father of the country" in that his writing frees readers to question their perceptions and enact positive changes in their lives, she also accuses him of lacking passion to "interpret" human life, an inability to connect to life that she believes reveals his own lack of balance. Though Fuller finds the *Second Series* better than the first in this respect, even it, she thinks, does not "produce on the mind the harmonious effect of a . . . tree in full leaf." Taken together, the essays "tire like a string of mosaics or a house built of medals." Playfully mocking her mentor's insistence in his essays on a man's maintaining "the erect position," she notes that Emerson had "raised himself too early to the perpendicular and did not lie along the ground long enough to hear the secret whispers" of "mother earth."[2]

In this first of her numerous *Tribune* columns, Fuller's irreverent tone lacked the deferential courtesy men then expected of women. Thus, though with her proud head and piercing blue-gray eyes she was easy to spot in a room packed with prominent literati, most of them, said Greeley, didn't bother to seek her out for conversation, put off as they were by what they interpreted as conceit in her columns. Lowell was so angry over her criticism that he later would parody her in his *Fable for Critics* as Miranda, whose whole being, he said, is "a capital I." And her criticism of Emerson's *Essays: Second Series* broadened the gulf between them. However, she found the writing of Herman Melville and Edgar Allan Poe of value, as she also did that of Cornelius Mathews and William Gilmore Simms.[3]

Fuller in her popular front-page essays and mass-appeal reviews allied herself with social misfits and political radicals. In a column she titled "Items of Foreign Gossip," she included information she had culled and translated from various European newspapers. Zwarg notes that Fuller in one of them offers "three cases of transgendered behavior," or of what Fuller apparently called an "exchange of parts between the two sexes." Fuller tells first about a man whose transsexual dress and actions the public had discovered and scorned. She next describes a woman who successfully dressed and behaved as a man and then chronicles the plight of another woman who, disguised as a man, served the French army under Napoleon with such distinction that when at her death her gender was discovered, the public was reluctant to condemn her. Fuller's skillfully written columns on such exotic subjects no doubt helped Greeley sell papers, even as her decision to write on such, for their time, "strange" topics reveals her own continuing fascination with men and women who cross gender lines and defy social conventions, like Europeans George Sand and Percy Bysshe Shelley. In an August 1845 review in which she defined socialism, communism, and humanism, Fuller even introduced her readers to Friedrich Engels and Karl Marx—whose radical writings were beginning to appear in Europe—by translating and publishing in her review a German immigrant newspaper column. Titled by Fuller "The Social Movement in Europe," the column, which took up half the *Tribune*'s front page, argued that social progress does not necessarily accompany political progress and included mention of Marx and passages from Engels's *Condition of the Working Class in England,* which had been published in Leipzig in March 1845.[4]

Fuller's columns reveal her divided interest, on the one hand in radical revolutionaries and materialistic idealists like Engels, Fourier, and the stormy Danish writer Harro Harring, and, on the other hand, in writers who endorse a vision of soul redemption like Emerson and the English Presbyterian Philip James Bailey. Fuller had already reviewed Bailey's best-selling epic *Festus* (1839) in the *Dial* and would review it again in the *Tribune.* Inspired by Goethe's *Faust* and *Wilhelm Meister,* Bailey tells about a young man named Festus who journeys in life from despair over the death of his beloved Angela, through a period of anguish in which Lucifer tempts him and he lusts after another woman, to spiritual redemption by way of repentance and acceptance of a Christlike savior. In her review, Fuller praises *Festus*'s theme of "the soul's progress" while criticizing Bailey for having failed not only to lay out the steps by which Festus progresses to spiritual perfection but also to develop Lucifer's character so he seems to embody evil. She also criticizes Bailey for relying on traditional church dogma in depicting Festus's redemption. Despite these criticisms Fuller loved this long pedantic poem and would give a copy of it to James Nathan, the German-born Jewish businessman with whom she would soon fall in love.[5]

That Fuller found this poem based on a Calvinist vision of temptation, sin, unmerited grace, and redemption so appealing suggests that, despite her fascination with gender complexity, class strife, and Fourierist socialism, she was not entirely free from her Puritan past. It also reveals how wrong she could be in her assessment of which literary works would have lasting value. She certainly missed the mark in praising Harro Harring's novel, *Dolores,* which had been rejected by Harper Brothers and would not have been published in English at all without Fuller's five-hundred-dollar loan to Harring for private publication. The book had no lasting value, and Harring never repaid her. Fuller had placed her faith in a man who misused her, a pattern she would repeat throughout her life.[6]

Though Greeley would come to appreciate Fuller, he was at first put off by what he thought was her inclination "to luxury." Greeley, after all, lived a Spartan life with his wife, Mary, in the large rented house in Manhattan's Turtle Bay neighborhood. The old yellow farmhouse sat isolated on a large tract of land between Thirty-fourth and Fiftieth streets. The front yard was a garden of flowers, shrubs, large vines, and trim box borders. A broad hall cut through the structure's center and at the back opened onto a piazza that stretched the width of the ruinous old mansion. Overgrown with wild vines and rosebushes, the piazza faced the bay and a distant tree-covered shore. No matter the weather while she was residing with the Greeleys, Fuller loved to stroll on this piazza, as she also did on the shrub- and tree-covered lawn located a step or two below it. Narrow paths leading down to the river wound through this rock-strewn, picturesque lawn. Lydia Maria Child recalled that the house was set so close to the water that it seemed "almost *on* the East river." Child, who visited Fuller there in February 1845, remembered the view from the piazza of Blackwell's Island with its notorious penitentiary that housed several hundred female inmates. Within this spacious but dilapidated house, the Greeleys lived as religious ascetics. Both believed in the cold-water cure, refused all medicines, and abstained from fine foods. In the months she lived there, Fuller dined on beans, potatoes, boiled rice, puddings, bread and butter, with no condiment but salt, not even a pickle. They preferred to keep no alcohol, tea, or coffee in their home.[7]

This last did not suit Fuller, who insisted they serve her tea. In Greeley's recollections of Fuller, which William Channing included in the *Memoirs,* Greeley recalls that when she complained one morning at the breakfast table of a headache and he suggested a connection between her headache and the strong tea she drank the night before, Fuller told him that she did not like being lectured to "on 'the food or beverage she saw fit to take." This disagreement, he observes, "created a perceptible distance between us."[8]

It took the tough-minded newsman some time to accept Fuller's eccentric approach to writing. He found her writing fresh and vigorous but not always clear.

He did not understand her need to wait to write until she felt "the flow" of the spirit moving through her, "or at least . . . relative health of body." To "the inveterate hack-horse of the daily press," the idea of waiting for "a happier frame of mind" to write seemed, he said, "absurd."[9]

Greeley tells how gradually, however, he found himself "drawn" into her "current." Fuller, in turn, grew to like—"nay more, love," she said—"Mr Greeley." She especially liked living rent-free at his house, which was convenient, she wrote her mother, to "the Haarlem omnibus" that ran hourly to and from the heart of the city. She in fact liked the house so much that, after getting the flu in January, she stayed there to write, a self-indulgence tolerated by Greeley after a fire at the Ann Street *Tribune* office in February 1845 forced the staff to move temporarily to Nassau Street. The house in Turtle Bay offered Fuller a relatively quiet place to write, though Mary hired and fired cooks and maids in accord with her volatile moods. During Mary's outbursts, Fuller would escape either to the study recess in her upstairs bedroom, which looked out upon a woody knoll over the river, or to one of the paths that led easterly through shrubs and trees to rocks that dropped abruptly to the water. During the spring, and especially at night, Margaret would climb down the myrtle-covered bank to the rocks below. There, seated on a rock and with a waterfall of blue flowers behind her, she watched the moon slip behind thin clouds and distant sails "glide sidelong" far out on the river.[10]

Fuller's affection for Greeley made the arrangement especially pleasant. A staunch Whig, Greeley nevertheless supported progressive causes. For instance, though he thought abolitionists divisive, he advocated using legal means to stop the extension of slavery into new territories. Moreover, although he was against unionism and strikes, he used his editorials to advocate improvement of the deplorable working conditions in factories. While he loved the common people, the worker, and democracy, he feared the masses. He also sympathized with Fuller's argument for greater liberty for women but supported neither women's suffrage nor divorce reform.[11]

Perhaps the two got along so well because they were so eccentric, which they both communicated in their attire. Fuller now made it a habit to attach a nosegay of natural flowers (often violets) to the bodice of the colorful dresses she wore in public, whereas Greeley invariably wore a cream-colored jacket and trousers. With his pale-blue eyes and towlike hair, the news editor looked benign, though his manners and language were as rough as a seaman's. And he had an eye for excellence. Unlike reviewers who had faulted Fuller for questioning women's assumed inferiority to men, Greeley found her frankness refreshing. But he was baffled by her insistence—so inconsistent, he thought, with her vision—that men should open doors for women and protect them when they walked home alone at night through streets only dimly illuminated by gaslights.[12]

Fuller's open adoration of him and affection for his toddler son, Pickie, and high-strung wife (who had already lost two children and suffered two miscarriages) made Greeley increasingly appreciate her. He came to learn, he wrote, what others fond of her always found out, "that her faults . . . were all superficial." He even went with Fuller to Sunday meetings of a reform-oriented society of "Christian Union," founded in April 1843 by William Henry Channing, now a leading activist in the American Union of Associationists in the city, where he preached Fourierist socialism.[13]

A former New Hampshire farm boy with a mystical bent, Greeley admired Fuller's faith in the immortality of the soul. He also came to appreciate Fuller's courage in defending radical writers in her reviews and articles along with whatever seemed to her good and true, even if it countered public opinion. While winning over Greeley, Fuller was losing touch with Emerson. She was becoming politicized and hopeful about the possibility of radical social change. The formerly skeptical Fuller was gaining faith in the ability of individuals to be reborn as changed souls who can rise above and take control of difficult circumstances. The once-optimistic Emerson, in contrast, was becoming increasingly skeptical about people's capacity to control fate, a skepticism evident in his essay "Fate," where he would write, "A little whim of will to be free gallantly contending against the universe of chemistry."[14]

Before moving to the city, Fuller in the summer of 1844 had visited Concord, staying first at what was known as the Parsonage (later called the Old Manse) on the Concord River with the Hawthornes—Nathaniel, Sophia, baby Una, and dog Leo—and then at her sister's. On 23 May, Margaret's birthday, Ellen had given birth to a baby she named Margaret Fuller Channing, nicknamed Greta. Concord that summer had been full of family life and babies. On 10 July Lidian had given birth to another son, whom she named Edward Waldo; and while Fuller had been at Lidian's bedside visiting, her golden-haired seraphlike daughter Edith—the third of Emerson's living children and now almost three years old—had knelt on the bed by her mother and gazed at the baby cradled in Lidian's arms. At the Hawthornes, Fuller had enjoyed boating with Hawthorne on the river and also seeing Una, who, as Margaret held her, had laid her head on Margaret's breast. Fuller thought the big-eyed, brunette Una the most beautiful baby she had ever seen, though she confessed that no child could take the place in her heart of little Waldo and resented the fact that his father had given his new baby the name of the beautiful boy who had died.[15]

As Hawthorne's wife played with and cared for the four-month-old Una, Fuller felt glad for the good mothering provided by Sophia, who was able to breastfeed not only Una but also Ellen's baby, who looked gratefully up into Sophia's eyes and cooed as she sucked Sophia's bountiful breast. Margaret was relieved that Greta had accepted Sophia's breast, since the tubercular Ellen, whose marriage was per-petually on the edge of dissolution, had been having trouble breastfeeding her baby, a sickly looking creature who seemed to her aunt to be sadly wise with a "premature intelligence" about male-female discord.[16]

With so much baby life about her, Fuller had felt a dangerous lethargy fill her. The draw of the babies seemed lethal to her, as if their smiles might lure her away from the work she now felt called to do. Concord was so quiet that one night she had gone out and lain in an avenue for hours, staring at the stars and listen-ing to the wind as it whispered through the fir trees. On the July night she had gone to stay at Ellen's, she had ridden through a violent shower. Met at the door by the "excellent sable 'help,'" the only person present except herself that night, Fuller went "to bed with a deep sense of pleasure." That night her dead kin's spirits seemed to hover in her room, their "faults," she confided in her diary, "vanished." She knew, however, that this sense of the perfection of the dead was an illusion, as was the "sweet smile" of her "fair Greek" Emerson, on whose lips she confessed she could almost taste "the perfumed honey of Hymettus." Tempted by visions she knew to be illusions, by Emerson's mellifluous voice as he read to her from his sec-ond series of essays, Fuller equated Concord with "Sleep & Death!" One July eve-ning as she lay on a rock near the Parsonage with only Leo as company, she looked up through the trees and drank in the night, but "ugly memories shed their bitter in the cup." Disturbing memories reminded her that with her words she had the positive power to motivate readers to change their lives to want to reach out and help the poor and oppressed.[17]

With this thought in mind, Fuller had fired off from Ellen's house a last letter to Emerson, who, in his 1 August 1844 address in Concord on the tenth anniversary of the emancipation of slaves in the West Indies, had addressed the slavery issue. In his talk he had referred to Africans as "Afrites," which is apparently a power-ful class of devils in the Muslim faith. In her wry letter, Fuller reminds Emerson that his silver-tongued aphorisms will make "none the better" in the actual world and will certainly not improve the dire living conditions of "hapless" enslaved "Africans."[18]

In October 1845, a year after this summer Concord visit and several months after the publication of *Woman in the Nineteenth Century*, Fuller paid a final visit to Concord. During it she noted the tension between them and attributed it to the fact that Emerson, who was preparing for his "Representative Men" lec-tures by rereading Plato, was still "with Plato," whereas she was now "with the instincts." Though Fuller still believed that the "Truth" must be pursued, Plato's idealism seemed a world apart from the hard problems of slum life in the "dirtiest of cities," New York.[19] For there women, men, and children slept in places so foul that, as Charles Dickens described it in 1842 after having visited the Five Points district of lower Manhattan with two policemen as bodyguards, even "dogs would howl to lie."[20]

Plato's vision did nothing to help the plight of the homeless people Margaret saw roaming New York streets and sleeping in doorways (three thousand of whom by 1850 were estimated to be children), or of the woman she saw reciting church liturgy while squatting in the corner of an insane asylum cell, a shawl wrapped about her head and chest "like a Nun's veil." In her 19 March 1845 column, Fuller observes that the sad story of a vagrant at the Bellevue Alms House does not lift the human spirit "as does the story of the Prodigal Son," which offers the wanderer hope of finding a home. Such Bible stories teach love and forgiveness, themes absent from Emerson's and Plato's idealism. The latter gave her no way to deal with the "stern realities" she daily faced in the city: the foul smell in the upper galleries of the Tombs, or the pink eye epidemic she saw in an orphanage. Such big-city problems seemed to have little meaning to Emerson, who was now enjoying the life of a country gentleman, thanks in part to the success of his lectures.[21]

Though Cary and Emerson remained close, Fuller felt the distance growing between her and her friends. In her 29 September 1845 letter to Emerson, Cary had asked if Margaret had arrived yet for her planned mid-October visit, then confessed: "I shall not wish to see her & she will not wish to see me." Back in July, just two months before Margaret had made this last trip to Concord from the city, her brother Richard had written from Cambridge, where he was in law school, to say, "Emerson is not your true friend. I know that thoroughly, & I rejoice you are away from him." "His influence is bad," he added, "& he does not know you." Richard was upset by what he had heard Emerson say about her book, "that you ought not to write, you talked so well."[22] If Emerson's criticism upset her, Fuller did not let on that it did—she still held the Socratic belief that a person must follow the path of her destiny and not that of another. And hers seemed to be leading her away from Emerson and the butter-cupped meadows of placid Concord.

In New York Fuller began to act in accord with principles she felt were hers; these represented a merging of Transcendentalism, European Romanticism, Boston Unitarianism, Jeffersonian democracy, and the Judeo-Christian ethic of justice and mercy she had inherited from her Puritan ancestors—though altered to include women as equals. Images from her Puritan past frequently surfaced in her mind. She would never forget her grandmother Crane "holding the 'Saints Rest' in her hand," her "trembling figure" bowed in humility before her God, who was Christ, her redeemer. Nor could she forget the poetic words her father's great-great-grandfather, Thomas Fuller, had bequeathed his descendants, that if through life they'll "fear the Lord," their "souls at death he'll save."[23]

Fuller in her writing and actions believed herself to be affirming what her friend Channing called "the Living God in the soul," whether that be in her own soul or in that of a person whose difficult childhood circumstances had led to a life of prostitution or crime. In visiting the schools for immigrant children, hospitals for the poor, insane asylums, and prisons for vagrants and women prostitutes, visits that provided her with the research material she needed to write about the social injustices wrought on the disadvantaged, Fuller saw scores of people who were homeless, sick, insane, and impoverished. For no matter how many institutions New Yorkers erected in the nineteenth century to house the indigent and poor—like the Bloomingdale Asylum for the Insane or the New York Orphan Asylum—there were still more people needing food, shelter, clothing, and medical care.[24]

Exposed through her work on the *Tribune* to people marginalized because of race and gender, Fuller became increasingly concerned for their welfare and began to focus less on writing literary criticism than she did on publishing essays on how to solve New York's many social problems. For she identified with these outcasts. In a December 1845 column, she would denounce the "unchristian" and "illiberal prejudice" of the New Bedford lyceum membership, which had voted to exclude "people of color" because members held that the "right to the privileges of a citizen consists" in "the color of the skin." These people knew, as did she who argued that women should be on a par with men, how hard it is "to lift one's head amidst" sneers and derisive laughter; they knew what it meant to have to earn a living, that is, to work for their survival.[25]

Money was always on Fuller's mind. As one of the first self-supporting female members of the working press, she was proud that the five hundred dollars Greeley paid her a year was what he paid men for similar work. Fuller's substantial income paid her bills and boosted her self-esteem. Though she had never wholeheartedly supported planned societies (she had visited Brook Farm but had not been an active member), Fuller agreed with Fourier's view that for a woman to be independent she needed to earn enough money to support herself.[26]

According to Fuller, Greeley paid her well because he believed in her abilities "to a surprizing extent." Indeed he did. For her daring essays on uncommon literary and social topics—such as those on a home for discharged female convicts, controversial French novelists, and "Items of Foreign Gossip"—were increasing the paper's circulation, which by 1847 would be, according to an auditor hired that year by the *Tribune,* about thirty thousand. She was arousing public interest in the social issues Greeley believed in. In her reviews and commentaries, Fuller wrote with the aim of enlightening her readers about the plight of the poor, insane, and outcast. In her featured front-page column, she used sensational language to move her staid, middle-class audience to care enough to act in behalf of members of society's underclass, people whom she felt to be equally "worthy" of being recognized as souls capable of being reborn into a higher, spiritual way of life.[27]

A prostitute, for instance, in Fuller's opinion, could wake up one day having decided to slough off her sinful ways and be born again with the strength "within" to resist the temptation to make money by selling her body for sex. Fuller's confidence in these "so-called worst" of women had been reinforced during her October 1844 visit to Sing Sing. There she saw a more humane atmosphere for women being created by Eliza Farnham and a woman Fuller knew from Brook Farm, Georgiana Bruce, an assistant warden of women prisoners and ardent admirer of Fuller.[28]

Fuller's efforts at making the comfortable classes aware of the ill effects of inequality and poverty on people, especially women, reflected her middle-class Protestant upbringing. Readers, for the most part, were not offended by her liberal social views. However, because in her early writing she had not yet formulated firm views on certain social issues, or a definite strategy on how to use her writing to reach across class lines and disrupt the prevailing ideological assumptions, she sometimes slid into sentimentalism. Sounding condescending, Margaret, after her 1844 visit to Sing Sing, wrote Richard how amazed she was to discover that these "women, some black and all from the lowest haunts of vice," nevertheless "showed the natural aptitude of the [female] sex for refinement."[29]

Despite the middle-class tendency—even her own—to typecast prostitutes as "polluted," Fuller was nonetheless touched by their stories. After a second visit to the women prisoners in Sing Sing at Christmas, she appealed in her column for funds to help women in their work on behalf of women prisoners, many of whom had been jailed for public drunkenness and prostitution. Her exposés of conditions at the city's so-called "*benevolent!*" institutions—its schools, prisons, and a lazar-house (a "cess-pool of . . . social filth" "mis-called 'hospital,'" according to Channing)—caused a furor among middle-class women active in public affairs. When enough money was raised to establish the first halfway house in New York State for women parolees, Fuller's appeals were credited.[30]

Fuller's columns defending controversial people and causes made her a celebrity. Fans piled into the Third Avenue stage that took them out to the Greeleys' farmhouse, where they had tea with this female phenomenon. Fuller, in turn, visited the residences of old friends, like the Unitarian minister Christopher Cranch, who had contributed to the *Dial,* and Lydia Maria Child, who had favorably reviewed *Woman in the Nineteenth Century.* She also made new friends, like the Quaker abolitionists and philanthropists Marcus and Rebecca Spring. And in the evenings she attended the literary salon of Anne Lynch, where she mingled with literati, including Edgar Allan Poe.

In a review Poe had praised *Woman in the Nineteenth Century* for its "unmitigated radicalism," as well as for its "nervous, forcible, thoughtful, suggestive, brilliant, and to a certain extent scholar-like" style. But he had printed in the *Broadway Journal* a two-paragraph lampoon beneath a comic caricature of Fuller by Boston artist Samuel E. Brown. In it, a frowning, ringlet-coiffed Fuller perches at a table reading a book she is holding quite close to her nearsighted eyes. Poe notes that the artist has not adequately "preserved" the "'fine phrenzy' of the eyes": "that the little finger of the left hand is too straight . . . —that the table is too round—the feather of the pen too feathery—and the ink, . . . too *blue*." Poe's parody of Fuller as a bluestocking captures in a playfully spiteful way what Channing would later call Fuller's "saucy sprightliness." To most people she met in New York, however, Fuller apparently seemed, as she had at first to Greeley, cold, abstracted, and scornful.[31]

Despite her professed spiritual rebirth, Fuller nonetheless sensed that at this time of public celebrity all was not right in her soul. She yearned for communication with friends from home to maintain her mental balance and feel emotionally whole. She had "no time" in the city, she wrote Cary in March 1845, to attain the mental tranquility she needed to make contact with the power she believed inspired her creative life. Whereas in Concord she had feared that her lethargy might cause a chrysalis to grow around her, in New York she produced numerous articles yet suffered, she said, "perpetual stress" from having to be writing all the time. It seemed to her "unnatural" to have "to keep at it" even in August, with no vacation allowed her. Seven months later she would say she felt "threatened with" an attack of "morbid suffering." For "the day is thronged a great deal too thick with tasks." She had "no chance for repose."[32]

Perhaps more perilous to her psychological health was the fact that she was now out of touch with Emerson, a man whose "shine" had guided her, in her words, "through all this fog" for almost a decade. With Emerson near in her periods of stress, the mere memory of his "sweet smile" was the lifeline she needed "to cling to."[33] Now without his support, despite her outward success, Fuller felt she was sinking.

Greeley, in commenting on her life in New York, says that Fuller lamented in her journal that she felt she had "no real hold on life,—no real, permanent connection with any soul." Elsewhere in her New York journal she notes that she feels like "a wandering Intelligence, driven from spot to spot"—"from home to home." After an 1845 Valentine party held in the parlor of the literary celebrity Anne Lynch, an acquaintance of Fuller was shocked when, "in the dressing-room preparing to go home," she heard Fuller sigh and say, "Alone, as usual."[34]

Fuller otherwise gave little outward indication of her psychological distress, especially after she had entered a clandestine romantic relationship with James Nathan. Unfortunately, in suppressing these emotions she also failed to deal with those chaotic creative energies that had fueled her writing of *Woman in the Nineteenth Century.* When Fuller started working for the *Tribune,* she had said, "All flows freely." Newspaper writing then had seemed to her, she confessed in her essay on American literature, "next door to conversation."[35] The frantic pace at the press, however, combined with its need for her to write primarily on impersonal public matters, prevented, she felt, her from expressing her innermost concerns.

Hence, writing for a newspaper did not relieve her unresolved narcissistic tensions; it did not satisfy her deepest need for love.

She observed that her life and writing seemed characterized now by superficiality without and a sense of loneliness within. Channing, who saw her often in New York, said that Fuller treated people she met at literary gatherings as if they were too "frivolous" and "conventional" to warrant her time. Yet her seeming conceit was the old queenly demeanor she defensively used against those who did not really like her and to whom her private thoughts would have seemed strange.[36]

In New York she felt shackled to the wall of public opinion. Aware she must write to a middle-class audience, Fuller knew she could be liberal when commenting on issues such as prison reform and halfway houses but had to be cautious when dealing with human psychosexual complexity—on the sex and gender issues that intrigued her. In his comments on her life in the *Memoirs,* Greeley notes that it was during this period of prolific productivity that Fuller confessed in the private pages of her journal, "Father, let me not injure my fellows during this period of repression. I feel that when we meet my tones are not so sweet as I would have them."[37]

Margaret Fuller now lived a divided life. In public she projected a persona full of confidence, control, supercilious charm. She enchanted, for instance, Mary Greeley's friends, who, when they came to Turtle Bay, viewed her with a "strangely Oriental adoration." In private, however, and alone at night, she lamented her lack of a complete love that would make everything right in her heart, mind, and soul. Rather than merging to form a synthesis in Fuller, these conflicting self-images persisted alienated from one another but side by side within her. In neither New England nor New York was Fuller able to reconcile the inner division she had acknowledged in the journal she had kept while vacationing with Cary at Fishkill Landing in the autumn of 1844: "The Woman in me kneels and weeps in tender rapture; the Man in me rushes forth, but only to be baffled." "Yet the time will come," she had said, looking forward to an imagined period of psychic harmony, "when, from the union of this tragic king and queen, shall be born a radiant sovereign self."[38]

37 ✑ Fallen Women and Worldly Men

Once settled in New York, Fuller had meant to leave behind her personal conflicts. But walled off and denied, deep-seated archaic needs and early acquired patterns of behavior did not just vanish. From beneath the cool facade of a public-minded newspaper columnist, the "many voices" of Fuller's "soul"—intense, passionate, anguished voices—twisted through her iron defenses and found an outlet in fantasy-filled letters to James Nathan.[1]

In contrast to these revealing personal letters, Fuller's public columns represent her attempt to channel her conflicted energies into a moral vision acceptable to both herself as a social liberal and her morally conservative readers. Her strategy worked, and after a year she had gained respect in New York as a public voice of moral authority. Rumor had it that she and Anne Lynch went to Poe's home to demand he return letters sent to him by the poet Frances Sargent Osgood, letters the women thought compromising to Osgood.[2]

While gaining respect as a moral authority on matters relating to sexual behavior, Fuller, though self-consciously professional in tone, was nonetheless unwittingly revealing in her writings her sexual yearnings. This dual message, expressive of the divided life she was living, is evident in both Fuller's public and private presentations and writings during the twenty months she lived in the city—from December 1844, when she arrived there, to August 1846, when she left for Europe. It is evident in her literary reviews as well as in her public pronouncements about prison reform for women; it is especially evident, as we shall see, in her letters to Nathan.

In her literary reviews the two sides of Fuller's personality compete for ascendancy. In her 1 February 1845 commentary on French novelists, Margaret, sounding eerily like Timothy, self-righteously condemns behavior in others toward which her own "shadow side" is drawn. Margaret deplores French novels that corrupt the young by showing them "pictures of decrepit vice and prurient crime, such as would never, otherwise, be dreamed of here"—in America. Young people are "more" easily corrupted than adults, she says, because "such knowledge is so precocious." A boy is more "deeply injured by initiation into wickedness than a man" because such an initiation robs him of virtue and keeps him from developing the inner strength "that might restore it." Still, "it is useless to bewail" the pouring of Europe's corruptions "on our shores, both in the form of books and of living men." "On the steamboats we" (by whom she presumably means herself and other unwary readers) "have seen translations of vile books" that make those who happen to cast "a cursory glance at their contents" blush with "shame." "Our only hope," she says, is in our community's ability "to cast off its contaminations."[3]

Fuller especially condemns Balzac's "passionless scrutiny" of the human heart and his soulless materialism. She appreciates that "touch of the demon" in Balzac that enables him to "read so well" others' hearts. But Balzac's "demon" is cold and destructive. In Balzac's works, "every good not only rises from, but hastens back into, the jaws of death and nothingness." She thinks Balzac is no genius: "For genius is ... positive and creative, and cannot exist where there is no heart to believe in realities." Yet Balzac can fortunately have a permanent influence, she believes, only on an already "thoroughly corrupt" person: "His unbelief makes his thought too shallow."[4]

Fuller contrasts what she sees as Balzac's corrupt disposition with Sand's integrity. Fuller thinks that Sand's spiritual vision enabled her to transcend a life of illicit passion. She attributes Sand's corruption to the difficult circumstances of her upbringing. Married to a man she did not love, Sand moved "from a convent where she had heard a great deal about the law of God and the example of Jesus, into a society where no vice was proscribed, if it would wear the cloak of hypocrisy." Unable to subscribe to a life of hypocrisy and "loudly called by passion," Sand "yielded" and broke "the marriage bond." She is a woman, notes Fuller, who "knows passion . . . at a *white* heat." Despite Sand's sexual intrigues, Fuller believes Sand has not sinned "against what she owned to be the rule of right, and the will of Heaven." Sand's "free descriptions, the sophistry of passion are, at least, redeemed by a desire for truth," by an insistence on what is "real."[5]

George Sand, she concludes, is hence a boon to her country, "both as a warning and a leader." She has probed France's "festering wounds," and, "if they be not past all surgery," she is one, as surgeon, who "helps toward a cure." And then, as if the thought occurred to her while writing, Fuller bizarrely exclaims: "Would, indeed, the surgeon had come with quite clean hands!" In this revealing image of the contaminated healer, Fuller exposes her own guilt-laden sense of herself as a sexual being. Near the end of her review, Fuller includes a prayer, ostensibly for Sand but also for herself: "May Heaven lead her, at last, to the full possession of her best self, in harmony with the higher laws of life!" When Sand reaches that point, says Fuller, "she will have clues to guide many a pilgrim" who could not be helped by "one less tried, less tempted than herself."[6]

In the extemporaneous talk she gave to the prostitutes and other women inmates in Sing Sing on Christmas Day 1844, Fuller made a similar plea and revealed in the process her uncertainty about her own sinful state. This speech reads like the prayer of a woman who feels that she herself has been too close for comfort to the dark "gulf of sin and sorrow, towards which," as Fuller put it to the inmates, temptations "would hurry you." Fuller's identification with what Channing later called "her fallen sisters" underscores Fuller's suspicion that being a spiritually reborn (for Fuller not necessarily Christian) person provides no guarantee that one's life will be thereafter completely "pure" and righteous. As her Puritan ancestor Thomas Fuller wrote about his own strictly Christian rebirth, such an experience may, instead, merely mark the start of an arduous struggle with, as Fuller told the prisoners, "the temptations that await you in the world."[7]

Fuller in this talk reveals her ambivalent feelings for these "fallen" women. Part of her speaks as a traditional female reformer, a proper middle-class lady conditioned since childhood to see prostitutes as having "descended" to a lower order of being, a kind of vermin that can of course be studied and even potentially redeemed. This part of Fuller liked to believe that a fallen woman could be "saved" if she would confess her sins and pledge to live virtuously. Yet another part of Fuller suspected that such women were beyond redemption, that their horrific childhoods and subsequent crimes "for the sake of sensual pleasure" damned them to despair and early death, as she had predicted that her own unnatural childhood must "bring" her "to a premature grave." In this part of her being—what Emerson saw as "the quality of darkness" in her—she believed that women like the Sing Sing prostitutes had entered a dark sphere of desire that had forever stained them and from which they could not return to the upper world of sexual restraint and purity. It seemed to her that the circumstances of their lives denied such women, as girls, their virtue. She feared that since boys initiated into wickedness lacked the inner strength to "restore" their virtue, these women, too, could never lift themselves up.[8]

In this talk, both sides of Fuller speak—the optimist who believes that fallen women can be redeemed, and the cynic who sees the dark circumstances that have produced them. Thus Fuller tells them that though they may be born of "unfortunate marriages," "neglected in childhood," or be "so faulty, by temperament or habit" that they "can never on this earth lead a wholly fair and harmonious life," they are still "fitted to triumph over evil."[9]

Appearing perhaps in a full-skirted black silk gown, with her long hair arranged in ladylike side ringlets and a braided knot in back, the carefully manicured Fuller with her proper Cambridge accent and prim New England style may have seemed to the inmates like some "other" order of being. Lifting her upper lip to enunciate each word clearly and making "prominent use" of her smooth white hands as she talked, Fuller probably spoke with the same conviction as when she talked in Boston to the well-to-do matrons who attended her Conversations. "Be inwardly, outwardly true," she advised the inmates. "Then you will never be weakened or hardened by the consciousness of playing a part," as Fuller knew she herself was prone to do. "And if, hereafter," she said, someone "unfeeling or thoughtless" should attempt to push "back a soul emerging from darkness" (as she felt Emerson had done when she was emerging from her 1839–41 crisis), and especially, she added, if someone you love should "give you pain," then, no matter what that person or others might say about you, "you will feel" within yourself, she said, "the strong support of a good conscience."[10]

Admonishing herself as much as the inmates, a theatrical Fuller then urged her "fallen sisters" to "never be discouraged; never despond; . . . even if you relapse again and again." Should "you fall, do not lie grovelling; but rise upon your feet once more, and struggle bravely on."[11]

What Greeley later called the "frank compassion" of this talk to the "outcast portion of the sex" shows Fuller's determination in New York to teach women through her writing and lecturing to live a self-reliant and moral life. Her intention was "to expose the restrictions upon mental freedom" which kept a woman, she thought, from being in "full possession of her best self." In her relationship with James Nathan, such "restrictions" upon her mental freedom, among other things, certainly kept Fuller from being in possession of her own "best self," as we shall see when we examine her letters to Nathan that stretch from late February 1845 to September 1846.[12]

ℂℂℂ ℂℂℂ ℂℂℂ

Fuller felt fortunate to be able to share her views with the public through the *Tribune* even as she increasingly feared being locked into lonely spinsterhood. As the principal actor in her life's drama, a single female pilgrim on her way to an as-yet-unknown destination, she felt, in the fashion of a Psyche and Wilhelm Meister, that she now needed to move beyond erotic love and unite in blessed wedlock with an ideal companion. Unfortunately, many of her favorite models from literature did not offer positive examples of people who had successfully moved forward on their pilgrimage to maturity. After all, even Sappho, at least as Ovid told her story, had fruitlessly pursued the ferryman Phaon. In *Woman in the Nineteenth Century*, Fuller alludes to Ovid's story of the Lesbos poet's "unrequited" passion for Phaon and laments, probably with herself in mind, that Sappho's "great impulses" were not "suitably met" in her own time. Though in her New York letters Fuller does not refer to Sappho, as she does to both Psyche and Wilhelm Meister, the passionate poetess was surely in Fuller's mind as she pursued the handsome Nathan. Not lost on Fuller was the life-negating image of the heartbroken, forsaken Sappho—"all [her] genius . . . halted by [her] woes"—drowning "in the Leucadian wave" at the foot of the high cliff from which, as Ovid tells it, "fate" led her to leap.[13]

Despite Sappho's tragic end, Fuller still hoped she might enter a fulfilling relationship with a man. Emerson later recollected that Rebecca Spring had told him that Fuller in New York had said, "I am tired of these literary friendships, I long to be wife & mother." Yet Fuller's reservations about the institution of marriage remained, and she wrote in her journal at about this time the remark of a female friend: "God marries women, before they know what they are about. . . . If they waited long enough to think about it they would never marry." She thought her loneliness was "nothing" when compared to the miserable lives of men and women who enter into relations with mates who only "*seem* husbands, wives, & friends." Still, at almost thirty-five years old, Fuller knew her time for childbearing was running out, and she very much wanted a child of her own.[14]

For Fuller adored children. As the eldest child she had helped raise her siblings for her frequently ill mother, who had put her in charge of raising Edward Breck, the baby born on Fuller's eighteenth birthday that had died in her arms when he was sixteen months old. He was "a beautiful child," she wrote, and she "mourned for him much." Of all her friends' children, she had most loved little Waldo, who had also died. Next in her affection was the Hawthornes' dark-haired Una, who, when Fuller had visited with her parents in Concord in July 1844, had acted "like a little wild thing," leaning toward Margaret and stretching out her arms to her.

Now, in New York, Fuller lavished affection on Pickie, Greeley's son, as well as on Eddie Spring, son of Rebecca and Marcus Spring, who would soon invite her to travel with them to Europe as Eddie's tutor. Although Eddie was fond of Fuller, Pickie, who was only eight months old when she arrived in New York, grew to love her, and Fuller spent much of her time entertaining him when she lived at Turtle Bay. Greeley recalls that she "was never lofty, nor reserved, nor mystical" with Pickie; she became "his teacher, playmate, and monitor; and he requited her with a prodigality of love and admiration."[15]

In recalling Fuller's affection for his son, Greeley told of an episode that took place on the eve of Fuller's departure for Europe. Pickie had been napping in his father's office. Awakened before he was ready, a crying Pickie refused to be pacified. When Fuller entered the office, she went at once to him "in perfect confidence" that she could quiet him. Yet all Fuller's tender attempts to quell the toddler's rage failed. "At last," wrote Greeley, she "desisted in despair; and, with the bitter tears streaming down her face, observed:—'Pickie, many friends have treated me unkindly, but no one had ever the power to cut me to the heart, as you have!'"[16]

∽∂ ∽∂ ∽∂

Behind Fuller's grief here lay her heartache over her broken romance with James Nathan. Fuller immediately felt a strong attraction to the German-born Nathan when she met him at a New Year's party shortly after she moved in with the Greeleys. This smooth-talking yet intense, thirty-four-year-old romancer seemed interested in developing a serious relationship with Fuller, who thought he offered the prospect of a reciprocal relationship between equals, as she had depicted in *Woman in the Nineteenth Century,* then in press.

Not long after meeting Fuller, Nathan, an educated man who was employed at a textile import house, was taking the Haarlem omnibus to Forty-ninth Street to visit her at the Greeleys'. He courted Margaret with an ardor no man had ever shown her, playing his guitar and singing to her in the parlor. Fuller found him irresistible. She thought she saw in Nathan—a burly, bearded man with dark hair and sparkling blue eyes—the same combination of worldliness and sensitivity she had seen in Sam Ward. It seemed to her that Nathan's "feminine sweetness and sensibility" offset her masculine ambition.[17]

The Jewish Nathan thus seemed the perfect mate for her. In response to his chivalric gestures, her vivid imagination conjured images of their journey through life together. With Nathan she believed she might form a friendship that would eventually lead, as in the story of Cupid and Psyche, to wedded love. She thought reality would be just as she imagined it. A believer in signs and premonitions, Fuller interpreted their meeting as an act of fate. After accompanying Nathan in early February to view a panorama of Jerusalem, she wrote him that she saw in their meeting the fulfillment of her long-held "presentiment that I should meet, nearly, one of your race, who would show me how the sun of to-day shines upon the ancient Temple." She confesses, however, that she had never expected to find "so gentle and civilized an apparition and with blue eyes!"[18]

Fuller fell with all her heart for Nathan, an adept salesman and natural charmer who in turn saw in this woman an opportunity to advance in his career. After she gave him a copy of *Woman in the Nineteenth Century*, billed in the city as the "Great Book of the Age," he eagerly agreed to more meetings, as well as to exchanges of letters and to all the courtesies of an apparent romantic attachment. Encouraged by Mary, who had at first objected to Nathan's visits but relented since she wanted Margaret to find a man, Nathan visited her often at Turtle Bay. They attended the same afternoon teas, went together to a performance of Handel's *Messiah,* and secretly met downtown, sometimes at Lydia Maria Child's rooms on East Third Street or at the office of Fuller's hypnotist and magnetic healer, Dr. Theodore Leger, who seemed by means of a mysterious magnetic power that radiated from his hand to have alleviated her back pain.[19]

Nathan's presence in Fuller's life may have had something to do with Leger's alleged magnetic cure of her spine, since, as even she confessed, though she spent hours each morning in the mesmerist's office, he did not have the power to put her in a trance. But James Nathan did. Indeed, no man had ever treated Margaret so sweetly, and if her back troubled her less while she was in New York, her improved state may have had more to do with how Nathan made her feel than an actual spinal cure. Nathan's image was always in her mind—his expressive eyes, his compelling, sweet smile. She replayed in memory each of his courtly gestures toward her. She hummed the songs he sang to her and recalled his "words," which she thought "most unusual," so she always closely and "willingly listened" to him. She interpreted his behavior as indicating a deep and lasting affection. Nathan, after all, had told her his hard-luck story as a penniless immigrant who had come to America in 1830, and he had seemed genuinely appreciative of her sympathy and understanding. Fuller believed that he intended to marry her, noting that he had shared his "deep wants" with her and had responded enthusiastically to her thoughts on Panthea, whose story she calls in *Woman in the Nineteenth Century* "the most beautiful picture presented by ancient literature of wedded love." Panthea's story, after all, is about a wife so devoted to her husband that, when he dies in battle, she kills herself rather than live without him, an idea that Fuller absorbed so deeply that it may have contributed to her death aboard the *Elizabeth.*[20]

Nathan no doubt liked Margaret Fuller a great deal; he respected her work as a journalist and enjoyed getting her letters when they could not meet. Yet they inhabited different worlds: he was a profit-minded businessman, she a Romantic idealist and Puritan moralist. Nathan was a man of the earth; he wanted a woman to give him sexual pleasure without the bother of marriage. Fuller yearned for "pure soul communion."[21]

And even if she was "self-deceived" on occasion, as Emerson said, "by her own phantasms," Fuller appreciated the importance of using words precisely to arrive at a truth about reality, whereas Nathan twisted words to get from others what he wanted. No doubt he played on Fuller's affection, seeing in her proximity to power an opportunity for himself. Before he left for Europe in early June, Fuller had promised Nathan that she would secure for him, as she did, a letter of introduction from George Bancroft, President Polk's secretary of the navy. Through Fuller, moreover, Nathan made arrangements to get his letters from abroad published in the *Tribune*.[22]

What Fuller failed to see was that in Nathan she had met a man as histrionic as she was, a shrewd actor in the world who wanted sex and material success and was not hamstrung by Puritan moral scruples in his run to get them. As Fuller perceived reality, she was the principal actress in the ongoing drama she made of life. But Nathan had his own play in mind. He shuffled his cards with a slight of hand that hid from Fuller his private dealings as well as his motives for behaving so gentlemanly toward her.

Fuller's first hint of Nathan's deception was gossip she heard from a landlady in his neighborhood linking Nathan romantically with an Englishwoman. At the very time Nathan was seeing Fuller and letting her believe that he loved her, he was, so the landlady said, keeping this other woman as his mistress. When Fuller confronted Nathan in a 2 April 1845 letter with the rumor that he was already involved with an "English maiden," he lied. Playing back to Fuller her own argument about society's need to reform prostitutes, Nathan implied that his friend had been a woman of the streets whom he was trying to "rehabilitate."[23]

Wishing it so, Fuller believed him, even though she "felt" his "falsity" and acknowledged he "had acted a fiction" with her. Her sense of his duplicity was so painful to her that it made her feel faint. The shock of discovery as she read his ambiguous confession that, yes, there was another woman, made all things seem to swim before her. She impulsively took off the brightly colored flowers she had pinned to her bodice that morning, which had expressed her feelings up to the moment she read his letter, and she gave them to a blind girl whose "shut up state" she almost envied.[24]

She was able to understand, Fuller explained to Nathan in her 6 April letter, how an attractive man like him could be "tempted by the romance of the position." Fuller chose here to use the word "tempted," for it carried great moral weight for her— though in these exchanges of letters, both writers were, in a sense, double talking. In mid-March she had noted to Nathan that, while she could not ask it in the speech of God's "chosen people," she nonetheless thought "the prayer which He of Nazareth gave is true for the heart of all nations—'Lead me not into temptation and deliver me from evil.'" Fuller's deliberate substitution of "me" for "us" surely suggested to the sexually experienced Nathan how powerfully she was attracted to him.[25]

As a way of excusing Nathan's behavior, Fuller in her 2 and 6 April letters recalls how he had told her that he "had 'only broken through the conventions of this world.'" Yet even as she wrote "only," she made it clear to him that this word, too, carried great weight for her. Although she had defended in print the unconventional behavior of George Sand, Fuller suggests that she does not approve of Nathan's unconventional behavior toward a prostitute. She tells him how she had thought of taking such a woman on an outing with her yet had decided not to do so when she considered the potential damage to her own reputation. Here Fuller hints to Nathan that he ought to be more discreet, though she had also conceded to him in these letters how easy it is to act "unwisely." Seemingly alluding to her own similarly indiscreet behavior toward a person she once loved, Fuller confesses: "Also there have been circumstances in *my* life, which if made known to the world, would judged by conventional rules, subject me as probably to general blame, as these could you." Although these instances "will, probably, never be made known," she says she is "well prepared" to pay the price of public censure should they come to light. For she believes she has done no real wrong and has "too much real weight of character to be sunk" by the judgment of others, "unless," she adds, "real stones of offense" were "attached to me."26

In her 2 and 6 April letters, as elsewhere in the letters she wrote Nathan between March and May 1845, Fuller conveys a mixed message, hinting heavily that she, like Nathan, has defied sexual moral convention, even as she condemns his indiscreet behavior with, she says, "an injured woman." That a woman who is sexually active outside of marriage is, in Fuller's eyes, *injured*—an unconventional use of the word we will want to remember and a term she uses to describe a prostitute's fallen state—hints at the dark view she had of premarital or extramarital sex. At times she thus played the part of the conventional pious Puritan who considers all sex outside marriage to be a sin and is devoted to her "heavenly father." At other times she hinted that, as Hawthorne wrote in *Blithedale Romance* about Zenobia (who, in a nod to Fuller's well-known inclination to don a fresh flower every day, as well as her obsession with Nathan, always wore a flower and was obsessively in love with a man who rejected her for a reformed girl of the streets), "There is no folded petal, no latent dew-drop, in this perfectly developed rose!"27

38 ∽ The Garden's Desecration

Fuller in her letters frequently hinted that it would give her pleasure to receive Nathan's sexual advances. On 31 March 1845, after she had learned that Nathan planned to go abroad, she wrote him that she had "a strong desire" to be with him: "To feel that there is to be so quick a bound to intercourse makes us prize the moment." She responds to his warning that she may never know him "wholly" by telling him that it is important "to know the natural music of the being." These

---

comments, along with others, made Nathan think she wanted to close their friendship in America with a sexual connection.[1]

On 9 April, a week after she had discovered his liaison with the "injured" English maiden, Fuller wrote Nathan how his "sweet ray touches" her life and how she wishes "it might call out full" with "splendid blossoms, like the pink cactuses" we see "in the windows . . . these bright spring days"—an image suggestive of sexual readiness. "I am with you," she croons, "as never with any other one": "I like to be quite still and have you the actor and the voice." She writes that she hopes he will "indulge" her in this "repose," as she says another man once did—and here she doesn't identify the man—on whose "pure altar" there "sometimes" "burnt" a fire "too fiercely," while at other times, it lay "desolate with ashes."[2]

We cannot know if that other man to whom Fuller refers—that man on whose "pure altar [her 'little birds'] could always alight"—is Emerson, with whom she had a hot-cold relationship, or Sam Ward, George Davis, or even William Clarke. Whatever her intentions, Nathan, whom she had been meeting (sometimes secretly), thought she meant that she had already been with a man sexually. When Nathan thus took Fuller's words to mean that she wanted to fulfill his own "*hope*" for sex with her outside of marriage and apparently propositioned her during an 11 April encounter, Fuller wrote him three days later fervently denying ever having suggested that she was looking for a relationship based on sexual gratification. Bewildered, she asks how a "most trusted friend" could "be '*hoping*' about such things?" In her 14 April letter she tells Nathan that he has misread her words. She accuses him of letting "the hoofs of the demon" trample and desecrate "the sweet little garden, with which my mind had surrounded your image."[3]

The garden to which Fuller alludes has two likely literary sources, Milton and Shelley. In a late May letter she will misquote a phrase from the end of *Paradise Lost* when she confesses to Nathan that had they "been alone" after one of their emotional meetings, she should have "dropped a few [natural] tears." By alluding to Milton's epic, Fuller in this May 1845 letter reveals her guilt over having felt lust for Nathan. The image of a sweet little garden conveys a wish she could go back to a time in her mother's garden before she became conscious of sexuality and death: Paradise/Eden before the serpent.[4]

Confessing to Nathan in early May her "need of escaping from this overpowering" attraction she feels for him when she is with him, Fuller retreated, as was her pattern, to fantasy and literature, especially to poems by Shelley. Indeed, Shelley's "The Sensitive-Plant" is another probable source for the image of the "sweet garden." In that poem, a self-pitying and pathetic flower grows in an "undefiled Paradise," a garden tended by a gentle woman who resembles Fuller's mother and who dies. In the perfect world of the garden prior to the death of this unfallen Eve, the sensitive plant thrives in this "garden sweet" in "Air" that is "all love." The sweet garden of her letter thus comes from this poem by Shelley, whom Fuller once confessed *stirred* her mind more than Milton and whose poetry she was rereading that May.[5]

The "garden sweet" suggests an enclosed imaginary space where love is "undefiled." It conjures Margarett Crane's Cambridgeport flower garden and a time when Margaret as a small child was alone there with her mother, prior to the death of her infant sister and her father's domination over her life. That Fuller depicts herself in these letters as a violet as opposed to a rose, a flower we know she associates with her lovely mother, makes sense when we note how pathetic is the flower of Shelley's poem.[6]

But these letters about a defiled garden were written in a period of panic and depression after her unnerving 11 April sexual encounter with Nathan. On 15 April 1845, the day after she accused Nathan of desecrating her garden—alluding apparently to his crude sexual overture ("a sadder day," she says, "than I have had in all my life"), she wrote him an angry letter wherein she claims that it was no "act of 'providence,'" after all, "but of some ill demon" that had "exposed" her to what is, "to every worldly and womanly feeling," an insult.[7]

Evidence indicates that Nathan did indeed press Fuller to engage in a sexual relationship with him and that in doing so he touched her in a way that distressed her. This intimate contact made her feel as if her mind was "enfolded" in his "as a branch with flame." What seems to have happened here is that Fuller linked Nathan—the kind of worldly "man of business" she depicted Timothy as being in her untitled autobiographical romance—with her father, who, when she was a child, looked forward to "folding to his heart his long-lost daughter" when she jumped up to greet him when he returned from a trip. By linking James Nathan with Timothy and hence the past, she unconsciously transferred her archaic feelings for her father onto Nathan and consequently behaved toward him, as she herself said, "like a child."[8] And, childlike, she trusted him. She believed his words even when he lied.

Fuller "wanted" Nathan, then, not just because she felt a strong adult attraction to him. She wanted him also because his sexual advance had stirred to life in her, as an adult, "a feeling of childhood" that she liked, intense "feelings" that had of necessity—as she herself said of her feelings in childhood—sunk "deep within" her when she was a child.[9]

It seems the feelings were attached to events she could not quite remember. Hence Fuller could describe the suffusion of emotion she felt in Nathan's presence only as "a feeling of childhood," of being "led by the hand," of being "gently drawn near to the realities of life." Whatever the case, that Nathan was *not* the "noble" or "honorable" man Fuller imagined him to be, was not, after all, of great significance. For what counts in a transference interaction such as this Fuller was experiencing in relation to Nathan is not the actual object, who went on his way, but instead, as Roland Barthes has said, *"the transference itself."*[10]

To make excuses for Nathan, Fuller blamed his behavior on a "demon," on that evil yet fascinating power to which she had earlier confessed that she was herself sometimes "mysteriously" drawn, a "power most obvious in the eye." Where was God, she wonders in her letter, when she, "poor child," needed him? To Nathan's contention that it was not he but she who "sinned" against him by pretending to want him sexually, only then to assault him with insults and disdain, Fuller replied: "Not one moment have I sinned against you; to 'disdain' you would be to disdain myself." If she could be "deceived" as was Eve by Satan, then she is, herself, at her core, "impure!"[11]

"Self-conscious now" in a way she has not been before as a sexual human being, Fuller defensively attests to Nathan: "You have touched my heart, and it thrilled at the centre, but that is all." Here Fuller reveals that it was not an entirely pleasant sensation she felt when Nathan aroused her sexually. Yet, to feel a thrill for Fuller was *truly* to feel—something that it had been difficult for her to do since her childhood when, to survive psychologically, she had buried her "true life" "deep within." Trying to further explain her reaction, Fuller says that if she has expressed herself more frankly than most, then he must know that "she has been in her way a queen and received . . . guests . . . of royal blood." In a distant queenly voice she notes that Nathan's "past conduct" has not been "*severely* true," and with her, "truth is the first of jewels,—."[12]

39 ∽ Narcissistic Wounds and Imaginary Mystic Entities

"Truth at all cost" was Fuller's maxim. And the truth is that Fuller's past holds the reasons that her heart "thrilled" at Nathan's touch and that she was shrill in her reaction to him. That she felt her mind folded into his and her body hence eerily out of her control "exposed" her to herself, it seemed, as being no better than the prostitutes to whom she had lectured on their need for moral redemption, women whose "lonely hours" were "haunted," she thought, by "painful images" of their "contamination." Afraid that she might actually be as great a sinner as they, Fuller confessed to Nathan eight days after her traumatic encounter with him on 11 April that she has long suspected she "was not really good at all." The "feeling" of being mentally out of control, of being "alienated from *myself*," she wrote him, was "dreadfully unnatural to me."[1]

In projecting her childhood feelings onto Nathan, Fuller felt "alienated" from her vital "I" as an agent for social change and a spokeswoman for the living God in her soul—a "god," as we know, that she tended at this time to fuse and confuse with her father, an ideal being she defensively sought to find in Nathan. Thus in her 19 April letter she expresses her thanks not only to Nathan for pardoning her for her sins, but also to "our father for making thee [Nathan] the instrument of good to me." The way to "repose," she wrote this worldly man whom she is attempting to turn into a savior, is to be "God[']s good children," to be childlike in ways other than in expressing "impulses and childish longings."[2]

Nathan, however, was no god; in his needs he was, as she herself noted, "*manly*." And this manly man was baffled by a woman who wrote him letters hinting she wanted to consummate their relationship, yet who, when he actually tried it, accused him of letting a demon defile her. Not long after Fuller's traumatic mid-April 1845 encounter with him, Nathan lost romantic interest in her even as he continued to send her notes and, in some ways, to encourage her, perhaps because he still wanted her help in his career. When he, then, failed to give Fuller the "reverent love" she said she was seeking, she panicked. The thought of the loss of this man she mentally linked with her father caused her "unspeakable" pain.[3]

Fuller in New York had intended to give up childish illusions. But that was not easy, for the intense emotions stirred in her by Nathan's sexual assertiveness toward her had suffused her body with feeling like water through a gully after rain. These emotions were so strong that when he was near and they surfaced in her it made her feel "in a sort of trance," a state of mind that gave her pleasure.[4]

Recollecting this feeling in fantasy was hence preferable for Fuller than acknowledging she had been betrayed by a man she loved but lost. Such a conscious recollection of betrayal brought with it a memory from the past and the pain she had felt in relation to her father, who had left her each year to go to Washington and who had died before she had reconciled outstanding issues with him. So emotion builds on emotion, as Wordsworth said—except that, for Fuller, this accumulative emotional process did not always lead to self-enrichment through memory; sometimes it led to self-dissolution through dim reminiscences of past painful scenes of betrayal, loss, and trauma.[5]

In a December 1843 letter to Anna, Fuller had talked about her "inward conflict" as well as about her "powerful imagination," which, "at the least touch of an old wound," was able to retrace and concentrate "into a moment of perception the long scene of strife and pain where it was made." Though her recollection of such a scene would have been corrupted by the effects of time and memory, still, the specific "moment of perception" Fuller refers to here was apparently so fraught with pain for her that recalling it threw her back into childhood. This process of recollection thus kept her, she said in her letter, from ever being able to rise "entirely above childishness."[6]

In such a way Nathan's "touch" without love reopened in Fuller "an old wound," one even deeper than the cut made by her father's abrupt death, or by what she felt was her mother's neglect of her when she was a child. Both these old hurts, however, contributed to her retreat to fantasy at the mere thought that Nathan might abandon her. This retreat of the "too sensitive" soul is familiar to students of the Romantics, especially admirers of Shelley. Enchanted with Shelley's poetry, Fuller presented a volume of his poetry to Nathan as a "parting gift" when he left in early June 1845 for Europe.[7]

This pattern in Fuller's life of idealizing an object of love and obsessing on it to the point of psychic inertia and instability is not unlike the emptying of self into death evident in several of Shelley's poems, where the protagonist vainly searches to reacquire an ideal lost love. That Fuller at this point was so taken with the life-negating poetry of Shelley suggests the power of the written word to reinforce both good *and* bad behaviors. That she so easily absorbed certain images from his poems shows how unstable her ego was when she was in New York. Shelley's poems like "The Sensitive-Plant" and *Alastor; or, The Spirit of Solitude* appealed to Fuller's narcissistic "dark side," her tendency to retreat to fantasy, even though she knew that "careless excursions into the realms of fantasy" could corrupt her "virginity of heart."[8]

Each of these poems features a lonely, betrayed, misunderstood person trapped in a magical world of angels and demons that seem to determine the direction of his life in the same way Fuller blamed Nathan's behavior on an "ill demon" and prayed for a "guardian Angel" to care for her. Though she may be referring here to the angel who guarded Festus from the devil as he journeyed through sin and temptation in Bailey's epic (a copy of which she also gave Nathan), Fuller's fantasy pursuit of Nathan follows more nearly the pattern of Shelley's *Alastor.*[9]

In *Alastor* a solitary poet wanders in quest of perfect love. The poem's persona is a wounded narcissist who follows a self-projected ideal female from his "cold fireside and alienated home / To seek truths in undiscovered lands." Perhaps Shelley's "soul out of my soul" motif came to Fuller's mind when Nathan told her that he, like she, was a poet; perhaps she thought of it when she called them "twin spirits." Certainly it moved her to refer to Nathan later as "brother of my soul."[10] And her decision to follow Nathan to Europe was likely in part influenced by the flight of Shelley's poet/persona, who sailed the sea in search of love as well as of the truth of his being. The truth he discovers, however, unlike that of the returning prodigal son, is that only in death can he recover his dream maiden, the original object of his love: his mother.

Fuller might have been thinking of the poem's images of an absent mother when she wrote Nathan. The "veiled maid" the poet has seen in a dream vanishes the moment that she "Folded his frame in her . . . arms." This loss generates in him a desire to pursue this vision that Shelley depicts as "two starry eyes, hung in the gloom of thought," an image suggesting an infant's memory of a mother's eyes. Crying out, "Alas! alas! . . . Lost, lost, for ever lost," the poet sets out on a quest that takes him over untamed seas in a "little boat" that is "driven" by his desire to recover his lost love, by a power seemingly greater than his capacity to control it.[11]

The surreal setting through which the poet travels is the manifestation of his troubled mind, much as Fuller's letters to Nathan display her anxiety. The poet rides the outer edge of a black womblike whirlpool in a boat that takes him steeply down to a stream in a "labyrinthine dell." It comes to rest on a green recess at the top of a precipice that drops down into an "immeasurable void," symbol of the poet's empty soul. The powerless poet lies down in this cradlelike recess to die. The sense that only in death can he recover the mothering love he has lost is conveyed by Shelley through the image of a horned moon that "hung low" and heavy in the sky, "two lessening points of light" that fade as the poet dies. Two starry eyes, a cradlelike green recess, a heavy horned moon like a mother's full breasts and taut nipples: all these, the poet dreams, will be his when he enters "the dark gate of death"—an image that appears in Fuller's later letters from Europe.[12]

In this poem where erotic desire leads to death and the natural setting is a projection of the poet's vacant soul, the reader hears the despair of the poet who has never been able to resolve his intense ambivalent feelings for his mother. According to critic Barbara Schapiro, the fantasy-maid is an image of the self-made-whole by a love "never bestowed by or received from the mother." Such a fantasy of regressive fusion is like that to which Fuller retreated when experiencing stress or degrading rejection. Yet the cry of victimization of the "too sensitive soul"—of the poet in *Alastor* and of Fuller in her letters to Nathan—only thinly conceals a grandiose fantasy of secret superiority and power. This fantasy of godlike power harbors within it the illusions that the self is so special that it cannot die and that its purity propels it beyond good and evil.[13]

This description so far fits Fuller, who felt she had mystical powers. She tells Nathan in early May that she has "deep mystic feelings" in herself "and intimations from elsewhere," as if a god has "*chosen*" her to speak on behalf of nineteenth-century women as the Greek gods spoke through the Pythia at Delphi. If her priestly interpreter had been Emerson, then maybe her "spirit-facts" would have grown wings. But by projecting her feelings onto a man who used her, she gave him—or his specter—power over her ego, or, as Emerson would say, over her "soul." Like a modern follower of a neopagan mystery cult or self-serving charismatic leader, Fuller gave control of her soul to a mystic-romantic entity that subsumed her individuality and hence took from her the agency necessary for independent, life-affirming action. In early May she thus wrote Nathan, "I hear you with awe assert the power over me." Five days later she tells him she feels as if she has "never been able to go a step where you did not take me." And on 15 May she writes, "You have force; and take with you the sense that I am thus deeply in your debt"—as she still felt "indebted" to her dead father, a powerful man by whom she felt, as she had written him when she was nine, "possessed."[14]

In her relationship with Nathan, Fuller's Romantic imagination set an ordinary businessman "all aglow" with an aura of power not his own and let her "self" become "enslave[d]" to a man who saw her affection for him as a way to forward his profession. In such a way James Nathan became Fuller's fantasy-maid, a being spun from her own emotions and needs and hence misperceived by her as "feminine," an object she would futilely pursue, not just in New York, but over the ocean to Europe.[15]

40 ∞ Romantic Obsession

Fuller's letters to Nathan show how beneath the seemingly self-possessed presence of a highly visible public figure there can exist a separate self obsessed with a destructive private fantasy, which in Fuller's case was fed by her reading of the Romantics, especially the poetry of Shelley. Though she occasionally saw Nathan in May, when he did not come to comfort her she could not sleep, her head ached, her neck hurt, and it seemed that she cried all the time. "Mein liebste," she wrote him 7 May, "you tell me to rest, but how can I rest when you rouse in me so many thoughts and feelings?"[1]

To escape the pain, Fuller lay in her darkened room overlooking the river, shut out "outward objects," and turned to fantasy. Recasting disturbing sexual impulses into spiritual terms acceptable to her punitive conscience, Fuller appeals in a May letter for mercy to the Zeus-like power from which, she says, like Athena, she "sprang": "O Heaven, O God, or by whatsoever name I may appeal; surely, . . . O All Causing thou must be the . . . *All-Fulfilling* too." Please satisfy my desire, she prays to this power. May the "magic of its touch" throw open "the treasure chambers of the Universe."[2]

Fuller tells Nathan of her need to escape "this overpowering sense" of connection to a mystical power. She confesses in her early May letters that the feeling Nathan has a similar power over her "causes awe, but not dread," such as she has felt in the past at the approach of such a power. Apparently unaware of the sexual imagery in her words, she notes that, though "the first turnings of the key were painful, yet the inner door makes rapturous music too upon its golden hinge." She writes that Nathan reads her "so deeply" that it seems he must know the "secret" that "hides" behind that inner door. "Sometimes" he makes her "tremble too." So deep is the "secret" he reads that the mere "sense" that his "thoughts" are "pour[ing] upon" her takes from her "all power of thought or motion." "Then comes the painful retrograde motion." She deludes herself into believing that Nathan will "lead [her] on in a spirit of holy love."[3]

Yet even as Fuller gained pleasure from such fantasy fusions with Nathan, another part of her knew that this pleasure-giving state of mind was the product of illusion. Psychologists say that such a mystical feeling is typical in narcissistic people whose lovers have disappointed them. Triggered by the loss of the narcissistic union with the idealized self-object, the insecure subject compensates by investing his or her feelings in archaic forms of idealization—in ecstatic religious visions, trancelike states, autoerotic sexual practices, or dreams of merging with

"god," as Fuller does here. She imaginatively transforms Nathan into Cupid, noting how Psyche, too, was "but a mortal woman." Yet as Love's bride, she became
"divinely human," as Fuller desires to be.[4]

In his replies Nathan corrected her German grammar in the same condescending way Timothy had done when she was a child, thus reinforcing the negative
transference of feelings for her father onto him. She defended her error on Monday,
26 May, writing him that when she wrote "Mein liebste" (feminine) for "Mein lieb-
ster" (masculine) she was "seeking the woman" in him, a comment that the "manly"
Nathan surely thought odd. Anticipating his negative reaction, Fuller claims that
such outpourings are not, as he might think, unnatural. "If a flow of gentle love be
natural," such as she had felt for him when they were together Sunday evening,
then "surely there was nature." At the end of May she misquotes Wordsworth to
him, "Nature *never* did deceive The heart that loved her" (original emphasis).[5]

In another end-of-May letter, which reached Nathan before he left on 1 June for
Europe (taking his English mistress with him), Fuller wrote that she "naturally"
wished in these parting hours to do all she could for him. But her, he complained,
"babbling of green fields," her self-confessed need to retreat to "this region of beautiful symbols" wherein she was "nourished," she said, "as the infant from the mother's breast," repelled him. Perhaps it has likewise repelled historians and Fuller
biographers, for they all but ignore the letters and hence deny a partitioned yet significant part of Fuller's personality. To do so, however, is a mistake. For while our
sense of self and identity, as psychologist Daniel Schacter has said, is indeed dependent on our explicit recall of verifiable events from our past, the idiosyncrasies that
make us who we are may in fact be more closely tied to what Schacter describes as
"implicit memories," memories of past experiences we cannot remember explicitly that "unconsciously influence our perceptions, thoughts, and actions." I would
argue that these letters to Nathan reveal that experiences from Fuller's past that
she cannot recall clearly—that she describes only as "a feeling of childhood"—are
influencing Fuller's perceptions of Nathan as well as her actions in relation to him.
In Fuller's case, it may be that what she thought she felt for Nathan was in fact a
misreading of the reason he had such a "powerful magnetic effect" on her. The
"flow" of her emotion, which she called natural, may in fact not have been natural
at all; thus nature does deceive the heart that loves her.[6]

As Fuller was thus increasingly retreating into "this region" of illusion, part of
her was dealing with reality. In late June when Margaret's mother came to visit,
she played the dutiful daughter. The Greeleys' home at the time was in more than
its usual state of disarray: Margaret had quarreled with Mary over Josey, the New-
foundland puppy that Nathan had left with her. Mary liked Nathan, but she did
not want a dog in her house and scolded Margaret, who had never owned a pet,
for deficiency in caring for it, though the maid was bathing it daily and Margaret
took it with her at night when she went for a swim in the river. The puppy "swims

nobly," she wrote Nathan in July, even though, because he does not like water, she had to get some boys to throw him in. The puppy, unlike Nathan, is fond of her regardless of her "faults."[7]

In the same letter Fuller confesses to Nathan that it gave her "a strange kind of pleasure" when he called her his "little girl." For she has no memory of having been regarded that way by her parents, only of having been "called on for wisdom and dignity long before my leading strings were off." Even now she was being asked to exhibit a maturity she did not feel, since she was having to deal with her mother, who "could not fully see" how she could be "content" living in a house where servants quit rather than tolerate Mary's moods. Mrs. Fuller had apparently decided that it is better to live in a house with a facade of calm than acknowledge underlying "dissensions"—which is precisely the way this quietly dignified woman had chosen to run her home in the face of her absent husband's lascivious behavior in relation to pretty women in Washington.[8]

After her mother's visit, the "only drawback" of which was that it was apparent to her that her mother did not "fully" comprehend her daughter, Fuller spent hours looking out her upstairs bedroom window with its view to the river. Distressed over Nathan's indifference, Fuller that summer turned, as she had in the past, to the alluring gentleness of flowing water for relief from her anxiety. The week after her mother left, she wrote Cary about a "charming" spot she had found "on the edge of the rocks" where "a wall of . . . rock rises behind me." It was like the spot the poet-protagonist of *Alastor* had found in his lonely quest for love. When the summer heat became intense, Fuller liked to sit there at night with Josey as companion and the water rustling up to her feet. Other nights she liked to lie in the hammock on the piazza. It is "like being in a cradle," she tells Nathan. She wishes he were there to play his guitar and sing to her.[9]

In the same way the poet of *Alastor* found peace in a green recess described by Shelley as nature's "cradle," so Fuller during this New York interlude found peace lying in a hammock overlooking the East River and dreaming of Nathan singing to her like a mother to her baby.[10] Her letters suggest the extent to which her porous ego at this time had absorbed the poetry of Shelley; in them, as in many of his poems, we hear the lament of a wounded narcissist who has never resolved her ambivalent feelings for the mother.

Fuller's ambivalent feelings for the feminine figure had been intensified by her mother's continuing failure to understand her as well as by Cary's newly cool attitude toward her, which was caused in part by Cary's growing interest in William Tappan, a young man Emerson had been urging her to meet. Cary had also distanced herself from Fuller after reading *Woman in the Nineteenth Century*. Its style and content annoyed Cary, as did an article Fuller published in the *Tribune* about their visit together to the Bloomingdale Asylum for the Insane on Valentine's Day. In it Fuller suggests that only a hairsbreadth separates the sane from the insane.

She praises a Dr. Earle and the asylum for providing a "house of refuge" for "those too deeply wounded or disturbed in body or spirit to keep up that semblance or degree of sanity which the conduct of affairs in the world" demands.[11]

She notes in her article how pleased she was to see at a Valentine's dance at the asylum "people who, half a century ago, would have been chained in solitary cells, screaming out their anguish," now restraining "their impatient impulses." Their conduct convinced her "that the power of self-control is not lost" in the "sick in mind," "only lessened." Fuller notes how in a famous painting in Munich of "a mad house" the artist has represented in it "the moral obliquities of society exaggerated into madness; that is to say, self-indulgence." In our self-indulgence, she says, "we are all mad, all criminal." In the voice of a Christian reformer she urges her readers not to despair, for "the Ruler of all" could never "permit such wide-spread ill" if it were not for the good end of giving us "a field to redeem it."[12]

This 22 February article, which pleased social reformers, had upset Cary, for in it Fuller had casually mentioned something private in their past. Cary had been offended by Fuller's remarks about how a "companion," presumably Cary, "of that delicate nature by which a scar is felt as a wound, was saddened by the sense how very little our partialities, undue emotions, and manias need to be exaggerated to entitle us to rank among madmen." Having made the comment privately to Fuller, Cary felt her older friend had violated her trust when she printed it for all New York to read.[13]

In a letter she wrote Cary four months later when she was in anguish over Nathan, Fuller recalls the peace she had felt the previous summer when she and Cary had vacationed together at the beach and were once again dear loving friends. "Do you remember that night last summer when we fell asleep on the bed and were like Elizabeth and Mary[?]" she asks Cary.[14]

In stressing the purity of their love, Fuller in this July 1845 letter noticeably did not tell Cary about the dark dreams that had haunted her when they had gone together to the beach the summer before: in one Fuller had fallen off the rocks into the sea, and in another it seemed "great spiders [were] running over me." Even more terrifying had been the nightmare she had had that September (1844), the one in which she saw Cary drowning in the ocean and was unable to save her because her feet felt frozen to earth and her "cloak of *red silk* kept falling off" whenever she reached out to help her. At last Cary's body had washed up on the sand, only to have the waves draw it back again. "It was a terrible dream," wrote Fuller, as disturbing as the one she had while lying in bed beside Anna in October 1842 when Sam was away. In that one, too, the price her punitive conscience had made her pay for her desire was death by drowning in the cold waves, though in the 1842 dream it was Fuller who had drowned. The night after her nightmare about Cary being washed up dead on shore, Fuller had dreamed her mother was dead. In her journal Fuller wrote that the "pathos" of these dreams left her "sobbing."[15]

Though Fuller loved both women deeply, maybe the dreams also left her feeling a bit relieved. For in them she conveniently obliterated the two bothersome females who had failed, she felt, to love her adequately. However one interprets them, Fuller's nightmares about her mother and friend reveal the depth of her ambivalent feelings for the feminine figure whose love she craved yet whom she still was not sure she could deal with in a balanced way.[16]

During that summer of 1845, Fuller found Nathan's silence even more trying than her mother's failure to understand her or Cary's coolness to her. Her anxiety mounted when through June and most of July she had not heard from him. After seven weeks of silence he finally wrote her. In return she sent him a morbid letter telling about "the great fire" of 19 July, which had ravaged the business district of New York City. Amid the "still smoking" ruins she saw a man searching for his wife. She heard of a girl who had lost everything and wandered to the Fulton ferryhouse, where she managed "to kill herself" by taking laudanum, and of a corpse they found still "grasping in one hand charred ledgers."[17]

Against this bleak backdrop, Fuller imposed an image of the absent Nathan as a bright godlike being, insisting, as she did in mid-August, that theirs was an "*immortal love.*" Three weeks later, like Shelley's heartsick poet, she cried out "where art Thou!" Obsessed with an idealized image of Nathan as a man of "great experience, great ideas, [and] religious heart," Fuller ended her Sunday, 15 September, letter with a prayerful confession, "last moon at Rockaway on the noble beach with the surf rushing in, I thought of thee, every night and in a sense all the time, so near wast thou And . . . I . . . pray that life may purify and perfect thy noble nature." Exhibiting symptoms characteristic of a person whose frustrated obsessive love for an idealized object has led to a sense that his or her "self" is dissolving, Fuller notes that her head constantly "throbs" and her hand "trembles." Only in dreams, she says, do "I feel quite happy." In dreams, says she in language the sexual nature of which a man like Nathan would not have missed, "I have you with me as a river that has passed through another rushes joyous and enriched on its course."[18]

41 ∽ A Soul-Paralyzing Pain

That Fuller in his absence identified keenly with Shelley's self-pitying protagonists, Nathan acknowledged by sending her a rose from Shelley's tomb in Rome. The role of an obsessed narcissist who feels betrayed and abandoned, however, only loosely fit her. Shelley's typical protagonist, who tends to be colorless and amoral, never locates the source of his rage and aggression in himself but blames other people for his troubles. In fact Fuller had more in common with the flamboyant Byron and his defiant, passionate characters: the Byronic hero is a clear-cut figure with a highly developed moral sense who accepts responsibility for the act of defiance that destroys him or others.[1]

Fuller likewise had a highly developed moral sense, and the guilt she felt when she defied what she believed were divine laws was excruciating, especially, as we know, when it came to sex. Though in New York she had intended to control her emotions, Nathan's allure made her feel as if an invisible magnetic power were pulling her to him even as her conscience insisted on her sexual purity.[2] The inevitable clash within her produced the shrillness we hear in Fuller's letters to Nathan, a passionate appeal for sensual love cut off by a zealously punitive conscience.

Underlying Fuller's obsession with Nathan was, as we have seen, a soul-paralyzing "hysteria." "Hysteria" was nineteenth-century society's term—one critics now decry as "more than a little misogynistic"—for a woman's expression of panic, pain, and anxiety "at the least touch," as Fuller put it, "of an old wound," one often connected in some way to her sexuality. It is a pain unintelligible to those who have not felt it—so inexplicably jarring that it can make a woman feel faint and certain rational men, unable to comprehend it, dismiss it as imagined. Even Emerson, after her death, in reading Fuller's journals of her New York period, disparagingly described the anguished cries in them as "hysterical."[3]

Relevant to Fuller's obsession with Nathan is Freud's observation in an 1896 paper that in the cases of obsessions he had studied, he invariably found a substratum of what he called "hysterical" symptoms, such as those Fuller exhibited in relating to Nathan. Evident in her letters to Nathan is the (so-called) "hysterical" personality's usual fascination with sex and "mental 'sensitiveness,'" as well as a barely repressed erotic tension that might be read by their recipient as a sexual advance. Apparent also is such a person's shrill response to a sexual touch, the denial of a desire for sex, and the theatrical appeal to an idealized dead father for protection. All this is linked to an increasing tendency to fantasize, pass into trancelike states, and exhibit other symptoms of what Harvard medical researchers now call "chronic pain syndrome." The latter includes headaches, backaches, sleeplessness, trembling hands, a general inertia, and malaise. Researchers list factors known to predispose people to developing chronic pain syndrome: "a compulsive personality, constant stress, and a history of physical or sexual abuse."[4]

In contrast to one scholar's claim that this litany of symptoms was well known by clever nineteenth-century women like Bertha Papenheim (Anna O.), who played sick to get attention, Fuller's retreat to fantasy and her self-described "soft trances," though hyperbolic and theatrical, do not seem to be part of a self-conscious act. In her brief but painful relationship with Nathan, Fuller instead acted out a script that had been written for her in her childhood during which she had acquired a set of behaviors she now unconsciously replayed in relating to Nathan. Her feeling that he had power over her thus gave her, as she said, "a *strange* kind of pleasure" (emphasis added). It was the kind of uncanny power she had written about in her notes on the demonical in which she says that such "unconscious" power is often conveyed by "the eye" of those who "mysteriously control." We dread it, she says, yet we approach "nearer, and a part of our nature listens, sometimes answers to this influence," as part of Fuller's nature now answered to Nathan's. In late July she wrote Nathan how she longs to be "summoned by your voice catch animation from your eye." As a child, she had similarly anticipated being summoned by her watchful father to recite for him.[5]

Fuller in these letters was predictably exhibiting profound dedication to the idealized memory of her dead father. She recalls in her 30 September 1845 letter to Nathan, which she wrote the night of the anniversary of Timothy's death, how at "just about this time he left us and my hand closed his eyes."[6] Her father had abandoned her before she had had a chance to resolve her conflicted feelings for him, a pattern now being repeated with Nathan.

As a child Fuller had felt her father's absence with the same intensity she now felt Nathan's. She found herself longing to hold Nathan's hand and crying all the time, as tears had sprung to her eyes when her father had failed to mention her in letters he sent his wife from Washington. Three months after Nathan left, Fuller wrote him an anguished letter asking, "Why, why, must you leave me? If you had staid, I should have been well and strong . . . and had so much natural joy and so many thoughts of childhood!" Has she not been, she asks him on 29 September, a "sweet companion" eager to be "upborne" in his "strong arms[?]"[7]

Lost in illusion, Fuller in the 29–30 September letter wherein she appeals to her father for a blessing evokes an image from *Oberon*. In *Oberon* the Christian knight Huon and his pagan lover Rezia consummate their love outside of wedlock. In her letter, Fuller sees herself and Nathan, like Huon and Amanda (Rezia's Christian name), united finally by "holy vows" "within the pure white veil." Fuller's reference here is to both the silvery veil cast over Amanda by her good Angel at *Oberon*'s end and an actual white veil Nathan had given Fuller as a parting gift. It is also to the white veil—a "pure silver haze," according to Fuller here—that hides divine Truth and is purportedly lifted from the eyes of those who have died who have given their lives to the Lord (2 Cor. 3:7–18; 4:3). Joined with Nathan in "holy" wedlock, notes a pain-filled Fuller, there would be "no more [pain] or sin or sadness."[8]

In this letter in which she recollects how she had closed her dead father's eyes, she wonders if, "from that home of higher life" her father now inhabits, his "blessing" would "still accompany" the hand that closed his eyes. She thinks "he thus far would bless his child."[9]

Not to the historical Nathan but to an idealized father-god-lover Fuller thus penned her letters. And in direct proportion as her obsession with Nathan grew, so her various illnesses—what scientists today might consider the result of a "conversion disorder"—hindered her work so that Greeley had to reprimand her for falling behind in her writing. In such a way her childhood need for love now began to undercut her ability to work. Whether pouring out "childish" feelings in letters to Nathan or writing daring articles for the *Tribune*, Fuller in New York was unable to reconcile the conflicting sides of her self.[10]

This inner division stayed alive when she moved out of the Greeleys' chaotic house and into quieter quarters in the city, first into a boardinghouse on Warren Street and then, until 12 March, into rooms she rented from a widow at 4 Amity Place. After that, to save money, she stayed in the homes of various friends in Brooklyn. Torn between a fantasy she was afraid to abandon and a reality she could not deny—that Nathan's "love" was, at best, "cold and scanty"—Fuller tried harder to fit her unorthodox self into the narrow conventions that Americans saw as feminine. When she attended parties or entertained, she put on her "prettiest dresses." One light green silk dress, which she had "trimmed with blonde lace" and adorned with "natural flowers," she wore to a party she gave at Amity Place. As the feminine woman that both her father and Nathan preferred, she now defers to Nathan in letters as her "strong man."[11]

In return for her letters, Nathan sent travel letters she published in the paper as a Wayside Notes Abroad column. Still, she kept writing him obsessively. She did so even though at the end of December 1845 she confessed that the "image" of him that would suddenly rise before her—even while "in the presence of others" such that she was "suddenly lost to them"—left her feeling as if there were a "void" in her. Although such empty "communion" depressed her, as is evident from her letters to Nathan, friends in New York did not see her depression, and not even Mary Greeley knew how greatly Fuller suffered after Nathan's departure. In January 1846 Fuller got a brief letter from Nathan—the one with a rose from Shelley's grave in it—but in April when she had not heard further from him she panicked and wrote him an acutely humiliating letter. Echoing the anguish of the poet-persona of *Alastor,* she cries, "Alas! and Alas! and once again Alas!" "Where are you? What are you doing?" Is their failure of love, she wonders, "the will of the Angels[?]"[12]

42 ∞ A Trust Betrayed

What could make such an intelligent woman behave as irrationally as Fuller did when Nathan left her? Knowing that when under stress she retreated to fantasy and her childhood pattern of yearning for her mother's love and needing to please her father does not get to the root cause of her obsessive behavior toward Nathan, the reason she felt he had touched her "inmost life."[1]

Maternal neglect can turn a child into an adult who continues to crave the mothering love he or she was deprived of as an infant. Yet, though the letters to Nathan exhibit such a tendency in Fuller, she was not entirely a narcissist. Margarett Crane, after all, had been a good mother until the death of Julia Adelaide in October 1813. At that time—just when the three-year-old Margaret was being

---

drawn into the "deathly, deserted universe" of her mother's depression and absence—Timothy began to impose his presence on her. Margarett Crane did not interfere, confessing to Margaret later, in a February 1847 letter, that she regretted having ignored the effects on Margaret's "physical being" of her husband's attempts to turn her daughter into a "genius." The mother's memory of Margaret's upbringing thus concurs with her daughter's memory.[2]

We have already seen that Timothy did indeed make great demands on Margaret. Although Capper notes that encouragement of children's intellectual precocity was common in Cambridge in the post-Revolutionary years, most children taught by their fathers did not grow up exhibiting the "extravagant tendencies" of thought and manner that Fuller's friends attributed to her having been "overtasked by her father." One such tendency was a need to please any man who awakened in her memories of her father, as happened with Emerson and then Nathan.[3]

Yet Fuller's feeling for Nathan had a shrillness to it that was absent in her relationship with Emerson. It was as if, to use her words, a "shadow side" of her personality was powerfully drawn to Nathan. "Absent or present," he stirred in her that "impulse" she "hated," which "showed" her "a slave," "a child—an infant still."[4] Yet for all of this strong, intelligent, publicly celebrated woman's conscious efforts at controlling her childish reactions, this impulse persisted, and she threw herself into self-destructive relationships.

The pattern of a person in an abusive relationship is like that Fuller established in relation to Nathan. She acknowledges as much in her 15 April 1845 letter to him, suggesting that she knows how it feels to love someone who mistreats her, and how that person's cruelty somehow stirs feelings in her so deep that the cruelty makes her love him all the more. She compares her love for him to a sadistic interaction between a nursemaid and child, telling Nathan how, like "the child, even when its nurse has herself given it a blow, comes to throw itself into her arms for consolation, for it only the more feels the nearness of the relation. . . . so I come to thee."[5]

When Fuller first met Nathan, she instinctively felt a strong attraction to him. He awakened in her an agitated sense of excitement, especially when he said to her, in words similar to those we know Timothy once wrote her but of which she seems to have no memory, "You must be a fool, little girl." Still, from the first, she sensed something was not right about the relationship. Before she let him embrace her, she had to overcome doubts and fears. On 9 April she had written to say that she would "trust" him "deeply," even though he "roused" in her disturbing "thoughts and feelings," a need so deep she obsessively wrote him letters. She sent him flowers when he did not appear at the farm on May Day as planned. Hoping to get a glimpse of him, she wrote telling him when she intended to stroll along Wall Street or amble about the neighborhood of the Battery, places she thought he might appear.[6]

In June 1845, after he had been gone only two weeks, she wrote him how she liked to lie in her room with "no lamp lit," and, in a trance, dream of him. In her letter she tells him how, on the ferry ride home from Staten Island, "though people were ta[l]king to me and I answering mechanically, I was really conversing with you." In late July, she notes how, in a room with people, "other voices are silent, yours is soon heard." When she is in this trancelike state, it is as if Nathan were "entirely with" her.[7]

If at these times her eyes seem empty to others, it is because, she wrote him, "your look fills my eye, . . .your voice my ear." In his absence, his "gaze," seems "present" to her. Fuller seems here to have been recalling not just Nathan but Timothy. Yet it seems nature did deceive her: trusting instinct, she had consciously linked Nathan with a memory of her "upright and pure" father who had long ago held her by the hand. Yet the behavior of the object she now loved, Nathan, was so painful to her that her awareness of his betrayal had almost made her, we recall, faint.[8]

Not just pleasurable but painful images relating to Nathan thus haunted her "lonely hours." They remained fresh in her mind a year after Nathan had left for Europe. In late April 1846, she would write him, "I have felt, these last four days, a desire for you that amounted almost to anguish." "How unnatural!" she cries, for such "darkness to follow on such close communion."[9]

In trusting "Instinct," Fuller now found herself behaving like a child in a relationship that gave her pleasure but also made her feel guilt, pain, and also, alas, "unnatural." After all, it was not a "host of golden daffodils" bouncing in the breeze that had earlier made her think of Nathan. Instead, it was tulips; "the crimson ones," she wrote him, "seem to me like you." She associates Nathan with the color crimson: a deep purple-red, or blood-red, as in the wings of the giant butterfly that in dream had "plunged his feet, bristling with feelers," deep into her brain, causing her pain, or as in the sea of blood that threatened to suffocate her in a dream she had had as a child in which she "walked and walked and could not get out."[10]

This nightmare of smothering in blood, we recall, had followed what Fuller was later to see as "spectral illusions" of faces with "loathsomely" swelling features that advanced toward her until they seemed about "to close upon her." She had a "peculiar horror," she wrote in her notes on her childhood, of eyes coming at her. Whatever the cause—whether nightmares of detached eyes coming at her or a peculiarly intense display of "fatherly tenderness" from a man who by day insisted that his children "correctly" "hug & kiss" him so as not to "offend" him yet at night rewarded his children's goodness by visiting their beds "and pressing a kiss upon their unconscious lips"—Margaret remembers how as a child she had walked in her sleep. In an account written when she was thirty, she bitterly accuses her father of being "the cause" of "these horrors of the night."[11]

The cause? How so? In Fuller's fifty-odd letters to Nathan—letters remarkable for both their number and intensity—are hints of the sad reality of Fuller's childhood that provoked her night terrors and sleepwalking. In her letters to and about Nathan, Fuller associates sex with fear, panic, pain, and betrayal. In an anguished March 1846 letter to Sam and Anna Ward, she mentions her "painful youth" that, as she had confided to Clarke, had made her "transition state" hateful for her to remember. That transition, presumably, was into puberty, which for her apparently began early; as a child of ten she was already "five feet two inches high," almost her full adult height. When Fuller tried to explain to Nathan why his sexual overture had so unnerved her, she had said that she had wanted to trust "nature and providence" but "felt afraid lest pain should ensue," which her heart knew not how to bear from a "cherished hand."[12]

She was thinking of Nathan's hand, how safe she had felt when she held it, but also of her father's, whose "cherished hand" she had held as a child in faith it would not harm her. In her letters and published writings, Fuller frequently focuses on the hand as a synecdoche for the way one person relates to another. A man with a "pure hand" is hence one who acts honorably toward others, as Fuller had read in the Bible about the "mighty works" wrought by Christ's pure hands, such as how he had saved a man's daughter from death by "taking her by the hand" (Luke 8:53–54). In *Woman in the Nineteenth Century,* Fuller herself had noted how even "very vulgar men become refined to the eye when leading a little girl by the hand," for "at that moment the right relation between the sexes seems established." The image here of a vulnerable girl being led by a possibly vulgar man is, however, problematic. It reveals Fuller's mental conflict in that she idealizes here a little girl's subordination to a "vulgar" man. On the positive side it suggests that Fuller considers the proper way for an "upright" father to relate to his daughter is for him to lead her "by the hand," and in this context the effect of the man's hand is calming and curative.[13]

The concept of a pure hand was thus important to Fuller. Time and again she insists in letters that her hand is "pure," as she did in her 30 September 1845 letter to Nathan wherein she soliloquizes to her father on the anniversary of his death. The hand with which she had closed his eyes, she assures him, is pure "thus far from evil," unlike that, say, of Sand, whose sexual passion, as Fuller had written in her February 1845 essay on French novelists, had soiled her hands. It was, in contrast, with a "pure hand" that Margaret had "hid[den] the sad sights of this world from [her father's] eyes which had begun to weep at them."[14]

Fuller here is referring to her father's failed political ambitions. She also, however, has in mind the chaos at the farm in Groton that, as we recall, had caused the older brothers to battle with their father and leave home in a pattern like that of their prodigal Uncle Peter. The younger sons, Richard and Arthur, had then worked the fields with their father, only to come quickly to see how unsuited they were for farming, not to mention for the bizarre routines their father forced on them—like running barefoot with him through the snow, or bathing in ice water and then drying themselves with "rough towels" because their father thought such punishing routines had medicinal value. Not to forget that health manuals were then touting these as ways to quell sinful sexual impulses.[15]

Timothy's obsession with controlling his children's errant impulses seems less odd when we recall not only that the experts of his day—preachers and writers of child-rearing manuals—were harping on the need for parents to control their sons' sinful tendency to masturbate, but also that Lloyd, who was seven when Timothy moved his family to Groton (1833), may already have been exhibiting signs of mental instability, one of which was to be to masturbate compulsively. Given Timothy's need to be in control of his children's actions, Lloyd's behavior must have been a challenge. Perhaps Lloyd and her father had been on Margaret's mind when, in her comments on Goethe's *Iphigenia* in the essay on the Classical and Romantic that she had written in Groton while her father was still alive, Fuller had hinted at just how bad things were there. In it she argues how important it is to the play's progress that the "*mind*" of Iphigenia, Agamemnon's virgin eldest child whose life he was willing to sacrifice to save Greece and the classical heroine with whom she most closely identified, "be kept unsullied" so "that she may be a fit intercessor to the gods in behalf of her polluted family." We will recall that "pollution" is a word Fuller associates with prostitutes, women "sullied" by illicit sex.[16]

Yet now, twelve years later, Fuller felt that Nathan had sullied her mind by having tempted her to participate with him in "an act" (presumably sexual intercourse) to which she "had always attached importance." In the same April 1845 letters to Nathan in which Fuller exclaims that she has been "violated," she laments that God was not there "as a Father" to save her from Nathan. Nathan's sexual gesture, coming as it did from "a cherished hand," had delivered a lethal message by undermining her "heavenly trust" in the God-father-figure she had made of Timothy. This trust in a "heavenly father," however, was based on an idealized memory of Timothy that had previously protected her from facing the fact that people are capable of committing heinous crimes, even against their children.[17]

In reading Fuller's many letters to Nathan (from the day after he propositioned her, 12 April, to the day he left for Europe on 1 June, she wrote him twenty-one letters) one becomes aware that it was of utmost importance to her that he had *not* betrayed her trust, that his touch was motivated by pure love, not lust. For, as she wrote Nathan on 15 April, just "one grain of distrust or fear is poison to a good nature." Her ability to reconcile her behavior demanded that she wash this "earth-stain . . . quite away." The "barb" in her heart caused an unbearable hurt.[18]

43 ∞ The Dark Side of Her Lot

Hints abound in Fuller's writings that all was not right in the Fuller house when Margaret was a child. Indeed, it is unlikely that Fuller's erotic encounter with Nathan would have so unsettled her had she not linked it with an emotionally loaded memory of an experience so painful to her that it was "unspeakable." In her 8 October 1833 letter, Fuller, who had been visiting her Uncle Henry in Boston, tells James Clarke how her attention that morning had been "recalled to some painful domestick circumstances." She asks him please to "pray for me." For, "the part" in life "I have had to act" is far harder "than you ever knew" and "is like to become much more difficult." She asks that he pray to God that "any talents" she has been "endowed" with will not be "wasted in fruitless struggles with difficulties" that she "cannot overcome." "I think I am less happy in many respects than you," she had confided to Clarke in this letter written just two months before mentioning the "secret trials" she had suffered during her transition to adulthood. She concedes that he will "*need* the skill of Champollion to decipher" her letter, "particularly," she had said, since he could speak "freely" to her of all his "circumstances and feelings," whereas: "It is not possible for me to be so profoundly frank with any earthly friend." "Thus my heart," she had said, "has no proper home."[1]

Unlike Emerson, who had asserted in an October 1840 letter to Cary that he had no secrets, Fuller admits she has secrets that make her feel she cannot be "profoundly frank" with any friend, though she had mistakenly believed that Nathan had read her "so deeply" that he had intuited the "secret" hidden behind her "inner door." That she must conceal a secret even from her closest friends makes her lament "the appalling power" of "circumstances," her lack of a "proper home." In the memoir Fuller wrote in 1840 about the 1831 Thanksgiving service she had attended with her parents when she was twenty-one, she found herself envying "all the little children; for I supposed they had parents who protected them." At that age she "knew not," wrote Fuller, "that I was not the selected Oedipus, the special victim of an iron law."[2]

In her recollection Fuller confesses that she had not yet learned that she was "not the *only* lonely one" selected by fate to suffer as did the mythical Oedipus, who had murdered his father and committed incest with his mother. Indeed, no matter how—to use Margaret's word—"proper" Timothy Fuller's family appears in the public record, his children's adult difficulties suggest there was, as Fuller described her own life to Nathan, a "dark side" to their "lot."[3]

Timothy's offspring bore throughout their lives the scars of their traumatic childhoods. The oldest of Margaret's siblings, Eugene (b. 1815), a Harvard graduate and avid theatergoer, lost his job as a teacher in Stow, northwest of Boston, after swallowing lamplighter fluid. He then suffered "a softening of the brain" during a sojourn in New Orleans and ended his life at age forty-four by either falling or jumping from a boat bound for Boston from New York. The hot-tempered Ellen (b. 1820) gave birth to five children in her brief life, had a tempestuous marriage, and died of tuberculosis at age thirty-six. Arthur (b. 1822), who had become a Unitarian preacher, during the Civil War was a chaplain in the Sixteenth Massachusetts Regiment and, despite an honorable discharge for illness, "impulsively grabbed a musket and answered a call for volunteers to cross the Rappahannock," even though he knew that "he would not be exchanged if taken prisoner," and that "if he were killed his family would not get a pension." In what Capper has called "one of the more peculiar martyrdoms of the Civil War," Arthur rushed forward into the battle and soon fell, pierced by two bullets, after entering Fredericksburg. William Henry (b. 1817), the most likable of the boys, did not attend college and failed several times before finally establishing himself in business in Cincinnati. After graduating from Harvard, Richard (b. 1824), who among his siblings seems a solid survivor, entered his Uncle Henry's law firm but discovered that his melancholic temper unsuited him for the partnership. The youngest of Margaret's living siblings, Lloyd (b. 1826), who as we know had mental and emotional problems, was institutionalized and outlived his four brothers and two sisters, while Margaret (b. 1810) suffered through life the dire consequences of her difficult childhood.[4]

⤳ ⤳ ⤳

Twice in her writings Fuller compares herself to Oedipus. She does so in an undated letter to William Channing wherein she says she must follow her own law even if she returns blind and outcast like Oedipus. Then, writing about that Thanksgiving Day, 1831, she also makes the comparison by noting that at age twenty-one she had not yet learned that she was not the only "special victim."[5]

A popular theme in nineteenth-century Romantic literature was incest, the crime committed by Oedipus. The idea of incest was not just a fanciful conceit concocted by Sophocles, Byron, and other writers. Historian Linda Gordon, for instance, without referring to Margaret Fuller, found that cases of father-daughter incest reported in Boston from 1880 to 1930 indicate that such a tragic violation of healthy human relationships was not uncommon. While studying the case records of family violence kept by three child-welfare agencies in Boston over these fifty years, Gordon found a family pattern dominating such reported cases, not unlike the pattern that Timothy established half a century earlier in relating to his wife and elder daughter. In the case records she examined, Gordon discovered that "the incestuous relationships grew out of and appeared to participants as part of an overall family pattern of turning girls into second wives."[6]

I am *not* implying here that Timothy Fuller in fact committed incest with any of his children. Yet I do think that the "unnatural stimulation" Fuller experienced as a child in relation to her father had a libidinal element—that Timothy's late-night tutoring of his daughter, given his dominating personality and her emotional vulnerability, as Capper has speculated, probably did instill these lessons with what he calls "a certain erotic content." Timothy's behavior in relation to his family fits the pattern Gordon found of men reported to have formed incestuous relationships with their daughters in Boston.[7]

In this pattern, according to Gordon, there generally was a period when the mother was either weakened or absent altogether and the eldest daughter, a responsible girl, filled in for the mother by assuming her domestic duties, including supervising the other children. Gordon in her research also found that the father in these cases was invariably dependent on his family yet rigid in his refusal to do the "drudgery" of housework and in his expectation of being waited upon. Notably, says Gordon, when the mother was absent, the father did not become a mother; that is, he did not do domestic chores nor offer his offspring nurturing love.[8]

In families like these, according to Gordon, the fathers "often" hypocritically "voiced moralistic attacks on loose sexual morals in the community." They were "unusually tyrannical; the mothers, when present, self-effacing." This is the pattern that family acquaintance Thomas Wentworth Higginson remembers in the Fuller household where, in his words, "the whole punctuation was masculine" and where, as we know, Margarett Crane self-consciously chose to obey her husband's decrees no matter how irrational they might be or how disconsolate his rakish behavior made her. Margarett Crane was "*dutiful*" to her husband to the point that family members called her "a perfect recluse." Many nineteenth-century wives remained thus blindly loyal to their husbands, thereby alienating daughters from mothers, who sometimes even, according to Gordon, "colluded in this domestic incest." After all, she says, the daughter's compliance with the father's commands provided relief from the mother's own hard life "as housekeeper and as sexual servant." Yet, the "most consistent participation of mothers appeared to operate at a deeper level: they promoted within the family a view of the father's needs, however brutal, as legitimate and deserving sympathy."[9]

Despite this abuse of parental power, all was not negative for the daughter. Had it been, she would not have felt bound to a person whose existence denied her individuality. Using the same metaphor Fuller used in the letter wherein she talks about the barb in her heart from a childhood wound, Gordon notes: "The barb on this domestic hook in the flesh of the girl was that there were often emotional rewards for her." She felt prized by the father as "special." The saddest consequence of such an interaction was that the daughter, who may in fact have adored and idealized this same distant parent and even felt a peculiar pleasure in being the recipient of intense albeit inappropriate affection, was left, as she grew older, feeling conflicted over how to deal with this bewildering situation. For it simultaneously represented the ultimate fulfillment of a little-girl's desire to be the center of her father's attention (as Margaret as a child desired to be), and the ultimate betrayal of her trust, a betrayal that crippled the girl's later capacity to love naturally as an adult (Margaret, age twenty-three, noted about her childhood self: "a natural human—I know I was not"). Feeling it was their duty to comply with the wishes of their tyrannical fathers, many of the girls in the cases Gordon examined "had internalized slave-like images of themselves." Others, however, found creative ways to rebel—as Fuller did in writing *Woman in the Nineteenth Century,* in which she stresses male brutality and hypocrisy, and as she would also do by participating in the 1849 revolution of the Italians against their betraying "father," Pope Pius IX, and the armies of invading and occupying tyrants.[10]

Fuller's rebellious anger is understandable when we recall how sadistic, humorless, "unkind" and controlling her hot-tempered father could be in relating not just to her but also to her mother. Even as he insulted his wife in letters—accusing her once, she said, of "*stupidity*"—and even as he flirted with pretty women in Washington and sent his wife shamelessly detailed accounts of these encounters, he kept close tabs on her. In the pattern of men driven by a need to control and exert power over women, Timothy—especially in the letters he wrote from Washington during the 1819–20 session of Congress—made it clear that Margarett Crane would pay severely if she were to so much as look at another man. And though he enjoys watching beautiful women in Washington (especially the "engaging handsome" Mrs. Deforest), he is nonetheless, even while in Washington, *always,* he wrote her, watching her. We recall Timothy's warning to his wife not to flirt, for his eye, even in absence, is on her: "And what I say to you, I say to all—watch." "Take care," he had cautioned his wife in his memorable December 1819 letter, "to explain in your [reply] all your wayward movements." He orders her not to let "even a whisper or a smile be forgotten": "If any thing is suppressed, I shall certainly know it."[11]

This was Timothy's pattern of conduct with women: to demand they do as he commands even when he is not behaving honorably toward them, then self-righteously to lecture and threaten them if they defy him. Margarett Crane had soon caught on. And she dealt with Timothy's controlling, hypocritical ways by shifting her focus from him to her wifely job of managing his household. No doubt she loved him, even as she expressed a wish in her early letters to him that he consider her "sensibility" when writing her on this subject he so loves "to *enlarge* upon"—that is, "the Ladies." When he continued writing her about their beauty, she pleaded: "Whom shall I depend upon to . . . preserve your feet from falling and *my eyes* from tears?" When even this appeal to him to stop writing her about women failed, she resorted to irony. We recall her strong January 1819 response to his cruel condemnation in a letter of all he found "censurable" in *her* "disposition," that, unlike him, "my *conduct* & *principles* generally coincide."[12]

Doubting her husband's ability to remain faithful, Margarett Crane, right after he had left by stage for Washington in December 1818, had a dream she then wrote Timothy about. In it the two are together at a party and he introduces her "to the young Ladies" he has "been acquainted with for several years." He then tells his wife he is sorry he could not have married one of them instead of her, a remark she tells Timothy that she really "resented." Margarett Crane's dream perhaps expressed her concern that her husband regretted having married her. "The dream was so fresh," she says, that if she had been favored with an opportunity, "I should have behaved with great dignity," a phrase that captures the way Margaret's mother thereafter dealt with her husband's rakish behavior.[13]

This tension between husband and wife may have contributed not only to Margaret's sense as a young woman that she had no "proper home" but also to the emotional distress that made her as a child sleepwalk and have terrifying dreams. Her father's treatment of women may also underlay her distrust of Nathan years later. After all, as a child she had read "several times" each of her father's letters addressed to her mother and commented on them. About his 15 February 1818 letter, Margarett Crane had reported to Timothy that, "S. M. observed after reading it that she thought it the most affectionate letter Pa had ever written me." But that was before Timothy had met Mrs. Deforest and before Margarett Crane had written him that she found some of his remarks and behavior "outrageous."[14]

Indeed, as tension between husband and wife increased and with it the distance between Margaret and her "*really* suspicious" mother, so the latter's mention of Margaret in her letters to her husband had decreased. So noticeable was her silence on the subject of her daughter's well-being that Timothy in April 1820 would note to Margarett Crane that his daughter "seems quite a stranger." She was silent about their daughter even though Timothy in his letters was increasingly asking about Margaret's progress in her studies. Meanwhile, Margaret's wish to please her father, who in letters was hinting he was finding his wife inadequate as a companion, had become an obsession by the time she was ten.[15]

Timothy in turn at this time was showing increasingly intense interest in his daughter, expressed primarily as an obsessive need to teach her. While his daughter was fantasizing about her powerful father and the glamorous life he lived in Washington, he in fact was spending boring hours shut up in his boardinghouse room where he wrote his wife daily letters, organized hers into neat piles, angrily complaining when she skipped a day, and fantasized about both wife and daughter. We recall that in a February 1820 letter he had confessed to his wife how in daydream he would try "the memory & judgment of my daughter by questions in chronology, history, Latin &c." This focus on her in her father's letter had surely made Margaret feel special when she heard her mother read these words aloud to her and Eugene in the parlor.[16]

The girl, whose eyes "sparkled with pleasure" to hear her father say he was thinking of her, "now," indeed, began to feel, as Fuller, looking back, would later phrase it, that "all [my father's] feelings were now concentred on me." Sensing his intensity of feeling for her may have put her in that kind of autohypnotic trance that she later confessed she felt when she thought of Nathan "thinking," she said, "of me," as if he were *in* her and she, herself, floated over her body. As if she were, as she said, alienated from herself. As a child, Fuller had sensed this division within. There was the "real Margaret" whose true feelings were buried deep within her, and the superficial but bright good girl who strove for perfection in her studies and performed brilliantly in an attempt to please her ever-critical father. She worked so hard to excel intellectually that he even complained to his wife that Margaret was frequently so "absorbed in reading" that she no longer jumped up to hug and kiss him when he entered a room.[17]

Despite the maturing daughter's new reticence, which was in part the result of a natural and necessary maturation process, both father and daughter nonetheless gained a strange pleasure from their late-night sessions. And Margaret now felt the same way in relation to Nathan, to whom she felt drawn, she wrote him on 6 April 1845, "like a child" who creeps close to the side of her companion to listen in awe "to his stories of things unfamiliar," as little Margaret must have sidled up to her congressman father. It was a kind of pleasure that had "over-excited" her as a child, who, though mature for her age, had still only reluctantly by candlelight made her way to her room on the second floor, where she eventually passed into a troubled sleep, one disrupted by Timothy, who came in to kiss her on the lips as a reward for her good behavior, and by remembered images from the *Aeneid, Oberon,* and other adult-level books she had been reading.[18]

∽ ∽ ∽

In her childhood dreams the horses trampled over her. The trees and rocks streamed blood on her as huge shapes, usually faces, advanced from the corners of the room and pressed upon her, faces that grew larger and larger until they seemed about to crush her. The blood filled a pool that threatened to drown her while detached eyes came at her. Calling up similar images of being crushed, the grown-up Fuller in the letter she wrote Nathan three days after he made a sexual pass at her merges past with present, recalling how the demon "desecrated and trampled" her "sweet little garden" and pelted "with his cruel hail-stones me, poor child, just as I had laid . . . open my soul in a heavenly trust."[19]

44 ∽ "Possessed of" Her Father

In the narratives Fuller created about her past that letters and other evidence suggest are emotionally if not factually true, she sees herself as a sensitive child taught by a severe, tyrannical father. In her 1840 autobiographical romance she calls herself "Poor child!" even as she acknowledges that "no one understood" back then that to force a child to perform beyond her development level could cause the permanent emotional damage that she felt had been done to her. Since Fuller's time, psychologists and psychiatrists have documented the negative effect on a child of the kind of emotional and mental trials to which Timothy subjected his daughter, which today one might even see as abusive. Writing from a late-twentieth-century perspective, psychiatrist Leonard Shengold says that child abuse is "the abuse of power." It is about control; and, as we know, Timothy insisted on maintaining absolute control over the emotions of both his wife and elder daughter.[1]

Psychologists today know that people who were abused as children have to deal with issues pertaining to anger, abandonment, boundaries, and identity, including sexual identity. Such adults have to overcome feelings of guilt and shame, of having no power and feeling "like a victim," as well as of needing "to be perfect." Most abuse victims suffer throughout their lives from painful memories of "over-stimulating events in childhood" that cannot be erased entirely from consciousness. Memories of these events live on in symptoms associated with conversion disorder and chronic pain (headaches, sleeplessness, panic attacks, trembling, and other stress-related and nervous diseases) and in certain aspects of their behavior, especially relating to sex. Psychologists and psychiatrists alike say that a feeling of being "alienated" from one's body—exactly the way Fuller said she felt in relating to Nathan—can be produced not just by overtly incestuous relationships but also by covertly incestuous ones. Moreover, according to Shengold, victims of abuse "are under a powerful unconscious compulsion to repeat the circumstances of their own childhood." In "Not in This House: Incest, Denial, and Doubt in the White Middle Class Family," Elizabeth Wilson quotes Peter Gay's apt paraphrase of Freud's astute perception: "The finding of a love object . . . is always a refinding. . . . The pull of early incestuous attachments is invisible, unacknowledged, and tenacious."[2]

If it is hard for women today to talk about what happened to them as children, how much harder it must have been for Fuller, who as an adult felt she had no one with whom she could be "profoundly frank" and, as a child, found that the one person on earth she most loved and hoped to please was also guilty—to paraphrase what O'Brien said Big Brother aimed to do to Winston in Orwell's *1984*—of squeezing her being empty and then filling it with himself, of possessing, so to speak, her soul. Yet try as she did to suppress them, "ugly memories" of childhood events kept intruding in adulthood. In late May 1844, just seven months before she met Nathan, she wrote in her journal that she saw "no hope that this story can be made beautiful to me, that I can ever be wholly reconciled with the Past."[3]

Though we likely will never know what trauma beyond the death of a sister happened to Fuller as a child, two facts allow us to say with some certainty that *something else happened* to this "child" who, in her own words, "already kept up so late" by her father, "was still unwilling to retire." First, in both narratives written by her as an adult during her major psychosexual spiritual crisis (one she wrote in 1839 when she was twenty-nine, the other in 1840) she says that she was traumatized. Second, the excruciating pain Fuller felt in her relationship with Nathan—a shrill thrill like a dentist's drill on a nerve evoked, as she wrote him in August 1845, by "thoughts of childhood!"—was quite "real."[4]

The pain evident in Fuller's letters to Nathan and her compulsive need to repeat the circumstances of her childhood—the early fixation on her father and now on Nathan—suggest not only that Fuller's attachment to her father probably did have an erotic element, but also that she was aware of this. Fuller's psychological profile suggests the same. There is the precocious intelligence; the piercing nature of her gaze; the erotic intensity of her love for Nathan; her sense of herself as "outcast" yet "special," a sibyl in touch with unseen powers; her confusion about her sexual identity; her tendency to sink into trancelike states when threatened by situations that triggered painful feelings. Added to this is the sense, reported by psychoanalyst Michelle Price, that women who were sexually abused feel they are living a split existence (though evidence in Margaret's case suggests Timothy possessed not her body but her soul). There is the daytime "Margaret Good child" who performs adeptly in public, her bright smile concealing behind it the nighttime Margaret's "dark side," as she referred to it.[5]

And, of course, threading darkly through it all is the persistent theme that she is so sinful and twisted that she is not "worthy" of love or, as she put it in her 1838 flower garden memory: "I cannot get over this feeling of being unworthy to be a part of nature." Addressing the asters, roses, and lilies—flowers she identifies with her mother—she says, "ye know nothing of the blights, the distortions, which beset the human being."[6]

Shengold uses the dramatic phrase "soul murder" to designate "a certain category of traumatic experience: instances of repetitive and chronic overstimulation, alternating with emotional deprivation, that are deliberately brought about by another individual." This frightening overstimulation of a child "inevitably leads," he says, "to rage and an overwhelming mixture of sexual and aggressive feelings" that continue to torment the child who is too young to understand or adequately deal with them and who "may later succumb to an inner need for annihilation." Such "victims of soul murder remain in large part possessed by another, their souls in bondage to someone else" in much the same way that Fuller as a child had felt "possessed of," she said, her father, whose "spirit" living in her she struggled with all her life.[7]

45 ∾ Yearning to Wash Her Soul of Sin

In an 1839 fragment about her friend Elizabeth Randall, whose physician father had similarly subjected his daughter to an "unnatural taxing of her faculties," Fuller says that if only Elizabeth had "grown up an unmolested flower by the side of some secret stream she had been a thing all natural . . . bloom and fragrance." That is, if only Elizabeth (by extension, Fuller, too) had never been mistreated, then she would have been a "natural" woman, like Fuller's mother, whom Fuller depicts as a rose. Along this line of thought, Fuller will protest in a 30 May 1845 letter to Nathan that a lowly violet has a right to grow "lovely and *innocent*," despite the fact "she is not a rose" (emphasis added).[1]

Though the word "molest" did not convey in the nineteenth century the negative sexual connotation that it does today, that Fuller through the mask of her friend Elizabeth suggests that she would have been a "natural" woman had she not been "molested" as a child, taken in combination with the violent content of Fuller's dreams and the fact that her father had "frequently" sent her to bed "several hours too late" while expecting his wife to retire "early" when he is home from Washington certainly does, as Fuller herself said, "cast a deep shadow over her young days."[2]

On the scrap of paper about her own life that she had attached to her dark remarks about Elizabeth's, Fuller wrote that when she tried to tell "these things sometimes," that is, about her dread of going to bed, "little notice was taken." Worse, her mother "seemed ashamed" of her sleepwalking. On the scrap of paper Fuller notes that her mother's shame gave her "an idea" there was "something ridiculous . . . attached to it." Because of the unbearable feelings her father awakened in her, coupled with her mother's apparent shame at her behavior, Fuller retreated from feeling, as is typical of children who have been deprived of love. Later she would confide to a friend, "those who live would scarcely consider that I am among the living,—and I am isolated, as you say."[3]

Indeed to some extent she was emotionally isolated from others. Then in New York she met Nathan, whom she consciously linked with her father and whose "root," she said, cut to the quick of her being. This piercing phallic image shows the strength of her reaction to Nathan. Instinctively she had dropped her defensive "reserve," which is why the relationship brought her so much "pleasure"—as well as pain. Perhaps it was something he said during their first long conversation, his gaze at her from across the room at the New Year's party where they met, or a touch of his hand or the brush of his sleeve that had brought them that night into momentary contact. Whatever it was, it had triggered in her a flood of feelings. Perhaps in the flood was some of that "erotic content" Capper surmises was part of her childhood feeling for her father. Underlying that was what the late Christopher Lasch described as "this boundless need that drew people to her in the first place[,] but [that] also drove them away, in droves," as she initially drew Nathan to her, only eventually to drive him away. Indeed, Fuller's "insatiable craving for love and admiration" gave her, wrote Lasch, an "almost grotesque power" to charm others. Thus Fuller at first felt "vibrations" pass between her and Nathan, and for a brief time the electricity between them was exhilarating—as the "excited beginning of the seduction" is always, says Shengold, "easier to repeat" than is "the subsequent terror, overstimulation, and rage."[4]

In a September 1845 letter to Nathan wherein she endows Nathan with the power to cast out "sin," Fuller depicts her father as "upright and pure," a godlike being who is watching her "from that home of higher life" he now inhabits.[5] In deifying not just Nathan but her father thus, she behaves like other people who have been mistreated as children by a parent. We have already seen how she defensively assumes her father's identity as a mask to protect her "true" self from pain. In "A Rose for Emily" William Faulkner presents a parallel case. In that story, Emily, after the death of her tyrannical father who had stood between her and the men who might have loved her, assumes his identity. In such a way, says Faulkner, Emily clung "to that which had robbed her, as people will." According to Shengold, children who are left alone with an adult who exercises an absolute power over them are prone to do this. Since the child has no one to turn to but the all-powerful parent for rescue and relief, he or she for survival not only must assume the identity of the abuser (since to be the abuser is not to see him and therefore is to be in control) but must also register the tyrannical parent as good. Faulkner offers insight into this aspect of an abused child's mind when in "Barn Burning" he has Sarty Snopes, whose pyromaniac father habitually beats him, proudly exclaim at the moment he thinks his father is dead, "He was brave! . . . He was!"[6]

When Margaret was seven, Timothy had sent kisses through the mail "for my girl," Margaret, in letters addressed to his wife. But by the time she was eleven, instead of transmitting innocent kisses, the letters were filled with his obsessive corrections of her "defective habits"; he also repeatedly reminded her, as he coldly criticized her, that his "remonstrances" were the "best evidence" he could give of his "affection." That is, he kept that tense distance between himself and his daughter that suggests the erotic is possible—that electrically charged feeling that can tie a child to a sadistic adult in what we might call a trauma bond. In such a relationship the love-hungry child behaves as did Margaret, who, like "a slave," she said, "gave [her] heart's blood unpaid" in an attempt to satisfy the desire of her seemingly all-powerful parent.[7]

In the role of "good girl" she strove to do perfect work at school, and later, as we have seen, for Nathan she would don her "prettiest dresses" in an attempt to please him in the way that ladies in Washington had pleased Timothy. Moreover, like the fictional Beatrice in Hawthorne's 1844 "Rappaccini's Daughter," Fuller as a child had sought love from the flowers in the garden behind her father's house. In

Hawthorne's dark story, the father uses his daughter as a subject for a deadly scientific experiment. He controls her and poisons her so no man can touch her without becoming infected, while Rappaccini himself is careful when working in the garden or approaching Beatrice to wear thick gloves and a mask to prevent his own contamination. Hawthorne, who seems to have modeled Beatrice's relationship with her father on Margaret's with Timothy, hints that the relationship between father and daughter is darker than his pen dares report when he has the learned professor Baglioni say to Giovanni, who is enchanted with Beatrice: "I know little of the Signora Beatrice save that Rappaccini is said to have instructed her deeply in his science, and that . . . she is already qualified to fill a professor's chair. . . . Other absurd rumors there be, not worth talking about or listening to"—rumors, perhaps, not only about Rappaccini's sacrifice of his daughter to science but also about how, in Fuller's words, he had "devoured" much of her life "in the bud."[8]

❧ ❧ ❧

In Hawthorne's story, one senses the "all-pervasive presence" of Rappaccini "within the shadow" from which he peeps and controls every scene Beatrice takes part in.[9] In a manner similar to Rappaccini, Timothy had "insinuated" himself into his daughter to the point she felt his eye on her even after he was dead. To some extent, he had behaved in accord with the advice of experts who advised that, like the squire Sherasmin in *Oberon* who watched Huon with "Argus eyes" to make sure Huon stayed "spotless" (chaste) until marriage, parents should keep an Argus eye on their children. So Timothy had kept a watchful eye on Margaret, obsessing in letters to her that she keep her "person" "neat and *spotless*." Indeed, far more effective in making a child behave than the threat of being whipped by a riding stick—like the one Timothy used to whip his sons—was the fear of being caught committing a sin by the peering eye of the parent. The all-powerful eye was particularly effective when it belonged to a rigid, controlling, self-righteous man like Timothy Fuller, heir of Puritans and hence, like his wife, of strict Calvinists. Though Timothy had raised his children in the Unitarian Church, he was nonetheless imbued with the spirit of Calvin, who preached that to feel a sexual impulse outside the bond of marriage or to exhibit pride was to sin.[10]

Parents were to keep an eye on their children especially to see if they were committing the sin of pride or, worse, as noted, "self-pollution," the sin Lloyd would be guilty of committing. In this "culture of surveillance," Timothy (who age twenty-two had "peep[ed] at" another "Margt") had always kept an eye on Margaret, who confesses in her notes on the demonical to being drawn to those who "mysteriously control" through a power "in the eye." Aware at age eight that her father's eye was on her, Margaret had written him that if he had "spies" they would find she was "not very dissipated." And when she was ten and visiting in Boston, Timothy had written his wife—in a letter Margaret no doubt later read—that he hoped his daughter would not be gone long, "as she needs a parent's eye now as much as any part of her life."[11]

By age ten her childhood had been thus sufficiently distorted that she believed she was "foredoomed to sorrow and pain." And by the time she arrived at the Prescotts' school, she was convinced she was a terrible sinner. In Mariana, Fuller created a fictional alter ego who, mocked by classmates, had "let the demon" rise "within her." The principal calls Mariana to give an account of her behavior but, determined to die, she throws herself on the hearth so hard that she is knocked unconscious. In response to this suicidal gesture, the teacher—who sees "how stained!" is her soul—rescues the "sin-defiled" child by assuring her that "one great fault," presumably disobedience or pride, "can[not] mar a whole life!"[12]

The pattern here is of someone's cruel behavior prompting a "prodigal" child to retaliate with wayward behavior, followed by the child expressing remorse. That pattern appears in a plea Fuller wrote Nathan four days after her 15 April letter accusing him of letting an "ill demon" assault her. Like a bewildered child pleading with an inscrutable, fearful father to forgive her for some great "fault" (a favorite term of Timothy) or sin she feels she has committed, Fuller wrote Nathan, "I will now kneel, and, laying thy dear hand upon my heart, implore that, if pride or suspicion [of his motives] should hide there again," then she will do all she can "to drive them out." She asks Nathan to have patience with her "impulses and childish longings."[13]

Like the child certain that his or her bad behavior has provoked the adult's anger, so Fuller sees clearly now, she wrote Nathan on 19 April, that "it is then, indeed, myself who have caused all the ill." In the pattern of women accustomed to abuse, Fuller confesses in this letter, now eight days after Nathan had approached her sexually—in the same way she was to blame herself again three weeks later—that she believes in her heart she has deserved his disrespectful treatment of her. Secretly fearing her soul is "stained," she tells him she has "longed for a *baptism without* to wash off the dust of the world, *within, a deep rising of the waters* to purify them by motion" (original emphasis).[14]

46 ∽ The Ties That Bind

Fuller's need to please Nathan ("I am desirous to do as you desire," she wrote him in May, after she knew he had deceived her) is reminiscent of her need as a child to please Timothy. That and the pain-riddled quality of her love for him suggest that scenes "of strife and pain" occurred in Fuller's childhood—as does a cryptic remark she made about her childhood in her suggestive 7 October 1833 letter to Clarke: "—It was not time; I had been too sadly cramped—I had not learned enough and must always remain imperfect."[1] Fuller's words here seem to echo the view of her critical father, who, in his numerous letters to her, never seems pleased with her.

Her terrifying fear of being imperfect—her desperate need to be blessed by her cruelly vigilant congressman father—is especially evident in her letters to Nathan, onto whom she transferred not just her positive feelings for her father but also her doubts and dark misgivings regarding his character and motivation. In the process of writing these letters Fuller almost seems to have been reliving painful scenes from her past, even repeating words and phrases she might have said in her inter-actions with Timothy. One can almost hear the dutiful daughter say, "I have not been good and pure and sweet enough." "Your hand removes at last the veil from my eyes. It is then, indeed, myself who have caused all the ill." "My heart . . . knows not how well to bear [pain] from a cherished hand." But, you "are noble." "I have paid dear for your love. . . . It was pure." "I do not mind the pain."[2]

Given Nathan's deceitfulness and sexual aggression toward Fuller, her repeated assertions that he is noble and that their love "was pure" make suspect the accu-racy of her perception in her 30 September letter to Nathan of Timothy as "upright and pure." Lending support to this suspicion is Fuller family friend Higginson, who in his biography of Margaret describes the "high pressure by candle-light" lessons as a "serious additional evil" to the generally "ruinous" tutoring relation-ship he had established with her. In a fictional caricature of the vaguely unsavory relationship between Fuller and her father, Hawthorne named the female charac-ter in "Rappaccini's Daughter" Beatrice. In that story the name alludes not only to Dante's Beatrice but also to the historical Beatrice Cenci, who had a violent and cruel father who developed an incestuous passion for her.[3]

ᔕ ᔕ ᔕ

In light of the kind of man Timothy was and of Margaret's veiled comments in let-ters, it seems likely that this man whose life was riddled with contradictions did love his children even as he subjected them to some unpleasant scenes, as Fuller in 1843 cryptically wrote Anna Barker Ward about her past, "of strife and pain" in order to fulfill his need for "pleasure" as well as self-corrective piety. In *Woman in the Nineteenth Century* his daughter would bitterly castigate men as having "eyes clouded by secret sin" and as being "incapable of pure marriage; incapable of pure parentage," but specifics elude us.[4]

Whether it was merely, as Freud would say, the "unwitting" arousal of his daughter that caused her to develop a fixation on her father, which she then trans-ferred to other men who awakened her past feelings for her father, or an impul-sive—innocent, even—gesture on Timothy's part that hinted of incestuous desire, the fact is that Timothy loomed so large a figure in his young daughter's life that he invaded her sense of self, the private chamber of her heart. And a result of this intrusion, this desecration of her "little garden," is evident in the adult Fuller's shrill reaction to Nathan's sexual touch. Even after that demeaning incident she asserted her "confidence" in him, somehow convincing herself "that," as she indicated in what she wrote Nathan in May 1845, "he will lead me [by the hand] in a spirit of holy love, and that all I may learn [from him] of nature and the soul will be legitimate." To think of him in any way other than "with deep affection," she had already confessed to him, "was suicide."[5]

One reason for Margaret's loaded feelings for her father might have been that he disappeared for half of each of her formative years (1817–25), leaving her alone as a child in a house full of sharp-tongued aunts and overbearing uncles, one of whom, the bachelor Abraham, she calls "sordid" in a later letter to her mother, the one wherein she expresses her rage at the man's unwillingness to use money from the estate for Ellen's education. Yet that interpretation places the blame for Margaret's anguish where it does not primarily belong. No doubt Abraham was, as Margaret also said, "vulgar." Still, the night horrors might never have happened had Timothy not insisted on "thrusting" (her word) on her a love that was not, as she herself later said, "natural," a love so intense she would later see it as a betrayal. It was, after all, with the Greek heroines Antigone and Iphigenia—not Electra— that Margaret most closely identified; "my sisters!" she calls them in *Woman in the Nineteenth Century,* depicting herself in the company of Antigone and Iphigenia: women whose "forms" have been "dwarfed and defaced by a bad nurture."[6]

Iphigenia is the dutiful eldest child of Clytemnestra and Agamemnon whom, to save Greece, Agamemnon sacrifices to Artemis, the goddess who turns Iphigenia into a sibyl-like priestess. In *Woman in the Nineteenth Century,* Fuller claims to understand Iphigenia—this ill-fated daughter of a man whom she describes as "strong in will and pride, weak in virtue"—"better than she understood herself." According to Fuller, although Agamemnon "suffers" over the sacrifice he feels he must make, "it requires the presence of his daughter to make him feel the full horror of what he is to do." Still, despite Iphigenia's pleas for pity, Agamemnon sacrifices her anyway. Fuller highlights Agamemnon's hypocrisy, noting how "noble" he seems when he holds his daughter in his arms, "as if he never could sink below the trust of such a being!" But he does. And when Iphigenia sees that her appeals are falling on her father's deaf ears, she willingly gives her life for Greece. As well she might have. For "the 'truth' about Iphigenia," as John Prudhoe writes, "is not that her father decided one day to sacrifice her, but that she was born into a [family] pattern . . . so complex . . . that to stress any incident in it is to distort the significance of the whole."[7]

In her comments about Iphigenia in her essay "Classical and Romantic," comments she wrote while living in Groton and with which Prudhoe might agree, Fuller had observed how important it was that Iphigenia keep her mind "unsullied" so she might "[intercede] to the gods in behalf of her polluted family." These are strong words coming from a woman who saw her own fate depicted in that of this doomed heroine and for whom the word "polluted" meant sexually "stained"—as Fuller makes glaringly clear in *Woman in the Nineteenth Century* when she says about Beatrice Cenci that "the tender relations of nature" had "been broken and polluted from the very first." In a later reflection on her near-death in Groton from a mysterious, perhaps psychologically induced disease, Fuller hints at how bad life had become for her when she says that when she "remembered how much struggle" awaited her if she recovered, she "felt willing to go."[8]

It may be true, as noted in chapter 10, that angry public reaction to a story she published in August 1835 featuring "a sneering . . . womanizer" prompted her despair. But what made her "vaguely suicidal" back then was, we recall, the soul-trying circumstance of being stuck in the country with her father, with whom she increasingly found herself in contention; the stress of having to teach her younger siblings, which left her little time for reading; the bad behavior of her rebellious older brothers; and her mother's frequent illnesses. Her father's praise of her when he thought she was dying only exaggerated her guilt after his death at not having expressed gratitude for the reading seat he had built for her.[9]

This emotional burden shows in her reaction to a scene she witnessed shortly after his death. We recall that Margaret had spent a night in a cottage belonging to a girl from Groton who was dying from consumption, the girl she had described in a letter to Cary as sunk "into that abyss lowest in humanity of crime for the sake of sensual pleasure." In her letter Fuller tells how, as she returned with the morning star to their house, then empty of everyone but herself, through "the shadows of that night ghost-like with step unlistened for, unheard assurance came to me." Compelled by the dead, she unlocked the door into the silent room that had "but late" belonged to her father. There, as if in a trance and hence unaware of passing time, she lay on his bed, a self-conscious act of surrender suggesting the unfathomable depth of her identification with the sexually stained dying girl, as well as with her father.[10]

ℒℛ ℒℛ ℒℛ

The ties that had bound Margaret to Timothy now bound her to James Nathan and compelled her—in the pattern of the Romantic poet in *Alastor* and Indiana in Sand's novel—to follow this phantom. It felt to her as if some great destiny were driving her to flee "across the sea" over which her beloved Ellen Kilshaw had sailed so many years before, the "wide waters" that had earlier called her seductively to come, to succumb to the peace they offered in their "white arms." Psychiatrists such as Leonard Shengold tell us now that a deep need for annihilation is typically present in people who were abused or neglected as children.[11]

Despite her private anguish, Fuller continued to do her work adeptly for the paper. She walled her problems off in a separate fantasy life she kept apart from the

PROFESSIONAL WOMAN, PRIVATE PASSION

public eye and her public role as a professional writer for the *New-York Daily Tribune*.[12] Few, if any, saw her anguish. She could survive and even thrive in this fantasy as long as she could communicate with the abusive but badly needed Nathan because such fantasy contact made her feel, sad to say, alive. Thus the touch from a hand that had misused her paradoxically had the power to release her hidden springs of feeling and to draw her over the sea.

Fuller also knew that in order to find what she was seeking, as well as to gain the right as a woman to express herself freely, she must leave America. When her wealthy philanthropist friends, Rebecca and Marcus Spring, proposed that she accompany them to Europe in the summer of 1846, Fuller jumped at the chance. To help pay her way she borrowed money from friends, including the Wards, and she eagerly accepted the Springs' offer that she tutor their eleven-year-old son, Eddie. She was keenly aware that at this juncture in her life she traveled less as a tourist than as a celebrated journalist. As an indication of his faith in her, Greeley promised to pay Fuller ten dollars for each article she sent to the paper. Meanwhile, ever present in the back of her mind, even as she acted as an ambitious newspaper columnist, was the hope that in Europe she might recover Nathan.

The cataclysmic public events Fuller was thereafter to witness in Italy, in tandem with her agonizing personal trials, would compel her while in Europe to enter a new phase of her life in which she would move forward on her path as a pilgrim to gain possession of her soul. Before she entered that phase, however, she was to find herself alone on the top of a mountain in a life-and-death struggle to save her soul from giving in to suicidal despair. In Europe, Fuller was not only to take a positive step forward in her pursuit of Truth, but also to embrace, in her final act, the tragic idealism she saw embodied in her "darling sister," Antigone, whose "straight forward nobleness," she wrote Nathan, "led her to Death."[13]

PART SEVEN

The Rising Tide of Revolution

While Fuller was packing her bags for England, most of the European countries from France eastward to Russia were on the brink of revolution, an uprising of the people against their autocratic rulers. The two years leading up to the revolutions of 1848 were to see reform banquets and the incendiary effects of socialist writings on the intelligentsia in France, a constitution and United Diet in Prussia, a civil war in Switzerland, a political awakening in the Italian states led by the exiled Romantic radical, Giuseppe Mazzini, as well as the rise to popular power of the Polish poet and activist Adam Mickiewicz, a messianic-Romantic nationalist set on redeeming Poland from the ravages of foreign invasion and domination. In sympathy with the quickly unfolding events abroad, Fuller wrote in her 1846 "First of January" article that the "cauldron simmers, and so great is the fire that we expect it soon to boil over, and new Fates appear for Europe."[1]

Fuller's millennial language indicates her eagerness to enter the theater of revolutionary action, the explosive social and historical conditions of which provided the scenic backdrop for her actions and interactions with key players—players and conditions the reader needs to be familiar with in order to comprehend fully the transformation of Margaret Fuller from a reform-minded, middle-class American journalist into a radical revolutionary.

47 ✑ Passionate Players and Incendiary Social Conditions

As Fuller's ship sailed into Liverpool on 12 August 1846, the peoples of Europe were preparing to overthrow the despots imposed on them by not only the combined powers of Austria, Prussia, and Russia, but also the Roman Catholic Church. The recently deceased Pope Gregory XVI had been an aristocrat determined to suppress democratic reforms.[1] Pope Gregory had wanted to quash reform, which, having grown up during the French Revolution, he equated with revolution. As well he might have. For the 1848 European revolutions, like the French Revolution, had their origins in liberal Enlightenment thinking that argued the existence of universal laws regarding basic human rights. Yet the 1789 revolution had ended in a bloodbath, further tyranny, and a general sense of disillusionment when Napoleon rolled over Austrian, Prussian, and Russian forces in 1805–7, only to be defeated at Waterloo. The 1814–15 Congress of Vienna divided his empire among the old absolutist powers in their effort to suppress nationalism and democracy. Still, by 1840 the ideas that the French Revolution had let loose upon the world—that all *men* are born free and equal and, when given the right circumstances as well as the free use of their reason, will progress to a state of moral perfection and the recognition of their common humanity—were deeply embedded in the minds of many of Europe's intellectual leaders, as they were in Fuller's. These "liberal" ideals fed the fires of the 1848 revolutions.[2]

The causes of the fifty revolutions that erupted in Palermo and Paris and spread through most of the countries to the east of France—through the German states, the Austro-Hungarian Empire, and then the rest of the principalities and states that constituted Italy, igniting finally the papal states—were complex and at times conflicting. In many of these revolutions, constitutional, national, and social issues became intricately intertwined and, in the end, undermined each other, as the social revolution in France was to undermine the Constitutionalists. Only Russia, which Czar Nicholas I controlled with an iron fist and a network of spies, as well as England, where reform measures and the use of thousands of special constables and troops defused a potentially explosive April 1848 Chartist demonstration, escaped these revolutions that ended in failure and sidelined for the time not just liberal dreams of political freedom, but also many nineteenth-century totalistic Romantic notions about transforming society.[3]

Not all who rebelled against their repressive monarchs wanted a total change in political and social arrangements. Nearly all, however, did want a constitution to limit the monarch's power by expanding the franchise and permitting more people to take part in their government. Political moderates who fought for parliamentary reforms tended to be suspicious of Romantic radicals like Fuller who sided with them in revolution but who dreamed not just of political change but also of change in social relations. In France, for example, the reasonable leadership of the moderate republican Alphonse de Lamartine, whose propagandistic 1847 *History of the Girondists* inspired the revolution that led to the creation of the French Republic after King Louis-Philippe's February 1848 abdication, ended abruptly in June when hundreds of students and destitute workers erected barricades and were gunned down by government guardsmen. Blaming Red Republicans (with whom many Americans by 1850 would identify Fuller), most American papers proclaimed how glad they were that "Communism, Socialism, Pillage, Murder, [and] Anarchy" had been quickly quelled by the forces of "Law and Order, Family and Property."[4]

In the kingdom of Poland, which was ruled by the Russian Czar, the revolutionary leader and poet Adam Mickiewicz, who saw himself as spiritual leader of the Poles, was gaining visibility. In his Paris lectures of the 1840s, the charismatic and mystical Mickiewicz horrified both monarchists and democrats with his vision of a unified, independent Poland as the New Israel chosen by God to lead other Slavic, and indeed all Christian, nations to a collective salvation. He appealed to other oppressed European nations to follow his lead to create a brotherhood of nations based on the ethos of activism and moral perfectionism. Mickiewicz believed that people of different ethnicities and inherited traditions in Poland could be united by their common history as well as by their common will to regain their independent statehood and to establish the divine order on earth. Seeing charisma as "the only legitimate source of power," Mickiewicz rejected the rationalism of the West, arguing instead for a society "based entirely and exclusively upon the gifts of the Holy Ghost."[5]

This kind of uplifting millennial message as conveyed by Romantic radicals impatient with the slow progress of reason and parliamentary change appealed to the masses in nineteenth-century Europe, who were afraid of the rapid changes brought about by urbanization and industrialization. They were more attracted to the earnest passion of Mickiewicz's messianic exhortations and the strong religious coloration of Giuseppe Mazzini's radical message regarding Italy's Risorgimento (rebirth). While the religious tone of Mazzini's call to arms repelled many democratic intellectuals, it enchanted young Italians, who en masse joined Young Italy, Mazzini's secret society dedicated to making Italy a unified, democratic republic. As a Romantic spiritualist, Mazzini spoke in terms of his nation's regeneration, redemption, and salvation while rejecting the traditional Christian doctrine of redemption through Christ and divine grace as well as the authority of the Roman Catholic Church; he believed, instead, that "the People" were to be saved by understanding their nation's mission through studying its particular historical development. The ideal nation as depicted in the poetically inspired speeches of Mazzini or Mickiewicz was more palatable to idealistic yet traditionally religious men and women than was a purely rational argument in behalf of human liberty that smacked to them of atheism. This was the case even though Mazzini himself was as persistently anti-Catholic as the French democratic intellectuals who considered themselves atheistic rationalists and who were feared by many of Mazzini's followers.[6]

In this Romantic era—when men and women dreamed of regenerating the human race and of resolving the problem of human evil—the rationalist outlook of eighteenth-century philosophers, statesmen, and politicians yielded to the emotional radicalism of women and men who questioned authority and traditional institutions and focused poetically on the plight of the poor. One such was the Abbé Félicité-Robert de Lamennais, an advocate of democracy and social equality whom Fuller would meet in Paris. Inspired by Mickiewicz, Lamennais in his biblically rhapsodic 1834 booklet, *Words of a Believer* (which influenced Mazzini), called on the upper classes (the "great" people) to create a society based on brotherly love by breaking down the barriers between themselves and the "little" people who labored in the factories and fields.[7]

In Germany many of the poets and philosophers whose writings had intrigued Fuller were now emphasizing the individual's capacity through intuition to come in direct contact with the great creative power, what Friedrich von Schlegel saw as the "Ur-Ich" (or "Primordial I"), the ground of all being, a unifying spiritual force whose electriclike energy could fill even the lowliest of tinkers with godlike power and thus the capacity to create his own paradise on earth. In a world now empty, as Novalis said, of the "gods . . . with their retinues," the German Romantic writers were basing many of their poems and epics on the paradigm underlying Fuller's life, that of the prodigal son; that is, on the glory to be obtained on earth if only each searching pilgrim can return to the land that was once home, where he or she and those like him or her might live in peace as a family or nation. This desire to realize the kingdom of God on earth was what drove the radical Romantics of Europe to provoke revolution.[8]

Disillusioned with the rationalists' arguments for objective universal truths, and especially with the concept that analytic reason can in time right wrongs and adequately deal with human pain and evil, many of Europe's Romantic revolutionaries turned not only to the thinking of the French utopian dreamers Charles Fourier and Henri de Saint-Simon, but also to the subjective idealism of some of the same German Romantics who had influenced Fuller—Schlegel, Novalis, Johann Gottfried von Herder, and Friedrich Schelling. Whereas Schelling in his cosmic philosophy posited the existence of an essential unity underlying the chaos of the empirical world, Herder (1744–1803) has been called the father of the idea of national unity, or nationalism, which inspired both Mazzini and Mickiewicz. Herder argued that individuals need to belong to an identifiable group with its own outlook, traditions, and historical memories. According to Herder, each such collective body has its own special *Volksgeist* (national soul) and must be understood and judged in accord with its own set of values and beliefs and not in terms of an abstract set of universal laws and rules, like those advocated by the scientifically minded men of the French Enlightenment.[9]

Idealizing the common man and woman—the peasant, the day laborer, the old-fashioned artisan, and the sexual outcast—and holding to their belief that a political nation is made up of a community of men and women bound by ties of territory, culture, and common history, some of the more romantic-minded leaders of the 1848 revolutions fought not for a contractual, constitutional conception of the state but for the sense of power and identity they derived from seeing themselves as an integral part of a unique nation. The "nation" in this vision is an almost mystical body of people who possess the imagination and will to remake society into a paradise on earth wherein all people are equal and free and live in harmonious relation to the almighty One.

Two such leaders were Mazzini and Mickiewicz, men who would soon become Fuller's friends and who had reason to dream of a radical transformation of society. For they were keenly aware of the overwhelming social problem of those living on the edge of destitution and who in the 1840s made up nearly a third of Europe's population. The Industrial Revolution with its machines that competed with and made obsolete traditional home industries, coupled with overproduction, crop failures, and a sudden upsurge in population in 1815–48, had left millions of agrarian laborers as well as unskilled workers and craftsmen unemployed and hence without sufficient income to feed themselves and their families. The potato blight in Ireland, poor wheat harvests, the high price of bread on the Continent, a slump in manufacturing, and the economic depression of 1841–42 exacerbated this already-dire situation by spreading famine across Europe in the 1840s, and with it destitution, disease, and despair.[10]

Aware of the deplorable conditions in which masses of European workers lived and worked, Karl Marx estimated that in 1845 one in every ten Europeans was a pauper dependent on relief; in Britain one in six was unemployed. The unemployed streamed into industrial cities, where work was scarce and living conditions crowded. In Manchester, which Fuller would visit after arriving in England in August 1846, reliable reports indicate that 50 to 75 percent of all workers were unemployed in 1841–42. In both Manchester and Liverpool, where Fuller's steamer docked, those of the lowest classes—primarily the Irish—lived hovelled together like animals in cellars for warmth in winter. Historians agree that Europe's common people in the 1840s were hurting, and that, apart from makeshift charity and meager public relief plans, Pope Gregory and the monarchs had done little to reduce their suffering.[11]

Worst hit, and of special interest to Fuller, were women and children, who flocked to mills to weave, which took little skill and hence attracted the untrained, who worked from dawn to dusk at one-fourth to one-half the wage paid to men. The British Government had passed the Factory Acts of 1833 and 1844 to mitigate the specter of brutality. These forbade the employment of children under the age of nine in textile mills (excluding silk and lace) and set limited hours for those older. They also prohibited employers from tying women and boys younger than ten to carts that they pulled up steep inclines through dark, low-ceilinged, coal mine tunnels, often on their hands and knees.[12]

Fuller visited a Newcastle coal mine in 1846, after the Factory Acts had been enacted and so was spared the sight of such an egregious use of human labor. In Manchester, Glasgow, and London, however, she would not have been spared the sight of prostitutes sitting at night in windows with their breasts bared to solicit clients. Driven to prostitution to supplement their meager earnings, laundresses, domestics, mill hands, and seamstresses strolled streets scandalously bareheaded at night and solicited men. In a Victorian world where morality was preached by the upper-middle classes, where birth control was barely used, yet where hunger drove an untold number of women to prostitution, illegitimacy was rampant. In the 1840s in the larger cities of Europe, illegitimate births were estimated to be anywhere from a third to a half of all births, a fact that makes Fuller's later out-of-wedlock pregnancy less startling. Infanticide among the poor was widespread, while newborns who escaped being murdered by their mothers or dying of malnutrition or disease (Fuller's baby would suffer from both malnutrition and disease) were often left in doorways or on the streets. Although middle-class churchgoers were appalled at the numbers of abandoned infants, few offered to care for the babies or to welcome into their churches their unwed mothers, who were viewed as anathema.[13]

Radical Romantics in Europe dreamed of a revolution that would transform society by eliminating such human injustice and suffering. They spoke of their fight in language that came from the Bible, particularly from the Book of Revelation, in which a vengeful Christ returns to save the poor from their oppressors. After all, most of the revolutionaries, even those like Mazzini who rejected traditional Christianity, still interpreted historical and political events—as did Fuller—through the frame of biblical prophecy. And the book of the Bible most frequently cited by radical Romantics like Mazzini and Fuller was the apocalypse of St. John, which promised the poor and oppressed that they would be first in heaven. The Book of Revelation thus filled Romantic prophets and the poor with hope through a set of symbols that promised that their hard lives were worth living, and that death was not the end but merely a transition to paradisiacal peace. In this place of peace there would be "no more death, neither sorrow, nor crying, [nor] any more pain."[14]

To Romantics like Mazzini and Fuller, however, men and women who did not expect what one critic has called "an apocalyptic relief expedition from the sky" suddenly to alleviate the suffering of the poor but instead dreamed that people might love one another as brothers and sisters in their own time on earth, revolution seemed the most efficacious way to make the world conform to their ideal of it. Their appeal for an actual revolution contrasted starkly with the view held by many Romantic writers, who transferred the theater of events in Revelation from the external world to the mind of the single believer where they sought a personal, not political, redemption.[15]

The nineteenth-century revolutionary Romantics of Europe were nonetheless idealists, and as such they inevitably misjudged the real needs of destitute workers. While these radical dreamers wanted to create a world in which all people are free and equal, the hungry masses wanted foremost bread to eat and a bed to sleep on.

Moreover, in idealizing the lower classes, messianic Romantic nationalists failed to foresee the factional strife that arises when people who do not speak the same language and are products of different ethnic, religious, and cultural backgrounds are forced to share a common homeland.[16]

They also failed to take into account the terrible insecurity that was to well in the hearts of Europeans of the lower classes when threatened with the destruction of the traditional patriarchal hierarchies and orders of social life that had given their lives meaning and constancy. Particularly unsettling to them was the assault on their traditional vision of God, on the one hand by the scientific-minded Enlightenment thinkers and on the other by the Romantics. The latter believed in a spiritual power, but one they frequently figured in abstract or maternal terms and not as the ultimate father-lawgiver of the Judeo-Christian tradition. Mickiewicz, who in 1841 had been influenced by the Lithuanian mystic Andrzej Towiański, famously argued in his Paris lectures at the Collège de France (1840–44) that in a restored historical and political Polish nation there would be no need for political or civil laws, nor, for that matter, for any codified, written law at all, since to gain a sense of identity and direction, the people needed only to follow their own intuition as well as the leadership of a God-inspired, charismatic, national leader.[17]

Their faith in innate human goodness prevented nineteenth-century radical Romantics such as Mickiewicz and Mazzini from seeing the need of the masses to cling to the traditional symbols and codified laws provided them by institutions like the Roman Catholic Church. They did not foresee that the sinister end of their attempt to uproot traditional religious rituals and myths as well as to question the validity of the laws ("the rules," as political theorist-philosopher Isaiah Berlin has put it, "supposedly enjoined by God or by nature or by the prince") would be to leave ordinary men and women with no veil between them and the reality of human aggression, suffering, and death. Moreover, religious radicals such as Mazzini did not foresee that by taking the supernatural element out of Christ and his mission, many people, in their need for an incarnated god and symbols to believe in, would in time be driven to fill the vacuum left in their absence with what Berlin has called a "*Gemeinschaft*—symbols and agencies which proved far more powerful than either socialists or enlightened liberals wished to believe," that is, with the idea of the nation as supreme authority and symbols of a sort that advocated a reality (as happened in Germany) just the opposite of what these Romantics with their dreams of individual and national redemption had intended.[18]

Fuller, too, failed to see this need, mocking in some of her *Tribune* dispatches the Catholic emblems and rituals that gave meaning to the lives of poverty-stricken Europeans. In place of traditional Christian images and sacraments, Fuller, we recall, during her mystical phase had generated her own rituals and symbols. In the pattern of ancient women initiated into the mystery cults surrounding Demeter, Dionysus, and Orpheus, she had attempted to teach women to reach the god

THE RISING TIDE OF REVOLUTION

"within" by purifying their lives. She taught this process in her Boston Conversations as well as in *Woman in the Nineteenth Century,* the heart of which is a wish for redemption, and for which she had originally submitted a mandala-like design for its frontispiece. Fuller chose a mandala because in Hindu and Buddhist Tantrism its shape, a circle containing a blazing sun or star (Fuller's mandala contained a blazing star), was considered a symbol of the cosmos, a collection point for all universal forces. The psychoanalyst Carl Jung, who drew his first mandala in 1916, said that the mandala represents the inner core of one's personality and that individuation involves a descent within the self. There, Jung believed, one comes in contact with "the inner sun as the god within."[19]

Fuller, too, believed that by delving "within" and communing with this electromagnetic core of "Power," a woman might be filled with its vital life force and hence be reborn as a spiritually pure person capable of entering a perfect marriage with a man, and also of saving men from sin. In a poem about her mandala that appears in her 1844 scrapbook, Fuller eagerly anticipates the era of social harmony, "When the perfect two embrace, / Male and female, black and white." In this poem she notes that then, at that precise moment in time, the "Soul" will receive saving grace, not from Christ, but "in space," and the darkness will be made "fruitful by the light," not of God the Father, but of "the diamond Sun." Then, says Fuller, "Time, eternity are one."[20]

Thus even in this poem describing her mandala, we see the glow of the apocalypse coloring Fuller's perception as she looks toward that critical moment when history as we know it will end. Although this suicidal or millennial wish for personal obliteration appears throughout Fuller's life, this side of her personality was not altogether negative. The positive aspect for Fuller of her millennial mystical vision is that she felt it let her bypass the law of the fathers and go right to what she imagined to be the source of life. This feeling of direct communion with the genderless almighty One filled Fuller with the courage to challenge in her writings and actions what she, along with students and workers all over Europe, saw as unjust and repressive patriarchal structures. Her fervent desire to overthrow Europe's authoritarian leaders caught the attention of Mickiewicz and Mazzini, both of whom also dreamed of ridding Europe of its tyrant-fathers and of creating a confederation of nations based on the liberal vision of universal liberty and justice. These spokespersons for the rights of "the people" believed they had been chosen by God, Providence, or some other form of higher power to fulfill on earth their "sacred" mission. This fervid faith in their chosen status enhanced their popular appeal and power; it underlay their charisma.[21]

The negative side of such a messianic vision was that its extremism prevented revolutionaries like Mazzini and Mickiewicz from being able to realize an all-inclusive and harmonious brotherhood. These Romantics not only failed to take into account ordinary people's fierce loyalties to family members and friends as well as humanity's often brutish nature; they also failed to see that the same Romanticism that preaches man is god by his ability to fuse with the almighty One also demands that a person relinquish control of "self" and hence the capacity to make rational decisions and moral choices.[22] He or she relinquishes possession of his or her soul. Such a state was anathema to Fuller, who considered soul-possession the privilege of the pilgrim who has completed the journey of life to maturity. Thus for Fuller the idea of soul-possession had a pragmatic American side. Heir to the Puritans and, in her words, "the fathers of the revolution," men willing to die to secure for themselves the right of self-rule, Fuller when faced with the reality of the Roman Revolution would hold as "her standard," as Ann Douglas has said, "that set by the American Revolution."[23]

The fortuitous intersection of Fuller's strong American personality with the charismatic personalities of Mickiewicz and Mazzini along with that of the caring yet politically radical Giovanni Angelo Ossoli, as well as with the violent upheaval of the 1848 revolutions, made possible Fuller's final step forward on her life journey from *Tribune* reporter to heroine of history.

48 ∞ Entering the European Stage

Before leaving for Europe on the Cunard steam packet *Cambria* with her reform-minded philanthropist companions, Rebecca and Marcus Spring, Margaret wrote Cary on 20 July 1846 that she went "with a great pain" in her "heart." Though such pain was "nothing new," and nothing she could "evade by staying," seeing Cary before she sailed from Boston on 1 August might help. But if Cary could not come, "know me more than ever yours in love Margaret." Since she planned only a brief 30 July stopover in Cambridgeport, where her mother was now renting a house, Fuller feared she might similarly not have a chance to say good-bye to Emerson. But Emerson appeared in Cambridgeport with letters of introduction, including one to Thomas Carlyle in which he calls Fuller "an exotic in New England, a foreigner from some more sultry & expansive climate."[1]

As a child, Fuller had imagined herself a changeling, a European princess whose real home lay across the sea. This childhood dream was linked in her memory to Ellen Kilshaw, whose return to Liverpool when Fuller was seven had depressed her. After that Margaret had associated her absent friend with a gift Ellen had given her before she left for Liverpool, a bunch of dried golden amaranths from Madeira, a place the child imagined as a "fortunate isle" set "apart in the blue ocean from all of ill or dread." Whenever Margaret thereafter saw a passing sail, her thoughts returned to Madeira and to the feminine figure for whom she yearned. Ellen's image merged in memory with an idea of home as a happy place where parents unconditionally loved their children.[2]

Another draw to Europe was Nathan, whose departure for Europe had similarly upset Fuller. So, too, had her mother's decision not to visit her a last time
in New York before she left the States. Margaret feared her mother might be in
Canton on the day of her departure from Boston and that she thus might not see
her mother or, for that matter, any of her family again: like her prodigal Uncle
Peter, she might not return from her "pilgrimage." In early June her dark mood
had momentarily lifted when she at last received a note from Nathan promising
her that either he himself or a letter would greet her in London when she arrived
in September. Hope of seeing Nathan again kept her looking forward through the
summer of 1846, when continuous rain kept her head hurting.[3]

Depressed and unwell yet hopeful she might see Nathan in London, Fuller
had boarded the *Cambria*. Though the trip to Liverpool was made in a record ten
days, sixteen hours, and the weather and "all circumstances [were] propitious," the
steamer's constant rocking, combined with "the smell and jar of the machinery,"
had made her feel nauseous and her already-aching head throb with pain. She
"enjoyed nothing," she wrote home, "on the sea" and was glad when she saw tall
crags, circling seabirds, and then the green fields.[4]

Arriving on 12 August 1846, Fuller discovered shortly that the land of her childhood fantasies clashed dramatically with the reality of a modern European city.
Liverpool, like Manchester where Fuller went next, was a large town whose textile industry had attracted masses of field hands to work in its factories, including thousands of refugees from the Irish famine. Laborers lived there in dirty,
crowded tenements and dark, damp cellars—several families sometimes sharing
one room and all the families on a block sharing a single privy and water pump.
But the deplorable living conditions of the poor were not immediately visible to
Fuller, whose first dispatch is full of the high-minded moralizing of an American, middle-class woman seemingly more concerned with her writing's impact on
readers than she is with those swarming around her. She is morally condescending
when she writes of the "coarse, rude" girls from the Manchester mills who stroll
the streets at night attempting to pick up men, of, as she put it, "the squalid and
shameless beggars of Liverpool," and of the unkempt older women whose heavy
drinking, mostly in gin-joints, had made them "too dull to carouse."[5]

Fuller was shocked to see women she thought ought to be the "warder" of home
life thus drinking in bars and soliciting sex on the street. She was equally shocked
to find that in England's industrial cities it seemed "None but the sick ever bathe."
In neither Liverpool nor Manchester had she found a public bath. And when in
Chester Fuller asked the chambermaid about getting a bath, she replied that there
might be one at the local infirmary. She was soon, however, to be impressed by
the public bath in London, which had an adjoining facility where poor women
could rent for relatively little money all they needed to wash clothes: good tubs,

heated water, and an apparatus for rinsing, drying, and ironing. It was thrilling to see women do in three hours a load of wash that at home would have taken them three or four days.[6]

In that first dispatch, Fuller caught, as if on camera, striking images of such strangeness and uncommon beauty that they underline the distance she has traveled. She mentions, for instance, how in Liverpool she had seen women carrying an infant corpse to the grave. She notes the beauty of the "custom here that those who have fulfilled all other tender offices to the little being, should hold to it the same relation to the very last." She captures in writing the fleeting image on a canal boat, a few days later, of a young man of such "pure East-Indian" beauty that she felt compelled to gaze at him. With his black satin cap, his richly embroidered coat, and bare throat graced by a heavy gold chain, he looked, wrote Fuller, like "Love asleep, while Psyche leans over him with the lamp."[7]

At Ambleside in the Lake District, where Harriet Martineau had arranged for them to stay in a stone cottage with a mountain view, Fuller and the three Springs spent eight days boating on the lakes and visiting notable people. Though the English authoress had found the cottage for the travelers, Martineau was cool to Fuller, who had been critical of her book *Society in America*. Martineau later said of the visit that Fuller was only happy when she could "harangue the drawing-room party." Yet visiting the Lake District was worth it, for there Fuller met Wordsworth, a reverend but kind old man dressed in black who walked "with cautious step along the level garden path." The seventy-six-year-old Tory poet spoke with more liberality than Fuller had expected regarding the necessity of repealing the Corn Laws. She was struck by his fondness for hollyhocks and in her *Tribune* dispatch says that though the poet's neighbors value him as a kind neighbor, they lament his ignorance "of the real wants of England and the world." Wordsworth, she says, hears not "the cry of men in the jaws of destruction" that "will not be stilled by sweet, poetic suasion."[8]

Fuller was hardly one to criticize Wordsworth for his ignorance of "real wants," for she was still harboring her own poetic suasion about Nathan. After delightful visits in Edinburgh with "the English Opium-Eater" Thomas De Quincy, author of *Suspiria de profudis* (1845), a recent psychological inquiry into dreaming, and Dr. Andrew Combe, an even-tempered man, phrenologist, and editor of the *Phrenological Journal*, Fuller wrote Thomas Delf, a London book dealer who was acting as liaison between her and Nathan. She asked Delf to tell Nathan either to join her in Scotland or, if that was not possible, to forward to Edinburgh letters to her from him. In reply she got a note from Nathan saying he intended to marry another woman.[9]

She panicked at this news. Her pain at the thought of the loss of this man she imagined she loved was so great that, as Rebecca Spring tells it, she fell into a depression so deep that she acted in an unusually imprudent way. During a two-week tour of north-central Scotland that took the travelers by coach from Edinburgh to Perth and on to Rowardennan by way of Loch Katrine, a "deeply despondent Fuller," according to Rebecca, rode outside alongside the driver, even in a driving rain. And after having been rowed across Loch Katrine, Fuller insisted on walking through the pass that led from Loch Katrine to Loch Lomond, a distance of six miles.[10]

Fuller's pain is apparent in her 30 September dispatch to the *Tribune*. She tells readers the tragic story of Queen Mary of Scots, who "had never possessed or could not retain . . . the love of the men she had chosen." She also tells how "touching" she found a "wild and plaintive air" sung by a handsome young boatman who had rowed them across Loch Lomond to their inn at Rowardennan. It was a Gaelic song, she says, about "a girl whose lover has deserted her and married another."[11]

Without a guide Margaret hiked with Marcus up the four-mile trail that led from their inn at the bottom to the top of "the lofty Ben Lomond." They reached the peak in the evening, whereupon both were moved by the beauty of the scene before them. "Peak beyond peak," wrote Fuller, had "caught from the shifting light all the colors of the prism." Viewing the distant scene, Fuller thought of death. She reported to her readers how she had felt that moment on top of the mountain like an actress on a stage and concluded that if climbing Ben Lomond had been "the last act" of her life, it would have been a fine one.[12]

It almost was. In what may have been, as Robert Hudspeth says, "a suicidal gesture," Fuller on the way down in the gathering darkness became separated from Marcus and was forced to spend the night alone on the mountain. "Imprisoned" on "a little perch of that great mountain," she recalled how Psyche, whose parents had abandoned her on a mountain, had thought she was destined to marry "Death." Fuller at first felt the same, telling *Tribune* readers how she had with her that night no coat, no food, no hand to hold. The thick mist hid the stars. Around midnight she thought she saw on the hillside floating white phantoms, but it was only the mist, which gave her "a kiss pervasively cold as that of Death."[13]

Yet when Fuller faced "Death," she chose not to embrace it. She figured her only hope "lay in motion," her "only help," she said, "in myself." She kept moving "the whole of that long night." Though later she learned that twenty men with dogs had been searching for her, she heard no sound except the rush of the waterfall, the sigh of the night wind, and, once or twice, the startle of a grouse in the heather. "It was," she wrote, "a never-to-be-forgotten presentation of stern, serene realities."[14]

That night on the lonely mountainside, no Cupid had come to save her. But, then, neither had Death claimed her as his bride. Instead, Fuller had let her "Yankee method" guide her. At the first light of day when the little flies "arose from their bed amid the purple heather" to bite her, she climbed down the mountain to where she was found by shepherds, who carried her to the inn. There she was met by the relieved Springs and hotel staff. In describing the event in her dispatch, Fuller presented her adventure as a struggle between herself and Death, thus transforming her "hair-breadth" escape with life into a drama, its backdrop being the Grampian Mountains.[15]

Confronted with the possibility of death, Fuller had done what was required to survive and was thus briefly freed from the illusion of Death as a comforting lover. In her next dispatch she would begin to exhibit a new alertness to real human suffering. She sent this dispatch from Paris, having traveled by coach to London and stopped there from October 1 until mid-November, when she went to Paris. In it Fuller recalls the deplorable living conditions of the women and children standing in doorways of cottages in Glasgow or leaning on gates near the road. Never before had she seen so many poor people living together in such cramped conditions, nor had she seen people drinking so much alcohol as their only means of coping with poverty and pain. The sight of impoverished women especially upset her; they were "dressed," she says in her dispatch, "in dirty, wretched tatters" and had on their faces a look of "unexpecting woe" "far more tragic than the inscription over the gate of Dante's *Inferno*."[16]

Fuller was relieved in Edinburgh to meet the philanthropist James Simpson, whom she praises in her November dispatch for his work in behalf of popular education and in particular for having induced the erection of public baths in Edinburgh. Given that no European city at that time had an adequate or sanitary water supply and that Fuller thought physical cleanliness essential for "progress in higher culture," she was grateful to Simpson for making it possible for working people—as well as herself who had witnessed so much poverty and filth—to take a bath.[17]

On their journey from Loch Lomond to London, Fuller and the Springs had visited Scott's tomb at Abbotsford, then traveled by coach in heavy rain to Newcastle, where, in their petticoats and fine clothes, Fuller and Rebecca Spring descended by bucket into a coal mine. After traipsing half a mile underground by tallow candlelight, they begged to turn back along the wet and dirty path and be lifted by bucket up to fresh air. With blackened face and hands, Fuller left Newcastle thinking about the miners' "poor horses" that were doomed to "see the light of day no more" once they had "been let down into these gloomy recesses," there to "pass their days in dragging cars along the rails of the narrow passages." She did not comment that, until the passage of the Factory Act of 1844, the horse-drawn coal carts had been hauled by harnessed women and children. Still the middle-class American sightseer, Margaret noted tartly to her brother Richard in her 27 September letter that she thought her descent into a coalmine a "rare feat for a lady."[18]

49 ∾ Mazzini Enters

On 1 October Fuller arrived in London to find no letters awaiting her. Her mood darkened further over the next six weeks for she could not see the sun for the coal smoke and fog hanging over the city. She was also depressed that she and the Springs could afford no more than "fourth or fifth" class lodgings. Such matters increased her awareness of the abyss separating the "parade of wealth and luxury" from the misery that "stares one in the face in every street and hoots at the gates of her palaces." Fuller wrote in her December dispatch from Paris how poverty in England holds "terrors" of a sort she "never dreamed at home." She pities the homeless, whose plight warrants "a speedy solution," and also the middle class. "Too close, too dark," she says, "throng the evils they cannot obviate, the sorrows they cannot relieve."[1]

In London Fuller met social activists—Hugh Doherty, editor of the *London Phalanx*, a paper that forwarded a Fourierist view of socialism; Mary and William Howitt, the main supporters of John Saunders's *People's Journal*, which advocated workers' rights; and, Dr. Thomas Southwood Smith, an expert on fever and infectious diseases and a philanthropist who built "good tenements" for working people. She met various writers but missed Tennyson, who was out of town, and Elizabeth Barrett, who had eloped to Italy with Robert Browning. She did meet Henry George Atkinson, a phrenologist she describes as the "Prince of the English Mesmerizers," a man "in the fulness of his powers" with a "head of the Christ-like sort as seen by Leonardo."[2]

And she met Thomas Carlyle, who invited her to spend an evening with him and his wife, Jane, at their home. At first she admired him and the way he sang "his great full sentences." During a second visit, however, she found that his haranguing wearied her "mind," which, she wrote Emerson on 16 November, "disclaimed and rejected almost everything he said." His hatred of democracy enraged her. "The worst of hearing Carlyle," she told Emerson, is not "that you cannot interrupt him" but that in his presence you become a "prisoner." Carlyle, in turn, begrudgingly praised her to his brother, writing that he found her a "strange *lilting* lean old maid, not nearly such a bore as I expected."[3]

Fuller liked Jane Carlyle, who admired George Sand; and she greatly enjoyed meeting Jane's friend Giuseppe Mazzini, the exiled leader of the Italian democratic republican movement whose slim figure, fine forehead, olive complexion, short-cropped beard and moustache, and sonorous voice made him seem to some Italians like a messiah come to save their nation. Mazzini was a Romantic radical committed to winning national independence for his country by freeing it from the temporal power of the pope and a system of governments run by foreign despots and regional autocratic rulers. Through a massive propaganda effort to educate Italians about Italy's history and the importance of freedom, Mazzini hoped to spark a revolution that would engulf Europe and overturn the 1815 Congress of Vienna settlement. The latter had divided historical nations into regions controlled by the powers of the ancien régime, a move that prevented each nation from asserting its independence. Mazzini knew that educating Italians about the past was essential if Italy was to regain its identity and freedom.[4]

At the time Fuller met Mazzini, Italy was a complex mosaic of eight sovereign states, each with a reactionary and absolutist government. Though nominally independent, each acknowledged dependence on Austrian protection. In the Piedmont region from which Mazzini had fled in 1831, Victor Emmanuel I had abolished the Napoleonic Code, restored feudal privileges to dispossessed nobles, reinstituted the old system of law and penal procedures, and annexed Genoa, where Mazzini had been born in 1805. Son of a Genoan physician who had been a member of the government under the pre-1815 Ligurian Republic, Mazzini at the age of sixteen had been moved by the sight of the ragged Italian patriots who had flocked to Genoa to escape to Spain after the Austrians crushed their insurrection in Piedmont. Mazzini then had dedicated his life to freeing his nation from foreign despots as well as from the pope, who ruled the Papal States where the Inquisition had been restored, the position of the Jesuits had been reestablished, and laymen were forbidden participation in government. As a twenty-four-year-old lawyer and advocate for the poor, Mazzini had joined the Carbonari, a quasi-Masonic group of secret societies that saw Christ as the first victim of tyranny and aimed to overthrow both priestly and royal absolutism. Arrested on a charge of conspiracy, he was released for lack of evidence and fled to France.[5]

Thus began Mazzini's long exile, first in Marseilles, where in 1831 he drew up the manifesto for his new society, Young Italy. In it he outlined a plan to restore national unity and set up a republican government in Italy, as well as to agitate for political equality, social justice, and self-determination for Europe's oppressed peoples. By means of the often unrealistic, sometimes even false, yet always eloquent propaganda he smuggled out of France and distributed throughout the Italian states, Mazzini educated Italians about their rights and history and thus inspired idealistic young men. He believed his dream of freedom and democracy could come true only if these men were willing to die for it in armed insurrection. Driven by his radical dreams, Mazzini was seen by Austrian police as one of Europe's most threatening revolutionaries.[6]

When an attempted 1833 military coup in Piedmont was betrayed and King Charles Albert of Sardinia, a one-time Carbonari sympathizer, executed twelve revolutionaries, a despairing yet not defeated Mazzini had sought sanctuary first in Switzerland, where he continued to plot strategies for popular uprisings. He then went to London in 1836. The propaganda he poured into Italy from England inspired two Austrian naval officers, Attilio Bandiera and Emilio Bandiera, to defect and attempt to initiate an uprising in the Kingdom of Naples in 1844, a failed effort for which they were executed. Despite this setback, Mazzini continued writing, publishing *Memoir of the Bandiera Brothers* and *Scheme of 1844*. In the latter he laid out a plan for an insurrection in the Papal States. A tireless crusader, Mazzini in London also ran a night school for poor Italian boys. And it was in London at the Carlyles' that he met Fuller, who was immediately drawn to this man who was willing to give his life for the idea of a republican and unified Italy.[7]

In Mazzini, Fuller found a fellow Romantic. An admirer of Rousseau, Shelley, Byron, Burns, and Wordsworth, Mazzini believed there to be an underlying unity among the people of the eight Italian states: their shared but dormant sense of national identity that, once awakened, would inspire diverse Italians to fight together for their freedom. He believed, as he would put it in an 1845 letter, that "unity was and is the destiny of Italy," and that through his propaganda he could make people see "the indissoluble *co-partnery* of all generations and all individuals in the human race." Mazzini believed in this "impulse towards harmony" despite the fact that 95 percent of the people on the Italian peninsula spoke distinct dialects that prevented them from understanding one another. Mazzini himself, moreover, had never traveled farther south than Livorno (Leghorn) and hence had no current experience on which to base his theory, though historically Greeks, Celts, Arabs, and Lombards had lived harmoniously together in Italy for centuries.[8]

A Romantic messianic nationalist, Mazzini had been influenced by Herder's idea of a national soul as well as by Mickiewicz's vision of each nation having a special mission to contribute to the cause of humanity. But he condemned the kind of nationalism that involved imperialistic encroachment on other peoples' rights. He defined nationality as "the role assigned by God" to a specific group of people "to the end that God's thought may be realized in the world."[9]

Mazzini's faith in liberty—in an individual's capacity to understand that his or her worth rests in responsible action in relation to "the collective whole"—was so great that he criticized not only the Risorgimento liberals who aimed to replace the authoritarian old regime with a constitutional monarchial government and narrow parliamentary representation, but also those who put class economic interests over individual human rights. He was therefore an early opponent of Karl Marx. Echoing Saint-Simon and Lamennais, Mazzini argued that maintaining individual freedom depended on "the People"—"great" and "little"—working together in accord with the principle of "association." By this he meant for the people of the eight nation states of Italy—no matter their social class—to work together to forge their collective destiny.[10]

Though the ethic underlying Mazzini's vision was Christian, the radical movement he led, Young Italy, was committed to the secularization of Italian culture. Contending that the Christian religion had deviated from its original mission, Mazzini, like other spiritually inclined nineteenth-century Romantics, aimed to teach people to channel their religious impulse away from rituals and denominational differences toward a new faith that allowed "the People" to come face to face with God. "He had taken for his motto," Fuller later wrote, "GOD AND THE PEOPLE, and believed in no other powers."[11]

In her 16 November letter to Emerson, Fuller noted that Mazzini had been in the group one evening when the Carlyles came to visit the Springs and Fuller, and it had been Mazzini, not Carlyle, who had impressed her. For Carlyle's words that night had been "a defence of mere force,—success the test of right;—if people would not behave well, put collars round their necks;—find a hero, and let them be his slaves, &c." With Mazzini there the conversation had turned "to 'progress' and ideal subjects, and C.," wrote Fuller, "was fluent in invectives on all our 'rose-water imbecilities.'" As Carlyle mocked Romantic revolutionaries, Rebecca Spring, an ardent abolitionist, had stood staring at Carlyle, and an increasingly agitated Mazzini had paced the floor, his hands clasped behind his back.[12]

Rebecca had apparently held her composure until she heard Carlyle say, "If people consent to be slaves, they deserve to be slaves! I have no pity for them!" At that point, as she tells it, she started toward him, angrily denouncing the severity of laws against teaching slaves to read, yet proclaiming how they still found ways to learn. Rebecca recollects how her passion had made Fuller laugh and exclaim, "I have been wondering how long Rebecca would bear it!" Noting Mazzini's agitation, Jane had said in an aside to Margaret, "These are but opinions to Carlyle; but to Mazzini, who has given his all, and helped bring his friends to the scaffold, in pursuit of such subjects, it is a matter of life and death."[13]

As indeed it was, and soon would be for Fuller, too. Shortly after meeting her, Mazzini, who approved of her views on women, wrote her, "You do not know how much I esteem and love you." He invited her to speak at his evening school for Italian boys. Fuller warmed to this man who showed a kind of dedication to the cause of human freedom that she had seen before in Emerson and Alcott—though Mazzini, unlike them, was a man of action. What drives Mazzini, she wrote to the *Tribune*, is "an understanding of what *must* be the designs of Heaven with regard to Man, since God is Love, is Justice."[14]

In that December dispatch, Fuller compares the attempts by oppressed Europeans to throw off the control of foreign despots to America's fight for freedom from England. To this declaration of liberation on behalf of a united and republican Europe she added a millennial call for Europe's spiritual salvation, noting, "there can be no . . . salvation for any, unless the same can be secured for all." She depicts Mazzini as a messiah and his school for boys as "a planting of the Kingdom of Heaven" on earth where "poor boys, picked up from the streets, are redeemed from bondage and gross ignorance." In Mazzini's ideas and actions, Fuller found an embodiment of the union of socialistic and religious thought for which she had been searching. Mazzini gave her a theoretical frame for her own visionary writings and revolutionary actions during the last years of her life.[15]

Mazzini's impact on Fuller's mind and imagination was so great that her dispatches to the *Tribune* would begin to unfold as a drama detailing the events leading up to the European Revolutions of 1848. And in this drama she and Mazzini would each play major parts: he as hero, she as the spirit of liberty. In both her public and private letters a violent rage now begins to appear. She directs this rage at all the men who have wronged her and pilgrims like her by making them feel their humiliating subjugation. She reserves her greatest rage, however, for deceitful men like Nathan who betray people's trust in them. Playing Dido to Nathan's Aeneas, Fuller on 25 October 1846 from London wrote Nathan a blistering letter congratulating him on his marriage and demanding he return her letters. Yet as coolly as Aeneas asserted to Dido that they had never exchanged legitimate wedding vows and hence his leaving her was not a betrayal, so Nathan on 6 November wrote Fuller that he had promised her nothing. When he received her irate reply accusing him of duplicity and again demanding her letters, Nathan wrote denying that he had ever been deceitful. He even suggested that maybe Delf had forged the letter signed by him in which he says he intends to marry another woman. He accuses Fuller of lacking "experience of life," of judging him "without a hearing," and hence of insulting him.[16]

With that last cruel retort, Fuller realized she could be done with this man who insulted her. She had a cause to fight for now, and it left no room in her life for the scurrilous Nathan.

ﾒ ﾒ ﾒ

Fuller's letters to friends now glow with new faith, affection, and daring. She wrote Emerson that she felt in her element in European society: "It does not indeed come up to my ideal; but so many of the encumbrances are cleared away that used to weary me in America, that I can enjoy a freer play of faculty, and feel, if not like a bird in the air, at least as easy as a fish in water." She wrote Cary: "I find how true for me was the lure that always drew me towards Europe. It was no false instinct that said I might here find an atmosphere needed to develope me in ways *I* need." She tells Cary to read an essay in "Sanders People's Journal" headed "Italian Martyrs" by Mazzini, in whom "holiness has purified, but nowhere dwarfed the man."[17]

It was important to Fuller that Mazzini ardently supported women, in particular Sand, whom he had been defending since 1839 when he published in the *People's Journal* what has been called the "first friendly review" of her work. This was no small feat, since Sand was seen in England as an outlaw. Englishmen linked her with the socialism of Saint-Simon, who envisioned a kind of Christianity that blended mysticism and rationalism and also a world without a military system, inherited wealth, or competition in business and industry. Saint-Simon, who influenced Mazzini, argued in behalf of human rights for both male and female workers, and he denounced the hypocrisy of a Christianity that allowed men "the right of 'scortatory love'" while damning women who did not meet the high—but double—standard of Victorian sexual morality. Most Englishmen feared Sand because they saw her as a threat to the traditional patriarchal family structure.[18]

Mazzini liked Fuller's writing and kept in touch with her after she left London. While still in London, she wrote home that an English edition of her *Papers on Literature and Art* had "been courteously greeted in the London journals" and that *Woman in the Nineteenth Century* "has been read and prized by many," including Mazzini. By mid-November she was in Paris carrying letters of introduction from Mazzini to his friends there, including the dissident French priest Lamennais, the Polish patriot and poet Mickiewicz, and the controversial Sand.[19]

50 ∞ Mickiewicz Enters

Paris was vibrant in December 1846 with middle-class discontent with the "citizen king," Louis-Philippe, who had come to power in August 1830, as well as with worker enthusiasm for the socialist schemes of Saint-Simon and Fourier. Trudging through the mud coating the sidewalks and clinging tenaciously to the cobblestones of Paris's narrow streets, Fuller sensed the same glaring disparity between the lives of the rich and the poor as she had seen in London. During a dreary winter of mud and mist, she found that the ladies she saw at balls, lectures, art galleries, and the theater were generally so well dressed that the effect was "of a flower-garden."[1]

Casting a shadow over the "graceful vivacity" of these lovely French ladies was, in Fuller's mind, the mass of the poor whose suffering had not been relieved by the fat bourgeois king, Louis-Philippe. The poor in their tattered clothes made Fuller self-conscious about the luxury of her room in the Hôtel Rougement, just off the boulevard des Italiens near the theaters and exclusive cafés. It is small, she wrote her mother, but "very pretty, with the thick, flowered carpet and marble slabs; the French clock, with Cupid, of course, over the fireplace."[2]

In this "city of pleasures" Fuller met people who defied convention in their public politics or private lives and influenced her, as did the radical feminist and socialist Pauline Roland. Roland, who had translated and published Fuller's "Essay on American Literature" in *La revue indépendante,* a socialist and literary review Sand helped found, openly opposed marriage, and had conducted a school at Leroux's Fourierist commune at Boussac near Sand's country home at Nohant. Roland liked Fuller's work and urged her to keep submitting to the review after she returned to America.[3]

Though she had found Roland a woman of interest, she had become "engrossed" with the French actress Rachel (Élisa Félix). Writing to Cary, Fuller confessed that she went to the theater whenever Rachel performed. In her dispatch Fuller says she liked her most in *Phèdre,* in which the actress expresses "guilty [incestuous] love ... with a force and terrible naturalness that almost suffocated" Fuller as "beholder." After Phèdre "had taken the poison, the exhaustion and paralysis of the system—the sad, cold, calm submission to Fate," the price Phèdre must pay for incestuous love, seemed to Fuller "still more grand."[4]

In November she wrote Cary, "there is nothing like [Rachel's] voice; she speaks the language of the Gods." Then adds offhandedly, "She has a really bad reputation as woman." A liberal Frenchman had told Fuller that "M[adam]e *Sand* has committed what are called errors, but we doubt not the nobleness of her soul, but it is said that the private life of *Mlle Rachel* has nothing in common with the apparition of the Artist." "Do not speak of this," Fuller warns Cary, "in America."[5]

Intrigued as she was with the great actress's "dark side"—her reckless sexual life—Fuller now, since meeting Mazzini, increasingly made it her public mission to alert her U.S. readers to the plight of Europe's poor. Sitting before a bright wood fire in her cozy Rougement room on Christmas Eve 1846, Fuller wrote in the dim lamplight about her visit that day to the great Roman Catholic cathedral, Saint-Roch. There she heard "beautiful music to celebrate the birth of Jesus" yet also saw inscribed on faces in the crowd "the woes and degradation" of which there were "glaring evidences on every side." When she then spied the gilt coaches of royalty leaving the door, she marveled at men's faith that, at the end of eighteen hundred years, "they would still be celebrating a fact" which "has produced so little of the result desired by Jesus."[6]

Struck by the disparity between upper-class ease and lower-class poverty, Fuller foresees an era of revolutionary reform. "While Louis Philippe lives," she says, "the gases, compressed by his strong grasp, may not burst up to light; but the need of some radical measures of reform is not less strongly felt in France than elsewhere, and the time will come before long when such will be imperatively demanded." Though eager for this era to begin, Fuller is critical of Fourier, whose socialism she thinks is anchored in "gross materialism" and hence "commits the error of making soul the result of health of body, instead of body the clothing of soul." Still, she is pleased that Fourier's doctrines are making progress in Paris, since in their "practical application ... the precepts of Christ, in lieu of the mummeries of a worn-out ritual, cannot fail to be felt."[7]

In Paris Fuller had attended discussions at the Athénée Théâtre Louis-Jouvet on the Crusades and also on suicide. She was annoyed when, on account of her gender, she was denied entry to the Sorbonne to hear the astronomer Leverrier lecture, but delighted when she was admitted into the Chamber of Deputies where she touched the manuscripts of Rousseau, the great Romantic whose "soul," she tells *Tribune* readers, has so "pervaded this century" that he is "the precursor of all we most prize." In the Chamber of Deputies she also heard speeches but missed at the Collège de France hearing two of its more charismatic speakers: Jules Michelet, a French historian who wrote romantically about the glorious days of 1789–90 and was a popular proponent of a Republican France, was ill; and Adam Mickiewicz, the Romantic poet and advocate of Polish messianism, had been banned two years earlier from the college due to his heretical views and because his rhapsodies on Napoleon and the messianic calling of France had roused among his followers (especially women) hysterical reactions. Dark-eyed with thick graying hair, the charismatic albeit aging Mickiewicz—a friend described him and his looks at this time as "podupadly" ("deteriorating")—was still attractive to women.[8]

Though she missed seeing Mickiewicz at the college, after Christmas she met a man he had influenced, the former priest turned Christian Socialist, Félicité-Robert de Lamennais. In dispatch 10 she calls him "the apostle of Democracy." Fuller admires Lamennais, whose argument for democracy, à la Mickiewicz, grew out of his wish to realize on earth the Christian ideal of brotherly love, liberty, and social justice. Writing about Lamennais made her think of Mazzini. She had hoped she could get him to come to Paris. On Christmas Eve, however, he wrote to say it was too dangerous, noting he hoped to be able soon to return to Italy, not as a hunted revolutionary but as a free man.[9]

Still, as Mazzini had hoped, Fuller continued to spread the Italian leader's message as she reported to the *Tribune* on the revolutionary changes taking place in Europe. At the "Evening Schools of the *Frères Chrétiens*" she had been impressed with the progress of young working men in acquiring basic reading and writing skills. Increasingly she was agreeing with Mazzini on the need for people to live not as isolated individuals as Emerson argued but in associations. Fuller liked the French system of parish crèches, or community day-care centers, for working women.[10]

Fuller was impressed with the Deaconess Home in Paris where the poor could take their sick children to be cared for by nurses. Unlike these caring nurses, the people running the refuge centers in Paris for society's "most unjustly treated class"—prostitutes and abused women—seemed ignorant of human nature. She thought they lacked the warmth of women in New York who had done similar work. In dispatch 12 she vents her rage over the heartless way society's "more favored" and "protected" women treat wayward women, naively writing that she hopes to awaken such women to the facts about what drives innocent girls into prostitution.[11]

Near Paris Fuller visited the School for Idiots, where mentally backward boys were living like animals. When she was told of the violent and grossly sexual behavior of one boy committed to the institution three years earlier, she might have thought of Lloyd, whom Arthur and Richard were contemplating committing to the Brattleboro Asylum in Vermont. Ever hopeful that Lloyd and other such "Pariahs of the human race" might be "saved," Fuller in her column notes how, through the patient efforts of his physician, the French boy "has been raised from his sensual state" and now "is partially redeemed."[12]

In her *Tribune* pieces Fuller maintained the voice of a female crusader for social justice, but in private letters to friends she continued to reveal her fascination with the lives of outsiders, for example women like Rachel and Sand who defied conventional morality. Indeed, within this seemingly free Parisian society, where illegitimacy was common and women lived with men outside of marriage, Fuller felt no need to conceal her admiration for Sand. She tells Elizabeth Hoar in a January 1847 letter that Sand "takes rank in society like a man." She defends Sand's leaving her "stupid, brutal" husband and taking "a series of lovers," telling the socially conservative Hoar that Sand, who is forty-three and in the prime of her power, now has a lover, Frédéric Chopin, "with whom she lives on the footing of combined means, independent friendship!" Apparently Fuller did not know that Chopin, the Polish exile and composer, had already separated from Sand, though both still had residences on the Place d'Orléans.[13] Whatever their living arrangements, the idea of a strong older woman loving a younger man took root in Fuller's mind, just as Sand herself, when Fuller at last met her at her Paris home, left a lasting imprint.

Mazzini had written Sand and paved the way for a meeting of the women. Thus the minute Fuller in February learned that Sand had returned to Paris from her château in Nohant, she wrote asking if she might visit her. Fuller went alone to the writer's house on the Place d'Orléans because Rebecca, who objected to Sand's "low" moral life, had refused to accompany her.[14]

In her journal Fuller describes meeting Sand. She was standing in Sand's anteroom having trouble communicating in French with the maid when Sand opened the door and stood looking at her. The "doorway made a frame for her figure," which was "large, but well-formed." Sand's abundant black hair matched a black mantle she had thrown over her shoulders and a robe of dark violet silk. Her dignified appearance presented "an almost ludicrous contrast to the vulgar caricature idea of George Sand." Her face, says Fuller, is "finer" than depicted in portraits: "the upper part of the forehead and eyes are beautiful, the lower, strong and masculine, expressive of a hardy temperament and strong passions, . . . the air of the whole head Spanish."[15]

As their eyes met, Sand said, "'C'est vous,' and held out her hand." Thus hand in hand they walked into Sand's study. As soon as the two were seated, Fuller said: "*Il me fait de bien de vous voir*" (it does me good to see you). Later Fuller reflected that she said this with all her heart, for it had made her very happy to see such a woman, "so large and so developed a character, and everything that *is* good in it so *really* good." "I loved, shall always love her."[16]

In Sand, Fuller saw a confident woman who combined what Americans then considered a "masculine" mind with a "feminine" style. She saw that Sand's "position" as an intellectual woman and friend in her circle was like her own. Realizing the great range of Sand's intellect and emotions, Fuller could understand how she had "naturally changed the objects of her affection, and several times." Feeling an affinity with Sand, Fuller confided to her journal that "there may have been something of the Bacchante in [Sand's] life, and of the love of night and storm, and the free raptures amid which roamed on the mountain-tops the followers of Cybele, the great goddess, the great mother."[17]

Fuller "heartily enjoyed" being in the presence of this woman of genius who seemed to have reconciled her private and public selves in a strong yet feminine personality. "I liked the woman in her, too, very much; I never liked a woman better." Despite the fact Sand smokes, breaks with friends, and lacks "an independent, interior life," Fuller feels she "needs no defence, but only to be understood, for she has bravely acted out her nature."[18]

Through another acquaintance Fuller met Chopin, who had had a stormy relationship with Sand. Ill at the time, he seemed "frail as a snow-drop" yet still "an exquisite genius," wrote Fuller after hearing him play. It was then indirectly through Chopin that Fuller met his friend Adam Mickiewicz, who she knew had responded so wholeheartedly to Emerson's First Series of *Essays* that he had cited him often and called him "the American Socrates" in his 1843–44 Collège de France lectures. What she probably did not yet know about Mickiewicz was how profoundly he was committed to a mystical vision. In fact, Mickiewicz had lost his professorship at the Collège de France in 1844 for having fallen under the spell of the Lithuanian mystic and religious reformer Andrzej Towiański. During Mickiewicz's last two terms at the college, he had rhapsodized in his lectures on Towiański and his sect, known as the Circle of God. Calling Towiański "Master," Mickiewicz had announced that the man was a prophet and that the exiled Napoleonic dynasty was destined to play a key role in the realization of a coming new age of spiritual elevation and social justice. So, too, he thought, was Poland. The epoch's most urgent need, he argued, was for a messiahlike hero who combined "the Christian spirit" with the charisma necessary to lead the Polish people through a catastrophic period of revolutionary wars to a military victory and the introduction "of the 'Kingdom of Heaven on Earth.'" In Mickiewicz's envisioned kingdom, Christian morality would permeate politics and all people would see themselves as members of a community greater than that of their individual historical nations or ethnic cultures.[19]

Through his poetry, Mickiewicz had moved the minds and hearts of some of Europe's greatest reformers, including Mazzini and Lamennais. In 1832 the poet had published *The Books of the Polish Nation and of the Polish Pilgrims,* an idealized history of the Polish nation. And in the fall of that year he had returned to his epic poem *Pan Tadeusz,* which he wrote in honor of the Polish people's courage in their unsuccessful 1830 fight for freedom from Russian rule. Now, however, as 1847 was beginning, he was still spellbound by the blind illuminist Andrzej Towiański and hence still believed what he had taught in his 1844 lectures at the college: that Poland must play a messianic role as the leader nation in a series of sweeping revolutions that would restore exiled Poles and other wandering pilgrims of Europe to their rightful homes in their respective free nations. At the time Fuller met him, Mickiewicz, who, after a break with Towiański, was leading a Circle in his home that enabled him to remain true to the philosophy and mission of the Lithuanian "master."[20]

Though Mickiewicz and Mazzini were both progressives, they had different aims and styles. Mazzini dreamed of restoring unity to the Italian nation as a multiethnic, democratically governed, free political entity. But in his Towiański-inspired vision, Mickiewicz combined a belief in progressive reincarnation with Romantic antirationalism and a Carlylean kind of antidemocratic hero-worship in which a superior man and nation (Poland) would lead the fragmented European nations to a collective and terrestrial salvation. Unlike the ascetic anti-Catholic Mazzini, who championed the cause of national liberation, Mickiewicz was a tempestuous, heterodox Catholic who had an earthy passion for people.[21]

A loving man with a broad open smile and thick unruly hair, Mickiewicz quickly won Fuller's heart. Not only was he charismatic, but also, for a brief time, he had revered Emerson in a way Mazzini never did. Though Mickiewicz misread Emerson—having only skimmed some of Emerson's essays to take from them what he could insert into his own largely improvised ("God-inspired," he said) lectures he gave at the college—he found one or two of Emerson's ideas compatible with his own. Mickiewicz liked the American prophet's early emphasis on intuition (or feeling) over intellect, as well as on the superior active capacity of the "soul" ("*duch*" or spiritual being) to raise itself up toward the "Over-Soul" (God). However, far more than did Emerson, Mickiewicz insisted on preserving the virtues of hope and love for humanity, tying these virtues to his messianic vision of the Polish agrarian folk as a moral force that would redeem the world.[22]

Admiration for Emerson had moved Mickiewicz to seek out Fuller, who confessed in a letter to Emerson regarding her 15 February 1847 meeting that she had enticed the Polish poet to come to see her by sending him Emerson's poems. "He came," she wrote Emerson, "and I found in him the man I had long wished to see, with the intellect and passions in due proportion . . . a soul constantly inspiring." She felt the "relation" to be "real and important."[23]

Before meeting Mickiewicz Fuller had lamented to Emerson that she needed to find in Paris a friend who could "initiate" her into "little secrets of the place and time." She found that friend in Mickiewicz, who was married to a beautiful woman who had borne him six children before succumbing to mental illness. With Mickiewicz she felt a connection she had missed in other relationships. During her last days in Paris, Mickiewicz spent many evenings with her and the Springs.[24]

In Mickiewicz, Fuller found a man whose ideas coincided with hers. Both believed in the immortality of the soul and in the individual's capacity to progress steadily upward to moral perfection. This view was not shared by Emerson, who had come to believe that the "mysterious ladder" by which a man makes his way to heaven, his "consciousness," is "a sliding scale, which identifies him now with the First Cause [the power that generated 'the miracle of life'], and now with the flesh of his body." Thus while at one moment a man might feel he "fills the sky," at the next he might feel like "a weed by the wall." Also unlike Emerson, both Fuller and Mickiewicz argued the necessity of sweeping social reforms. Fuller sympathized with Mickiewicz's religious views, which grew out of a fusion of Christian principles with the ethereal spiritualism of medieval and pagan mysticism. According to Mickiewicz, who incorporated into his religion Lithuanian folk beliefs regarding the migration of souls, God was to be experienced through mystical vision and political action, a view in tune with Fuller's. Sensing their compatibility, Mickiewicz invited her to take part in the Circle of God meetings he led in his home. So entirely did Fuller feel she had found in Mickiewicz a soul mate—and, she perhaps hoped, a lover, too (an eyewitness later confessed that "eroticism sneaked into [sect members'] spiritual exaltations")—that the experience of hearing Mickiewicz talk overwhelmed her, and, as the eyewitness said, she "fainted on the sofa." Unlike so many American men, Mickiewicz was not afraid of her genius and intensity.[25]

Fuller was so excited by the vital life she found in Paris—in this city where the vital "I" of her being was seeking, now, release—that she could barely sleep while she was there. Though the French in general seemed "slippery" to her, she nonetheless felt irresistibly drawn to Sand, Rachel, and Mickiewicz. While in personal letters Fuller tells of her continuing fascination with Rachel, in her carefully crafted *Tribune* dispatches she complains that the actress "can only express the darker passions." In the seven performances she has seen, there is, she declares, "too much pain." Fuller speculates that a passionate woman like Rachel cannot "live long," for she "expends force enough upon a part to furnish out a dozen common lives."[26]

51 ∽ On to Lyons and Italy

Though Fuller liked the "great focus of civilized life" in Paris, she still felt like a stranger in "this region of wax lights, mirrors, bright wood fires, [and] shrugs," in the perpetually overcast city with only one day of nice weather from mid-November until late February 1847, and where her French teacher teased that she spoke and acted like an Italian.[1]

Perhaps in Italy, Fuller had written Emerson in January, "I shall find myself more at home." But she had not yet met Mickiewicz. An affectionate, sensual man whose charisma sometimes spilled over into ecstatic expressions of sexual love for beautiful women (unbeknownst to Fuller, when she met him he was involved with his children's governess, who would bear him a daughter), Mickiewicz had little patience with Fuller's puritanical attitude toward sex, and he set out to alter it.[2]

Adam Mickiewicz touched Fuller in a down-to-earth way she had never experienced. He openly admired her and, in his fashion, loved her, too. He saw in her the superior woman he believed could lead other women to their political and sexual liberation, since, according to him, historical progress depended on a few God-chosen, superior people leading lesser beings to a state of moral perfection. In a frank letter Mickiewicz admonished Fuller. Casting her as a woman "who has sinned in the old world" yet who is striving to create a "new world," he tells her that her special "mission is to contribute to the deliverance of Polish, French and American womanhood." "You have acquired the right to know and to maintain the rights and the obligations . . . of virginity," he says, then adds: "the first step of your deliverance and of the deliverance of your sex (of a certain class) is to know, whether you are permitted to remain a virgin." "Give of your spirit," he proclaims, "and to those who are prepared to receive it, give it all with / Thy brother A——"[3]

In Mickiewicz Fuller found a soul mate who shared her belief that she was destined to do great things. He was her Dionysus, exhorting her to sow her wild oats, to free herself from all those inhibiting American conventions that held her down, like the chain around the talon of the broken-winged eagle she had seen in the museum as a child. To Fuller, Mickiewicz's words were an elixir; in drinking them in she felt herself metamorphose into Cybele, the great goddess of fertility and life, the mother of all who took as her lover the handsome young Attis.[4] After all, to Mickiewicz, Fuller was a supernatural being with an enormous mind and both the will and power to alter the course of human history.

Thus Mickiewicz's words had a life-altering impact on the mind and imagination of this gifted yet vulnerable descendant of Puritans. Here was a man who, as he spoke, made no bones about it: he detested Puritanism and was even suspicious of Fuller's Quaker friends, the Springs, for their conformity to the parochial mores of American middle-class society. Certainly Mickiewicz was correct to suspect that the initiation into "secrets" Fuller sought could not be enacted so long as she stayed the Springs' traveling companion. Fuller began to resent them because their ever-watchful presence inhibited her from at last releasing her pent-up Bacchante energy. She wrote Cary she "felt at times a wicked irritation against them," especially after they took her from France and, so she may well have imagined, a liaison with Mickiewicz.[5]

When she left France at February's end, Fuller took with her letters Mazzini had secretly given her to deliver to his mother in Genoa, and also Mickiewicz's positive words that reinforced her self-image as a woman chosen by Providence to deliver women from bondage. Endowed with a new sense of power, Fuller began depicting herself in her dispatches as the heroic figure Mickiewicz envisioned, a champion of the poor, especially of women whose lives had been ravaged by the effects of the industrial revolution, whose suffering she now saw firsthand.

On their way to the Mediterranean, the Springs and Fuller stopped at Lyons, center of the French handloom-weaving industry and site of a major uprising in 1835. The new technology had recently hit home weavers hard. Technological improvements, combined with a slackening of demand and the flood of unskilled and unwanted laborers who had turned to weaving and piecework in hopes of earning money enough to live on, meant for them falling wages and high unemployment. One source reports that sixty percent of the weavers (half of whom were women) had no work.[6]

Fuller's heart went out to the Lyons silk weavers. She reported to the *Tribune* about a "sweet little girl" who was their guide: the mother of two "sickly looking children," she thought only of finishing a piece of work so she could pay her rent. The Springs and Fuller had followed the young woman up a winding path to a building in which each weaver with his or her family lived and worked in a single room. Fuller described the weavers' scant living and work conditions: "On one side were the looms, nearer the door the cooking apparatus, [while] the beds [reached by ladders] were shelves near the ceiling." As their guide opened the doors into "those dark little rooms," Fuller heard her sigh and say, "Ah! we are all very unhappy now."[7]

Regarding the plight of girls like her, Fuller reported the observation of a gentleman of Lyons that girls of her economic class had but two ways "to gain their bread," either "of weaving or prostitution." To this an angry Fuller in her column retorted that "there are those who dare to say that such a state of things is . . . what Providence intended for man—who call those who have hearts to suffer at the sight, energy and zeal to seek its remedy, visionaries and fanatics!"[8]

Fuller wanted to lift these women from their degrading lives, and in her *Tribune* dispatches she reminded readers of the benefits of crèches that provide day care for workers' children or offer wet nurses for their infants. She thought these Fourierist schemes, if enacted, might "save the mothers from too heavy a burden of care and labor." Fuller hoped to awaken in staid New York social reformers an interest in seeking ways to free such women from having to work to earn money while raising their children, that "heavy burden of care" she felt her father had saddled her with when he died.[9]

Mickiewicz, in the meantime, hoped to free Fuller from the prison of her Puritan conscience. Like a Polish Whitman, in his letters he was thus exhorting Fuller to cast off the trappings of her social inhibitions and to trust the prompting of her sexual passion. In a March 1847 letter, Mickiewicz tells Fuller that her mind cannot be truly free until her body too is free. He says she needs to pass as much of the strength and life of her soul into her body as she can. Influenced by the provocative suggestions of this virile Emerson enthusiast, she too began to think that it was "high time" she fled what Emerson, writing in April, called the "coup" of "our bigoted" American society.[10]

She thus began asserting her independence shortly after she and the Springs arrived in Rome in late March. Before then, they stopped at Avignon, where they waded through melting snow to the tomb of Petrarch's Laura. They also stopped at Arles, where Fuller saw "saxifrage blossoming on the steps of the Amphitheatre," fruit trees flowering amid the tombs, and an old woman knitting where once twenty-five thousand people gazed down on men fighting lions. The trip to Genoa by steamer through a cutting wind gave her a headache and kept her from appreciating Genoa's palaces, though she enjoyed meeting Mazzini's friends and family, especially his mother, Maria, whose son had told her to be kind to the American correspondent as well as to keep track of where she was staying as she traveled throughout Europe. Mazzini, after all, continued to count on Fuller to help spread his message of Italian liberation. He had even arranged with editors at Saunders's *People's Journal,* which published his writing, to publish her work in progress on the Italian fight for freedom. This arrangement, along with requests for her writing from the Howitts in London and from Pauline Roland in Paris, led her to consider extending her stay in Europe.[11]

Though the path on which destiny was now leading her seemed to her clear, an incident on the way to Naples from Leghorn unnerved her. On a clear night, her English boat had been rammed by a French mail steamer. The incident ended with the mail steamer returning the traveling party—which now included George Palmer Putnam of the publishing firm Wiley and Putnam, and his wife, Victorine—to Leghorn on a night when Mother Nature, as she had in the past, seemed to Fuller hauntingly seductive. The sea was as calm as a lake, the sky was full of stars, and the mail steamer with its smoke and lights circled round to them "like the bend of an arm embracing." In less poetic terms Fuller wrote Emerson, "Between Leghorn and Naples, our boat was run into by another, and we only just escaped being drowned."[12]

52 ∞ On to Rome

Fuller enjoyed the boat ride down the coast from Leghorn to Naples, especially since on it she happened to meet "a Polish lady," one of Mickiewicz's former lovers, of whom there was apparently an impressive number. One suspects it was in part Fuller's meeting Countess Zaluska on the boat that made her conclude upon arriving at Naples: "Only at Naples have I found *my* Italy."[1]

From the Kingdom of Naples and Sicily (also called the Kingdom of the Two Sicilies), which was ruled by the tyrannical Bourbon King Ferdinand II, the traveling party went north toward the Papal States by coach on a bumpy road that had been built in the first century A.D. and that joined with the Via Appia Antica, which had been built in 312 B.C. Though the coach was bulky and the six horses that pulled it heavy and slow, Fuller preferred this mode of travel to the railroad, which she thought a "convenient" but "stupid way of traveling." Since the Papal States had no railroad, it was fortunate she liked to travel by coach, which gave her a chance to view the villages she saw nestled in the hills where olive trees guarded the entrance to Rome.[2]

In Rome Fuller was soon to discover the land she had imagined while sitting at the window in her father's book closet and reading books like the *Aeneid*, with its bloody battle scenes, and *Oberon*, wherein the Christian knight Huon and pagan princess Rezia defy Oberon's decree not to consummate their relationship before being blessed by a priest in Rome. When compared to such childhood dreams, Rome at first did not live up to her ideal of it. For, unlike Rezia, Fuller had no companion with whom to share its pleasures.

Without such a friend, she found Rome's magnificent temples and tombs disappointing. In her May 1847 dispatch she complains that of the once-great City of the Caesars there remained standing only a few ruins. There was, for instance, the Colosseum, where she heard owls hoot by moonlight. With the tourists she had seen the pomps and shows of Holy Week in St. Peter's and "ascended the dome and seen thence Rome and its Campagna." She had even been in the cathedral undercroft, where she saw "by torch-light the stone Popes" lying "on their tombs, and the . . . Virgins with gilt caps."[3]

In her dispatch she suggests she was not impressed by the artwork she saw in studios in Rome. Of the sculptors' work, she preferred Joseph Gott's groups of young figures connected with animals to the grand marble sculptures then in fashion. One was Hiram Powers's bulky statue of John C. Calhoun, which she was soon to see in Florence and which would play a role in her destiny. Of current work in Rome by European and American painters, Fuller mentions as "charming" a half-length portrait of an Italian girl holding a mandolin by the American landscape and portrait painter Thomas Hicks, who would also play a part in determining her destiny.[4]

It pained Fuller to see the poor condition of Raphael's frescoes in La Farnesina, the villa that contains Raphael's *The Triumph of Galatea*. With her red veil blowing backward in the wind while a circle of Cupid-like boys points arrows at her heart, the nymph Galatea in this fresco seems to be turning and looking wistfully over her shoulder, as if in an effort to hear the strange love song of the clumsy giant Polyphemus. That this fresco was on Fuller's mind is evident in that she saw it—apparently in bad condition—in the Villa Farnesina, which is located across the Tiber from the Farnese Palace, where the frescoes of Carracci and his scholars were to her, she wrote in her May 1847 dispatch, "a source of the purest pleasure." Moreover, from Rome she would later mention in a letter to Richard the *Galatea* that Goethe had "beautifully described." In this same letter she curiously refers to "the portrait of the Cenci," which hangs in the Barberini Palace.[5]

In Rome she came to appreciate the works of Titian, whose portraits spoke to her "things new and strange." She especially liked Titian's painting illustrating the same woman in two strikingly different poses. In the left of the painting she sits finely dressed in white, apparently for her wedding. She leans casually back on a classical sarcophagus, which doubles as a fountain. Above her gloved left hand a sliver of wrist is revealed, suggesting the sexual ecstasy she expects to experience in wedded love. On the sarcophagus's right side, the same woman sits boldly forward and upright, exposing—except where her red robe hangs casually over her upper arm and a loose white cloth drapes across her groin—her smooth, nude body. Perhaps the figure is Venus, as some speculate, or maybe the stone coffin as fountain is meant to hint that sensual pleasure poisons life's waters and leads to death. Fuller noted only how entirely the (presumably) seated figure in this painting, *Sacred and Profane Love,* "has developed my powers of gazing to an extent unknown before." As the title hints, it is almost as if the woman dares the viewer to object to her double life as saint and sinner, a divided state of mind with which Fuller identified.[6]

Of all the artwork she saw in Rome, it was this two-pose painting of a confident woman that captured her imagination, as did Michelangelo's grand sculpture of a fiercely strong and dynamic sitting Moses, who clasps at his side the tablets containing the ten commandments. This stone statue of a judgmental father "is the only thing in Europe, so far," she wrote home to an approving American audience, that "has entirely outgone my hopes."[7]

Yet Rome would grow on her. As spring came that year and she looked about at the abundant life about her, she came to love the ancient city as an earthly paradise. For in Rome beneath the bright spring sun where spotted lizards basked on the walls of ruins, where olive trees burst with blossoms and orange trees hung heavy with fruit, and where marble statues of nude ancient gods and heroes towered over sober Christian saints, Fuller felt at home. Despite two millennia of Christianity, Romans in their behavior expressed a reverence for the human body, as was apparent to her not only in their art, but also in the attitude of Italians everywhere she went. On public benches, lovers caressed and kissed. Men walked arm in arm. Women nursed their babies unabashedly in public.[8]

Moreover, in Rome the Madonna—a figure with whom Fuller had often identified—was adored. Thus while in her heart she saw herself as Titian's boldly sensuous physical female, she also saw herself as the Madonna, a comparison encouraged by Mickiewicz. In a March letter, which was waiting for her on her arrival in Rome, the Polish poet urged her to see her Madonna-like beauty. He also urged her to "live" in Italy as much as she could "with nature." Enjoy now, he tells her, "what surrounds you. Breathe the life in through all your pores." Alluding to the era he hopes revolution will usher in, Mickiewicz says: "The time is coming when inner beauty, inner spiritual life will become the first and essential quality of a woman." Mickiewicz assures Fuller that without inner beauty a woman cannot exert a beneficial "physical influence," and that in her he feels he has found such a beautiful woman, "a *true* person": "Such an encounter on life's journey consoles and fortifies." He ends his letter by commanding Fuller to learn to appreciate herself "as a beauty and, after having admired the women of Rome," to say, "And as for me, why I am beautiful!"[9]

Here was a man of warmth and genius affirming Fuller's existence as beautiful. He meant what he said, and she knew it. She had been so touched by his presence in Paris that even before she left there, she determined to see him again before she sailed for the States. Intending to return to Paris for that future meeting, she had left with an American acquaintance there, a Miss E. Fitton, her fur muff, velvet bonnet, and brown merino dress, as well as a watercolor of Faust and Marguerite.[10]

The ardent attention Mickiewicz had paid Margaret upset the staid Rebecca, who in the strongest terms possible told her not to return to Paris to see him and quizzed her late one night as to whether or not she were in love with the Polish revolutionary. Before dawn on 10 April Fuller wrote the Springs a twenty-four-page letter, which she handed to Rebecca as she was leaving their hotel for the Villa Borghese on the Pincian Hill, where she intended to sit and contemplate things. It was only a short walk from the hotel to the gallery, which houses Bernini's baroque statues of *David* and of *Apollo and Daphne,* as well as a Greek bronze statue called the *Dancing Satyr* and Bernini's provocative marble statue, *Rape of Proserpina.* Upstairs in the villa, Fuller passed quickly by Raphael's oils, noting in her May *Tribune* dispatch that she gained nothing from them. She was pleased with the work of Domenichino, whose grand and free style, she wrote, "perfectly satisfies," and she was enthralled by the most famous painting of the Borghese collection, Titian's *Sacred and Profane Love,* identifying with the beautiful woman in it.[11]

Later that morning Fuller was joined in the garden at the Villa Borghese by Rebecca and Eddie. While she sat thinking, Eddie gathered flowers and made garlands with them. Lost in her daydreams, Margaret, who had allowed Eddie to follow her as she went on a path apart from Rebecca, failed to notice that Eddie had wandered off, until a splash and a cry made her realize that Eddie, who had been sailing his garlands in one of the great fountains, had fallen in and was sinking and rising, gasping for air. Fuller rushed to the fountain and was about to plunge in fully dressed when she caught hold of a toy stick the panicked boy was still clutching in his hand. Thus she saved from drowning this child she had once playfully called her "little lover."[12]

Though Rebecca later credited Fuller with saving "our little boy from drowning in the great fountain" at the Villa Borghese, the Springs saw her as inching toward improper behavior they could not condone. Fuller, in turn, displayed increasing impatience with them and began to assert her independence, to the point they thought her "quite insupportable." In the long letter she had given the Springs early that April morning of Eddie's accident, Fuller contends that she was by "nature destined to walk by the inner light alone." On this, her journey of life: "It has led, will lead me sometimes on a narrow plank across deep chasms, if I do not see clear, if I do not balance myself exactly I must then fall and bleed and die." Aware that pain may result from her effort, she also knows that if she wishes to be true to who she is, she must not be "afraid of it."[13]

"From infancy," writes Fuller, " I have foreseen that my path [toward truth] must be difficult." Alluding to Nathan, Fuller vows to avoid "frivolous" infatuations. Claiming never to have "sought love as a passion" or to have clung "to a tie which had ceased to bind the soul," she concedes she has never loved "in the sense of oneness." She says she has, however, loved enough "to feel the joys of presence the pangs of absence." And more than once, she says, "my heart has bled." As for Mickiewicz, when she was with him, "my heart beat with joy that he . . . felt beauty in me. When I was with him I was happy." "Still," says she, "I do not know but I might love . . . better tomorrow." She tells the Springs that she has never loved anyone as much as she has loved the music of Beethoven, though "at present" she is "indifferent to it," just as, the other day, she had expressed little interest in seeing the forms that Michelangelo "had traced on the ceiling of the Sistine." However, she confesses, whenever in the past "I loved either of these great Souls I abandoned myself wholly to it, I did not calculate." She now vows to do so again, "if I love enough."[14]

53 ✑ Ossoli Enters

It was springtime in Rome, where a pagan earthiness exudes from every rock and ruin, and Fuller, in tune, felt her body pulsate and open to the sun, like the orange blossoms whose fragrance lay heavy in the air. On her journey through life she had at last attained "an awesome clarity" about herself, and she was ready now for an adult relationship. She had had enough of airy transcendentalism, of translating every erotic impulse into moral vision. She now wanted for herself something real, reciprocal, and earthy. That Fuller had already found somebody she felt she could "love enough" is suggested by a 23 April 1847 letter she sent the Pennsylvania-born artist Thomas Hicks, who at age twenty-four (thirteen years younger than she) was already an associate member of the American National Academy.[1]

Fuller had met Hicks through her friend Christopher Cranch, who had brought his family with him to Italy when he left the ministry to join the expatriate artists' colony there. Fuller felt drawn to this bearded, melancholic stranger who had entertained her and the Springs in his studio and whose youth and artistic sensibility had awakened in Fuller her feminine need to nurture as well as her masculine urge to dominate. Thinking the physical attraction was mutual, she wrote Hicks to ask him why he does not come to see her: "I want to know and to love you and to have you love me. . . . Very soon I must go from here, do not let me go without giving me some of your life." She hopes he might be that "congenial" companion for whom she has been searching and regrets she could not meet him in the "Palazzo Borghese," where Titian's great *Sacred and Profane Love* was exhibited.[2] Hicks politely declined her offer of love in early May.

But sometime around the first week of April—Holy Week—Fuller had met another man, a handsome Italian either in St. Peter's Basilica or in the magnificent piazza it faces, the colonnades of which seem like loving arms welcoming wandering pilgrims. Whether she met him on Maundy Thursday after attending vespers at St. Peter's, which was on 1 April, or on Easter Sunday, which was 4 April, is not clear to Fuller scholars. What is clear is that she had gone to St Peter's with the Springs and had somehow got separated from them in the church and become confused. At that point, according to Emelyn Story, she was approached by the dark-haired, well-bred Giovanni Angelo Ossoli, who asked in Italian if he might secure a carriage for her. Although not yet conversant in Italian, she understood his courteous gesture. Thus began a friendship that would soon—in the context of pagan Rome where the warm spring wind carried with it the musky odor of urine-stained ruins mixed with the sweet scent of orange blossoms and jasmine—blossom into love.[3]

Giovanni Angelo Ossoli was the youngest of four sons of Filippo Ossoli, a high functionary at the papal court who had recently left the Vatican because of illness. A younger brother in a land of primogeniture, Filippo did not inherit the title of marchese (marquis), so his son Giovanni was not "authorized to inscribe himself as a Marquis," contrary to what Ossoli (as Fuller came to call him) seems to have let Fuller believe. Filippo's older brother, Antonio—deceased since around 1842–43 and father of a celibate son, Francesco—instead had held the title. After the later deaths of Francesco and Ossoli's eldest brother, Allesandro, the title marchese apparently passed to Ossoli's elder brother, Ottavio, and then to Ottavio's son, Pietro, who would play a vital role in the lovers' lives.[4]

When Fuller met him, Ossoli was living in a first-floor flat in the family home— a "standard Roman house, Via Tor di Specchi"—and caring for his dying father. Though a devout Catholic, the independent-minded Ossoli did not approve of the pope's temporal power. His elder brothers, Alesandro and Ottavio, were currently serving in the pope's Guard of Nobles, the "armed force" of the Vatican State. Most tightly bound to the papacy was the third son, Giuseppe, who, following in their father's footsteps, was a high papal functionary. Giuseppe had little tolerance for the rebellious ways of his younger brother, who wanted a united Italy free from the rule of Austrian overlords, foreign rulers, and Roman Catholic pope and instead run as a republic. In a letter to their sister, Angela, Giuseppe would later rage against Ossoli's "outrageous 'deeds against religion.'" Indeed, Ossoli was a great admirer of Mazzini, and when he learned Fuller was Mazzini's friend, he was impressed.[5]

In Angelo Ossoli—a sweet-tempered, reserved, and delicate Italian from an aristocratic Italian family with a distinguished history of papal service—Fuller would find fulfilling love. Ossoli was gentle, courteous, selflessly kind, and responsive to her every need—at one point he set off with "knightly zeal" on an errand to have her parasol's handle repaired. What made him especially appealing to Fuller was that in looks and manner, as well as in his rebellious ways, he reminded her of her tall, lean, sweet-tempered, "pretty" (she called him) brother Eugene. "How all but infinite the mystery by which sex is stamped on the germ!" she had once exclaimed: "Here am I the child of masculine energy, & Eugene of feminine loveliness." Five years younger than Margaret, Eugene was the only sibling old enough to have remembered Timothy's late-night recitation demands on his daughter. He was certainly the sibling to whom she felt closest in her adolescent years, when Eugene was just beginning to rebel against their father's rigid commands.[6]

Like Eugene, Ossoli was lovely and uninterested in books. Perhaps because she associated him with her brother, Fuller felt safe in the company of this quiet but able young man (born 17 January 1821, he was eleven years Fuller's junior). Though lacking formal education, Ossoli had skills that would prove useful in the coming revolution. He knew how to tend to his stallions and ride them with grace, as well as to use firearms. Keenly aware of Ossoli's lack of an education, Fuller later half-apologetically wrote her mother that Ossoli was "absolutely ignorant" of books and had "no enthusiasm of character." Emelyn Story, the wife of lawyer-turned-sculptor William Wetmore Story and a good-natured woman soon to become Fuller's close friend, responded positively to Ossoli, recalling that his manner toward Fuller had been "devoted and lover-like." He had nursed her when she was ill "with the tenderness of [a] woman." His tenderness as a nurse and fondness for flowers were traits Margaret lovingly associated with her mother.[7]

In Ossoli, Fuller thus gained not only the safe love of a brother she intuitively knew she could trust but also the nurturing love she missed as a child. In Fuller, Ossoli in turn gained a guiding force to give him the direction he lacked, as well as the mothering he had lacked since childhood. Ossoli's mother had died when he was five, and ever since the motherless son had prized a "scar on his face, made by a jealous dog, when his mother was caressing him as an infant." That Fuller was a virgin increased her value in the eyes of the devoutly Roman Catholic Ossoli.[8]

These two adults, neither of whom fit stereotypical gender definitions, thus had much to offer each other. As a mother figure, Fuller was able to comfort this younger man whose adored mother had been dead two decades. As an aggressive and hence "masculine" intellect, she guided him. And as friend and confidante she was soon to join with him and other Italians in their "struggle," as she will say in a later *Tribune* dispatch, "between the principle of Democracy and the old powers" of monarchs and papal authority.[9]

Before the revolution, however, in carefree springtime Rome in 1847, the two were simply happy together touring, taking carriage rides out into the country, and learning, in general, what they could about each other, though Fuller spoke Italian only in broken phrases and Ossoli no English at all. Yet Fuller was so proper in public with him that even the Springs believed that he was no more to her than Thomas Hicks, who was also now a close friend and, like Ossoli, brought her fresh flowers and went sightseeing with her. When she met Hicks on the Via Condotti at the Café Greco—an untidy, dark place where speakers harangued while artists and writers drank coffee and carried on theoretical discussions about the coming revolution—it is very possible that Ossoli was there, too. In a room thick with cigar smoke, they heard news about events taking place in the other Italian states as well as elsewhere in Europe. Though the relationship with Ossoli was still in the early stages of intimacy, Fuller's happiness was nonetheless evident in her laughter. When sometime in the late spring of 1847 she visited the Capuchin monastery at Castel Gandolfo with the Springs and Hicks, Margaret delighted Rebecca by making friends with the monks. She joked with them in broken Italian as well as in fluent Latin, which impressed them. The monks invited the party to a picnic of strawberries and cream, during which Margaret's further jokes and anecdotes made the strangers feel as if they had been friends for a long time. Rebecca recalls that on that day Margaret was "radiant."[10]

Fuller knew that loving a younger man placed her in the position of guide and aggressor. She also knew that in most Americans' eyes the reversed age difference would seem unnatural. But, then, she had long felt that she was no "natural human." At the age of nine, instead of finding a role model in the feminine antagonist Isador Argyle in Mrs. Ross's "moral-novel" *Hesitation,* Fuller had no doubt found such a model in the Comtesse de Pologne, a forty-something conversationalist who formed relationships with younger men. Why should not Fuller in pagan Rome behave like the Comtesse de Pologne, who appeared, in Ross's words, "no unfit companion for the youngest and gayest"? Had not also Cybele, "the great mother," as Fuller had referred to her, fallen in love with the handsome Attis, a man young enough to have been her grandson?[11]

Far now from America, Fuller nonetheless knew that her "singular conduct" would eventually make her seem to Americans like a wanderer off "the beaten path" tread by most women. For she felt she had more in common with Sand, whom Fuller had compared to Cybele in her writing, than she did with conventional American women. Sand, for instance, had had as her companion in Paris the delicate Chopin. Six years younger than Sand, Chopin was rumored to be only Sand's friend, though it was also said that he would have preferred "to be a lover." With Sand and Chopin in mind, Fuller felt more urgently than ever, as she had put it in her letter to the Springs, the need "to be free and absolutely true to my nature." "And if I cannot live so," she had said, "I do not wish to live."[12]

According to Emelyn Story, Ossoli, after his father's death in February 1848, would ask Fuller to marry him. She would say "no." She had long sought a companion to satisfy her needs, which Ossoli did—emotionally, though not intellectually. Besides, she remained ambivalent about marriage. In *Hesitation: or, To Marry, or Not to Marry?,* the novel she had liked so much as a child, the heroine faces the same perplexing question. In novels of manners, however, men and women end up happily united in marriage. Yet as Fuller knew, Ossoli's proposal represented a crucial life choice with real consequences. Back in New York she had even praised Sand in print for "systematically assail[ing] the present institution of marriage and the social bonds which are connected with it."[13]

In her journal Fuller had been critical of marriage, noting in contrast her own fortunate and free situation. In one entry she had questioned the wisdom of a powerful woman entering marriage, predicting it would end in divorce, since "social wedlock is ordinarily mere subterfuge & simulacrum." In his diary on 26 February 1847 Alexander Chodzko, Mickiewicz's friend, wrote an account of a conversation Mickiewicz recalled in which Fuller swore "never to marry." If Chodzko's account is accurate, then Fuller apparently was prepared not to let marriage stand in the way of her freedom as a woman, even with a man who loved her.[14]

Fuller's wish for personal freedom reflected the larger dream of the Italian people that they might win freedom from their Austrian overlords and foreign rulers. This dream had been generated in part by Mazzini's propaganda efforts, but also by the June 1846 election of Giovanni Maria Mastai-Ferretti to the apostolic throne left vacant by Pope Gregory's death. A big, handsome, charismatic man, who at age fifty-four was comparatively young, Pope Pius IX had been inspired by Abbé Vincenzo Gioberti's 1843 book, *Concerning the Moral and Civil Primacy of the Italians,* which rejected the radical philosophy of the French Revolution and dismissed Mazzini's vision of a centralized republic as "a solemn utopia." Although he did not defend liberalism, Gioberti supported the idea of a national federation led by the pope as moral leader, and he insisted that peaceful reform was the only way to resolve the Italian problem. As if in answer to reformers' dreams, Pope Pius IX thus initiated a series of reforms in Italy in an attempt to diffuse tensions between the people and their oppressors.[15]

Still "long[ing] for hero-worship," the Italian people, Fuller wrote the *Tribune,* thunderously applauded Pius IX each time he announced a new reform, as he did when he had the cardinal secretary publish a circular on 19 April establishing a representative council of laymen from the various provinces. Whereas Fuller saw that nothing could be more limited than this improvement, she also conceded in her May 1847 dispatch that "it was a great measure for Rome." She describes how, on the night of 19 April, the Via del Corso where she was living had been illuminated by the torches carried triumphantly by thousands of people who turned out to celebrate this slight concession in the direction of self-rule. Fuller tells how the people assembled at the Piazza del Popolo and formed around its fountain "a great circle of fire," until, "as a river of fire, they streamed slowly through the Corso, on their way to the Quirinal to thank the Pope, upbearing a banner on which the edict was printed."[16]

Fuller's words created a scene her American readers could see, thus helping Greeley sell papers and earning for herself even greater respect as a reporter. "The stream of fire," she wrote, "advanced slowly with a perpetual surge-like sound of voices; the torches flashed on the animated Italian faces": "Ascending the Quirinal they made it a mount of light. Bengal fires were thrown up, which cast their red and white light on the noble Greek figures of men and horses that reign over it. The Pope appeared on his balcony: the crowd shouted three vivas; he extended his arms; the crowd fell on their knees and received his benediction; he retired, and the torches were extinguished." The multitude then, according to Fuller, "dispersed in an instant."[17]

It was no doubt an impressive show, but show it was. Fuller feared that the pontiff's enthusiasm for reform, his eagerness to do "something solid for the benefit of Man," would evaporate like the crowd the night of 19 April. On 23 May, her birthday, Fuller wrote Eliza Farrar's aunt, her New Bedford friend Mary Rotch, "The tendency of the present Pope to Reform . . . draw[s] out the feelings of the people, but it is not sufficient to affect importantly the state of things in Italy."[18]

Mazzini's friends invited Fuller and the Springs to attend an open-air dinner in the Baths of Titus organized to celebrate the restoration of municipal government. It was attended by several returned exiles. With the Colosseum and Triumphal Arches as their backdrops, speakers heralded the pope as a noble founder of a new state. One of them, the son-in-law of the writer Alessandro Manzoni, even suggested that God did not give Italy to the Austrian emperor "*that you might destroy her,*" a remark Fuller knew would provoke a negative reaction. As it did: the Austrians seized the paper that published the speech. When plans for a dinner for the pope's fete day were dropped for fear "something too frank should again be said," Fuller's suspicion increased that Pope Pius IX was a man more carried along by popular sentiment and current events than he was the master of them. She suspected that he did not have the fortitude to declare war on Austria or concede the pope's temporal power to a republican form of government. At one of the events Fuller attended with the Springs celebrating the Italian people's hope that the new liberal pope would restore their ancient liberties, Margaret turned to Rebecca and said sadly, "He is not great enough. He can never carry out the work before him."[19]

54 ∾ To Marry, or Not to Marry?

Fuller thought she "saw the future dawning" in Rome and was excited by what she saw. She felt so well emotionally that she suffered only two headaches during her two-month stay. Still, by late May 1847 she knew she must leave the city, not only because she was committed to the Springs as Eddie's tutor, but also because her relationship with Ossoli was growing too intense. Though part of her wanted to be daring like George Sand or the Comtesse de Pologne, her Puritan conscience damned her for her daring. Echoing terms she had internalized as a child from *Hesitation* by Mrs. Ross, who calls "unfit" any (to her) "unnatural" sexual "connexion," Fuller will later tell her sister that she "felt very unhappy to leave [Ossoli], but the connexion seemed so every way unfit." While needing and appreciating Ossoli's caresses, she also saw how inappropriate the relationship must seem from the perspective of, as Emerson would say, the "thousand-eyed" public. It was not just that she was older than Ossoli—as Sand was older than Chopin and the Comtesse de Pologne was older than the young men who adored her—but that she and Ossoli were products of such different cultures, religions, and social classes that she knew the relationship might seem ridiculous. Moreover, how could she explain having fallen in love with a man who was, as she later said, "ignorant of books," especially since in *Woman in the Nineteenth Century* she had stressed the importance of "intellectual communion" in marriage, that "pilgrimage towards a common shrine" ideally undertaken by soul mates?[1]

Then, of course, on another and deeper level, there was the question of pain. After all she had been through, how could she trust anyone? With so much pent-up pain, did she dare again risk loving a man? Or, like her beloved Emerson, who had shut his heart's door to penetrating love, was it forever her destiny to flee it?—to write, to teach, to participate nobly in history and care in an abstract way for her "fellow man" yet never *really* to touch or be touched by another loving human being?

As she traveled with the Springs through northern Italy that summer, Fuller pondered the problem of marriage. She was not sure she believed in marriage as an institution. The future she saw "dawning" she thought "in important aspects" was "Fourier's." Fourier appealed at this time to Fuller because he called not only for the emancipation of women but also for the liberation of human instincts and passions. In Fourier's Utopian scheme, the wage system would be abolished and all social classes would unite and live freely together in associations in which men and women would do chores in accord not with their gender but with their impulses and preferences. Though Fuller had written Channing in May that she was finding most Fourierites in Europe "wearisome," she nonetheless liked Fourier's idea of abolishing not only work for profit but also marriage as an institution.[2] Thus though she yearned to return to Rome, it would not have been with a wish to marry Ossoli.

Fuller in letters to family members struggled with the question of whether she should separate from the Springs, and how she would get enough money to survive on her own in a foreign country if she did. The Springs planned to travel north that July before heading home, but Fuller did not wish "to fly" through Germany in the same way she felt she had hurried through Italy, her two months in Rome now seeming to her "but a moment." She thought she might go with them as far as Switzerland and then hire a servant to accompany her back to Rome for at least the autumn. If she did not do this, she wrote Richard from Florence on 1 July, then all her life she would "suffer the pain of Tantalus thinking of Rome." However, if she did part ways with the Springs, she knew that, should something go wrong, being a single American woman traveling alone would put her in a desolate condition. She thus hopes Richard will persuade her mother to advance her five hundred dollars from the large sum of money she mistakenly thinks her recently deceased Uncle Abraham has left her, for Arthur had written she could expect money. Before she learned of Abraham's April death, she had written her mother asking for a hundred dollars, but now she imagined she was going to inherit a substantial sum. It seems that Fuller's decision to leave the Springs may have been based partly on her expectation of being left enough money to allow her to live independently in Europe.[3]

The thought of financial independence may indeed have emboldened her, as did the memorials she saw in her travels through northern Italy dedicated to Italians who had had the courage to follow their vision. Everywhere she went she saw signs of the soul's capacity to rise above social convention and attain greatness. One such soul was St. Francis of Assisi. She was awed when touring the underground chapel where his bones were "saluted by the tears of so many weary pilgrims" who had come "to seek strength from his example." She notes the influence that "flows from a single soul, sincere in its service to Truth." St. Francis's example lifted her spirits in "clean" and free Assisi, where on every wall she read "*Viva* Pio IX."[4]

In Florence the atmosphere was the opposite. Leopold II, Grand Duke of Tuscany, had ordered "his people to keep still." The result, according to Fuller, is that "they *are* still and glum as death." Despite his concession of a free press, the duke's grip on his people made the environment seem unbearably oppressive, even though it was full of flowers, which made Margaret think of her mother. It made her uneasy to be in a region controlled by not only an untrustworthy ruler who issued irrational commands but also Austrian overlords who lacked the imagination to understand the Italian character. But she loved Bologna, where women seemed to be "the soul of society" and were honored in both a monument and a portrait bust. Fuller was heartened that the commemorated women were professors at Bologna's university. "A woman should love Bologna," she wrote, "for there has the spark of intellect in Woman been cherished with reverent care." In Milan, too, she was heartened to see "the bust of a female Mathematician" in the library.[5]

Glad to be in a country that seemed to appreciate intellectual women and hoping she would soon inherit money enough to travel on her own, Fuller in Venice at last parted with the Springs. Venice alone lived up to Fuller's ideal. Gathering her energies, she enjoyed on her own this gem of a city set in the sea. She visited St. Mark's Cathedral, went to market by gondola, sipped coffee at an outdoor café, and watched from "amid the mob" as decorously dressed nobility seemed to rise from the water as they arrived by gondola for a night of entertainment at the palace of Madame de Berri on the Grand Canal. The palace was so full of light that from the canal Fuller could see even the paintings on the walls. As she took pleasure in such scenes that seemed from "fairy land," she thought of Ossoli and wondered if their feelings of affinity were not, after all, the product of "a momentary dream." Her head, after all, said the relationship was unfit, even as her heart warmed at the recollection of this young man's tender touch. Reinforcing her wish to follow her heart's desire were words Mickiewicz sent her on 26 April: "Do not leave lightly those who would like to remain near you. This is in reference to that little Italian you met in the Church."[6]

Fuller was grateful to the Springs, whose generosity had enabled her to fulfill her lifelong dream of seeing Europe, even as she was glad that they now were gone. She wrote Richard in late July that despite having been ill her first week alone in Venice, she had spent, since then, "happier and more thoughtful hours than all before in Europe." To Cary in late August from Lake Como she wrote how, when she had been with the Springs, "I was always out of the body": "Since I have been alone . . . I seemed to find myself again."[7]

Fuller wistfully recalls in a letter to Cary her last glorious nights in Rome, wandering among the old walls and columns and sitting by the fountains in the Piazza del Popolo or by the Tiber River, which made all the pain she had suffered "both after and before" worth it. Only, she adds, "one hates pain in Italy." In letters to Cary and Elizabeth Hoar, Fuller tells about a new confidante whose friendship has given her "great pleasure." That confidante was the politically active and internationally renowned Marchesa Costanza Arconati Visconti, who bore one of the most distinguished names in Italy. At seventeen, Costanza had married the Marchese Giuseppe Arconati Visconti of the ancient and splendid Visconti family. In Milan as dukes, they had built the grandest palace, collected the finest library, begun a great cathedral, and held the most lavish court in all Europe.[8]

After touring on her own Vicenza, Verona, Mantua, Lago di Guardia, and Brescia, Fuller in August spent a fortnight in Milan. There she found the marchesa preoccupied with her nephew's death and hence with little time for her American friend, who had just received a letter from Mickiewicz scolding her for wasting energy in "romantic reveries" and "melancholy." In his letter, Mickiewicz tells Fuller not to confine her life to books and dreams but instead to live and act as frankly "as you write." "Literature," he says in another letter, "is not the whole life." Noting that she is seeking refuge from pain in unrealistic dreams, he urges her to anchor the happiness of her inner life in her body. He then accuses Fuller of still living mentally "in bondage worse than that of a servant" to the same repressive patriarchal order that in her published writings she has effectively argued against. He exhorts her to remember that even in her private life "*as a woman*," she has "rights to maintain."[9]

Costanza, though consumed with family problems, nevertheless let Fuller know that she was concerned that Mickiewicz's influence was having a negative effect on her friend. Fuller, in turn, felt disappointed with the marchesa when the latter cautioned her not to listen to Mickiewicz. As a political moderate recently returned to Italy after a twenty-five-year exile forced on her by the Austrians because of her work in behalf of Italian independence, the marchesa was still no admirer of Mazzini or Mickiewicz. Like Pius IX, she admired Abbé Gioberti, who championed an Italian federation of states united under the pope's moral leadership. In accord with Gioberti, she believed that the state's executive authority should be placed in the hands of a college of princes. As she saw it, charismatic radicals like Mickiewicz threatened European stability by undermining the class structure in which educated aristocrats like her controlled the ignorant masses. Costanza instead favored a step-by-step advancement under the leadership of the pope to an Italian constitutional monarchy. Mickiewicz's extravagant talk of a coming millennium was heresy to the devoutly Catholic Costanza, whose range of experience gave her an insight Fuller would not yet have had: that despite the seeming free environment for women in Europe, in reality women of Fuller's financial status and social class had no more freedom in Italy than in America. It was a tight society, and only wealthy, bold, aristocratic women like Sand dared defy European social convention without paying a heavy price.[10]

Still, Fuller found Mickiewicz's words compelling: "I tried to make you understand the purpose of your existence.... Your mind still does not wish to believe that a new epoch commences and that it has already begun. New for *woman* too." In glorious Italy, Fuller had met women who embodied his ideal of this new era, women whose beauty radiated from within. Costanza was one such woman. In September from Florence Fuller wrote Elizabeth Hoar that while the Marchesa Visconti lacks "physical beauty, the grace and harmony of her manners produce ... the impression of beauty." More impressive to Fuller is the fact that she also has "a mind strong clear, precise and much cultivated by intercourse both with books and men." Vacationing with Costanza at the Visconti villa at Bellagio on Lake Como at August's end, Fuller had met the brilliant and widowed Polish Countess Radzivill. In a mid-November letter she describes the princess as "one of the emancipated women," as handsome "in the style of the full-blown rose."[11]

Fuller had spent wonderful hours with these women, many of whom owned charming villas and gardens on the lake, where she went boating with them. In a high gale on Lake Lugano, she felt in direct communion, she said, with the "Creative Spirit." Despite Costanza's warning about Mickiewicz's mad revolutionary views, Fuller felt happy and free, in near-perfect harmony with Mickiewicz and his mystical vision of a "new era, of the Kingdom of Heaven on Earth." As it had Rebecca, the vision made Costanza "uneasy." She was convinced that Mickiewicz was leading Fuller astray.[12]

But Fuller seemed only to hear words that reinforced her sense of herself in Europe as a woman who might do as she pleases. To Emerson she wrote of the poet and novelist Alessandro Manzoni, whom she had met in Milan, that after the death of his wife, whom in *Woman in the Nineteenth Century* she had idealized as a perfect marriage partner, Manzoni had quickly "taken the liberty to marry a new wife for his own pleasure and companionship." He had married Borri Stampa, a woman Costanza thought a difficult recluse. He had married her even though "the people around him do not like it," Fuller confided to Emerson. Fuller, however, liked Stampa, and she understood "why" Manzoni had "married her."[13]

For herself, Fuller still had doubts about marriage, and especially about the appropriateness of her marrying a young man with whom she had little in common. Her continuing doubts about marriage appear in letters she posted to Richard from Milan. Richard had become engaged to a woman Fuller did not think right for him. In late July, she had cautioned him that "in the present arrangements of society a choice of a companion for life acts as a Fate on the whole of life." She asks him to let his engagement "rest private for awhile" so that the couple might "try how deep the affinity is, before rivetting the bond." Contemplating the unhappy marriages of people she cared about—her parents, Jane Tuckerman King, Almira Penniman Barlow, Ellen Sturgis Hooper, and her sister Ellen—marriages Fuller believed had compromised them "fatally for life," she would note to Richard from Florence on her way back to Rome: "I have dreaded for you that life-long repentance of a momentary dream, that slow penance of years wasted in unfit relations."[14]

Margaret's letters to her brother reflect her concern not merely that Richard might marry someone he hardly knows but that Margaret herself might forge a too-hasty union with the dark, appealing stranger who had courted her in Rome. She feared that a decision to follow the call of her heart and return to Rome might act "as a Fate" on the whole of her life, "fatally" limiting her options and compelling her to behave in ways that would never have occurred to her before. Thus she knew her decision to return to Rome would be a turning point in her life, just as she now realized that, in having chosen not to go on with the Springs into Germany and then home, she had abandoned the Germany of her youthful dreams as well as the Boston of her rigid New England upbringing to embrace a future that fate would unfold for her in Italy.

Fuller felt that destiny was compelling her to return to Rome to enact an as yet unspecified part in the revolutionary events unfolding there. Her wish to participate is evident in her 9 August *Tribune* dispatch from Milan. Excitedly Fuller tells readers how a "supposed" Austrian spy "has been assassinated at Ferrara, and Austrian troops are marched there." Her words capture the moment: "It is pretended that a conspiracy has been discovered in Rome; . . . The National Guard is forming.

All things seem to announce that some important change is inevitable here, but what?" She confesses she is still "too much a stranger to speak with assurance of impressions" she has "received." Still, she declares, "it is impossible not to hope."[15]

Back in Milan, Fuller saw the September arrival of a new pro-Italian archbishop, an event greeted with parades and feasts. But the crowd's elation turned quickly to outrage when Italian youth who were attempting to sing the "Hymn to Pius IX" in celebration of the archbishop's pro-Italy position offended the Austrian police, which responded by wounding several spectators—in the back. In the two dispatches she wrote in October, Fuller argues that such incidents prove that Austria's policy is too set "to change except by revolution." Austria's policy, she says, offers the Italian people "physical" good while denying their deeper wish for spiritual rebirth as an independent nation. Fuller dreams of "a new great covenant of brotherly love," a unified Italy "composing all differences between cities, districts, and individuals," where "all strifes" are reconciled, all petty, local differences are dropped, and "all stains" are washed away. Here Fuller's thinking reflects not only the imprint of her Puritan heritage and the recent influence of Mickiewicz's messianic vision, but also the impact of Mazzini's call for Italians to unite as a nation in a risorgimento. In his writings and speeches of 1847 in behalf of the "People's International League," Mazzini had loosely defined a "nation" as all classes of people united harmoniously in a distinct historical region identifiable by geographic characteristics, shared traditions, and a single language that encompassed different dialects.[16]

In her October dispatches Fuller contends that Austrian rule makes class differences "more glaring" by allotting the lower classes "a degree of material well-being" while denying them freedom. She castigates rich Americans abroad who sympathize with the Austrians "who think that a mess of pottage can satisfy the wants of Man." Such Americans, she says, are so enchanted with "the equipages, the fine clothes, [and] the food" that "they have no heart for the idea, for the destiny of our own great nation." They cannot feel the spirit of liberty now "struggling" to be reborn in Italy and in other nations of Europe.[17]

In these dispatches about Europe's fermenting revolutions, Fuller assumes the role of liberty. In her 18 October *Tribune* letter she prophesizes that "our age is one where all things tend to a great crisis, not merely to revolution but to radical reform," thereby tying the idea of social reform to a vision of popular liberty. Countering the view of Costanza, who wanted a federation of states under the pope and a college of princes with executive authority, Fuller contends: "From the people themselves the help must come, and not from princes." For there will be only "natural princes, great men," in "the new state" Fuller envisions. Help must come, she says, "from the teachings of conscience in individuals, and not from an old ivy-covered church." "Rome," she insists, "to resume her glory, must cease to be an ecclesiastical Capital."[18]

THE RISING TIDE OF REVOLUTION

Vehemently opposed to the Roman Catholic Church holding political power in civil society, Mazzini had hoped that Pius IX would act as a positive force in promoting the people's drive to free and unify Italy. In early September he had thus written the pope, begging him to unite Italy as a democracy based on spiritual sanctions. A friend threw his letter into the pope's passing carriage. That act had outraged many Catholics, including Costanza, but it inspired Fuller. And her dispatches now glow with new confidence not only in her own capacity to effect change through her writing, but also in the power of the people in the kingdoms, Papal States, foreign-occupied territories, and other regions that together constituted Italy to free themselves from their repressive overlords, local rulers, and papal authorities.

The quilt of regions that constituted Italy was complex. In northern Italy, Piedmont was still ruled by its vacillating hereditary king, Charles Albert, who had dreams of national leadership and kept hinting he wanted Italy to be free of Hapsburg rule, yet who persistently refused to let Mazzini return from exile and was known for his swift changes in political opinion. While this fickle Italian controlled a large army in Piedmont (though only by the grace of Austria), Leopold II was allied by marriage to Austria, which held power over him and also occupied the regions of Lombardy and Venetia. Meanwhile, in southern Italy, the Bourbon King Ferdinand II lorded over Naples and Sicily, while Pius IX as temporal ruler controlled the Papal States, which stretched from Ferrara in the north to Terracina in the south, as well as from sea to sea, effectively, as Joseph Jay Deiss put it, cutting the peninsula in two.[19]

Despite the powerful presence of foreign-backed monarchs in Italy, Fuller was optimistic about Italy's move toward democracy and unity. For Italians everywhere were responding positively to Mazzini's idea of throwing off Austrian rule. In mid-July the Austrians sent troops into Ferrara, angering the Italians, who remembered well that the previous November the Austrians had sent arms to the minority of Catholic cantons in Switzerland with the intention of inciting a civil war. Moreover, in annexing the Polish republic of Cracow (now Krakow) in November 1846, Metternich, the Roman Catholic minister to Austria's emperor Ferdinand I, had violated the public law of Europe and aroused patriotic fervor among the Slavs. Mazzini had potential allies in the Poles, Czechoslovaks, and southern Slavs, which together made up half the population of the Austrian Empire. By September 1847, when Fuller was in Milan—where Lombard patriots were boycotting tobacco and thus using it as an economic weapon against their Austrian overlords, who held a monopoly on it—and Florence, Prince Metternich saw that the balance of power in Europe was shifting. He feared local revolutions would break out in both Rome and Tuscany, which, as Mazzini knew, would ignite a major European war.[20]

And everywhere it seemed powerful people were playing with matches. On Fuller's return trip from Venice through Florence in September, she learned that

Leopold II was busy realizing Metternich's fears. Indeed, he had "dared to declare himself '*an* **Italian** *Prince*'" and to grant the formation of a national guard, an armed unit under the command of the Tuscan government and not that of Rome. The guard's formation was hence hailed as "the first step toward truly national institutions and a representation of the people." Fuller was also thrilled to see that a free press was now making possible public meetings and the free exchange of ideas between social classes that Mazzini saw as essential for the forging of a nation out of a people who not only were of different social classes and nationalities but also spoke in so many different dialects—as a frustrated Fuller had found out in her travels—that people from even neighboring regions could not understand one another. Aware of these complexities and tensions, Fuller was thus glad to see that the duke's recent reforms had brought hope to the Tuscan heart.[21]

Fuller felt it her duty to educate American readers about the Italian people's fight for freedom and rebirth as a unified nation. Thus she tells readers in dispatch 17 how she has seen a new spirit of unity expressed at fetes in Tuscany celebrating the new national guard. And she calls on Americans to remember their own country's fight for freedom, the "ground-work" for which "is the assertion . . . that all men have equal rights, and that these are *birth*-rights, derived from God alone."[22]

Believing that the Italians' struggle represented "the cause of all mankind at present" and seeing herself as a key player in it, Fuller felt more than ever as if some higher power were drawing her to Rome. She also felt the power of Ossoli's physical self pulling her to pagan Rome and to the joys of a mutually satisfying and loving sexual union. All things seemed to be headed toward revolution, resolution, and a final apocalyptic melding not only of Italy's divergent regions into one harmonious whole, but also of male and female—Ossoli and Fuller—into a new union. "Enough, to say," she wrote Elizabeth Hoar in the September letter she posted on her way back to Rome, "Italy receives me as a long lost child and I feel myself at home here, and if I ever tell . . . anything about it you will hear something real and domestic."[23]

55 ∽ Do As the Romans Do

On her return to Rome in early October 1847, Fuller missed the red poppies that had brightened the fields on her trip north in June, but the grapes hung heavy now; they were "full of light and life," ripe and ready for picking off the vine. Though the fields were brown and sere, the heavens seemed serene to Fuller. It was the best time to visit Rome, before the winter rains, while the climate was still mild.[1]

Traveling the timeworn Perugia route into Rome, Fuller felt she was entering not only an ancient city, but history. She felt, moreover, as if she were entering the most important phase of her life. She was living in vital relation to two of the most extraordinary men of her age, Mickiewicz and Mazzini, both of whom were profoundly committed to a vision of human liberty and to attacking tyranny. These men had charisma, which in Greek means "divine gift."[2]

To their followers both Mazzini and Mickiewicz seemed appointed by God to redeem their countries from tyranny and oppression. Mickiewicz was driven by his vision of a long-suffering Poland as a new Messiah. The more sober though no less Romantic Mazzini believed his mission to be guided by God's Providence. Certainly the success of the Risorgimento can be attributed in part to Mazzini's belief that he could see "the finger of God in the pages of the world's history." Fuller, herself, we know, felt *"chosen among women"* to be the oracle through whom the spirit spoke to nineteenth-century women. And Mickiewicz, as we also know, was feeding her belief that her mission was divine. Though Fuller had once confessed to having "no confidence in God as a Father" or as "an over-ruling Providence," she did not doubt that a higher power was now directing her back to Rome to live and act in relation to Mazzini, Mickiewicz, and Ossoli.[3]

Indeed, she professed to Marcus Spring in an October 1847 letter that "all mean things were forgotten" in the joy that rushed over her as her coach reentered Rome. Perhaps as her horse-drawn coach bumped and swayed its way into the city she thought of what Mickiewicz had written her: that she had wasted precious time trying to escape both history and pain through what now seemed, even to her, like infantile dreams. All that self-indulgent yearning now seemed oceans apart. For here in Italy were vital individuals who sympathized with her character, she wrote her mother, "as no other people ever did." Here in this city where Romans committed to an ideal of civic liberty still revolted against the invasion—as she put it in a *Tribune* dispatch—"of trampling emperors and kings,"[4] she felt connected to a reality bigger than herself, to a rich historical past that made hurts and conflicts from her personal past fall into perspective. Even as she acknowledged this, she also knew that her ability to identify with a nation suffering under a tyrant's rule derived from her blighted childhood in which she had been deprived by her domineering father of the right, she felt, to develop naturally.

In Rome Fuller felt part of an ongoing drama of an ancient people whom she had idealized in her youth as soldiers who stood firm on the ground. Yet it was here, too, in Rome, as she knew, that Christian martyrs had laid down their lives for a vision taught them by a charismatic Jew named Jesus: that through faith, love, and self-sacrifice for the good of one's fellow man—especially in behalf of the oppressed, hungry, and outcast—one would gain a reward greater than earthly riches or power. One would acquire peace of mind on earth and glory forever hereafter.

Fuller was thus glad to be working with men whose ethical base was not coldly Platonic but, she thought, "truly Christian," men who recognized the value of women and whose ideas stressed not Emersonian self-reliance but relationship. In her undated "New and Old World Democracy" dispatch, which was published in the *New-York Daily Tribune* on 1 January 1848, she notes how blessed are those who can keep that portion of "generous love with which they began life" and have enough "to spare for the thirst of others." When such appear on earth, she says, thinking not just of Christ but of Mazzini and Mickiewicz, "we must arise and follow."[5]

Contemplating the planet's history, Fuller observes how "little has been achieved for Humanity as a whole." She thinks of England with "its monstrous wealth and cruel poverty"; of France, "so full of talent" yet so "shallow"; of "lost Poland" and "Italy bound down by treacherous hands"; and, worst, of "Russia with its brutal Czar and innumerable slaves"—not to forget "Austria and its royalty that represents," to her, "nothing!"[6]

How sad it seemed to her that for all the words of truth spoken in the world, the public failure should be thus "monstrous." "Still," says Fuller, as if glimpsing on the horizon the galloping horses of the apocalypse, "Europe toils and struggles with her idea, and, at this moment, all things bode and declare a new outbreak of the fire, to destroy old palaces of crime!" From the ashes of the coming clash of the people with outdated authoritarian structures, Fuller sees a "new world" emerging. This world will be based on Mazzini's notion of "voluntary association," a way of relating that will "combine a deep religious love with practical development" to give "a nobler harmony to the coming age." She ends her dispatch by calling the United States "the darkest offender" for supporting the "cancer of Slavery" and fighting the Mexican War to extend slavery. She calls on American youth to "give soul" to their country and to treasure those moments when they have "been truly human—not brutal." Then they will be on the path to a "genuine Democracy" where "the rights of all men are holy."[7]

Although in her dispatches she predicts this bright new era, Fuller's personal letters suggest she is aware it might not be so easy to remake reality to fit her ideal of democracy. She had already learned how hard it was going to be for her as a woman to travel alone in Europe. In Rome in the spring she had been remarkably healthy. But in the summer as she traveled north, she had often been ill. Without the Springs to turn to, she had suffered without medicine and had had to rely on the help of people she did not trust. In Brescia she had been too ill to eat without being sick and was able to travel to Milan only because a servant made a bed for her in a carriage. She had become ill again after returning to Florence and had been forced to rely on the charity of Vermont banker turned sculptor, Joseph Mozier, and his kind wife, Isabella.[8]

Not just illness but a shortage of money made life hard for her in Europe. Early in 1847, before she had learned of her Uncle Abraham's 6 April death, she had written to ask her mother to give her a hundred dollars from a loan Eugene had just repaid, suggesting in her letter that she felt the money was due her since her mother had been so negligent in caring for her as a child. Upset, Margarett Crane had sent the money, regretting in her letter that she had not been more to Margaret throughout her life. She then promised that should the two ever be "reconciled in future years," she would try "to redeem the past."[9]

That hundred dollars, however, had hardly been sufficient to enable Margaret to live on her own for any length of time in Europe. To complicate her situation, the inheritance of several thousand dollars Fuller had thought she was getting from Uncle Abraham did not materialize. Although he had left bequests of a thousand dollars to various relatives and friends, to Margaret Abraham left $214.28—"not enough," she wailed to her mother in October. In letters thereafter to friends and relatives, she begged for money to allow her to extend her stay. She had even hinted she needed money to Emerson, who sent a letter—but no money—encouraging her to stay abroad. Richard in February 1848 came up with five hundred dollars as a gift from the family, noting in a letter that they felt it was due her "as the bright ornament of our family." Even Greeley's New York Associationist friends, Mary and Richard Manning, sent money as a loan. Greeley sent word that he would pay ten dollars for each letter she sent to the *Tribune*. He also gave Fuller permission to draw on the *Tribune* account when she needed money.[10]

Even when she was able to cajole American friends and family into sending her money, once it arrived in Italy it was subject to diminishment before it reached her. Fuller's courier had not been helpful; he had deflated her romantic view of lower-class folk by charging her huge fees for his services and spending her money without her permission. Fuller wrote her mother that he was "a brutal wretch who robbed and injured" her "under the mask of obsequiousness" when she had been sick in Brescia. He was so untrustworthy she feared that should she "die on the road," no one in America would ever know about it.[11]

As her situation in Europe worsened, reminders of family discord at home reached her in waves in letters posted two months earlier. There had been the news of Richard's first, hasty proposal, and of his misery working as a lawyer for his domineering Uncle Henry. There was also troubling news of the threat of William Henry failing again in business in Cincinnati; of Ellen's tumultuous marriage, along with that of Horace and Mary Greeley, whose baby, Mary Inez, had died in May. Then, too, there was the unstated but ever-present tension in letters between Margaret and her mother. Margarett Crane had been hurt by her daughter's remark that Margaret's emotional problems stemmed from her mismanaged childhood. Margaret made matters worse when she wrote her mother to thank her for her "prompt attention" to her "wishes about money" and then added flatly an ambiguous remark that surely shook her mother: "You are always the same." Perhaps her cool tone stemmed in part from her mother's offhand remark in an earlier letter that Nathan intended to marry and return to New York, where he and his bride hoped to rent rooms in the Greeleys' home at Turtle Bay.[12]

Surely this news upset Margaret, as did news about Lloyd conveyed in her mother's distraught 8 October letter. Margaret had held out hope for Lloyd, believing that if he lived at Brook Farm he might be redeemed. Yet even Brook Farm failed to reform him. While there Lloyd had written hateful notes about the residents and scattered them about the farm. In her October letter, Margarett Crane confides to Margaret that she tries to look on the "beautiful side of things" when it comes to Lloyd, but when she learned that Arthur and Richard had put him in the Brattleborough Asylum for the Insane, she had "wished to die." "His brothers," she says, "feel sure that the habit which has grown from a solitary life, and early companionship with one vicious person, is the cause of his present melancholy condition."[13]

Margaret's mother in passing mentions "one vicious person" as being the cause of Lloyd's problems but she gives no name nor does she specify what problems she means. Yet even this indirect reference to Lloyd's embarrassing "habit" (presumably connected in some way to masturbating) no doubt disturbed Margaret, just as Margarett Crane's detailed account of events at the Greeleys' must have hurt her. Mrs. Fuller informed her daughter that "beautiful" Pickie Greeley, who was often ill, had grown into a spiteful child who battled with his mother. In May while Mrs. Fuller was there, Pickie had refused to take a bath. His mother had then been violent with him, and he had hit her. It was a "frightful scene," says Margarett Crane, who, when she brought up the problem, was told by Mary that she was keeping her son for Margaret, "as no other person can take care of Pickie."[14]

To this painful reminder of Mary Greeley's inept mothering of a child Margaret loved, Margarett Crane added that, when she was at the Greeleys', Pickie had handed her "two pale carnelians given him by Mr. Nathan" and said, "Mrs. Fuller, I wis[h] to give these pretty stones to you because they are 'so pretty.'" Unaware of the power of her words, Mrs. Fuller continues: "Mrs. G. says Mr. Nathan married his wife for her love & knowledge of musick, and that he wishes her to teach after she recovers from the birth of her child."[15]

Such pain does the blundering mother here unintentionally inflict on her daughter: Fuller, having once hoped to be Nathan's wife, now learns that his wife is pregnant with their child. This news must have indeed been painful to that part of Fuller that yearned for a child.

The news no doubt sealed her decision to return to Rome, where bankers helped her find an affordable second-floor furnished apartment in a stone house at 514 Corso. In mid-October, Fuller wrote her mother that the bankers who chose it for her did not object to the fact that it was run by a woman who carried the title of marchioness but is "not received into society." She is not a member of the nobility but came by her title by having been the mistress of "a man of quality" who then married her "before his death." Margaret notes that this woman, who has "black eyes and red hair like Aunt Martha," now has another lover, an artist who is an officer in the newly organized people's militia, a part of the civic guard of Rome. The pope had permitted the formation of the civic guard in July, though battalions of men wearing the guard's red-corded dark coats had begun to form in mid-October. Fuller assures her mother that her own apartment is entirely "separate" from that of the marchioness and that she (Margaret) pretends "to ignore all these circumstances; [the lover] appears here only as a friend and visitor."[16]

Fuller does not add that the marchioness's lover probably knows Ossoli, who on 15 November was to be commissioned a sergeant in the Fifth Company of the Second Battalion of the Civic Guard. When Fuller writes that in "glorious Rome . . . all the pleasures I most value . . . are within my reach," it is perhaps the marchioness's situation—and its application to her own—that she is referring to: an illicit sexual relationship under the guise of the man being merely "a friend and visitor." More revealing is her remark in a letter to the editor of the *People's Journal* containing a poem she submitted praising the woman who plays her part to "rouse" the "soul of man" to fight for "injured Italy." In it she says "that in Rome it is well to do as the Romans do."[17]

That autumn she let it seem she had only a friendship with Ossoli, such as she had with Hicks, who included her in parties attended by well-to-do, young, expatriate painters and writers. On Monday evenings Fuller, in turn, entertained visitors. Too poor to serve a meal, she filled her book-lined drawing room with soft candlelight and fresh-cut flowers. Her guests included Christopher Cranch and his wife Elizabeth, William Wetmore Story and his wife Emelyn, and the American sculptor Thomas Crawford. Fuller liked him because he had joined the civic guard and also sculpted Orpheus, he who, she wrote the *Tribune*, "shamed Hell itself into sympathy with the grief of love."[18]

Other nights when she stayed in, Fuller immersed herself in histories of Italy as well as in recent writings about Italy's politics and potential for rebirth, like Abbot Gioberti's *Il Gesuita moderno* (*The Modern Jesuit*) and articles in *Il risorgimento*, the newspaper founded by Count Camillo Benso di Cavour, who was to become the chief architect of the Kingdom of Italy. While this research aided her in writing her *Tribune* dispatches, it also gave background information she needed to write a history of the Roman Republic. On some of these nights she was not alone. With her was Ossoli.[19]

Fuller had never been so happy as she was in the period she spent with Ossoli in Rome between mid-October and the end of 1847. Italy was the dream of her heart come true. Her apartment was near the Pincian Mount, the Piazza del Popolo, the French Academy, and the artists' studios. When she opened her window, she looked out on the Corso, the narrow street that served as Rome's main thoroughfare for carnivals, parades, and demonstrations. One crisp October day, she laughed to see a troop of the Trasteverini dancers parade by with their tambourines jangling and colors flying. The bright colors of these flamboyant dancers from the poor west section of Rome contrasted sharply with the brown robes of

the chanting monks that had passed by minutes earlier. On the numerous beautiful days that fall, she went by way of the Corso to the nearby Villa Borghese. There
she saw "races, balloons, and, above all, the private gardens open, and good music
on the little lake."[20]

Walking along the Corso and through the gardens of the Villa Borghese was
especially pleasant due to the presence in her life of Ossoli, whose red-corded uni-
form of the civic guard identified him with the cause of Italian liberty. Fuller wrote
Emerson at October's end that she lived, ate, and walked alone, but by December
Ossoli was her frequent companion, and walks in the garden were paradise for her
with him at her side. In an early December letter, she wistfully says in a letter to
the Springs, "On the road from Bologna here I seemed to see Eddie running lightly
before me with his stick always! and also in the Villa Borghese running." She notes
she has been to the fountain where Eddie fell in, but instead of the music of the
water, there is only silence. "It is covered with dead leaves now, and there are no
flowers to make garlands of."[21]

That autumn Fuller became Ossoli's lover. Her "fall" into sensual pleasure, what
her Puritan conscience damned as "sin," helps explain how, amid her joyful excla-
mations—such as this to her mother on 16 December: "I have not been so well
since I was a child, nor so happy ever as during the last six weeks"—a note of sadness creeps in as she laments the absence of flowers and innocent Eddie in the
villa's gardens. She wrote the Mannings that day that she experienced at times a
foreboding "sense of exile and loneliness, a sense that if you die, or fall sick or sad,
the smiles of all . . . may be withdrawn like a mask, and a painful cold indifference
be left staring you into stupefaction, . . . without a tear to hallow [your dust]."[22]

But most of the time morbid thoughts like these were countered by an "unexpected remembrance from some friend," such as a kind word from the Mannings
assuring her of their continuing concern for her, or a thoughtful gesture on the
part of Ossoli. She would later tell her mother about a happy time when she went
by carriage with Ossoli and one of his friends to the Villa Correggi, where she was
given a bouquet of crimson flowers. When she was poor after the war, Fuller would
consider such carriage rides a "luxury." But now it seemed to her that such rides
in the country were paradise and that no one but Ossoli could share with her so
entirely in her communion with nature. Emelyn Story remembers the couple in a
carriage coming down the Corso—a laughing, bonneted Fuller and a mustached,
attentive Ossoli in a fitted jacket and flowing cravat, his hand atop a bamboo cane:
"What a beautiful picture is that of their return to Rome after a day spent on the
Campagna!"[23]

An intelligent, plump, pretty woman with dangling ringlet curls and a spirit
unsuppressed by a Puritan past, Emelyn in her recollections reflects on Fuller's
demeanor at this time. Though she had not known Fuller personally in Boston,
nonetheless, "through her friends, who were mine also," says Emelyn, "I learned to

think of her as a person on intellectual stilts, with a large share of arrogance and little sweetness of temper. How unlike to this was she now—so delicate so simple confiding and affectionate."[24]

During this bright moment in Fuller's life her private and public selves were in harmony. She was in a loving relationship with a gracious, devoted, unpuritanical Italian. She was, at the same time, doing work she loved: writing about Italy's politics for the *Tribune* and making a living of it. Moreover, as Mazzini's correspondent and friend, she was allied with the core power of Mazzini's party. According to Emelyn, Fuller had access to privileged inside information about the papacy that had to have had "highest value in [an] age of incorrect report and perverted statement." To her, says Emelyn, "he carried all the flying reports of the day, such as he had heard in the café, or through his friends." They attended meetings together. And in late October she watched the civic guard maneuvering—a martial drill that surely included Ossoli—in the great field full of ruins near the tomb of Cecilia Metella. Fuller thought the "effect was noble, as the band played the Bolognese march, and six thousand Romans passed in battle array amid these fragments of the great time." On Christmas Eve they watched the pope on his way back to the Quirinal Palace from the church of the Santa Maria Maggiore, where he had officiated. In her 30 December dispatch Fuller tells how, "as he returned, the moon looked palely out from amid the wet clouds, and shown upon the fountain and the noble [statues] above it, and [on] the long white cloaks of the Guardia Nobile who followed his carriage on horseback." Darker objects "could scarcely be seen, except by the flickering light of the torches, much blown by the wind." The lovers were glad for the dark, which hid them from Ossoli's brothers, who rode proudly on their prancing stallions behind the pope's carriage.[25]

During this idyllic interlude, Fuller suspended her disbelief in the duplicitous father and in her *Tribune* dispatches expressed faith in the pope. Identifying with the Italian people, she shared their faith in Pius IX and his potential to change the rigidly conservative papacy. In her 18 October 1847 dispatch, she calls the pope "a father" to the Italian people, who have "showed themselves children, eager to learn, quick to obey." On 17 December she confesses that she, too, is "happy to be for once in a place ruled by a father's love," which she had missed as a child. "It is a real pleasure," she says, to see the pope "in the thoroughfares, where his passage is always greeted as that of *the* living soul." She believes that as pope he has shown "wisdom, clear-sightedness, bravery, and firmness," though it is his "generous" heart that gives him "power over his people." When she watched him arrive in state at the Church of St. Carlo on the Corso, his face seemed bright with the faith of a man "sure of support from a higher Power." While riding on the Campagna, she had seen him in a flowing white robe walking rapidly on foot. Two young priests in spotless purple walked on either side of him and "gave silver to the poor who knelt beside the way, while the beloved Father gave his benediction."[26]

In her personal letters, too, Fuller idealizes the pope. She tells the Mannings to assure their daughter that she is in "no danger," for the pope "is so kind he would not willingly hurt a fly." In an otherwise depressed 20 December letter to Emerson, she calls Pius IX "a real great heart, a generous man." She says she likes being "within" the influence of his love.[27]

All this adoration of the pope as a kind father took place while he was instituting liberal reforms and she was seeing things, she wrote Richard, not as a sightseeing stranger but as Italians see things, that is, "in the natural manner." Fuller closes this 29 October letter with a blessing and an expression of hope that heaven will show her brother "how to act" in regards to marriage. Surely she is thinking here of herself, hoping heaven will show her the way to respond to the experienced Ossoli's persuasive caresses.[28]

In a culture where women as different as George Sand and Fuller's landlady took lovers and where out-of-wedlock pregnancy was common, Fuller felt, she told her brother, happy and free. Yet as Emerson had observed thirteen years earlier, Margaret was "by no means so free with all her superiority." In her 17 December dispatch, written after Ossoli and Fuller had consummated their relationship, she reveals her first intimation that in having behaved so freely she may have closed the door to her freedom. While visiting the Santo Spirito cemetery in the first week of November, she saw painted on a wall the stations in the Passion of Jesus. At each, people knelt to pray: "here a Franciscan, in his brown robe and cord; there a pregnant woman, uttering, doubtless, some tender aspiration for the welfare of the yet unborn dear one; there some boys, with gay yet reverent air, while all the while ... fresh young voices were heard chanting." These particular images relay to the reader Fuller's suspicion that the issue of her union with Ossoli will be—as happened in the union of Rezia with her noble knight Huon in *Oberon*—a baby. Touched by the spirit of the gay boys chanting and of the fatherly friar and pregnant woman praying, Fuller prayed. She noted also praying for the dead that day were "many lovely, warm hearted women!" Though women in Italy were "intellectually in a low place," Fuller says she believes that "they will be yet the mothers of a great and generous race."[29]

She was pregnant, and for a few days it seems she let herself relish the thought of being such a mother, noting to her own mother on 16 December that Rome is so dear to her now that "I do not know how I can ever ... live anywhere else." After all, people there addressed Ossoli as a marquis; his seventeenth-century Roman forebears, dealers of wheat, had built up a thriving bakery business that served local monasteries. When he sold the business in 1659, family founder Giovanni Angelo Ossoli had first bought "the territory of the Marche ... of Pietraforte" and in so doing acquired the family title. A few years later he purchased the great castle at Pietraforte. Now fallen in fortune, the Ossoli family nonetheless had a chapel in the fifteenth-century Church of the Maddalena, near the Pantheon. On the Ossoli crest appears a gold-crowned black eagle. An eagle to Fuller symbolized freedom—not only America's but her own—as in the wild eagle she said she had seen flying free and high above the White Mountains on an 1842 trip. Yet the Ossoli family was profoundly Roman Catholic, a people who would never approve of a son and brother living out of wedlock with a free-spirited, middle-class American woman. The Romantic dream of bearing a noble Italian son was wonderful; the reality of being an unwed mother in a conservative world of censuring Catholic fathers, not to mention of unforgiving Puritans back home, was hell.[30]

Winter set in and the bleak rains began to fall. Fuller, pregnant and alone with her secret except for Ossoli, entered a period more difficult than any since she was a child unloved in a threatening world of forbidding adults. To Emerson on 20 December she wrote: "Nothing less than two or three years, free from care and forced labor, would heal all my hurts, and renew my life-blood at its source. Since Destiny will not grant me that, I hope she will not leave me long in the world, for I am tired of keeping myself up in the water without corks, and without strength to swim. I should like to go to sleep, and be born again into a state where my young life should not be prematurely taxed." Fuller's words are reminiscent of the nightmare world that had haunted her sleep in 1842. In that dream she was on a sinking ship but had no energy to swim, and no one came to help her, a dream that evokes images of the near drowning of the Christian knight Huon and pagan princess Rezia in *Oberon*. Being thrown into the tumultuous sea was the price the lovers paid for having defied Oberon by consummating their relationship before marriage in Rome. In her letter to the fatherly Emerson, Fuller confesses she has had in Italy some "blessed, quiet days," but now "I must begin to exert myself, for there is this incubus of the future, and none to help me, if I am not prudent to face it." Fuller laments to the clueless Emerson, "So ridiculous, too, this mortal coil,—such small things!" "And yet," she might have added, "so final!"[31]

56 ∽ Roman Winter

From 16 December 1847 until mid-March 1848 rain fell in torrents, making it seem like night in Fuller's apartment on a street of high houses that blocked such scant light as might otherwise have crept in through her window; she found she needed to light the lamp when she arose in the morning. In daylight hours, a lethargic Fuller had barely enough energy to make her way through the muddy street and sidewalks of the Corso. She spent hours lying on her sofa and dreaming of riding in a chaise in the hills and fields of New England, though she knew that she could not return in her condition. In her letters and dispatches she explained how, "after a month of continuous rain," she felt as if "the weight of the world" was pressing her and her high aspirations down to earth, where they then dissolved in the thick mud that lay outside the door to her house.[1]

It was tempting to think of death, as if destiny were drawing her rapidly along the waters of life to "the gate of death" in the way the spirit of death had drawn the poet in his boat in *Alastor* along tumbling waters to a quiet death in a cradlelike recess atop a precipice that dropped, suddenly, into nothingness. While lying half asleep on her sofa, Fuller had a vision of Richard, she wrote Richard on 1 January 1848, "six or seven years hence" with "honors already gained" and "your true wife at your side, . . . perhaps visiting my grave."[2]

Margaret had earlier preached to Richard on his need to be more careful in choosing a mate for life. Now, in light of her own predicament, she began to exhibit a new sensitivity to others' odd choices and mistakes. "God knows," she wrote Richard in her 1 January letter, "I have not myself been wise in life."[3]

Sadness pervaded her heart whenever she thought of the fate of her siblings. It is as if, she wrote Richard two months later, they are "never wholly sunk by storms," although "no favorable wind ever helps our voyages to surprizing good results." In these 1 January and 17 March letters to Richard she stresses the hardship they each have suffered. She feels badly for Richard, whose fiancée ran off and who cannot work peaceably with their domineering Uncle Henry. She worries about William Henry, who "gets along, but seems likely never to do more"; about Eugene "after all his tribulation"; about Arthur, whose "calamity" of a permanently damaged eye, "hangs on him like a cloud"; and about Ellen, who "has wed herself to difficulties from which only the death of her husband could free her." Then, too, there is the persistent problem of "poor Lloydie," whom she hopes "is not unhappy" in the asylum. Margaret now feels sorry for them all.[4]

Her new humility permeates a January 1848 letter to Cary, as does her despair, the cause of which she does not reveal. After a year's silence, Cary had sent Margaret a letter in which she failed to mention a fact Fuller found out secondhand, that Cary had married William Aspinwall Tappen of New York in December 1847. On 11 January Margaret replied, saying that she rejoices that Cary has cast her lot with another person, that they shall live "in a house I suppose; sleep and wake in unison with humanity," a pleasure denied the illegitimately pregnant Fuller, whom Americans would damn if they knew of her condition. Skirting the personal, Margaret says she is glad that Cary has found an island in the river of life. The "union of two natures for [even] a [brief] time," she says, "is so great."[5]

Hearing Cary's news fills Margaret with "certainty that there is love, is realization, hope and faith" in her friend's life. She hopes Cary will hang the gifts she intends to send her, a medallion of "Raphael's Poesy" and a rosary, above her bed. She then tells Cary what she dared not tell anyone else: how much she hated having to travel with the Springs, even though she knew her bitterness was less against them than against "the destiny which placed me with them, instead of those who fancied they loved me."[6]

Fuller tells of pleasant hours boating on Lake Como, where "red banners floated; children sang and shouted; [and] the lakes of Venus and Diana glittered in the sweetest sunshine." She tells also of her day in Parma where she saw the vaulted chamber of the Abbess Giovanna da Piacenza of the convent of San Paolo, the architecture and frescoes of which were so brilliantly fashioned that Fuller concluded that the Renaissance artist Correggio "deserves all his fame." As she stood in the abbess's parlor and saw above on the frescoed vault a leafy bower of forest green, a pagan wood pierced by portholes through which she could see frolicsome cupids playing, it seemed, she says in this 11 January letter, that paradise had been opened before her. "Sweet soul of love!" exclaims Fuller regarding the unabashedly sensual figures appearing in the convent's frescoes painted expressly for the Abbess and her friends by Correggio, who recast pagan figures to serve as symbols in Christian scenes of religious rapture.[7]

Tucked between her glowing accounts to Cary of boating and sightseeing, Margaret hints of her situation: "I have known some happy hours; but they all lead to sorrow, and not only the cups of wine but of milk seem drugged with poison for me. It does not seem to be my fault,—this destiny: I do not court these things, they come. I am a poor magnet with power to be wounded by the bodies I attract." Here Fuller links her magnetic power over people with a retributive bodily wound. After all, Cary had been one of the "bodies" she attracted that had wounded her—both earlier during their traumatic encounter at Nahant and now. She will later confess to Cary that she was hurt to have had to learn "through others first" the "great fact" in Cary's life, that is, the birth of her baby.[8]

She feels that Ossoli, too, has wounded her. By having had sex with him, she both opened herself to an emotional wound and entangled herself in a net of ties that might, she felt, kill her. Revealing her pain to Cary yet not the cause of it, she tells about a day crossing the Apennines: "The young crescent moon rose in orange twilight, just as I reached the highest peak. I was alone on foot; I heard no sound; I prayed." In telling Cary about the ill effect of the Italian weather on her health, Fuller cryptically alludes to her unmentioned condition. "I feel," she writes, "as if I had received a great injury." To Cary she confesses, "I was at first intoxicated to be here." But "with this year, I enter upon a sphere of my destiny so difficult, that I, at present, see no way out, except through the gate of death."[9]

Although Fuller has written that "this destiny does not *seem* to be [her] fault" (emphasis added), she accepts responsibility for her fate, telling an undoubtedly baffled Cary: "I have no reason to hope I shall not reap what I have sown, and do not. Yet how I shall endure it I cannot guess; it is all a dark, sad enigma. The beautiful forms of art charm no more, and a love, in which there is all fondness, but no help, flatters in vain." "I am all alone," she adds, "nobody around me sees any of this." In becoming pregnant out of wedlock, Fuller had defied the law of the father who lived in her and demanded of her "clear judgment" and "fidelity." This tangible result of her rebellious behavior cast her in the very role of the "outlaw" stained "by passionate error" about whom she had written in *Woman in the Nineteenth Century* that "society has a right" to condemn until "she has revised her law." Although Fuller noted in that expanded essay that it "ought not" be that a woman of great intellect should find herself, by birth, "in a place so narrow, that, in breaking bonds" she becomes, in society's eyes, an outlaw, still, as she was aware, that was reality.[10]

In following her own law, however, Fuller had cast her lot with Oedipus, who, as she had earlier acknowledged to William Channing, paid for his transgressions of murder and incest by being forced to "return [home] a criminal, blind and outcast." That the price Oedipus paid for his sin of incest was on Margaret's mind is evident in a remark she added the next day in an addendum to her letter to Cary, as well as in remarks she made to Ellen in a letter also dated 12 January. After comments to Cary about the suffering the French actress Rachel endured for her wayward sexual life, Margaret ends her letter by referring to a historical figure made wayward by a father who forced her into incest: "Yesterday I saw Beatrice Cinci's [sic] prison and the place where she was tortured so long and never [like Oedipus] blinded." About herself in her 12 January letter to Ellen she says that she hopes God grants "the grave may prove a door to some real peace." Until then, however, she hopes Ellen will continue to send news about herself and her children. Thinking clearly of her own thwarted childhood, Margaret exclaims about Greta, the baby: "Dear child! I think her circumstances happy in the country and with a mother she loves so much and who will take care that she is not forced or injured in any way."[11]

What is not said here is as important as what is. Contained in this coded remark to Ellen is Margaret's awareness that the young Margaret Fuller, who was born on the elder Margaret's birthday in 1844, is protected by a loving mother in a way she felt that she, like Beatrice Cenci—who was on her mind that day—had not been by "parents who protected" her as a child. Margaret suggests that Ellen's protective love could create for her daughter "circumstances" conducive to a happy childhood such as she, the older Margaret, was denied, circumstances in which Greta is not "injured," a word that she has earlier associated with sexual activity.[12]

Set in her negative view that her "birth-star was not a kindly one," Fuller was unwittingly helping to shape the dark fate she feared. In a letter she wrote at this time to Jane Tuckerman (who, she says, never "wounded me"), she compares her life to a storm-tossed ship at sea: "the drama of my fate is very deep, and the ship plunges deeper as it rises higher." Here Fuller seems to surrender her freedom to the fatalistic vision of her life she had earlier limned in her untitled 1840 autobiographical fragment, wherein she noted she was destined for a "premature grave." Sensing that death is near, Fuller now felt an urgent need to share her vision of the coming kingdom of liberty, love, and justice with her New York readers.[13]

With winter rains pounding the earth outside, Fuller sat by her fire and poured out letters to the *Tribune* giving her account of events leading up to the 1848 revolutions. Her aim was to offer analyses of the coming revolutions, which, she hoped, would "democratize Society at a blow." Representing her best writing, these letters also reveal her yearning for a catastrophic confrontation between the powers of heaven and hell that will purge people of their sins and hence redeem humanity. Invoking the water imagery she has used in the past, Fuller expresses in these letters a longing for a breaking down of old institutions and "a pouring out of the heart" until "the flood-gates" burst open and salvation, like a freed mighty river flows over the people of each European nation that suffers under a tyrant's oppressive rule.[14]

Fuller wanted to be purged of "sin" because she was in pain. Yet flooding waters were more now to her than a metaphor of her female power and spirituality; they were her daily reality. So constant was the rain that her health gave way "entirely," she said, "beneath the Roman Winter." Nothing, she thought, could compare with "the dirt, the gloom, the desolation of Rome" when viewed through heavy sheets of rain, the weight of which gave her a "constant . . . headache."[15]

A suffering Fuller thought of Pius IX's kind face as he blessed the poor that day she saw him walking on the Campagna. Wanting for the pope to be a just and caring father, she persisted in misperceiving him, projecting onto him her needs. In dispatches she thus continues to defend him as a reliable leader and Italy's friend. She did so even after receiving from Mazzini a letter telling of an irreparable breach between him and Pius IX, whom he calls "the Louis XVI of the Papal Rome" and whose job, he says, is "*to give the last blow to the papacy.*" Mazzini also says he fears that Emerson, who had been in London lecturing, "will lead man too much to contemplation." Though such may be needed in America, "in our own old world we stand in need of one who will . . . inflame us to the Holy Crusade and appeal to the *collective* influences . . . more than to individual self-improvement."[16]

Fuller continued to defend the pope despite mounting evidence that he lacked the spine to defy the Jesuits, who had secured power positions at the highest levels of government in the Roman Catholic countries of Austria and Italy and were persuading the pope that liberalism was a product of Protestant defiance of the Roman Catholic Church and hence incompatible with "true religion." In dispatch 19, Fuller tells of the pope's 1847 Christmas gift to the people: the creation of a cabinet council of ministers, to include only one cardinal, as the secretary of state. She fails, however, to mention that this council, unlike the representative council established the previous April, would consist all of ecclesiastics, since the pope did not specify to the curia that lay people should be on it. Thus two days after Christmas, the people, still fearful of the Jesuits, sent the pope a list of demands through a popular tribune, a wine and horse dealer called "Big-boy" Ciceruacchio because of his girth. In it they demanded the immediate suppression of the Jesuits—to which the pope did not concede.[17]

In her mid-December dispatch Fuller notes how, nevertheless, on the day the council was to be inaugurated, people from across Italy converged on Rome to wave their regional flags in joyful anticipation of what Fuller calls "the dawn of an epoch" of freedom. She tells how some rash young Americans, convinced "that the cause of freedom was the cause of America and her Eagle at home," made a red, white, and blue silk flag. But just as people readied their banners to wave as a sign of national unity, a Jesuit-inspired ordinance appeared, decreeing no flag could be flown but that of Rome, a pronouncement that chilled Italian hearts.[18]

Fuller lauded Pius IX's "excellent intentions." Even when in his speech receiving the councilors the pope said he meant "not to *reform*" but to "keep things *in statu quo*," Fuller heard his words as an attempt to placate "Czars, Emperors and Kings," not as revealing his soul. She ends dispatch 19 by describing the funeral procession of a councilor who had died shortly after being inaugurated. Led by a single horseman, among others marched the councilors and "the Civic Guard with drums slowly beating." Finally came the state carriages with their liveried attendants. Like shadows passing, all moved in the dark night along the Corso, banners drooping, torches dim—a scene presaging dark times for Rome, tumultuous waters yet ahead.[19]

Also foretelling dark times ahead was the rain that threatened to extinguish the torches during a procession to the Quirinal Palace on the evening of the day that the civic guard leaders had paid their respects to the pope, who had expressed his satisfaction with them. That night there was to be a procession to celebrate the occasion. But due to the rain, says Fuller, "the Pope could give but a hasty salute under an umbrella, when . . . a cataract of water" descended on the people and "drove both man and beast to seek the nearest shelter." A further disappointment was that the pope, Fuller notes in her New Year's letter, failed to appear on New Year's Day when the people, as was their custom, went to the Quirinal to receive his benediction. There the cardinal in charge denied them access. Ciceruacchio stopped a riot by suggesting an emissary be sent to Pius IX, who was ill. The pope promised to pass among the people through the streets of Rome the next day. He kept his promise, says Fuller, even though the day was rainy and cold. In anticipation of his arrival Italians had thrown open their windows despite the weather and hung out red and yellow tapestries to honor the father. As he passed, people along the thoroughfare knelt and cried out, "O Holy Father, don't desert us." In response Pius IX wept and said, "Fear nothing my people, my heart is yours." Again defending the pope, Fuller notes that whenever he directly shows himself in such a way to the people, "his generous affectionate heart" dissipates "the clouds which others have been toiling to darken."[20]

Although Bell Gale Chevigny sees this displacement of "her orphaned feelings of dependency" onto Pius IX as "the last" such instance of Fuller expressing "the fervent spirituality of her adolescence,"[21] the increasing stridency in her *Tribune* letters suggests that in abandoning her adolescent idealizations and yearnings she is becoming more committed to an apocalyptic vision in which a radical Christ defends with sword in hand the poor and oppressed and denounces all forms of injustice.

In the 1 January 1848 dispatch wherein she laments the absence of a "genuine Democracy" in the world, Fuller affirms that there are in Europe men capable of leading mankind into an era in which the rights of all people will be "holy." She says that the sight of such triumphant souls "gives a meaning to life." In the United States, however, she sees no such leaders. Though she finds much to praise about her home country, she wonders if she can say that the American men "of most influence in political life are those who represent most virtue, or even intellectual power?" At least, she says, the abolitionists, who had earlier seemed "tedious" and "narrow" to her, have attained an idea "worth living and dying for[,] to free a great nation" from slavery.[22]

To Fuller, Italian liberty was worth living and dying for. Though she continues to defend the pope, an unapologetically Protestant Fuller was upset by scenes of Roman Catholic ritual. With great dismay Fuller one day watched an elegantly dressed twenty-six-year-old prepare to take the veil of a nun. This involved having her hair cut short and her clothes exchanged for the nun's vestments, "the black-robed sisters" looking to Fuller "like crows or ravens at their ominous feasts." Fuller, who had earlier advocated virginity as a means for women to attain power, found the scene "revolting." To the American-raised Fuller, the sight of the new municipal officers in their white-collared, black velvet gowns kneeling to kiss the foot of the pope in his gold and white robe was likewise repugnant, as was the hypocrisy of a priest who claimed to represent Christ yet who made an orphan pay "a scudo" and "seven baiocchi" before he would say six masses for the soul of the boy's dead uncle.[23]

Disgusted with church ornamentation bought with money she thought should have been spent on the poor, Fuller in her dispatches began a relentless attack on the Roman Catholic Church, especially on Jesuit institutions. She tells her readers that in every instance when a riot had been incited by inflammatory handbills, by false rumors, or by even the pope's failure to appear, as on New Year's Day, the Jesuits had had a hand in it, their aim being to arouse suspicion of the anti-Catholic radicals.[24]

Determined to see Pius IX as a "good MAN," Fuller was nonetheless forced to concede that he was too bound by his belief that he must be the "Pope of Rome" rather than "a Reform Prince, and father to the fatherless," to be man enough to alter history. Yet even if Pius IX lacks the perspicacity "to hear the signs of the times" about democracy being trumpeted at his palace door, still, says Fuller, again eerily foreshadowing her own tragic fate, "A wave has been set in motion, which cannot stop till it casts up its freight upon the shore."[25]

57 ∞ More Rain and Revolutionaries' Conflicting Aims

The wave of revolutions that hit Europe in the winter and spring of 1848 was tidal; sweeping over the countries of Europe, it lifted ordinary people like pebbles to great heights of excitement and fervor before it dropped them abruptly on reality's shore a year later. Caught up in the wave was Fuller, who sent dispatches home with news of revolution. In Milan, where the Austrian occupation of Venetia and Lombardy was headquartered and where the people had been boycotting tobacco to diminish Austrian tax revenues, Field Marshall Joseph Radetzky, who had earlier seized the northern city of Ferrara, on 1 January 1848 ordered his troops and other paid agitators to taunt Italian men by blowing smoke in their faces. When the provoked Italians expressed their rage in outright rebellion, the troops charged into the crowd, wounding sixty-four people, some of whom died.[1]

There were similar outbreaks of violence all over Italy. In Venice, police feared that Mazzini was planning a national rebellion. Both Costanza Arconati Visconti and King Charles Albert attributed a 4 January attack on the Jesuits in Genoa to Mazzini's influence. Meanwhile, in Tuscany rioters in Leghorn expressed their rage against the repressive policies of Grand Duke Leopold. With the death of Napoleon's second empress, the Archduchess Marie-Louise von Habsburg, who had been given the duchy of Parma in 1830, the region fell to the duke of Modena. The latter replied to the people's petition protesting their former ruler's police state tactics by, in Fuller's words, "crowding his dominions with Austrian troops."[2]

In this incendiary situation, Sicily on 12 January erupted into full insurrection with the successful rising of the people in Palermo against Naples and Ferdinand II. However, as was true for most of the European revolutions that year, the people's motivations were diverse: some, inspired by Mazzini's propaganda, fought for national unity; others, happy in victory, raised the yellow-and-red flag of Sicilian separatism, while a group of mafioso gang leaders plundered the city and paraded a policeman's head on a stick.[3] Mazzini was unable to focus the people on a vision of national unity, and their varied purposes helped undermine the drive for liberty.

The immediate result of these rebellions was that the people of each region were granted a constitution. Thus Ferdinand's example in January of granting his subjects a constitution and representative assembly was soon followed by Grand Duke Leopold of Tuscany and, in March, by Pope Pius IX as well as by Charles

Albert of Piedmont. Such constitutions, however, hardly gave to Mazzini and his followers the liberties they sought. Each limited the religion of the state to "Roman Catholic Apostolic" and declared that "the King shall be forever sacred, inviolable, and not subject to responsibility." Even when granting what seemed to be freedom of the press, a restriction was invariably attached, such as article 2 of the constitution King Charles Albert presented: "The press shall be free, but subject to repressive laws."[4]

Fuller could report only what news she heard. And from her perspective it seemed the wave of the future was with Mazzini and democracy and against despotic rulers and a church "encumbered with the remains of Pagan habits and customs." There was "soul in the religion," she wrote, "while the blood of its martyrs was yet fresh upon the ground," a soul, now, "fled elsewhere." When attending the Feast of the Bambino in late December, Fuller had been put off again by Roman Catholicism. Approaching the Church of S. Maria d'Aracoeli (the altar of heaven), she was astounded to see that its staircase was "flooded with people," and that "the street below was a rapid river also, whose waves were men." Inside she found the church packed "with contadini [peasants] and the poorer people." Fuller's failure to understand Italians' love of a religion laden with remains of pagan ritual suggests how profoundly Protestant she still was despite her penchant for falling into pagan mystical trances and wearing a seal ring of the flying Mercury when writing friends. She sardonically says that she wished "the ugly little doll" they worshipped with "its gilded robes and crown," symbol to Roman Catholics of Baby Jesus, could do them good.[5]

This remark in a late January dispatch reveals Fuller's ignorance of the depth of the need of Europe's uneducated poor for the traditional patriarchal hierarchies and religious symbols that lent meaning to their hard lives. This typical failure of revolutionary visionaries like Fuller and Mazzini contributed to the Roman Republicans' defeat. In her dispatch, Fuller accuses the priests and people who participated in the Feast of the Bambino of failing to see "that the Christ who is to save men is no wooden dingy effigy of by-gone superstitions, but . . . a Child, living, full of love, prophetic of a boundless Future." He is "a Man," she says, "acquainted with all sorrows that rend the heart of all, but only loving Man, with sympathy and faith death cannot quench." She assures her American readers that "*that* Christ lives" and orders poor Italians to "burn your doll of wood."[6]

Fuller's prophetic tone echoes that of Mazzini in his September 1847 letter to Pope Pius IX, which she had translated and included in her New Year's Eve dispatch. In it Mazzini says that he writes in behalf of "an idea" that he feels God has ordained him "to realize here on earth": to make Italy a model of moral unity and progressive civilization for all the nations of Europe to imitate. Loathing, he says, the vices of materialism, egotism, and reaction, which he concedes "contaminate many of our party," Mazzini asserts that he is "not a subverter, nor a communist, . . .

or exclusive adorer of [any] system" that is not a part of God's design. Mazzini then asks the pope to help him to realize God's design on earth by seeing himself, not as the head of the Roman Catholic Church, but as an Italian prince and moral leader of a united nation. He contends that "the moral Unity of Europe" depends on the unity of Italy, and affirms that his faith in this idea has never wavered though all his years of exile, poverty, and grief. As a radical democrat who sees all people as equal, he adds: "I speak to you as I should speak to God beyond the sepulchre." He blames the lack of genuine religious feeling in Italy not on Pius IX but on his predecessors and the church hierarchy. The result, he says, of this "crisis of doubts and desires" in Europe is that "Faith is dead, Catholicism is lost in Despotism; Protestantism is lost in Anarchy." "Nobody," according to Mazzini, "*believes.*"[7]

Instead of Emersonian self-reliance, Mazzini in his letter to the pope stresses the Christian concept of self-sacrifice, arguing that nobody now is willing "to sacrifice" himself "for the good of all." Putting forward a very un-Emersonian notion, Mazzini says people must believe in the idea of heaven (a concept Emerson found cold and barren) in order for a civilized society to exist, the "idea of Society" being, in his opinion, "only a consequence of the idea of Religion." As a revolutionary Romantic, Mazzini then suggests that, since "we have no more a Heaven," it is man's, as well as the pope's, *duty* to realize the "idea" of heaven on earth. Only then can there be a truly human "Society" in which people love each other, since "Love" is "the soul of all religions." He thus declares that the pope's mission is twofold: "to be a believer, and to unify Italy." Mazzini ends his letter by affirming that a free and democratic Italy is "part of the design of Providence."[8]

The responses this letter provoked illustrate the complexity of the revolutionary movement in Italy, where most Italians wanted increased liberty, though in different degrees. Some, like the aristocratic Costanza, wanted merely a constitutional monarchy; others, like Mazzini, wanted a republic where "the people" would be in control of their government, while Fuller was among those who also wanted a radical change in basic social relations. In a 12 January letter in which she expresses her fear that Mazzini was behind attacks on Jesuits in Genoa, Costanza tells Fuller that she does not like Mazzini's "presumptuous" manner of addressing the pope: "Mazzini has the air of treating [Pius IX] as from power to power." Fuller replied: "What black and foolish calumnies are these on Mazzini!" Fuller felt "that he speaks as he should,—near God and beyond the tomb; not from power to power, but from soul to soul, without regard to temporal dignities."[9]

When she wrote Margaret on 12 January, Costanza confessed she did not know but had been told that her friend "had a lover in Rome, a member of the Civic Guard," a fact Mickiewicz later discreetly shared with her. Though at first, wrote Costanza, she had not "wanted to believe it," the socially prominent and poised Costanza had room in her heart for her intriguing friend. She felt differently, however, about the Princess Cristina Trivulzio Belgioioso. To Fuller the princess seemed a beautiful woman of noble birth but republican sympathies. She was the queen Fuller as a child had dreamed of being, and Fuller was soon to feel honored by being chosen by Belgioioso to serve as a nurse in the war. Like George Sand, Belgioioso was a scholar and political activist as well as the center of a brilliant salon in Paris, where she had lived in exile from 1830 to 1847. Also like Sand, Belgioioso had been influenced by Saint-Simon's thinking. Fuller would later note in a dispatch how on her estate near Milan, before the Austrians confiscated it in the 1820s, she had made some "experiments in the Socialist direction with fine judgment and success." Unlike Sand, however, Princess Belgioioso had a wraithlike beauty. Two years older than Fuller, her fair, oval face—with its sharply chiseled features and wide-set, dark expressive eyes—seemed untouched by age, just as her hair, which she wore pulled into a braided bun, was still rich and full and raven black. The princess was a powerful presence, and the minute they met in December in Rome Fuller fell under her spell.[10]

In a February 1848 letter to Richard, Fuller compares Sand unfavorably with Belgioioso, noting that though both women have no doubt "had several lovers," the "public life of the Princess has been truly energetic and beneficient." Though Fuller still likes, even loves, Sand, whose unorthodox relationship with the young Chopin surely encouraged hers with Ossoli, she no longer wishes "to know her more." Fuller lost respect for Sand when she learned that Sand thought women in general too mean spirited and treacherous to be trusted with the vote, and that only a total transformation of society would enable them to participate in politics. In contrast to such cynicism about women, the princess's politics and lifestyle pleased Fuller. At age sixteen Cristina had entered a marriage doomed by the hot temper of her husband, the twenty-four-year-old Principe Emilio Belgioioso, whom she soon left, even though as Roman Catholics they could not divorce. Exiled from Italy for her anti-Austrian activities, the princess entertained artists, musicians, and politicians—including Liszt, Balzac, Lafayette, and Heine—in her Paris salon, where it was rumored she also entertained her lovers. Her fierce independence as an intellectual, a radical, a feminist, and—though married—an aggressive lover of men, may have influenced Fuller's decision at this time not to marry Ossoli, whom she was fond of yet considered "unfit" to be her husband.[11]

Costanza in the meantime let Fuller know that she did not approve of the strong-willed, free-living Belgioioso, writing Fuller on 7 February: "I understand your attraction for Madame Belgioioso. She is a woman of superior intellect & who has the art to captivate, as you are—but morally she is of little worth."[12]

Whatever the reality of the Princess Belgioioso, she was useful at this point to Fuller as a positive model for her own rebellion, something she badly needed since she was having grave misgivings about her ability to handle her illegitimate pregnancy. Constant nausea and a Puritan conscience had intensified her anxiety. Then, too, the relentless rain still pounded the earth from a blank gray sky, whose lack of light seemed to mock Mazzini's Romantic dream of turning earth into heaven. Life for Fuller these rainy months was miserable. Even when the rain let up briefly, her nerves were aggravated by an organ-grinder playing "Home, Sweet Home" beneath her window. Meanwhile, in the cold, dark, damp apartment, the landlady's three small black dogs, fidgety at missing their daily walk, yapped at Fuller's friends. The grating noise of the organ-grinder, the toxic smell of a cheap cigar from a peddler who insisted she view his cameos, and the reeking odor of the "horrible cabbage, in which the Romans" so "delight," combined to give Fuller a three-month headache. She felt so unwell that after January she did not send out another dispatch until 29 March.[13]

58 ∽ Personal and Political Rebellions

"Pour, pour, pour again, dark as night," Fuller lamented near the end of her January 1848 dispatch. Bored with the rain, people came to her parlor to visit, such as Henry Hedge in early March. Hedge, who knew Fuller when she was spending hours dressing—even using a horsehair pad to minimize the disparity in shoulder heights—might have suddenly noticed the difference if, depressed and sick, Fuller was now forgoing efforts to look more attractive. Shocked at her appearance, he later said he thought she had developed a "spinal disease" that made her look "like a humpback." Both the pain in her spine and nausea brought on by her pregnancy (as well as by migraines, aggravated by the weather), contributed to her feeling of illness.[1]

A nineteenth-century American woman, even Fuller, would have been unlikely to have explained to a minister friend like Hedge the cause of her miserable condition, particularly since her pregnancy would hardly have been evident yet. As the two parted, Fuller uncharacteristically threw her arms about his neck and "burst into tears." Afterward Fuller sent him a note, attaching letters of introduction she had written for him. One was to the Princess Belgioioso. In her note to Hedge Fuller confesses that in her "sick moping moods" she fancies she will "never get back" to America; "it seems so far off; you must write a good verse to put on my tomb-stone."[2]

Another visitor was Mickiewicz, who had come to Rome in early February. He had taken rooms near hers and had been with her in mid-February during Carnival Week when, through torrential rain, they had watched a "tide of gay masks" parade down the Corso. Fuller noted that the servant girls, now dressed in white muslin and roses instead of drab winter woolen, seemed happy as they threw flowers at the carriages containing richly dressed dukes and princes with their consorts. In her shawl and boa Fuller shivered and inhaled the sepulchral air as she and Mickiewicz viewed the papal procession from her open window and applauded the bravado of the working girls, who seemed not to mind the drenching rain.[3]

Emerson meanwhile in London had been made uneasy by Fuller's account of her health in her December letter. Concerned, he wrote suggesting she meet him in Paris, return home with him, and rent a house near his in Concord. On 14 March Fuller replied that though she had hoped to return to Paris, she now did not feel well enough to do so. She noticeably did not mention either Ossoli or the cause of her ill health. When not busy with the civic guard, he apparently spent winter days moping about her flat because Fuller would not agree to marry him. She may have felt it pointless to do so until she knew that she and the baby would survive childbirth. Puerperal fever, after all, had killed Mary Wollstonecraft, whose out-of-wedlock sex with Gilbert Imlay Fuller in *Woman in the Nineteenth Century* had called "repulsive." Indeed, in the Benjamin Disraeli novel that Fuller liked—one involving a contested marriage in Venice between the Protestant Contarini Fleming and his Roman Catholic cousin Alceste Contarini—Alceste dies in giving birth to a stillborn son.[4]

Fuller also foresaw that marriage to Ossoli would create problems with Ossoli's family and with his inheritance. His papal functionary older brother, Giuseppe, who assumed the role of family patriarch after their father's February death, disapproved of Ossoli's republican sympathies yet would not have cut him out of the family unless he did something outrageous, like marry a Protestant radical republican. Since Fuller was also a friend of the despised Mazzini, a publicly known marriage for them, at this time, was unthinkable.[5]

There was apparently then no legal restriction in Italy preventing a Roman Catholic from marrying a non-Catholic. For such a marriage to occur, however, certain conditions had to be met: both parties had to be baptized (as were both Fuller and Ossoli), the priest had to be "convinced of the good faith of the request," and the couple had to promise to raise the child in the Roman Catholic Church. Fuller, who loathed Catholicism, would surely not have agreed to that last point; she also knew that, should the marriage prove impossible, her Roman Catholic husband would never agree to a divorce, nor could they seek one in Italy. With her own situation in mind, Fuller in February advised Richard, who had been thinking of leaving his uncle's law firm, not to take "rank" and "means" "lightly or rashly." Such aids to advancement "are not to be despised in this difficult world." In March she wrote him again: "I feel afraid you may sometime love in a quarter that will make you regret having made choice of this narrow path when it is too late to change."[6]

Certainly it was too late for Fuller to turn back on the labyrinthine path that had led her to the corner where she now felt "nailed."[7] She only knew that, at this time, she must not marry Ossoli. The price of his being disinherited and hence losing his claim to a share in the Ossoli property was too high. If Ossoli were cast out of his family, then their child could not claim financial backing from or legal connection to its uncles and cousins. Besides, as she began feeling better later in her pregnancy, Fuller knew that as a single professional woman she always had her writing to turn to, and the prospect of that was exciting.

For these were "stirring times," Fuller said in letters to friends. Not even "piping times" but "great times" when a "good loud swell of the trumpet" roused her each morning out of bed, along with the "rub a dub" of the drum as the men of Rome marched out into Lombardy. It seemed a glorious dawn to be alive, when war was everywhere and a brave new world seemed within the reach of Fuller and her European friends. Late in March as she sat down to write again for the *Tribune*, Fuller felt that the gods themselves walked on earth.[8]

Fuller's heart swelled with the rapidity and grandeur of the events taking place. In a 29 March letter to William Channing, Fuller confesses: "It is a time such as I always dreamed of, and for long secretly hoped to see." There had been the victorious rising of the Sicilian people at Palermo in January against Naples and its Bourbon king, followed by the revolution of Naples and the granting of constitutions by regional sovereigns all over Italy—from Ferdinand II in the south to Charles Albert in the north. Meanwhile, most Europeans had been caught off-guard when, on 22 February, a two-day revolution of French workers fighting alongside students and members of the bourgeoisie, in particular urban artisans, forced Louis-Philippe to flee. Two days later France had been proclaimed a republic and a provisional government had been set up headed by poet-statesman Alphonse de Lamartine. On the heel of this event, on 13 March, in Vienna, capital of the ancien régime, another insurrection had taken place, one that forced Prince Metternich into exile and the emperor to renounce his absolute power. Also, in Prussia, an uprising was reported to have begun against King Friedrich Wilhelm.[9]

Shortly after Fuller posted her 14 March letter to Emerson, Milan experienced one of the most remarkable instances of street fighting in European history. On the morning of March 18, the Milanese people, using barricades and homemade weapons to attack Radetzky's sixteen thousand soldiers, began a fight in the streets that drove the Austrians out of Milan. Five days later Radetzky's army retreated to the Quadrilateral, a section in the north made up of four fortified cities. Located between Lombardy and Venetia, the Quadrilateral provided a passageway through which Austria could pour arms and soldiers into Verona. While Radetzky was withdrawing his troops toward Verona, emboldened Venetians ejected the Austrians and declared St. Mark an independent republic, and the people of the duchies of Modena and Parma ousted their Austrian princes. By the end of March, most of northern Italy had declared its independence. Italian national unity and freedom now depended on the unstable Charles Albert of Piedmont, who had supported the people with his professional army but could not be trusted, and the pope, who, if only he would do as Mazzini advised, could use his power to unite Italy and drive the Austrians over the Alps.[10]

In Rome, Fuller and Mickiewicz delighted in seeing Italians celebrate the success of the revolutions in France and Austria as well as of Italian victories in Milan and Lombardy by setting the city ablaze at night with the twinkling lights of the thousand floating tapers they carried along the Corso. As Fuller watched rapturous men and women hugging, dancing, and casting wood into the great bonfire made from burning Austrian arms in the Piazza del Popolo, she felt certain that the march to liberty was unstoppable. But news from France was unsettling because the political struggle was being merged in the social. Despite this precipitous move toward social change, Fuller on 29 March declared that such insurrections of the people are good, no matter that blood is shed. For, as Fuller sees it, Europe's "tremendous problems MUST be solved," despite the pain the people suffer in making a just world happen. Sounding like Marx, whose *Communist Manifesto* had just been published in February, Fuller says she hopes Americans will "learn," before it is too late, "the needs of a true Democracy." She hopes they "may in time learn to reverence" and "guard, the true aristocracy of a nation . . . —the LABORING CLASSES."[11]

In this same March dispatch, Fuller describes the people's rapture as they pulled down the double-headed eagle of Austria from the portal of the Palazzo di Venezia and replaced it with the white-and-gold eagle of Italy, "inscribed with the name ALTA ITALIA." Delirious Italians fed the flames with yet more wood when they heard that Milan was fighting her tyrants, that the Venetians had driven out their Austrian overlords, and that even the people of Modena and Parma were freeing themselves from tyranny. In a jubilant letter to Channing wherein she says that her friends have reclaimed Milan, Fuller notes, "there may be need to spill much blood yet in Italy": "A glorious flame burns higher and higher in the heart of the nations." As if anticipating the millennium, she exclaims, "It is a time such as I always dreamed of, and for long secretly hoped to see." "Perhaps," she adds, "I shall be called to act."[12]

While depicting herself in public as a woman eager for action, Fuller in private confided to Mickiewicz her fears about her pregnancy. He consoled her and told her not to despair of her "very natural" condition. Besides, even if Americans now spurned her for her defiance of social convention in becoming illegitimately pregnant, Mickiewicz was sure that the world was on the verge of a great revolution that would inaugurate a new era in which people would break free from both political and social oppression.[13]

In this glorious spring when new life was blossoming on every bush and tree, Fuller, briefly, found it easy to believe Mickiewicz. On a 1 April visit by carriage to the sea—to Ostia, the ancient port of Rome, and then on south to the Castle Fusano, a villa surrounded by rolling dunes—her heart revived as she heard the birds singing and saw the green sod growing "over the graves of the mighty Past." As sea breezes burnt her face and the surf rushed in on the shore, Fuller felt "the sublime hopes of the Future, Nature, Man." More hope filled her heart when back in Rome she learned that Archduke Rainier, Habsburg viceroy of Lombardy and Venetia, had capitulated at Verona and that "Italy is free, independent, and One."[14]

Fuller feared this might be mere "April [First] foolery." It seemed "too speedy a realization of hope." Yet there was reason for such hope. On 7 April 1848, Mazzini arrived in northern Italy after a seventeen-year exile. He was greeted in Milan with bands and a popular demonstration. Shortly after Mazzini's arrival in Milan, Mickiewicz left Rome with the company of the Polish Legion. In mid-April he gave an electrifying speech in Florence. Despite the man's magnetism, neither Mazzini nor Fuller was convinced that the revolution could be carried off as speedily as the relentlessly romantic Mickiewicz wished. Mazzini was aware of the conflict within republican ranks, as well as of the persistent anger directed at him and his friends from Charles Albert, who loathed republicanism and believed monarchist or republican France to be as great an enemy to him as imperial Austria. Charles Albert had supported the people's revolution in Milan. But he had done so to achieve recognition as a leader in the Italian fight for independence and hence gain the backing of the patrician class. His long-range goal was not to help the liberals further their dream of unifying and freeing Italy but to annex Lombardy, with himself as king over the region and a governing body dominated by his most ardent supporters: a semifeudal aristocracy and reactionary clergy. While Charles Albert smiled and offered the republicans his support, he worked behind their backs to undermine their efforts. Several of Italy's most respected republican leaders later attributed the revolution's ultimate failure to King Charles Albert of Piedmont and his divisive drive to annex Lombardy.[15]

Meanwhile Fuller in dispatch 24 praised Mickiewicz's assertions in the address he gave in Florence that the "will of God is that the nations should act toward one another as neighbors," and that Tuscans and Poles are "One" in "Christian brotherhood." She heralded him and his Polish Legion as "pilgrims" willing "to defy the greatest powers of the earth." Still, she had doubts about the outcome of a republican revolution. She feared that even the Genoa-born Mazzini, who had been absent from Italy for so long and had never traveled in southern Italy, lacked practical knowledge of the people's real wants. In her April dispatch she praises Mazzini for having "a mind far in advance of his times" and of skillfully riding "the advancing wave of his day," while conveying her reservation. Mazzini, she observes, aims at political, not economic, emancipation. Fuller refers to events that "even now" in Europe "begin to work their way," momentous events she believes "Mazzini sees not." "Suffice it to say," she says, apparently unaware of the unnerving effect of her words on Americans, "I allude to that of which the cry of Communism, the systems of Fourier, &c. are but forerunners."[16]

Fuller here predicts the rise of communism in Europe, even as it was the soft-spoken Mazzini who saw beyond the immediate horizon to the powerful appeal in the future of democracy and the liberal republican principle to people everywhere in Europe. He also saw that for true internationalism to exist, people and nations with different ethnic and cultural identities must respect one another. Fuller nonetheless was prescient in foreseeing the imminent rise in her era of communism, of a totalitarian system that promises people economic stability and equality over liberty. Fuller herself, as we know, felt drawn to Fourierism and other utopian socialist schemes. She was intrigued by them to the extent that she omitted the word "liberty" in advocating at this time a vision of "true Democracy" that promised humanity, as she put it in her 29 March dispatch, "FRATERNITY, EQUALITY." She felt such schemes could put an end to the suffering of workers everywhere.[17]

Yet Fuller, who called herself a "Socialist," was not a Marxist socialist. Her view of reality and human progress was opposite that of Marx, who based his system on the tenet that matter, not spirit, is the driving force of life. Fuller as a Romantic thought that the Great Spirit spoke through her as she wrote and that this unseen "higher power" operates "in the seeming chaos of human history" to give order and moral meaning to an otherwise empty universe.[18]

Fuller's writings at this time reveal her now-familiar dual view of reality. As an American pragmatist she predicts that a republican form of government based on reason and logic and personal accountability for individual actions will eventually prevail in Europe. But as a revolutionary Romantic she continues to yearn in letters for a world purged of sin that will result from an apocalyptic confrontation between the forces of good and evil. In her vision, such a final confrontation will morally and socially transform the people of Europe, who will thereafter embrace as their way of life "voluntary association in small communities." This kind of "socialist" community had in fact been rejected by Marx in the *Manifesto* as bourgeois and insufficiently revolutionary. For it posited a right that Fuller, like the authors of the U.S. Declaration of Independence, saw as inalienable: the right of the human individual to choose whether or not to join such a socialist association. Thus while on one hand she believed that the Great Spirit was leading her and her friends to revolution and the creation of God's kingdom on earth, on the other hand she was fundamentally American in her insistence on the right of individuals to determine the path they take in life and on their need to accept responsibility for their actions. Before embarking on the *Elizabeth,* as we shall see, she will accept responsibility for the impulsive act she committed that will bring her, as she had predicted, "to a premature grave."[19]

✑ ✑ ✑

Fuller's American friends and readers had trouble seeing Fuller's Americanism because they increasingly linked her with the "red" republicans, the radical faction in France that wore red sashes and caps and that flew, instead of France's tricolor flag, a red flag as symbol of their support for violence and terrorism. Such red symbols were associated in the minds of people in England and the United

---

States with the blood that had flowed during the Reign of Terror. Elizabeth Barrett Browning would later speculate that Fuller's work on the revolution could not "have been otherwise than deeply coloured by those blood colours of Socialist views." Americans like Barrett Browning associated red flags with socialist radicals who advocated class struggle and worker domination of society through violence. Such a violence-based socialist vision contrasted sharply with the peaceful Christian Associationist vision advocated by, say, William Channing.[20]

That Fuller's friends in America were beginning to gossip and wonder why she was writing about the brotherly scope of socialism and advocating workers' rights in the *Tribune* is not surprising when her words are considered in the context of events unfolding abroad. The dispatch she wrote from 19 April to 13 May 1848, the one in which she predicts the rise of communism, did not appear in the *Tribune* until 15 June, just eight days before the outbreak of the Bloody June Days in Paris. Angry at France's newly elected government for having abolished the socialistically inspired national workshops that had promised jobs to all citizens willing to work but had turned out to be nothing but charities, fifty thousand workers rebelled. Three thousand insurgents were cut down, while twelve thousand more were arrested, tried, and imprisoned. Headlines appearing in U.S. newspapers were compiled from articles in conservative London papers as well as from France's newly elected conservative government. The latter had been voted into office on 23 April in accord with a plan of direct and universal suffrage proposed by the provisional French government. To the consternation of industrial workers, conservative peasants in the provinces had sided with the privileged classes and thus elected a government hostile to both the French and the Italian republicans.[21]

Liberal dreams seemed even less likely to be realized when Pius IX issued on 29 April an allocution disavowing the war in behalf of Italian liberty and rejecting Mazzini's proposal that, as an Italian prince, he let himself be named head of the republic. Fuller's fear that the pope lacked spine proved justified when Pius IX failed to contradict the influence of his corrupt counselors regarding an incident in Ferrara. After learning that Austrian soldiers stationed there had hung "as a brigand" a member of the Roman Civic Guard, the Roman people had gone to the pope to demand he stand decisively for the war. In response, Pius IX convened a consistory. He then shocked his followers by issuing a second allocution, this time disclaiming any part he had played in fanning the flames of rebellion, saying that he had "only intended local reforms" and regretted "the *mis*use that had been made of his name" toward encouraging them to fight the Austrians.[22]

Deeply distressed when Pius IX betrayed the people's trust in him, Fuller was forced to concede that the pope had set himself up as "the foe" of the people as well as of her own liberal dreams about human rights and equality between men and women. Without the pope's leadership, says Fuller, the "responsibility of events now lies wholly with the People and that wave of Thought which has begun to pervade them."[23]

Aware that Pius IX's "final dereliction" to "the cause of Freedom, Progress, and of War" has signaled the beginning of the end of any real hope for victory through revolution, a despairing Fuller will begin to affirm even more fervently that out of the chaos of the coming war a new man and woman will emerge on an earth that is a restored paradise. "All lies in the Future," she will write in her 7 May dispatch, "and our best hope must be that the Power which has begun so great a work will find due means" to bring "a year of true jubilee to Italy; a year . . . of recognized rights . . . founded not on compromise and the lying etiquettes of diplomacy, but on Truth and Justice."[24]

Fuller tells her *Tribune* readers that she intends to stay in Italy to celebrate this new year, despite pleas from family and friends that she return to America. For in Europe, "amid the teachings of adversity," Fuller sees "a nobler spirit . . . struggling," a spirit, she says, which is not "spoiled by prosperity" and "soiled" by slavery. In Europe she hears "earnest words of pure faith and love." She sees "deeds of brotherhood," as she does not in the United States where, at present, it seems to her that "the spirit of our fathers flames no more." Noting that there are events taking place in Europe at that very time that are "worth recording," Fuller says that she will "gladly be" their "historian." "Meanwhile," she adds, in the voice of a Romantic prophet-priestess, "the nightingales sing; every tree and plant is in flower, and the sun and moon shine as if Paradise were already reëstablished on earth."[25]

59 ∞ A Love Higher than Law or Passion

After sending off dispatch 24 in May 1848, Fuller prepared to leave for the Abruzzi Apennine mountains to wait out her pregnancy and write a history of the Italian revolution. Before leaving she wrote Emerson she was sorry that he would miss meeting Mazzini and Mickiewicz, though she doubted he would find "common ground" with either of them. On 19 May she wrote again. Responding to Emerson's late April letter from London telling her she is imprudent to stay in Rome "with so much debility & pain" and ordering her to "come to Paris, & go home with me," she lied only slightly. She said she "should like to return" with him but felt she had "much to do and learn in Europe yet": "I am deeply interested in this public drama, and wish to see it *played out*." She thinks she has her "*part* therein, either as actor or historian."[1]

Returning to America with Emerson was not an option. She had crossed what most Americans would see as the line between eccentric and errant behavior. In declining Emerson's invitation she hints there are reasons other than wanting to record history that she is not yet ready to head home. In her 19 May letter she tells him she wants "scenes of natural beauty, and, imperfect as love is, I want human beings to love," while in the earlier letter she says that she has heard his boy is fine, then adds: "Children, with all their faults, seem to me the best thing we have."[2]

In letters to other friends, however, Fuller made a point of evading what Costanza Arconati Visconti in April had referred to as the "mystery" of Fuller's increasingly elusive life. Fuller had not written her in two months, not even to acknowledge money Costanza had sent her. Caught in a net of lies because of her relationship with Ossoli, Margaret in a 20 May letter to Richard gives "the agitated state of Europe," along with limited finances and poor health, as her reasons for retiring to the mountains, where she hopes to find uninterrupted time to write. She also wrote Eliza Farrar's aunt Mary Rotch, strongly hinting she needs money. In her note Fuller tells Rotch that she is mistaken in her belief that Uncle Abraham has bequeathed her (Margaret) a sizable sum of money. On the contrary, she says, her "hard-hearted" Uncle Abraham, who in 1837 had refused Margarett Crane's request for funds for Ellen's education and "against [whose] rude tyranny" she (Margaret) "for eleven years" had "defended [her] mother," has left her no grand legacy. In fact, adds Fuller, "if his ghost knows any of my plans have been aided at all through him, it sighs at the thought."[3]

Fuller's long-simmering rage at tyrannical fathers blazed into the late May letter she wrote Costanza on the subject of Gioberti, whose vision of a confederated Italy challenged Mazzini's dream of Italian unity. In it Fuller calls Gioberti a man of straw, "whom the fire [of God's holocaust] already kindled will burn into a handful of ashes." To the moderate Costanza, who has pledged to remain a "faithful" friend even when "opinions do not agree," Fuller wrote, "Everything confirms me in my radicalism." Evoking a water metaphor, Fuller says she is glad "to see [war events] rush so like a torrent, . . . tending to realize my own hopes."[4]

Those hopes would come to nothing if she died in childbirth, which was apparently much in her thoughts. She sent gifts home by way of acquaintances: a cameo for Ellen, a coral cross for Greta, a mosaic for her mother. Moreover, before she left Rome she let Hicks paint her portrait. In it she is wrapped in a white shawl and sits before a Titian-like Venetian scene. Behind her on a pedestal is a statue of Eros, and to her right in the background can be seen the shadows of lovers, reminiscent of the shadowy shepherd lovers who can be seen embracing to the right in the background of Titian's *Sacred and Profane Love*. The setting strongly suggests that Hicks knew Fuller's secret, as does the fact that she entrusted him with a sealed box to give her mother should she die. In it were trinkets, a letter, and a lock of her hair. Attached to the box was a note instructing Hicks to tell those she left behind that she was willing to die, for she has suffered more in life than she has enjoyed: "I have wished to be natural and true, but the world was not in harmony with me— . . . I think the spirit that governs the Universe must have . . . for me a sphere where I can develope more freely, and be happier." After giving Hicks the box, Fuller packed a trunk with her clothes, a daguerreotype of Ossoli, and research materials for her book. On 29 May she set out with two servants and Ossoli—looking very much like a married couple and their household awaiting the birth of their first child—for Aquila, a mountain village about fifty miles northeast of Rome.[5]

⁂

During her mountain retreat—spent first in Aquila and then in nearby Rieti— Fuller felt anxious and alone. It was hard for Ossoli, a sergeant in the civic guard, to get away to visit. She depended on him to bring her letters as well as news of the war's progress, though what she heard made her still more anxious. Against Mazzini's advice, the provisional government of Milan wanted to forge an alliance with Piedmont and had thus in late May held a plebiscite that resulted in an overwhelming vote for fusion with the Kingdom of Piedmont-Sardinia. Though the move pleased Charles Albert, Fuller thought it unwise.

In letters to friends Fuller posits that she has isolated herself in order to write her book on the revolution. On 22 June she wrote Emelyn Story that it would take about "three months to write out what has passed . . . before my eyes for two years"—about the time that would elapse until the birth of her child with a few additional weeks for her to recover enough to travel. That same day she wrote a friend at Brook Farm confessing that at times she has "fits of deep longing to see persons and objects in America." She knows, however, that she has "no 'home'" in America to return to where she can "repose in the love" of her kindred free from "friction."[6]

In this letter Fuller says she likes being in a hill town full of churches with faded frescoes over the arched portals. The pictures in them, "not by great masters," are "sweetly domestic." One depicts "the Marriage of the Virgin," another "the Virgin offering the nipple to the child Jesus." Fuller notes how "his little hand is on her breast, but he only plays and turns away." Music and flowers fill these churches, "and the mountain breeze sweeps through them." In Aquila a woman cooks turnips for Fuller, scrubs her clothes on a rock in a stream, and murmurs so Fuller can hear, "'Povera, sola, soletta,' poor one, alone, all alone!"[7]

Her letters to Ossoli say little of the beauty of the countryside or her excitement about "wars and the rumors of wars" evident in letters to friends and family. Instead, to Ossoli she notes she feels "lonely" and "imprisoned." She complains of headaches, nosebleeds, and teeth that ache; her spirits are tried by this condition Italian women call "a martyrdom." To the gallant young man whom in late June she is still addressing in letters as "my friend," she says that if he fails to come see her on Saturday, she will die. She is so tired all the time that she cannot concentrate to work on her book manuscript. How much she would write, she laments in August, if only she had "force!" Fuller's ambition to write was thus undercut by the fatigue and anxiety of a pregnant woman nearing the age of forty.[8]

She is uneasy about the imminent establishment of the Kingdom of Northern Italy under the rule of the untrustworthy Charles Albert. She is even more anxious about the Neapolitan soldiers stationed in Aquila who are on their way home from Lombardy to Naples to help Ferdinand II, king of the Two Sicilies, a tyrant his people would soon nickname King Bomba for turning his cannon on his own people. In order to put down the insurgent liberal faction in his Kingdom of Naples, Ferdinand had unexpectedly called his troops home from the war in Lombardy against the Austrians, an act Fuller in December 1848 would call "the first great calamity of the war." In July on their way to Naples, Ferdinand's troops had arrested six liberals in Aquila. Fuller had real reason to feel scared.[9]

Desperately short of funds, Fuller appealed to Greeley for money. Though financially strapped himself (he had recently sold part of his interest in the *Tribune*), he sent money with a letter of credit, though to the wrong Paris bank. Alone in Aquila, Fuller was left to think that he had not sent it, and she began to lose trust in him. She had funds enough to get by, she wrote Richard from Rieti in mid-August, but not enough to get the research books she needed or to travel to Lake Facino and "the birth-place of Ovid." She complains bitterly in letters about Greeley's apparent refusal to further her plans by sending her the necessary money.[10]

Unaware of the mix-up, Greeley was baffled by Fuller's complaints but nonetheless sent her money, even though she had written him that she would not be sending another dispatch for an indefinite period of time, claiming illness as an excuse. Fuller dared not tell Greeley about her out-of-wedlock pregnancy. Despite the miscommunications, Fuller managed to make do on her scant funds and a hundred-dollar loan acquired for her by a bank employee in Rome on her "word merely," as she noted in a letter. Greeley, in turn, was understandably angry over her seeming ingratitude.[11]

∽ ∽ ∽

Fuller did not write another dispatch until two months after the birth of her son, Angelino (Nino) on 5 September 1848 in Rieti, where she moved to escape the Neapolitan soldiers. She loved the mountain-encircled town, whose ancient Umbrian dwellings bore timeworn red-brown tile roofs, and whose ripening vineyards were draped with amber and emerald grapes in late July when Fuller arrived there. Unlike the region near Aquila, where the scorching summer sun had left fields brown and dry and where the dust in the air made breathing difficult, the Rieti plain had rich soil and invigoratingly clean air. Abundant rain had turned the valleys of the Abruzzi Mountains yellow with saffron flowers; the fields seemed to be "carpets of grain," richly patterned with scattered cornflowers and red poppies.[12]

Fuller had moved into a private apartment on the second floor of a house on a quiet street. Her rooms opened onto a long wooden loggia, a covered porch that looked over the rapid river Velino. On nights she could not sleep, which were increasingly frequent, Fuller paced this porch, breathed in the mountain breezes, and was calmed by the steady rush of the stream and the chime of a bell from a convent of Cappucins high among the mountains. Fuller's upper-level apartment had three rooms: a small one for eating, a chamber for her servant, and her own "brick paved" room with drafty windows and "simplest finish and furniture." For only pennies a day she had plenty of fresh fruit and salad, as well as help from the two servants who had come with her from Rome, Maria Bonani and Giuditta Bonani. Giuditta, who had the room in Fuller's apartment, cooked, sewed, and ironed for her. All this made life in Rieti pleasant. Not to mention it was closer than Aquila to Rome and hence to the action and also Ossoli, whose stagecoach she could watch from her loggia as its horses trod the Via Salaria and crossed the ancient Roman bridge over the river.[13]

In Rieti Fuller came to distrust the family of her landlord—Giovanni Rossetti—and the local people, even as she grew in self-understanding. In Aquila she had begun to see the insufficiency of her earlier mystical rebirth. In July she had written Emerson, who had been in Europe when the February 1848 revolution in Paris broke out but was now home in Concord: "Some years ago, I thought you very unjust, because you did not lend full faith to my spiritual experiences; but I see you were quite right." At the time it seemed she "had tasted of the true elixir." She sees now, however, that there was "too much taint of weakness and folly" in those seeming "glorious hours," "so that baptism did not suffice." She makes "acquaintance" now with mountain peasants, whom she thinks ignorant yet blessed with simple luxury for little money. In their eyes, she tells Emerson, she seems an "instructive Ceres" come to tell them "tales of foreign customs." Subtly alluding to Emerson's view that the bread and wine of communion should be "freely dealt to all creatures," Fuller affirms that it would "suffice" her to eat "bread and grapes among them."[14]

Alone in Aquila she had grown reliant on Ossoli not just for news of the revolution but for emotional support as well. His letters say little about himself but are full of encouragement for Fuller. He tells her not to be sparing in giving "exact accounts of yourself." He writes that he looks forward to the time "I [can] come to thy arms." Ossoli's consistent solicitous concern, what Fuller felt she had missed as a child, tapped into a reservoir of trust that had been instilled in her by her mother at a time before Margaret could remember, before Margarett Crane, depressed over Julia Adelaide's death, had become withdrawn. Added to that, Ossoli's looks and gentle demeanor reminded her of her beloved Eugene. Hence the tone and content of Fuller's letters to Ossoli were to change over time from shrill complaints about her suffering into tender expressions of respect and regard for a man she loves more each day. No longer does she address Ossoli merely as "my friend." Instead, as in her letter of 13 August from Rieti, she tells how his visit has calmed her and how grateful she is that "at least we have had some peaceful hours together." She ends her note with, "Goodbye my love, I always embrace you and pray for your well-being."[15]

And as Fuller's love for Ossoli deepened, she longed to have him nearby, especially when news about the war's progress upset her. In mid-July the Austrians had crossed the Po River separating Lombardy from the Papal States, after which they pressed into service the people of Ferrara to resupply their troops. King Charles Albert of Piedmont-Sardinia, who in the spring had led his troops into Lombardy and pursued the Austrians all the way to Verona, in late July retreated to Milan. There he suddenly surrendered the city to Field Marshall Radetzky on 5 August, thus negating the March victory of the people, their famous "five days" of fierce street fighting. In a last attempt to deter the Austrians before Charles Albert retreated with his troops, effectively ending Piedmont's war with Austria, a Piedmontian ambassador at Paris appealed to the French to send sixty thousand troops to support their war, but to no avail. Instead, all of Lombardy was quickly occupied by Austrian soldiers.[16]

To complicate matters, just three days after Charles Albert's retreat, a detachment from Radetzky's army attacked Bologna, which was within the papal domains. But Bolognans, who hated Austrians even more than they hated the pope, drove the Austrians away in a hard-fought victory that temporarily boosted Italians' spirits. When news of Bologna's victory reached Rome on 11 August, a call went out for volunteers to join Rome's civilian army. There was talk of Pius IX encouraging the civic guard to defend the city. Instead, when he appeared before the civic guard, which had been called to Monte Cavallo, they "got only," wrote Fuller, "benediction."[17]

Everywhere in Italy lay reasons for Fuller to be concerned: She was distressed over both Charles Albert's failure of will and the Austrian occupation of Lombardy; fearful for friends in Milan; and depressed because fighting in Bologna and Milan meant Ossoli might soon have to fight for his people. She had mixed feelings about his eagerness to leave her so near her due date. Because their letters were crossing, she sometimes reacted to dated information. Unaware the pope had not called up the civic guard, as expected, to defend "his state," Fuller wrote Ossoli on 13 August to say that if he felt it necessary for his honor to fight, then she would "try to be strong." Still, she was glad when she learned that Pius IX had not asked the civic guard to fight. But "ah!" she says, "how contemptible is the pope" for *not* having done so. As for the betraying Charles Albert, a furious Fuller will write in her 19 January 1849 dispatch: "Had the people slain him in their rage, he well deserved it at their hands." About such duplicitous father figures as Charles Albert and Pius IX, she confides to Ossoli: "they will be cursed for all ages to come."[18]

The pope's failure to call up the civic guard did not deter Ossoli's ambition to sign up with the volunteer civilian unit preparing to fight for Italian liberty. In a letter she received 17 or 18 August, Ossoli tells Fuller he is suffering continual "inner struggle": he wants so much to fight for his country and also leave Rome, where he hates living among his "hated brothers." But he feels he "cannot go so far from you, my dear love."[19]

In reply Fuller wrote that it is a bad time for him to enter the volunteer army. In his work as an agent for family properties he has a steady income, something the two badly need. If France and England do not intervene, and if the war does not continue, then, she wrote him, "you leave Rome and the employment with your uncle for nothing." She tells him to wait three weeks before entering active service. Then both the public situation and her private one—whether she and the baby survive childbirth—"also will be decided." As for now, she advises him not even to ask his uncle for a day off from work, since doing so would arouse suspicion.[20]

In these letters to Ossoli before the baby's birth, a bossy Fuller tells her patriot lover how she thinks he should direct his life, while betraying an uncertainty that her young lover might not, after all, do her bidding. A softness hence enters her plea, a gently hinted wish that Ossoli might be with her mornings in Rieti to drink coffee and read news of the war in the Roman papers, the *Epoca* and Mazzini's *Italia del Popolo*. Though daily she trusts him more, Fuller's unstated fear that Ossoli might yet betray her or leave her, as others she has loved have done, resonate in these appeals. On Tuesday, 22 August, she wrote him, "when I think that it is possible for me to die alone without touching a dear hand, I prefer to wait" for "this ordeal" to pass. To wait, that is, until Ossoli can be with her as she gives birth and, perhaps, dies. But Fuller's doubts, fortunately, this time were unfounded. At about the same time she was penning this mournful missive to Ossoli, his own crisis of conscience had passed, for on Friday, 25 August, he posted an urgent note to her, saying, "Dear—Tomorrow I leave Rome, and I hope to have you in my arms Sunday. . . . Addio until then."[21]

A change came over Fuller when she received this missive the following day; something in her said that this was a man she could rely on, someone she might even trust enough to marry. In response to a note he wrote her on Wednesday, 23 August, she wrote: "I will wait for you on Sunday morning and again I will have your coffee ready." "Near here there is a beautiful place where we can go together if I am able to go out when you come." Ossoli is indeed there that Sunday, and he is in Rieti on 5 September for the birth of their son, though shortly after he had to return to Rome. In her 7 September letter to Ossoli, back in Rome, Fuller for the first time refers to him as "Consorte" (husband). At least that is the word that the landlord Giovanni Rossetti—to whom Fuller dictated letters of 7 and 10 September to Ossoli because she was too weak to read or write after the birth—used in the salutation of these letters addressed to Ossoli. It is possible that the landlord used the word "Consorte" sardonically: indeed, a cryptic remark in a 4 June 1849 note from Fuller to Ossoli suggests that that might be the case. In the 4 June note, Fuller bitterly recollects how "that wicked Ser. Giovanni always wrote" (presumably in the salutation of the notes he transcribed for her) "dear *Consorte*" (emphasis hers), apparently meaning to insinuate he thought either that the two were not legally married or that it had been a shotgun marriage. If Giovanni Rossetti meant the latter, then we can speculate on when and where in Rieti Fuller and Ossoli exchanged private vows or were married by a local priest prior to the baby's baptism, as Joan von Mehren believes they were. If Giovanni thought the former, then we might surmise that the couple simply felt that—recognized or not by church or state—they were indeed married. Despite the excellent detective work done by von Mehren in her attempt to answer the questions surrounding the legality of Fuller's "marriage," the fact remains that Fuller herself never clarified the point in any extant letter or other writing.[22]

Perhaps as von Mehren speculates the lovers did officially marry sometime around Angelino's birth and just pretended to their landlord prior to that time—perhaps in order to rent the apartment—that they were already married. From a letter Ossoli wrote Fuller in early October concerning Angelino's baptism, it is clear that it was important to them that their landlord—Giovanni Rossetti was also the bishop's chancellor—thinks they are married, even if it was merely a shotgun marriage. In this letter Ossoli says: "Ser Giovanni told me that while he was in Rome he could arrange for a *procura* [similar to a power-of-attorney] to baptize the baby by a person of my choice." Ossoli adds: "Use caution—don't tell him what I have written because he might get to know our situation too clearly." In short, Ossoli, who is aware that the landlord has read his letters and hence called Fuller "wife" in the salutation of his 8 September letter, does not want Giovanni Rossetti to know his and Fuller's "situation," which may be that they recently married or have not yet officially married. Perhaps they feared that if Rossetti knew for certain the real situation, then he would realize that the baby had been conceived "in sin," out of wedlock. If he were then to gossip, the news might reach Ossoli's brothers, a situation Ossoli and Fuller dreaded.[23]

Whatever the reason, Fuller and Ossoli address each other as "husband" and "wife" in the salutations of the aforementioned letters. Fuller says nothing political in them, and she pointedly speaks graciously about her landlord and his family. Ossoli, in turn, asks her to let him know when she can read again, "which I hope will be soon." It is revealing that a note of 9 September in her own hand is addressed not to "Dearest Husband" but to "Mio bene" [My love]). When she was strong enough to resume reading and writing on her own, both she and Ossoli in their letters' salutations use terms of endearment such as "Mia Cara" / "Mio caro" [My dear], or "Mio amore" [My love].[24] One could speculate, however, that Fuller and Ossoli did not use terms of endearment simply as a matter of decorum out of respect for Rossetti as an older male and as an official in the church.

Indeed many have considered the question of their marriage. Although von Mehren speculates that the Rieti priest who baptized Nino, Father Giovanni Battista Trinchi, might have performed the ceremony, when friends back home heard about her relationship with Ossoli, they speculated that she had, in the words of one friend, "connected herself with a young man" in a "Fourierist or Socialist marriage, without the external ceremony." That friends would assume that Ossoli and Fuller had joined in such a union prior to the baby's birth is not unexpected. Such a union seems plausible in light of the abundant evidence suggesting the powerful impact on Fuller of Fourier's views of marriage. Sarah Clarke, when told of Fuller's "connection," even wrote Fuller that she thinks her friend is "more afraid of being thought to have submitted to the ceremony of marriage than to have omitted it." After her death, Fuller's friend William Channing contended she never married, arguing "that a legal tie was contrary to her view of a noble life." Emerson, however, countered that Fuller would have married, since, "against the theorist was a vast public opinion, too vast to brave."[25]

Perhaps Emerson was right. We recall how sensitive Fuller finally was to the way people in New York would view her if she appeared publicly with a woman "upon whom public odium had been thrown," the kind of sexually "injured woman" Nathan was supposedly helping. To avoid public censure, Fuller had chosen "another escort." Moreover, Fuller might well have eventually united with Ossoli in a church-sanctioned marriage, if only out of respect for her mother. To support her view that the two were married prior to Nino's 6 November 1849 baptism, von Mehren refers to an 1833 journal entry in which Fuller wrote that, having read Benjamin Disraeli's novel *Contarini Fleming* (1832), she identified with the novel's fanatically ambitious Protestant hero, who impetuously married his Catholic cousin, Alcesté Contarini, in Venice.[26]

Von Mehren has a point, for we have seen how closely Fuller identified as a child and young adult with the heroes and heroines of the many books she read. Yet even if before the baby's birth Fuller and Ossoli had not exchanged traditional vows, this does not mean that Fuller did not already feel married to Ossoli. After all, that was the way it was done in the literature Fuller most loved. We recall that the Carthaginian queen Dido had called her union with Aeneas "marriage" and given herself and her kingdom wholly to him, though Aeneas did not accept as legitimate his mountain-cave "marriage." Moreover, in Southeby's *Oberon*, the fairy tale Fuller read as a child, Huon and Rezia had likewise called each other husband and wife before a priest had blessed their union. Friends in America had done the same; Sophia Peabody and Nathaniel Hawthorne had addressed each other as "husband" and "wife" months before their marriage.[27]

In the letter Fuller wrote Cary in March 1849 revealing the "secret" of her baby to Cary, Margaret evades the subject of her and Ossoli participating in a marriage ceremony. Instead she wrote about how the ancient Umbrians were married in Rieti. "In presence of friends," she says, "the man and maid received together the gifts of *fire and water*. The bridegroom then conducted to his house the bride. At the door he gave her the keys and entering threw behind him nuts as a sign that he renounced all the frivolities of boyhood." Of course, witnesses ("friends") to attend such a ceremony for Fuller and Ossoli would have been hard to find. There were the servants, Giuditta and Maria. There was also a midwife, as well as the doctor, Camillo Mogliani, whom Fuller felt at first she could trust. That would have been enough people to participate in such a ceremony. Buttressing this theory is the fact that, as von Mehren could have predicted, in Disraeli's *Contarini Fleming* where a Catholic and Protestant marry hastily in Italy "by the forms of the Catholic church," "two servants were the only witnesses."[28]

Whatever the way—whether pagan ceremony, Fourierist union, or sacred marriage by a priest—Fuller felt she was not lying when she professed later that she was married. She will later say as much in a letter to Emelyn Story in which she asks the latter to disregard the unkind things being said about her and Ossoli. She tells Emelyn she feels certain that Emelyn's "affection" for her will prompt her friend to say to the gossips that she is "confident [that] whatever I have done has been in a good spirit and not contrary to *my* ideas of right." Hawthorne, as noted may have thought of Fuller and her "ideas of right" when he wrote *The Scarlet Letter* (1850), saying of Hester, perhaps with Fuller in mind: "The world's law was no law for her mind."[29]

Fuller's life was shaped to a great extent by books she had read when she was young, like the *Aeneid* and the Bible. The actions of characters in Disraeli's *Contarini Fleming* or in Sotheby's *Oberon* might have influenced her behavior in Italy. In *Oberon,* we recall, the pagan Rezia and Christian Huon tend to their out-of-wedlock baby, Huonet (the diminutive of Huon, as Angelino is of Angelo) on an isolated island, where they come to appreciate a higher love than passion.[30]

We have already seen how the pattern of Fuller's life is like that of the lovers in *Oberon.* Both feature a dictatorial father, forbidden sex, escape to isolation in nature, and emotional growth through pain and deprivation along with a claim to marital status in the absence of an official ritual, followed by the birth of an illegitimate infant. The story underlying the journey motif of *Oberon* is the biblical parable of the prodigal son, but Fuller's story does not end happily, as do those of Huon and the prodigal son. Instead her story will end more like that of Xenophon's Panthea, who chooses suicide rather than live her life without her beloved warrior husband, who because of her urging has gone into battle, where he dies.[31]

As some claim, the editors of Fuller's *Memoirs* imposed on Fuller's papers and letters the pattern of ancient tragedy with "the barely hidden moral that her fate was the price" she paid for defying social convention. Yet by self-consciously patterning her life after the lives of tragic heroes and heroines she admired, especially Iphigenia and Antigone—whom she calls "my sisters" in *Woman in the Nineteenth Century*—Fuller had made that easy for them to do. In that sense, Fuller was the ingenious creator of the tragic drama of her life.[32] Perhaps Fuller's lasting literary masterpiece is her extraordinary life story.

Instead of the Romantic revolutionary persona Fuller self-consciously presented to *Tribune* readers, a selfless heroine that represents a merging of the personal and political emerges in the letters she wrote to family members and friends both during and after the Roman revolution.[33] This enduring figure is also evident in the written remarks of those in Europe who had come to know and love her. In these letters and observations we see the physically plain Margaret Fuller metamorphose into the beautiful queen she, as a small child, had imagined herself to be.

PART EIGHT

Apocalyptic Dreams
and the Fall of Rome

The conflicting sides of Fuller's personality—the millennial-minded mystic and the pragmatic pilgrim set on soul- or self-possession—persisted in her as the situation in Rome grew increasingly tense. Confronted with the reality of revolution, she was divided between her need as an individual to act as an independent center of power and her yearning to be totally absorbed within an all-consuming "Dionysian power of fluidity."[1]

This division is particularly apparent in the contrast between the apocalypse-tinged vision she sent home from Rome in her letters to the *Tribune* as the Italian Republic was collapsing around her, and the realistic news she shared with family members and friends in private letters wherein she told not only about the Roman Republicans' fight for freedom but also, finally, about Ossoli and the baby. As we follow Fuller on the path she traveled during these last difficult months of her life, we will see how writing her passionate *Tribune* dispatches becomes for her a form of action, an aggressive weapon into which she will pour her soul and with which she will attack Europe's tyrant-fathers. If the Romantic writer's aim is to defeat death by the power of the poetic imagination, then Fuller in these dispatches succeeded.[2]

Scholars have acknowledged the power of Fuller's dispatches about the revolution in which she rages against the patriarchal powers of emperor, king, and pope and articulates her radical desire to turn earth into Eden through violent revolution. Yet the less-noticed private letters she sent to family and friends in Europe and America reveal a down-to-earth, loving Margaret Fuller. In these letters we see Margaret the woman dealing with the conflicting demands of child and career. We see how the demands of the love that offered her hope and happiness amid war's death and destruction contributed to a drain on her energies already overtaxed by her prolific writing about the revolution as well as by her work as a nurse to the war's wounded. The private letters also show how, after Rome's defeat, Fuller maintained her courage and sense of balance by grasping one last illusion: that in New England she might yet live harmoniously with her family and friends in a small, Fourierist community. These last "romantic chapters" in Fuller's life story come to their dramatic end, as we shall see, with her ill-fated attempt to return to the States, in particular to her mother, as Romantic pilgrims often attempt to return home and to reconcile, not with the father, against whom they have rebelled, but with the mother, for whose love, throughout life, they have yearned.[3]

60 ∞ Harsh Reality and Apocalyptic Dreams

Alone with a baby in Rieti, Fuller found that reality fast dispelled any romantic notion of the bountifulness of the female breast: because of milk fever she was unable to breastfeed her son and had to engage a wet nurse. She dismissed Giuditta, who could not breastfeed. And Chiara Fiordiponte, whom she hired to replace her, soon left when her own baby became ill. Even after Chiara's return, Fuller still fretted about having been left alone and ignorant with a baby the first days of his life. Had she been in Boston and properly married, she would have been surrounded with women friends and kin who would have taught her how to handle a newborn baby. They would have relieved her when they found she was unable to supply her baby with milk, as Sophia Hawthorne had breastfed Greta when Ellen's milk proved insufficient.[1]

Also soon dispelled was her romanticized notion of the natural goodness of "simple" mountain folk. Now the "lower" people of Rieti seemed to her, she wrote Ossoli in October, "the worst people" she had "ever seen." She compares interacting with Giuditta and her brother Nicomedi to dealing with "a den of foxes." She complains that her privacy is constantly invaded by Giovanni's "detestable" and meddling sisters. As for the bishop's chancellor, her landlord Giovanni Rossetti, Fuller is convinced he is attempting to sexually "*corrupt Chiara*," Nino's pretty wet nurse. But then Chiara, who had seemed at first "so lovely and innocent," turned out to be no saint, either: Fuller will later accuse her of stealing money and giving Nino red wine, reserving her milk for her own baby. In a letter to a friend she will complain that Chiara had "betrayed" Nino "for the sake of a few scudi."[2]

With no reliable wet nurse and unable to breastfeed Nino herself, Fuller found that he screamed constantly. Even with servants to cook, iron, and sew, during the day she was too tired and distracted to work on her book. At the time there was also a smallpox epidemic in the region. In late October Fuller had taken Nino for a stroll to the bishop's garden, thinking it a safe place, only to learn that the week before, she wrote Ossoli, "a child died there from small pox." After that she dared not leave her rooms until the doctor, Camillo Mogliani, came with the necessary vaccine to inoculate Nino. Confined to her apartment and Nino, Fuller felt "like a prisoner." She wrote Ossoli on 20 October that she could not sleep at night and cried all day. But he could not help; he was "too far away." When the overworked Mogliani did not arrive when he said he would to vaccinate Nino, Fuller began to think him as "detestable" and "untrustworthy" as Giovanni, Giuditta, and all the other people of Rieti. On 28 October she wrote Ossoli that if she does not continue "spying on all these people, they will take advantage of me." She was "beginning not to trust anybody." Fuller feels she is being "abused by everybody."[3]

Having idealized for so long the Virgin Mary and Baby Jesus, Fuller was shocked to find mothering so difficult. Still, Nino seemed so happy when he finally fell asleep on her breast that she felt "no one else can take care of him as well as I." Yet she also knew that to resume her career as a journalist, she had to return to Rome. Ossoli, who had only the money he earned from his uncle, was always short of cash. Fearing his conservative brothers might disinherit him were they to learn that he had fathered an illegitimate child with a liberal Protestant American, Ossoli had outright rejected Fuller's idea that they hire a nurse for Nino in Rome. For the sake of "secrecy," he said, she must leave the baby with someone in Rieti when she returned to work in Rome.[4]

Fuller felt divided. Early in October she confessed in a note to Ossoli that she was "tired of taking care of [Nino]." She yearned to be near the action in Rome. She also wanted to be near Ossoli, just as she wished, as well, "to be free to come back here" quickly should she feel "too anxious . . . about [Nino]." "Oh dear," she had written Ossoli, "how hard life is!"[5]

In late October when Fuller's departure was delayed by Mogliani's continuing inability to locate smallpox serum to inoculate Nino, she wrote Ossoli of her conflicted feelings: "On the one hand I am happy to spend another week with my baby. He becomes more interesting every day. On the other hand I feel the need to spend some time with you and to go once again into the world from which I have been apart now for 5 months." Just as she was hoping to reestablish her career as a newspaper columnist, Fuller was experiencing the guilt that inevitably accompanies a woman's attempt to be both a good mother and an able career woman. She was beginning to feel less like the bold Romantic persona she presented to her New York readers than an ordinary working mother. Words Fuller later wrote about her predicament express the sentiment of every hard-working mother: "God be merciful to me a sinner comes so naturally to the mother's heart."[6]

It seemed with a child there were always pressing problems. Ossoli came up with solutions to two of them. He located the smallpox vaccine, which by 29 October had been administered. Next was the problem of having the baby baptized as a Roman Catholic. Tantamount to a birth certificate, a certificate of baptism was essential in Italy at the time. Without it the child would be considered stateless or, worse, nonexistent. With it he would inherit the Ossoli name and thereby remain legally connected to the noble Ossoli family. In order to have Nino baptized and thus insure his claim to such property as his father might be heir to, it was now in Fuller's interest to be legally married to Ossoli. That the obligatory note "Non Legittimo" does not appear on the baptismal record—which does have on it the word "coniugi" (married) in front of Ossoli's name—does suggest, as von Mehren argues, that "a secret marriage" might have taken place shortly before Nino was baptized on 6 November. To have Nino baptized without his brothers knowing, Ossoli had himself named as proxy to baptize his own child, and his nephew Pietro Ossoli served as the baptism's authorizing agent and godfather.[7]

Before, however, they were able to celebrate Nino's baptism, in late October the autumn rains began to fall. Though the days were still glorious, nights in Rieti brought "rain, always rain," wrote Fuller on 1 November. She worried now how her baby would fare in her absence, and how he would stay warm in her breezy apartment since her room had neither a fireplace nor a rug on its brick floor. She began to ponder where she could move him to ensure he would stay warm and dry. As Fuller fretted, Chiara's baby fell ill, and Fuller had to tend to Nino again on her own. Refusing her breast, Nino cried in the night. Weather permitting, she would walk on the loggia above the river, her son in her arms. It was peaceful those autumn nights when, just before a storm, lightning illuminated the river that gnawed at the bank below.[8]

Constant rain, however, made her head hurt, as did troubling news about the war. Fuller's hope for the success of the republican cause had made her months of mountain seclusion bearable. She was already angry over Charles Albert's surrender of Milan and thus Lombardy in August to the Austrians when she heard that, during the week of Nino's birth, Ferdinand II had his troops attack his own people, "subjects he had deluded," as an irate Fuller would note in her first of two 2 December 1848 dispatches, "by his pretended gift of the Constitution."[9]

As war's reality—a ruthless king's massacre of his own people and a derelict pope's betrayal of the "liberal party"—became daily more apparent to Fuller, her dispatches and her letters home became increasingly biblical in their urgency. Having left Nino in Rieti with Chiara, who took Nino with her to stay with her and her extended family, Fuller in November will write a friend from Rome: "It is a time such as I always dreamed of; and that fire burns in the hearts of men around me which can keep me warm." Yet she concedes that her "private fortunes are dark and tangled;" her "strength to govern them . . . much diminished." Perhaps, she says, "[God] will make my temporal state very tragical." Even if "he" does, Fuller believes God has given her a mission: "to cheer on the warriors, and after write the history of their deeds." The first she has done. She feels "blest" in having the capacity to write words that impel others to action.[10]

This same revelatory tone is evident in a letter she was to write her mother from Rome later that fall, on 16 November 1848.[11] Still saying nothing about Ossoli or her baby, she instead early in the letter describes her room. Located high up in a house on a corner near the Quirinal, it has a view on one side to the pope's palace and gardens, on the other to the Piazza Barberini. Unlike her dark apartment on the Corso, this large room floods with sunshine daily. Also, unlike in Rieti where only the kitchen had a fireplace, here she has an "excellent chimney" kept lit by her delightful old landlady, Antonia, or by a priest who lives in the attic. Antonia grows flowers on her balcony and keeps Fuller's room filled with fresh-cut flowers in a way, writes Fuller, that reminds her of her mother.

In this loving yet apocalyptic letter, Fuller paints a graphic picture of the assassination of Count Pellegrino Rossi, a moderate nationalist whom Pius had appointed prime minister of the Papal States on 16 September. Opposed to the republican cause, Rossi was hated by the Italian people for his opposition to a proposed plan to draw up a constituent assembly from all parts of Italy. "Yesterday," says Fuller, as Rossi exited his carriage to enter the Chamber of Deputies, the crowd jostled him, and "a sure hand stabbed him in the back." The silence that purportedly followed suggested to Fuller that those present approved the death. As a Romantic radical glad at the death of a tyrant, she says: "I never thought to have heard of a violent death with satisfaction, but this act affected me as one of terrible justice." She repeats a line from a song she heard sung by people as they passed that night on the street: "Happy the hand which rids the world of a tyrant!"

Fuller then tells her mother of that morning's events when a crowd of ten thousand marched along with Rossi's once-loyal troops to the Quirinal Palace to demand that the pope form a constituent assembly and relinquish temporal power. They found instead the Swiss Guard ready to defend him. When angry demonstrators attempted to storm the palace door, nervous members of the Swiss Guard fired into the crowd. Viewing events from a safe distance, Fuller saw a wounded man borne by and heard the drum call out the National Guard. Later that afternoon, snipers fired into the pope's antechamber, killing Monsignor Palma, a bishop serving as papal secretary.

Into this November 1848 letter to her mother Fuller—who in March will confess to Channing that she lacks "faith in the paternal love, I need" and in an earlier dispatch had railed against the "bloody tyranny" of "trampling emperors and kings"—now poured her rage not only at the pope, whose betrayal made the people feel they had "lost their father," but at all the tyrannical fathers whom she felt had done violence to the poor and vulnerable, especially to women. In a dispatch she will write just two weeks after she wrote this long November letter to her mother, she notes how she feels such violence is being done now to women in Italy—and even in "privileged America"—where "mothers and wives" are unable to protect themselves from abusive "sons and husbands" because of a social system that deems them second-class citizens and uses intimidation and deception to conceal the "giant wrongs" done to women by men who beat them at night for "diversion after drinking." It almost seems she thinks that, by identifying with the radicals who have struck out at the "deceptive" patriarchal powers—the traitorous pope, invading emperors, and false and cowardly kings—she can free herself from pain and regain control of her life, in particular, her soul. Moreover, when she says she is now certain that her mother "will always love" her, it is as if she believes that with this show of defiance against these abusive "old powers" that she will at last be worthy of her mother's love. Indeed, as a mother herself now, she concedes to her mother that she once "dreamed of doing and being much, but now am content with the Magdalen to rest my plea hereon, '*She has loved much.*'" In the letter, which shows a new appreciation of her mother, Fuller evokes the image of the end of time and tyranny as depicted in Revelation when she excitedly says, it is near "the hour" when the pope is to be "stripped of his temporal power," the republic proclaimed, Mazzini returned to Rome, and the people freed at last "to act."

In this same 16 November epistle, Fuller tells of her "strange escape" from being carried away by the rain-swollen Tiber. Fuller had decided at the last minute not to take the early-morning coach from Rieti to Rome. She later learned that it "had been seized by a torrent; the horses up to their necks in water": "The door of the diligence could not be opened, and the passengers forced themselves, one after another [through the windows], into the cold water,—dark too." "Though all escaped with life[,]" says Fuller fatalistically, "had I been there I had fared ill."

Two days later two more coaches arrived to take Fuller and the other stranded travelers to Rome along a route where the ravines and mountains were shrouded in snow. The going was rough, and the conductor, in attempting to urge his team along the snow-crusted road, hurt his leg under a wheel, leaving Fuller to sympathize with the pain of his suffering and to hear his curses—"Blood of Jesus," "Souls of Purgatory"—pierce the icy air. When they learned that the inn along the route was full, the travelers kept on through the night rather than risk stopping alongside the road to sleep. The full moon was half-draped in a mist that drew over her face a thin white veil. As the coaches neared the Tiber, "the towers and domes of Rome" could be seen "like a cloud lying low on the horizon" above "a sheet of silver," like the "sea of glass" of Revelation, the book of the Bible to which Fuller alludes in her letter. And as the "noble horses" plowed knee-deep through the Tiber's overflowing waters, she and her fellow travelers were indeed like pilgrims making their way into the kingdom of God as envisioned in Revelation. It was a moving and beautiful scene, Fuller wrote her mother.

Despite the dangers around her, Fuller tells her mother she has no plan to come home. Ever since as a child she had read the *Aeneid,* she had sought for signs in the heavens of her chosen status. Her miss with death on the road must have seemed a sign to her that God meant to spare her, as God had spared the woman described in Revelation who had borne a male child and had escaped the flood after being given the wings of an eagle with which she flew away. Fuller felt God meant her to stay in Europe to fulfill her destined mission. Were she to return at this moment, "I should feel as if forced to leave my own house, my own people, and the hour which

---

I had always longed for." She closes her letter by asking her mother not to "feel anxious about" her: "Some higher power leads me through strange, dark, thorny paths . . . . If God disposes for us, it is not for nothing."

In accord with the "romantic" story she sees her life to be, Fuller here records her confidence that she is an integral part of a divine plan that will culminate in a cataclysmic war that will once and forever transform reality into a paradise wherein there will be no more death, nor pain, nor sorrow.

Thus even if Rome should fall in her fight for freedom, Fuller sees the struggle as "paving" the way for the "final triumph" on earth of biblical prophecy, of the realization of a dream of a genuine democracy in which all people have a right to liberty and dignity, that is, to possess their souls. Not only in her letter to her mother but also in her two December dispatches Fuller expresses a wish for this kind of ideal earth, where truth and God—not princes and precedents—reign supreme. In this world, even a woman such as she, says Fuller in her New Year's Eve 1849 dispatch, "might ask to be made Ambassador" and thereby be able to act to alleviate "the ills of Woman's condition" worldwide.[12]

∽ ∽ ∽

In these December 1848 dispatches, Fuller tells of the cowardice of the pope, who fled Rome for fear of the violence to follow. Dressed as a priest, he donned thick glasses and escaped during the night of 24 November to Gaeta, where, says Fuller, he threw "himself in the arms of the bombarding monarch," Ferdinand II of Naples, blessing him and his soldiery "for preserving that part of Italy from anarchy." From there Pius IX sent word to the world that his earlier promises of liberal reform were now "null and void," that they had been "extorted" from him "by violence," a proclamation Fuller sees as "strange" coming from the "representative of St. Peter!" Rome, she notes, is full of the effigies of martyrs, people over whom "violence had no power to make [them] say what [they] did not mean." Unlike the pope, "they could be done to death in boiling oil, roasted on coals, or cut to pieces; but they could not say what they did not mean." In the role of Romantic liberator, Fuller praises these martyrs who disseminated "the religion of Him . . . who died a bloody death of torture between sinners, because He never could say what He did not mean." She reminds her readers of Peter, who, alarmed over the persecution of the Christians, was fleeing Rome when he "recognized his Master traveling toward Rome":

> "Lord," he said, "whither goest thou?"
> "I go," replied Jesus, "to die, with my people."
> Peter comprehended the reproof. He felt that he must not . . . deny his Master, yet hope for salvation. He returned to Rome to offer his life in attestation of his faith.

Fuller here suggests that she, like Peter, has returned to Rome to offer her life in attestation of her faith in her own radical vision of liberty, adding that "the only dignified course for the Pope to pursue was to resign his temporal power."[13]

Sounding much like a messianic radical, Fuller in her dispatches calls for the realization through revolution of humanity's redemption. She exhorts her readers to heed Christ's message and expresses her disdain for those who adhere to Christian rituals—especially those "under the old regime" who worship "the Madonna and Saints"—yet remain "ignorant of the precepts and life of Jesus." Like Emerson, she accepted as "Truth" the radical implications of Jesus's message—that all people are blessed in the eye of God and hence should have an equal right to partake of the "corn and the wine." Upon this belief that she made the central tenet of her dispatches home—that "Mankind is one, / And beats with one great heart"—Fuller based her "faith" in the revolution. Realizing that to many Americans her appeal might seem foolishly romantic, she nonetheless will appeal to them in an 1849 dispatch to support the revolution and let "loose" their tongues to cry: "'Long live the Republic, and may God bless the cause of the People, the brotherhood of nations and of men—the equality of rights for all.'—*Viva America!*"[14]

61 ∞ The Lull before the Storm

In contrast to the messianic tone of so many of her later *Tribune* letters, most of the personal letters Fuller wrote after returning to Rome late in 1848 convey a calm humility. Even in the visionary letter she wrote her mother in November about Rossi's assassination can be heard a plaintive note. She would if she could, she confesses, confide in her mother, whose trials as a mother she is beginning to appreciate. "The thought of you, the knowledge of your angelic nature," says Margaret, "is always one of my greatest supports. Happy those who have such a mother! Myriad instances of selfishness and corruption of heart cannot destroy the confidence in human nature."[1]

Margaret acknowledges that her "heart" is now "in some respects better" and "more humble." Her letter reveals that she no longer suffers the illusion that, to be a good person, she needs to be sexually "pure." She no longer feels a need to distance herself from Byron, whom she had earlier condemned as a "cankered" soul guilty of "moral perversion." She thus tells how her heart now swells "to tears" in tune with Byron's cry, "O, Rome, *my* country, city of the soul!" Though she does not dare tell her mother about her "fallen" state, Margaret indirectly does so when she compares herself to the Magdalen, who "*loved much.*" And whereas in New York her Puritan palate could scarcely tolerate a glass "of ruby wine," she confesses she now finds "the grape-cure" to be "more charming than the water-cure."[2]

Fuller could now understand her mother's treatment of her as a child. Not unlike her mother, who had abandoned Margaret at age three to the care of nursemaids and Timothy, Fuller had left her two-month-old son in Rieti in the care of Chiara. Also like her mother, Margaret thought her baby not as pretty as she had hoped. He looked nothing like his slim, dark-haired, Italian father; Nino's skin and wispy hair were fair. Alas, instead of Margarett Crane's loveliness, Nino had apparently inherited the appearance and "obstinate" personality of Margaret and Timothy. Still, for all her new appreciation of her mother, Fuller did not yet share news of Ossoli and the baby with her or with her friends back home for fear, no doubt, of bringing on herself American moral censure and thence a feeling of being even more alone in Rome than she already was—most Americans had fled the city for fear of contracting malaria or of Rome being invaded.[3]

The exit of Americans and the pope and his retinue left Fuller and Ossoli free to enjoy a glorious, sunny winter, going about together without fear of encountering censure. Though unable to pay for a carriage, the couple relished this honeymoon period uninterrupted by sounds of drums and baby's cries. It was an easy walk to the Villa Albani where they could view its collection of antiquities, to the Church of St. Lorenzo with its early mosaics, and to the vineyards near the Porta Maggiore. The unseasonably warm air allowed them an evening visit to the Forum and Monte Cavallo, "now so lonely and abandoned," she wrote Emelyn's husband, William Story. In this 9 December letter Fuller tells him how she and her "congenial companion" Ossoli go out in the morning on the Campagna, "carrying the roast chestnuts from Rome." They drink wine and eat bread "in some lonely little osteria," and in the evening reach Rome "just in time to see it . . . gilded by the sunset." And, though she does not share this private thought with Story, in the warm glow of the setting sun, her love for Ossoli deepened.[4]

At Christmas Fuller went to Rieti. There she found Nino recovering from being covered with spots from "a dreadful pox." Though Fuller wrote Ossoli that Nino has had "small pox very badly," it was "probably," as one scholar surmises, "chicken pox." Fortunately, his face was not scarred. In March she would describe to Cary what it was like to return to her baby at Christmas:

> The weather was mild when I set out, but by the fatality that has attended me throughout, in the night changed to a cold, unknown in Italy and remained so all the time I staid. There was . . . no fireplace except in the kitchen. I suffered much in my room with its brick floor, and windows through which came the cold wind freely. My darling did not suffer, because he was a little swaddled child like this and robed in wool beside, but I did very much. When I first took him in my arms he made no sound but leaned his head against my bosom, and staid so, he seemed to say how could you abandon me, what I felt you will only know when you have your own.

Fuller does not think or write in terms of tomorrow or of Nino's "manly life." For "it is *now*" she wants to be with him, "before passion, care, and bafflings begin." She imagines that with a little money she might go into "retirement for a year or two and live for him alone." However, this she cannot do because "all life that has been or could be natural to me is invariably denied."[5]

A heavy silence pervaded Rome when Fuller returned there after Christmas, as if the apocalypse were near. On 20 December, a provisional junta in Rome had named a new minister, declared its intention of forming a constituent assembly, and dissolved the rump parliament. On 29 December the junta announced that it would hold a 21 January election calling for a national assembly, direct universal suffrage, and a secret ballot. It set 5 February as the tentative date for the first meeting of the Constitutional Assembly. As her carriage rolled into Rome on 29 December, Fuller felt the tension surrounding the announcement of these radical alterations in the way Romans were to be governed. She was excited to play a role as historian of the momentous changes taking place in Italy. On New Year's Day she thus began recording events pertaining to the formation in Rome of a republican form of government. Using the Romantic liquid metaphor regularly now in her writings, she notes that there are "many breakers yet before that shore is reached."[6]

One such breaker, she knew, was the formidable "power of the priests." Thwarting Italians' hopes that the pope would return to Rome for the 6 January celebration of the Epiphany, Pius IX instead issued from Gaeta a monitory condemning the proposed election for a general national assembly and threatening Catholics with excommunication if they took part in events leading to its formation. When his condemnatory monitory appeared on city walls, irate Romans ripped them off. Some stuffed copies in privies.[7]

Such gestures by rebellious youth and idealistic revolutionaries were insignificant when compared to the threat to the pope's temporal power of a constituent assembly elected by a direct and universal suffrage for all adults. Determined to stop the election, Pius IX sent out from Gaeta appeals for help—not only to his Bourbon host Ferdinand II and the heads of state of France, Spain, and Austria, but even to the president of the United States, asking each "to bring his weight to bear in this calamitous time for the preservation of the temporal power of the Holy See." About the pope's power to rally the western powers to his defense, Fuller in her 20 February dispatch will note how a "host of enemies without are ready to levy war against this long-suffering people, to rivet anew their chains." Still, she contends, there is "an obvious tide throughout Europe toward a better order of things, and a wave of it may bear Italy onward to the shore." Fuller notes that "waters that had flowed so secretly beneath the crust of habit . . . have suddenly burst to light" and "all rush to drink the pure and living draught."[8]

Once unrestrained, however, bursting waters turn chaotic and destructive. So it was to be with this revolution. For not only were various foreign powers gathering their military forces to advance on Italy, but within republican ranks there was grave dissension. Fuller knew of Mazzini's differences with Gioberti, who wanted a confederation of Italian states and was suspected of sympathizing with the pope and the imperialist ambitions of Charles Albert. She was not, however, fully aware of the irreparable rifts in the republican ranks in northern Italy, where few republican leaders shared Mazzini's dream of a unified Italy. Dreading democracy as a threat to private property, members of the high aristocratic party (which included Costanza Visconti) preferred to see Lombardy and Piedmont united under the monarchy of Charles Albert. A middle-class group led by Giuseppe Ferrari and Carlo Cattaneo admired Mazzini and desired a republic but were against complete unification, fearing it would produce an overcentralized state and exaggerated nationalism. Ferrari and Cattaneo thought a federation of Italian states would better protect personal liberties and a pluralistic society. They thus tried in vain to persuade Mazzini to help them overturn Milan's moderate provisional government by enlisting the French military to help them set up a separate Milanese republic.[9]

So set was Mazzini on his dream of Italian unification that he had feuded with these republican leaders. In the spring of 1848 he had even yielded briefly to Charles Albert, saying he would ask his followers to support the monarchy at Turin if the king would agree to Italian unification. Though Charles Albert refused this concession, Mazzini's offer had further enraged republicans while pleasing many Milanese who saw in Mazzini a man working not so much for revolution as for reconciliation.

Unaware of these divisions in republican ranks, Fuller nonetheless sensed that Rome would not stay calm long and hence cautioned friends who wanted to visit. To Emelyn Story in early January 1849 she wrote that Rome is now "the centre of the Italian movement," that she lives in one room and does not entertain, and that a neighbor's apartment was recently robbed. Hoping that Emelyn and William still might come, she wrote later that month that she expected Rome to stay calm during the opening of the Constitutional Assembly in early February and probably through the carnival on the tenth. The city will stay calm unless Louis Napoleon, the anticlerical nephew of Napoleon I who had been elected president of the French Republic on 10 December 1848, should betray the Roman Republic and join the pope in the latter's drive to regain power, a betrayal Fuller fears. When Sarah Clarke wrote she wanted to visit, Fuller replied bluntly, "the Austrian seems likely to conquer Hungary and . . . pursue his murderous work here," while France cannot be depended on, and the pope is now "a traitor." On 26 January she portends in her journal: "the French will soon be at Civita Vecchia [the Port of Rome] and with hostile intentions. Monstrous are the treacheries of our time."[10]

When friends at home learned of events unfolding in Europe, they urged Fuller to return to the United States. Eliza Farrar and Elizabeth Hoar sponsored a plan to give Fuller an annual annuity of three hundred dollars if she would return to the States and sever herself from what Eliza thought to be an evil spell that Rome had cast over Fuller. Margaret wrote her mother on 19 January that if ever she could make it home, then the annuity offered her hope "of repose in the future," something Fuller had hoped might happen after the death of Mary Rotch in New Bedford. But Rotch bequeathed her fortune to her female companion and her lawyer. Still, the thought of the annuity made home seem temptingly sweet. Her brother Arthur, who had recently been ordained as a preacher in Manchester, New Hampshire, had invited Margaret to visit. What a joy it would be for her to hear New England Sunday morning bells, sit in a pew with her mother and Lloyd, who were both now living with Arthur, and listen to him preach. In her 20 January reply to Arthur's invitation, she asks her brother, who has himself been ill with a lingering cold and lung trouble, to take care of their "precious" mother, since "the flesh is weak."[11]

"Death begins to play its part in my absence," she wrote Arthur as she thought of the flesh's frailty. Recently there had been the deaths of Uncle Abraham, Mary Rotch, Eugene's first baby, as well as of Cary's sister Ellen Sturgis Hooper, whose poems Fuller had published in the *Dial* and who had been married to a man so inferior to her and who had suffered so much in life that Fuller thought her death "an excellent thing." She wrote Sarah Clarke that she regretted not having been there to kiss Ellen's face and hands before her interment. With her mind set on death, she asks Sarah to write and describe Ellen's "last days, if you saw her often and how she died, and how her face looked under the last impress." She is relieved that Ellen is dead and "unoppressed by unfit ties."[12]

To James Clarke, who had written pleading with Margaret to come home, Fuller replied: "What come back for? Here is a great past and a *living* present. Here men live for something else beside money and systems. . . . 'Tis a sphere much more natural to me than what the old puritans or the modern bankers have made." For this 19 January 1849 letter Fuller copied out Mickiewicz's February 1847 letter to her describing what he sees to be Fuller's "mission." She confesses to Clarke that, while it may be true as Mickiewicz says that she has "sinned in the old world," she is "also," she says, still "purely idealist."[13]

And as sinner and idealist Fuller was committed to Mazzini, who had sought sanctuary in Switzerland after the Austrians defeated Charles Albert at Custoza on 25 June 1848 but who had returned to Italy on 8 February 1849, the day the Roman Republic was declared. In a 20 February dispatch, Fuller tells about the bells ringing over Rome in the early hours of 9 February and the republic's tricolor flag surmounting the Palace of the Senator. Romans that day heard a reading of the Fundamental Decree of the Constitutional Assembly of Rome in which the temporal power of the papacy was declared ended and the Roman government instituted as "a pure Democracy" under "the glorious name of Roman Republic."

For Fuller the celebration was tempered by news she received the next day of the flight from Tuscany of Grand Duke Leopold II, who said he feared he might be excommunicated. Though in her dispatch Fuller mentions Garibaldi walking arm in arm in the celebratory procession with Carlo Luciano Bonaparte, a nephew of Napoleon, it is not the great freedom fighter Garibaldi she heralds as "the idol of the people," but Mazzini.[14]

On 9 March she wrote Marcus Spring how Mazzini had been received "like a prince" when he reentered Italy at Leghorn, and how he had quietly entered Rome the night of 5 March on foot as a Roman citizen and member of the assembly, by declaration of the newly elected assembly on 30 February. Mazzini, who had visited Fuller in her apartment the night before she wrote Marcus, seemed to her "more divine than ever." She sees him as Christlike, a savior come to free his people from their poverty and enslavement, a soulful man whose thoughts she saw springing up all over Italy. With William Channing and Emerson, Mazzini is one of her holy "triad." She tells Marcus she believes that "if any one can save Italy from her foes, inward and outward, it will be [Mazzini]," and that she would "freely" give her life to aid him, hoping only for a quick death since, "I don't like slow torture." That same day she wrote her mother saying she fears Mazzini's "entrance into Jerusalem may be followed by the sacrifice."[15]

To Cary in the mid-March letter in which she tells of her Christmas visit to Rieti, Fuller describes in holy terms her love for Mazzini: "Dearly I love Mazzini, who also loves me. He came in just as I had finished this first letter to you. His soft radiant look makes melancholy music in my soul; it consecrates my present life that like the Magdalen I may at the important hour shed all the consecrated ointment on his head." As "the Magdalen," a sinner, Fuller would, if she could, wash Mazzini's feet with her tears, then wipe them with her loosened hair before pouring "ointment on his head" in preparation of his sacred body for burial.[16]

Beneath the dream of Italian liberty is Fuller's awareness that human aspiration can never meet the ideal except perhaps in death. One must keep one's faith, she thus advises Cary, as did Mary Magdalen and Mary, mother of James, who, in confronting the crucified Christ's empty tomb, affirmed a vision that enabled them to transcend the limits of their mortality.

Mazzini has such faith, says Fuller in her 20 March dispatch to the *Tribune*. Though he "is not an orator," the "powerful and first impression from his presence must always be of the religion of his soul." Fuller elsewhere again compares him to Christ, who had "spoken and acted as much truth as the world could bear." Men like Christ and Mazzini, she says, "conquer in defeat."[17]

Fuller thus sees in Mazzini the strength and faith of a hero. She fears, however, that she lacks the courage to "bear" the "anguish incident to the struggle" for one's "principles." She begins her 10 March letter to Channing with "clumsy lines from some hymn" that keep "recurring," lines she "learned in childhood": "Father of light, conduct my feet / Through life's dark, dangerous road; / Let each advancing step still bring / Me nearer to my God." Yet, no sooner had Fuller recalled the good "Father" than memories of the bad father surfaced. She regrets that all the "precious first feelings" of her life "were wasted," that, because of her unhappy childhood, "I am not what I should be on this earth. I could not be."[18]

A "kind of chastened libertine," she roves "pensively, always, in deep sadness, often O God help me; is all my cry." To her trusted friend William Channing, a Christian socialist, Fuller confesses she does not have "faith in the paternal love" she needs; "the government of the earth does seem so ruthless or so negligent." She takes interest in some plans, "*our* socialism, for instance, . . . but the interest is shallow as the plans." Although such plans "are needed," still, says she, "man will . . . blunder and weep, as he has done for so many thousand years." Fuller suggests in her 20 March dispatch that American patrons of the arts and merchants should act like the Christ who drove the money changers from the temple instead of seeking "bargains for [their] own advantage at the expense of a poorer brother."[19]

Despite her anger at the "American Maecenas" for his selfish materialism, Fuller in her dispatches expresses her continuing faith in America. In her 20 March dispatch she tells readers that, in "seeing the struggles of other nations, and the deficiencies of the leaders who try to sustain them," one comes to appreciate "the wonderful combination of events and influences that gave our independence so healthy a birth." Even in her personal letters with their hints of her own deficiencies and "fallen" nature, Fuller stresses to those she loves, as she did to Richard in her 19 January letter, how important it is for them to remember what a "vast blessing [it is] to be born in America."[20]

In this January 1849 letter to Richard she had noted the selfless nature of the "courageous youth" of Italy, as well as of Mazzini. The latter she had observed when she attended two sessions of the general assembly. He had sent her tickets in early March to hear him speak in Rome, which, according to Denis Mack Smith, was the only conceivable "capital for his idealised Italy." There she heard Mazzini make his now-famous prophecy: "After the Rome of the Emperors—after the Rome of the Popes, will come the Rome of the People."[21]

Unlike the speech of the passionate Mickiewicz, Mazzini plainly and without drama affirmed that the only powers he acknowledged were "*God and the People.*" He called on Romans to show the world that true patriotism is not hostile to religion, and that freedom and equality can coexist in a republic. He declared that liberty of conscience and speech are human rights to be enjoyed equally by all people and that in an Italian republic there should be no hatred of political opponents or intolerance of people from different ethnic backgrounds or regions, but only a united effort to win national independence. Quoting Oliver Cromwell, Mazzini urged all who heard his words to "put your trust in God and keep your powder dry." Although he knew that "many sincere men" viewed his hopes "as Utopian," he nonetheless called on such men—Italians who participated not only in divisive interregional rivalries but also in feuds over territorial rights within their regions—to unite in an effort to end the Austrian occupation of Italy.[22]

Like Mazzini, Fuller sensed that Italian unity probably was at that point in history mere romantic dream. Still, both believed that the dream would eventually be realized, though each dreaded "the holocaust of broken hearts" that must attend the fight of idealistic youth to achieve it. Both Mazzini and Fuller also knew that in the pursuit of their dream of freedom, they might die. When Fuller shared her dark foreboding with Marcus—not about her fate but Mazzini's—he wrote her not to despair, for "you will meet him in heaven." In reply, Fuller dredged up that weighted word used not only by Virgil in referring to Dido's spurious "marriage" but also by Timothy when criticizing her as a child: "This I believe will be, despite all my *faults*" (emphasis added).[23]

Aware now of what even she deemed to be her "faults," Fuller despaired in letters to her trusted friends. One such fault was made glaringly apparent by James Russell Lowell. Offended by Fuller's earlier criticism of his poetry as shallow, Lowell in *A Fable for Critics* mocked Fuller as "Miranda," a woman who corners "terrified victims" for the purpose of "unfolding a tale (of herself, I surmise, / For't is dotted as thick as a peacock's with I's)." On 8 March she sent Cary "a sad cry" from her "lacerated affections" over Lowell's caricature of her. A distraught Fuller tells Cary that this "last plot" against her "has been too cruel"; if only she could have "remained in peace," she "should have felt overpaid for all the pains and bafflings" of her early, "sad," "difficult," "broken" life. She tells Cary how badly she needs the love she has given "other sufferers." A week later she wrote Cary the long 16 March letter about her baby, confessing: "all the solid happiness I have known has been at times when [Nino] went to sleep in my arms." Yet even this happiness is compromised by guilt; for it seems that when she first held Nino on her return to him at Christmas, "he made no sound but leaned his head against my bosom, and staid so, he seemed to say how could you abandon me." Fuller reflects in this important letter not only on the fate of her baby but of the war she knows must soon be waged by republican Rome against her enemies, the combined power of the well-armed fathers—of pope, priests, emperors, and kings. Sadly she says: "how it will end, I do not know."[24]

On 18 March she wrote Anna Ward Barker about a dream she had in which Barker had treated Margaret's suffering lightly. She pleads with Anna not to be so careless of her feelings should she in fact come home. For she is "weary," she says, "of striving in the world," more weary than she ought to be, but her strength, she explains, was "prematurely exhausted"—alluding here, presumably, to the "unnatural" behavior demanded from her as a child by her own controlling, all-powerful, fault-finding father.[25]

All indeed would not end well for Fuller or the Roman republicans. Even as she prepared to leave for her March visit to Rieti, Fuller was twining with her duplicitous words a net of lies about herself from which there would be no exit. For under the Roman Republic, Fuller had to obtain from the Office of Public Security a document that was in effect a passport. One biographer says she gave her name as Margherita Ossoli and her place of birth as Rome, implying that Ossoli was her maiden name and that she and Ossoli were blood kin. This lie suggests either that Ossoli and Fuller were not yet officially married or—and more likely—that Ossoli wanted to hide from the public his marriage to a heterodox who was also a radical republican. On the document Fuller also claimed to be twenty-nine years old, when in fact she would be thirty-nine in May 1849.[1]

While she was deceiving the Italians, the French were setting a trap for the Roman republicans. Fuller intuited this, noting in her Roman journal on 17 March: "It appears that the Roman ambassadors have not been received in Paris, [and] that the French government will not be friendly to the Italian republics." Ten days later she noted other ominous signs that the Roman Republic would be short lived. On 12 March 1849, Charles Albert had again led the Piedmontese in an attack on the Austrians; on 23 March he was decisively defeated at Novara, after which he abdicated in favor of his son, Victor Emmanuel II, and fled to Spain. Genoa, which had refused to join in Victor Emmanuel's proposed capitulating armistice with Austria, in the meantime was besieged and bombed by Sardinian troops. With a reactionary ministry in power in Piedmont, Fuller laments that "Genoa, Piedmont are all submissive, the press is muzzled, the clubs shut up." In Florence a similar conservative reaction had set in. From Rieti in early April she wrote Ossoli that she is "disgusted" even with the *Epoca,* which she says "has become a reactionary's paper." With only Mazzini's paper to counter conservative propaganda now, Fuller thinks the republican cause doomed, especially since France is now "sending her troops [to Rome] to restore the pope." About France's betrayal, Fuller says, "she can sink no lower."[2]

But the French republicans could and would sink lower, systematically weaving their own net of lies with which to deceive naive Romantic republicans like Mazzini and thereby hasten the fall of Rome. Louis Napoleon, a former liberal and Carbonaro who had once fought tyranny in the Papal States, announced that he was sending an expeditionary force to stabilize the region. This was in fact a calculated effort to get himself promoted from "prince" president to emperor (for which he needed the pope's blessing), for his military expedition was really planning to attack and defeat the Italian republicans. Like the Greek Sinon who in Virgil's *Aeneid* sidled up to the Trojans with his gift of a giant wooden horse, General

Nicolas Charles Victor Oudinot, whom Louis Napoleon had put in charge of this expedition, was to pretend to be a friend of the republicans while secretly implementing Louis Napoleon's plan to enter Rome and establish there French military power. Oudinot was to buy time to allow the French to send enough reinforcements to accomplish this ambitious mission.[3]

While this was transpiring, Fuller was heading in a carriage to Rieti, where she arrived on 27 March. That she did not trust their landlord Giovanni to keep Nino's existence a secret, Giovanni's sisters meddled in her affairs, and the rooms she was renting from him were brutally cold: all these negative factors had made Fuller decide to move Nino to a place she thought would be better. She would rent an upstairs bedroom in the home of Nino's wet nurse, Chiara, and her husband, Niccola.[4]

When Fuller arrived that rainy March day at their house, she found Nino in good health, although she did wonder why he had grown so fat while not growing in length in the three months she had not seen him. She also began to wonder about the people from whom she now rented. She was resting on the third day of her stay after having bathed Nino when she heard a drunken Niccola shouting downstairs at his brother Pietro. When she went to see what was going on, Pietro threw a piece of wood at Niccola that whizzed by her head. Though neighbors broke up the fight, Fuller dramatically wrote Ossoli that if Nino had been downstairs he could have been killed. She wonders if they should just tell their "secret," then nixes the idea, noting that "our whole future lives depend upon the discretion of this moment."[5]

Whatever the reason for their continuing wish to dissemble—whether it was the couple's wish to keep secret the fact of their marriage or the absence of one and presence of a baby—it meant they had to keep Nino hidden in Rieti even though Fuller did not feel he was safe there. More Neapolitan troops had arrived just over the border in Aquila, while approximately a thousand of Garibaldi's guerillas were now stationed in Rieti, waiting to be called to fight for the Roman Republic. Fuller's fear increased when Garibaldi's long-bearded men arrived in town. Unlike "legion" officers, who still wore Garibaldi's trademark red tunics, the soldiers, who up until then had looked like brigands, now dressed in dark blue great coats with green collars and matching trousers. Over their long, unkempt hair they wore tall Calabrian hats with turned-down brims with cockerel feathers and bands. These savvy guerrilla fighters carried any manner of weapon available: musket, lancet, bayonet, or saber. Near the end of the siege of Rome, they would all proudly don red shirts to identify themselves with their leader. To a mother protecting her infant, however, they seemed "desperadoes." Rumors they had raped women and killed a priest and nine civilians scared Fuller. It was also said that two corpses had been found in the river on Palm Sunday, which was on 1 April.[6]

On 4 April 1849 she wrote Ossoli that she was scared to go out alone. She also said she regretted they could not be together that day, an expression of regret one scholar says suggests that she and Ossoli had been married in a ceremony on 4 April the year before. This theory, however, is not supported by the content of the letters they exchanged in April 1848. These indicate that Ossoli, as late as mid-August 1848, was avoiding in writing making a commitment, while Fuller that spring was still referring to Ossoli as "friend" or "dear," not as "love" or "husband." Ossoli, moreover, who lived with his sister, Angela, in 1847–48, still listed his married state as bachelor, just as Fuller in letters tells Ossoli that she sees no reason for them to take action until they know that she and the baby will survive childbirth. Thus it is more likely, as has also been theorized, that Fuller is referring to her desire to celebrate the anniversary of the day they met, Easter Sunday 1847, which fell on 4 April. This is likely since Fuller in another instance will mark as important the day she first met someone she liked, that someone being Lewis Cass, U.S. chargé d'affaires in Rome, whom she will soon meet on 30 April. Whatever the reference in her 4 April letter, Fuller is now glad Ossoli did not arrive the night before, because Nino had cried all night, and it had rained all day and was still raining hard.[7]

And it continued to rain in torrents during Fuller's three-week stay in Rieti. Still, she cherished her time with Nino, as well as with Ossoli, who got a day off from work. By mid-April, however, she was eager to return to Rome. On a cold and rainy April day, she kissed Nino good-bye and set out in a carriage for Rome. On the way she and her fellow travelers stopped at an inn for lunch, where they encountered Garibaldi's soldiers. Rather than panicking, Fuller pragmatically decided that "courtesy was the best protection from injury" and thus treated the legion to lunch "at her own expense," despite her own near poverty. Emelyn Story tells how, as the men "came boisterously into the *osteria*," Fuller stood and said to the padrone, "Give these good men wine and bread." The noise subsided, the men bowed respectfully to her, and Fuller sat and listened to an account of their journey, "wondering," according to Story, "how men with such natures could have the reputation they had."[8]

Back in Rome, Fuller found that a dreaded nightmare had come true. On the day she arrived, the French Chamber of Deputies authorized the government to send troops to Italy. The Rome to which Fuller returned was thus quickly becoming, as one scholar has said, "a circle within a circle of enemies—a Catholic noose gradually being drawn tight about the center of the Catholic world." To the south the Neapolitan armies of Ferdinand II were moving across the frontier. From the north and east Austrian armies advanced, reclaiming as they did the land they had lost. To the west at sea waited ships with troops loyal to both the king of Spain and the pope. Most surprising to the Italian people, though not to Fuller, was the news that a French military expedition, estimated to be about ten thousand men strong, was expected soon to arrive at Civitavecchia, the port of Rome forty miles northwest of the city.[9]

The pope's appeal had been effective. Aware of the support pouring in for him, he issued another allocution. In it he said that Rome had become "a den of wild beasts, overflowing with men of every nation, apostates, or heretics, of leaders of communism and socialism and animated by the most terrible hatred against Catholic truth." The pope's accusation confirmed suspicions of many American readers of Fuller's dispatches that she had allied herself with the "reds," and the gossip began to circulate in the United States about Fuller's allegiances.[10]

But Fuller had by now identified entirely with the Italian people's fight for freedom from authoritarian control. While she was in Rieti, the Roman Assembly had voted to place Rome under the leadership of a triumvirate with Mazzini at its head. Members of the new government had immediately instituted progressive reforms; they initiated tax and land reforms, declared freedom of the press and religious equality, and abolished the death penalty and the right of primogeniture while steering clear of making promises of guaranteed work and wages. It had been the failure to follow through on such socialist measures that had undermined the French Republic. Though the liberal Mazzini had rejected such socialist proposals, he was still depicted in the conservative London *Times* and similar papers as a dangerous radical.

The next days brought further fast changes as ships of the large French fleet sailed into Civitavecchia off the Tyrrhenian coast on 24 April. General Oudinot, second duke of Reggio, then issued the first of many duplicitous messages, saying that the government of France is "animated by liberal and friendly motives" and that it "will respect the wishes of the majority of the Roman nation." Oudinot never doubted that the Romans would "welcome deliverance from the communists, atheists and mercenary soldiers" he saw as running the republic. Even his troops believed that they were coming to help the Roman people. When Fuller heard that the French had disembarked at Civitavecchia, she sensed war was imminent and went with Emelyn to the Piazza del Popolo. There they met the Princess Belgioioso, who was standing on a bench and looking, according to William Story, "much older and negligently dressed." On 26 April Oudinot sent an aide to Rome to declare that France's aim was to block Austrian and Bourbon aggression and restore harmony between the Roman people and the pope. Since the last thing the Roman republicans wanted was the pope's return to temporal power, the Roman Assembly rejected the proposition. Backed by the triumvirs, the assembly voted to fight to save the Roman Republic. As soon as its members passed this unanimous declaration, barricades began going up all over Rome. Excited youth prepared for war; everyone wanted to fight. Even women were drilled in the use of firearms. On 27 April Garibaldi's troops marched from Rieti into Rome. There they prepared to meet the French forces sent to restore the pope.[11]

The last day of April proved to be fateful for Fuller: the French first assailed Rome; Fuller began her work as a wartime nurse; and she first met Lewis Cass, the new U.S. chargé d'affaires. Fuller initially did not trust Cass because she knew he had predicted that within a month the Roman Republic would be defeated and the pope restored to power. Acting on U.S. orders, in early April he had not recognized either papal authority or the republican government, but by 30 April that stand was reversed. On 21 April he wrote Secretary of State John M. Clayton that the republicans in the assembly were not "an ultra-democratic faction" but a group of "moderate, educated, and comparatively wealthy men" who "abhor communism," want "protection of property," and believe "no right or freedom" is possible under a government run by cardinals. Unfortunately Cass's communication arrived too late in the States to have any effect on the rapidly accelerating roll of events that catapulted Rome into war on 30 April.[12]

With war now imminent and American lives in jeopardy, Cass that day had come to Fuller's apartment on the Piazza Barberini to urge her to move to the Casa Diez in the Via Gregoriana. There, she and other Americans still in Rome were to be placed under the protection of the U.S. flag. Cass's admonition was timely. The French, who were sighted at nine in the morning on the Via Aurelia five miles from Rome, attacked Roman defenses that day outside of Rome. The war had begun.

Early that morning of 30 April Fuller had received a note from Princess Belgioioso, now directress of hospitals in Rome. In it she named Fuller "Regolatrice of the Hospital of the Fate Bene Fratelli" on Tiber Island. She told Fuller to go there at noon and direct the women who came to attend the wounded. Before leaving for the hospital, Fuller had visited Ossoli, who was stationed on the walls above the Vatican gardens where the French led their attack. On those walls, the first Roman volunteer fell, a university student majoring in philosophy and mathematics. After seeing Ossoli, Fuller had returned to her apartment. It was in that interval before she left for the hospital that Cass had arrived to urge her to move. From the loggia and windows of the Casa Diez, the Storys and other Americans—like the ancient Latins who Virgil says pressed "toward the rooftops and the towers" of Latinia to watch the Trojans and Ratulians battle—watched the Roman republicans and the French battle. The fighting commenced about noon with French cannons bombarding the Vatican, destroying a coffered ceiling decorated by Michelangelo and a fresco in the Cappella Paolina; it ended in the afternoon about five when Garibaldi repulsed the French, who then retreated on the road to Civitavecchia.[13]

Around noon that same day Fuller first made her way to the Hospital of Fate Bene Fratelli. She went again that night to the hospital, where she found war "more dreadful" than she "had fancied it." In her 27 May dispatch, Fuller confesses she saw for the first time that night the "agonies of those dying or who needed amputation." She felt their pain and longing for "loved ones who were away." She later wrote how strange it had seemed—having "passed the night amid the groans of many suffering, some dying men"—to walk 1 May in the first light of day through a Rome "shorn of [its] locks," the plantations of trees that had "lent grace to her venerable brow." Seeing blood on the walls of the Vatican gardens, she felt as if Rome had been "profaned." It must have seemed as if her childhood nightmare of trees dripping blood had come true.[14]

Even the trees of the Villa Borghese had been "laid low" for barricades. In her dispatch she notes how "the fountain, singing alone amid the fallen groves," seemed an "innocent infant calling" amid "the bodies of those that once cherished it." And there were plenty of bodies, for the French had abandoned five hundred dead and wounded. Three days after that first battle, as the Storys walked on the wall where members of the civic guard had fought, Emelyn was struck by the sight of monks under a black flag "looking for the unburied dead."[15]

For a moment it *seemed* as if no army could stop the Roman republicans' drive to liberty. In reality, however, the republican army was so ill equipped and inadequate that, despite its fervor, it could not resist the well-armed and professionally trained French. To complicate matters, Ferdinand II of Naples with nine thousand troops was moving up from the south with the intent of also attacking Rome, which would mean the city had to defend itself on two fronts. Aware that the French were vulnerable, Garibaldi asked the triumvirs if he might pursue them to the sea. But Mazzini, assuming a truce had been declared between the Romans and the French and hoping the French would finally rally in defense of the Roman Republic, sent Garibaldi south to fight the Neapolitans. Garibaldi thought the command naive and resented Mazzini for it, even as he forced Ferdinand II's troops back across the border, defeating them on 19 May.[16]

Meanwhile, throughout May, Mazzini and Oudinot parleyed back and forth regarding French intentions—Mazzini believing Oudinot's promises while in reality the general awaited reinforcements to carry out Louis Napoleon's orders to defeat the republicans and take Rome. Between "the heaves of the storm," Fuller wrote her 27 May *Tribune* letter wherein she accuses the French of being so "entangled in a web of falsehood" that they had underestimated "the sincere movement of the Italian people." She celebrates the "struggle" now "commenced between the principle of Democracy and the old powers, no longer legitimate." Though the struggle "may last fifty years," she predicts that in the next century all Europe will "be under Republican Government."[17]

As for now, however, Fuller tells readers, she and her friends at the Casa Diez can see from the loggia the French troops encamped on the hills outside Rome, and as they watch their night fires, they wonder, "what will they do?" If the Austrians attack, will the French troops fraternize with them "after pretending and proclaiming that they came here as a check upon [Austrian] aggressions?" "Ah!" she exclaims, "the way of falsehood, the way of treachery, how dark—how full of pitfalls and traps!"[18]

The way of treachery was dark, indeed, in a world where men's words did not match their actions and hence were empty of meaning. Expecting the worst, Fuller on 22 May (the day before her thirty-ninth birthday) wrote a dolorous letter to Richard noting that—despite Garibaldi's having driven back the Neopolitans— "the French seem to be amusing us with a pretence of treaties, while waiting for the Austrians to come up." The Storys, she says, fearing Rome is to be bombarded, are going away as soon as they can find horses to carry them to Germany. Fuller, however, intends to stay "in the house, under our flag, almost the only American, except the Consul and Ambassador." Aware of the widening chasm between herself and Richard, Margaret asks him nonetheless to see how much she needs his love. Aware she might die during the assault on Rome, she sends "Love to dearest Mother, Arthur, Ellen, Lloyd," and adds that, "should any accident, possible to these troubled times, transfer me to another scene of existence, they need not regret it. There must be better worlds than this,—where innocent blood is not ruthlessly shed, where treason does not so easily triumph, where the greatest and best are not crucified." She hopes that, should she die, he will "keep this last word from your sister."[19]

63 ∾ The Fall of Rome

Alone in Rome in "these troubled times," Fuller at night felt the presence of ghosts in the now empty rooms of the Casa Diez. "Strange noises," she wrote Emelyn on 29 May, "haunt the rooms. I start from my book and my sleep, seeming to hear the rustling of garments and the opening of doors, then all is silent." In the dark, she says, "black shadows here and there seem about to take form and advance upon me." She felt the same terror she had as a child when, alone in her room at night with the candle out, colossal faces seemed to advance on her from the corners of the room.[1]

In the dark world Fuller now inhabited, however, people lied, waged war, and died. Fearing her own death, Fuller had shared part of her secret with Emelyn before the Storys left for Germany, swearing her to secrecy. Fuller said that she and Ossoli had married and that they had a child. As evidence, Margaret showed Emelyn a document "given by the priest who married them, saying that Angelo Eugene Ossoli was the legal . . . heir of whatever title and fortune should come to his father." Emelyn asked no questions but promised that, if Ossoli and Margaret died in the revolution, she would get Angelino and the documents to America and into the care of Fuller's mother and her friend Caroline Tappan.[2]

Sensing French deception, Fuller correctly assessed that the French were merely "amusing" themselves that May when they sent Ferdinand-Marie de Lesseps to Rome as minister plenipotentiary to arrange a peace agreement with the Republican government. During a twenty-day armistice made possible by de Lesseps's well-intended negotiations, Mazzini and the republicans trustingly released hundreds of French soldiers, a goodwill gesture ironically seen in Paris as an insult. Fuller thought the republicans dangerously naive. She saw that the French were playing a game with the Romans: pretending to protect the republicans, the French were cleverly leading them to their destruction.[3]

Unaware of Louis Napoleon's strategy, de Lesseps on 31 May presented the republicans with a plan that allowed the French to occupy the Roman territory to defend it against other invading armies. In return the French would not contest the Romans' right to choose their form of government. De Lesseps's proposal, however, was hollow. On the same day that he made another and still more liberal offer, one that the Romans accepted, Oudinot denounced de Lesseps's pledges and the latter was recalled to Paris. With the malaria season fast approaching and both Spanish and Austrian troops threatening to move on Rome, Oudinot was eager to act. During the truce he had situated his troops in a commanding position atop one of the hills dominating Rome. On 1 June, the day de Lesseps sailed for France, Oudinot—who now commanded thirty thousand infantry, four thousand cavalry, as well as an ample supply of field artillery, howitzers, and mortars—announced in writing his intention to attack the city on Monday, 4 June. Foreign nationals in theory would be given enough time to leave the city. Like the Greek Sinon, however, Oudinot had strategically lied: he began the attack at three in the morning of Sunday, 3 June, thereby catching Rome's defenders—excepting its sentries—asleep.[4]

Fuller witnessed the battle from the balcony of the Casa Diez. She watched as casualties mounted. As an Italian band on the walls played the *Marseillaise* in an attempt to shame the French for their treachery, the Italians—once Garibaldi arrived that morning at half past five at the Porta San Pancrazio just 250 yards from the Villa Vascello—fought like cornered cats. Three times that day the Italians reclaimed the Casino dei Quattro Venti, a building on the grounds of the Villa Corsini, which was located between the Villa Pamfili and the Vascello, all of which were outside the walls of Rome. The French had seized the Corsini before dawn and knew if they could occupy the Vascello, which was nearest the walls, then they could gain access to the city though the Porta San Pancrazio. Only the will of the idealistic young Italians kept their ragtag army fighting that day, charging in groups of as few as twenty directly into intense fire from French sharpshooters planted strategically along the narrow lane leading to the Casino dei Quattro Venti. There the corpses piled up, yet still the Italians charged. At the day's end, the republicans held only the Villa Vascello, having yielded the Villa Corsini to the French.[5]

In a 6 June letter to Emelyn, Margaret told how she viewed from her loggia at the Casa Diez this "terrible," this "real battle," which began about "four in the morning" and "lasted to the last gleam of light": "The musket-fire was almost unintermitted; the roll of the cannon . . . most majestic. As all passed at Porta San

Pancrazio and Villa Pamfili, I saw the smoke of every discharge, the flash of the bayonets; with a glass could see the men." The result of these volleys was horrific: three hundred "on our side," she says, "killed and wounded; theirs must be much greater." In one casino "have been found seventy dead bodies of theirs." Fuller was aware that the Italians had, in fact, taken a terrible loss. Garibaldi's division had lost a thousand men, a hundred of them officers. The French lost only about 275 men. Perhaps the most grievous wound of all was to Italian pride: the Romans had trusted the French soldiers who had fought them with such ferocity that all in Rome, wrote Fuller, think the French soldiers to be as "false as their general, and cannot endure . . . talk of brotherhood."[6]

Fuller, who went daily to the hospital on Tiber Island as well as to the wards set up in the Quirinal Palace, was relieved not to find Ossoli on a cart among the wounded and dying. In the hillside garden of the Quirinal Palace, she walked with wounded soldiers—"one with his sling; another with his crutch"—or she sat with them as they told bright-eyed boys about their bravery in battle. But such idyllic moments were rare. In her 6 June letter to Emelyn, she says the French throw rockets into the town: "one burst in the court-yard of the hospital, just as I arrived there yesterday, agitating the poor sufferers," who "said they did not want to die like mice in a trap."[7]

Seeing the carnage, Fuller worried about Nino and also about Ossoli, who was stationed on the walls of the Vatican garden. With death as the backdrop to their lives, Fuller truly felt wedded now to Ossoli. Though Ossoli had survived the battle, Fuller feared neither of them would live through an all-out assault on Rome. So she sent Ossoli a note saying that she had "left a paper with Angelino's birth certificate and a few words praying the Sto[rys] to take care of him." She adds: "Should I by any chance die you can take back this paper from me, if you want, as from your wife." The "as" in this sentence is troublesome because it suggests likeness, not fact: that Ossoli can retrieve the paper she has given Emelyn Story in the same way he would *if* she were his wife, which here her wording suggests she is not. Though the surviving baptismal certificate does provide compelling evidence that Fuller had married Ossoli before 6 November 1848 (providing Ossoli did not collude with Father Trinchi in legitimizing the baptism), it is nonetheless troublesome that in this brief message Fuller fails to mention their marriage certificate. Such an important document she presumably would also have wanted to be left with the Storys. Despite her embarrassment that the date on it might have revealed that it had been a shotgun marriage, Fuller still knew that a marriage certificate would have been necessary in America not only to spare her mother embarrassment but also to prevent the stigma of illegitimacy falling on Nino and the rest of the Fuller family. Officially married or not, a stressed-out Fuller penned a loving postscript to Ossoli, "If you live and I die, be always very devoted to Nino. If you ever love another woman, always think first of him, I beg you, beg you, love." On

17 June from war-torn Italy she wrote Elizabeth Hoar, advising her to "prize" the peace of Concord.[8]

Her letter to Hoar had been prompted by one she had received on 3 June from Emerson, the day the French began their attack on Rome. On 10 June she wrote Emerson: "I received your letter amid a round of cannonade and musketry." Though "a terrible battle," the "Italians fought like lions": "It is a truly heroic spirit that animates them. They make a stand here for honor and their rights, with little ground for hope that they can resist, now they are betrayed by France."[9]

In this letter to a man who—as she had written him five months earlier—she hopes will always "think of M." and "how much she loves you," Fuller, too, makes a stand for honor. She expresses her faith that Emerson, once he finds out about her situation, will not betray her love; "I am caught in such a net of ties here,—if ever you know of my life here, I think you will only wonder at the constancy with which I have sustained myself." "Meanwhile, love me all you can; let me feel, that, amid the fearful agitations of the world, there are pure hands, with healthful, even pulse, stretched out toward me, if I claim their grasp."[10]

But the increasingly socially conservative Emerson was in no mood to reach forth his hand to a woman already rumored in Boston to be in some sort of "Fourierist or Socialist marriage." From Emerson she hence received no words of support, and neither did "Elizh" respond to Fuller's appeal for love and understanding. She now understood that her defiance of middle-class social conventions had evoked censure from those she most loved at home. She was in a sense alone in Rome, one American woman fighting on the side of the oppressed Italian people for their freedom from tyranny, a fight she knew they were certain to lose.[11]

While the French bombarded Rome, Fuller, now chief assistant for a sick and feverish Cristina Belgioioso, worked long hours at the hospitals. Far more now than merely a reporter, or an incendiary revolutionary persona on the front page of an American newspaper, Fuller—in the view of those who knew and loved her in Rome—was a heroine fighting for her home. As Fuller watched the dream of Italian liberty crumble around her, as she agonized in letters to friends about her capacity to endure this defeat, she grew in stature in the eyes of Lewis Cass Jr. The young American envoy later recollected that, though the weather was intensely hot, though her health was "feeble & delicate" and "the dead & dying were around her in every form of pain & horror," still "she never shrank from the duty she had assumed." For Fuller's "heart & soul," he wrote, "were in the cause for which these men had fought," and she did all that could be done to comfort them. To the wounded Fuller was an inspiration; to some, it seemed, she was a queen. Walking with Fuller through the wards, Cass recalls seeing "the eyes of the dying, as she moved among them . . . meet in commendation of her . . . kindness." He later heard many of the recovered "speak with all the passionate fervor of the Italian nature, of her, whose sympathy and compassion throughout their long illness, ful-filled all the offices of love & affection."[12] Fuller, who as a child had cherished her mother's tenderness in nursing her children through their illnesses, now became in the eyes of the wounded men a similar nurturing goddess, a beautiful woman like her mother.

Emelyn, who had fled Rome before the June bombardment, recollected about Fuller's work at the hospital in May, how, with little money or resources, Fuller gave the wounded her "time and thoughts" instead. Emelyn remembers "how comforting was her presence to the poor suffering men." Moving among the sol-diers' beds, Fuller gave to one a book; to another she told the news of the day. They were appreciative, recalls Emelyn, "rais[ing] themselves up on their elbows, to get the last glimpse of her as she was going away."[13]

Moving amid rows of men dying agonizing deaths from "gunshot-wounds and wound-fever," Fuller for a moment was not so sure if fighting for one's principles was worth it. The sight of "the beautiful young men, mown down in their stately prime," made her "forget the great ideas" and sympathize with the women, moth-ers "who had nursed their precious forms, only to see them all lopped and gashed." "You say," she will write William Channing from Ricti on 28 August, long after the French entered Rome, that "I sustained them; often have they sustained my courage: one, kissing the pieces of bone that were so painfully extracted from his arm, . . . mementoes that he also had done and borne something for his country and the hopes of humanity."[14]

France's final assault on Rome began 20 June and lasted until the Romans sur-rendered on the last day of the month. Anxious about Ossoli and her baby, she would wake up and seem "to hear [my little boy] call me," and, always, "he seemed to be crying." With bombs falling around her, Fuller went every day to wait in the crowd for letters about Nino. She saw blood streaming on the Pincian wall close to where Ossoli was. She picked up a piece of bomb that had burst close to him. Wit-nessing so much destruction—even the death by a cannonball near the Porte San Pancrazio of a twenty-one-year-old woman who was there that day handing her husband ammunition—made Fuller first doubt, then reaffirm, her conviction that the republican principle was worth dying for. To the Quaker Springs, Fuller will later write that what they say "about the peace way being the best" is "deeply true": "If any one see clearly how to work in that way, let him in God's name. Only if he abstain from fighting against giant wrongs let him be sure he is really and ardently at work undermining them or better still sustaining the rights that are to supplant them. Meanwhile I am not sure that I can keep my hands free from blood." She confesses that though she has never pretended to be a Christian "except in dabs and sparkles," she now keenly feels "the agonies of that baptism of blood . . . oh how deeply in the golden June days of Rome." She adds: "Christ did not have to see his dear ones pass the dark river; he could go alone." Fuller had to stay and watch the soldiers whose wounds she could not heal as they passed over that "dark river"—Styx or Jordan she does not say—into the realm of death.[15]

The number of the dying multiplied after the French made a breach in the Aurelian Wall at two on the morning of 22 June, "the fatal hour," Fuller called it in the *Tribune,* after which hand-to-hand fighting persisted until it spread down the Janiculum Hill and into the Trastevere district. For eight miraculous days the republicans kept fighting—with their bare hands when their weapons failed; yet it was, lamented Fuller, a "slaughter." Vastly outnumbered, the idealistic young artists and other such volunteers were "uniformly heroic." Meanwhile Fuller was increasingly seeing "subjects for amputation" among the "grievously wounded" men at the hospital. The Casa Diez, where Fuller usually stayed at night, was bombed late on 28 June. As cannonballs and bombs showered the building and whizzed and burst near her, she prayed that if a bomb struck her "much-exposed apartment" she might instantly die and God would transport her "soul to some sphere where Virtue and Love are not tyrannized over by egotism and brute force."[16]

The following night a violent storm shook Rome, forcing the French to pause in their bombing, only to resume it at two in the morning. After a night of shells and grenades raining heavily over the city, Lewis Cass, concerned for Fuller's safety, on 30 June went to her apartment at Casa Diez. He found her lying on her sofa. Exhausted and pale, she told him that she had a child and was married to Ossoli, who was now in command of a battery of soldiers on the Pincian Mount, the most exposed position in Rome. She also told Cass that she wished to join her husband there to die with him if fate demanded, and she asked him to deliver to her family the packet of papers in her hand.[17]

As they talked, however, the war was ending. With the stench of rotting corpses drifting down the Janiculum and into the city, the assembly voted that day to surrender. On 2 July the French prepared to take possession of the city. That evening Fuller went to the Corso in a carriage that stopped to let the lancers of Garibaldi gallop by. She followed them to the piazza of St. John Lateran. "Never," she wrote home, had she "seen a sight so beautiful, so romantic, and so sad": the "solemn grandeur of that piazza," "the magnificence of the 'mother of all churches,' the Baptistery with its porphyry columns, the Santa Scala" that legend says Christ climbed before his death, "the view through the gates of the Campagna," "so richly strewn with ruins." Fuller watched as the sun went down, the crescent moon rose, and the Italian youth were marshaled into order. Conspicuous among them were the Legionnaires: the tunic of bright red cloth, the Greek cap or round hat with Puritan plume. "Their long hair was blown back from [their] resolute faces"; they "all looked full of courage." These brave young soldiers, wrote Fuller, "had counted the cost before they entered on this perilous struggle": "they had weighed life and all its material advantages against Liberty, and made their election; they turned not back . . . at this bitter crisis." Called by Garibaldi to follow him to the hills and continue the fight, four thousand men followed him—all of them to suffer, most to die. They left behind them thirty-five hundred dead and wounded, the cost of a month's defense of the Roman Republic.[18]

Fuller, too, suffered. But now she was able to see that she had suffered nothing compared to Mazzini. She saw him on 3 July before he escaped by way of Marseilles to Switzerland. He had sent her a note conceding "friend, it is all over," and now he was eager to find passports to help Ciceruacchio—the republican believed to have engineered Rossi's assassination—escape Italy with his son. Fuller wrote Channing about her meeting with him in the home of his friends, the Modenas, noting that Mazzini, who had watched "his dearest friends perish," had not slept for nights: his eyes were "blood-shot; his skin orange." Of "flesh he had none; his hair was mixed with white; his hand was painful to the touch." Yet still full of "fiery purpose," he "had protested in the last hour against surrender." "In him," says Fuller, "I revered the hero, and owned myself not of that mould."[19]

In this world where the "bad side triumphs," Fuller had conceded in a 19 June letter to her sister, Ellen, she wished she might just lie down and sleep her "way into another sphere of existence" where she could be at peace with "one or two that love and need me." Having identified with the Italians in their fight against invading emperor, local kings, and a betraying pope, Fuller had warred with the fathers and "lost." On 8 July she wrote Richard: "Private hopes of mine are fallen with the hopes of Italy."[20]

Life for Fuller was indeed now "difficult." Ossoli's participation in the "democratic movement" had cost him his family's support, especially that of his brother Giuseppe. Equally offensive to Giuseppe was Ossoli's relationship with Fuller. Ossoli was seen as a traitor by his brothers, one of whom had hidden in his home's cellar while republican troops quartered there. Not only could Ossoli expect no financial support from them; they now shunned him. Worse, even if the couple left Rome, no matter where Ossoli went in Italy he would be in danger of harassment and arrest by the police.[21]

With the collapse of the republican cause went Fuller's hope of making her home in Rome, where she had lived, she wrote an American friend, "in a much more full and true way than was possible in our country." In Italy she had been respected, whereas by her own countrymen she was now being talked about and condemned as a social outcast, an eccentric rebel. In December 1849, three months after Fuller and her family had moved for safety to Florence and almost six months after the war had ended, Frederick Gale, brother of one of Fuller's Greene Street pupils, wrote from Italy to his sister about having met there "the quondam Margaret Fuller—now transformed, by marriage": "Now that the scornful, manhating Margaret of 40 has got a husband, really no old maid need despair, while there is life in her body!" In his journal he noted how he had found "*Madame Ossioli*"

[sic] to be "much older & uglier than I had anticipated," with "wrinkles & lines in her face, old enough for 60!" After noting her "ardor" for "that vulgar . . . beverage—so unfashionable for Boston blues, *the whiskey punch*," Gale concedes that he "danced two cotillions with her & found her none the worse for the liquor." Although Gale found Fuller's "ardor" for liquor amusing, whispered rumors were circulating back home about her outlandish behavior.[22]

Both friends and enemies were now linking her name with terms that to most provincial middle-class Americans were contemptible—"Red Republicanism," "Socialism," "Communism." These accusations were more damning to Fuller than were accounts about her unorthodox marriage, for contemporary periodicals were using "the terms as synonymous with each other and with 'anarchism,' 'terrorism,' and 'Jacobinism.'" Fuller was hence now seen as "a Red," a view confirmed when, in her November 1849 dispatch from Florence, she heralded socialism as the inevitable ideology for Europe in the coming era and prophesied that it would lead to "vast changes in modes of government, education and daily life," to "an uncompromising revolution."[23] Fuller's prediction that Europe in the future would embrace what American readers saw as a communist vision to solve its frightful social problems, as well as her illicit family, meant she could not expect a warm welcome should she return to the States, just as she also knew that in Rome her family no longer had a home.

Before leaving for Rieti where she and Ossoli went right after the fall of Rome before going to Florence by route of Perugia, Fuller paid a last visit to the Vascello Villa, where the fighting had been heaviest. She describes in her 6 July dispatch what she saw: "A marble nymph, with broken arm, looked sadly . . . from her sun-dried fountain, some roses were blooming still, some red oleanders amid the ruin. The sun was casting its last light on the mountains on the tranquil, sad Campagna, that sees one leaf turned more in the book of Woe." All this, she says sadly, was in the ruined Vascello. She "then entered the French ground, all mapped and hollowed like a honey-comb. A pair of skeleton legs protruded from a bank of one barricade; lower a dog had scratched away its light covering of earth from the body of a man, and discovered it lying face upward all dressed; the dog stood gazing on it with an air of stupid amazement." Following this account, Fuller appealed to Americans to "*do something*" to help the defeated Italian republicans as well as the heavily outnumbered Hungarians, who were fighting to defend their recently declared Hungarian Republic against Austrian and Russian aggression. She pleaded with her readers not "to sneer at all that is liberal." She hoped that her fellow countrymen—"lovers of freedom, lovers of truth"—would "rest not supine in your easier lives, but remember 'Mankind is one, / And beats with one great heart.'"[24]

64 ✑ Last Illusions

Despite the death and destruction in Rome, Fuller was able to hold fast to a few illusions. Like any mother, she had her hopes for her baby. No sooner had Rome fallen than she was writing Cass pleading with him to give her counsel as to how to escape Rome. She felt she would die "to be again separated from what I hold most dear." But for Nino, she would not leave, she said, until she knew if "some men, now sick," shall "live or die." Since the French had ordered the transfer of the wounded to the Termini prison, she feared the worst for them; some had lost limbs, one a right arm and leg. In the *Aeneid,* she had read about terrible war wounds, but even that blood-soaked text had not prepared her for their reality. Fuller wished she could stay and comfort the men near death. But an edict had been issued on 9 July that republican sympathizers who did not leave Rome within twenty-four hours were to be "shot here and there, when caught, or driven from port to port"; "they are the saddest exiles, since Troy fell," said Fuller in her August 1849 dispatch. She warns the French their triumph is temporary; the "exiles of Ilium founded a new world," and "He that had [no] where to lay His head . . . conquered the world." She felt she might yet conquer through her son. Before Rome fell she wrote Ellen congratulating her on her son's birth: "every mother is delighted by the birth of a man-child." Each "hopes to find in hers an Emanuel."[1]

But this dream about Nino fast faded when Fuller and Ossoli arrived in July in Rieti to find Nino almost dead. Because communication between Rome and Rieti had been severed, letters with Chiara's pay had not reached Rieti. Letters from Chiara's family, in turn, went unanswered. Thinking Nino had been abandoned, Chiara had fed the baby, instead of breast milk, a little wine and bread. Thus Fuller found in the Fiordiponte home no fat baby as she had during her March visit to Rieti. Rather she found Nino this time "wornd to a skeleton"—his life, according to Fuller, hanging "over the abyss." She vowed in a letter to Cass that "if he dies, I hope I shall, to[o]. . . . this last shipwreck of ho[pes] would be more than I can bear."[2]

But Nino survived, and a humble Fuller wrote friends to tell them about Ossoli and Nino, whom she now knew she must take to Boston. In her letter to William Channing revealing her son's existence she says that Nino's smiles "give my heart amid the cries of carnage and oppression an even bird like joy." Regarding his father, Fuller concedes: "If earthly union be meant for the beginning of one permanent . . . we ought not to be united. . . . Yet I shall never regret the step which has given me the experience of a mother and satisfied domestic wants in a most sincere and sweet companion."[3]

In August to Costanza from Rieti, Fuller similarly noted that she has "united" her "destiny" with that of "an obscure young man" who lacks "intellectual culture." She concedes that "you will see no reason for my choosing"—except that "we have with us our child, of a year old." She tells Costanza that if she feels she must tell her friends, then "it will be true to say that there have been pecuniary reasons for this concealment. But to *you* in confidence I add, this is only half the truth." However, since they must necessarily meet and speak, says Fuller, "in the midst of 'society,'" it would be wise for her "to enquire for me now as *Margaret Ossoli* that being done, I should like to say nothing farther on the subject." Despite her wish that Costanza hereafter pass over the subject in silence, Fuller insists that she is "more radical than ever." Her affirmation of her radicalism suggests that Fuller's omission of a mention of marriage was intentional. To Channing she was more candid, saying that the "tie" (and again she avoids mention of marriage) leaves her "mentally free," as she wants Ossoli "also to remain." On the subject of children she says: "in the midst of a false world . . . truth is easier to those who have not them."[4]

No matter how bold she might be in interacting with trusted friends like the worldly Costanza and the socialist Channing, as a member of middle-class American society—what she cynically in her letter to Channing calls "this corrupt social contract"—Fuller knew she must play her womanly part in accord with certain rules. Or she must at least provide society with a reason to overlook her wayward behavior. Fuller hoped by means of her book on the Roman revolution to "refute," as a friend would later put it, "the calumnies and falsehoods" with which her name as well as those "of the Republican leaders" had "been blackened . . . throughout the civilized world." To realize this second dream—that she might save herself and her family through the publication of this history—would be difficult, especially since she was writing it without a contract with a publisher. The London firm to which Fuller had sent the raw material for the book had rejected it. Their negative assessment not only added to her doubts about the future but also called into question her writing ability. In December from Florence she wrote Caroline that of "at least two volumes" produced during her "vehement efforts . . . to redeem the time" after Nino's birth in Rieti, "no line seems of any worth." When on 5 September 1849, Nino's first birthday, Fuller received the letter of rejection, she had not been surprised. She had "foreseen" it, she wrote Cass, "from a feeling of fate."[5]

For her small family's financial security, Fuller had to earn money from her writing. In late August Ossoli had tried to get money from his brothers in return for renouncing claims on Ossoli property connected to the Castle of Pietra-forte in the Sabine Hills, but his brothers had repudiated him. Equally troubling, while Ossoli was checking on these properties he had crossed into the Kingdom of Naples and was arrested on suspicion of being a Garibaldi supporter. He was apparently released only because he was carrying a letter for the Marchese Ossoli. A Bourbon regimental chaplain recognized the Ossoli name as being connected with the Guard Noble of the pope. Fuller in the meantime visited a local official to make sure Ossoli's papers were in order for his release.[6] Ossoli's encounter with Ferdinand's soldiers reinforced with the couple the importance of Fuller earning enough to pay their way to America.

Yet it seemed to Fuller that fate was determined to keep her from making money from her writing. In September she and Ossoli rented a small apartment in Florence on the third floor of a house with windows looking out over the piazza of the Santa Maria Novella Church, but the only room with a stove was the small dining room with its frescoed ceiling and polished tiled floor. When a cold spell "unknown before to Italy" brought Florence to a standstill in December, the room where she had hoped to write became uninhabitable and she was unable to work for about seven weeks. She had tried writing by oil light on the oval dining table. But in that crowded room she spent so much time tending to Nino that she was generally too tired at night to do anything but read. In such a way "all the little daily things" cut into her writing. Yet even before the cold spell had come, she had written Channing not to "expect any thing very good of [my writing]." Writer Elizabeth Barrett Browning, who had supported Italian unity and over "a great gulf of differing opinion" had become Fuller's friend, said after Fuller's death about the book that, "nothing was finished."[7]

Still, even with the difficult circumstances and an unfavorable exchange rate, Fuller thought she and Ossoli could make it through April if they lived simply. Despite disappointments—the promise of the American artist Joseph Mozier to secure for her some financial compensation for a series of Letters from Florence fell through; her living quarters remained cramped and cold; and she continued to have doubts about her writing—Fuller believed that once back in the States she could assemble a manuscript that would attract a publisher.[8]

Fuller's success at revision depended, however, on her ability to realize a third dream. During a winter when Rome was buried beneath two feet of snow, when Florence was so cold that even the oil congealed in the closet by the fire, as did the water in bed chambers in houses "as yet uncomforted with furnaces," and Nino suffered "with chilblains," this last illusion helped Fuller keep going. In it she saw herself as a prodigal child returning home to discover an "obscure" yet redemptive community in which she and her little family would be joyously received by charitable friends, as well as by her loving and forgiving mother. This Bible story to which she had often alluded—as she had the previous winter in a letter to Richard from Rome—for her now involved a scene of recognition and reconciliation between not father and son but mother and daughter. She hoped that such a harmonious return to her mother's home, in particular to the loving arms of her mother, would be the way her story as a wandering pilgrim would end.[9]

In the August letter wherein she finally tells her Calvinist mother about Ossoli and Nino, she noticeably does not mention a marriage, perhaps because to do so would be to reveal that Nino was illegitimate. Instead she says: "The first moment, it may cause you a pang to know that your eldest child *might* long ago have been addressed by another name than yours, and has a little son a year old" (emphasis added). But the kind and generous Margarett Crane asked no questions: rather, she sent her "fervent blessing" to her grandson, along with an assurance to her daughter of her continuing love, support, and sympathy. The mother advises her prodigal daughter: "Let us hold fast our faith in the good providence of God, who has led us gently thro' all our darkest days, wiped away our tears . . . and showed us the light of His countenance when we were ready to faint by the way." A joyous Margaret in December replied: "Dearest Mother, of all your endless acts and words of love, never was any so dear to me as your last letter so generous, so sweet, so holy! What on earth is so precious as a mother's love; and who has a mother like mine?"[10]

Sitting in her cold and barely habitable room, with the earth outside "shrouded" in snow, "I have thought a great deal of you," Margaret confessed to her mother in February 1850, "remembering how you suffer by cold in the winter and hope you are in a warm comfortable house, have pleasant books to read and some pleasant friends to see." She says that in Florence she and Ossoli have a new close friend: "Horace Sumner youngest son of Father's [friend] Charles Sumner." She notes how odd this friendship seems, since "not one of Father's friends ever became mine," though she thinks that might be because she was, herself, so "odd" a child. In the evenings Horace sits in the dining room by the fire with Ossoli. There they exchange instruction in English and Italian. She says that Horace, whom she calls "slow," has spoken warmly of Lloyd, whom he had known at Brook Farm. Her mother, her sister, her brothers, and a few friends like Horace are all Fuller feels she needs to live a rich life at home.[11]

Fuller believed that within such a community, she would "be welcome with my treasures, my husband and child." To her trusted friends Sam and Anna she had written in October to say that she and Ossoli were married. Trying to explain her odd choice of a mate she says, "it is for my heart that he loves me." Still, if only they could be "sure of a narrow competency" in the United States, then they could be happy; "however . . . life itself is so uncertain."[12]

A fact her friend Costanza, who had lost a teenage son, understood. To Costanza, who at age thirty-eight had given birth to another son, Fuller wrote in October how Nino is for her a source "of ineffable joys, far purer, deeper than any thing I ever felt before." To Emelyn in November she wrote: "What a difference it makes to come home to a child." Before Nino she "used to feel sad" coming home. But "now" she never feels lonely or sad, "for even if my little boy dies, our souls will remain eternally united." For him she feels "*infinite* hope" he will "serve God and man" more loyally than has she.[13]

Yet Fuller knew how perilous are the hopes parents pin on their children. The previous August she had received from Greeley his grieving 23 July letter. "Ah Margaret!" he had written, "You grieve, for Rome has fallen; I mourn, for Pickie is dead." Greeley tells Fuller how his life has been too busy to include in it "an intimate friend." Yet, since Pickie's birth, he has had "no hope, no dream of personal good or distinction" of which his son's "advantage, was not the better part." "Ah! my friend!" he keens, "he was a dear child, and it is very hard to leave him in the cold earth."[14]

In the image of Pickie in the cold earth, Fuller saw Nino. "Bitterest tears alone can answer those words—*Pickie is dead,*" she wrote Greeley on 25 August. She confesses in her letter that she has "suffered not a few sleepless hours thinking of our darling, haunted with fears never again to see his sweet, joyous face which on me, also, always looked with love and trust." And her "heart," in return, "always was open to him." Only once before had she "so loved" a child, and that was "little Waldo Emerson."[15]

In this letter Fuller had revealed Nino's existence to Greeley, noting that while he grieves to relinquish Pickie to the earth, "my heart is bound to earth as never before"; "for I, too, have a dearer self—a little son." But she has already been warned that she must be prepared to relinquish him. For after the war, when their "dearest friends" had been "laid low," she had found her baby in Rieti "wasted to a skeleton." Remembering "what Mrs. Greeley did for Pickie" when he was ill, she was "able to restore him." She knows, however, that she holds Nino "by a frail tenure."[16]

Nino had become Fuller's lifeline. Regarding Pickie's death, she confessed a week later to her mother: "One would think I might have become familiar enough with images of death and destruction; yet somehow the image of Pickie's little dancing figure, lying, stiff and stark, between his parents, has made me weep more than all else." "Earth, our mother," she says, "always finds strange, unexpected ways to draw us back to her bosom."[17]

In December 1849 she wrote Ellen and Cary about her agony when she had returned to Rieti after Rome's fall to find Nino almost dead. To Ellen she confesses that, when she really saw him lingering "between life and death, . . . I resolved to live day by day and hour by hour for his dear sake." If he is to be only a "treasure lent," then she "at least" has these "days and hours with him." To Cary at Christmas she wrote how nothing had prepared her for "this kind of pain." Yet having experienced it: "This much I do hope, in life or death to be no more separated from Angelino. . . . The position of a mother separated from her only child is too frightfully unnatural."[18]

❦ ❦ ❦

Fuller found herself in an ironic situation. Though in Italy she had affirmed her sense of herself as a woman, her defiance of the fathers—both Puritan and Roman Catholic, including those of Ossoli's family who had cut him off financially and emotionally—made "imperatively necessary" her return to an America that now viewed her as a pariah. In Italy where she had felt at home, she thus no longer had a home. Even in Florence, where the imprint of the more liberal-minded Leopold could still be felt, Ossoli, now using an American passport, which marked him as a republican fugitive, was harassed by police who would have sent both Ossoli and Fuller out of Tuscany had friends not intervened in their behalf. Fuller appealed to Cass, who helped secure the paperwork necessary for them to extend their stay in Florence. Ossoli in the meantime wrote an influential Roman friend, Gaeto Suárra, pleading with him to intercede by getting for him an official pontifical passport to make it safe for "Gio Angelo Marchese Ossoli with wife and family" to stay in Florence. In his letter requesting the passport, Ossoli warned his friend not to try to obtain one from officials in his home parish because, he said, "I never told them that I had married an American woman outside of Rome." Instead of proof of marriage, Ossoli enclosed in his letter the passport he had used earlier to travel the year before to Aquila, along with Fuller's. The friend replied by telling Ossoli "that his wife should go to the American ministry immediately," that "they are extremely interested." In the meantime Fuller had contacted Cass. Three weeks later Ossoli was granted a permit allowing him to extend his stay in Florence for two months with the possibility of extension. That their friends were able to secure for him the required permit but not an official pontifical passport indicates, as von Mehren says, that the "pontifical authorities were not inclined to be lenient to those who had fought on behalf of the Roman Republic." It also suggests "that Ossoli was probably unable to produce evidence of a marriage recognized by the Catholic church."[19]

Knowing Ossoli was under surveillance in Florence and that reactionary forces were gaining strength in Piedmont, Tuscany, and Rome, made Fuller and Ossoli turn their eyes ever more eagerly, confessed Fuller, "towards *America*." So, too, did their need of money. Ossoli's brothers rejected his appeals for money, and what was due him from the Ossoli estate he was not likely to see for years. To help tide them over, Joseph Mozier in January gave Ossoli a job as an assistant in his art studio, and he was also paying Fuller to tutor his daughter. But their combined income was hardly enough to allow them to plan for the future. Fuller wrote a friend back home that now she is a mother, she feels "poverty a great evil." Desperate for money she wrote the Springs, now in New York, asking them to go to the publishers of her miscellanies to see if they can "squeeze" any money out of them.[20]

Thus Fuller's need to return home to earn money and ensure her and Ossoli's freedom was drawing her and those she loved to destruction. About her decision to leave the Springs in Venice in July 1847 and go back to Rome and Ossoli, Fuller in a 29 November 1849 letter had said she had "no regrets." To Ellen in the December 1849 letter in which she does not mention marriage, she echoes terms from the novel *Hesitation* she had loved as a child. In it she says that Ossoli is Roman Catholic and she hence does not know how to explain a "connexion" that to friends at home must seem "so every way unfit." "I acted upon a strong impulse," she says. "I could not analyze at all what passed in my mind." Then in words similar to those

　APOCALYPTIC DREAMS AND FALL OF ROME

with which she had defended George Sand, she says: "I neither rejoice nor grieve, for bad or for good I acted out my character Had I never connected myself with any one my path was clear, now it is all hid, but in that case my development must have been partial." To Channing on 7 December she admitted that no one—except, perhaps, children and her mother—has ever loved her as "genuinely" as does Ossoli.[21]

Though her "path" through life was now not "clear," Fuller did not "regret the step" that made her a mother because, as she had written her mother: "In [Ossoli] I find satisfaction, for the first time, to the deep wants of my heart." Moreover, it was the experience of being a mother that had made possible a loving reconciliation with this good woman Margaret now knew she had never sufficiently appreciated. Still more, in connecting with Ossoli in "marriage," however unorthodox it might be—and even *if*, as Hawthorne would say of Hester Prynne's connection with Dimmesdale, "unrecognized on earth"—Fuller became, in her own and others' view, a marchesa. Thus she became the queen that as a child she had imagined herself to be. In her December letter to Cary in which she tells how her mother "blessed" her and "rejoiced" that "she should not die feeling there was no one left to love" her daughter, Fuller notes that "St Peters is like Rome, mixture of sublimest God, with corruptest Earth." In St. Peter's Basilica she had met Ossoli. Hence "no place" on earth could be to her "like St Peters, where has been the splendidest part of my life": "My feeling was always perfectly regal, on entering the piazza of St Peters."[22]

But rude reality dispels illusions. Fuller's poverty made her unsure how she would ever "get across the great water" to America. A despairing Fuller shared with Cary before Christmas what seems to have been a fleeting suicidal thought: "There is snow all over Florence in our most beautiful piazza. La Maria Novella, with its fair loggia and bridal church is a carpet of snow and the full moon looking down, I had forgotten how angelical all that is, how fit to die by."[23]

At about the time that Fuller was sharing with Cary not just her despair but also her joy in watching her boy playing naked on the sofa with the toys he had received for Christmas—his mouth making "a little round O" as he happily regarded a toy bird, a horse, a cat—she was also writing what would be her last and most utopian letter to the *Tribune*. In it she transmutes despair over the failed revolution into prophecy by envisioning for her readers the coming millennium when time itself will be forever altered. Fuller predicts that the Italian people's failure through armed revolution to overcome tyranny has sown the "seeds for a vast harvest of hatreds" that cannot "be extirpated, till the wishes of Heaven shall waft a fire that will burn down all, root and branch, and prepare the earth for an entirely new culture." The result of this "radical" revolution is to be a new culture wherein not just Jesuits but even the "Pope cannot retain . . . his spiritual power." To achieve this ideal state, "not only the Austrian, . . . but every man who assumes an arbitrary lordship over [his] fellow man, must be driven out." From her despair Fuller thus generated a vision of a world wherein authoritarian fathers no longer rule and men (and women) are "represented"—not as physical beings with errant passions—but "as souls . . . and governed accordingly."[24]

In projecting a vision that damns what seemed to her to be "a prostituted civilization" wherein men and women sell their souls for gold, Fuller embraced a radical Romantic ideal that offended her American readers in its total rejection of authority—be it that of king, pope, or authoritative father. From the perspective of her primarily Christian, socially conservative yet reform-minded middle-class American audience, it seemed the vision of a deluded woman who had wandered, to use Fuller's own words, "quite off the beaten track" and embraced, not a life-saving faith in God, but anarchy and death in its denial of the everyday ceremonies, civilities and rituals that make life in common possible.[25]

In the States, public feeling for Fuller had grown so negative that, months before she left from Leghorn, her return was indeed as if ill-fated. In the same way as Dido's love affair in the cave with Aeneas made Rumor (Fama) run rampant through northern Africa, so Rumor now raced over the ocean ahead of Fuller, gathering strength as it traveled. Though in Europe it had seemed to Fuller but a small thing, by the time it reached America, Rumor, as Virgil depicts it in lines Fuller had quoted from memory to Henry Hedge years earlier, "walked upon the ground," "its head in the cloud-base." Fuller knew this was the price she must pay for her outré behavior. In her 6 March 1835 letter to Hedge, Fuller had noted her "great partiality" for the Roman goddess Fama that was now ruining her reputation. And it was being ruined in the eyes not only of conservative New York Catholics, but also of New England Puritans she loved. With gossip all around them, Elizabeth and Waldo still did not find time to write. Even the exceedingly open-minded William Channing, who was seeing the Springs regularly at Associationist meetings and his New York church, was worried that Fuller had at last crossed a line of propriety in the eyes of certain people who would not—could not—now forgive her.[26]

Aware of the damage to her reputation, Fuller Dido-like appealed to Channing. In letters she affirms her faith that he will understand when she at last tells him "things" she does not "wish to put on paper." Alluding to the lines from Virgil about rumor she knew well, on 6 February she wrote him: "I know there must be a cloud of false rumors and impressions at first, but you will see when we meet that there was a sufficient reason for all I have done, and that if my life be not wholly right, (as it is so difficult to keep a life true in a world full of falsities,) it is not wholly wrong nor fruitless." Fuller continues: "But I have too much to tell you of all that, in which others are also interwoven. My life proceeds so regularly, far more so than the fates of a Greek tragedy, that I can but accept all the pages as they turn." In seeing herself as a character caught in the inevitable events of a tragedy, she ironically surrendered her freedom to what seemed to her to be a prewritten script and fatalistic power, as Oedipus had felt compelled to "return a criminal, blind and outcast"—words Fuller had once written in regards to herself. Indeed, that power now seemed to be compelling her to return to America where—except for her mother who loved her, faults and all—as a prodigal daughter she was not welcome.[27]

What Cary had written her about "the meddling curiosity of people" in New England repelled Margaret. In a letter to Emelyn she angrily labeled all the gossips with their prying eyes "the social inquisition of the U.S." and asked what right had any of them "to know all the details of my [private] affairs?" "You and I," she says, "know enough of the U.S. to be sure that many persons there will blame whatever is peculiar . . . whatever is mysterious must be bad." "It is so different here," Margaret wrote Cary. When she appeared in Florence with a husband and a son of a year old, "none asked or implied questions." Even she had been surprised and pleased when both Europeans and "the little American society of Florence" had greeted her and her unsuspected "underplot" with a "warmth of interest," since, she wrote Costanza, as "Goethe says, there is nothing men pardon so little as singular conduct for which no reason is given."[28]

Trying to explain Fuller's "singular conduct" to their mutual friends at home, Emelyn wrote Maria Lowell in Boston saying that she had known about the "marriage" for more than six months and that the "Marquis Ossoli" was a decent man whose participation in the Italian Revolution had prompted his family, which supported the pope, to disclaim him. She said these family difficulties had prevented Fuller and Ossoli from announcing their marriage earlier. Margaret was grateful to Emelyn for attempting to ameliorate the situation at home since she was set on returning. A descendant of Puritans, as well as a child raised on Romantic literature, Margaret felt returning home was the way the story was supposed to go. Like both Huon in the fairy tale *Oberon* she had loved as a child and the prodigal son with whom she identified, she had left home, sinned in the world, become penniless and now, humbly, longed to return home to receive her parent's blessing. Fuller, who had literally journeyed into a far country and was now considered a sinner and outcast in American public opinion, longed with all her heart to return to her mother, to be "embrace[d]" by this good woman who, after Margaret had told her about Ossoli and the baby, had lovingly responded, "how dearly I shall love him if he brings you safe to me."[29]

Although her pious Puritan fathers would, Fuller knew, condemn her defiance of social convention, her loving mother eagerly awaited her arrival. In a June letter that Fuller was never to see, her mother will say that she is waiting in America to bless her "beloved child" and receive her "treasures" when she returns with them to her "native home." Fearing she is mailing her letter too late, Margarett Crane will "grieve" in it that it cannot reach her "beloved Daughter" in time "to confer" her "blessing" on her wandering child's journey. "We have a good & rich girl," Fuller's mother will say in a 28 June letter to Richard, "and if those we love return to us all seems to promise well." Margarett Crane is thinking here of her prodigal brother Peter, that sweet-tempered yet presumptuous youth who had left home without his parents' blessing to seek a distant Eldorado, only to die there in poverty and thus break his mother's heart, Margaret's pious grandmother, who had waited long fruitless years for her only son's return.[30]

Apart from wanting to see her mother, other reasons were drawing Fuller home that summer. She wanted to see Eugene, who was coming to New England that summer. She also wanted to find a publisher for her "history of the late Italian revolution." A new regulation in England prohibiting foreigners from holding copyrights now left her sole publishing options in the States, where she wanted to be "on the spot" to negotiate a contract with a publisher. She had received in the mail an offer from a U.S. publisher, but it was unsatisfactory to her.[31]

For all these reasons, Fuller felt she had to sail home that summer, despite Joseph Mozier's attempt to convince her to stay in Florence longer. But it was Mozier, then, who arranged passage on the "Elisabeth," a small but nearly new and well-kept three-masted merchantman. It was scheduled to leave Leghorn (Livorno) in northern Italy for New York in May 1850 on a voyage that would take about sixty days. Fuller dreaded it. Her head hurt so much at sea that the thought of being on it for two months was distressing. But traveling by merchantman from Leghorn cost about half as much as going to Le Havre and taking a packet, which took half the time and was safer.[32]

Aware of the risks, Fuller worried about her young son becoming ill or malnourished at sea. The travelers would be gone so long that it would be hard to stock enough supplies—not to mention she was going to have to bring along a nursemaid—a young woman from Rome named Celeste Paolini—for the baby as well as a goat to supply fresh milk. In her last letter to Channing, Fuller confessed that, for Nino, she had become a "miserable coward." She loves her son too much, she says, but feels she has no other options. In an early March letter to the bachelor Cass, she says, "nothing else" but one's love for one's child "can take the worst bitterness out of life: nothing else can break the spell of loneliness."[33]

Fuller wrote this letter to kind Lewis Cass from Florence on a "divine day" in March when the winds were blowing gently and the crows were "cawing and searching in gay bands; the birds twittering their first notes of love" and "the fields" flowing "with anemones, cowslips and crocuses." It was a lovely Italian spring, as good as paradise before the fall. Fuller tells Cass that she has never felt "so near happy as now," when "I find always the glad eyes of my little boy to welcome me home." She confides: "I feel the tie between him and me so real, so deep-rooted, even death shall not part us. I shall not be alone in other worlds, whenever Eternity may call me." Unlike the too intense "love" that had existed between her and her father, this "unimpassioned love" between her and her son "knows not dark reactions, it does not idealize and cannot be daunted by the faults of its object."[34]

Was this, then, the all of paradise she was to know?—the glad eyes of her little boy welcoming her home on a glorious, sunlit Italian day? Apparently so. For on the first of April the rain began to fall, incessant heavy rains that made her head hurt and filled her with a dark premonition about the approaching voyage. Always seeking signs in the skies of her chosen status, Fuller felt as if God himself had cast his wrath upon her planned voyage home. "Various little omens" gave her a dark feeling and made her "absurdly fearful about this voyage," she wrote Costanza on 6 April. "Among others just now, we hear of the wreck of the ship Westmoreland, bearing Powers's Eve"—an ill omen if ever there was one. For with this damage to Powers's statue of "Eve," it did seem as if God as father meant, again, to curse mankind through woman. It was especially scary for Fuller, who knew that the *Elizabeth,* which bore the name of a queen, was carrying Powers's heavy statue of the American politician John C. Calhoun, in addition to 150 tons of Carrara marble. "Perhaps," Fuller writes to Costanza, "we shall live to laugh at these [omens], but in case of mishap, I should perish with my husband and child perhaps to be transferred to some happier state; and my dear mother, whom I so long to see, would soon follow, and embrace me more peaceably elsewhere." This written vow to die with her husband and son should her ship meet with mishap, she repeats in another letter to Costanza two weeks later.[35]

In that 21 April letter Fuller notes she has just read about the wreck of the *Argo,* the packet ship she had considered sailing on out of France. In the same paper there were also notices "of the wreck of the 'Royal Adelaide,' a fine English steamer, and of the 'John Skiddy' one of the fine American Packets." Since "it seems safety is not [to] be found in the wisest calculation," she writes, "I shall embark more composedly in my merchant ship; praying, indeed, fervently, that it may not be my lot to lose my babe at sea, either by unsolaced sickness, or amid the howling waves." Should that happen, she prays "it may be brief anguish, and Ossoli he and I go together."[36]

All through April friends came by and tried to persuade her not to sail on a merchantman, saying that she had no idea how much she would suffer on so long a voyage, and how terrible it would be if the baby should become ill:

That the insecurity compared with packet ships or steamers is so great; that the cabin being on deck will be terribly exposed in case of a gale; that I cannot be secure of having good water to drink, far less to wash clothing, and therefore must buy an immense stock of baby-linen; that I cannot go without providing for us poultry, a goat for milk, oranges and lemons, soda hardbread, and a medicine chest, all things which in the passenger line are . . . a matter of course if you want them . . . ; that these things will cost as much as the difference of going round by France, while I shall suffer much more, and be exposed to greater risk.—

For these many reasons, her friends contended, Fuller should go to Le Havre and travel by packet. Yet nothing now could change her mind. Fuller chose to go home on the *Elizabeth* with a full understanding of its dangers. She also knew that, in having given birth to a baby without having written home specifics about a marriage, she had, as she says in a 10 May letter to William Story, "acted with great carelessness"—"carelessness" being, as she was well aware, the "one fault" her father "often mentioned, as the source, the very fountain" of *all* her "others."[37]

It was thus as if Fuller were courting a dark destiny she had felt since early childhood that fate had preordained for her. On 2 May she explained in a letter to Cass how she could have lived happily "always" in Italy. But "destiny," she says, did not permit it.[38]

Though Fuller thought it to be destiny's design that she return home after her years of wandering, the "unpropitious weather" seemed determined to hinder her departure, for heavy rain delayed the loading of the cargo of marble and rags. Fuller was so anxious about the trip and so sad at leaving Italy that she seemed, she told William Story in her 10 May letter, "paralyzed." And in a letter to her mother dated four days later, she fatalistically notes that should they never meet "on earth again," then "think of your daughter as one who always wished at least to do her duty, and who always cherished you." She asks her mother to give her love to her sister, aunts, cousin, and brothers, but "first my eldest, and faithful friend, Eugene, God bless him." She hopes she and her mother will meet again, "but if God decrees otherwise,—here and hereafter, My dearest Mother," then signed her letter—"Your loving child, Margaret."[39]

Fuller's anxiety had been fed by a prophecy that Ossoli had been told by a fortuneteller when he was small, as Elizabeth Barrett Browning recalled the account, a prophecy "talked of jestingly" on that last night in Florence when the Brownings had come to say good-bye, "that [Ossoli] should shun the sea, for that it would be fatal to him." That night Fuller had thus given as a parting gift—from her child to theirs—a Bible inscribed with: "*In memory of* Angelo Eugene Ossoli."[40]

65 ∞ A Wayward Pilgrim Journeys Home

Before she boarded the *Elizabeth* on 17 May in Leghorn, Fuller received a last packet from home containing separate letters from Marcus and Rebecca Spring, as well as one from Emerson, offering unbidden, even cruel, words of advice. Writing from Rose Cottage on 14 April, Rebecca hedges in her letter as she tells Fuller "my most important thing. . . . And that is that much as we should love to see you and strange as it may seem we, as well as all your friends who have spoken to us about it, believe it will be undesirable for you to return at present." After all, Fuller's writing would be more valuable telling about events in Italy. Moreover, "your friend (whom with much pleasure we now learn from Hicks is your old friend Giovanni) would not—and could not—be so happy here as in his own beautiful Italy." "It is," then, says Rebecca, "because we love you" that "we say—stay!—It is because we believe it best for you—and in thus advising you, you have a proof of the true friendship and affection of Rebecca." Marcus was abrupt. All her friends, even "Wm Channing," with whom "we had a good long talk about your affairs," argue "in favor of your remaining abroad." Listing a dozen reasons why everyone thinks this best for her, Marcus tells Fuller that she could be a kind of "outside barbarian," continuing to send news of Europe home to America. Marcus stresses how glad they were to learn that she and the Marquis Ossoli "had married," glad that "now it all turns out right," after all. Playing on Fuller's vision in *Woman in the Nineteenth Century* of "the purity of love, in a true marriage," he ends his epistle with a cunning benediction: "I cordially wish you both a long life of constantly increasing & deepening love, which I believe must result from the *true* marriage. Marcus" (original emphasis).[1]

Even her beloved Emerson, whom she had asked to stretch forth his pure hands so she can claim their grasp to save her from despair, wrote finally in mid-April, urging her not to return. He assures her he will do all he can to get the best terms for her with a U.S. publisher. Ill at ease in the part he feels obliged to play, he sent word in this last letter to his "dearest" friend Margaret: "It is certainly an unexpected side for me to support,—the advantages of your absenteeism,—I, who had vainly imagined that one of these days . . . our little Concord would draw you to itself, by the united claims of four families[,] of your friends,—but surprise is the woof you love to weave into all your web."[2]

Emerson here compares Fuller to the mythical Arachne—a Lydian weaver who rouses Athena to such wrath by producing so perfect a tapestry in a weaving duel with her that the goddess destroys it, causing the despairing girl to try to hang herself, whereupon Athena saves her by turning her into a spider that continues to spin and weave. Emerson thus sees Fuller as an Arachne-like spider weaving her destiny in a design quite at odds with what conventional friends back home expect (the "net of ties" she herself had written him she was "caught in"), and one he suspects will lead to tragedy. He suggests that he hopes that the design she weaves will again surprise them and not lead her home. But Fuller remained determined to return home, "prepared to expect," she had confided to Emelyn, "everything that is painful and difficult." For she knew that she was taking Ossoli to a society that would reject him. To both her mother and sister she had written that Ossoli would be "among strangers" in whose estimate ("Mr Emerson['s]," she said, "for one") "he will be nothing." Such friends will see only the "unfit and ill-fated outwardly . . . externals of our relation." But then she knew that she, too, had been and would continue to be after her return, as Sophocles' Antigone had said of herself, "a stranger . . . in my own land."[3]

As Antigone's "unnatural" life had ended in tragedy, so it now seemed to Fuller that hers might also, especially after the *Elizabeth*'s Captain Seth Hasty was struck down with smallpox after their departure from Italy. In two 3 June letters posted from Gibraltar where the ship stayed anchored for a week flying the quarantine flag—one to Marcus wherein she also tells him that she has drawn on him financially in order to fund her trip home, and another to the parents of Mrs. Hasty—Fuller details the captain's horrific death. They had been at sea only a week when Captain Hasty—who Fuller remembers had played with Nino—went to his cabin to lie down after complaining of violent pain in his head and back. The next day the fever began. Fuller at first mistook it for a "nervous fever" and hence had spent a great deal of time nursing him as best she could. But on the following Saturday a red eruption had showed itself, first on the forehead and hands, until gradually it covered his body. Everyone saw that it was smallpox; but since harbor authorities allowed no physician onboard, night and day the captain was nursed by his wife, and then by Fuller when Catherine Hasty grew too tired to tend to him. Though the fever diminished enough to deceive the women into thinking he was through the worst of the disease, the drop in fever was in fact followed by an "extreme, a convulsive and constant cough" that deprived him of sleep. "Then," writes Fuller, "his throat became [so] swollen and irritated that it was impossible for him to swallow." By this time the pustules covering his body had turned black and become "very painful." In this frank letter, the last Fuller would write, she tells how, at death's door, Captain Hasty expressed hope "to recover and live with [his wife], and see again their dear parents and friends." Yet "*still* he said," adds Fuller in words that reveal her own state of mind, "though I wish to live, if God wills it otherwise, I am resigned."[4]

On Sunday morning, 2 June, after ten days of unbearable pain, Captain Hasty died. His death was considered a "mercy" by all who had witnessed his suffering, especially, says Fuller, since "his face assumed immediately that hallowed calmness, peculiar to the death of those whose spirits have been good and not evil." Hasty's death had been wretched to witness. The strain of smallpox virus was so virulent that, according to Fuller, it reduced "the once fair and expressive mould of man" in a mere ten days to an abscess-covered mass of flesh.[5]

Fuller suggests in her letter to Marcus that looking on Hasty during his last days—days "truly terrible with disgusts and fatigues"—made her contemplate her own mortality. All her life she had evaded the pain of reality and death through escaping into beautiful illusions, yet here she was now, as in her nightmare, "imprisoned in a ship at sea" with death, so to speak, as her fellow traveler.[6]

That Sunday at six the crew buried their captain in deep water. Fuller wrote Marcus how "a divinely calm soft glowing afternoon had succeeded a morning of bleak cold wind." Numb from the sad scene she has witnessed yet ever the vigilant journalist, she describes "how beautiful the whole thing was—the decent array and sad reverence of the sailors—the many ships with their banners flying, the stern pillar of Hercules all veiled in roseate vapor, the little angel white sails diving into the blue depths with that solemn spoil of the poor good man—so still who had been so agonized and gasping as the last sun stooped." "Yes!" she confesses, "it was beautiful but how dear a price we pay for the poems of this world."[7]

On 8 June the *Elizabeth* set sail from Gibraltar with First Mate Henry Bangs as acting captain. Nino, whom Fuller had taken into the captain's cabin before the nature of his illness asserted itself, came down with smallpox two days out of Gibraltar. His body broke out in a rash that progressed to small blisters and then to pustules that covered his face so as to swell his eyelids shut. Sitting beside his son's sickbed in their cabin, Ossoli, who had already had the disease and thus was immune, gave Nino up to God. But Fuller, who in letters to friends had intuited that she and her child might die on this voyage, would not let Nino go. If ever a mother's care has had the power to deter death, then Margaret Fuller's love and good nursing kept her child alive, and on the ninth day the fever broke. Nino's "glad eyes" opened and greeted his grateful mother.[8]

But all Fuller's efforts to deter death were to come up against a destiny that seemed to have singled her out Oedipus-like as an example and instrument of instruction to others. Everything she feared was coming true. As if fated, shortly before four in the morning of 19 July 1850, while the ship was sailing north off course in gale winds not more than fifty yards from Fire Island, the thirty-mile sandbar along Long Island's south side, it struck the sandbar. Mr. Bangs, an inexperienced navigator, had underestimated the danger they were in by miscalculating the ship's position; he thought the ship was positioned somewhere between Cape May and Barnegat, New Jersey. Nor could he have known that the storm that had suddenly come up and blown him off course was of hurricane strength. It had earlier that day made its way up the Atlantic Coast, flooding the streets of Richmond, Virginia, washing away the Cumberland Valley railroad bridge, grounding the schooner *Adelaide* with its 126 tons of coal near Lewis, Delaware, and filling the Susquehanna River with downed trees and debris. According to Mrs. Hasty, at about half past two in the morning Mr. Bangs, the mate in charge, took soundings, and held course. Meanwhile the passengers, having packed in preparation for landing in the morning, were asleep in the cabin with "the storm howling fiercely" outside. They were asleep when the ship sometime after three-thirty hit head-on the sandbar in the shallows of Fire Island. The bow stuck as towering powerful waves swung the ship broadside to the beach. The sudden jolt threw the 150-ton marble cargo—Powers's statue of Calhoun and heavy rough blocks—against the ship's hull, tearing a hole in it. "Canted on her side," wrote the reporter who recorded Mrs. Hasty's account, the *Elizabeth* "stuck fast" while "the mad waves" made "a clear sweep over her, pouring down into the cabin through the skylight, which was destroyed."[9]

With half the cabin under water, the passengers—Ossoli, Fuller, Nino and his nursemaid Celeste, Horace Sumner, and Catherine Hasty—huddled together in a dry spot against the windward wall. Meanwhile, the crew stayed safe and dry across the waist of the deck in the forecastle, which still remained above water. Through sheets of rain and the waves that pounded water down on the deck that separated the passengers' cabin from the forecastle, Mrs. Hasty called to the crew, who could not hear her over the shrieking wind and snarling sea. Around seven in the morning, when it became apparent that the cabin "must soon go to pieces," the second mate, Charles Davis, gingerly made his way to them over fallen timber and debris on the deck. One by one he led the passengers across the deck, imperiling his own life each time he did so. With Nino in a bag slung around his neck, Davis led Fuller and the rest to the relative safety of the forecastle, where the crew wrapped the passengers in blankets, gave them wine and food, and waited with them for someone from shore to launch a lifeboat.[10]

Fuller had had two life preservers, but one had proved unfit to use. Soon after light she had given the other one to a sailor so he could swim to shore to see that a lifeboat was launched to save them. Those stranded on the sinking ship saw the sailor make it safely to shore and waited anxiously for a lifeboat to be launched. When, however, after more hours had passed and they saw that no rescue mission had been undertaken (a lifeboat was seen on the shore, but no effort by anyone to launch it), the sailors and passengers discussed how they might best save themselves before the tide began to rise around the stricken ship.[11]

Meanwhile, the carpenter, wary of the sea's ever-increasing swells, "cut loose some planks and spars" and advised Fuller to grab one and make for shore; knowing she would not go without Nino, Henry Bangs promised to go in advance with the boy. Fuller, who was athletic, nevertheless "refused" his offer, wrote a *Tribune* reporter, "saying that she had no wish to live without the child, and would not, at that hour, give the care of it to another." The second mate Davis, at great risk to himself, held onto Catherine Hasty's plank and helped her reach the shore. Horace Sumner, encouraged by the success of two sailors and Davis, jumped into the sea. According to William Channing, who says his account in the *Memoirs* is "as accurate, even in minute details, as conversation with several of the survivors enabled me to make it," Acting Captain Bangs again appealed to Fuller to try to escape, saying "it was mere suicide to remain longer." Bangs said that he could not sacrifice the lives of his crew, and that he himself would take the child, but again Fuller declared she would not be separated from her husband and child. Bangs then gave the order for the men to try to "save themselves." Having been told by Fuller to go on without her or the boy, Bangs grabbed a hatch for buoyancy and, though badly bruised, also made it alive to land.[12]

As the forecastle filled with water, Fuller and the rest of "the helpless little band were driven to the deck." Dressed in a long white shift, her hair loose and raked by the wind, Fuller clung with one hand to the foremast and clutched Nino to her breast with the other. At her side stood Nino's nurse, weeping, while Ossoli, resigned to death, no doubt prayed beside them. When Fuller had written Ossoli from Rieti after Nino's birth about how anguished she was when Nino refused her breast, Ossoli in response noted how "So Sad" her "dear letter" had made him. Urging her to have courage and be strong for the sake of "our baby," he nonetheless conceded: "How much we continually have to make us unhappy. . . . But do what we will, it [suffering] is our destiny and we must resign ourselves to it." Likewise, when Nino almost died from smallpox, Ossoli, unlike Fuller, had no hope for his recovery: he instead had prayed in preparation for his son's death.[13]

Stranded on the deck now twelve hours after the *Elizabeth* had struck the sandbar, the howling waves washing round her, Fuller was surely living her nightmare from years before when she had stayed with Anna while Sam Ward was away. It was as if the gods had sent the dream to forewarn her of her fate. For in the dream she was stranded on a wrecked ship. Friends had come to the ship and seemed at first glad to see her. But when she let them know her situation, with a cold courtliness they had glided away. Similarly, when friends in America had found out about her plight in Italy, they had written to tell her not to come home. "Oh it was horrible," Fuller had earlier written about her dream, "these averted faces and well dressed figures turning from me, from captive, with the cold wave rushing up into which I was to be thrown." Even Emerson had not responded to her latest appeal that he stretch forth his "pure hands" for her to claim their clasp should she need them to lift her from despair.[14]

With Nino crying, Fuller crouched and desperately clung with one hand to the foremast, with the other, to Nino. There was no gentlemanly Montague to rescue her from drowning as there had been for Isadora in the novel *Hesitation,* nor was there a magical ring to save her and her family in the way such a ring had saved Huon and Rezia from drowning in *Oberon.* There was only the moaning sea and its cold spray that—like the mist at night when she had been lost on Ben Lomond—came on her "with a kiss pervasively cold as that of Death."[15] There, in Death, was a lover who would not leave her.

In a letter to Channing years earlier, Fuller had described a night at the beach when she and Cary had stayed too late far out on the rocks. The moon had risen red and kept "hiding her head" behind dark clouds. Seized with a "terrified feeling," Fuller thought she heard the damp wind sobbing and the waves wailing as the red moon gave her up to the demons of the rock. As the waves moaned "a tragic chorus," she had "felt a cold grasp." That night she had wondered if that "was a real voice from Nature," and she had asked herself, "what did it say?" Stranded now on the water with the wind mercilessly whipping the waves, she must have known: it was "Death," that night, she had heard nature say.[16]

From the first that day, as she and the other passengers in the forecastle waited vainly for help, Fuller had said that she did not want to live without her husband

and child. She knew that if she grabbed a plank and swam with a seaman behind her, the odds were good they could make it to shore. After all, about the night she had spent alone on Ben Lomond, she had confessed in a letter to her brother Richard that she would have died "*if* I had not tried" to survive. Back then, however, she had no real reason to wish to die. To save only herself now meant she would have to forfeit what gave her life meaning: her manuscript, Ossoli, and, of course, her son. Though the second mate had gone back to the cabin to get Captain Hasty's watch, some jewelry and money-drafts of Fuller's, and a hoard of figs and wine, Fuller, according to Channing, told Mrs. Hasty that she would not ask him to return for her manuscript. Moreover, Ossoli, who had knelt in prayer beside her, could not swim and hence was doomed. She had surely watched as their friend and fellow passenger, Horace Sumner, who was young and slender like Ossoli, disappeared beneath the waves in his attempt to reach the shore.[17]

Still, though "entreated by the sailors to leave the vessel," Fuller, clasping her baby close to her breast, "steadily refused." Describing the pain of finding Nino almost dead in Rieti after the war, Margaret had written Cary at Christmas that she wanted "in life or death to be no more separated from Angelino." And again, in April, just a month before they set sail, she had conjectured in a letter to Emelyn how Maria Lowell was doing since her first child, Blanche, had died, and added, "I could not, I think, survive the loss of *my* child."[18]

That one frail line holding Fuller to life was snapped when the steward, George Bates, trying to save the baby, yanked him from her arms, then disappeared into the sea. Now there was nothing left for her to do but to fulfill the fate her recent words had suggested in the letter she had written Costanza shortly before sailing, that, "in case of mishap, I should perish with my husband and child perhaps to be transferred to some happier state; . . . ," and also in her December 1849 letter to her sister about her son: "I could not let him go unless I would go with him."[19]

After witnessing the burial at Gibraltar, Fuller had written Marcus Spring: "It is vain by prudence to seek to evade the stern assaults of Destiny. I submit." According to the cook, who was the last person to reach the shore alive, Fuller's words to him as he left the vessel were, "I see nothing but death before me,—I shall never reach the shore."[20]

✧ ✧ ✧

The wreck lay "but a quarter of a mile from the shore—so close," as one eyewitness said, that "it seem[ed] as if a dozen oar-strokes would carry a boat alongside" it. Like Sophocles' Antigone, whose "straight forward nobleness," Fuller had said, "led her to Death," Margaret Fuller yielded to the cold embrace of the storm-tossed sea.[21]

Although to some it seemed that she had recklessly thrown "away her own life, out of her resolve not to be [sundered] from her husband & their boy[,]" William

Channing later argued in a letter to Fuller biographer Higginson, "What else could such a grand, majestic, self-sacrificing, tenderly loving woman do, than what she did amidst that awful tragedy?" Indeed, rather than throwing away her life, Fuller's final actions were her acknowledgment of the power of the word over her life. She had said that in case of mishap she would die with her husband and child, and so she did. In her steady refusal, as one survivor said, "to be separated from her husband and child"—or, in Channing's words, to "*desert* them even if she had seen the smallest *chance of her being saved* herself!"—she expressed her "contempt" for those at home who were "so easily disconcerted" by news of her liaison and baby. Before she set sail, she had angrily written Emelyn: "I was not a child; I had lived in the midst of that blessed society in a way that entitled me to esteem and a favorable interpretation, where there was doubt about my motives or actions."[22]

In the manner of an Italian marchesa or the classical heroine Antigone, Fuller chose to die with those she loved rather than to live without them in a nineteenth-century American society that damned her. After Margaret's death, Cary speculated about Fuller's life had she lived: "The waves do not seem so difficult to brave as the prejudices she would have encountered if she had arrived here safely." As had Antigone, Fuller, an American woman of intellect and passion in a provincial Puritan society, had been "unjustly judged" by her country, which, "to the last," as Emerson wrote in his journal after hearing of her death, "proves inhospitable to her."[23]

At the time of her death it seemed "that blessed society" was to have the last word on Margaret Fuller. Though Emerson also wrote in his journal about how to mark her death, "there should be a gathering of her friends & some Beethoven should play the dirge," there was to be no such gathering of her friends on the shore. There was no funeral service. Her body never washed ashore. Emerson sent Thoreau to the scene of the wreck to scout for "fragments of manuscript or other property." He returned five days later with little to show but a button he had ripped from a coat he had found on the seashore that had belonged to the Marquis Ossoli, an object that interested him less, he said in his journal, "than my faintest dream." Not such objects but "our thoughts," he wrote, "are the epochs in our lives." Emerson asked Fuller's friends to send him their thoughts about her. Almira Barlow's was apt: "Her life was romantic & exceptional: So let her death be."[24]

At Margaret Fuller's death no Beethoven played a dirge. No eagle soared suddenly free, high up into the sky. There was no parting of the clouds, no seventh trumpet sounding the end of the world and the advent on earth of a New Jerusalem. After the hurricane had passed, there was only the sound of the wind moving over the waters that caressed the wreck-strewn shore like the "sweet white arms" of a mother welcoming her wandering child home.

Notes

Abbreviations

Works frequently cited in the notes have been abbreviated as follows (see bibliography for full data).

Barry: *IW*	Joseph Barry, *Infamous Woman: The Life of George Sand.*
Bean: *MF,C*	Judith Mattson Bean and Joel Myerson, eds. *Margaret Fuller, Critic: Writings from the "New-York Tribune."*
B: *MFTtoR*	Paula Blanchard, *Margaret Fuller: From Transcendentalism to Revolution.*
C: *MFPY*	Charles Capper, *Margaret Fuller: An American Romantic Life, The Private Years.*
C: *TW&TM*	Bell Gale Chevigny, *The Woman and the Myth: Margaret Fuller's Life and Writings.*
D: "LCS-MF"	Francis B. Dedmond, "Letters of Caroline Sturgis to Margaret Fuller."
Deiss: *RYMF*	Joseph Jay Deiss, *The Roman Years of Margaret Fuller.*
E: *ELofRWE*	Ralph Waldo Emerson, *Early Lectures of Ralph Waldo Emerson.*
E: *E&L*	Ralph Waldo Emerson, *Essays and Lectures.*
E: *J&MN*	Ralph Waldo Emerson, *Journals and Miscellaneous Notebooks.*
E: *LofRWE*	Ralph Waldo Emerson, *Letters of Ralph Waldo Emerson.*
FAB: "HN"	Arthur Buckminster Fuller, "Historical Notices of Thomas Fuller and His Descendents."
FE: "HC"	Edith D. Fuller, "Her Childhood." Paper on the early life of Margaret Fuller read at Normal State College, Albany, New York, Feb. 1900. In *Fuller Family Papers.* bMS AM 1086 (B). Houghton Library, Harvard University, Cambridge, Mass.
FE: "EDTF"	Edith Davenport Fuller, "Excerpts from the Diary of Timothy Fuller."
F: *EMF*	*The Essential Margaret Fuller*, ed. Jeffrey Steele.
FFP: HM	Fuller Family Papers: Houghton manuscripts, fMS AM 1086. Twenty-two Manuscript Volumes and Four Miscellaneous Boxes. Houghton Library, Harvard University, Cambridge, Mass. Citation of materials from this collection is by permission of the Houghton Library, Harvard University.
"FJ42"	Joel Myerson, ed., "Margaret Fuller's 1842 Journal: At Concord with the Emersons."

FL	Margaret Fuller, *Letters of Margaret Fuller.*
F: *MFCritic*	Margaret Fuller, *Margaret Fuller, Critic: Writings from the New-York Tribune.*
FR: *CF*	Richard F. Fuller, *Chaplain Fuller.*
FR: *RRF*	Richard F. Fuller, *Recollections of Richard F. Fuller.*
FRob: *MACS*	Robert C. Fuller, *Mesmerism and the American Cure of Souls.*
F: *SL*	Margaret Fuller, *Summer on the Lakes, in 1843.*
F: "TGL"	Margaret Fuller, "The Great Lawsuit."
F: *TSBGD*	Margaret Fuller, "*These Sad But Glorious Days*": Dispatches from Europe.*
F: *WNC*	Margaret Fuller, *Woman in the Nineteenth Century: A Facsimile of the 1845 Edition.*
Hig: *MFO*	Thomas Wentworth Higginson, *Margaret Fuller Ossoli.*
KJV	King James Version (Bible).
Langer: *PSU*	William Langer, *Political and Social Upheaval, 1832–1852.*
MC: *MF'sNYJ*	Catherine C. Mitchell, *Margaret Fuller's New York Journalism.*
MJ: *CEonMF*	Joel Myerson, ed. *Critical Essays on Margaret Fuller.*
O: *AH&A*	Margaret Fuller Ossoli. *At Home and Abroad.*
O: *AL&D*	Margaret Fuller Ossoli, *Art, Literature, and the Drama.*
OM	Margaret Fuller Ossoli, *Memoirs of Margaret Fuller Ossoli.*
R: *EMoF*	Robert D. Richardson Jr. *Emerson: The Mind on Fire.*
R: *ER*	Larry J. Reynolds, *European Revolutions and the American Literary Renaissance.*
RSV	Revised Standard Version (Bible).
Shengold: *SM*	Leonard Shengold, *Soul Murder: The Effects of Childhood Abuse and Deprivation.*
S: *Mazzini*	Denis Mack Smith. *Mazzini.*
Virgil: RF	Virgil, *The Aeneid,* trans. Robert Fitzgerald.
Virgil: AM	Virgil, *The Aeneid of Virgil: A Verse Translation,* trans. Allen Mandelbaum.
V: "EtF"	Joan von Mehren, "Establishing the Facts on the Ossoli Family."
V: "MF&MQ"	Joan von Mehren, "Margaret Fuller, the Marchese Giovanni Ossoli, and The Marriage Question."
V: *M&TM*	Joan von Mehren, *Minerva and the Muse: A Life of Margaret Fuller.*
Wellisz: *FMF-AM*	Leopold Wellisz, *Friendship of Margaret Fuller D'Ossoli and Adam Mickiewicz.*
W: *SRWE*	Stephen E. Whicher, ed. *Selections from Ralph Waldo Emerson.*
Wieland: *SO*	C. M. Wieland, *Oberon, a Poem,* trans. William Sotheby.
Zwarg: *FC*	Christina Zwarg, *Feminist Conversations: Fuller, Emerson, and the Play Of Reading.*

People frequently cited in letter sources have been abbreviated as follows.

AF	Arthur Fuller
CS	Cary Sturgis
EH	Elizabeth Hoar
FHH	Frederic Henry Hedge
GAO	Giovanni Angelo Ossoli
JFC	James Freeman Clarke
MCF	Margarett Crane Fuller
MF	Margaret Fuller
RFF	Richard Frederick Fuller
RWE	Ralph Waldo Emerson
SMF	Sarah Margaret Fuller
TF	Timothy Fuller
WHC	William Henry Channing

A Comment on Note Style

Material from manuscripts contained in the four miscellaneous boxes and twenty-two manuscript volumes (the final five being copybook volumes [called "Works"]) that are a part of the Fuller Family Papers housed in the Houghton Library, Harvard University, are hereafter identified by information pertaining to the particular item (author of letter or journal, recipient of letter, date, etc.) followed by the abbreviation HM and either a shelf mark bMS Am 1086 and a box number (A, B, C) or a call number (fms Am 1086) and item number. Thus TF to MCF, 30 Jan, 1820, FFP: HM (fMS Am 1086 [3:102]) is Timothy Fuller to Margarett Crane Fuller, 30 Jan. 1820, Fuller Family Papers, Houghton Manuscript (fMS Am 1086), volume 3, page 102. FFP: HM (bMS Am 1086 [B]) is Fuller Family Papers, Houghton Manuscript, Miscellaneous Box B. Other common scholarly abbreviations (not always Chicago style) are used throughout the notes, such as: n for note and nn for notes (used immediately after the number of the page containing the text of the note or notes); qtd. for quoted; trans. for translated, and so on. Moreover, because the notes list so many citations from letters and journals that appear in two or more volumes, I likewise veer in them from traditional Chicago style. In citing these, I first give the source's abbreviated form (*FL,* for instance, for *Fuller Letters*). I then put a comma followed by volume number in roman numerals, which I follow with a *comma* and then the page number in arabic numerals. Thus *Fuller Letters* volume 5, page 205 followed immediately by *Fuller Letters* volume 6, page 109 appears as: *FL,* V, 205; *FL,* VI, 109. In citing the multivolumes of Houghton materials and also from one particular volume only in a series, I use traditional Chicago style, which is to separate volume from page number with a colon.

Prologue

1. In her May 2001 paper at the American Literature Association, Joan von Mehren noted that in Italy in the 1840s an official marriage between a Catholic and Protestant could take place without a papal dispensation if both parties were baptized and promised to raise the child in the Roman Catholic Church, "so any parish could celebrate the marriage with no particular formalities." Thus Fuller might have married Ossoli with the church's approval. See V: "EtF," 4, 7; V: "MF&MQ" 123. See also *FL,* IV, 82; *FL,* V, 42, 261; and *OM,* I, 15.

2. *FL*, V, 146, 150, 145; *FL*, I, 331.

3. *FL*, V, 150; *FL*, II, 173; *FL*, I, 331; and *OM*, I, 141.

4. See M. Fuller, "Goethe," 8, 4; *OM*, I, 244; P. Miller, ed., *Margaret Fuller*, 77; C: *TW&TM*, 63.

5. T. R. Mitchell, *Hawthorne's Fuller Mystery*, 1–11. And see C: *MFPY* and Zwarg: *FC*.

6. James, *William Wetmore Story and His Friends*, I, 127–31. And see O: *AH&A*, 447–48. In the Fuller Family Papers housed in Harvard's Houghton Library is a letter claiming Fuller's and Ossoli's bodies were buried on Coney Island. See C: *TW&TM*, 401n45. And see Sophocles, *Antigone*, 183–238; and F: *WNC*, 185.

7. See Novak, *Margaret-Ghost*. Hudspeth, intro. to *FL*, I, 53. And see *FL*, I, 192, *FL*, VI, 231, 99.

8. See *OM*, I, 139–40; *FL*, VI, 99. For James's explicit and Hawthorne's implicit allusions to Beatrice Cenci in a story inspired by Fuller's relationship with her father, see James, *William Wetmore Story*, I, 126, 131; and Hawthorne, "Rappaccini's Daughter," in *Nathaniel Hawthorne's Tales*, 188, 188n7, 192–93. Beatrice Cenci, youngest daughter of a sadistic Italian nobleman who forced her into an incestuous relationship, with her brother and stepmother's help, murdered "their common tyrant." For Fuller, as well as the poet Shelley on Beatrice Cenci, whom Pope Clement VIII beheaded, see F: *WNC*, 199, and the preface to Shelley's "The Cenci," in *Shelley's Poetry and Prose*, 238. See also Reynolds, ed. Fuller, *Woman*, 134n3. And see F: *EMF*, 4.

9. TF, diary, 16 Jan. 1814, FFP: HM (fMS Am 1086 [2:8]); *OM*, I, 13, 156; Kelley, intro. to *Portable Margaret Fuller*, xii; C: *MFPY*, 32; Ernest Becker qtd. in Wessell, *Karl Marx, Romantic Irony, and the Proletariat*, 25.

10. *FL*, I, 268–69.

11. See Schneiderman, *Jacques Lacan*, 6, 146–47, 148–52.

12. M. H. Abrams in conversation with the author 31 May 1991, Ithaca, N.Y. And see Luke 15:11–32; Abrams, *Natural Supernaturalism*, 191, 255, 194; and Wieland: *SO*.

13. *OM*, II, 7, 337; *FL*, VI, 85, 70, 74, and 81. See also Kelley, intro. to *Portable Margaret Fuller*, x.

14. *FL*, I, 331; *FL*, VI, 99. Myerson, ed., *Transcendentalism*, 280; R: *ER*, 18, 45; and see Sophocles, *Antigone*, 220.

15. Fuller, "Palmo's—The Antigone," *New-York Daily Tribune*, 16 April 1845. See item C119 on the CD-ROM version, which is included in F: *MFCritic*. And see M. Fuller, "Goethe," 27. In alluding here to a "blind" tyrant, Fuller merges Creon with Oedipus.

16. See Lear, *Love and Its Place in Nature*, 20–23.

Part One. "No Natural Childhood"

1. *OM*, I, 16; FAB: "HN," 3–5; FR: *CF*, 5–6; Hig: *MFO*, 3–5.

2. C: *MFPY*, 5–6; FE: "EDTF," 34–35; Hig: *MFO*, 7–10.

3. Hig: *MFO*, 12, 16–17; C: *MFPY*, 5–6; FAB: "HN," 6–7.

4. C: *MFPY*, 13; Hig: *MFO*, 11–12.

Chapter 1. Her Father's House

1. FR: *RRF*, 12–13; FAB: "HN," 9; Timothy Fuller, journal, 12 May 1800, FFP: HM (bMS Am 1086 [A]); Hig: *MFO*, 13.

2. RF: *RRF*, 12–13; FAB: "HN," 9; *OM*, I, 17; TF to MCF, 30 Jan. 1820, FFP: HM (fMS Am

1086 [3:102]); TF to MCF, 22 Jan. 1820 , FFP: HM (fMS Am 1086 [3:94]); TF to MCF, 16 Jan. 1820, FFP: HM (fMS Am 1086 [3:89]).

3. FR: *RRF*, 21; C: *MFPY*, 8, 124; Comfort, *Anxiety Makers*, 39–41; FR: *CF*, 30–33. See also Kincaid, *Child-Loving*, 174–75, and 1 Cor. 6:9–10 KJV. On this notion regarding masturbation see G. J. Barker-Benfield, *Horrors of the Half-Known Life*, 155–96, 223–26.

4. TF to MCF, 12 Feb. 1818, FFP: HM (fMS Am 1086 [3:34]); FE: "EDTF," 42, 37–38, 45; Timothy Fuller qtd. in C: *MFPY*, 14–15.

5. Timothy Fuller, journal, 4 March 1800, 12 July 1801 & 29 July 1800, FFP: HM (bMS Am 1086 [A]).

6. TF, diary, 5 Aug. 1801, 19 Aug. 1802, 22 Aug. 1801, FFP: HM (fMS Am 1086 [2:2]); TF, diary, 12 Sept. 1801, 14 Nov. 1801, 25 Dec. 1801, FFP: HM (fMS Am 1086 [2:3]); TF, diary, 19 and 15 Feb. 1802, FFP: HM (fMS Am 1086 [2:3]). And see Timothy Fuller qtd. in C: *MFPY*, 14–15.

7. Anthony, *Margaret Fuller: A Psychological Biography*, 8; C: *MFPY*, 17; V: *M&TM*, 7–8; *FL*, I, 79n; Timothy Fuller, diary, 7 July 1802, FFP: HM (fMS Am 1086 [2:4]).

8. TF to MCF, 13 May 1801, FFP: HM (fMS Am 1086 [3:1]).

9. See Hig: *MFO*, 11–12. And C: *MFPY*, 15.

10. See *OM*, I, 23; C: *MFPY*, 26–27; and MCF to TF, 25 Jan. 1821, FFP: HM (fMS Am 1086 [6:119]).

11. On TF see V: *M&TM*, 14; C: *MFPY*, 8, 15; FE: "HC," FFP: HM (bMS Am 1086 [B]). The portrait Hudspeth titled Timothy Fuller in *FL*, VI, 269 (see the gallery) does seem to be Timothy. Though the black tie suggests the portrait may have been painted later, the tie's elaborate knot and the shirt's starched, sharp, turned-up collar points seem to follow Beau Brummell fashion (c. 1811–20). Perhaps the portrait was painted in the 1830s (TF d. 1835) and, in the fashion of the Alonzo Chappel portrait of Margaret, romanticized. On Margaret lifting her lip, see Poe in the *Broadway Review* (Aug. 1846) repr. in C: *TW&TM*, 162.

12. The fireplace in that room almost certainly identifies it as Timothy and Margarett Crane's bedroom. See "Report on Restoration Potential Completed in the 1970s," which was sent to me in a packet of materials about the house by Angelique Bamberg, Historic Marker Program Coordinator for the Cambridge Historical Commission. Useful photos of the house appeared in Cambridge Historical Commission, *Survey of Architectural History in Cambridge*, 48. A two-story ell (right when facing the house) was added in 1827, a year after the Fullers moved out ("Report on Restoration," 3).

Names and dates of Margaret and her siblings are: Sarah Margaret[t] (1810–1850); Julia Adelaide (c. 1812–1813); Eugene (1815–1859); William Henry (1817–1878); Ellen Kilshaw (1820–1856); Arthur Buckminster (1822–1867); Richard Frederick (1824–1869); Lloyd (1826–1891); Edward Breck (23 May 1828–15 Sept. 1829). Margaret's father, Timothy (1778–1835), was the fourth of eleven children born to the Reverend Timothy (1739–1805) and Sarah Williams Fuller (d. 1822). Margarett Crane (1789–1859) outlived her elder daughter by nine years. See *FL*, I, 79; *FL*, II, 187.

13. C: *MFPY*, 27; TF to MCF, 7 Sept. 1800, FFP: HM (fMS Am 1086 [3:5]); *FL*, V, 299; V: *M&TM*, 10. See also FR: *RRF*, 10–11.

14. Brigham, *Remarks on the Influence*, 36; *OM*, I, 14–15; TF to MCF, 11 March 1813, FFP: HM (fMS Am 1086 [3:6]); TF to MCF, 26 April 1814, FFP: HM (fMS Am 1086 [3:7]); TF to MCF, 12 July 1814, FFP: HM (fMS Am 1086 [3:9]); TF qtd. in C: *MFPY*, 30, and see 34.

15. Timothy Fuller, diary, 16 Jan. 1814, FFP: HM (fMS Am 1086 [2:8]); MCF to TF, 8 Feb. 1818, FFP: HM (fMS Am 1086 [6:113]); TF, diary, 16 Jan. 1814, FFP: HM (fMS Am 1086 [2:8]).

16. On the "dead mother complex," see André Green in Doane and Hodges, *From Klein to Kristeva*, 56–59.

17. *OM*, I, 13–14.

18. TF, diary, 16 Jan. 1814, FFP: HM (fMS Am 1086 [2: 8]); *OM*, I, 11, 23, 235; and Margarett Crane Fuller qtd. in Hig: *MFO*, 18–19.

19. Margarett Crane Fuller qtd. in V: *M&TM*, 16, 21. And see C: *MFPY*, 28, 38, 67; *FL*, I, 95, 154, 155n2. On such experts' views on "sexual precocity" see Comfort, *Anxiety Makers*, 38–39 ff. On the danger of precocity, as well as on early nineteenth-century women scribblers' tendency to compare raising children to caring for plants, see Kincaid, *Child-Loving*, 64–80, 90–93, 120–24. Such topics are the subject of a book by Fuller's friend, Lydia Maria Child, whose second edition of the *Mother's Book* Carter and Hendee issued in Boston in 1831. On Fuller's wish to be called "Margaret," see Douglas, *Feminization of American Culture*, 261.

20. TF to SMF, 4 Jan. 1818, FFP: HM (fMS Am 1086 [5: 1]); TF to SMF, 20 Jan. 1818, FFP: HM (fMS Am 1086 [5: 2]). And see *OM*, I, 17–18.

21. Brigham, *Remarks*, 74, 64, 44–45, 55; Samson Reed, "Oration on Genius," in Myerson, ed., *Transcendentalism: A Reader*, 21. And see R: *EMoF*, 16; and Porte, *In Respect to Egotism*, 14. Porte quotes A. W. Schlegel, who says that organic form "unfolds itself from within, and reaches its determination simultaneously with the fullest development of the seed."

22. Comfort, *Anxiety Makers*, 38–39; Kincaid, *Child-Loving*, 64–79; Rousseau qtd. in Wilson, "Not in This House," 42. See also *OM*, I, 15–16, 17–18, 40; C: *MFPY*, 91; and Brigham, *Remarks*, 72–73.

23. See Zaretsky, *Secrets of the Soul*, 41; J. R. Martin, "Contradiction of the Educated Woman."

24. See Zaretsky, *Secrets of the Soul*, 41–45; J. R. Martin, "Contradiction of the Educated Woman."

25. See Zaretsky, *Secrets of the Soul*, 42–43; Welter, "Cult of True Womanhood," 21–41; C: *MFPY*, 68, and *OM*, I, 17–18, 32.

26. TF to SMF, 13 April 1820, FFP: HM (fMS Am 1086 [5: 6]).

27. *OM*, I, 18–19; *FL*, I, 81, 81nn2–3.

28. *OM*, I, 28; TF to MCF, 11 Dec. 1820, FFP: HM (fMS Am 1086 [3: 199]); TF quoting MCF in his letter to MCF of 12 Jan. 1820, FFP: HM (fMS Am 1086 [3: 86]); TF to MCF, 15 Feb. 1818, FFP: HM (fMS Am 1086 [3: 37]). In his need to control women, Timothy was like a womanizer. See Hedaya, "The Womanizer," 113–14.

29. TF to MCF, 12 Feb. 1818, FFP: HM (fMS Am 1086 [3: 34]); TF to MCF, 18 Jan. 1818, FFP: HM (fMS Am 1086 [3: 21]); TF to MCF, 18 March & 11 April 1820, FFP: HM (fMS Am 1086 [3: 144 & 165]); TF to MCF, 30 Jan. 1818, FFP: HM (fMS Am 1086 [3: 102]; TF to MCF, 9 Jan. 1820, FFP: HM (fMS Am 1086 [3: 83]).

30. MCF to TF, 28 Jan. 1818, FFP: HM (fMS Am 1086 [6: 10]); TF to MCF, 4 Feb. 1818, FFP: HM (fMS Am 1086 [3: 29]); MCF to TF, 13 March 1818, FFP: HM (fMS Am 1086 [6: 30]).

31. MCF to TF, 30 Dec. 1818, FFP: HM (fMS Am 1086 [6: 46]). Mrs. Deforest was the American consul to Brazil's wife. And see MCF to TF, 29 Dec. 1818, FFP: HM (fMS Am 1086 [6: 45]).

32. MCF to TF, 29 Dec. 1818, FFP: HM (fMS Am 1086 [6: 45]); MCF to TF, 24 Jan. 1819, FFP: HM (fMS Am 1086 [6: 63]).

33. TF to MCF, 15 Jan. 1820, FFP: HM (fMS Am 1086 [3: 88]); TF to MCF, 16 Dec. 1819, FFP: HM (fMS Am 1086 [3: 63]).

34. MCF to TF, 27 Dec. 1818, FFP: HM (fMS Am 1086 [6:44]); MCF to TF, 22 Feb. 1818, FFP: HM (fMS Am 1086 [6:20]).

35. TF to MCF, 10 Feb. 1818, FFP: HM (fMS Am 1086 [3:33]); MCF to TF, 15 March 1818, FFP: HM (fMS Am 1086 [6:30]); MCF to TF, 26 Jan. 1818, FFP: HM (fMS Am 1086 [6:9]); TF to MCF, 19 Jan. 1818, FFP: HM (fMS Am 1086 [3:21]); MCF to TF, 13 Dec. 1818, FFP: HM (fMS Am 1086 [6:36]).

36. MCF to TF, 26 Feb. 1818, FFP: HM (fMS Am 1086 [6:22]); MCF to TF, 1 Jan. 1819, FFP: HM (fMS Am 1086 [6:47]); TF to MCF, FFP: HM (fMS Am 1086 [3:86]); TF to SMF, 22 Feb. 1820, FFP: HM (fMS Am 1086 [5:4]); TF to SMF, 3 Dec. 1820, FFP: HM (fMS Am 1086 [5:7]); *FL*, I, 150n2; TF to SMF, 3 April 1824, FFP: HM (fMS Am 1086 [5:15]). And see *FL*, I, 97n7, 137n1.

37. *FL*, I, 102.

38. See C: *MFPY*, 31–32; MCF to TF, 20 Jan. 1818, FFP: HM (fMS Am 1086 [6:7]); *OM*, I, 18.

39. *OM*, I, 15, 62n, 31, 21; TF to MCF, 8 Dec. 1819, FFP: HM (fMS Am 1086 [3:58]); Virgil: AM, 316; and FE: "HC," 2.

40. See "Report on Restoration Potential completed in the 1970s," Cambridge Historical Commission, 3; *OM*, I, 15–17. On Betsy getting Margaret to bed see MCF to TF, 8 Jan 1819, FFP: HM (fMS Am 1086 [6:53]). On Timothy urging his wife to retire early see TF to MCF, 17 Jan. 1820, FFP: HM (fMS Am 1086 [3:90]). And for Fuller on understanding "Hades" see *FL*, II, 69.

41. *OM*, I, 15–16; F: *EMF*, 4–5; Virgil: RF, 87–88; TF to MCF, 16 Dec. 1819, FFP: HM (fMS Am 1086 [3:63]). See also Virgil: AM, 77. On nightmares and night terrors see Hartmann, *Nightmare* (1984); and Kellerman, *Sleep Disorders* (1981). On trauma causing dreams of drowning and being crushed see Hartmann's *Dreams and Nightmares*, 61–75; and Terr, *Too Scared to Cry*, 110–11, 272.

42. F: *EMF*, 5; Virgil: AM, 316–36, 77, 136, 230, 58. On images appearing three-dimensional in the reader's mind see Scarry, *Dreaming by the Book*.

On a possible source of these dream images, see Jeffrey Steele, *Transfiguring America*, 37. Though Steele thinks they come from the sack of Troy in the *Aeneid*'s book 1, the *Aeneid* is so bloody it is hard to determine origin.

43. See Rev. 8:8, 16:3, 16:17 RSV; *OM*, I, 21; Ovid, *Ovid's Metamorphoses*, 1: 119–24, 319–25, 862–63. Fuller may have read a translation of "The Story of Pyramis and Thisbe" in *Of Ovid's Metamorphoses, Book IV*, in Johnson, ed., *Works of the English Poets*, 20: 455–56. See also "The Story of Erisichthon" and "The Description of Famine," *Of Ovid's Metamorphoses, Book VIII*, in Johnson, ed., *Works of the English Poets*, 20: 497–98. For other texts that may have made Fuller dream of trees dripping blood and severed heads see Shakespeare's *Macbeth* 5.8.54–59, where Macbeth is beheaded. And see *Julius Caesar* 2.2.75–79, where Calpurnia dreams Caesar's statue spouts blood.

44. Johnson, "Transformations of Erisichthon's Daughter," *Of Ovid's Metamorphosis, Book VIII*, in *Works of the English Poets*, 20: 498. See also Ovid, *Ovid's Metamorphoses*, 1: 323–25; and Price, "Incest and the Idealized Self," 22–24.

45. On how the mind turns the past into a coherent narrative see Eakin, "Autobiography, Identity, and the Fictions of Memory," 290–305. See especially how "parental intervention" influences a child's creation of a "story line" (296). See also Schacter, "The Sin of Bias," in *The Seven Sins of Memory*, 138–160; and Lowen, *Narcissism*, 136–37.

46. *OM*, 1, 15–16, 28; FR: *CF*, 14. On recurrent dreams and how dreams connect traumatic events and other materials see Hartmann, *Dreams and Nightmares*, 11–16, 17–35, 48–50, 116–

17. See also Green on the "dead mother" in Doane and Hodges, *From Klein to Kristeva,* 56–59.

Chapter 2. Hungry for Love

1. See *OM,* 1, 12–13, 28; V: *M&TM,* 10; C: *MFPY,* 27, 31, 55; Hig: *MFO,* 17; B: *MFTtoR,* 17–18; and MCF to TF, 3 March 1818, FFP: HM (fMS Am 1086 [6: 25]). And see Blackstone qtd. in Beard, *Woman as Force in History,* 89–90.

2. TF, diary, 19 Jan. 1802, FFP: HM (fMS Am 1086 [2: 3]); TF to MCF, 18 Jan. 1818, FFP: HM (fMS Am 1086 [3: 21]); MCF to TF, 26 March 1820, FFP: HM (fMS Am 1086 [6: 85]); V: *M&TM,* 14.

3. MCF to TF, 13 Jan. 1818, FFP: HM (fMS Am 1086 [6: 6]); TF to MCF, 11 April 1820, FFP: HM (fMS Am 1086 [3: 165]); TF to MCF, 13 Dec. 1819, FFP: HM (fMS Am 1086 [3: 61]); TF to MCF, 28 March 1820, FFP: HM (fMS Am 1086 [3: 154]); TF to MCF, 29 April 1820, FFP: HM (fMS Am 1086 [3: 175]); TF to MCF, 6 May 1820, FFP: HM (fMS Am 1086 [3: 178]).

4. MCF to TF, 26 Feb. 1818, FFP: HM (fMS Am 1086 [6: 22]); MCF to TF, 5 March 1818, FFP: HM (fMS Am 1086 [6: 26]).

5. MCF to TF, 8 Jan. 1819, FFP: HM (fMS Am 1086 [6: 53]); MCF to TF, 28 Jan. 1821, FFP: HM (fMS Am 1086 [6: 120]). And see Johnson, "Transformations of Erisichthon's Daughter," *Of Ovid's Metamorphoses, Book VIII,* in *Works of the English Poets;* Ovid, *Ovid's Metamorphoses,* I: 324–25; and *FL,* V, 145.

6. *OM,* I, 16, 17; *FL,* I, 84 & 84n1; MCF to TF, 21 Jan. 1819, FFP: HM (fMS Am 1086 [6: 62]); MCF to TF, 24 Jan. 1819, FFP: HM (fMS Am 1086 [6: 63]); MCF to TF, 27 Dec. 1818, FFP: HM (fMS Am 1086 [6: 44]). Schacter says traumatized children retain "'burned-in' visual impressions" that may last a lifetime. Dreams like Fuller's of her mother in a coffin Schacter sees as visual renderings of "worst fears." See *Searching for Memory,* 202, 207–8. And see Hartmann, *Dreams and Nightmares,* 1–35; and Doane and Hodges, *From Klein to Kristeva,* 56–59.

7. *OM,* I, 23–24.

8. Ibid., 23; Hig: *MFO,* 20; C: *MFPY,* 27.

9. *OM,* I, 62n, 23–24; *FL,* I, 96, 97n3, 161n. And see Scarry, *Dreaming by the Book,* 40–71.

10. *FL,* I, 103; Hig: *MFO,* 18; *OM,* I, 91. And see C: *MFPY,* 17; and Margarett Crane Fuller qtd. in V: *M&TM,* 20.

11. MCF to TF, 26 Feb. 1818, FFP: HM (fMS Am 1086 [6: 22]); *FL,* IV, 137. And see Sulloway, *Born to Rebel,* 69; and Sifford, "First-born Children Often Succeed," sec. D1.

12. MCF to TF, 28 Jan. 1821, FFP: HM (fMS Am 1086 [6: 120]); MCF to TF, 20 Jan. 1821, FFP: HM (fMS Am 1086 [6: 117]).

13. Schapiro, *Romantic Mother,* ix–xvi. For a summary of objects-relations theory see Doane and Hodges, *From Klein to Kristeva,* 41–42. On attachment theory see Ainsworth and Marvin, "On the Shaping of Attachment Theory and Research," 3–21. See also Oppenheim and H. S. Waters, "Narrative Processes and Attachment Representations," 197–215; Owens et al., "Prototype Hypothesis and the Origins of Attachment Working Models," 216–33; and "Introduction to Part 2," in Waters et al., *Caregiving,* 25.

On the "self" as "a kind of fiction" see Eakin, "Autobiography, Identity, and the Fictions of Memory." And see John Shotter qtd. in Eakin, 290–91; Doane and Hodges, *From Klein to Kristeva,* 45; and Jane Loevinger qtd. in Hauser, "Loevinger's Model," 24–25. "Framework of meaning" is Hauser's phrase.

14. TF, diary, 16 Jan. 1814, FFP: HM (fMS Am 1086 [2: 8]). And see Lowen, *Narcissism*, 7; André Green qtd. in Doane and Hodges, *From Klein to Kristeva*, 58. And on Fuller as a "good child" who buried her "true" self "within" see *FL*, VI, 232; *OM*, I, 18; and Fuller, 1833 journal, FFP: HM (bMS Am 1086 [A, file 8]). On "defensive isolation" see Shengold: *SM*, 30. On mother-infant interaction and narcissism see Lasch's *Culture of Narcissism*—esp. 31–51. And see Klein, *Love, Guilt and Reparation and Other Works*; Klein, *Envy and Gratitude and Other Works*; Kohut, *Analysis of the Self*; and Kernberg, *Borderline Conditions and Pathological Narcissism*.

15. See "Narcissus and Echo" and "Narcissus," in Ovid, *Ovid's Metamorphoses*, I: 96–104. See also Sandys, *Ovid's Metamorphosis*, 138–41. In Providence Fuller would teach Ovid's "Narcissus."

16. *OM*, I, 236; *FL*, I, 172. And see Lasch, *Minimal Self* (1984); and Schapiro, *Romantic Mother*, 13–14.

17. TF to MCF, 3 Jan. 1820, FFP: HM (fMS Am 1086 [3:77]); TF to MCF, 12 Jan. 1820, FFP: HM (fMS Am 1086 [3:86]).

18. Hig: *MFO*, 27–29; *OM*, I, 15. And see V: *M&TM*, 12.

19. See Margarett Crane Fuller qtd. in V: *M&TM*, 12; TF to SMF, 29 Dec. 1819, FFP: HM (fMS Am 1086 [5:3]); TF to SMF, 13 April 1820, FFP: HM (fMS Am 1086 [5:6]); C: *TW & TM*, 50–51. And see C: *MFPY*, 40; and J. R. Martin, "Contradiction of the Educated Woman," 4–9.

Chapter 3. "Gate of Paradise"

1. C: *MFPY*, 41; *OM*, I, 32–34; *FL*, I, 85n2. On Kilshaw see B: *MFTtoR*, 27–29. And see Fuller's notes for "Lillo," a romanticized first sight of Kilshaw in FFP: HM (bMS Am 1086 [A]).

2. Ellen Kilshaw to MCF, 20 July 1818, FFP: HM (fMS Am 1086 [2: 25]); *OM*, I, 17, 33–35.

3. *OM*, I, 35. And see Price, "Incest and the Idealized Self," 26–28. The influence of *Paradise Lost* is obvious.

4. *FL*, I, 88–89. And see TF to MCF, 13 May 1809 ("Angel"), FFP: HM (fMS Am 1086 [3:1]); C: *TW & TM*, 51 ("unconscious wants").

5. *OM*, I, 35–37.

6. *FL*, I, 94.

7. See Price, "Incest and the Idealized Self," 23–24; Shengold: *SM*, 5.

8. *FL*, I, 89, 94. Timothy never mailed Fuller's 20 Nov. 1819 letter to Kilshaw. See *FL*, I, 89n.

9. For examples of "possess" in the novel, see Ross, *Hesitation*, I: 11, 38, 41, 43, 53, 56. And see *FL*, I, 91, 92n5, and V: *M&TM*, 15.

10. TF to SMF, 29 Dec. 1819, FFP: HM (fMS Am 1086 [5:3]); 25 Jan. 1820, FFP: HM (fMS Am 1086 [5:5]); and 22 Feb. 1820, FFP: HM (fMS Am 1086 [5:5]); *FL*, I, 84, 84n2. See also V: *M&TM*, 21, 13; C: *MFPY*, 33, 43, 55, 87, and *FL*, I, 87n1, 93–94.

11. C: *MFPY*, 8; *FL*, I, 89; *OM*, I, 25, 235.

12. *FL*, I, 88; *OM*, I, 40. And see Price, "Incest and the Idealized Self," 32–34.

13. *OM*, I, 40–41.

Chapter 4. The World of Books

1. See *FL*, I, 90–91; Hig: *MFO*, 24; C: *MFPY*, 45. On Timothy's youngest brother, Elisha (1794–1855), see *FL*, I, 87n2.

2. *FL*, I, 91, 92nn3 & 5; Ross, *Hesitation*, I: 36.

3. *FL*, I, 94, 106; TF to SMF, 25 Jan. 1820, FFP: HM (fMS Am 1086 [5:5]).

4. Ross, *Hesitation*, I: 15; ibid., II: 239, 242, 243. On "connexion" as "unfit" see *FL*, V, 283, 292.

5. Ross, *Hesitation*, I: 15–16, 42; ibid., II: 229; TF to SMF, 25 Jan. 1820, FFP: HM (fMS Am 1086 [5:5]).

6. Ross, *Hesitation*, I: 21, 35–36, 26, 104, 173–75, 267, 270; ibid., II: 245. In her autobiographical romance, Fuller refers to herself as cold and haughty. See *OM*, I, 41–2, 65.

7. Ross, *Hesitation*, II: 254–55; ibid., I: 18.

8. Ibid., I: 259–60, 262–63; *OM*, I, 91, 206, 280. And see *FL*, I, 94, 106.

9. Ross, *Hesitation*, I: 17–18, 263–64.

10. *FL*, I, 104, 94–95; F: *SL*, 101.

11. *FL*, I, 95. In bk. IV, lines 233–144, Virgil attributes Dido's fate to her impulsive union "that day" in the cave with Aeneas. See Virgil: *RF*, 101–2. My translator here was my daughter Allie Murray in 1999. It seemed to me that a translation by Allie, who was then a senior in high school, would be more nearly like a translation by a young Fuller than would a translation by a sophisticated Latin scholar. The lines in an 1833 edition, *Works of P. Virgilius Maro, Including the Aeneid, Bucolics and Georgics,* read: "That day first has been the cause of death to Dido, and first the cause of her woes; for Dido neither is moved by the appearance of her crime or by honour, nor now does she meditate a secret love; she calls it marriage; with this name she screens her fault" (101).

12. See *FL*, I, 226, for Fuller's 6 March 1835 letter to Hedge wherein she quotes the lines from memory from bk. IV of the *Aeneid* about the goddess Fama. Fama, frequently translated as Fame, means Rumor, as Fuller knew. See also the lines as they appear in the Latin text used by my daughter in high school, *Vergil's Aeneid,* by Clyde Pharr, 210. The lines about Fama as Fuller misremembers them ("vires acquirit eundo / parva metu primo; mox sese attollit in auras, / et caput inter nubilia condit") have been translated into English here by my daughter. See also Virgil: *RF*, 101–2, as well as Fitzgerald's translation of bk. IV, lines 465–68, which read: "Do not think / I meant to be deceitful and slip away. / I never held the torches of a bridegroom, / Never entered upon the pact of marriage" (Virgil: *RF*, 107). The translation that appears in my text of these lines wherein Aeneas denies he has married Dido is once again that of my daughter Allie in 1999 from bk. IV, lines 337–39 of *Vergil's Aeneid: Books I–VI,* 222.

13. My translator is, again, my daughter Allie. See bk. IV, lines 322–23 of *Vergil's Aeneid: Books I–VI,* 221. See also Virgil: *RF*, 107, and Virgil: *AM*, 91; *FL*, I, 96, 97n7; and TF to SMF, 22 Feb. 1820, FFP: HM (fMS Am 1086 [5:5]).

14. *FL*, I, 86; TF to MCF, 10 Feb. 1820, FFP: HM (fMS Am 1086 [3:113]).

15. *FL*, I, 115, 131.

16. TF to MCF, 7 March 1820, FFP: HM (fMS Am 1086 [3:136]); and see FAB: "HN," 9–10.

17. *OM*, I, 91. On Fuller's eyes see V: *M&TM*, 18; and Dall, "Reminiscences of Margaret Fuller," 422. See also FE: "HC," 4.

18. *OM*, I, 24–25, 22. In the text I describe the actual room, closet, and window; it is possible that by "book closet" Fuller meant the entire room.

19. Frye, *Great Code*, 96–97; *OM*, I, 20–21.

---

20. *OM*, I, 26–27; V: *M&TM*, 13.

21. Ibid., 25, 27–29, 31, 235. In his 25 Dec. 1820 letter to Margarett Crane, Timothy says he wants Sarah Margarett to "attend to the rules" of "good writing." FFP: HM (fMS Am 1086 [3: 206]). On "burden of existence," see Cavell on Hamlet in "Being Odd, Getting Even," 26.

22. *FL*, I, 98.

23. Ibid., 98; TF to MCF, 27 March 1820, FFP: HM (fMS Am 1086 [3: 153]); Wieland: *SO*, I, 2. For instance, on 13 May 1809, two weeks before marrying Margarett Crane, Timothy wrote her he wants them "to be united in indissoluble bands," words Rezia uses to describe her out-of-wedlock union with Huon. See FFP: HM (fMS Am 1086 [3: 1]); Wieland: *SO*, II, 45, 211.

24. Wieland: *SO*, I, 193.

25. Ibid., I, 96–98, 104, 105, 108; TF to MCF, 27 March 1820, FFP: HM ([3: 153]).

26. Wieland: *SO*, I, 109–111. See "Dreaming with Anna, [30 Oct.] 1842," in Fuller, "Margaret Fuller's Journal for October 1842," 290; and repr. as "Dreaming with Anna" in C: *TW&TM*, 532.

27. *OM*, I, 17; *FL*, I, 98; Wieland: *SO*, I, 155, 160–61.

28. Wieland: *SO*, I, 185, 190; Wieland: *SO*, II, 2. To see how Wieland's language became so integral a part of Fuller's mind that she unconsciously repeats phrases from *Oberon* in letters years later, compare language in Fuller's 13 Nov. 1834 letter to James Clarke to Oberon's command to Huon to "grave it in your brain" to as "brother and . . . sister chaste remain!" See *FL*, VI, 245 and Wieland: *SO*, I, 185. And see Scarry, *Dreaming by the Book*, 3–9.

29. Wieland: *SO*, II, 6–9; and see Wieland, *Oberon: A Poetical Romance*, 161–62.

30. Wieland: *SO*, II, 9, 13.

31. Ibid., 17, 124, 227; Wieland, *Oberon: A Poetical Romance*, 204. And see A. B. Faust, intro. to *Oberon*, by Wieland, lxxxiv, lxxxviii. On exemplary and cautionary fairy tales see Tatar, *Off with Their Heads!*" 42–43 ff.

32. Wieland: *SO*, II, 45, 77, 103, 211, 227, 232, 234.

33. *OM*, I, 31, 43; Wieland: *SO*, I, 57–58, 160–61; ibid., II, 218.

34. See *FL*: I, 91, 92n5; TF to SMF, 25 Jan. 1820, FFP: HM (fMS Am 1086 [5: 5]); *OM*, I, 15; Wieland: *SO*, I, 185; ibid., II, 9.

Part Two. The Transition Years

1. *OM*, I, 41–42; C: *MFPY*, 82–83; *OM*, I, 41–42; Timothy Fuller qtd. in C: *MFPY*, 82.

2. *OM*, I, 41–42; C: *MFPY*, 92–93; *FL*, I, 201, 217; Hig: *MFO*, 27.

Chapter 5. Boston Schooling

1. *OM*, I, 40–41; *FL*, I, 103–4, 106. Fuller's language here reflects that of the health manuals of her time that advised: to prevent "unnatural" urges in a child parents should immerse the child's body in ice water and/or have the child engage in "violent exercise." See Comfort, *Anxiety Makers*, 40.

2. *FL*, I, 107, 109, 111, 110.

3. See TF to SMF, 22 Jan. 1822, FFP: HM (fMS Am 1086 [5: 9]); C: *MFPY*, 56, 60–61; *FL*, I, 108n2, 110, 103n2, 124; and V: *M&TM*, 22–24.

4. TF to MCF, 19 Dec. 1820, FFP: HM (fMS Am 1086 [3: 203]); Peabody qtd. in E: *J&MN*, XI, 482.

5. *FL*, I, 113–14, 117–18, 116n1. And see C: *MFPY*, 59, 64; V: *M&TM*, 24–25.

6. Ibid., 117; Hedge's account appears in *OM*, I, 91–93; *OM*, II, 5.

7. TF to SMF, 24 Dec. 1823, FFP:HM (fMS Am 1086 [5:12–13]); TF to SMF, 22 Jan. 1822, FFP:HM (fMS Am 1086 [5:9]); and TF to SMF, 3 March 1822, FFP:HM (fMS Am 1086 [5:10]).

8. See Hedge qtd. in Dall, "Caroline Dall's Reminiscences," 427; and see Hedge in *OM*, I, 92–93; and FE: "HC," 4.

9. Hig: *MFO*, 36–37, 29; C: *MFPY*, 46, 63.

10. See C: *MFPY*, 54. And see Hig: *MFO*, 23; *OM*, I, 92; *FL*, I, 125.

11. *FL*, I, 127, 132–33, 116; TF to SMF, 3 Dec. 1820, FFP:HM (fMS Am 1086 [5:6]).

12. *FL*, I, 126.

13. Margarett Crane Fuller qtd. in C: *MFPY*, 66, and see 72–73; TF to SMF, 24 Dec. 1823, FFP:HM (fMS Am 1086 [5:13]); and 3 April 1824, FFP:HM (fMS Am 1086 [5:15]). And see Timothy Fuller qtd. on his high expectations for Margaret in *FL*, I, 131n1, 137n1.

14. See TF to SMF, 22 Feb. 1820, FFP:HM (fMS Am 1086 [5:5]); Dall, "Caroline Dall's Reminiscences," 421; and TF to SMF, 3 April 1824, FFP:HM (fMS Am 1086 [5:15]). And see *FL*, I, 97n7 where Hudspeth quotes from Timothy's ultracritical 22 Feb. 1820 letter to Margaret.

15. *FL*, I, 132. George B. Emerson ran this innovative and prestigious school for girls that had just opened on Beacon Street. See C: *MFPY*, 71.

16. See *FL*, I, 132–33, 135.

17. See Bradford qtd. in R. C. Carter, "Margaret Fuller and the Two Sages," 198. And see Felman, *Jacques Lacan*, 123.

Chapter 6. Boarding School at Groton

1. *FL*, I, 87 n2. And see "Mariana," in F: *SL*, 82, and in *OM*, I, 42–52. See also C: *MFPY*, 71.

2. See F: *SL*, 82–83, 86.

3. Ibid., 82, 84–85.

4. Ibid., 87–89, 90–91, 93.

5. *FL*, I, 160.

6. Ibid., 139, 142, 143.

7. Ibid., 145–46. And see Shengold: *SM*, 20.

8. *FL*, I, 145–46.

9. Margarett Crane Fuller qtd. in C: *MFPY*, 67, 72–73.

10. *FL*, I, 151; Ariosto, *Sir John Harrington's Translation of Orlando Furioso*, book 25, stanza 24, line 1.

11. *FL*, I, 148.

12. Ibid., 146, 151–52, 148; E: *J&MN*, XI, 484–85. See also Fuller, "MS Journal," FFP:HM (bMS Am 1086 [A]).

Chapter 7. Metamorphosis in Her Young Adulthood

1. *FL*, I, 151; Hig: *MFO*, 23–24.

2. Hig: *MFO*, 24–25, 30; *OM*, I, 92; *OM*, II, 6; and see Wade, *Margaret Fuller*, 16.

3. Hig: *MFO*, 25.

4. Ibid., 26.

5. Ibid., 27, 31, 22.

6. Ibid., 28–29. And see MCF to TF, 11 Dec. 1818, FFP: HM (fMS Am 1086 [6:34]). Capper questions Higginson's interpretation, noting how letters show Margaret's mother's participation in making day-to-day decisions about Margaret's activities and her concern "about Margaret's morals and 'deportment.'" All this is so. However, in the life of a father's daughter like Fuller, it often feels as if the mother is not emotionally present. Besides, Higginson, a shrewd observer, was there. See C: *MFPY*, 66–67.

7. See Fuller qtd. in Hig: *MFO*, 21. And see *OM*, I, 138; FR: *RRF*, 13, and FR: *CF*, 16–17. And see Erikson, *Young Man Luther*, 65. Erikson's account of how the important parent's choice of one particular child to justify his or her existence is relevant even today to an interpretation of Fuller's life.

8. *OM*, I, 70; *FL*, III, 105; C: *MFPY*, 92–93; FR: *CF*, 15, 17.

9. *FL*, I, 154–55, 156–57; C: *MFPY*, 91–92.

10. *FL*, I, 154; Wade, *Margaret Fuller*, 68.

11. *FL*, I, 154. In "Literature, Psychoanalysis, and the Re-Formation of the Self" (343), Alcorn and Bracher discuss "identity theme," as does Norman Holland in *Five Readers Reading*, 60, 227–28. And see Shengold: *SM*, 5–6, 14–17.

12. *OM*, II, 6–7. Expecting Fuller to be "a 'sneering and critical dame,'" Emerson found "this new Corinne." See P. Miller, foreword to P. Miller, ed., *Margaret Fuller*, xix; E: *J&MN*, XI, 496; Gutwirth, *Madame de Staël, Novelist*, 157, 259.

13. See Gutwirth, *Madame de Staël, Novelist*, 27–30, 45–9; Doyle, *Oxford History of the French Revolution*, 28–9, 61 ff.; and Posgate, *Madame de Staël*, 23–4, 39–48. De Staël qtd. in Posgate, *Madame de Staël*, 47.

14. Posgate, *Madame de Staël*, 24–28; Gutwirth, *Madame de Staël, Novelist*, 31; FAB: "HN," 10.

15. Necker and de Staël qtd. in Gutwirth, *Madame de Staël, Novelist*, 31, 42. The reference is to Rousseau's *Émile: Or, On Education*.

16. Gutwirth, *Madame de Staël, Novelist*, 261, 157–61; Posgate, *Madame de Staël*, 2–3, 112, 115, 137–39.

17. See de Staël, *Corinne*, 18 ff.; Porte, *In Respect to Egotism*, 26–30; MCF to TF, 14 Jan. 1821, FFP: HM (fMS Am 1086 [6:114]).

18. C: *MFPY*, 93; Hig: *MFO*, 27, 29–30, 37; and see FR: *CF*, 18.

19. David Barlow, a classmate of Edward Emerson who died in Puerto Rico in October 1834, wrote "Lines to the Memory of Edward Bliss Emerson." Almira, who married David in 1830, separated from him in 1840, after which she lived with her children at Brook Farm, Mass. Although Zenobia's personality in *Blithedale Romance* was based on Fuller's, Almira was the model for her beauty. *FL*, I, 93n, 154, 155n, 170–72, 212n; C: *MFPY*, 97–98.

20. Hig: *MFO*, 35; C: *MFPY*, 95; MCF to TF, 25 Nov. 1820, FFP: HM (fMS Am 1086 [6:92]).

21. Hig: *MFO*, 35–36; B: *MFTtoR*, 61–64; Dall, *Reminiscences*, 424; C: *MFPY*, 95–97; *FL*, I, 181n.

Chapter 8. The Influence of the Harvard Romantics

1. From Ralph Waldo Emerson, "Historic Notes of Life and Letters in New England," in P. Miller, ed., *Transcendentalists*, 501–2. And see Frye, "Drunken Boat," and Eichner, "Rise of Modern Science."

2. See Abrams's discussion in *Correspondent Breeze* of the indelible imprint upon Westerners of biblical imagery and thematic patterns, "outside of which," as the nineteenth-

century radical economist and social theorist Pierre Proudhon said, "we can neither speak nor act, and without which we do not even think" (qtd. 226). Essays in Abrams's collection I have drawn on for insights are: "The Correspondent Breeze: A Romantic Metaphor," "English Romanticism: The Spirit of the Age," and "Two Roads to Wordsworth." See also Abrams, *Natural Supernaturalism,* and Abrams, *Mirror and the Lamp.* And see Coleridge, *Biographia Literaria,* I, chapters 12–13, esp. pp. 164–69.

3. E: *E&L,* 407. Recall "Lines: Composed a Few Miles Above Tintern Abbey": "And I have felt / A presence . . . a sense sublime / Of something far more deeply interfused, / Whose dwelling is the light of setting suns[.]" Wordsworth, *Wordsworth,* 164. The young Emerson loved Wordsworth's poetry, including "Tintern Abbey." See R: *EMoF,* 149.

4. See Porte, *Representative Man,* 66, and Porte in general on Emerson's *Nature,* 69–86; and E: *E&L,* 10, 411.

5. See Eichner, "Rise of Modern Science," 8–30 (esp. 16–17); Wessell, *Karl Marx,* 26–40; and Porte, *In Respect to Egotism,* 17–19.

6. See W. E. Channing, "Unitarian Christianity," 4, emphasis mine; and Aaron, *Men of Good Hope,* 18.

7. E: *E&L,* 407; Steele, *Representation of the Self,* 101; *FL,* I, 154.

8. *OM,* I, 27, 43, 46.

9. Ibid., 62, 62n; *FL,* I, 96, 97n3; and C: *MFPY,* 98–99, 104–06.

10. Clarke qtd. in C: *MFPY,* 105, 100.

11. See P. Miller, ed., *Transcendentalists,* 43, 66–67; Frye, "Drunken Boat," 13; and Aaron, *Men of Good Hope,* 18.

12. See *FL,* I, 163–64; *FL,* VI, 187.

13. *FL,* I, 163–165, 165nn1&2. The Judge was Nathan Weston (1782–1872). Fuller mentions Moore's "Tyrolese Song of Liberty," which appears in *Works of Thomas Moore* (New York: 1825), 3: 65–66, and in the 1829 Philadelphia edition, both of which she had access to, just as she surely had located Moore's edition of *Life, Letters, and Journals of Lord Byron,* which originally appeared as two volumes early in 1830. I refer to a 1972 reprint of the two volumes in one, which was published by John Murray in London (1920).

14. *OM,* I, 114, 242; *FL,* I, 177; *FL,* VI, 187. Clarke (*OM,* I, 114) says Fuller began studying German in 1832. According to Hudspeth, Fuller had access to *Goethes Werke: Vollstandige Ausgabe letzer Hand* (Stuttgart: 1827–30). See *FL,* I, 178n3.

15. *OM,* I, 18; *FL,* VI, 195–96, 139, 164; and see Margarett Crane qtd. in C: *MFPY,* 72. Fuller's "two souls" echoes Faust to Wagner in part 1 of *Faust,* lines 1,112–17: "Two souls alas! are dwelling in my breast, / And one . . . Unto the world in grossly loving zest, / With clinging tendrils, one adheres; / The other rises forcibly in quest / Of rarified ancestral spheres." See Goethe, *Faust,* 145.

16. *FL,* VI, 160, 185; *FL,* III, 156; C: *MFPY,* 102–4.

17. *FL,* I, 163.

18. Ibid., 170–72; and see *OM,* I, 95.

19. *FL,* I, 171; Rebecca Clarke recalling her father's words in C: *MFPY,* 106.

20. See B: *MFTtoR,* 210, and *FL,* VI, 169–70. And see Shengold: *SM,* 30.

Chapter 9. The Search for Self

1. See Steele, *Representation of the Self,* 1, 13, whose words I echo.

2. See Hartman, "Romanticism and 'Anti-Self-Consciousness,'" 54.

3. *OM*, I, 137–38, 26; *FL*, VI, 139. Capper identifies the friend with whom Fuller had the conversation as Eliza Farrar. See C: *MFPY*, 112–13.

4. *OM*, I, 139–42.

5. Ibid., 139–40.

6. Ibid., 140–41.

7. *FL*, I, 159, 185–86; *FL*, VI, 139. And see Shelley's "Hymn to Intellectual Beauty" in *Shelley's Poetry and Prose*, 93.

8. *OM*, I, 80, 138; *FL*, I, 158.

9. See P. Miller, ed., *Transcendentalists*, 8; *FL*, I, 158–59; *FL*, VI, 161; *FL*, I, 159.

10. Frye, "Drunken Boat," 16; Schapiro, *Romantic Mother*, ix–xvi.

11. See Steele, *Representation of the Self*, 10–11; *OM*, I, 238. For a young Fuller on her "superficial brilliancy of expression," see *FL*, VI, 195.

12. *FL*, VI, 174–75, 176; and see C: *MFPY*, 108, 376n41. Fuller here anticipates Freud, who read dreams not as messages from the gods, as did Clarke, but as a register of personal feelings. See A. Alvarez, *Night*, 119. And see Zaretsky, *Secrets of the Soul*, 41–63.

13. Capper says we "can only guess what [Clarke] had to say" in reply to "such a strangely impassioned, paranoid, and (to a modern Freudian reader) sexually tempting dream." See C: *MYPY*, 108.

14. *FL*, VI, 140; C: *TW&TM*, 61.

Chapter 10. The Farm in Groton

1. Steele, *Representation of the Self*, quoting Wolfgang Iser, 8.

2. FR: *RRF*, 26; C: *MFPY*, 119.

3. *FL*, VI, 186, 190, 192–93, and 194n1, for Ralph Manheim's translation of the lines Fuller quotes from Novalis in German; Hig: *MFO*, 40–42.

4. *FL*, VI, 192–93.

5. Ibid., 192–94, 190, 196.

6. FR: *CF*, 18–19, 31; FR: *RRF*, 15–16, 21, 35; C: *MFPY*, 119, 121. It is mere coincidence that Timothy bought his two grand homes from men whose last names happened to be Dana: Chief Justice Francis Dana had built and owned the Dana mansion in Cambridge, whereas Judge Samuel Dana sold Timothy the Groton farm.

7. *FL*, VI, 200, 203, 205; *OM*, I, 27. On Fuller's translation of *Tasso* see Zwarg: *FC*, 59–62, 67–79.

8. *FL*, VI, 205, 203.

9. Ibid., 210. See Schlegel qtd. in Wessell, *Karl Marx*, 26–27. And see C: *MFPY*, 128–29. And for Fuller on Novalis (Freiherr von Hardenberg [1772–1801]) see *FL*, I, 177; for Hudspeth on same see 177n1.

10. *FL*, I, 185, 186n2. See Schleiermacher qtd. in Wessell, *Karl Marx*, 25, and 24–28.

11. *FL*, I, 182, 183n5, 245; *OM*, I, 165; Wessell, *Karl Marx*, 24–27; C: *MFPY*, 173.

12. *FL*, VI, 201–2. On Clarke's feelings for Fuller see *FL*, VI, 276, 277nn1&2; C: *MFPY*, 140–42.

13. *FL*, VI, 202. And see, for instance, Gen. 1:1–3 RSV; Acts 1:6–8 RSV; Matt. 5:14–17 RSV; John 1:1–17 RSV. The conduit metaphor was used in a 30 May 1996 sermon, "Where the Son Shines," by Dr. William Bryant, executive director of the Outreach Foundation of the Presbyterian Church USA, at the First Presbyterian Church in Columbus, Ga.

14. *FL*, VI, 216, 221, 223.

15. *FL*, I, 188–89, 218; *FL*, VI, 216, 215, 223. In "The Legend of Hitler's Childhood," Erikson says about the nineteenth-century German youth's yearning for a real home that in "the Reichs-German character, this peculiar combination of idealistic rebellion and obedient submission led to a paradox. The German conscience is self-denying and cruel; but its ideals are shifting and, as it were, homeless" (Erikson, *Childhood and Society*, 335–36).

16. *FL*, I, 192: *FL*, VI, 231, and 211n1, for Clarke's lack of luster as a preacher. The idea of a "transition state" was important to Fourier, whose thinking influenced Fuller. It seems she meant by the phrase what Fourier did, since for him a transition state is "like a growth crisis 'similar to the onset of puberty.'" See Zwarg: *FC*, 116–17, 204, and Jonathan Beecher, *Charles Fourier*, 338.

17. *FL*, VI, 241, 216; *FL*, I, 201; *FL*, III, 85. On Fuller's grandmother's Calvinism see C: *MFPY*, 16.

18. FR: *RRF*, 21; FR: *CF*, 26, 21, 23–25; FE: "HC."

19. *FL*, I, 195; FR: *CF*, 34, 29–30; *FL*, VI, 130; FR: *RRF*, 23.

20. TF to MCF, 10 Feb. 1820, FFP: HM (fMS Am 1086 [3:113]). And Timothy Fuller qtd. in C: *MFPY*, 14, 29. And see 1 Cor. 6:9–10 KJV.

21. Comfort, *Anxiety-Makers*, 40–41, 56, 93; Kincaid, *Child-Loving*, 174–75; C: *MFPY*, 168; *FL*, I, 201. On "violent bodily exercise" as a way of relieving Fuller's "nerves" see *OM*, I, 41.

22. Frye, "Drunken Boat," 11, 22; *FL*, VI, 235; *FL*, I, 224.

23. *FL*, III, 85; *FL*, I, 180; FR: *CF*, 44–45; Fuller qtd. in C: *MFPY*, 124. And see FR: *RRF*, 25–26.

24. See *FL*, I, 213; *FL*, VI, 130; and Fuller's journal cited in C: *MFPY*, 133–34.

25. Fuller qtd. in C: *MFPY*, 134; *FL*, VI, 232, 215; and *FL*, I, 218.

26. FR: *RRF*, 25; FAB: "HN," 9.

27. See C: *MFPY*, 144–45.

28. See Fuller, "Classical and Romantic," in P. Miller, ed., *Margaret Fuller*, 40–41.

29. Ibid., 43, 46; C: *MFPY*, 149–50. And see Goethe, *Iphigenia in Taurus*.

30. *FL*, I, 214n2, 229–30, 231n2.

31. Ibid., 230, 231n3. And see C: *MFPY*, 11–12. Emerson had preached on 31 May in Charles Robinson's First Parish Church in Groton. When the church called the liberal Robinson to be its minister, the orthodox minority formed the Union Congregational Church, whose first minister, John Todd, served 1827–33. Todd, who wrote on the necessity of sexual abstinence, apparently stayed through the summer of 1833. This means Margaret, who moved to Groton in April, would have had time to hear about the controversial Todd, if not also to hear him preach.

32. C: *MFPY*, 157–58.

33. Ibid., 155–58; FR: *RRF*, 25; *OM*, I, 154–55.

34. *OM*, I, 154; FR: *CF*, 31–33. On bad drinking water as the cause of cholera in 1830s Great Britain see Vachon, "Doctor John Snow Blames Water Pollution."

35. *OM*, I, 156; FR: *RRF*, 35; Hig: *MFO*, 54.

36. *OM*, I, 156; C: *MFPY*, 167–68.

37. FR: *CF*, 32; *FL*, I, 237; *FL*, III, 85–86.

38. *FL*, I, 236n1; C: *MFPY*, 161–65.

39. *FL*, I, 254, 243, 224, 182; *OM*, I, 153; C: *MFPY*, 153.

Part Three. Emerson, Epistolary Friend and Guide

1. *FL*, VI, 195, 223; *OM*, I, 153; C: *MFPY*, 153. *FL*, I, 254, 199, 210; *FL*, VI, 219. On Dewey see R: *EMoF*, 157, 160; and *FL*, I, 208n2.

2. *FL*, I, 212n6, 213, 206–8; *FL*, VI, 193. On Fuller's 1833 translation of Goethe's *Torquato Tasso* see Zwarg: *FC*, 67–79.

3. FR: *RRF*, 29, 37; FR: *CF*, 46–47, 49; *FL*, I, 319.

4. R: *EMoF*, 37, 224; Bishop, *Emerson on the Soul*, 169.

5. On the grieving process and the human tendency to seek to find "new relationships to substitute for the lost ones" see Terr, *Too Scared to Cry*, 100–102.

6. See Zwarg: *FC*, 42, 29; R: *EMoF*, 24–25; and RWE to MF, 11 April 1850 (Philadelphia); E: *LofRWE*, IV, 198–199; *FL*, V, 239–40.

Chapter 11. The Search for a Guide

1. See Whicher, *Freedom and Fate*, 50–71; W: *SRWE*, 9; Buell, *Emerson*, 14; R: *EMoF*, 36–37, 185; and E: *E&L*, 91.

2. See Porte, *Representative Man*, 89, 215; E: *LofRWE*, VII, 539; R: *EMoF*, 190–93; Buell, *Emerson*, 13–15, 15n, 22–23.

3. *OM*, I, 203; Sealts and A. R. Ferguson, eds., *Emerson's Nature*, 23; and see Bishop, *Emerson on the Soul*, 181, where Bishop sums up the perception of John Jay Chapman.

4. See Whicher, *Freedom and Fate*, 4; W: *SRWE*, 7; R: *EMoF*, 19; Porte, *Representative Man*, 214–15; Buell, *Emerson*, 14, 15n; and Bishop, *Emerson on the Soul*, 182. For Emerson on "defect of character" see E: *J&MN*, II, 238. For RWE's 8 March 1848 letter to Lidian Emerson see E: *LofRWE*, IV, 33; and Porte, *Representative Man*, 214.

5. W: *SRWE*, 1–4; R: *EMoF*, 23, 27; Barish, *Emerson*, 19–23, 44–45.

6. Cheyfitz, *Trans-Parent*, 161; R: *EMoF*, 18; Barish, *Roots of Prophecy*, 55, 61–62.

7. E: *E&L*, 76; R: *EMoF*, 33, 34.

8. On the Common Sense School of "Scottish philosophy" see R: *EMoF*, 29–33, and Hondrich, ed., *Oxford Companion to Philosophy*, 815–16.

9. See Cayton, "The Socratic Response" and "Spiritual Laws and Natural Organicism" in *Emerson's Emergence*, 33–56, 57–79; Reed qtd. in R: *EMoF*, 71. Calvin thought Scripture's written law to be "nothing but a witness to the law of nature by which God recalls to our memories what has been inscribed in our hearts" (Bouwsma, *John Calvin*, 75).

10. E: *E&L*, 20. A "straight and narrow" path suggests the natural and right way to travel, as opposed to the crooked way taken by those who stray from accepted morality, like "wayward women." Calvin, whose thinking through Aunt Mary influenced Emerson, "saw God's law," notes Bouwsma, "as a narrow path; only if we stay within its boundaries, straying neither to the right nor to the left, will we be safe" (Bouwsma, *John Calvin*, 49). On the origin of the idea of sexual perversion as wayward and hence "evil" behavior see Dollimore, *Sexual Dissidence*—esp. 103–47, where he discusses the "The Wiser, the Waywarder," "the holy sinner," and "the straight and narrow."

11. Cayton, *Emerson's Emergence*, 66–68; W: *SRWE*, 219; E: *E&L*, 282, 409; and Zwarg: *FC*. For Calvin on the necessity of keeping an "erect posture" in life, of maintaining "*uprightness*," and of controlling one's passions, see Bouwsma, *John Calvin*, 71, 80. Calvin said passions express themselves in excess and resist vehemently the control of the soul: "they are 'vicious and perverse because they burst out and endure no restraint.' . . . they make us worse than beasts." Martha Nussbaum's discussion of Socrates' attitude toward "virtue" in

her review, "Chill of Virtue," gives insight into how Emerson came upon his own particularly rigid definition of what makes for moral "uprightness" (34–40).

12. See Porte, *Representative Man*, 117; and E: *E&L*, 75.

13. See G. J. Barker-Benfield, *Horrors of the Half-Known Life*, 182; Fowler qtd. in Aspiz, "Walt Whitman," 380; Stern, "Margaret Fuller and the Phrenologist-publishers," 230; Porte, *Representative Man*, 259–60; and B. Barker-Benfield, "Spermatic Economy," 336–72.

14. G. J. Barker-Benfield, *Horrors of the Half-Known Life*, 135–62; Cheyfitz, *Trans-Parent*, 161; Porte, *Representative Man*, 259–60, 280–82. See also Comfort, *Anxiety Makers*, 69–113. The Fullers moved to Groton in early April 1833. See C: *MFPY*, 120. The Rev. Charles B. Kittredge replaced Todd in October 1833. On Richard and Arthur attending Kittredge's church and Todd's ministry in Groton see *FL*, I, 230, 231n3.

15. W: *SRWE*, 186; Aspiz, "Walt Whitman," 380–81.

16. Zwarg: *FC*, 37; Cheyfitz, *Trans-Parent*, 165; Bishop, *Emerson on the Soul*, 153.

17. Porte, *Representative Man*, 89; W: *SRWE*, 186; B: *MFTtoR*, 122; *FL*, II, 58; *OM*, I, 202. On Fuller's 21 July to 11 Aug. 1836 visit, see *FL*, I, 255n1.

18. *OM*, II, 35; *OM*, I, 202–3; *FL*, IV, 61n7; B: *MFTtoR*, 122. For a description of Fuller see Dall, "Caroline Dall's Reminiscences," 422. For Fuller on her "brown" hair see her 7 Dec. 1848 letter to RFF from Rome, *FL*, V, 160.

19. *OM*, I, 227; Emerson, "Address at the Woman's Rights Convention," in *Later Lectures of Ralph Waldo Emerson*, 2: 19; and Douglas, *Feminization of American Culture*, 273.

20. *OM*, I, 202–3, 229; R: *EMoF*, 224. On Emerson and laughing see B: *MFTtoR*, 103.

21. *OM*, I, 202–3.

22. Ibid., 229; *FL*, I, 258. Though *Nature* was published 9 Sept. 1836, Fuller did not read it until 1840. We know Emerson read *Nature* through a draft of "Prospects" to her during her July–August 1836 visit (see *FL*, II, 128, and Sealts and Ferguson, *Emerson's Nature*, 43–44). See also B: *MFTtoR*, 105; and R: *EMoF*, 241. Fuller's calico dresses were perhaps what made some men say she dressed "dowdily." See E. H. Miller, *Salem Is My Dwelling Place*, 232.

23. Emerson's study has been preserved in the Concord Free Museum. A recorded voice reads a note of Fuller to Emerson. In it Fuller says how much she likes "to be in your library when you are out of it." See MF's October 1841 note to RWE, *FL*, I, 234. See also RWE's March? 1880? letter to William Allen Wall in E: *LofRWE*, VI, 322, and his April 1833 letter to Charles (E: *LofRWE*, I, 374, 374n40), wherein he says he is leaving "next Tuesday . . . for Florence in company with [the New Bedford painter] 'Mr Wall.'" Wall's copy of the original painting, *The Three Fates*, by the Florentine mannerist Cecchino Salviati hangs in Emerson's study. And see Robert D. Habich, 15 Feb. 2000 letter to Mr. David F. Wood, curator of the Concord Museum, regarding Salviati, sent to me by Judy Fichtenbaum of the Concord Museum.

24. B: *MFTtoR*, 105; Sealts and A. R. Ferguson, *Emerson's Nature*, 5; Francis Bowen in P. Miller, ed., *Transcendentalists*, 174; Cheyfitz, *Trans-Parent*, 1; *FL*, II, 128; *FL*, I, 261. And see W: *SRWE*, 89.

25. See Sealts and A. R. Ferguson, *Emerson's Nature*, 5, 7–8.

26. See ibid., 5, 7–9; Buell, *Emerson*, 92–94.

27. Buell, *Emerson*, 92–94; *FL*, II, 128; Sealts and A. R. Ferguson, *Emerson's Nature*, 30–31.

28. Zwarg: *FC*, 45; Sealts and A. R. Ferguson, *Emerson's Nature*, 33–37, 43–44; E: *E&L*, 46–47. Bowen says "the highest praise" he can accord *Nature* is "that it is a *suggestive* book." See P. Miller, ed., *Transcendentalists*, 174. Emerson uses Shakespeare, Angus's remarks on Macbeth: "Now does he feel his title / Hang loose about him, like a giant's robe / Upon a dwarfish thief." See *Macbeth* 5.2.20–22. See also R: *EMoF*, 237–41.

Chapter 12. A Fluid Friendship

1. See "Modern British Poets," in O: *AL&tD*, 90, 86. And see C: *MFPY*, 177.

2. See "Modern British Poets," in O: *AL&tD*, 91, 90, 103, 100; E: *E&L*, 47. On Fuller, Fourier, and "transition-state," see Zwarg: *FC*, 118–19, 204, 208–10.

3. See W: *SRWE*, 186; Aspiz, "Walt Whitman," 381; and Bishop, *Emerson on the Soul*, 148–49.

4. *OM*, I, 156; *FL*, I, 224.

5. *OM*, I, 156, 280.

6. See Schneiderman, *Jacques Lacan*, 151–52; *OM*, I, 219, 18; *FL*, VI, 223; C: *MFPY*, 176. And see Fuller, 1833 ("Pearl"), FFP: HM (bMS Am 1086 [A]). See also FFP: HM (fMS Am 1086 [Works V: 17]).

7. E: *LofRWE*, III, 376; *FL*, VI, 206; *FL*, I, 174, 175n1; Hig: *MFO*, 44–45.

8. G. J. Barker-Benfield, *Horrors of the Half-Known Life*, 136. Lloyd was nine when Todd's book appeared. Capper implies that Lloyd picked up his habit "later." Some things we cannot know. See C: *MFPY*, 168.

9. *FL*, I, 225, 248, 248n2; Zwarg: *FC*, 5. Hudspeth says that Goethe took Vulpius as a mistress in 1788 but married her in 1806, "thus legitimizing an affair that had scandalized the Weimar court" and made the "righteous" in America scorn Goethe.

10. P. Miller qtd. in Keller, "Puritan Perverse," 143. *FL*, I, 224; R: *EMoF*, 207–8. On Emerson's home see also *Emerson House in Concord*, a pamphlet available at the house.

11. *FL* I, 262, and see Fuller, "Modern British Poets," O: *AL&tD*, 86–88, 90.

12. *OM*, I, 203.

13. Ibid., 18, 196. And see Mark 6: 1–6 RSV, where the Bible says that Jesus "laid his hands upon a few sick people and healed them."

14. *OM*, I, 18, 202, 213, 227–28; E: *J&MN*, XI, 500. And see Porte, *Representative Man*, 219.

15. E: *J&MN*, XI, 500; Porte, *Representative Man*, 219; E: *J&MN*, V, 188, 190.

16. *OM*, I, 228; E: *J&MN*, XI, 500; Schneiderman, *Jacques Lacan*, 56–59.

17. See Anthony, *Margaret Fuller*; and Hardwick, "Genius of Margaret Fuller," 14. In *Remembering Anna O.*, Borch-Jacobsen discusses the "hysteric" "Anna O." and her interaction with Freud. On narcissism, Ann Douglas says Fuller's "narcissism" was "born of utter necessity" (271). And see Schapiro, *Romantic Mother*, ix–xvi; Steele, *Representation of the Self*, 9–11; Kohut, *Analysis of the Self*, xiv.

18. *OM*, I, 197; Zwarg: *FC*, 41; R: *EMoF*, 25. In 1988 Porte wrote me, "If Emerson was ever 'in love' with anyone (excluding Ellen Tucker and later his obvious passion for Anna Barker—everybody was in love with her!) I am convinced Margaret Fuller was the one." See Porte to author, 30 June 1988.

19. *OM*, I, 78; E: *LofRWE*, II, 328. And see Zwarg: *FC*, 32–43.

Chapter 13. A "Forlorn" Boston Winter

1. *OM*, I, 298; *FL*, I, 254; B: *MFTtoR*, 101.

2. See P. Miller, ed., *Transcendentalists*, 150–56, 170; *FL*, I, 256n; Wordsworth, "Ode: Intimations of Immortality," *Wordsworth*, 460–62.

3. *FL*, I, 260–62.

4. Ibid., 260–62. For examples of MF's letters to TF see *FL*, I, 96, 136, 137n1.

5. See William Ellery Channing, "Unitarian Christianity" and "Likeness to God," in *Uni-*

tarian Christianity and Other Essays, 3–38, 86–108. See also Miller, *Transcendentalists*, 21; and *FL*, I, 263 n1.

6. See P. Miller, *Transcendentalists*, 21–22; B: *MFTtoR*, 110–11.

7. See P. Miller, *Transcendentalists*, 150–56; B: *MFTtoR*, 107–16; and C: *MFPY*, 195, 198–200.

8. *FL*, I, 278–79.

9. Ibid., 266, 288, 278.

10. Relevant here is Lacan's "The Empty Word and the Full Word," in *Language of the Self*, 9–27.

11. B: *MFTtoR*, 107–16; *FL*, I, 268–69.

12. Ibid., 272, 265n.

13. Ibid., 272; *FL*, II, 234.

14. *FL*, I, 283; *FL*, VI, 209; *FL*, I, 268.

15. *FL*, I, 272, 273, 273–74n. The phrase "vale of tears" is used by Ralph, loyal lover of Indiana, who almost threw her life away in pursuit of the unfaithful Raymon in George Sand's *Indiana*, a favorite novel of Fuller, which she read in 1835.

Chapter 14. Providence, Pain, and Escape into Illusion

1. *FL*, I, 267n1, 280; C: *MFPY*, 204; C: *TW&TM*, 151; E: *J&MN*, XI, 491. Fuller never wrote a biography of Goethe, but she wrote an analysis of the poet's work for the July 1841 *Dial*. See *FL*, I, 280n1; *OM*, I, 96, 243–44.

2. *FL*, I, 288, 289–90; B: *MFTtoR*, 120–21; Fergenson, "Margaret Fuller as a Teacher in Providence," 62–63; Shealy, "Margaret Fuller and Her 'Maiden,'" 51.

3. *FL*, I, 284, 322; Emerson qtd. in C: *MFPY*, 206–7.

4. *FL*, I, 286, 284, 316, 317n2. And see Fergenson, "Margaret Fuller as a Teacher in Providence," 73; Shealy, "Margaret Fuller and Her 'Maiden,'" 63n15; C: *MFPY*, 207.

5. Kopacz, "School Journal of Hannah (Anna) Gale," 82; Fergenson, "Margaret Fuller in the Classroom," 139; Fergenson, "Margaret Fuller as a Teacher in Providence," 62–63; *FL*, I, 288, 328; B: *MFTtoR*, 120–21.

6. See Stern, "Margaret Fuller and the Phrenologist-Publishers," 229–31; C: *MFPY*, 221; and *FL*, I, 313, 303. And see R. C. Fuller, *Mesmerism and the American Cure of Souls*, 2–5, 13, 26, 30–31. Surely Fuller's headaches were migraines. That she had only a lorgnette to help her see did not help, as Myerson notes in Dall, "Caroline Dall's Reminiscences," 428n32.

7. *FL*, I, 305n7, 316, 317n2; Stern, "Margaret Fuller and the Phrenologist-Publishers," 229–31; C: *MFPY*, 221. Orson Fowler would become Fuller's bookseller-publisher. And see R. C. Fuller, *Mesmerism and the American Cure of Souls*, 2–5, 13, 26, 30–31.

8. *FL*, I, 278; *OM*, I, 18, 57; B: *MFTtoR*, 135. Numerous friends commented on Fuller's public style. For instance, see Hoar's remark in a 3 April 1839 letter to Hannah L. Chappell regarding Fuller's "*superficial* manner," in C: *TW&TM*, 89–90.

9. Fergenson, "Margaret Fuller as a Teacher in Providence," 74; *OM*, I, 181; *FL*, I, 303; B: *MFTtoR*, 132; C: *MFPY*, 220–21, 229–31; Stern, "Margaret Fuller and the Phrenologist-Publishers," 230–31.

10. See Shealy, "Margaret Fuller and Her 'Maiden,'" 56, 53, 48, 62; B: *MFTtoR*, 121; Fergenson, "Margaret Fuller as a Teacher in Providence," 89; Kopacz, "School Journal of Hannah (Anna) Gale," 71, 76; C: *MFPY*, 229–231; V: *M&TM*, 90–91; Fuller, [On Her Childhood],

"Journal, March 1839," in F: *EMF,* 4–5; and Fergenson, "Margaret Fuller in the Classroom," 134–35. And see *FL,* I, 91, 97n7, 137n1.

11. See Fergenson, "Margaret Fuller in the Classroom," 134–35, and C: *MFPY,* 229–31.

12. *FL,* I, 327, 289, 311. And see C: *MFPY,* 211, and Fergenson, "Margaret Fuller as a Teacher in Providence," 62–63; *OM,* I, 228.

13. *FL,* I, 283; *Hamlet* 3.1; the accurate quotation is "The heartache, and the thousand natural shocks / That flesh is heir to. 'Tis a consummation / Devoutly to be wished." And see Baker, *Emerson among the Eccentrics,* 247, where Emerson in 1843 similarly paraphrases Shakespeare.

14. See *FL,* I, 283; *FL,* VI, 145, 206. See also MCF to RFF, 28 June 1850, FFP: HM (fMS Am 1086 [16:164]).

15. *OM,* I, 181.

16. C: *MFPY,* 32; *OM,* I, 14; *FL,* I, 248n2, 292–93, 293n2.

17. *OM,* I, 181; C: *MFPY,* 220; FL, I, 283, 278, 294–95.

18. Hig: *MFO,* 28; Kohut, *Analysis of the Self,* 12; Porte, *Representative Man,* 278–79; W: *SRWE,* 186.

19. See Zwarg: *FC,* 24. And see *FL,* II, 128; *FL,* I, 284; E: *E&L,* 7, 21, 38, 40; Cheyfitz, *Transparent,* 41; R: *EMoF,* 262. "Seminal thought" is Warfel's phrase in "Margaret Fuller and Ralph Waldo Emerson," 577. On Emerson's voice see "FJ42," 338.

20. E: *LofRWE,* II, 94–95; E: *E&L,* 54, 57, 60, 63–66, 70–71.

21. E: *E&L,* 60–65, 70–71. Bishop stresses the "new self" Emerson hoped and expected to generate in his auditors. See Bishop, *Emerson on the Soul,* 150–51. See also Cheyfitz, *Transparent,* 41.

22. *FL,* I, 277n; E: *LofRWE,* II, 47, 88, 94–95; *OM,* I, 279, 280. And see E: *J&MN,* XI, 471; and TF to SMF, 22 Feb. 1820 ("many . . . mistakes"), FFP: HM (fMS Am 1086 [5:5]).

23. *FL,* I, 297. On Cary Sturgis see *FL,* I, 273–74n; and D: "LCS-MF," 201–51. And see Burrill Curtis qtd. in E: *LofRWE,* VIII, 41n136.

24. See *FL,* I, 303–5, 306–7, 310–12, 313–15; and D: "LCS-MF," 205–6.

25. *FL,* I, 306, 312–13, 313–15.

26. Ibid., 322–23, 324n4; C: *MFPY,* 217–18, 220.

27. *FL* I, 327. And see Matt. 6:24 RSV: "No one can serve two masters."

28. *FL* I, 327–28; E: *E&L,* 71; Kohut, *Analysis of the Self,* 12, 25. And see RWE's 1 Sept. 1840 journal entry: "Gladly I learn that we have these subterranean—say rather, these supersensuous channels of communication, and that spirits can meet in their pure upper sky without the help of organs" (*Emerson in His Journals,* 244). See also W: *SRWE,* 134.

29. See C: *MFPY,* 249.

30. *FL,* I, 331; E: *LofRWE,* II, 128–29; D: "LCS-MF," 206; Alexander, *Women in Romanticism,* 8.

31. E: *LofRWE,* II, 143, 163, 168–69; Porte, *Representative Man,* 218, 277; E: *E&L,* 345. And see W: *SRWE,* 134.

32. E: *LofRWE,* II, 70; Steele, *Representation of the Self,* 7–9.

33. E: *LofRWE,* II, 197; E: *E&L,* 265; *FL,* I, 332, 159; *OM,* I, 42, 203. And see Fuller qtd. in Hig: *MFO,* 118; Kohut, *Analysis of the Self,* 72; and the comment of Boston biographer Gamaliel Bradford (b. 1863) that "Margaret had so many selves you could peel her like an onion" (R. C. Carter, "Margaret Fuller and the Two Sages," 198).

34. D: "LCS-MF," 204. And see Fuller qtd. in Porte, *Representative Man,* 219.

35. *OM,* I, 289, 230; *OM,* II, 11, 98–99, 106; E: *LofRWE,* II, 88.

Chapter 15. "Drawn" by Fuller's Siren Song

1. Fuller qtd. C: *MFPY*, 246, and see 249.
2. *FL*, II, 48; C: *MFPY*, 253. On Fuller's translation of Eckermann's *Gespräche mit Goethe*, see Zwarg: *FC*, 79–82.
3. See *FL*, II, 55 n1; R: *EMoF*, 37.
4. E: *LofRWE*, II, 173, 191.
5. E: *J&MN*, XI, 457; *OM*, I, 219; and Emerson, "Demonology," E: *ELofRWE*, III, 151–70.
6. Buell, *Emerson*, 22–31; E: *ELofRWE*, 151, 167–68, 162, 165, 156, 159; *OM*, I, 218–19. When Emerson suggests that demon-possessed people are unable to steer their "rudder true," he may have had in mind a passage from Goethe's *Tasso* as translated by Fuller in which "rudderless" suggests "a suspension of mastery and control between men and women." For a translation see Zwarg: *FC*, 83.
7. E: *ELofRWE*, III, 152, 153, 155, 156, 162. And see MF's 2 Nov. 1830 letter to JFC in *FL*, VI, 176.
8. E: *ELofRWE*, III, 160; *OM*, I, 219; *FL*, II, 168.
9. E: *ELofRWE*, III, 168, 169, 162, 163.
10. Ibid. 164–65, 167, 170. And see F: *WNC*, 90–93.
11. E: *ELofRWE*, III, 164–65, 167, 170. And see F: *WNC*, 90–93. Running after a ghost or dream appears in E: *ELofRWE*, III, 170.
12. *FL*, II, 54; E: *LofRWE*, II, 173.
13. *FL*, II, 54; E: *LofRWE*, II, 192.
14. C: *MFPY*, 257; B: *MFTtoR*, 139; E: *E&L*, 79–80, 88, 90–91. For Emerson on "Cultus, or established worship of the civilized world," see E: *E&L*, 79, 91.
15. E: *E&L*, 80, 88–89; E: *LofRWE*, II, 197.
16. *FL*, II, 68, 70n1. And see MCF to TF, 8 Jan. 1819 ("arbour"), FFP: HM (fMS Am 1086 [6:53]). Emerson notes in his journal that *"lyrical glances"* was a favorite phrase of Fuller and that she got it from George Sand. In "Demonology" he makes light fun of those who see meaning in "the glance of a dog." See E: *J&MN*, XI, 497; and E: *ELofRWE*, III, 154.
17. *FL*, II, 68–69; *FL*, I, 135. And see E: *ELofRWE*, III, 155; and Vanita, *Sappho and the Virgin Mary*, 51.
18. E: *LofRWE*, II, 201–3, 208–9, 211.
19. *FL*, I, 331; *FL*, II, 79, 105.
20. E: *LofRWE*, II, 238–39. And see ibid., III, 164.

Chapter 16. Retreat from Her Siphoning Sea

1. See Reynolds, "From *Dial* Essay," 19–21. Emerson qtd. in Reynolds, "From *Dial* Essay," 21; E: *LofRWE*, II, 253. And see C: *MFPY*, 340–50.
2. See Hig: *MFO*, 152–53; *FL*, II, 95n1; Myerson, *New England Transcendentalists and the "Dial"*; and C: *MFPY*, 348–50.
3. On the *Dial* see Hig: *MFO*, 154–72; C: *TW&TM*, 153–55; B: *MFTtoR*, 154–60; and Myerson, *New England Transcendentalists and the "Dial."* And see Carlyle qtd. in E: *LofRWE*, VII, 443.
4. See Hig: *MFO*, 154–72; C: *TW&TM*, 153–55; B: *MFTtoR*, 154–60; and Myerson, *New England Transcendentalists and the "Dial."*
5. *FL*, II, 86–88; Capper, "Margaret Fuller as Cultural Reformer," 512–15; B: *MFTtoR*, 144–49; C: *TW&TM*, 210–13; C: *MFPY*, 292–96; Marshall, e-mail to author, 4 Sept. 2007.

6. See Abrams, *Correspondent Breeze*, 77, 80–83.

7. Wordsworth, *Prelude*, Book XII, ll. 269–77 in *Wordsworth: Poetical Works*, 578.

8. For Peabody on the March 1841 conversations, which included men, see C: *TW&TM*, 226–28. For Hoar on the same see E: *LofRWE*, VII, 445n18. See also E: *LofRWE*, II, 234; and Capper, "Margaret Fuller as Cultural Reformer," 516.

9. E: *LofRWE*, II, 197; *OM*, I, 339–40; *OM*, II, 20–21; *FL*, II, 98, 184. See also C: *TW&TM*, 237; E: *J&MN*, XI, 476.

10. On Fuller's dress and performance see C: *MFPY*, 298–300; B: *MFTtoR*, 148–50; *OM*, I, 336–37; *OM*, II, 19–21; E: *LofRWE*, VII, 445; and Dall, "Caroline Dall's Reminiscences," 422. Bombazine is a twilled cloth of silk with worsted or cotton. Dyed black, it is often used for mourning.

11. Dall, "Caroline Dall's Reminiscences," 417; *OM*, II, 19–21. And see Hig: *MFO*, 115–18.

12. See Sarah Ann Clarke, James Freeman Clarke's older sister, qtd. in Hig: *MFO*, 117.

13. *OM*, I, 337; Clarke qtd. in Hig: *MFO*, 117–18.

14. *FL*, II, 101; Clarke qtd. in Hig: *MFO*, 117–18. For accounts of Fuller's violent headache attacks see, for instance, *FL*, II, 152; and *FL*, III, 55.

15. E: *LofRWE*, II, 245–46.

16. *OM*, I, 215; E: *LofRWE*, II, 70, 254–55, 261.

17. C: *TW&TM*, 76.

18. *FL*, II, 127, 125, 131; *OM*, I, 296; C: *MFPY*, 336.

19. See Hig: *MFO*, 159–64; B: *MFTtoR*, 154; E: *J&MN*, XI, 471; *OM*, I, 296. For the full text of the last entry, see Fuller's journal, FFP: HM (bMS Am 1086 [C]).

20. *FL*, II, 111, 121.

21. Ibid., 133, 135, 137n1; E: *LofRWE*, II, 299, 304, 306; Porte, *Representative Man*, 220.

22. *FL*, II, 152; and *OM*, I, 292.

23. *OM*, I, 288; E: *LofRWE*, II, 325.

24. *FL*, II, 157; E: *LofRWE*, II, 328 ("solitary"), 332 ("suck . . . dry").

25. See Porte, *Representative Man*, 217; E: *J&MN*, IX, 115. "Effeminating effects" are Porte's words.

26. E: *LofRWE*, II, 336.

27. E: *J&MN*, VII, 400. See Strauch, "Hatred's Swift Repulsions," 70–71.

28. *FL*, II, 159–60; E: *E&L*, 350–51. And see C: *TW&TM*, 76–79.

29. *FL*, II, 159–60.

30. Ibid.; E: *LofRWE*, II, 319; Sarah Clarke qtd. in Hig: *MFO*, 117; Bean: *MF,C*, 4; Cheyfitz, *Trans-Parent*, 158.

31. E: *LofRWE*, II, 337; *FL*, II, 160.

32. See Emerson, *Emerson in His Journals*, 91; and Steele, *Representation of the Self*, 120–21.

33. *OM*, I, 230; E: *J&MN*, IX, 115; Porte, *Representative Man*, 217; "FJ42," 339; and Plutarch, *Plutarch's Moralia*, 5: 45–47.

34. E: *LofRWE*, II, 345; Cheyfitz, *Trans-Parent*, 158; Bishop, *Emerson on the Soul*, 153, 45; Porte, *Representative Man*, 217.

35. E: *E&L*, 282, 267; E: *LofRWE*, II, 340, 349; *FL*, II, 167; *OM*, II, 104. In his study of hysteria, Freud wrote about "Dora," who saw herself in a dream as the Madonna. See *Dora*, 125–26.

36. E: *LofRWE*, II, 352–53.

37. Ibid., 364, 373–74; E: *LofRWE*, VII, 429, 431–32.

38. E: *LofRWE*, II, 270; Zwarg: *FC*, 14; Abrams, *Correspondent Breeze*, 80–83; Steele, *Representation of the Self*, 5.

39. *FL*, II, 213; and see the original letter in FFP: HM (fMS Am 1086), where Fuller had struck through "Margaret."

40. See Peabody qtd. in C: *TW&TM*, 226–28; and Clarke qtd. in C: *MFPY*, 314.

Part Four. The Seductive Lure of Nature

1. *FL*, III, 55; *OM*, II, 99; *FL*, II, 110. And see *FL*, III, 56n1.

2. *FL*, II, 40, 110. And see Bunyan, *Pilgrim's Progress*; and *FL*, VI, 124.

3. *FL*, II, 66; *FL*, I, 347. On the shadow self see Hartman, "Romanticism and 'Anti-Self-Consciousness,'" 47–51. See also Fuller's 1844 prayer: "Lead me through the labyrinth till I face the monster whose presence I feel in the secret depths," in C: *TW&TM*, 538.

4. *FL*, II, 66.

5. Ibid., 105, 107. In his 18 March 1991 letter to the author, Joel Porte wrote that Fuller's "psychic/psychosexual energies were enormous and radica lly a part of her genius." He compares her to Whitman, whose sexual energies similarly gave life to visceral images of love in *Leaves of Grass*.

6. Sealts and Ferguson, *Emerson's Nature*, 5, 35, 27, 28; *OM*, II, 34; *FL*, II, 106; and Hartman, "Romanticism and 'Anti-Self-Consciousness,'" 47.

7. Keller, "Puritan Perverse," 143–44. And see Porte, *Representative Man*, 268.

8. *FL*, II, 185. Mary Kelley notes Fuller's ability "to gather ideas from disparate sources and weave them together in a tapestry of larger meanings." See Kelley, intro. to *Portable Margaret Fuller*, xvii.

Chapter 17. Religious Crisis

1. *FL*, III, 219, 220n2.

2. *OM*, I, 183–84, 197; *FL*, I, 323, 324n4.

3. *OM*, I, 308–9, 289, 279.

4. See Tyler, *Freedom's Ferment*, 185; Hardman, *Charles Grandison Finney, 1792–1875*, 35–36; and *OM*, I, 139–42. In *Woman in the Nineteenth Century*, Fuller seems to have fused Samuel Richardson's fictional character "Sir Charles Grandison" and Finney when she says, "Let Sir Charles Grandison preach to his own sex" (F: *WNC*, 137). Fuller had read at least *Clarissa*. See C: *MFPY*, 104, and *FL*, VI, 159–60, 161n11. About a Finney sermon Emerson wrote Lidian, "The preacher had extolled God's heart at the expense of his head." See Cross, *Burned-Over District*, 314–15, in Porte, *Representative Man*, 266–70.

5. *FL*, I, 219; *FL*, II, 93, 157, 167.

6. *OM*, I, 308–9. Zwarg: *FC*, 32, notes the "flood of words" exchanged between Emerson and Fuller.

Chapter 18. A Divine Madness

1. *FL*, I, 183–84; *FL*, II, 54. For relevant insights on the *Symposium* and *Phaedrus*, see Nussbaum, "Chill of Virtue," 36, and Hackforth, intro. to *Plato's Phaedrus*, 3–18. See also *Symposium*, in Plato, *Five Great Dialogues*, 199–201; and *Plato's Phaedrus*, 92–95.

2. See Johnson, ed., "The Story of Orpheus and Eurydice" in *Of Ovid's Metamorphoses, Book X*, in *Works of the English Poets*, 20: 506–8. See also Hackforth, intro. to *Plato's Phaedrus*, 14; Russell, "The Pre-Socratics," *History of Western Philosophy*, 3–37; and Cavendish, ed. *Illustrated Encyclopedia of Mythology*, 132–33, 144–50.

3. See Johnson, ed., *Of Ovid's Metamorphoses, Books III* and *XI,* in *Works of the English Poets,* 20: 452–54, 515–16; Russell, *History of Western Philosophy,* 3–37; Cavendish, ed., *Illustrated Encyclopedia of Mythology,* 148–50; and *OM,* II, 92–93, 93n.

4. See Euripides, *Bacchae* and *Iphigenia in Aulis.* Fuller discusses the latter in the appendix to *Woman in the Nineteenth Century.* See F: *WNC,* 185–95; and Cavendish, *Illustrated Encyclopedia of Mythology,* 133.

5. See Russell, *History of Western Philosophy,* 14–24; *FL,* II, 215.

6. Xenophon qtd. by Russell, *History of Western Philosophy,* 90; *OM,* II, 87; Nussbaum, "Chill of Virtue," 34–36; Hackforth, intro. to *Plato's Phaedrus,* 13–15. On Fuller seeing herself as "strange," see *FL,* I, 331.

7. See Abrams, *Correspondent Breeze,* 147; *FL,* I, 242; *FL,* II, 169.

8. *FL,* II, 123; Porte, *Representative Man,* 183.

9. See Abrams, "*The Prelude* and *The Recluse,*" 163; *FL,* II, 167–68; *OM,* II, 11. Fuller's journey involved a metaphorical dive into what Frye calls "a sea of libidinous impulse." See Frye, "Drunken Boat," 22. Abrams, too, in "*The Prelude* and *The Recluse*" notes that "the vehicle" in Romantic writing for the poetic journey through the mind is often "a voyage at sea" (163). See also Hudspeth, intro. to *FL,* I, 53; Kohut, *Analysis of the Self,* 234–35.

10. See Schapiro, *Romantic Mother,* x; Lacan, "The Function and Field of Speech and Language in Psychoanalysis," in *Écrits,* 45.

11. *FL,* III, 47. See also E: *LofRWE,* II, 197, and Hartman, "Romanticism and 'Anti-Self-Consciousness,'" 54.

Chapter 19. The Siren Song of Nature

1. See *FL,* II, 206; *FL,* I, 249–50; Wordsworth, "Lines Composed a Few Miles above Tintern Abbey" and "Ode: Intimations of Immortality," in *Wordsworth: Poetical Works,* 164, 462; and Bloom, *Map of Misreading,* 13–14. The preacher is Theodore Parker.

2. *FL,* I, 249, 324n4; *FL,* II, 66, 68, 75–76. And see Sand, *Indiana,* 247.

3. *FL,* II, 75, and 79n1.

4. Ibid., 79n1, 83–84. And see "The Correspondent Breeze" in Abrams, *Correspondent Breeze,* 25–43.

5. *OM,* II, 93, 93n.

6. *OM,* I, 114; *FL,* I, 220; Sand, *Lélia.* Paul Blount says Sand's works were "frequently reviewed" in the "leading British periodicals." An 1833 article Fuller probably read is "French Literature, Recent Novelists." See Blount, *George Sand and the Victorian World,* 5–6, 172, where Blount lists in his bibliography "French Literature, Recent Novelists" from the *Edinburgh Review* (Am. ed.: vol. 57 [1833]: 330–57), a publication that Fuller at this time was avidly reading. And see C: *TW&TM,* 57; and Dickenson, *George Sand,* 56.

7. Barrett Browning qtd. in Blount, *George Sand,* 37–38.

8. Howe qtd. in Blount, *George Sand,* 13. See also Richards and Elliott, *Julia Ward Howe,* I, 67–69; Clifford, *Mine Eyes Have Seen the Glory,* 48–49.

9. *OM,* I, 250–51; Hudspeth, intro. to *FL,* I, 38.

10. *OM,* I, 248–50, 229; *FL,* II, 99, 100n5; and see Barry: *IW,* 141.

11. See Fuller's review, "French Novelists of the Day," *New-York Daily Tribune,* 1 Feb. 1845; reprinted in Bean: *MF,C,* 54–66; *OM,* I, 229.

12. See C: *TW&TM,* 57–58; and Steele, *Representation of the Self,* 9–11, 106–8.

Chapter 20. The Seductive Sand

1. Henry James qtd. in Barry: *IW*, 155.

2. Sand, "Preface to the Edition of 1832," *Indiana*, 21. And see Faderman, *Surpassing the Love of Men*, 151, 159; Cott, "Passionlessness," 219–36; Pagels, *Adam, Eve, and the Serpent*, 3–31.

3. *OM*, I, 250. And see *FL*, II, 123.

4. Sand, *Indiana*, 220–28, 270–72; F: *WNC*, 64.

5. *OM*, II, 36; Hig: *MFO*, 44–45.

6. E: *ELofRWE*, 164–65; and Sand qtd. in Barry: *IW*, 200–201.

7. Barry: *IW*, 12, 18–19, 36; *OM*, I, 11.

8. *FL*, I, 163; Barry: *IW*, 16, 28, 34–35.

9. Barry: *IW*, 50–51, 54, 56–57; *OM*, I, 139–41.

10. Balzac describes Félicité des Touches, a character based on Sand in his novel *Beatrix*. See Balzac and Musset qtd. in Barry: *IW*, 239–40, 190.

11. Fuller, "French Novelists," in Bean: *MF,C*, 60.

12. Sand qtd. in Barry: *IW*, 219.

13. *OM*, I, 248–49; and Sand qtd. in Barry: *IW*, 181–82.

14. Faderman, *Surpassing the Love of Men*, 238, 254–76. And see Balzac, *Girl with the Golden Eyes*, 27, 33, 84, 88, 115–16. On Fuller's daily fresh flower see *FL*, I, 56.

15. *OM*, I, 254; Bean: *MF,C*, 55; Barry: *IW*, 145, 148. For de Vigny's damning assessment of Dorval in his journal see Dickenson, *George Sand*, 94.

16. Barry: *IW*, 144; Pulchérie qtd. in Barry: *IW*, 157. And see Sand, *Lélia*, 102–3; and Faderman, *Surpassing the Love of Men*, 263–64.

17. E: *LofRWE*, II, 235; Hawthorne, *Blithedale Romance*, 48, 15, 42, 202–3. Though a model for Zenobia's beauty was Almira Cornelia Penniman, in Zenobia's exotic personality Hawthorne meant to depict Fuller.

18. Hawthorne, *Blithedale Romance*, 15. Exotic/erotic is Joel Porte's wordplay in a 18 March 1991 letter to the author. And see *FL*, I, 56, 93n1, and Emerson qtd. in Wade, *Margaret Fuller*, 186. And see Faderman, *Surpassing the Love of Men*, 254–68.

Chapter 21. Demonic Desires

1. See Plato, *Symposium (The Banquet)*, in *Great Dialogues of Plato*, 86–88; and *FL*, II, 39. The volume Fuller borrowed from Emerson was in French.

2. W: *SRWE*, 219; Ariosto, *Sir John Harrington's Translation*, 290–94.

3. *FL*, II, 39; Plato, *Symposium (The Banquet)*, in *Great Dialogues of Plato*, 86–88.

4. D: "LCS-MF," 202, 203; and *FL*, I, 273–74n.

5. D: "LCS-MF," 203.

6. Ibid., 204. The poet Ellery Channing was apparently for awhile in love with Cary, who, according to Joel Myerson, was "deeply disappointed" when he married the traditionally pretty Ellen Fuller. Sturgis was plain. Channing once said after taking her rowing and not hearing a word from her the entire time: "Here have I wasted this evening in rowing a girl who won't talk to me—and not so very good looking either." See Myerson, *New England Transcendentalists and the Dial*, 206, 283n7.

7. D: "LCS-MF," 214, 212; Smith-Rosenberg, "Female World of Love," 2–8, 16–22, 27; E: *LofRWE*, VII, 407, 406, 456, 400, 404, 413. And see Faderman, *Surpassing the Love of Men*, 147–60; Sahli, "Smashing," 17–27; Cott, "Passionless," 219–36; and Taylor and Lasch,

"Two 'Kindred Spirits,'" 23–41. See also Strout quoting George Dimock on the "importunate intensity" of Fuller's feelings for Sturgis in *Making American Tradition*, 47.

8. On homosocial female passions being typical of the time, see Smith-Rosenberg, "Female World," 1–14. However, for a good discussion of Fuller's "erotic self-consciousness" that put her "far beyond the pale of most Anglo-American friendship writings," see C: *MFPY*, 281–82. On how Fuller was viewed as "masculine" by men, see Emerson, *OM*, I, 280; Hedge, *OM*, I, 95; and Channing, *OM*, II, 21.

9. See Smith-Rosenberg, "Female World," 9–10; W: *SRWE*, 219; *OM*, I, 297; E: *J&MN*, XI, 472; C: *TW&TM*, 24; Plato, "Myth of the Soul: The Charioteer and Two Horses" and "The Subjugation of Lust" in *Plato's Phaedrus*, 69, 105–6.

10. On Fuller's comparing herself to Sappho see E: *J&MN*, XI, 502. For Sappho as "fair" see Plato, *Phaedrus*, in *Dialogues of Plato*, 1, 240. See also Higginson, "Sappho," in *Studies in History and Language*, 168–199; Ovid, "Sappho to Phaon," in *Heroides and Amores*, 181–97; Wharton, *Sappho*, 26–27; Bloom, *Anxiety of Influence*, 31.

Works by and about Sappho available to Fuller would have included Alexander Pope's 1707 translation of "Ovid's Heroic Epistle, XV," *Sappho to Phaon;* Ambrose Philip's translation of Sappho's second ode, published in the *Spectator,* no. 229; and "The Works of Sappho," trans. Francis Fawkes, in Johnson, ed., *Works of the English Poets,* 20: 369–78. Pope's translation appears in Wharton's *Sappho,* 187–97, while Philips's translation of Sappho's second ode appears in Philips, *Poems of Ambrose Philips,* 162, and is reproduced by Vanita in *Sappho and the Virgin Mary,* 43. Fuller's remark about Sappho in F: *WNC* ("The youth here by my side cannot be weary of . . . Sappho," 36) suggests she knew Philips's translation, the second line of which reads, "The Youth who fondly sits by thee . . . ." For Fuller's view of Sappho as a person see C: *MFPY,* 281.

11. Wharton, *Sappho,* 26–27; Sappho, *Sappho,* 8. And see Higginson, "Sappho" (1871), in *Studies in History and Language,* 183–86.

12. See "The Life of Sappho," in Johnson, ed., *Works of the English Poets,* 20: 371.

13. *OM,* II, 93; *OM,* I, 281.

14. *OM,* I, 281; *FL,* II, 43. And see Kohut, *Analysis of the Self,* 234–35; and *Plato's Phaedrus,* 103–6.

15. *FL,* II, 35, 40.

16. Ibid., 40, 44n1. On "the wise charioteer" see "The Charioteer and Two Horses" and "The Subjugation of Lust," *Plato's Phaedrus,* 69–71, 103–6. The Drachenfels was a legendary mountain on which maidens were sacrificed to a dragon, symbol of "unmanageable instincts." See Steele, *Transfiguring America,* 98.

17. *FL,* II, 42, 47.

18. *FL,* I, 331.

19. *FL,* II, 76–77.

20. *FL,* II, 77. And see Hartman, "Romanticism and 'Anti-Self-Consciousness,'" 53–54.

21. *OM,* I, 282; *FL,* II, 105; *FL,* III, 72.

22. See *FL,* II, 79, 81, 81–82.

23. Ibid., 82–83, and 69, 93. Emerson had presented his "Demonology" lecture on 20 Feb. 1839. See E: *ELofRWE,* III, 167–70. See also Hartman, "Romanticism and 'Anti-Self-Consciousness,'" 46–52, 47n2.

24. *FL,* II, 82–83.

25. Ibid., 81, 81n2. And see F: *WNC,* 136.

26. *FL,* II, 81; Crompton, *Byron and Greek Love,* 12. And see Hartman, "Romanticism and 'Anti-Self-Consciousness,'" 47.

27. Crompton, *Byron and Greek Love*, 11; Knight, *Lord Byron's Marriage*, chapters 1, 5, 7; Moore, *Life, Letters and Journals of Lord Byron*, 22, 31–32, 41, 53, 54–55. And see *Byron's Letters and Journals*; see esp. vol. 1 (1798–1810), 107, 124–25; vol. 8 (1821), 24; and vol. 9 (1821–22), 44.

28. *FL*, I, 151; *OM*, I, 15; Grebanier, *Uninhibited Byron*, 23–25, 27–33; Macdonald, "Childhood Abuse as Romantic Reality," 24–28.

29. *FL*, I, 163–64.

30. Ibid., 159; *FL*, II, 82–83, 93; O: *AL&D*, 86–87; Hartman, "Romanticism and 'Anti-Self-Consciousness,'" 47, nn1–2.

Chapter 22. "The Daemon Works His Will"

1. E: *ELofRWE*, III, 164, 167; FRob: *MACS*, 2–3, 26. And see *FL*, I, 317n2; and C: *MFPY*, 221. In *Mesmerism and the American Cure of Souls*, Robert Fuller discusses Franz Anton Mesmer's *Reflections on the Discovery of Animal Magnetism* (1779). See FRob: *MACS*, 4–6.

2. FRob: *MACS*, 2–9; *FL*, VI, 261.

3. FRob: *MACS*, 9–15; E: *ELofRWE*, III, 153; W: *SRWE*, 134.

4. See C: *MFPY*, 32; *FL*, VI, 141; E: *J&MN*, XI, 477; W: *SRWE*, 134; Hartman, "Romanticism and 'Anti-Self-Consciousness,'" 46–56; Alcorn and Bracher, "Literature, Psychoanalysis, and the Re-Formation of the Self," 348; Sappho, *Poems of Sappho*, 129; Ariosto, *Sir John Harrington's Translation of Orlando Furioso*, 292. For Fuller on every man having "a daemon," see *FL*, III, 163; and Steele, ed., *Essential Margaret Fuller*, 442n12. Fuller also valued Socrates' view of the "daimon" as a guardian spirit. See *OM*, I, 219. On Socrates' "*daimon*" see, too, Russell, *History of Western Civilization*, 90.

5. E: *E&L*, 7; *OM*, I, 225; *FL*, VI, 141–42.

6. Emerson qtd. in FRob: *MACS*, 34; *OM*, II, 94; *FL*, III, 163; *FL*, VI, 141.

7. *FL*, VI, 141. And see Fuller, "[A Dream]," in F: *EMF*, 6–7; Maria Espinosa, intro. to Sand, *Lélia*, xv; *FL*, II, 40, where Fuller associates "the butterfly" with "Idealism" and Emerson; Wieland: *SO*, I, 109, 111; C: *MFPY*, 287.

8. See *OM*, I, 14–15.

9. Fuller, "[A Dream]," F: *EMF*, 6–7. On the mind's use of dreams to control a disturbing dream representation, to master some "overwhelmingly disturbing traumatic experience," or to work through "the experiences of the day," see Lewin, *Dreams and the Uses of Regression*, 25, 31; John Mack qtd. in Hartmann, *Nightmare*, 42–43; Schacter, *Searching for Memory*, 88, 266.

10. Fuller, "[A Dream]," in F: *EMF*, 6–7.

11. *FL*, II, 105, 107, 93.

12. Ibid., 93.

13. Ibid., 93 (italics mine); *OM*, I, 228; For Fuller on the ideal father see *FL*, II, 175. On transference love see Schneiderman, *Jacques Lacan*, 83–85, 148. For "soul out of my soul" see Shelley's *Alastor*, "Epipsychidion," and "On Love," in *Shelley's Poetry and Prose*—esp. pp. 74, 379, 473–74.

14. Sand, *Lélia*, 97, 102–3.

15. *OM*, II, 96; *FL*, II, 188; *OM*, I, 289. And see Plutarch on love in terms of vision in *Plutarch's Moralia*, 8: 423.

Chapter 23. Redeeming Her Friendships from "Eros"

1. *FL*, II, 90.

2. *OM*, II, 31–34; *FL*, II, 50, 51n5.

3. *OM*, II, 36–38, 92–94, 112–13; Hig: *MFO*, 30; *FL*, II, 81.

4. See *FL*, II, 86–89. And see Fuller qtd. in C: *MFPY*, 281; and the British historian John Addington Symonds's *Studies of the Greek Poets* (1873) cited in David Moore Robinson, *Sappho and Her Influence*, 25–26. See also Higginson, "Sappho" (1871), in *Studies in History and Language*, 184–86; Powell, "Afterwords: Sappho of Lesbos," in Sappho, *Sappho, a Garland*, 33–35. Though Symonds's book was published after Fuller's death, the views he presents therein were well known in her time by the literati, as they were, for example, by Byron, who sang praises of Sappho in his writings.

5. *FL*, II, 97–98, 118; and see Plato, *Plato's Phaedrus*, 93–95.

6. C: *MFPY*, 297–306 (Fuller qtd. 302); *FL*, II, 101–2, 118–19; *OM*, II, 92–93.

7. *FL*, II, 102. Hymettus is a mountain in southeastern Greece famous for its honey. Fuller not only alludes to the mountain but also means to evoke an image of the women attending her sessions as Bacchantes, since Bacchantes were known for the "miraculous draughts of milk and honey" they dispensed during their ecstatic worship of Bacchus. See Plato, *Plato's Phaedrus*, 100, 100n2.

8. Fuller had borrowed Emerson's French edition of Plato in January 1839, during which time we know she read *Phaedrus* and the *Symposium* ("The Banquet"). In December 1839 she borrowed an English version from George Ripley and read again *Phaedrus* and the *Symposium*. On Fuller's reading these dialogues see *FL*, II, 39–40, 54, 102, 104–6; and for "respite" from "suffering" see Plato, *Plato's Phaedrus*, 96–97, 99–101.

9. *FL*, II, 118. And see Solomon, *In the Company of Educated Women*.

10. *FL*, II, 106, 103–4, 104n4.

11. *FL*, II, 107, 102, 104, and see 147. See also Plato, *Symposium*, especially the speech of Aristophanes, in *Great Dialogues of Plato*, 85–89. Being on the Drachenfels apparently meant to Fuller having given in to the Titanic ("unmanageable instinct") in her. See Steele, *Transfiguring America*, 98.

12. *FL*, II, 105, 106–7.

13. Ibid., 105, 107; *OM*, I, 281–82. On Fuller's erotic self-consciousness going beyond expressions permitted in sentimental female friendships, see C: *MFPY*, 282.

Chapter 24. Mystic Cleansing

1. *FL*, II, 157.

2. See Socrates' comments in the *Symposium*, *Great Dialogues of Plato*, 95–96; and for Fuller, "On Anna Barker," see F: *EMF*, 23, and C: *TW&TM*, 112–13.

3. *FL*, II, 168.

4. *OM*, II, 38, 101. Fuller may be fusing Persephone's myth with that of Dionysus, who is linked not with Persephone but with Ariadne, whom he rescued from Naxos. See Grimal, *Dictionary of Classical Mythology*, 140, 359.

5. *OM*, II, 101. And see "The Birth of Bacchus," "The Story of Penteus," "The Death of Penteus," "The Rape of Proserpine," and "The Death of Orpheus," in Johnson, ed., *Of Ovid's Metamorphoses, Books III, V, and XI*, in *Works of the English Poets*, 20: 450, 452–54, 467–68, 515–16. On the mystery cults surrounding Orpheus and Dionysus, see Cavendish, ed., *Illus-*

trated Encyclopedia of Mythology, 147–50. See also Russell, *History of Western Philosophy,* 14–24; and Grimal, *Dictionary of Classical Mythology,* 138–40, 331–33.

6. *FL,* II, 146, 157–58, 158–59. For a wonderful account of the fun made of Alcott and his misty-eyed sayings, see Myerson, "In the Transcendental Emporium," 31–38.

7. *FL,* II, 34, 167; *OM,* II, 101; Grimal, "Zagreus," *Dictionary of Classical Mythology,* 466; Ferguson, "The Orphics," in Cavendish, ed., *Illustrated Encyclopedia of Mythology,* 148–50; Russell, *History of Western Philosophy,* 14–24.

8. See V: *M&TM,* 132. On Fuller's identification with "virginal heroines" like Goethe's Iphigenia and Otilla as a way of controlling sexual impulses see B: *MFTtoR,* 135–36, 220, and Steele, *Representation of the Self,* 108–9.

9. Ovid, *Metamorphoses* ii, 51, 57, 59–60. And see "The Fable of Iphis and Ianthe," in Johnson, ed., *Of Ovid's Metamorphoses, Book IX,* in *Works of the English Poets,* 20: 505–6. Fuller surely knew this tale since she said it was Ovid who gave her a view as a child into the enchanted gardens of Greek mythology. See *OM,* I, 21. Iphis, moreover, is closely connected with Isis, whose legend Fuller treasured. On Iphis's love for Ianthe see also Barkan, *Gods Made Flesh,* 70–71.

10. *OM,* I, 221, 229; *FL,* II, 167–69; Plato, "The Subjugation of Lust," *Plato's Phaedrus,* 106; C: *TW&TM,* 62. On Fuller and "the sistrum of Isis," see Steele, *Representation of the Self,* 114–121. Steele says Fuller knew of the sistrum "from her reading in Plutarch's *Morals,* which she borrowed from Emerson in 1837" (117; *FL,* I, 277). Yet Fuller was already familiar with the sistrum (or timbrel) of Isis from having read Ovid as a child. See *OM,* I, 21.

11. E: *LofRWE,* II, 345; *FL,* II, 168–69.

12. *FL,* II, 168–69.

13. For Channing and Emerson on Fuller as a "Sibyl" see *OM,* II, 22; E: *J&MN,* XI, 502. See, too, Socrates on love's fever, as well as Hackforth on the "delirious ravings" of a sibyl in *Plato's Phaedrus,* 60, 82–84, 87–91, 96–7. On the sibyl see also Grimal's *Dictionary of Classical Mythology,* 417–18.

14. See Socrates' fable of the good and evil horses in *Plato's Phaedrus,* 106, as well as Hackforth on Socrates' analysis of how sublimated erotic energies inspire religious vision in *Plato's Phaedrus,* 98. And see Fuller's 27 Jan. 1839 letter to Sturgis (*FL,* II, 40) wherein Fuller alludes to Plato's depiction of divine and carnal impulses as good and bad steeds.

15. *OM,* II, 104–6; *FL,* II, 173, 180.

Chapter 25. Paradise Regained

1. *FL,* II, 109–10.

2. Ibid., 170, 158, 170, 163, 164n2; E: *LofRWE,* VII, 421, 421nn179, 180.

3. *FL,* II, 158–59, 159–60, 166–67. See also Fuller's 18 Oct. letter to Sturgis, *FL,* II, 163.

4. *FL,* II, 167; *OM,* II, 98.

5. *FL,* II, 171–73, 175.

6. Ibid., 183, 202, 199.

7. E: *J&MN,* XI, 457; *FL,* I, 172, 172n5. Leila is the unfortunate heroine of Byron's dark tale of passion and revenge, *The Giaour.* See *Byron's Poetry,* 84–114. Aware of Byron's tale, Elizabeth Barrett Browning titled an early unpublished poem "Leila." See Mermin, *Elizabeth Barrett Browning,* 26. The name Leila, like Lélia, suggests Lilith, the Bible's original Eve, who was created Adam's equal but, dissatisfied with Adam, left him to seek her pleasure elsewhere.

8. F: *EMF,* 53–58.

9. Ibid., 56, 57.

10. Ibid., 56, 54–55. See also Barry: *IW*, 156–58; Dickenson, *George Sand*, 158; C: *MFPY*, 287; *FL*, I, 172; Espinosa, intro. to Sand, *Lélia*, xiii. On *The Giaour* see note 7 above.

11. *FL*, II, 220–21, 221, 223–24.

12. Ibid., 221–22, 224–25; Hawthorne, *Blithedale Romance*, 109–11.

13. *FL*, II, 109. And see Anthony Wilden, "Lacan and the Discourse of the Other," in Lacan, *Language of the Self*, 270.

Chapter 26. The Law of the Father and the Embrace of Mother Nature

1. See C: *TW&TM*, 544; E: *J&MN*, XI, 500; *FL*, I, 331; *FL*, II, 204; Plato, *Plato's Phaedrus*, 106; Bloom, *Anxiety of Influence*, 8–9, and *Map of Misreading*, 11.

2. *FL*, I, 139; Wieland: *SO*, I, 65, 185; Milton, *Paradise Lost*, 8.ll.588, 593–94; O: *AL&D*, 48, 78; Bean: *MF,C*, 57.

3. *FL*, II, 224–25. Fuller's words here seem like those in Whitman's "A Word Out of the Sea." See Whitman, *Leaves of Grass*, 269–77. Reynolds says that Whitman read Fuller's dispatches from Rome and that her writing influenced him. See R: *ER*, 137–39.

4. Fuller, trans., *Günderode*, x, 40, 65; *FL*, II, 86n1; Helps and Howard, *Bettina*, 10. And see Zwarg: *FC*, 82, 85–96.

5. *FL*, III, 91–92.

6. See "Dreaming with Anna, [October 30] 1842," in C: *TW&TM*, 532.

7. See Smith-Rosenberg, "Female World of Love," 21; *FL*, II, 77; Wieland: *SO*, I, 98–99, 185; Wieland: *SO*, II, 9, 15–16; Fuller, "[A Dream]," F: *EMF*, 6–7. See MF journal entry, 1833, FFP: HM (bMS Am 1086 [B]). In 1974 this manuscript was in the Fuller Family Papers in the Houghton but since then seems to have been misplaced.

8. See "Dreaming with Anna," C: *TW&TM*, 532; Wieland: *SO*, I, 108–9; Freud, *Dora*, 90; and F: *EMF*, 56. And see Fuller, "Margaret Fuller's Journal for October 1842," 290.

9. In the *Memoirs*, Emerson dropped the "S." from "C.S." In his notes for the *Memoirs*, the entry reads "In C.S. . . ." See *OM*, I, 221; E: *J&MN*, XI, 473. Emerson identifies the "A" in this 1842 journal entry as Amelia Greenwood. See Fuller's 24 Feb. 1840 letter to Charles Newcomb: "Would life indeed permit us to be purged by water instead of fire!" *FL*, II, 122–23.

10. *FL*, III, 81; Fuller qtd. in Hig: *MFO*, 21; and see Fuller, "Margaret Fuller's Journal for October 1842," 291.

Part Five. The "Fine Castle" of Her Writing

1. Plato, *Five Great Dialogues*, 200. Translator B. Jowett says that Diotima may have been "a figment of Socrates' or, more probably, Plato's imagination" (192n39). And see "FJ42," 332; and *FL*, III, 105.

2. Dall, "Caroline Dall's Reminiscences," 422; C: *MFPY*, 106; C: *TW&TM*, 544. On George Davis and Samuel Ward see *FL*, I, 161n2, 235n5.

3. "FJ42," 330–31, 332.

4. Ibid., 331; *FL*, I, 301; C: *MFPY*, 216–17; V: *M&TM*, 94; *FL*, III, 105.

5. E: *LofRWE*, II, 197; F: *WNC*, 162. Emphasis mine.

Chapter 27. A Time to Write

1. E: *E&L*, 263–64, 473.

2. Ibid., 473; W: *SRWE*, 121; E: *J&MN*, VIII, 205; "FJ42," 338–39. And see Jason in *Medea* qtd. in Nussbaum, "Chill of Virtue," 39, whose words on fate I echo here.

3. *FL*, III, 49; W: *SRWE*, 208; "FJ42," 334–35, 338–39; and *FL*, I, 294.

4. *FL*, III, 43; *OM*, I, 293.

5. *FL*, III, 67, 46.

6. Ibid., 64, 67; Plato, *Apology,* in *Great Dialogues of Plato,* 437, 445; Plato, *Plato's Phaedrus,* 81, 92–95; Russell, *History of Western Philosophy,* 90; Nussbaum, "Chill of Virtue," 35. On Fuller's "daemon," see *FL*, III, 163.

7. *FL*, III, 67.

8. See F: "TGL," 4; and Nussbaum, "Chill of Virtue," 34–40.

9. See Plato, *Apology* and *The Republic,* Books VI and VII, in *Great Dialogues of Plato,* 303–11, 312–41, 434–36, 440; Plato, *Plato's Phaedrus,* 106; and Nussbaum, "Chill of Virtue," 34–40.

10. *FL*, III, 93; Plato, *Plato's Phaedrus,* 106, 81; F: *WNC*, 90.

11. *FL*, III, 42–43; E: *LofRWE*, III, 8. For Fuller's habitual talk of destiny directing her life, see, for instance, *FL*, III, 56–57, and "FJ42," 329.

12. *FL*, III, 49–50. See Hudspeth on Fuller's wariness of Alcott, *FL*, III, 35n4.

13. "FJ42," 331, 338.

14. Ibid., 331, 326, 340; and *FL*, III, 96.

15. "FJ42," 338.

16. *FL*, III, 91, 96, and 98n3. RWE qtd by MF in her 25 Aug. 1842 letter to her friend William Channing, *FL*, III, 91.

17. Ibid., 105.

18. Ibid., 114, 118–19; and Plato, *Plato's Phaedrus,* 92–93. For Fuller alluding at this time to Plato's metaphor of the winged soul, see her January 1843 letter to Elizabeth Hoar: "perhaps" the "heart has folded its wings" (*FL*, III, 114).

19. *FL*, III, 97; E: *LofRWE*, II, 197, 201–2, 234; Sams, ed., *Autobiography of Brook Farm,* 78. And see E: *E&L*, 408, where Emerson says: "Conversation is a game of circles," and the *Apology,* in *Great Dialogues of Plato* (432–33), where Socrates is accused of playing a game with his interlocutors. Zwarg focuses on the conversations Fuller had with Emerson, Fourier, the women in her classes, and herself. She sees an "association between conversation and feminist agency." See Zwarg: *FC*, 163.

Chapter 28. Millennial Fever

1. See Robert Fuller, *Mesmerism and the American Cure of Souls* (1982); Gauld, *History of Hypnotism;* Mesmer, *Mesmerism;* Coale, *Mesmerism and Hawthorne.* For Mesmer on "the influence of planets on the human body" and "On Magnetism" and its "discovery," see *Mesmerism,* 3–22, 33–39, 43–78. On visions of the coming apocalypse in America and elsewhere, see Cross, *Burned-Over District,* 287–321; and "Apocalypse: Theme and Romantic Variations" in Abrams, *Correspondent Breeze,* 225–57.

2. Cross, *Burned-Over District,* 288–91; White, *Sketches of the Christian Life,* 13–65, 70–78; Bliss, *Memoirs of William Miller,* 41–80.

3. Cross, *Burned-Over District,* 287–88; *OM,* I, 183–84, 197–98. And see Maclear, "Heart of New England Rent," 43–65; and Hackforth, who, in his commentary on Plato's *Phaedrus*

notes that, whereas "man seeks communion with God, the mystics seek absolute union with Him" (98).

4. *FL*, III, 55; *OM*, I, 183–84, 197–98; E: *E&L*, 80, 92.

5. E: *E&L*, 92, 48, 78, 21; Winthrop, "Speech to the General Court," 341.

6. *FL*, III, 119–20. And see Cross, *Burned-Over District*, 293, 297, 291; Carlyle, "Signs of the Times"; F: "TGL," 14. On the Romantic creative spirit, see Frye, "Drunken Boat," 14–16.

Chapter 29. Fuller's Apocalypse

1. F: "TGL," 17, 6, 2, 14–15; *OM*, I, 246; Abrams, *Natural Supernaturalism*, 47; Mesmer, *Mesmerism*, 13, 19, 27; F: *WNC*, 27–28. And see *FL*, III, 114.

2. F: "TGL," 1–2, 4.

3. Ibid., 4, 6; "Apocalypse: Theme and Romantic Variation," in Abrams, *Correspondent Breeze*, 230. Fuller quotes ("purge") from the eighteenth-century French mystic, Louis Claude de Saint-Martin.

4. F: "TGL," 4, 5, 8. And see John 16:32 RSV.

5. F: "TGL," 6, 38, 7, 43, 46–47. See also FRob: *MACS*, 2, 4–5, 45–46, 55; Mesmer, *Mesmerism*, 13, 19–20, 27, 36, 46, 56–57, 81, 101, 107.

6. F: "TGL," 4, 9. See MCF to TF, 24 Jan. 1819, FFP: HM (fMS Am 1086 [6:63]).

7. Collyer, *Lights and Shadows of American Life*, 22; F: "TGL," 38; FRob: *MACS*, 26–28; Zwarg: *FC*, 177–79.

8. F: "TGL," 11, 14.

9. Ibid., 18, 14, 15–16.

10. Ibid., 20.

11. Ibid., 20. And see Grimal, *Dictionary of Classical Mythology*, 359, 395; Cavendish, "The Mystery Religions," in *Illustrated Encyclopedia of Mythology*, 144–50; Noll, *Jung Cult*, 173; and Zwarg: *FC*, 159–60.

12. Von Mehren aptly titled her Fuller biography *Minerva and the Muse*.

13. F: "TGL," 21, 18.

14. Ibid., 14, 24, 26.

15. Ibid., 27, 35.

16. E: *J&MN*, VII, 461. For Zwarg on Fuller and Emerson on marriage see Zwarg: *FC*, 25, 51–53, 55–56, and esp. 137–42, 152, 158.

17. F: "TGL" 20; *FL*, II, 230, 231n1; "FJ42," 331–32, 333–36.

18. F: "TGL," 34, 27, 32–33. Fuller plays on Emerson's "*Man Thinking.*" E: *E&L*, 54.

19. F: "TGL," 32–33. See also Bunyan, *Pilgrim's Progress*, 8–11; and Appiah, "Marrying Kind," 48. On husbands as their wives' masters, see 1 Tim. 2:11–15 RSV; and Eph. 5:22–24 RSV.

20. F: "TGL," 28, 32.

21. Ibid., 29–30. For Timothy's damning assessment of Wollstonecraft, see his 16 Jan. 1820 letter to MCF, FFP: HM (fMS Am 1086 [3:89]).

22. F: "TGL," 29, 30, 31.

23. Ibid., 30, 19.

24. Ibid., 34, 36.

25. Ibid., 37–38. And see "Demonology," in E: *ELofRWE*, 154, 169; Steele, *Transfiguring America*, 127–28.

26. "Demonology," in E: *ELofRWE*, 164–65; FRob: *MACS*, x–xiii, 22, 26, 33; F: "TGL," 36–38. And see *FL*, II, 170.

27. See Collyer, *Lights and Shadows,* 22; FRob: *MACS,* 22.

28. F: "TGL," 37, 38. And see FRob: *MACS,* 12–13.

29. F: "TGL," 40, 44, 47.

30. Ibid., 4, 43.

31. Ibid., 43.

32. Ibid., 44, 46.

33. Ibid., 37–38, 45.

34. Ibid., 44.

35. Ibid., 33, 47, 18. And see Virgil: RF, 101. On the influence of Fourier on Fuller's vision of marriage see Zwarg: *FC,* 25, 38–39, 139–42, 152–53.

36. F: "TGL," 46. And see *FL,* II, 110.

37. F: "TGL," 46–47. And see Mesmer, *Mesmerism,* 13, 18–19, 37–38, 81, 106–7, and so on.

Chapter 30. Contradictory Wishes and Dreams

1. *FL,* III, 124; E: *LofRWE,* III, 170. Fuller spells the Seeress of Prevorst's name Frederica.

2. E: *LofRWE,* III, 183.

3. F: "TGL," 14, 8.

4. See *FL,* I, 327. And see C: *TW&TM,* 60–62, for Fuller's fantasy letter to Beethoven; Miller, *Salem Is My Dwelling Place,* 232, for Miller on Fuller's fantasies about her father; and Izenberg, *Impossible Individuality,* 8, on the Romantic "I."

5. C: *TW&TM,* 60–62.

6. *FL,* II, 234; C: *TW&TM,* 61. See also *FL,* III, 53, 96; and Matt. 10: 5–13, 38 RSV; Luke 15: 11–32 RSV.

7. *FL,* III, 199n4; F: "TGL," 14, 15–16; *FL,* I, 149. And see Zwarg: *FC,* 186.

8. *OM,* I, 156; F: "TGL" 15–16, 45; B: *MFTtoR,* 215–18.

9. F: "TGL," 29–30, 44; F: *WNC,* 62–65, 92; B: *MFTtoR,* 215–18.

Chapter 31. Pilgrims and Prodigals

1. Hig: *MFO,* 7–8; *FL,* II, 110; *OM,* I, 132; F: "TGL," 4; *FL,* III, 67; *OM,* II, 143.

2. *OM,* II, 143; F: "TGL," 20. And see Dall qtd. in Steele, *Representation of the Self,* 115–16; Emerson on Fuller and Cupid and Psyche, in *OM,* I, 334. See also *FL,* IV, 95, 96n2.

3. F: "TGL," 32; Fuller, "Goethe," 21, 26, 27. And see F: *WNC,* 114.

4. F: *WNC,* 115–16; and see Lange, intro. to *Wilhelm Meister's Apprenticeship,* 7–14.

5. Luke 15: 11–32; Matt. 10: 5–13, 38 RSV; Alexander, *Poetic Self,* 91. And see Abrams, *Natural Supernaturalism,* 165.

6. For Fuller's references to the prodigal son cited in this paragraph see *FL,* II, 195; F: *WNC,* 1; *FL,* III, 165–67. And for Abrams on the prodigal son see *Natural Supernaturalism,* 165–66, 193–94, 183–84, 255. See also Wordsworth, *Prelude,* in *Wordsworth,* 535 (bk. VI, ll. 592–608), where Wordsworth celebrates the power of the "Imagination."

7. *OM,* I, 279. And see *FL,* II, 170, 188.

8. F: *SL,* 128; *FL,* III, 209; *OM,* I, 219. And see *FL,* III, 125, 126. Von Mehren says that William was a cofounder of Chicago's third drugstore (V: *M&TM,* 173); Hudspeth says William "was an assistant engineer for the Chicago Board of Public Works" (*FL,* III, 125n1). In *Mesmerism and the American Cure of Souls,* Robert Fuller notes of mesmerism that it "provided confused individuals with an intense experience thought to bring them into an interior harmony with unseen spiritual forces" (79).

9. *FL*, III, 142.

10. Ibid., 128, 130, 126, 137, 133; F: *SL*, 35–36; F: *EMF*, 90, 92, 444n1.

11. F: *SL*, 113; *FL*, III, 134–35. And see F: *EMF*, 137, and Zwarg: *FC*, 98–99.

12. *FL*, III, 135; F: *SL*, 120; F: *EMF*, 142; V: *M&TM*, 176.

13. *FL*, III, 134; F: *SL*, 114–15; F: *EMF*, 138.

14. *FL*, III, 129, 143, 142.

Chapter 32. Discordant Energies

1. *FL*, III, 145, 161, 200; F: *SL*, 3 And see Steele, intro. to F: *EMF*, xxii–xxxi; and Wordsworth, *The Prelude*, in *Wordsworth*, 535 (bk. VI, ll. 600–602).

2. F: *SL*, 5, 115; *FL*, III, 133; Fuller, *OM*, I, 15; Zwarg: *FC*, 100–102. Zwarg argues that Fuller, by starting her memoir with the Niagara Falls account, "found an economical way to establish how inadequately her reading had prepared her for her experience at the rim of Western culture" (102). She also speculates Fuller's fear may have been fed by having seen John Vanderlyn's 1804 *The Death of Jane McCrea*. Zwarg notes "the remarkable resemblance" between Fuller's hallucination and the scene in this famous painting in which the victim is kneeling with her arms upraised beneath two tomahawk-wielding Native Americans, one of whom is preparing to scalp her (100–101). And see Kolodny on *Summer on the Lakes* "as a type of 'captivity narrative'" in *Land Before Her*, 123.

3. F: *SL*, 6; *FL*, III, 41, 169, 188.

4. V: *M&TM*, 177; Hig: *MFO*, 194.

5. F: *SL*, 11–12, 8–9. See also Wordsworth, *The Prelude*, in *Wordsworth*, 506 (bk. II, ll. 287, 307); and Zwarg: *FC*, 99–108. The White Mountains run north and east from New Hampshire into Maine but do not extend into Massachusetts. Thus Fuller and her friends did not pass through the White Mountains during this trip. Presumably Fuller is recalling her July 1842 visit to the White Hills (and mountains), where, she wrote Richard, "the eagle soars." See *FL*, III, 77, 81.

6. F: *SL*, 8–9. On her "just budded" wings, see MF to CS (Jan. 1841), *FL*, II, 199. See also Plato, "Love as the Regrowing of the Soul's Wings," in *Plato's Phaedrus*, 92–93, 96–97; and C: *TW&TM*, 541.

7. See *FL*, I, 249.

8. See ibid., 249; T. R. Mitchell, *Hawthorne's Fuller Mystery*, 85 and 273n68; and "Fragments from Fuller's journal, [May 1?] to June 10, 1844," and commentary in C: *TW&TM*, 533–34, 537.

9. C: *TW&TM*, 536.

10. Ibid., 535.

11. See *FL*, III, 202, 202n1; Grimal, *Dictionary of Classical Mythology*, 412–13, 419; and Cavendish, ed., *Illustrated Encyclopedia of Mythology*, 148–49.

12. See *FL*, III, 196–97, 202; C: *TW&TM*, 536–37.

Chapter 33. Mesmerism and Romantic Yearning in *Summer on the Lakes*

1. F: *SL*, 81–102; *FL*, III, 198–99, 199nn4&5; C: *TW&TM*, 544; Grimal, *Dictionary of Classical Mythology*, 419–20, 340–41.

2. F: *SL*, 94–99. On Mariana see Zwarg: *FC*, 105–7, 111.

3. F: *SL*, 100–101; Wordsworth, *The Prelude*, in *Wordsworth*, 505 (bk. II, line 237).

4. F: *SL*, 100–102. Walt Whitman uses this image in "A Word Out of the Sea: Reminis-

cence," in *Leaves of Grass,* 272. An influence on Fuller may have been Bailey's *Festus,* 719. The protagonist Festus similarly appeals to death: "Open thine arms, O death! thou fine of woe, / And warranty of bliss!"

5. F: *SL,* 126–27, 129, 130, 131. And see Zwarg: *FC,* 117–18.

6. F: *SL,* 130, 128, 129, 127. And see FRob: *MACS,* 13.

7. F: *SL,* 127–28, 148, 164; FRob: *MACS,* 6; "The Villa of the Mysteries" in Cavendish, ed., *Illustrated Encyclopedia of Mythology,* 148. Fuller borrowed the notion of an "aromal state" from Fourier. See Zwarg: *FC,* 116–17.

8. F: *SL,* 131; *FL,* VI, 141; *OM,* I, 225; and see FRob: *MACS,* 30.

9. *FL,* VI, 141–42, 298, 299n6; *FL,* I, 305n7; F: *SL,* 132; *OM,* I, 226; "The Villa of the Mysteries," in Cavendish, ed., *Illustrated Encyclopedia of Mythology,* 148. On the danger of the occult, see Goodrick-Clarke, *Occult Roots of Nazism,* and Noll, "Cult and Charisma," in *Jung Cult,* 16–26, 46. Noll borrows from Max Weber, who discusses charisma in *Sociology of Religion,* 1–5, 29ff, and in his papers, ed. by S. N. Eisenstadt, *Max Weber on Charisma.* "Crystallized" in the concept of charisma, says Weber, is the notion that, because some unseen power works through the charismatic person, he or she is not responsible for his or her actions. Fuller had sessions with a private mesmerist in New York. See E: *LofRWE,* VIII, 10n27; and see FRob: *MACS,* 6.

10. *FL,* VI, 141–42.

11. André Green qtd. in Doane and Hodges, *From Klein to Kristeva,* 56–59. F: *WNC,* 115. And see Myerson, *New England Transcendentalists and the "Dial,"* 37. Myerson notes Fuller's "desire to be at the center of attention."

12. *FL,* VI, 141–42; Fuller, "Goethe," 27; R. Hackforth, *Plato's Phaedrus,* 81. And see *FL,* V, 42, where Fuller, pregnant out of wedlock, laments: "I am a poor magnet with power to be wounded by the bodies I attract"; Stark, *Rise of Christianity,* 23–27. And see note 9 above.

13. F: "TGL," 38. On the mesmerists Joseph Philippe François Deleuze and Charles Poyen see FRob: *MACS,* 13, 17–22, 29, 32–33. And see *FL,* I, 304, 305n7.

14. F: *SL,* 134, 98, 128, 135–36, 152, 156–57. In *Remembering Anna O.,* Borch-Jacobsen (51, 68) classes the Seeress of Prevorst with "hysterics" like Bertha Pappenheim (Anna O.). Zwarg sees Hauffe's trances as "a type of self-protective strategy." Zwarg: *FC,* 118–19. She notes that one of Mesmer's most ardent followers was Fourier. See Zwarg: *FC,* 116–19.

15. F: *SL,* 135–37.

16. F: *SL,* 137, Kerner qtd. 139. And see Schneiderman, *Jacques Lacan,* 58–59, 146–47. Von Mehren also calls the Seeress a "hysteric." See V: *M&TM,* 180.

17. Kerner qtd in F: *SL,* 139.

18. F: *SL,* 142–43, 147, 160, 149. And see Blakeslee, "Out of Body Experience?" *New York Times,* 3 Oct. 2006, sec. D1, 6. Blakeslee quotes Peter Brugger, a neuroscientist at University Hospital in Zurich, who says that there is "nothing mystical about these ghostly [so-called 'out-of-body'] experiences."

19. F: *SL,* 151, 153–54.

20. F: *SL,* 154. And see Zwarg: *FC,* 119; R. Hackforth, *Plato's Phaedrus,* 81; and Irigaray's *Speculum of the Other Woman.* On the image of Fuller's dead father see *OM,* I, 156; and on civilization as an "iron cage," see Noll, *Jung Cult,* 21.

21. See Zwarg, "Fatal Conflicts," in Zwarg: *FC,* 108–13.

22. F: *SL,* 182.

23. F: *WNC,* 115; Grimal, *Dictionary of Classical Mythology,* 268; Becker, *Denial of Death,* 151.

Chapter 34. Mother Power, Beastly Men, and *Woman in the Nineteenth Century*

1. V: *M&TM*, 189; *FL*, III, 234–35; F: *SL*, 41.

2. *FL*, III, 219.

3. Ibid., 220, 220n4 (Luke 1: 39–41 RSV). And see *FL*, II, 105, 107; C: *TW&TM*, 541; and Vanita, *Sappho and the Virgin Mary*, 28.

4. *FL*, III, 220, 221n5; Vanita, *Sappho and the Virgin Mary*, 51, 67–68; *Of Ovid's Metamorphoses, Book X*, in Johnson, ed., *Works of the English Poets*, 20: 467–68. Emerson connects Sturgis with Proserpina in a May 1845 letter. See E: *LofRWE*, VIII, 28.

5. *FL*, III, 225–27. On nineteenth-century women controlling their lives via virginity see Vanita, *Sappho and the Virgin Mary*, 25–28. And see C: *TW&TM*, 538.

6. See Fuller qtd. in Reynolds, "From *Dial* Essay to New York Book," 26.

7. *FL*, III, 232, 241.

8. F: *WNC*, v–vi, 1, 13.

9. Ibid., 35, 45, 138, 136–137.

10. Ibid., 81, 20–22, 62–65. On "liberty of law," see Zwarg: *FC*, 170–71.

11. F: *WNC*, 33–34, 36, 72–80, 74. And see *FL*, IV, 171.

12. Ibid., 22. And see Zwarg: *FC*, 12–14, 167—on agency and feminism.

13. F: *WNC*, 90–92; E: *ELofRWE*, 164–65; Smith-Rosenberg, "The Female World," 9. And see Noll, "The Mothers! The Mothers!" in *Jung Cult*, 161–76.

14. F: *WNC*, 136–39.

15. Ibid., 91–92, 93, 95. See Robert Fuller (FRob: *MACS*, 60, 67, 85–88), who quotes the American mesmerist John Dods, who theorized that the body when breathing takes in animal magnetism in its original state and transforms it into "nervo-vital fluid." See also Collyer, *Lights and Shadows*, 138.

16. F: *WNC*, 138, 122–23, and 131 for Adam and "*his* wife." And see Zwarg: *FC*, 171–74.

17. F: *WNC*, 120.

18. Ibid., 120, 139, 132–33, 137. And see Vanita, *Sappho and the Virgin Mary*, 25–26.

19. F: *WNC*, 137–38.

20. Ibid., 21, 134, 132–33; *FL*, III, 237, 238n. Fuller visited Sing Sing on 26 Oct. 1844 with Channing and Sturgis.

21. F: *WNC*, 154, and see 84. For Emerson on the "One Man," see E: *E&L*, 53–54. And see Aristophanes' speech in the *Symposium* in Plato, *Great Dialogues of Plato*, 86–87. On the mesmerists' body-soul views see FRob: *MACS*, 45–46; and Gauld, *A History of Hypnotism*, 145, 149.

22. F: *WNC*, 154–55. For Mesmer on "harmony" see *Mesmerism*, 19–20.

23. F: *WNC*, 145, 22–23, 29, 25, 119.

24. Ibid., 118–23.

25. Ibid., 126.

26. Ibid., 126, 108–9.

27. Ibid., 149–50. And see Comfort, *Anxiety Makers*, 34–37—on hygiene.

28. F: *WNC*, 39; Vanita, *Sappho and the Virgin Mary*, 51; Cavendish, ed., *Illustrated Encyclopedia of Mythology*, 148–49; Noll, *Jung Cult*, 173.

29. F: *WNC*, 149–50, 108–9, 93. The source of the poem is unidentified. See Fuller, *Woman in the Nineteenth Century*, ed. Reynolds, 62, 62n5.

30. Ibid., 93, 31, 51. For Emerson on "*lyrical glances*" see E: *J&MN*, XI, 497. And for Emerson on "perverted flashes" see E: *LofRWE*, II, 345.

---

31. F: *WNC*, 140, 153.

32. Ibid., 157, 27, 163.

Chapter 35. "What Is the Lady Driving At?"

1. *FL*, III, 241.

2. Locke, *Works of John Locke*, V, 385. See Blackstone qtd. in Beard, *Woman as Force in History*, 78–80. Timothy's diary reveals he was reading "Blackstone's Commentaries" while teaching women at Leicester Academy. See Timothy's 1801 diary (22 Aug. 1801), FFP: HM (fMS Am 1086 [2:2]).

3. See Beard, *Woman as Force in History*, 80–92. See Mansfield, *Legal Rights, Liabilities and Duties of Women*, 262–63, original emphasis. And see *FL*, I, 237; and C: *MFPY*, 162–63.

4. F: *WNC*, 69–70, 140. And see C: *TW&TM*, 112–13, and *FL*, II, 168.

5. E: *J&MN*, VII, 461.

6. Myerson, *Margaret Fuller*, 18–21. Myerson reports there were apparently two issues printed at the same time of the first edition, the cover of the second being a dark purple gray and "possibly a remainder binding." I refer here to the first issue. And for an image of a mandala drawn by Fuller with a snake and star design, see C: *TW&TM*, 545.

7. See Myerson, "Margaret Fuller: The American Years," 10; Myerson, "Margaret Fuller: An Exhibition," 6–7; Child, "Woman in the Nineteenth Century," in MJ: *CEonMF*, 7; V: *M&TM*, 195; and Peabody qtd. in V: *M&TM*, 195.

8. See Myerson, "Margaret Fuller: An Exhibition," 6; and anonymous, [review of *Woman in the Nineteenth Century*], *Ladies' National Magazine*, 7 (April 1845), 143–44, in MJ: *CEonMF*, 16–18.

9. See Myerson, "Margaret Fuller: The American Years," 11; Myerson, intro. to MJ: *CEonMF*, viii; Brownson, "Miss Fuller and Reformers," in MJ: *CEonMF*, 19–20, 22.

10. Brownson, "Miss Fuller and Reformers," in MJ: *CEonMF*, 23, 20–21; and see P. Miller, ed., "Orestes A. Brownson (1803–1876)," in *Transcendentalists*, 45.

11. [Briggs], review of *Woman in the Nineteenth Century*, in MJ: *CEonMF*, 8–10.

12. Ibid., 12–13.

13. Ibid., 13–14.

14. F: *WNC*, 136–38, 159.

15. *FL*, IV, 39.

Part Six. Professional Woman, Private Passion

1. *FL*, IV, 54; Reiss, *Goethe's Novels*, 96, 100; *FL*, III, 156; F: *WNC*, 160.

2. On Fuller's improved writing see R: *ER*, 54–78; MC: *MF'sNYJ*, 31; V: *M&TM*, 215–16. For a helpful discussion of Fuller's evolving identity as a political writer during her months working for the *New-York Daily Tribune*, see intro. to Bean: *MF,C*, xv–xl. Bean and Myerson offer a representative group of Fuller's *Tribune* essays, with a focus on her criticism of literature and culture. Many have never been published or are out of print.

Chapter 36. A Divided Life

1. *OM*, II, 153; V: *M&TM*, 222 (the *Tribune* had to move because of a fire in February 1845); *FL*, IV, 182. C. C. Mitchell argues Fuller wrote far more than the 250 starred articles attributed to her. See MC: *MF'sNYJ*, 3, 7, 25; Zwarg: *FC*, 190; E: *LofRWE*, II, 197. And see Greeley qtd. in MC: *MF'sNYJ*, 3.

2. See Wade, *Margaret Fuller*, 145–47; Fuller, "Emerson's Essays," *New-York Daily Tribune*, 7 Dec. 1844 in F: *MFCritic*, 2, 5; Zwarg: *FC*, 193, 204–5; and V: *M&TM*, 204.

3. *OM*, II, 166. And see Wade, *Margaret Fuller*, 147; and Hudspeth, pref. to *FL*, IV, 6.

4. See Zwarg: *FC*, 201–2, 6, 192, 192n8. Zwarg argues that in presenting her examples of transgendered beings in a progression that went from negative to positive, Fuller not only offered readers images of "alternate modes of behavior, but, more, importantly, alternative modes of interpreting that behavior" (202). See also C: *TW&TM*, 294; and Hudspeth, pref. to *FL*, IV, 7.

5. See Bailey, *Festus*; and Fuller, review of *Festus*, *Dial* 2 (Oct. 1841): 236, 244–49, 254, 257–59. Fuller's 8 Sept. 1845 *Tribune* review is reprinted in F: *MFCritic*, 211–19. And see *FL*, III, 195n2; *FL*, IV, 91, 92n3; and Bailey, pref. to *Festus*, 6.

6. For Fuller's review of *Dolores* see F: *MFCritic*, 410. On Fuller's view of Harro Harring and his fight with Harper Brothers, see *FL*, IV, 186n1, 210–11; and V: *M&TM*, 225. See also *FL*, V, 296; *FL*, VI, 369, 370n1; and *FL*, IV, 211n1, where Hudspeth details the Harper-Harring feud. And see "Harro Harring," 338–39.

7. *OM*, II, 150–51, 153; *FL*, III, 250; *FL*, IV, 45, 47n1, 55n1; B: *MFTtoR*, 228. Blackwell's Island became Welfare Island in 1921 and Roosevelt Island in 1973.

8. *OM*, II, 153–54.

9. Ibid., 154–55.

10. Ibid., 156, 150–51; *FL*, IV, 42, 44, 56–57, 67, 85, 86–87, 132; *FL*, III, 250; V: *M&TM*, 205. And see Gotendorf, "Prefatory Note," 3–4; Hig: *MFO*, 207–8.

11. C: *TW&TM*, 288–89; *FL*, III, 193n10; V: *M&TM*, 201–205; and see Hale, *Horace Greeley*, 111–13.

12. See B: *MFTtoR*, 226–27. On Fuller's attire see C: *MFPY*, 298; *FL*, II, 262; *FL*, III, 41, 208; *FL*, IV, 67, 181, 197.

13. *OM*, II, 156; V: *M&TM*, 177, 200–201; *FL*, IV, 174n3.

14. *OM*, II, 157. And see E: *E&L*, 957.

15. See "Fuller's scrapbook, June 17 to September 8, 1844," in C: *TW&TM*, 539–50, esp. 546–47, 549–50. See also *FL*, III, 209n1, 217. A daughter, whom Lidian named Ellen after Emerson's first wife, had been born in February 1839. See Porte, ed., *Emerson in His Journals*, 135. On Fuller's evolving relationship with Hawthorne, see T. Mitchell, *Hawthorne's Fuller Mystery*, 41–92.

16. "Fuller's scrapbook, June 17 to September 8, 1844," in C: *TW&TM*, 547–48; *FL*, III, 217.

17. "Fuller's scrapbook, June 17 to September 8, 1844," in C: *TW&TM*, 547–48, 550–51, 554; *FL*, III, 216, 217.

18. *FL*, III, 213–16, 216n1. And see Emerson, "Address Delivered in Concord on the Anniversary of the Emancipation of the Negroes in the British West Indies," in Emerson, *Complete Works*, XI, 99–147. And V: *M&TM*, 186.

19. *FL*, IV, 167, 169n1, 181.

20. See Dickens qtd. in MC: *MF'sNYJ*, 54.

21. See V: *M&TM*, 218; F: *MFCritic*, xxii, 98–104.

22. E: *LofRWE*, VIII, 56n193; *FL*, IV, 145n2. Cary wrote Emerson a few days later saying she was "sorry" she had said she "did not want to see [Margaret]" (E: *LofRWE*, VIII, 58n199).

23. See *FL*, IV, 173–74; C: *TW&TM*, 292–93; *OM*, I, 124; B: *MFTtoR*, 229; Hig: *MFO*, 8–9.

24. *OM*, II, 13; B: *MFTtoR*, 230; F: *MFCritic*, xxii; MC: *MF'sNYJ*, 5; C: *TW&TM*, 291–92.

25. MC: *MF'sNYJ*, 5; *FL*, IV, 175n2 (see *New-York Daily Tribune*, 9 Dec. 1845). And see *OM*, II, 139; and Bean and Myerson, intro. to F: *MFCritic*, xv–xvi.

26. See *OM*, II, 73; F: *WNC*, 110–11. And see MC: *MF'sNYJ*, 36–40.

27. *FL*, IV, 56; MC: *MF'sNYJ*, 9–10, 31. On Fuller's conscious development of a style at the paper and Greeley as teacher, see MC: *MF'sNYJ*, 31; and Bean and Myerson, intro. to F: *MF-Critic*, xxxii–xxxv. Bean and Myerson (xxii) say the circulation was two hundred thousand. Perhaps they refer to what the total circulation would become by the next decade.

28. *FL*, III, 237, 238; *OM*, II, 145, 147–49. And see B: *MFTtoR*, 211; and V: *M&TM*, 166, 189. See also Fuller's "Prison Discipline" in her 25 Feb. 1846 *Tribune* column, reprinted in MC: *MF'sNYJ*, 105–12.

29. *FL*, III, 247–48; *OM*, II, 144–45; C: *TW&TM*, 291–92; Zwarg: *FC*, 194–95, 211.

30. *FL*, III, 237; *FL*, VI, 357; *OM*, II, 145, 149; V: *M&TM*, 219. And see MC: *MF'sNYJ*, 77, 92–93, 94–96.

31. See Poe, "The Literati of New York City," in Reynolds, ed. *Woman in the Nineteenth Century*, 224; *OM*, II, 6, 167; Pollin, "Poe on Margaret Fuller in 1845," 47–50; C: *TW&TM*, 232–33, 501–3; and Wade, *Margaret Fuller*, 154–55. For the caricature, which was first published in the 8 March 1845 *Broadway Journal*, see the illustration titled "Portrait of a Distinguished Authoress," which was reprinted in Pollin, "Poe on Margaret Fuller," 49.

32. *FL*, IV, 60, 144, 192. And see "Fuller's scrapbook, June 17 to September 8, 1844," in C: *TW&TM*, 542.

33. *FL*, I, 341, 249; *FL*, III, 216.

34. For Greeley's report on Fuller see *OM*, II, 166–67, and see 136 for Fuller lamenting she is driven "from home to home."

35. *FL*, IV, 51. And see Fuller on "American Literature" in O: *AL&D*, 316. The essay appeared in her collection of essays titled *Papers on Literature and Art*, which was published by Evert Duyckinck in the fall of 1846.

36. See *OM*, II, 166. Leonard Shengold calls the technique of turning a superficial front to the world, "defensive emotional distance." See Shengold: *SM*, 178 and 30.

37. *OM*, II, 167.

38. Ibid., 156, 136. On "Fuller's ability to wall off parts of her experience," see Hudspeth, intro. to *FL*, I, 43. See also Shengold: *SM*, 26–31; and Kohut, *Analysis of the Self*, 185.

Chapter 37. Fallen Women and Worldly Men

1. *FL*, IV, 54; and *FL*, I, 163. Bean and Myerson note that in Fuller's 1845–46 columns, "hints of her personal life appear infrequently; . . . her essays rarely assume the private tone of writing for an imaginary individual friend." See Bean and Myerson, intro. to F: *MFCritic*, xxxiii.

2. See *FL*, VI, 357; V: *M&TM*, 225; Zwarg: *FC*, 189–220.

3. Fuller, "French Novelists of the Day," in F: *MFCritic*, 54–55. And see *FL*, IV, 46; and Bean and Myerson, who note how "publishers' crews raced out to meet ships before they docked, hoping to scoop competing newspapers and publishing houses for European news and pirated editions of literary works." See intro. to F: *MFCritic*, xxi.

4. Fuller, "French Novelists of the Day," in F: *MFCritic*, 56–57.

5. Ibid., 57–58, 60.

6. Ibid., 58, 61.

7. *OM*, II, 145–47.

8. Ibid., 145–46; *OM*, I, 15; *FL*, II, 168; Fuller, "French Novelists of the Day," in F: *MF-Critic*, 54; E: *LofRWE*, VII, 403. On nineteenth-century prostitutes as redeemable, see James Beard Talbot, *The Miseries of Prostitution*, 3rd ed. (1844), 43, qtd. in Kincaid, *Child-Loving*,

107–8. See also Gordon, "Incest and Resistance," 253–67, who discusses documented cases of girls who became prostitutes to escape incestuous situations at home.

9. *OM*, II, 145, 147–48.

10. Ibid., 148. And see C: *MFPY*, 298; Poe's description of Fuller in V: *M&TM*, 226; and Higginson's description of the same in Hig: *MFO*, 30.

11. *OM*, II, 145, 148.

12. Ibid., 159; *FL*, IV, 213. On Sand being someday in "full possession of her best self," see Fuller, "French Novelists of the Day," in F: *MFCritic*, 61; on herself, see *FL*, III, 91, and VI, 147.

13. See F: *WNC*, 36. And see Ovid, *Heroides and Amores*, 193–97.

14. See *OM*, I, 15; E: *J&MN*, XI, 500; Zwarg: *FC*, 140; C: *TW&TM*, 555, 551.

15. See *FL*, III, 197, 197n2; "Fuller's scrapbook, June 17 to September 8, 1844," in C: *TW&TM*, 549–50; *OM*, II, 160–61. And on babies and Una see *FL*, VI, 354–55.

16. *OM*, II, 161–62.

17. *FL*, IV, 75; V: *M&TM*, 206.

18. *FL*, IV, 47, 48n1.

19. Ibid., 59, 50, 61n7. And see B: *MFTtoR*, 228, 239–40; V: *M&TM*, 205–6, 209; and *FL*, IV, 48n2, where Hudspeth reports that Theodore Leger was a New York hypnotist who had just published *Animal Magnetism; or, Psycodunamy*, which Fuller would review on 30 May 1846 in the *Tribune*. Georgiana Bruce, who went with Fuller to one of her sessions, reported that Leger seemed to have straightened and lengthened Fuller's spine by moving his right hand upward in the air from the base of her backbone to her head.

20. *FL*, IV, 59, 61n7, 110, 50, 71, 55; F: *WNC*, 72–80.

21. *FL*, IV, 91.

22. *OM*, I, 279; *FL*, IV, 8, 133, 135, 140–41, 142, 146, 149n1.

23. Nathan quoted by Hudspeth, pref. to *FL*, IV, 8, and see 71n1.

24. *FL*, IV, 69.

25. *FL*, IV, 69, 63.

26. Ibid., 67, 69–70.

27. Ibid., 68, 90; Hawthorne, *Blithedale Romance*, 44; *OM*, II, 145. Zenobia, in despair over Hollingsworth's love for Priscilla (the "injured" woman he loved), took off the jeweled flower she had been wearing and told Coverdale to bid Priscilla to wear it for her sake. See Hawthorne, *Blithedale Romance*, 208.

Chapter 38. The Garden's Desecration

1. *FL*, IV, 64–65.

2. Ibid., 72.

3. Ibid., 76, 73.

4. Ibid., 110, 73. And see Milton, *Paradise Lost*, bk. XII, l. 645.

5. Shelley, *Shelley's Poetry and Prose*, 212, 213, 214, 215; *FL*, IV, 73, 95; *FL*, VI, 205.

6. Shelley, *Shelley's Poetry and Prose*, 214, 212; *FL*, IV, 50, 111.

7. *FL*, IV, 77.

8. Ibid., 83, 52, 70, 74, 76n1; *FL*, VI, 180; *OM*, I, 12. On Fuller greeting her father see TF to MCF, 25 Dec. 1819, FFP: HM (fMS Am 1086 [3: 71]).

9. *FL*, IV, 70, 74; *OM*, I, 18.

10. *FL*, IV, 70, 69, 82, 155. And see Barthes qtd. in Kincaid, *Child-Loving*, 31. See also Schacter, *Searching for Memory*, 173, 201–2.

11. *FL,* IV, 73, 77–78; *FL,* VI, 141–42.

12. *FL,* IV, 75–76, 78; *OM,* I, 18.

Chapter 39. Narcissistic Wounds and Imaginary Mystic Entities

1. *OM,* II, 7; *FL,* IV, 75, 77, 121, 82–83, 84n1.

2. *FL,* IV, 82–83. And see Zwarg: *FC,* 13, who calls Fuller's vital "I" a "radicalizing agent."

3. *FL,* IV, 75, 78, 87.

4. Ibid., 116.

5. See Wordsworth, *The Prelude,* bk. XII, ll. 269–71: "So feeling comes in aid / Of Feeling, and diversity of strength / Attends us, if but once we have been strong." And "Lines Composed a Few Miles Above Tintern Abbey," ll. 58–66 ff. in *Wordsworth,* 164, 578.

6. *FL,* III, 164–65.

7. *FL,* IV, 110, 111.

8. Ibid., 136; *FL,* VI, 148–49.

9. *FL,* IV, 77, 75, and on *Festus* see 91, 92nn1 & 3. In the epic, Festus has a "Guardian Angel."

10. *FL,* IV, 75, 162, and 78. See also Shelley, "Epipsychidion," "On Love," and *Alastor,* in *Shelley's Poetry and Prose,* 72, 74, 379, 473–74.

11. See Shelley, *Alastor,* in *Shelley's Poetry and Prose,* 74, 75, 78, 82; and Frye, "Drunken Boat," 16, 21–22.

12. Shelley, *Alastor,* in *Shelley's Poetry and Prose,* 75, 78–86. And see *FL,* V, 43.

13. Schapiro, *Romantic Mother,* 19. On Fuller as "too sensitive" see *FL,* IV, 93, 110, 136.

14. *FL,* IV, 95, 98–99, 100; *FL,* I, 97, 94. And see Erikson, *Childhood and Society,* 326–58, who years ago discussed the mystic-romantic element in Nazism and tied it to a patriarchal family structure wherein a harsh and aloof father lacks inner authority. On the self-negating Romantic notion of transcendent individuality, see Izenberg, *Impossible Individuality,* 1–17.

15. *FL,* IV, 75. And see Coleridge, *Biographia Literaria,* chap. IV, in *Samuel Taylor Coleridge,* 235.

Chapter 40. Romantic Obsession

1. *FL,* IV, 96, 100–101.

2. Ibid., 96, 94. On fantasy and regression see Lacan, *Language of the Self,* 14.

3. *FL,* IV, 95, 98–99.

4. Ibid., 95. On idealizing transferences and narcissistic mood swings, see Kohut, *Analysis of the Self,* 97–98.

5. *FL,* IV, 96, 107, 110, 109, 112, 112n2 (original emphasis). And see *FL,* IV, 75, . Fuller misquotes ll. 122–23 ("Nature never did betray / The heart that loved her") from Wordsworth's "Lines Composed a Few Miles Above Tintern Abbey." See *Wordsworth,* 165.

6. *FL,* IV, 111, 97–98, 70, 75, 109. And see Schacter, *Searching for Memory,* 9–10, 232–33.

7. *FL,* IV, 97, 71, 120, 114, 136–37.

8. Ibid., 137.

9. Ibid., 137, 132, 138. And see *FL,* I, 249.

10. Shelley, *Alastor,* in *Shelley's Poetry and Prose,* 80.

11. *FL,* IV, 137. For Sturgis's letter about *Woman and the Nineteenth Century* to Fuller see Reynolds, ed., *Woman,* 207. And see *FL,* IV, 60n2. For Fuller's account, "Valentine's Day at the Bloomingdale Asylum," see MC: *MF'sNYJ,* 79–82.

12. See MC: *MF'sNYJ*, 80–82.

13. *FL*, IV, 60n3; MC: *MF'sNYJ*, 81–82.

14. *FL*, IV, 132.

15. See Reynolds, "From *Dial* Essay to New York Book," 26–27; V: *M&TM*, 182–83; and B: *MFTtoR*, 210. Blanchard says Fuller had the dream about spiders while with Cary at Nantasket Beach at Hull. Fuller had proposed that they go to Naushon, one of the Elizabeth Islands just off Cape Cod. See *FL*, III, 220. And see *FL*, VI, 169, where a twenty-year-old Fuller writes James Freeman Clarke about Elizabeth Randall at the seashore standing with both hands holding "her red-cloak tight over her mouth lest that insidious East should seize the time to invade the soul's frail dwelling."

16. Capper says, "Both private pleasure and public success, it would seem, sadly required [Margaret's] mother's absence." See C: *MFPY*, 40.

17. *FL*, IV, 135–36.

18. Ibid., 147, 153, 147, 160, 156; and see Kohut, *Analysis of the Self*, 97–98.

Chapter 41. A Soul-Paralyzing Pain

1. *FL*, IV, 190. And see Schapiro, *Romantic Mother*, 16–18.

2. On Nathan's "magnetic effect" on Fuller see *FL*, IV, 75, 95.

3. See *FL*, III, 164–65; E: *J&MN*, XI, 500. And see Kinetz, "Is Hysteria Real?" In an article in the 11 March 2004 *New York Review of Books*, Frederick Crews attacks Freud's early theory that the "then fashionable complaint of hysteria" could be traced "to pathogenic hidden memories." He also attacks the work of Lenore Terr, who examines the devastating effects of trauma on children in *Too Scared to Cry*. See Crews, "Trauma Trap," 37–40.

4. Fuller acknowledges she is "too sensitive." See *FL*, IV, 136, 110, 93. And see Hudspeth, pref. to *FL*, IV, 8; and Burlet, "Headache," 13. For Freud on "mental 'sensitiveness' . . . among hysterical patients" see "The Aetiology of Hysteria" (trans. James Strachey), a paper read by Freud in Vienna, 21 April 1896, reprinted as appendix B in J. M. Masson, *Assault on Truth*, 278, 280. Crews in "Trauma Trap" is particularly critical of Masson.

5. *FL*, 137 (emphasis mine), 141; *FL*, VI, 141–42. See also Borch-Jacobsen, who discusses hysterics and their propensity for histrionics in *Remembering Anna O.*, 83–92. And Kinetz, "Is Hysteria Real?"

6. *FL*, IV, 163.

7. Ibid., 154, 162. On Fuller missing her father see *FL*, I, 113, 131.

8. *FL*, IV, 162–63. See Wieland: *SO*, II, 232–33. Recall Hawthorne's fun with the image of the silver veil in *Blithedale Romance*, 98–108, 179–88.

9. *FL*, IV, 163.

10. Ibid., 120, 138. For Fuller on being childish see ibid., 87, 93, 98. And see Kinetz, "Is Hysteria Real?"

11. *FL*, IV, 154, 148, 197, 155. For where Fuller boarded see ibid., 174, 193, 189; and V: *M&TM*, 221–23. And on the kind of empty interaction Fuller had with Nathan see Sartre, "Imaginary Life."

12. *FL*, IV, 179, 190, 205. On *Wayside Notes* see ibid., 146, 149n1, 156, 157n2, 159.

Chapter 42. A Trust Betrayed

1. *FL*, IV, 97.

2. Hig: *MFO*, 22–23. And see MCF to TF, 8 Feb. 1818, FFP: HM (fMS Am 1086 [6:13]);

MCF to MF, 7 Feb. 1847, FFP: HM (fMS Am 1086 [8:216]). And see V: *M&TM*, 259; and C: *MFPY*, 16–23, 27–28, 67–68. On "the dead mother complex," see André Green cited in Doane and Hodges, *From Klein to Kristeva*, 56–59.

3. See *OM*, II, 5, and C: *MFPY*, 31–32.

4. *FL*, IV, 46; *FL*, VI, 209.

5. *FL*, IV, 78. I am grateful to Kittye Robbins-Herring for this major insight about Fuller that radically changed the way I viewed her.

6. *FL*, IV, 137, 72, 96, 137; V: *M&TM*, 211–12. That Nathan embraced Fuller is evident from remarks such as that appearing in *FL*, IV, 154.

7. *FL*, IV, 116, 134–35, 116.

8. *FL*, IV, 97, 162–63, 141, 69. For Fuller recalling Nathan's image see *FL*, IV, 114, 116, 134–35. Worth noting here is Aragon's poem, "Contre-chant," cited by Lacan at the start of his lecture, "The Freudian Unconscious and Ours," in *Four Fundamental Concepts of Psycho-Analysis*, esp. 17.

9. *FL*, IV, 121, 204, 205.

10. E: *E&L*, 269; *FL*, IV, 205, 98; Wordsworth, "I Wandered Lonely as a Cloud," in *Wordsworth*, 149; F: *EMF*, 1–2, 5, 6–7; *OM*, I, 16. And see Plath, "Tulips," *Ariel*, 10–12.

11. F: *EMF*, 4–5; *OM*, I, 15–16; FR: *CF*, 14. And see TF to MCF, 16 April 1820, FFP: HM (fMS Am 1086 [3:167]).

12. On Fuller's letters to Nathan see Hudspeth, pref. to *FL*, IV, 7. And see *FL*, IV, 192, 74; *FL*, VI, 231. Zwarg notes that the phrase "transition state" comes from Fourier, who saw civilization's growth into maturity "as a growth crisis 'similar to the onset of puberty.'" See Beecher, *Charles Fourier*, 338; Zwarg: *FC*, 116–17, 204; and *FL*, I, 103.

13. *FL*, IV, 74, 90. And see F: *WNC*, 107. Instances in the Bible of the healing that came to "sick people" when Christ "laid his hands upon [them]" (Mark 6:1–6 RSV) are too numerous to cite. But the image of a pure, healing hand left a lasting imprint on Fuller. See *FL*, V, 240. For the effect of Leger's healing hand on Fuller, see *FL*, IV, 61n7.

14. *FL*, IV, 163; F: *MFCritic*, 58.

15. C: *MFPY*, 124; Kincaid, *Child-Loving*, 174–75; Comfort, *Anxiety Makers*, 40–41, 56, 93; FR: *RRF*, 18; FR: *CF*, 21, 26; and FE: "HC," 1, FFP: HM (bMS Am 1086 [B]).

16. FR: *RRF*, 21; C: *MFPY*, 168; P. Miller, ed., *Margaret Fuller*, 43, emphasis added. On the family's distress see AF to RFF, 16 Sept. 1847, FFP: HM (fMS Am 1086 [13:32]). And see *FL*, III, 237.

17. *FL*, IV, 75, 77, 74, 90, 73.

18. Ibid., 77; *FL*, VI, 140.

Chapter 43. The Dark Side of Her Lot

1. *FL*, IV, 87; *FL*, VI, 221, 223, 231.

2. E: *LofRWE*, VII, 419; *FL*, VI, 223, 231, 235; *FL*, IV, 95; *OM*, I, 139–40.

3. *FL*, I, VI, 223; *FL*, IV, 136.

4. For Eugene's "by mistake" swallowing "lamplighter" see V: *M&TM*, 64, and on his death see FAB: "HN," 12; *FL*, I, 79n2; and C: *MFPY*, 170. On Ellen see *FL*, I, 103n1. On Arthur's death in the Civil War see FR: *CF*, 298–302, C: *MFPY*, 170, and V: *M&TM*, 344–45. On William Henry see *FL*, I, 82n5. And on Richard see *FL*, I, 139n1.

5. *OM*, I, 139–40; *FL*, VI, 99.

6. Gordon, "Incest and Resistance," 254.

7. See C: *MFPY*, 32, and Gordon, "Incest and Resistance," 254–56. Capper is correct. A

child can experience such feelings for her father and remember that she did. In discussing this matter with me years ago, Harvard psychiatrist Leston Havens said that what matters in such a situation is how the father responds to the daughter's eroticized expression of affection.

8. Gordon, "Incest and Resistance," 255–56, 258.

9. Ibid. 256, 257–58; Hig: *MFO*, 28–29; and see MCF to TF, 27 Dec. 1818 (*"dutiful"*), FFP: HM (fMS Am 1086 [6: 44]). Capper questions Higginson's depiction of Margarett Crane's passive role. But Margarett Crane herself refers to her kinfolk thinking she lives like a "perfect recluse." See MCF to TF, 11 Dec. 1818, FFP: HM (fMS Am 1086 [6: 34]). See also C: *MFPY*, 66–67, and 20.

10. Gordon, "Incest and Resistance," 257, 254, 256, 259–66; *OM*, I, 14. And see *FL*, VI, 140. See also Fuller qtd. in V: *M&TM*, 58, and Timothy qtd. in C: *MFPY*, 35. On Fuller "attack[ing] the hypocrisy of men" in F: *WNC*, see Myerson, "Margaret Fuller: An Exhibition," 6.

11. MCF to TF, 22 Feb. 1818, FFP: HM (fMS Am 1086 [6: 20]); MCF to TF, 20 Jan. 1818, FFP: HM (fMS Am 1086 [6: 7]); MCF to TF, 30 Dec. 1818, FFP: HM (fMS Am 1086 [6: 46]); TF to MCF, 16 Dec. 1819, FFP: HM (fMS Am 1086 [3: 63]). Mrs. Deforest was the wife of the U.S. consul to Brazil.

12. MCF to TF, 26 Jan. 1818, FFP: HM (fMS Am 1086 [6: 9]); MCF to TF, 31 Jan. 1818, FFP: HM (fMS Am 1086 [6: 11]); MCF to TF, 24 Jan. 1819, FFP: HM (fMS Am 1086 [6: 63]).

13. MCF to TF, 11 Dec. 1818, FFP: HM (fMS Am 1086 [6: 34]). And see Hartmann, "The Nature of Dreaming," in *Dreams and Nightmares*, 1–35.

14. *FL*, VI, 223; MCF to TF, 26 Feb. 1818, FFP: HM (fMS Am 1086 [6: 22]); MCF to TF, 15 Feb. 1818, FFP: HM (fMS Am 1086 [6: 17]); MCF to TF, 1 Feb. 1819, FFP: HM (fMS Am 1086 [6: 69]).

15. MCF to TF, 4 Jan. 1819, FFP: HM (fMS Am 1086 [6: 49]); TF to MCF, 5 April 1820, FFP: HM (fMS Am 1086 [3: 159]). And see TF to MCF, 21 Jan. 1820, FFP: HM (fMS Am 1086 [3: 93]); and C: *MFPY*, 38.

16. TF to MCF, 10 Feb. 1820, FFP: HM (fMS Am 1086 [3: 113]). And see C: *MFPY*, 34, 38, 29.

17. MCF to TF, 26 Jan. 1818, FFP: HM (fMS Am 1086 [6: 9]); *OM*, I, 14, 18); *FL*, IV, 98–99, 83; *FL*, VI, 232; TF to MCF, 16 April 1820, FFP: HM (fMS Am 1086 [3: 167]); TF to MCF, 25 Dec. 1819, FFP: HM (fMS Am 1086 [3: 71]). And see Shengold: *SM*, 12, 20, 138–41.

18. *FL*, IV, 70; *OM*, I, 42, 17.

19. *OM*, I, 16; F: *EMF*, 4–5; *FL*, IV, 73.

Chapter 44. "Possessed of" Her Father

1. *OM*, I, 16, 14. And see *FL*, IV, 73; and Shengold: *SM*, 3. As noted earlier, that the adult Fuller exhibits the characteristics of someone who was abused as a child is the insight of feminist Kittye Robbins-Herring.

2. Wilson, "Not in This House," 45, 51–52; Shengold: *SM*, 3–4. And see Freud cited by Shengold: *SM*, 15, and Schacter, *Searching for Memory*, 232. And see Burlet, "Headache," 13.

3. *FL*, VI, 223; C: *TW&TM*, 554, 535. And see Orwell qtd. in Shengold: *SM*, 2.

4. *OM*, I, 15–16; F: *EMF*, 4–5; *FL*, IV, 154.

5. C: *MFPY*, 32; *FL*, VI, 232; *FL*, IV, 136; Shengold: *SM*, 1–12, 15, 20–21, 24, 138–44. And see Oppenheim and Waters, "Narrative Processes and Attachment Representations," 209. For Fuller on "unseen powers" see F: *SL*, 128. Compare Fuller's discussion of the power inherent for women in feeling possessed of "unseen powers" with Michelle Price's discus-

sion of female incest victims who defensively deal with their exploitation by saying they are "endowed with special powers" ("Incest and the Idealized Self," 24).

6. OM, I, 24; Fuller qtd. in C: MFPY, 41, 368n30. And see Brigham, Remarks, 55.

7. Shengold: SM, 16–17, 1–2, 6; FL, I, 94.

Chapter 45. Yearning to Wash Her Soul of Sin

1. OM, I, 15; F: EMF, 4; FL, IV, 111 (emphasis added). Fuller's thoughts on Elizabeth appear in "On Her Childhood," in F: EMF, wherein Fuller deliberately uses Elizabeth's situation as a means to reflect on her own.

2. OM, I, 15; F: EMF, 4; TF to MCF, 17 Jan. 1820, FFP: HM (fMS Am 1086 [3:90]). And see Kincaid, Child-Loving, 92, and 102n143. Kincaid quotes from a parent's manual of the time that notes how "the shadow" of a parent's influence is always "there."

3. Steele has published that scrap of paper under the title "[On Her Childhood]," in F: EMF, 4–5; FL, VI, 135.

4. FL, IV, 97, 78, 137, 74; C: MFPY, 32. And see Christopher Lasch's letter to the author, 1 Jan. 1991. On "the alliance of pain and eros," see Kincaid, Child-Loving, 255–61, 263–66. And see Shengold: SM, 143, and 30 on "defensive isolation." Emerson had also pierced Fuller's facade.

5. FL, IV, 163.

6. OM, I, 18; Shengold: SM, 5, 11–12, 22, 26–29. Faulkner, Collected Stories, 119–30, 3–25.

7. On Timothy sending kisses, see C: MFPY, 35. And see TF to SMF, 3 Dec. 1820, FFP: HM (fMS Am 1086 [5:6]); TF to MCF, 11 Dec. 1820, FFP: HM (fMS Am 1086 [3:199]); FL, VI, 209; Shengold: SM, 22–23; deYoung and Lowry, "Traumatic Bonding," 170; C: MFPY, 14, 32.

8. FL, I, 91; FL, VI, 232; FL, IV, 148; Hawthorne, "Rappaccini's Daughter," Nathaniel Hawthorne's Tales, 193; OM, I, 32; and see T. R. Mitchell, Hawthorne's Fuller Mystery, 93–124.

9. Hawthorne, Nathaniel Hawthorne's Tales, 200; Erikson, Young Man Luther, 67. And recall Timothy as a student peeping in a female friend's window, as he recorded it in his 1800 journal. See Timothy Fuller, journal, 4 March 1800, FFP: HM (bMS Am 1086 [A]).

10. Hawthorne, Nathaniel Hawthorne's Tales, 205; TF to SMF, 3 March 1822, FFP: HM (fMS Am 1086 [5:10]); MCF to TF, 13 Jan. 1818, FFP: HM (fMS Am 1086 [6:6]); FR: RRF, 15; FL, VI, 142. On Margarett Crane as a strict "Calvinist," see FL, VI, 145. And on female disobedience, pride, and infidelity as "sins," see Tatar, Off with Their Heads! 94–119. See also Wieland: SO, I, 198 and II, 2—where Huon was "worn by [the] vigilance" of his mentor Sherasmin's "Argus eyes." Language in Timothy's letters and diaries indicates he had read Oberon.

11. FL, VI, 142; FL, I, 84; on Timothy peeping at "Margt Rogers," see n9 above. And see TF to MCF, 2 Feb. 1820, FFP: HM (fMS Am 1086 [3:105]). And F: WNC, 126. Kincaid discusses the Victorian obsession with masturbation and cites advice of "experts" like phrenologist O. S. Fowler, whose lectures Fuller had attended in Providence. See Child-Loving, 122–23, 135, 164–65, 174–75. On the "culture of surveillance" and "the watchful parental eye," see Tatar, Off with Their Heads! 88–91, who cites Foucault, Discipline and Punish. On the danger of "experts" intruding into the family, see Lasch, Haven in a Heartless World.

12. Fuller qtd. in V: M&TM, 18; OM, I, 48–51. In reply to Fuller's assertion that she had committed no sin, her mother told her "disobedience was a sin." See MCF to TF, 18 Feb. 1818, FFP: HM (fMS Am 1086 [6:18]); and C: MFPY, 38. On the yearning of children who have been emotionally imposed upon or neglected for someone to rescue them from the unbearable intensities within them, see Shengold: SM, 28. And on female disobedience as a "sin," see Tatar, Off with Their Heads! 105–11.

13. *FL,* IV, 77, 82–83; *OM,* 51–52.

14. *FL,* IV, 82, original emphasis.

Chapter 46. The Ties That Bind

1. *FL,* IV, 97; *FL,* III, 165; *FL,* VI, 223. On her desire "to gratify all [her father's] wishes," see *FL,* I, 107.

2. *FL,* I, 93, 95; *FL,* IV, 83, 82, 74, 70, 190, 96.

3. *FL,* IV, 163; Hig: *MFO,* 22. For Fuller on Beatrice Cenci see F: *WNC,* 199.

4. *FL,* III, 164–65; *OM,* I, 42; F: *WNC,* 119. And see Shengold: *SM,* 28–29, 178–79.

5. Freud qtd. in J. M. Masson, *Assault on Truth,* 11–12; *OM,* I, 23; *FL,* IV, 73, 95, 77. Edwin Haviland Miller notes of Fuller's 25 November fantasy letter to Beethoven how "she kneeled" in it before Beethoven "and, her incestuous fantasies emerging, asked to be [Beethoven's/Timothy's] wife-mistress-daughter" (*Salem Is My Dwelling Place,* 232). Miller here suggests that Fuller harbors "incestuous fantasies," indirectly thereby placing the blame on Margaret, not her father, for whatever went wrong between them.

6. *FL,* I, 300, 301; *OM,* I, 28, 16; F: *WNC,* 185.

7. F: *WNC,* 186–87. And see John Prudhoe, intro. to Goethe, *Iphigenia in Tauris,* xii; and Hamilton, *Mythology,* 350–61.

8. P. Miller, ed., *Margaret Fuller,* 43; F: *WNC,* 199; *OM,* I, 155. And see *FL,* III, 237.

9. C: *MFPY,* 155, 158; *FL,* III, 85; *OM,* I, 154–56.

10. *FL,* II, 168.

11. *OM,* I, 39; *FL,* IV, 107; F: *SL,* 100; Shengold: *SM,* 6; and *FL,* I, 249.

12. See Shengold: *SM,* 30; and Hudspeth, intro. to *FL,* I, 53.

13. *FL,* IV, 77.

Part Seven. The Rising Tide of Revolution

1. R: *ER,* 1–3; Langer: *PSU,* 113; Walicki, "National Messianism," 135–39; Bean: *MF,C,* 327. Mickiewicz was born in Lithuania.

Chapter 47. Passionate Players and Incendiary Social Conditions

1. Langer: *PSU,* 519; Reynolds, F: *TSBGD,* 18; S: *Mazzini,* 18.

2. Berlin, *Against the Current,* 346–55, esp. 353; Langer: *PSU,* 519–20. My views on the 1848 revolutions reflect those of Professor Johnpeter Grill of Mississippi State University, who lectured on 4 April 1996 to my graduate seminar on the American Romantics and the 1848 European revolutions.

3. See R: *ER,* 1–5; Langer: *PSU,* 150–51; Grill, lecture.

4. Langer: *PSU,* 90, 330–34; R: *ER,* 3, 44–45.

5. Walicki, "National Messianism," 129–35, 137–38, 140; Langer: *PSU,* 245–49; and see Berlin on nationalism in *Against the Current,* 341.

6. Lovett, *Democratic Movement in Italy,* 1, 18–20; S: *Mazzini,* 17–19; Langer: *PSU,* 115–16.

7. Langer: *PSU,* 217, 248–49; Abrams, *Correspondent Breeze,* 28, 45–48, 230.

8. See Wessell, *Karl Marx,* who borrows from Becker's *Denial of Death* and also quotes from the writings of Novalis, Fichte, Schlegel, and Schiller, 21, 23–24, 26–27; Walicki, "National Messianism," 135, 137–38; Luke 17: 20-2 RSV; and E: *J&MN,* VII, 461—on "twilights of the gods."

9. See Berlin, "Herder and the Enlightenment," in *Vico and Herder*, xxi–xxiii, 145–52, 156. And see Langer: *PSU*, 238–39, 534–35; Abrams, *Mirror and the Lamp*, 174–75; Abrams, *Correspondent Breeze*, 252–53; and Abrams, *Natural Supernaturalism*, 355–56.

10. R: *ER*, 4. And see Langer: *PSU*, 181–98; Grill, "European Revolutions of 1848."

11. Carlyle, *Past and Present*, 3; Langer: *PSU*, 187–90; Grill, "European Revolutions of 1848."

12. Langer: *PSU*, 184–86, 210. And see ibid., ills. 21 and 22.

13. Ibid., 195–97; F: *TSBGD*, 47, 72.

14. See Abrams, *Correspondent Breeze*, 47–55, 231, 226; and Abrams, *Natural Supernaturalism*, 37–41.

15. Rufus Jones qtd. in Abrams, *Correspondent Breeze*, 234, and see 66; Abrams, *Natural Supernaturalism*, 47, 57; Grill, "European Revolutions of 1848"; Lovett, *Democratic Movement in Italy*, 18–20; S: *Mazzini*, 17. Both Mazzini and Fuller nonetheless believed in some sort of an afterlife.

16. Grill, "European Revolutions of 1848." And see Langer: *PSU*, 249.

17. Berlin, *Against the Current*, 351; Walicki, "National Messianism," 139; Emerson, "Divinity School Address," in E: *E&L*, 76; Wessell, *Karl Marx*, 85.

18. Berlin, *Against the Current*, 347, 351–52; and see Noll, *Jung Cult*, 262; Goodrick-Clarke, *Occult Roots of Nazism*, 4–6.

19. Noll, *Jung Cult*, 240–42, 89–90; C: *TW&TM*, 544–45.

20. C: *TW&TM*, 545.

21. Noll, *Jung Cult*, 89; Abrams, *Correspondent Breeze*, 57. And see Weber, *On Charisma and Institution Building*—esp. Eisenstadt's intro., xxiii–xxvi.

22. Izenberg, intro. to *Impossible Individuality*, 3–11.

23. See Fuller, "Goethe," 21, 27; Douglas, *Feminization of American Culture*, 272, 282. And see Chevigny, "To the Edges of Ideology," 179.

Chapter 48. Entering the European Stage

1. *FL*, IV, 220, 221, 221n; Wade, *Margaret Fuller*, 186; and Slater, ed., *Correspondence of Emerson and Carlyle*, 407.

2. *OM*, I, 11, 235, 36, 39.

3. *FL*, IV, 208, 209, 214–15, 218, 226, 227n1. And see *FL*, III, 165–66.

4. *FL*, IV, 217, 225; F: *TSBGD*, 39.

5. See F: *TSBGD*, 47; Langer: *PSU*, 190–91.

6. F: *TSBGD*, 47, 48–49, 102–3.

7. Ibid., 48, 50–51.

8. Ibid., 51; Martineau qtd. in B: *MFTtoR*, 249; F: *TSBGD*, 53, 57.

9. Ibid., 65, 67–68, 61; *FL*, IV, 226–27. And see Hudspeth, pref. to *FL*, IV, 10.

10. See Hudspeth, pref. to *FL*, IV, 10. And see F: *TSBGD*, 69, 73.

11. F: *TSBGD*, 71, 73.

12. Ibid., 74–75; *FL*, IV, 228.

13. F: *TSBGD*, 76. See Psyche's story in *The Golden Ass*, repr. in Biallas, *Myths*, 187–204; and Hudspeth on "suicidal gesture," pref. to *FL*, IV, 10.

See also F: *TSBGD*, 11n35, for the comments of Reynolds and Belasco Smith on Fuller's possible "suicidal state of mind."

14. F: *TSBGD*, 75–76.

15. Ibid., 76–77; *FL*, IV, 246.

16. F: *TSBGD*, 79.

17. Ibid., 81; Langer: *PSU*, 192.

18. F: *TSBGD*, 82–83; *FL*, IV, 228; Langer: *PSU*, 210.

Chapter 49. Mazzini Enters

1. F: *TSBGD*, 88; *FL*, IV, 229–230.

2. *FL*, IV, 236n5, 269n6, 240, 242n2, 235, 236n3; F: *TSBGD*, 91.

3. *FL*, IV, 246–49, 249n3.

4. Deiss: *RYMF*, 33; Lovett, *Democratic Movement in Italy*, 18; Reynolds and Belasco Smith, intro. to F: *TSBGD*, 13; S: *Mazzini*, 5–15; Mazzini, *Selected Writings*, 81, 135–37; Langer: *PSU*, 115–16.

5. S: *Mazzini*, 3–4; Mazzini, *Selected Writings*, 10, 41–48; Langer: *PSU*, 113–14.

6. S: *Mazzini*, 5–6, 7; Lovett, *Democratic Movement in Italy*, 9–10; Langer: *PSU*, 115, 113; Mazzini, *Selected Writings*, 51–53, 127–35.

7. S: *Mazzini*, 7–8; Langer: *PSU*, 116–17, 137; Reynolds and Belasco Smith, intro. to F: *TSBGD*, 13.

8. Mazzini, *Selected Writings*, 67, 237, 114–15; S: *Mazzini*, 12–14;

9. Mazzini qtd. in Langer: *PSU*, 115; S: *Mazzini*, 12–13; Mazzini, *Selected Writings*, 130.

10. See Mazzini, *Selected Writings*, 237, 33–34, 98–99, 137–41, 167, 98–99, 169–70; Lovett, *Democratic Movement in Italy*, 20, 34; S: *Mazzini*, 2, 15–16; Langer: *PSU*, 115, 216–17.

11. Lovett, *Democratic Movement in Italy*, 10–13, 18; Mazzini, *Selected Writings*, 69, 203–7; and see F: *TSBGD*, 254, 262.

12. *FL*, IV, 248–49. And see Reynolds, intro. to F: *TSBGD*, 10.

13. *FL*, IV, 248–49. And see Rebecca Spring qtd. in Reynolds, intro. to F: *TSBGD*, 10.

14. Mazzini qtd. in Deiss: *RYMF*, 33; F: *TSBGD*, 99. And see B: *MFTtoR*, 256.

15. F: *TSBGD*, 98–100; C: *TW&TM*, 298–99; Hudspeth, pref. to *FL*, IV, 15.

16. See Reynolds on Fuller as "Liberty" in R: *ER*, 74. On Nathan see Hudspeth, pref. to *FL*, IV, 11; and V: *M&TM*, 241–42.

17. *FL*, IV, 245, 239–40.

18. See Blount, *George Sand*, 11–12, 6, 18–19.

19. *FL*, IV, 10, 244, 234.

Chapter 50. Mickiewicz Enters

1. See F: *TSBGD*, 87, 108, 118–19, 119n3. See also Deiss: *RYMF*, 37–38.

2. F: *TSBGD*, 108; *FL*, IV, 253; V: *M&TM*, 242.

3. *FL*, IV, 252, 252n1, 253, 253nn1–2. See also V: *M&TM*, 242–43.

4. *FL*, IV, 250; F: *TSBGD*, 104–6.

5. *FL*, IV, 250–52.

6. F: *TSBGD*, 87, 105; V: *M&TM*, 243–44; Fuller qtd. in Deiss: *RYMF*, 38.

7. F: *TSBGD*, 119–20.

8. F: *TSBGD*, 108–9, 120–21; Langer: *PSU*, 249–50, 90, 77. And see V: *M&TM*, 244; and S. K. Martin, e-mail to the author, 11 Aug. 2006. Martin gives as her Polish source Jaroslaw Marek Rymkiewicz, "Mickiewicz: Encyklopedia." And see Mieczyslaw Jastrun qtd. in Martin, "Ralph Waldo Emerson," 20.

9. F: *TSBGD*, 110–11, 110n16; Deiss: *RYMF*, 38; Langer: *PSU*, 248–49.

10. F: *TSBGD*, 123–24; V: *M&TM*, 244.

11. F: *TSBGD*, 124.

12. Ibid., 124–25. And see *FL*, IV, 259; V: *M&TM*, 244–45.

13. *FL*, IV, 256. And see V: *M&TM*, 245–47.

14. See V: *M&TM*, 246.

15. *OM*, II, 194–95. And see *FL*, IV, 256n1; V: *M&TM*, 246.

16. *OM*, II, 195–96.

17. Ibid., 196–97. Recall how Channing in the *Memoirs* had unconsciously linked Fuller as "Bacchante" with Sand. See *OM*, II, 92–93, 93n.

18. *OM*, II, 197–98; *FL*, IV, 256.

19. *OM*, II, 198; V: *M&TM*, 247; Langer: *PSU*, 247–50; Walicki, "National Messianism," 136–38, 140; Weintraub, *Poetry of Adam Mickiewicz*, 11–21, 48; Deiss: *RYMF*, 42; Ordon, "Mickiewicz and Emerson," 34–35; S. K. Martin, "Ralph Waldo Emerson and Adam Mickiewicz," 20–22, 23–25, 25–30. On Fuller's first hearing Chopin play, see *FL*, IV, 262n2.

20. V: *M&TM*, 248; Weintraub, *Poetry of Adam Mickiewicz*, 50–51, 221; Langer: *PSU*, 247–50; S. K. Martin, "Ralph Waldo Emerson and Adam Mickiewicz," 25–30.

21. Walicki, "National Messianism," 135–38.

22. Ordon, "Mickiewicz and Emerson," 35–42; Wellisz: *FMF-AM*, 7; S. K. Martin, "Ralph Waldo Emerson and Adam Mickiewicz," 47–56; C: *TW&TM*, 300. For Emerson's essay "The Over-Soul" see E: *E&L*, 385–400.

23. *FL*, IV, 261.

24. Ibid., 259; V: *M&TM*, 247–48; S. K. Martin, "Ralph Waldo Emerson and Adam Mickiewicz," 20, 25–26.

25. S. K. Martin, "Ralph Waldo Emerson and Adam Mickiewicz," 25–26; Wellisz: *FMF-AM*, 4–6, 6–8, 9–10; E: *E&L*, 405, 485, 484, 406.

26. *FL*, IV, 258–59; F: *TSBGD*, 105–6. And see Alexander, *Poetic Self*, 95, 106, and *Women in Romanticism*, 8.

Chapter 51. On to Lyons and Italy

1. F: *TSBGD*, 87, 118; *FL*, IV, 253, 259.

2. *FL*, IV, 259; V: *M&TM*, 248.

3. Wellisz: *FMF-AM*, 12–13.

4. F: *SL*, 11–12, 8–9. And see *OM*, II, 197.

5. *FL*, IV, 259, 291; Wellisz: *FMF-AM*, 12–13. And see Deiss: *RYMF*, 43.

6. Langer: *PSU*, 82, 184–88; V: *M&TM*, 249.

7. F: *TSBGD*, 127.

8. Ibid., 128.

9. Ibid., 128; *FL*, III, 85–86.

10. Wellisz: *FMF-AM*, 17; E: *LofRWE*, III, 394.

11. *FL*, IV, 262, 267–68, 268n4; F: *TSBGD*, 128–29, 90, 90n5, 91, 99; V: *M&TM*, 252–53. Fuller refers to Laure de Noves of Avignon. See *FL*, IV, 262n3.

12. *FL*, IV, 262, 224n1; F: *TSBGD*, 130–31; V: *M&TM*, 253.

Chapter 52. On to Rome

1. Weintraub, *Poetry of Adam Mickiewicz*, 17; V: *M&TM*, 248; F: *TSBGD*, 129–31; Wellisz: *FMF-AM*, 19.

2. Deiss: *RYMF*, 45–46. And see F: *TSBGD*, 50; *FL*, V, 101.

3. *FL*, IV, 266; F: *TSBGD*, 135–36.

4. F: *TSBGD*, 133–34, 142–43.

5. Ibid., 135; *FL*, V, 181. Fuller's memory here, says Hudspeth, fails her: when Goethe visited the Barberini Palace he saw there not *The Triumph of Galatea* but Raphael's *La Fornarina; Galatea* is in the Villa Farnesina. See Hudspeth, *FL*, V, 182n4. See also Gombrich, *Story of Art*, 240–45; Hintzen-Bohlen, *Rome and the Vatican City*, 437–39; and Wright, *Renaissance Masterpieces of Art and Architecture*, 90–91.

6. F: *TSBGD*, 134–35; Wright, *Renaissance Masterpieces*, 116–17; G. Masson, *Fodor's Rome*, 241; Rowland, "Titian," 15–17.

7. F: *TSBGD*, 135; Wright, *Renaissance Masterpieces*, 76–77.

8. See Deiss: *RYMF*, 46–49.

9. Wellisz: *FMF-AM*, 17–18.

10. V: *M&TM*, 249.

11. *FL*, IV, 262–63, 263nn1–2; F: *TSBGD*, 134–35; Deiss: *RYMF*, 47, 66; G. Masson, *Fodor's Rome*, 235–41; V: *M&TM*, 257; Wright, *Renaissance Masterpieces*, 116–17, 122; Rowland, "Titian," 16.

12. *FL*, IV, 263n2, 312n2, 85.

13. Ibid., 262–63, 263n2, 291.

14. Ibid., 263.

Chapter 53. Ossoli Enters

1. C: *TW&TM*, 423–25; V: *M&TM*, 260; *FL*, IV, 269, 270, 271n1. These are Balzac's words about Sand, qtd. in Barry: *IW*, 240.

2. *FL*, IV, 269, 270, 271, 271n1; V: *M&TM*, 260.

3. See Hicks in C: *TW&TM*, 424. For the different accounts of Fuller's first seeing Ossoli see V: *M&TM*, 256. See also Deiss: *RYMF*, 53–55. And on St. Peter's see von Matt, *Rome*, 54; Hintzen-Bohlen, *Rome and the Vatican City*, 468–69. In another account, George Palmer Putnam said he recalled seeing Fuller meeting Ossoli the previous Wednesday outside on the piazza, though in a letter Mickiewicz wrote Fuller he recalled that she had said she had met "a little Italian" "in the Church." Wellisz: *FMF-AM*, 20.

4. The information about the path the title took through the Ossoli men is in von Mehren: see V: "EtF," 8; V: "MF&MQ," 135; and V: "MF&MQ," 138n18, where von Mehren says Antonio died in 1842; presumably it was 1842 or 1843.

5. V: "EtF," 8; V: "MF&MQ," 134–35, 130; V: *M&TM*, 256–57; Deiss: *RYMF*, 53–54, 56, 67–68; von Matt, *Rome*, 54–55 and plate 15; Georgina Masson, *Fodor's Rome*, 113, 98.

6. V: *M&TM*, 256–57; Emelyn Story qtd. in C: *TW&TM*, 409. On Eugene see Fuller's July 1844 journal entry in E: *J&MN*, XI, 502. See also *FL*, V, 261; C: *MFPY*, 44–45; *FL*, III, 85.

7. V: "EtF," 7–8; V: "MF&MQ," 134–35; C: *TW&TM*, 409. And see *FL*, V, 261, 299; and Deiss: *RYMF*, 47.

8. *FL*, V, 299; V: "EtF," 7; Deiss: *RYMF*, 71.

9. F: *TSBGD*, 277–78.

10. V: *M&TM*, 261, 271; Deiss: *RYMF*, 49. The date is approximate.

11. Fuller qtd. in V: *M&TM*, 58. And see Ross, *Hesitation*, I, 262–63; *OM*, II, 197; and *FL*, I, 91.

12. *FL*, V, 269; *OM*, II, 197–98; *FL*, IV, 262–63.

13. C: *TW&TM*, 405; Bean: *MF,C*, 57.

14. See, for instance, "FJ42–1," 331–32. For negative remarks by Fuller on "wedlock" see

C: *MFPY*, 288; C: *TW&TM*, 518; and Chodzko qtd. by Mickiewicz's son Wladyslaw Mickiewicz in Wellisz: *FMF-AM*, 10.

15. Langer: *PSU*, 138–41; V: *M&TM*, 255; Deiss: *RYMF*, 50–51; F: *TSBGD*, 136n18; *FL*, IV, 274n1.

16. F: *TSBGD*, 141, 136.

17. Ibid., 136–37.

18. Ibid., 136; *FL*, IV, 273; Langer: *PSU*, 141.

19. F: *TSBGD*, 137; and Fuller qtd. from Rebecca Spring's travel diary in V: *M&TM*, 254.

Chapter 54. To Marry, or Not to Marry?

1. *FL*, IV, 271, 274; Ross, *Hesitation*, I, 262–63, 36, 15; *FL*, V, 292, 248; E: *E&L*, 261; F: *WNC*, 69. Like Mrs. Ross, Fuller in her letter uses the British "connexion." By 1847 the word would carry a sexual connotation thanks to the 1845 book *Origin of Life: A Popular Treatise on the Philosophy and Physiology of Reproduction* by British physician and lecturer Frederick Hollick, who was a "sexual enthusiast" and "follower of Robert Owen." See Horowitz, *Rereading Sex*, 113–15.

2. *FL*, IV, 271; F: *TSBGD*, 139–41; Langer: *PSU*, 219–20. And for Fourier's influence on Fuller see Zwarg: *FC*.

3. *FL*, IV, 276–77.

4. F: *TSBGD*, 140–41.

5. Ibid., 141–42, 143; *FL*, IV, 284. And see V: *M&TM*, 261–62.

6. F: *TSBGD*, 144–45; *FL*, IV, 284, 296; Wellisz: *FMF-AM*, 20.

7. *FL*, IV, 291, 284.

8. Ibid., 290–91, 294; V: *M&TM*, 255; Deiss: *RYMF*, 73.

9. *FL*, IV, 287; Wellisz: *FMF-AM*, 23–24.

10. *FL*, IV, 286; V: *M&TM*, 255, 266; Deiss: *RYMF*, 73; Walicki, "National Messianism," 136–39; S. K. Martin, "Ralph Waldo Emerson and Adam Mickiewicz," 23–33; F: *TSBGD*, 156, 156n3; Deiss: *RYMF*, 73. And on Gioberti see Langer: *PSU*, 138–39, 254, 430.

11. Wellisz: *FMF-AM*, 25; *FL*, IV, 294, 290, 291, 311; V: *M&TM*, 265–66.

12. *FL*, IV, 292, 288; V: *M&TM*, 265–66; F: *TSBGD*, 148, 222–24; Wessell, *Karl Marx*, 24; Langer: *PSU*, 247–251.

13. *FL*, IV, 287, 287n3; F: *WNC*, 68–69; V: *M&TM*, 265.

14. Richard's engagement to Anna de Rose, a nineteen-year-old Canton teacher, "ended abruptly in 1848," says Hudspeth, "when she ran away from home 'with a female friend.'" See *FL*, IV, 282–83, 284n1, and 296. On 5 Feb. 1849, Richard married Sarah K. Batchelder, "a step" he "never" repented. See FR: *RRF*, 87–91. On Fuller's friends and family members' unhappy marriages see V: *M&TM*, 266–67, and *FL*, IV, 297n5.

15. F: *TSBGD*, 146.

16. Ibid., 154, 158. And see Mazzini qtd. in S: *Mazzini*, 52–53.

17. F: *TSBGD*, 154.

18. R: *ER*, 74; F: *TSBGD*, 155–56, 156n3; Langer: *PSU*, 254.

19. See Deiss: *RYMF*, 108–11. And see map in ibid., 113.

20. S: *Mazzini*, 50–51; Deiss: *RYMF*, 108–10.

21. F: *TSBGD*, 157, 158.

22. Ibid., 158–59.

23. Ibid., 165; *FL*, IV, 293.

Chapter 55. Do As the Romans Do

1. F: *TSBGD*, 139–40; *FL*, IV, 298.

2. F: *TSBGD*, 139; Stark, *Rise of Christianity*, 24.

3. S: *Mazzini*, 17–18, 51–52—Mazzini, qtd. 17; *FL*, IV, 95; Walicki, "National Messianism," 139–40; *FL*, I, 224. And see Abrams, *Correspondent Breeze*, 55–57.

4. *FL*, IV, 298, 299, 302; F: *TSBGD*, 169. And see *FL*, V, 86 for Fuller on the "taint" and "folly" of her earlier mystical dreams.

5. F: *TSBGD*, 163.

6. Ibid., 163–64.

7. Ibid., 163–66.

8. *FL*, IV, 285, 300. And see 278n3 and 297n2.

9. Margarett Crane qtd. in V: *M&TM*, 259. And see MCF to MF, 7 Feb. 1847, FFP: HM (fMS Am 1086 [8: 216]); and *FL*, IV, 278n2.

10. *FL*, IV, 278n2, 300; *FL*, V, 48, 48nn3 & 4; Deiss: *RYMF*, 82–83; V: *M&TM*, 258, 259. Richard (FR: *RRF*, 91) says that each sibling received from Abraham's estate $1,200. But much was in property and hence unavailable to Fuller in Italy.

11. *FL*, IV, 300.

12. V: *M&TM*, 259, 267; *FL*, IV, 283, 300.

13. Margarett Crane qtd. in Deiss: *RYMF*, 81; MCF to MF, 7 Oct. 1849, FFP: HM (fMS Am 1086 [8: 222]).

14. Margarett Crane qtd. in Deiss: *RYMF*, 81–82; MCF to MF, 7 Oct. 1849, FFP: HM (fMS Am 1086 [8: 222]). And see C: *MFPY*, 168.

15. Margarett Crane qtd. in Deiss: *RYMF*, 82. And see MCF to MF, 7 Oct. 1849, FFP: HM (fMS Am 1086 [8: 222]).

16. *FL*, IV, 299, 301–302; Deiss: *RYMF*, 84–85; F: *TSBGD*, 136n18. And see V: "MF&MQ," 135. Deiss: *RYMF* (85) says that Ossoli's coat as an officer of the civic guard was dark blue and red-corded, but a later observer describes it as the "dark brown, red-corded coat of the Guardia Civica." See C: *TW&TM*, 411. For Ossoli's possible part in securing Fuller an apartment see V: "EtF," 7.

17. V: *M&TM*, 269; *FL*, IV, 301, 297, 297n1.

18. V: *M&TM*, 269; F: *TSBGD*, 159; *FL*, IV, 312–13.

19. *FL*, IV, 301, 313; Deiss: *RYMF*, 89, 103.

20. *FL*, IV, 312, 301, 305, 306, 309, 298; F: *TSBGD*, 176n15.

21. *FL*, IV, 308–9, 312. Eddie (Edward Adolphus Spring [1837–1907]) with his stick suggests Randolph with his stick in Henry James's *Daisy Miller* (1878), just as Daisy's relationship with Eugenio resembles Fuller's with Ossoli. Their baby's name was Angelo Eugenio Filippo Ossoli. He was given the name Eugenio to honor Fuller's brother Eugene. See F: *TSBGD*, 74n9.

22. *FL*, IV, 312, 313.

23. Ibid., 313; *FL*, V, 299; C: *TW&TM*, 409; Deiss: *RYMF*, 54; C: *MFPY*, 298.

24. Deiss: *RYMF*, 86; C: *TW&TM*, 403–4.

25. C: *TW&TM*, 404–5; F: *TSBGD*, 178; Deiss: *RYMF*, 98–99; *FL*, IV, 309.

26. F: *TSBGD*, 155, 169, 172.

27. *FL*, IV, 303, 315.

28. Ibid., 310.

29. F: *TSBGD*, 170–71; E: *J&MN*, V, 188, 190.

---

30. *FL*, IV, 312; V: "EtF," 9; V: "MF&MQ," 134; Deiss: *RYMF*, 69, 116 (ill.). On soaring birds and Fuller see Steele, *Transfiguring America*, 95, 222.

31. *FL*, IV, 314–15; C: *TW&TM*, 532.

Chapter 56. Roman Winter

1. F: *TSBGD*, 177, 203, 206, 209; *FL*, V, 40, 46.

2. *FL*, V, 40, 43, 39; Shelley, *Alastor*, in *Shelley's Poetry and Prose*, 75.

3. *FL*, V, 40.

4. Ibid., 40, 40nn3–4, 57, 58nn1–5; *FL*, IV, 284n1.

5. *FL*, V, 41. And see V: *M&TM*, 276.

6. Ibid., 41–42.

7. Ibid., 42–43, 45n7; Rowland, "Genius of Parma," 4–6, 8–9; Wright, *Renaissance Masterpieces of Art and Architecture*, 108, 119–21.

8. *FL*, V, 42, 208; V: *M&TM*, 276; Deiss: *RYMF*, 129. And see *FL*, VI, 140; Shengold: *SM*, 6–7.

9. *FL*, V, 43; and see "gate of death" in Shelley, *Shelley's Poetry and Prose*, 75.

10. *FL*, V, 42–43; F: *WNC*, 65–66, 62.

11. *FL*, VI, 99; *FL*, V, 45–46.

12. *FL*, V, 46; *OM*, I, 139; *FL*, IV, 43n2. For Fuller's view of the woman she thinks is a prostitute, the one whom Nathan is supposedly helping but who is really his mistress, as "an injured woman," see *FL*, IV, 68. On Beatrice Cenci (1577–1599), the daughter of an Italian nobleman who forced her to enter into an incestuous relationship with him, see Reynolds, ed., *Woman*, 134n3.

13. *FL*, V, 51, 59; *OM*, I, 15; Shengold: *SM*, 6.

14. F: *TSBGD*, 229; R: *ER*, 62–63; Porte, *Representative Man*, 267.

15. F: *TSBGD*, 209.

16. Mazzini qtd. in Deiss: *RYMF*, 106–7; and V: *M&TM*, 273–74. And see F: *TSBGD*, 172; and Mazzini to MF, December 1847, FFP: HM (fMS Am 1086 [11:96, 97, 98, 99, MS copy]).

17. Deiss: *RYMF*, 101–2; F: *TSBGD*, 136n18.

18. F: *TSBGD*, 174–75.

19. Ibid., 175–76.

20. Ibid., 179, 187–88; Deiss: *RYMF*, 102.

21. See C: *TW&TM*, 378.

22. F: *TSBGD*, 163, 165–66.

23. Ibid., 179, 184, 186.

24. Ibid., 187, 187n4.

25. Ibid., 191, 189.

Chapter 57. More Rain and Revolutionaries' Conflicting Aims

1. *FL*, V, 59n2; Deiss: *RYMF*, 111; F: *TSBGD*, 146n18, 201–2.

2. S: *Mazzini*, 56; F: *TSBGD*, 183, 181n9; *FL*, V, 49n1.

3. S: *Mazzini*, 56; F: *TSBGD*, 202.

4. Quoted material appears in Deiss: *RYMF*, 110; And see S: *Mazzini*, 56–57.

5. F: *TSBGD*, 204–5, 204n11.

6. Ibid., 205.

7. See Fuller's translation of Mazzini's letter in F: *TSBGD*, 193–98.

8. F: *TSBGD*, 195–98.

9. *FL*, V, 49. And see Arconati Visconti qtd. in 49nn1–2.

10. See Arconati Visconti qtd. in V: *M&TM*, 283–84. On the Princess Belgioioso see F: *TSBGD*, 281; R: *ER*, 66. On her appearance see Deiss: *RYMF*, 119–20, 229.

11. *FL*, V, 51. On the Princess Belgioioso see Deiss: *RYMF*, 119–20, 121; V: *M&TM*, 278–79.

12. Constance Arconati Visconti to MF, 7 Feb. 1848, FFP: HM (fMS Am 1086 [11: 50]). And see R: *ER*, 66. See also Deiss: *RYMF*, 121 for Deiss's translation.

13. F: *TSBGD*, 203, 206.

Chapter 58. Personal and Political Rebellions

1. F: *TSBGD*, 206, 206n15; *FL*, IV, 61n7; *FL*, II, 58; B: *MFTtoR*, 122; Dall, "Caroline Dall's Reminiscences," 427.

2. Dall, "Caroline Dall's Reminiscences," 427; *FL*, V, 54–55.

3. F: *TSBGD*, 210.

4. *FL*, V, 55; E: *LofRWE*, IV, 25–28; C: *TW&TM*, 405; F: *WNC*, 62. The novel is Disraeli's *Contarini Fleming* (1832), which von Mehren notes in V: "MF&MQ," 117. On Alceste's death in childbirth see Disraeli, *Contarini Fleming*, 246–48.

5. See Deiss: *RYMF*, 97–98, 124–25. Von Mehren speculates regarding the possible influence of the behavior of the characters in Disraeli's *Contarini Fleming* on Fuller's own in deciding whether or not to marry. See V: "MF&MQ," 134.

6. *FL*, V, 51, 57. My information regarding the possibility of the Protestant Fuller marrying the devoutly Catholic Ossoli comes from V: "EtF," 4.

7. Ibid., 61.

8. Ibid., 60–61, 58, 59.

9. Ibid., 58, 59nn1–2; F: *TSBGD*, 209–10, 202n7; S: *Mazzini*, 56–58; Deiss: *RYMF*, 128, 130–31.

10. S: *Mazzini*, 57–58; Langer: *PSU*, 371–376; Deiss: *RYMF*, 130–31; *FL*, V, 59n2.

11. F: *TSBGD*, 210–11, 211n6. William Story describes the feast of the tapers in his diary, see ibid., 210n4.

12. Ibid., 212; *FL*, V, 58–59.

13. Wellisz: *FMF-AM*, 34, 28.

14. F: *TSBGD*, 216, and see 216nn12–13.

15. Ibid., 216. And see S: *Mazzini*, 58–62; Langer: *PSU*, 139.

16. F: *TSBGD*, 223–25. On the lasting effect of Fourier's thinking on Fuller, see Zwarg: *FC*, 13, 25–27, 52–55, 114–16, and so on.

17. F: *TSBGD*, 211; S: *Mazzini*, 218–20; Langer: *PSU*, 216. And see Wieseltier, "When a Sage Dies," 27–30. For Marx's influence on Fuller see Zwarg: *FC*, 6. For his influence on the 1848 revolutions, see R: *ER*, 2, 119–20.

18. See R: *ER*, 2; Russell, *History of Western Philosophy*, 782–86; *FL*, IV, 288; *FL*, V, 150; Abrams, *Correspondent Breeze*, 57; Langer: *PSU*, 216.

19. See *FL*, V, 71; R: *ER*, 2, 65, 74; Russell, *History of Western Philosophy*, 783–88; *OM*, I, 15.

20. See Fuller qtd. in C: *TW&TM*, 414. And see R: *ER*, 22–24, 56; *FL*, V, 71; Langer: *PSU*, 216.

21. F: *TSBGD*, 217n1; *FL*, V, 67n3; Langer: *PSU*, 346–50; R: *ER*, 32–33, 44–48.

22. See F: *TSBGD*, 225n5, 227–28 (original emphasis); *FL*, V, 65n3. Both Hudspeth and Reynolds use the term "Allocution."

23. F: *TSBGD*, 226–29, 231.

24. Ibid., 225, 230; and see Abrams, *Correspondent Breeze*, 57.

25. F: *TSBGD*, 230–31.

Chapter 59. A Love Higher than Law or Passion

1. *FL*, V, 63, 66; E: *LofRWE*, IV, 61.

2. *FL*, V, 66, 64. Recall Timothy harped on Fuller's "faults" as a child. See, for instance, *FL*, I, 97n7; TF to SMF, 12 Feb. 1824, FFP: HM (fMS Am 1086 [5:14]); and TF to SMF, 15 April 1824, FFP: HM (fMS Am 1086 [5:15]).

3. Costanza Arconati Visconti to MF, 13 April 1848, Milan, FFP: HM (fMS Am 1086 [11:50, MS copy]), and qtd. in V: *M&TM*, 283–84; *FL*, V, 68, 70–71. And see *FL*, IV, 47n on "Aunt" Mary Rotch.

4. *FL*, V, 69; Costanza Arconati Visconti to MF, 3 June 1848, Milan, FFP: HM (fMS Am 1086 [11:51, MS copy]).

5. F: *TSBGD*, 230; *FL*, V, 103, 66; V: *M&TM*, 282–83, 284. And see Rowland, "Titian," 15–16. As he painted Fuller's portrait, Hicks probably had in mind Titian's *Sacred and Profane Love*, the wedding portrait of the Paduan widow Laura Bagarotto, who married the Venetian official Nicolà Aurelio.

6. *FL*, V, 74–75, 76–77.

7. Ibid., 77.

8. Ibid., 78, 79, 85, 93, 101. Emelyn Story recollects how Fuller told Ossoli that she would be merely his "friend." See C: *TW&TM*, 405.

9. *FL*, V, 79, 83, 84n3, 87, 88; F: *TSBGD*, 234.

10. *FL*, V, 82, 83n2, 103–4.

11. On the Fuller-Greeley interaction, see *FL*, V, 83nn1–2, 90, 96–97.

12. Deiss: *RYMF*, 157; *FL*, V, 208, 101, 199; F: *TSBGD*, 237.

13. *FL*, V, 104, 98, 208; Deiss: *RYMF*, 157; V: *M&TM*, 284–86; F: *TSBGD*, 237. Deiss: *RYMF* says the landlord is Giovanni Papetti on Bondara Street; Hudspeth says he is Giovanni Fassetti on Vedana Street; and von Mehren says he is Giovanni Rossetti. See Deiss: *RYMF*, 160; Hudspeth's translation in *FL*, V, 98; V: *M&TM*, 286. The Houghton librarian I consulted thought it was Fassetti on Vendana Street. I refer to him as Rossetti on Vendana Street.

14. *FL*, V, 86; E: *E&L*, 75; F: *TSBGD*, 237. See Grimal, *Dictionary of Classical Mythology*, 97, 131–33, for information on Ceres, the Roman name for the Greek goddess Demeter, Mother Goddess of the Earth, "the Corn Goddess."

15. *FL*, V, 79, 100; and see the English translation of letter, GAO to MF, 13 June 1848, FFP: HM (fMS Am 1086 [Works II: 1]).

16. *FL*, V, 59n2, 97n1, 102n1; F: *TSBGD*, 236–37, 232, 232n3; Deiss: *RYMF*, 160; S: *Mazzini*, 62–63. And see D. M. Smith, *Making of Italy*, 155.

17. *FL*, V, 100nn1–2, 102n1; F: *TSBGD*, 232. Several volunteer divisions of troops apparently formed at this time to defend Rome.

18. *FL*, V, 99, 100n2, 102, 102n1; F: *TSBGD*, 236–37.

19. GAO qtd. in V: *M&TM*, 286. For a listing of various regular and volunteer units that formed to fight in behalf of the Republic see Viotti, *Garibaldi*, 52.

20. *FL*, V, 107; V: "EtF," 7; Deiss: *RYMF*, 159. Fuller says Ossoli was working for his uncle but does not give a name. Von Mehren says Ossoli's Uncle Antonio had been dead since 1842 (43?). See V: "MF&MQ," 135, 138n18.

21. *FL*, V, 108, 109; V: *M&TM*, 285; Deiss: *RYMF*, 165.

22. *FL*, V, 110, 111. On the marriage question in general see V: "EtF," 4–5; V: *M&TM*, 316; V: "MF&MQ," 123, 127, 129. And see FFP: HM (fMS Am 1086 [Works II: 137]). See also MF's 4 June 1849 letter to GAO, which, according to my Italian translator, reads: "How much I suffered yesterday, as you can believe, to see again [my] very dear *husband,* as the mean Giovanni used always to write" (*FL*, V, 237). Houghton's translation is similar: "How much I suffered yesterday you can believe. Till we meet again, dear *Consorte,* as that wicked Ser. Giovanni always wrote." See FFP: HM (fMS Am 1086 [Works II: 221]). See also the original in Italian in the Houghton: MF to GAO, 4 June 1849, FFP: HM (fMS Am 1086 [9: 215]).

23. E: *J&MN*, XI, 508; V: "MF&MQ," 127–29; Ossoli qtd. in Deiss: *RYMF,* 174–75.

24. See *FL*, V, 111, 113—and translated into English: GAO to MF, 8 Sept. 1848; MF to GAO, 7 Sept. 1848; MF to GAO, 9 Sept. 1848 in FFP: HM (fMS Am 1086 [Works II: 29–31, 137, 139–41]).

25. See V: *M&TM,* 316; V: "MF&MQ," 127; Fredrika Brener and Sarah Clarke qtd. in V: *M&TM,* 320, 324; WHC qtd. in C: *TW&TM,* 415; E: *J&MN,* XI, 463. Zwarg assumes Fuller's and Ossoli's was a "Fourieristic marriage." See Zwarg: *FC,* 244.

26. *FL*, IV, 68, 70; V: "EtF," 4; V: "MF&MQ," 134.

27. Virgil: RF, 107. And see Hawthorne, *Blithedale Romance,* 231–38.

28. *FL*, V, 208, 121; Deiss: *RYMF,* 153; V: "EtF," 4, 10; Disraeli, *Contarini Fleming* (1832), 237.

29. V: "EtF," 4; *FL*, V, 285. And see Hawthorne, *Scarlet Letter,* 163. Joel Porte long ago reminded me of Hawthorne's remark about Hester Prynne and Margaret Fuller. Numerous critics have, in Sacvan Bercovitch's words, "argued persuasively that [Fuller] figures" in Hawthorne's "portrait of the tormented radical, Hester Prynne." See Sacvan Bercovitch, "Hawthorne's A-Morality of Compromise," *Representations* 24 (fall 1988): 1–27. See also, for instance, Francis E. Kearns, "Margaret Fuller as a Model for Hester Prynne," *Jahrbuch für Amerikastudien* 10 (1965): 191–97; and Chevigny, "To the Edges of Ideology."

30. See Wieland: *SO,* 103.

31. See F: *WNC,* 72–79, for Fuller on Panthea's "true marriage."

32. See V: *M&TM,* 341; F: *WNC,* 185. And see Zwarg: *FC,* 11; Steele, *Transfiguring America,* 209–27.

33. See R: *ER,* 54–78, esp. 64 and 74.

Part Eight. Apocalyptic Dreams and the Fall of Rome

1. See Wessell, *Karl Marx,* 85; Becker, *Denial of Death,* 35–36.

2. Wessell, *Karl Marx,* 24.

3. R: *ER,* 62–78; *FL*, V, 145.

Chapter 60. Harsh Reality and Apocalyptic Dreams

1. *FL*, V, 112, 116, 115, 117.

2. Ibid., 134, 124, 124n1, 121, 98, 141, 249.

3. Ibid., 141, 135, 134, 121, 141. See also V: *M&TM,* 287–88.

4. *FL*, V, 118, 122n1.

5. Ibid., 127, 131.

6. Ibid., 139, 294.

7. Ibid., 143, 129. See V: "EtF," 4, 7, 10; E: *J&MN,* XI, 508; V: "MF&MQ," 123–25, 126–28. See also V: *M&TM,* 288; Deiss: *RYMF,* 170–71, and 174, 178–79.

8. *FL*, V, 144, 137, 118, 209, 157.

9. Ibid., 84n3, 102n1, 139; F: *TSBGD*, 232.

10. *FL*, V, 153–54; V: *M&TM*, 288. And see R: *ER*, 67, 74.

11. For Fuller's 16 Nov. 1848 letter, which is discussed in this and the next seven paragraphs, see *FL*, V, 145–50, 150nn3–4. For other citations see F: *TSBGD*, 169, 231, 245–46, 278; *FL*, V, 205; *OM*, I, 28; and Rev. 4:6, 12:3–17, 21:1–4 RSV.

12. F: *TSBGD*, 245–46.

13. Ibid., 243–44, 244n14. And see *FL*, V, 159n1.

14. F: *TSBGD*, 278–79, 271, 284; E: *E&L*, 75.

Chapter 61. The Lull before the Storm

1. *FL*, V, 145.

2. Ibid., 150, 147, 145; *FL*, IV, 45, 181; O: *AL&D*, 86.

3. *FL*, V, 218, 220, 117.

4. Ibid., 158, 159n1, 161, 163, 163n1; Deiss: *RYMF*, 189–90.

5. Ibid., 209, 210, 163–65. And see Fuller qtd. in Deiss: *RYMF*, 191. Both Hudspeth's and the Houghton's versions of this letter call Nino's disease smallpox, but if he had smallpox at this point, he would not again have had it on the *Elizabeth* sailing home. Deiss: *RYMF* calls it "a dreadful pox—probably chicken pox," which is more likely. See FFP: HM (fMS Am 1086 [Works II: 199]). Now missing (since 1973) is the original picture of Baby Jesus that Fuller had attached to the page. See MF to CS, 16 March 1849, FFP: HM (fMS Am 1086 [9:170]).

6. *FL*, V, 166, 170n2. And see Rostenberg, "Roman Diary," 211.

7. Rostenberg, "Roman Diary," 211–13; F: *TSBGD*, 251–53, 253n6.

8. F: *TSBGD*, 250. And see Deiss: *RYMF*, 196.

9. S: *Mazzini*, 58–63.

10. *FL*, V, 169–70, 188, 190n2, 171; Rostenberg, "Roman Diary," 215.

11. *FL*, V, 176–78, 179n1, 185–86, 187n1. And V: *M&TM*, 293.

12. *FL*, V, 186, 172. And see *FL*, V, 173n5, where Hudspeth notes that at the time of her death on 3 Nov. 1848, Cary's sister was married to Robert Hooper, a Boston physician. She was the mother of three children, the youngest of whom, Marian (called Clover), married Henry Adams in 1872.

13. Ibid., 174–75, 175n2.

14. S: *Mazzini*, 62–64, 64–65; F: *TSBGD*, 254–58, 255n4, 262; Rostenberg, "Roman Diary," 216–17. The Republic was declared on the evening of 8–9 Feb. 1849; Mazzini did not make it to Rome until 5 March.

15. *FL*, V, 201, 202.

16. Ibid., 210.

17. F: *TSBGD*, 264; *FL*, V, 198.

18. *FL*, V, 258, 205–6.

19. Ibid., 205–6; F: *TSBGD*, 271. For Fuller misquoting "chartered libertine" from *Henry V*, see Porte, *Representative Man*, 219.

20. F: *TSBGD*, 269, 271. And see MF to RRF, 19 Jan. 1849, *FL*, V, 179.

21. *FL*, V, 179, 201; Mazzini qtd. in S: *Mazzini*, 65; F: *TSBGD* 263.

22. F: *TSBGD*, 262, 264; Mazzini qtd. in S: *Mazzini*, 65.

23. F: *TSBGD*, 264; *FL*, V, 201, emphasis added.

24. *FL*, V, 198–99, 209; Deiss: *RYMF*, 204–5; V: *M&TM*, 295. Compare Fuller's language here with that she uses to tell about the "broken" life of Beatrice Cenci in the appendix of her tract. See F: *WNC*, 199.

25. *FL*, V, 216–17, 210; *OM*, I, 14–16.

Chapter 62. Deceit and Treachery

1. Deiss: *RYMF,* 211–12. Even if Ossoli had the document prepared for her, Fuller still colluded in hiding facts about her identity from bureaucrats in the Office of Public Security of the Roman Republic. Von Mehren offers another explanation; see V: *M&TM,* 299. And see V: "MF&MQ," 129.

2. Rostenberg, "Roman Diary," 219, 220; *FL,* V, 232n1, 223, 224n2.

3. *FL,* V, 12, 190n2; S: *Mazzini,* 69; Virgil: AM, 32–34.

4. For Fuller's reasons for moving see *FL,* V, 131, 166, 121. And see Hig: *MFO,* 264.

5. *FL,* V, 218, 220.

6. Ibid., 223; Deiss: *RYMF,* 212; V: *M&TM,* 298–99; F: *TSBGD,* 304–5. And see Trevelyan, *Garibaldi's Defence of the Roman Republic,* 100. See also Viotti, *Garibaldi,* 44, 48.

7. *FL,* V, 223. See Hudspeth on Madeline Stern's hypothesis about the marriage (*FL,* V, 224n1) and von Mehren (V: "MF&MQ," 118). For Fuller on Ossoli as "friend" in late June 1848 see *FL,* V, 79 and C: *TW&TM,* 405. For Fuller marking as important the day she first met Lewis Cass see *FL,* VI, 83. And see Deiss: *RYMF,* 162–63, 215.

8. See C: *TW&TM,* 406.

9. See Deiss: *RYMF,* 219, 224; V: *M&TM,* 300; S: *Mazzini,* 69–70; Viotti, *Garibaldi,* 48.

10. See Deiss: *RYMF,* 222; R: *ER,* 18, 22–24, 48–50, 76; C: *TW&TM,* 414; V: *M&TM,* 300; S: *Mazzini,* 69–70.

11. *FL,* V, 227n1; Oudinot qtd. in Deiss: *RYMF,* 224, 231–32; S: *Mazzini,* 70; Viotti, *Garibaldi,* 48–50; William Story qtd. in Deiss: *RYMF,* 231; F: *TSBGD,* 275, 285–86.

12. Deiss: *RYMF,* 223–24. And see Cass qtd. in V: *M&TM,* 301, and in Deiss: *RYMF,* 224.

13. S: *Mazzini,* 70; V: *M&TM,* 301; *FL* VI, 83; F: *TSBGD,* 275–76; Viotti, *Garibaldi,* 54; Virgil: AM, 309; Deiss: *RYMF,* 236–38.

14. F: *TSBGD,* 280; *FL,* VI, 83.

15. F: *TSBGD,* 280; Deiss: *RYMF,* 239, and Emelyn Story qtd. in Deiss: *RYMF,* 242.

16. *FL,* V, 227n1, 230n2; S: *Mazzini,* 70; Deiss: *RYMF,* 242–43.

17. Deiss: *RYMF,* 241; F: *TSBGD,* 277–78; S: *Mazzini,* 70–71.

18. F: *TSBGD,* 279–80.

19. *FL,* V, 229–30, 231; F: *TSBGD,* 284.

Chapter 63. The Fall of Rome

1. *FL,* V, 230, 232.

2. C: *TW&TM,* 407–408; Deiss: *RYMF,* 248; V: *M&TM,* 303–4.

3. *FL,* V, 229, 234n2; Deiss: *RYMF,* 243–45; S: *Mazzini,* 68, 70; Viotti, *Garibaldi,* 56.

4. S: *Mazzini,* 71–72; *FL,* V, 230n2, 234n2, 238; V: *M&TM,* 306; Viotti, *Garibaldi,* 59. And see Virgil: AM, 32–36.

5. *FL,* V, 238; Virgil: AM, 307–309; V: *M&TM,* 306–307. And see Viotti, *Garibaldi,* 60–61; Deiss: *RYMF,* 227, 229, 230 (ills.), and 253–57. For a detailed account of the 3 June battle, see Trevelyan, *Garibaldi's Defence of the Roman Republic,* 172–87, 124–25 (map), and map 173 ("Battle of Villa Corsini, June 3, and first part of siege, June 4–21").

6. *FL,* V, 238; V: *M&TM,* 307; Viotti, *Garibaldi,* 60–62.

7. *FL,* V, 239, 238.

8. FL, V, 236, 241. And see V: "MF&MQ," 122–23, 129; and V: *M&TM,* 304. Joan von Mehren, the source of my information about a marriage, was working in collaboration with Dr. Roberto Colzi (d. 2002), an Italian archivist-researcher who discovered "the record of the birth and baptism" of Fuller's son. See V: "MF&MQ," 104.

9. *FL*, V, 239.

10. Ibid., 187, 240. See Luke 5:12–13 RSV: "While he was in one of the cities, there came a man full of leprosy; and when he saw Jesus, he . . . besought him, 'Lord, . . . make me clean.' And he stretched out his hand, and touched him, saying, 'I will; be clean.' And . . . the leprosy left him."

11. See Virgil: AM, 87; *FL*, V, 293; Fredrika Bremer qtd. in V: *M&TM*, 320.

12. Lewis Cass Jr., U.S. chargé d'affaires, to Mrs. W. E. Channing, 10 May 1851, FFP: HM (fMS Am 1086 [Works I: 669–775]).

13. C: *TW&TM*, 405–6.

14. *FL*, V, 239, 258.

15. Ibid., 302, 258, 293, 241, 295–96.

16. F: *TSBGD*, 303; Deiss: *RYMF*, 264–66; Viotti, *Garibaldi*, 65–67. For Trevelyan's account, "The Siege of Rome, June 4–29," see *Garibaldi's Defence of the Roman Republic*, 194–216.

17. See Deiss: *RYMF*, 265–66; V: *M&TM*, 309.

18. F: *TSBGD*, 304; Trevelyan, *Garibaldi's Defence*, 229–34; Viotti, 67–68.

19. See Deiss: *RYMF*, 270, and Mazzini qtd, 269; *FL*, V, 247; V: *M&TM*, 310.

20. *FL*, V, 242, 244.

21. Ibid., 244, 260–61, 262, 267.

22. Ibid., 283. And see C: *TW&TM*, 410–11.

23. R: *ER*, 18; F: *TSBGD*, 320. And see 321.

24. F: *TSBGD*, 310–11.

Chapter 64. Last Illusions

1. *FL*, V, 243, 247, 259, 242; F: *TSBGD*, 308, 312.

2. *FL*, V, 249, 246. And see F: *TSBGD*, 308n7.

3. *FL*, V, 248.

4. Ibid., 269, 250, 248.

5. Ibid., 248, 303, 264. And see Mrs. Hasty's narrative in O: *AH&A*, 451.

6. *FL*, V, 253, 254; Deiss: *RYMF*, 285. And see V: "EtF," 3.

7. *FL*, VI, 58, 77; *FL*, V, 301. And see C: *TW&TM*, 411, 414; and Browning qtd. in V: *M&TM*, 321.

8. *FL*, V, 278, 283; *FL*, VI, 55.

9. F: *TSBGD*, 320; *FL*, VI, 58, 51. On Fuller's dream of returning to the U.S. and living "in obscure quiet" with her small family and mother see *FL*, V, 284, 298–99. For Fuller on her Uncle Peter's "prodigal" journey see *FL*, III, 165. See also *FL*, II, 195 on Lloyd as "our prodigal son." For Fuller on herself as a "returning prodigal," see "Mariana" in F: *SL*, 93. And see F: *WNC*, 1. See also the undated letter to Anna Barker Ward wherein she summarizes the parable, *FL*, VI, 122–23. See also her Dec. 1848 letter to Richard from Rome wherein she alludes to the prodigal son, *FL*, V, 160.

10. *FL*, V, 260 (emphasis added), 298; *FL*, VI, 145; Margarett Crane qtd. in Deiss: *RYMF*, 282–83. Fuller's mother had both Revelation and the story of the prodigal son in mind in this 3 Nov. 1849 letter. See Rev. 21:1–4 and Luke 15:18–24 RSV. See also *FL*, V, 304, where Margaret tells Cary how her good mother had "blessed" her.

11. *FL*, VI, 58, 59; F: *TSBGD*, 320. On Horace Sumner see *FL*, V, 277n4.

12. *FL*, VI, 86; *FL*, V, 271–73.

13. FL, V, 269–70, 280.

14. Horace Greeley to MF, 23 July 1849, FFP: HM (fMS Am 1086 [10:57]).

15. *FL*, V, 255.

16. Ibid., 257.

17. Ibid., 259–60.

18. Ibid., 293, 303.

19. *FL*, VI, 76, 52, and 52n1; *FL*, V, 267. These are von Mehren's thoughts and facts. See V: *M&TM*, 316, and V: "MF&MQ," 121–22, where von Mehren quotes from the letters of Ossoli and Suárra.

20. *FL*, VI, 52; *FL*, V, 283, 296–97. Her publisher was Wiley and Putnam. And see V: *M&TM*, 322.

21. *FL*, V, 283, 292, 300. And on Fuller and Ossoli as an unfit "connexion," see ibid., 283.

22. Ibid., 292, 248, 261, 304–5, 270; Hawthorne, *Scarlet Letter*, 80; V: "MF&MQ," 130–31.

23. *FL*, VI, 47; *FL*, V, 306.

24. *FL*, 305; F: *TSBGD*, 321–22.

25. F: *TSBGD*, 323, 316; *FL*, V, 251. And see *FL*, V, 251, 269.

26. See C. Day Lewis's translation of these lines from Vergil, *Aeneid*, 4: 175–77 in *FL*, I, 227n4. Fuller had cited these lines in Latin in her 6 March 1835 letter to Hedge: *FL*, I, 226. See also *FL*, V, 293, and V: *M&TM*, 328.

27. *FL*, V, 300; *FL*, VI, 57, 99.

28. *FL*, V, 303, 285, 269. And see James, *William Wetmore Story and His Friends*, I, 130.

29. Emelyn Story qtd. in V: *M&TM*, 324–25; Margarett Crane qtd. in Deiss: *RYMF*, 283. And see *FL*, VI, 74.

30. MCF to MF, 16 June 1850, FFP: HM (fMS Am 1086 [8: 223]); and MCF to RFF, 28 June 1850, FFP: HM (fMS Am 1086 [16: 164]). And see *FL*, III, 165–67. And on "pious" Puritan "fathers" see FR: *CF*, 21. Numerous authors write of the stern "Puritan fathers." See, for instance, Deiss: *RYMF*, 190.

31. *FL*, VI, 76, 51, 55, 64. And see Reynolds and Belasco Smith, intro. to F: *TSBGD*, 34.

32. Ibid., 60, 75, 66; V: *M&TM*, 330.

33. *FL*, VI, 66, 75, 70, 69; V: *M&TM*, 301. And see O: *AH&A*, 451, where the nursemaid's name is Celesta Pardena. Channing says the nursemaid's name is Celeste Paolini. See *OM*, II, 338.

34. *FL*, VI, 69.

35. Ibid., 79, 74, 81, 83. See also V: *M&TM*, 331.

36. *FL*, VI, 81.

37. Ibid., 75, 86. And see *FL*, I, 97n7, for Timothy on Fuller's major *fault*.

38. *FL*, VI, 83.

39. Ibid., 83, 85–86, 86–87.

40. Barrett Browning in C: *TW&TM*, 414. And see V: *M&TM*, 321.

Chapter 65. A Wayward Pilgrim Journeys Home

1. Rebecca Spring to MF, 14 April 1850 (Rose Cottage), FFP: HM (fMS Am 1086 [11: 136]); Marcus Spring to MF, 17 April 1850 (Brooklyn), FFP: HM (fMS Am 1086 [11: 136]), original emphasis. And see *FL*, VI, 88–89nn1–2; F: *WNC*, 74.

2. RWE to MF, 11 April 1850, E: *LofRWE*, IV, 198–99; *FL*, V, 240; and Hawthorne, *Scarlet Letter*, 251. Dimmesdale, in asking Hester Prynne to help him up onto the scaffold, "extended his hand to the woman of the scarlet letter."

3. *FL*, V, 240, 299, 291, 283; *FL*, VI, 76; Sophocles, *Antigone*, 220; Grimal, *Dictionary of Classical Mythology*, 51.

4. *FL*, VI, 76n1, 89–90, 91; V: *M&TM*, 333. On the deadly progress of a smallpox infection see Broad, "Smallpox: The Once and Future Scourge?" sec. D1.

5. *FL*, VI, 91, 89.

6. Ibid., 89. And see Fuller, "Dreaming with Anna," in C: *TW&TM*, 532.

7. *FL*, VI, 89–90.

8. Ibid., 69; O: *AH&A*, 448. From a reporter's conversation with Mrs. Hasty about "The Wreck of the Elizabeth." And see V: *M&TM*, 333.

9. See "Fatal Wreck: Dreadful Loss of Life—S. Margaret Fuller Drowned," *New-York Daily Tribune*, 27 July 1850. Reprinted as "Letter of Bayard Taylor," in O: *AH&A*, 444–48. And see Mrs. Hasty's account of "The Wreck of the Elizabeth," in O: *AH&A*, 448–51; V: *M&TM*, 334; Deiss: *RYMF*, 311; Baker, *Emerson among the Eccentrics*, 313. On the gods using Oedipus as an instrument and example, see Robert Fitzgerald's commentary on Oedipus at Colonus in Sophocles, *Oedipus Cycle*, 176.

10. O: *AH&A*, 449–50; *OM*, II, 343.

11. Ibid., 445, 449–50. Men on shore said they would have lowered a lifeboat had they known "persons of *importance*" were aboard the sinking ship. See WHC, "To T. W. Higginson," letter from London discussing the "details of shipwreck fatal to M.F.O.," 5 Jan. 1884. Fuller Family Papers. Boston Public Library. Quoted by permission of the Boston Public Library/Rare Books Department.

12. See "Letter of Bayard Taylor," in O: *AH&A*, 445; and *OM*, II, 338n, 346–47. Evidence indicates Fuller could swim. Surely no woman would go alone at night to "bathe" in New York's East River, as she did, unless she could swim. Fuller had written Richard asking him to send her "bathing dress" so she might go "bathing" in the river. And from New York, she wrote Nathan how his puppy had to be thrown in before it would swim. Fuller herself suggests she can swim when in her Christmas 1847 letter to Emerson she says, "I am tired of keeping myself up in the water without corks, and without strength to swim." See *FL*, IV, 137, 119, 114, 314.

13. *OM*, II, 348. And see the translation of the letter from GAO to MF, 16 Sept. 1848, FFP: HM (fMS Am 1086 [Works II: 35, 37]).

14. Fuller, "Dreaming with Anna," in C: *TW&TM*, 532. And see *FL*, V, 240.

15. F: *TSBGD*, 76.

16. *FL*, II, 224–25. And see Whitman, "A Word Out of the Sea," in *Leaves of Grass*, 277. Whitman was apparently influenced by Fuller, whose *Tribune* columns it is "likely," says Reynolds, he read. For certain, says Reynolds, Whitman read Fuller's account of her night on Ben Lomond. See R: *ER*, 137.

17. *FL*, IV, 228; V: *M&TM*, 335; "Letter of Bayard Taylor" in O: *AH&A*, 446; "The Wreck of the Elizabeth," O: *AH&A*, 450; *OM*, II, 345; Deiss: *RYMF*, 312.

18. "Letter of Bayard Taylor" in O: *AH&A*, 445; *FL*, V, 303; *FL*, VI, 77. And see "Fatal Wreck. Dreadful Loss of Life," and other articles on the wreck in *New-York Daily Tribune*, 24 July 1850, FFP: HM (bMS Am 1086 [B]).

19. *FL*, VI, 74; *FL*, V, 293; "Letter of Bayard Taylor," in O: *AH&A*, 446.

20. *FL*, VI, 90. And see "Letter of Bayard Taylor," in O: *AH&A*, 446; and "Fatal Wreck," FFP: HM (bMS Am 1086 [B]).

21. *OM*, II, 349; and see "Fatal Wreck," FFP: HM (bMS Am 1086 [B]); *FL*, IV, 77. And see WHC, "To T. W. Higginson," 5 Jan. 1884.

22. See WHC, "To T. W. Higginson," 5 Jan. 1884; "The Wreck of the Elizabeth; Mrs. Hasty's Narrative," in O: *AH&A*, 450; *FL*, VI, 76–77.

23. Cary Tappan qtd. in V: *M&TM*, 338–39; Sophocles, *Antigone*, 220; E: *J&MN*, XI, 256.

24. *FL*, VI, 77; E: *J&MN*, XI, 258; Emerson, Thoreau, and Barlow qtd. in V: *M&TM*, 337–38. On "white arms" as "death," see F: *SL*, 100.

Bibliography

Aaron, Daniel. *Men of Good Hope: A Story of American Progressives.* New York: Oxford University Press, 1951.

Abrams, M. H. *The Correspondent Breeze: Essays on English Romanticism.* New York: Norton, 1984.

———. "The Deconstructive Angel." *Critical Inquiry* 3 (1977): 425–38.

———. "Introduction: Two Roads to Wordsworth." In *Wordsworth: A Collection of Critical Essays,* edited by M. H. Abrams, 1–11. Englewood Cliffs, N.J.: Prentice-Hall, 1972.

———. *The Mirror and the Lamp: Romantic Theory and the Critical Tradition.* New York: Norton, 1953.

———. *Natural Supernaturalism: Tradition and Revolution in Romantic Literature.* New York: Norton, 1971.

———. "*The Prelude* and *The Recluse:* Wordsworth's Long Journey Home." In *Wordsworth: A Collection of Critical Essays,* edited by M. H. Abrams, 156–69. Englewood Cliffs, N.J.: Prentice-Hall, 1972.

———. "*The Prelude* as a Portrait of the Artist." In *Bicentenary Wordsworth Studies in Memory of John Alban Finch,* edited by Jonathan Wordsworth. Ithaca: Cornell University Press, 1970.

Acton, William. *The Functions and Disorders of the Re-productive Organs [in Childhood,] in Youth, in Adult Age and in Advanced Life, Considered in Their Physiological, Social, and Psychological Relations.* London: John Chandler, 1857.

Addison, John. *The Works of Anacreon, Translated into English Verse; with Notes Explanatory and Poetical. To Which are Added the Odes, Fragments, and Epigrams of Sappho. With the original Greek placed opposite to the Translation.* London: n.p., 1735.

Ainsworth, Mary D. S., and Robert S. Marvin. "On the Shaping of Attachment Theory And Research: An Interview with Mary D. S. Ainsworth (Fall 1994)." In Waters, Vaughn, Posada, and Kondo-Ikemura, 3–21.

Alcorn, Marshall W., and Mark Bracher. "Literature, Psychoanalysis, and the Re-Formation of the Self: A New Direction for Reader-Response Theory." *PMLA* 100 (1985): 342–52.

Alexander, Meena. *The Poetic Self: Towards a Phenomenology of Romanticism.* Atlantic Highlands, N.J.: Humanities Press, 1979.

———. *Women in Romanticism.* Savage, Md.: Barnes & Noble Books, 1989.

Allen, Margaret Vanderhaar. *The Achievement of Margaret Fuller.* University Park: Penn State Press, 1979.

Alvarez, A. *Night: Night Life, Night Language, Sleep, and Dreams.* New York: Norton, 1995.

Anthony, Katharine. *Margaret Fuller: A Psychological Biography.* New York: Harcourt, 1921.

Appiah, K. Anthony. "The Marrying Kind." Review of *The Case for Same-Sex Marriage,* by William N. Eskridge, and *Virtually Normal: An Argument About Homosexuality,* by Andrew Sullivan. *New York Review of Books,* 20 June 1996, 48–54.

Ariosto, Lodovico. *Sir John Harrington's Translation of Orlando Furioso.* Edited by Graham Hough. Carbondale: Southern Illinois University Press, 1962.

Aspiz, Harold. "Walt Whitman: The Spermatic Imagination." *American Literature* 56, no. 3 (1984): 379–95.

Bailey, Philip James. *Festus: A Poem.* London: George Routledge & Sons, 1901.

Baker, Carlos. *Emerson among the Eccentrics: A Group Portrait.* Introduction and epilogue by James R. Mellow. New York: Viking, 1996.

Balzac, Honoré de. *The Girl with the Golden Eyes.* Translated by Carol Cosman. New York: Carroll & Graf, 1998.

Barish, Evelyn. *Emerson: The Roots of Prophecy.* Princeton: Princeton University Press, 1989.

Barkan, Leonard. *The Gods Made Flesh: Metamorphosis and the Pursuit of Paganism.* New Haven: Yale University Press, 1986.

Barker-Benfield, Ben. "The Spermatic Economy: A Nineteenth-Century View of Sexuality." In *The American Family in Social-Historical Perspective,* edited by Michael Gordon, 336–72. New York: St. Martin's, 1973.

Barker-Benfield, G. J. *The Horrors of the Half-Known Life: Male Attitudes Toward Women and Sexuality in Nineteenth-Century America.* New York: Harper Colophon Books, 1976.

Barry, Joseph. *Infamous Woman: The Life of George Sand.* New York: Doubleday, 1978.

Bean, Judith Mattson, and Joel Myerson, editors. *Margaret Fuller, Critic: Writings from the New-York Tribune, 1844–1846.* New York: Columbia University Press, 2000.

Beard, Mary R. *Woman as Force in History: A Study in Traditions and Realities.* New York: MacMillan, 1946.

Becker, Ernest. *The Denial of Death.* New York: Free Press, 1973.

Beecher, Jonathan. *Charles Fourier: The Visionary and His World.* Berkeley: University of California Press, 1986.

Bercovitch, Sacvan. "Emerson the Prophet: Romanticism, Puritanism, and Auto-American Biography." In *Emerson: Prophecy, Metamorphosis, and Influence,* edited by David Levin, 1–27. New York: Columbia University Press, 1975.

———. "Hawthorne's A-Morality of Compromise." *Representations* 24 (fall 1988): 1–27.

Berlin, Isaiah. *Against the Current: Essays in the History of Ideas.* Edited by Henry Hardy. Introduced by Roger Hausheer. New York: Viking, 1980.

———. "Herder and the Enlightenment." In *Vico and Herder: Two Studies in the History of Ideas,* 143–216. New York: Viking, 1976.

Biallas, Leonard J. *Myths: Gods, Heroes, and Saviors.* Mystic, Conn.: Twenty-Third, 1986.

Bishop, Jonathan. *Emerson on the Soul.* Cambridge: Harvard University Press, 1964.

———. *Something Else.* New York: George Braziller, 1972.

Blakeslee, Sandra. "Out of Body Experience? Your Brain Is to Blame." *New York Times,* 3 October 2006, sec. D1, 6.

Blanchard, Paula. *Margaret Fuller: From Transcendentalism to Revolution.* New York: Delacorte, 1978.

Bliss, Sylvester. *Memoirs of William Miller: Generally Known as a Lecturer on the Prophecies, and the Second Coming of Christ.* Boston: Joshua V. Himes, 1853. Reprint, N.p.: AMS Press, 1971.

Bloch, Dorothy. *"So the Witch Won't Eat Me": Fantasy and the Child's Fear of Infanticide.* Boston: Houghton Mifflin, 1978.

Bloom, Harold. *The Anxiety of Influence: A Theory of Poetry.* New York: Oxford University Press, 1973.

————. *A Map of Misreading.* New York: Oxford University Press, 1975.

Blount, Paul G. *George Sand and the Victorian World.* Athens: University of Georgia Press, 1979.

Bobbé, Dorothie. *Mr. and Mrs. John Quincy Adams: An Adventure in Patriotism.* New York: Minton, Balch & Co., 1930.

Boiardo, Matteo Maria. *Orlando Innamorato.* Edited by Anne Finnigan. Translated by Charles Stanley Ross. Berkeley: University of California Press, 1989.

Borch-Jacobsen, Mikkel. *Remembering Anna O.: A Century of Mystification.* Translated by Kirby Olson. New York: Routledge, 1996.

Bouwsma, William J. *John Calvin: A Sixteenth-Century Portrait.* New York: Oxford University Press, 1988.

Braude, Ann. *Radical Spirits: Spiritualism and Women's Rights in Nineteenth-Century America.* Boston: Beacon, 1989.

[Briggs, Charles F.] Review of *Woman in the Nineteenth Century,* by S. Margaret Fuller. *Broadway Journal* 1, no. 8 (22 March 1845). In *Critical Essays on Margaret Fuller,* edited by Myerson, 8–15.

Brigham, Amariah. *Remarks on the Influence of Mental Cultivation and Mental Excitement on Health.* Boston: Marsh, Capen & Lyon, 1833.

Broad. William J. "Smallpox: The Once and Future Scourge?" *New York Times,* 15 June 1999, sec. D1+.

[Brownson, Orestes A.] "Miss Fuller and Reformers." *Brownson's Quarterly Review* 7 (April 1845), 249–57. In *Critical Essays on Margaret Fuller,* edited by Myerson, 19–25.

Bryant, William. "Where the Son Shines." Sermon, First Presbyterian Church. Columbus, Georgia, 30 May 1996.

Buell, Lawrence. *Emerson.* Cambridge: Harvard University Press, 2003.

Bunyan, John. *The Pilgrim's Progress from This World to That Which Is to Come.* Edited by Roger Sharrock. 2d ed. London: Oxford University Press, 1960.

Burlet, Peggy. "Headache: A Special Report." *The Harvard Health Letter.* Rev. ed. Cambridge: Harvard Medical School Publications Group, 1999.

Byron, Lord George. *Byron's Letters and Journals.* Edited by Leslie A. Marchand. 12 vols. Cambridge: Harvard University Press, 1973–82.

————. *Byron's Poetry.* Edited by Frank D. McConnell. Norton Critical Edition. New York: Norton, 1978.

Cambridge Historical Commission. *Survey of Architectural History in Cambridge.* Vol. 3, *Cambridgeport.* Cambridge: Massachusetts Institute of Technology Press, 1971.

Capper, Charles. *Margaret Fuller: An American Romantic Life, the Private Years.* New York: Oxford University Press, 1992.

————. "Margaret Fuller as Cultural Reformer: The Conversations in Boston." *American Quarterly* 39, no. 4 (1987): 509–28.

Cardiff, Ira D. *What Great Men Think of Religion.* New York: Arno Press and *The New York Times,* 1972.

Carlyle, Thomas. *Past and Present.* Introduction by G. K. Chesterton. 1909. London: Oxford University Press, 1965.

————. "Signs of the Times." In *Carlyle: Selected Works, Reminiscences and Letters,* edited by Julian Symonds, 19–44. Cambridge: Harvard University Press, 1970.

Carter, Jimmy. *Living Faith.* New York: Times Books, 1996.

Carter, Ray Cecil. "Margaret Fuller and the Two Sages." *Colby Library Quarterly* 6 (1963): 198–201.

Cavell, Stanley. "Being Odd, Getting Even (Descartes, Emerson, Poe)." In *The American Face of Edgar Allan Poe*, edited by Shawn Rosenheim and Stephen Rachman, 3–36. Baltimore: Johns Hopkins University Press, 1995.

Cavendish, Richard, ed. *An Illustrated Encyclopedia of Mythology*. New York: Crescent, 1980.

Cayton, Mary Kupiec. *Emerson's Emergence: Self and Society in the Transformation of New England, 1800–1845*. Chapel Hill: University of North Carolina Press, 1989.

Channing, William Ellery. "Unitarian Christianity: Discourse at the Ordination of the Rev. Jared Sparks, Baltimore, 1819." In *Unitarian Christianity and Other Essays*, edited and introduced by Irving H. Bartlett, 3–38. New York: Bobbs-Merrill, 1957.

Chevigny, Bell Gale. "Daughters Writing: Toward a Theory of Women's Biography." *Feminist Studies* 9 (1983): 357–79.

———. "To the Edges of Ideology: Margaret Fuller's Centrifugal Evolution." *American Quarterly* 38, no. 2 (1986): 173–201.

———. *The Woman and the Myth: Margaret Fuller's Life and Writings*. Rev. ed. Boston: Northeastern University Press, 1994.

Cheyfitz, Eric. *The Trans-Parent: Sexual Politics in the Language of Emerson*. Baltimore: Johns Hopkins University Press, 1981.

Child, Lydia Maria. *The Mother's Book*. 2d ed. Boston: Carter & Hendee, 1831.

———. "Woman in the Nineteenth Century." *Broadway Journal* 1 (1845): 97. In *Critical Essays on Margaret Fuller*, edited by Myerson, 7.

Clarke, James Freeman. *The Letters of James Freeman Clarke to Margaret Fuller*. Edited by John Wesley Thomas. Hamburg, Germany: Cram de Gruyter & Co., 1957.

Clifford, Deborah Pickman. *Mine Eyes Have Seen the Glory: A Biography of Julia Ward Howe*. Boston: Little, Brown, 1978.

Coale, Samuel Chase. *Mesmerism and Hawthorne: Mediums of American Romance*. Tuscaloosa: University of Alabama Press, 1998.

Cole, Hubert. *Beau Brummell*. New York: Mason/Charter, 1977.

Coleridge, S. T. *Biographia Literaria*. Edited by J. Shawcross. 2 vols. 1907. Reprint, London: Oxford University Press, 1965.

———. *Samuel Taylor Coleridge: Selected Poetry and Prose*. Edited by Elisabeth Schneider. New York: Holt, Rinehart & Winston, 1964.

Colin, Virginia L. *Human Attachment*. Philadelphia: Temple University Press, 1996.

Collyer, Robert H. *Lights and Shadows of American Life*. New York: Burgess & Stringer, 1845.

Comfort, Alex. *The Anxiety Makers: Some Curious Preoccupations of the Medical Profession*. Camden, N.J.: Thomas Nelson & Sons, 1967.

Cott, Nancy. "Passionless: An Interpretation of Victorian Sexual Ideology." *Signs* 4, no. 2 (1978): 219–36.

Crews, Frederick. "The Consolation of Theosophy." Review of *Madame Blavatsky's Baboon: A History of the Mystics, Mediums, and Misfits Who Brought Spirituality to America*, by Peter Washington. *New York Review of Books*, 19 Sept. 1996, 26–30.

———. "The Consolation of Theosophy II." *New York Review of Books*, 3 Oct. 1996, 38–44.

———. "The Trauma Trap." Review of *Remembering Trauma*, by Richard J. McNally and *Memory, Trauma Treatment, and the Law*, by Daniel Brown et al. *New York Review of Books*, 11 March 2004, 37–40.

Crompton, Louis. *Byron and Greek Love: Homophobia in 19th-Century England*. Berkeley: University of California Press, 1985.

Cross, Whitney R. *The Burned-Over District: The Social and Intellectual History of Enthu-*

siastic Religion in Western New York, 1800–1850. Ithaca: Cornell University Press, 1950. Reprint, Harper Torchbooks, 1965.

Cunnington, Phillis. *Costumes of the Nineteenth Century.* Boston: Plays, Inc., 1970.

Dall, Caroline. "Caroline Dall's Reminiscences of Margaret Fuller." Edited by Joel Myerson. *Harvard Library Bulletin* 22, no. 4 (1974): 414–28.

Dedmond, Francis B. "The Letters of Caroline Sturgis to Margaret Fuller." In *Studies in the American Renaissance 1988,* edited by Joel Myerson, 201–351. Charlottesville: University Press of Virginia, 1988.

Deiss, Joseph Jay. *The Roman Years of Margaret Fuller; A Biography.* New York: Thomas Y. Crowell, 1969.

DeYoung, Mary, and Judith A. Lowry. "Traumatic Bonding: Clinical Implications in Incest." *Child Welfare* 71, no. 2 (1992): 165–75.

Dickenson, Donna. *George Sand: A Brave Man—The Most Womanly Woman.* New York: St. Martin's, 1988.

Disraeli, Benjamin. *Contarini Fleming, a Psychological Romance.* New York: Knopf, 1934.

Doane, Janice, and Devon Hodges. *From Klein to Kristeva: Psychoanalytic Feminism and the Search for the "Good Enough" Mother.* Ann Arbor: University of Michigan Press, 1992.

———. *Telling Incest: Narratives of Dangerous Remembering from Stein to Sapphire.* Ann Arbor: University of Michigan Press, 2001.

Dollimore, Jonathan. *Sexual Dissidence: Augustine to Wilde, Freud to Foucault.* New York: Oxford University Press, 1991.

Douglas, Ann. *The Feminization of American Culture.* New York: Knopf, 1977.

Doyle, William. *The Oxford History of the French Revolution.* New York: Oxford University Press, 1989.

Drapes, David, and Jeremiah Abrams, eds. *Meeting the Shadow: The Hidden Power of the Dark Side in Human Nature.* New York: Jeremy P. Tarcher, Inc., 1992.

Eakin, Paul John. "Autobiography, Identity, and the Fictions of Memory." In *Memory, Brain, and Belief,* edited by Daniel Schacter and Elaine Scarry, 290–306. Cambridge: Harvard University Press, 2000.

Eichner, Hans. "The Rise of Modern Science and the Genesis of Romanticism." *PMLA* 97 (1982): 8–30.

Eisenstadt, S. N. Introduction to *Max Weber on Charisma and Institution Building,* by Max Weber. Chicago: University of Chicago Press, 1968.

Emerson, Ralph Waldo. "Address at the Woman's Rights Convention, 20 September 1855." In *The Later Lectures of Ralph Waldo Emerson: 1843–1854. Volume 2: 1855–1871,* edited by Ronald A. Bosco and Joel Myerson, 15–29. 2 vols. Athens: University of Georgia Press, 2001.

———. *The Complete Works of Ralph Waldo Emerson.* Introduction and notes by Edward Waldo Emerson. 12 vols. Boston: Houghton, Mifflin, 1903–4. Reprint, New York: AMS Press, 1974.

———. *The Early Lectures of Ralph Waldo Emerson.* Edited by Robert E. Spiller and Wallace E. Williams. Vol. 3. Cambridge: Harvard University Press, 1972.

———. *Emerson in His Journals.* Edited by Joel Porte. Cambridge: Harvard University Press, 1982.

———. *Emerson's Nature: Origin, Growth, Meaning.* Edited by Merton M. Sealts Jr. and Alfred R. Ferguson. New York: Dodd, 1969.

———. *Essays and Lectures.* Edited by Joel Porte. Library of America ed. New York: Viking, 1983.

————. *The Journals and Miscellaneous Notebooks of Ralph Waldo Emerson*. Edited by William H. Gilman et al. 16 vols. Cambridge: Harvard University Press, 1960–82.

————. *The Letters of Ralph Waldo Emerson*. Edited by Ralph L. Rusk and Eleanor M. Tilton. 10 vols. New York: Columbia University Press, 1939, 1990–1995.

Emerson House in Concord. Concord: privately printed, n.d.

Erikson, Erik H. *Childhood and Society*. 2d ed. New York: Norton, 1963.

————. *Identity: Youth and Crisis*. New York, Norton, 1968.

————. *Young Man Luther: A Study in Psychoanalysis and History*. Norton Library Edition. New York: Norton, 1962.

Ethridge, Willie Snow. *Strange Fires: The True Story of John Wesley's Love Affair in Georgia*. New York: Vanguard, 1971.

Euripides. *The Bacchae*. In *Great Books of the Western World: Aeschylus, Sophocles, Euripides, Aristophanes*. 2d ed. Vol. 4, 472–93. Chicago: Encyclopaedia Britannica, 1990.

————. *Iphigenia in Aulis*. In *Great Books of the Western World: Aeschylus, Sophocles, Euripides, Aristophanes*. 2d ed. Vol. 4, 606–33. Chicago: Encylopaedia Britannica, 1990.

Faderman, Lillian. *Surpassing the Love of Men: Romantic Friendship and Love between Women from the Renaissance to the Present*. New York: William Morrow, 1981.

Faulkner, William. *Collected Stories of William Faulkner*. New York: Random House, 1948.

Faust, A. B. Introduction to *Oberon: A Poetical Romance in Twelve Books*, by C. M. Wieland. Translated by John Quincy Adams. New York: F. S. Crofts, 1940.

Felman, Shoshana. *Jacques Lacan and the Adventure of Insight: Psychoanalysis in Contemporary Culture*. Cambridge: Harvard University Press, 1987.

Fergenson, Laraine R. "Margaret Fuller as a Teacher in Providence: The School Journal of Ann Brown." In *Studies in the American Renaissance 1991*, edited by Joel Myerson, 59–117. Charlottesville: University Press of Virginia, 1991.

————. "Margaret Fuller in the Classroom: The Providence Period." In *Studies in the American Renaissance 1987*, edited by Joel Myerson, 131–42. Charlottesville: University Press of Virginia, 1987.

Ferguson, John. "The Mystery Religions." In *An Illustrated Encyclopedia of Mythology*, edited by Richard Cavendish, 144–55. New York: Crescent, 1980.

Fitzgerald, Robert. "Commentary on *Oedipus at Colonus*." In Sophocles, *The Oedipus Cycle*, 171–81.

Foster, Vanda. *A Visual History of Costume: The Nineteenth Century*. New York: Drama Books, 1984.

Foucault, Michael. *Discipline and Punish: The Birth of the Prison*. Translated by Alan Sheridan. New York: Random House, Vintage Books, 1977.

Fourier, Charles. *The Utopian Vision of Charles Fourier*. Translated, edited, and introduced by Jonathan Beecher and Richard Bienvenu. Boston: Beacon, 1971.

Freud, Sigmund. *Dora: An Analysis of a Case of Hysteria*. Edited by Philip Rieff. New York: Collier, 1963.

Frye, Northrop. "The Drunken Boat: The Revolutionary Element in Romanticism." In *Romanticism Reconsidered: Selected Papers from the English Institute*, edited by Northrop Frye, 1–25. New York: Columbia University Press, 1963.

————. *The Great Code: The Bible and Literature*. New York: Harcourt, 1982.

Fuller, Arthur Buckminster. "Historical Notices of Thomas Fuller and His Descendants, with a Genealogy of the Fuller Family, 1638–1902." Reprinted from the *New England Historical and Geneological Register for October 1859*, with additions by Edith Davenport

Fuller. Cambridge, Mass.: n.p., 1902. In Fuller Family Papers, Houghton Library, Harvard University, Cambridge, Mass.

Fuller, Edith D. "Her Childhood." Paper on the early life of Margaret Fuller read at Normal State College, Albany, New York, Feb. 1900. In Fuller Family Papers, bMS AM 1086 (B), Houghton Library, Harvard University, Cambridge, Mass.

Fuller, Edith Davenport. "Exerpts from the Diary of Timothy Fuller, Jr., An Undergraduate in Harvard College, 1798–1801." In *Proceedings of the Cambridge Historical Society*, 33–53. Cambridge: Cambridge University Press, 1920.

Fuller, Margaret. (Ossoli, Margaret Fuller). *Art, Literature, and the Drama*. Edited by Arthur B. Fuller. Boston: Roberts Brothers, 1874.

———. (Ossoli, Margaret Fuller). *At Home and Abroad, or Things and Thoughts in America*. Edited by Arthur B. Fuller. 1856. Reprint, Port Washington, N.Y.: Kennikat, 1971.

———. "Goethe." *The Dial: A Magazine for Literature, Philosophy, and Religion*. 2, no. 1 (July 1841): 1–41.

———. "The Great Lawsuit. Man Versus Men, Woman Versus Women." *Dial: A Magazine for Literature, Philosophy, and Religion* 4, no. 1 (July 1843): 1–47.

———. *The Letters of Margaret Fuller*. Edited by Robert N. Hudspeth. 6 vols. Ithaca: Cornell University Press, 1983–94.

———. *Margaret Fuller, Critic: Writings from the New-York Tribune, 1844–1846*. Edited by Judith Mattson Bean and Joel Myerson. New York: Columbia University Press, 2000.

———. "Margaret Fuller's 1842 Journal: At Concord with the Emersons." Edited by Joel Myerson. *Harvard Library Bulletin* 21, no. 3 (1973): 320–40.

———. "Margaret Fuller's Journal for October 1842." Edited by Robert D. Habich. *Harvard Library Bulletin* 33, no. 3 (1985): 280–91.

———. *Memoirs of Margaret Fuller Ossoli*. Edited by R. W. Emerson, W. H. Channing, and J. F. Clarke. 2 vols. Boston: Phillips, Sampson & Company, 1852.

———. Review of *Festus: A Poem*, by Philip James Bailey. *Dial* 2 (1841): 231–62.

———. [Review of Philip James Bailey, *Festus*]. *New-York Daily Tribune*, 8 Sept. 1845. In *Margaret Fuller, Critic*, edited by Judith Mattson Bean and Joel Myerson, 211–19. New York: Columbia University Press, 2000.

———. (Fuller, S. M.). *Summer on the Lakes, in 1843*. Boston: Charles C. Little & James Brown, 1844.

———. *"These Sad But Glorious Days": Dispatches from Europe, 1846–1850*. Edited by Larry J. Reynolds and Susan Belasco Smith. New Haven: Yale University Press, 1991.

———. *Woman in the Nineteenth Century*. Edited by Larry J. Reynolds. Norton Critical Edition. New York: Norton, 1998.

———. (Fuller, S. Margaret). *Woman in the Nineteenth Century: A Facsimile of the 1845 Edition*. Introduced by Madeleine B. Stern. Textual apparatus by Joel Myerson. Columbia: University of South Carolina Press, 1980.

———. *The Writings of Margaret Fuller*. Edited by Mason Wade. New York: Viking, 1941.

———, trans. *Günderode*. Boston: E. P. Peabody, 1842.

Fuller, Richard F. *Chaplain Fuller: Being a Life Sketch of A New England Clergyman and Army Chaplain*. Boston: Walker, Wise & Co., 1864.

———. *Recollections of Richard F. Fuller*. Boston: privately printed, 1936.

Fuller, Robert C. *Mesmerism and the American Cure of Souls*. Philadelphia: University of Pennsylvania Press, 1982.

Gauld, Alan. *A History of Hypnotism*. Cambridge: Cambridge University Press, 1992.

Gil, Eliana. "Etiologic Theories." In *Sexualized Children: Assessment and Treatment of Sexualized Children and Children Who Molest,* 53–66. N.p.: Launch, 1993.

Gilbert, Sandra M. "The American Sexual Poetics of Walt Whitman and Emily Dickinson." In *Reconstructing American Literary History,* edited by Sacvan Bercovitch. Cambridge: Harvard University Press, 1986.

Gilligan, Carol. *In a Different Voice: Psychological Theory and Women's Development.* Cambridge: Harvard University Press, 1982.

Glaser, Daniel. "Sexual Trauma and Compulsivity: Dynamics and Treatment." Presentation at the Pastoral Institute, Columbus, Ga., 5–6 Oct. 1995.

Goethe, J. Wolfgang von. *Faust, Parts One and Two.* Translated by George Madison Priest. New York: Covici Friede, 1932.

———. *Iphigenia in Taurus.* Translated by John Prudhoe. New York: Barnes & Noble, 1966.

Gombrich, E. H. *The Story of Art.* 13th ed. New York: Phaidon, 1978.

Goodrick-Clarke, Nicholas. *The Occult Roots of Nazism: Secret Aryan Cults and Their Influence on Nazi Ideology—The Ariosophists of Austria and Germany, 1890–1935.* Washington Square: New York University Press, 1992.

Gordon, Linda. "Incest and Resistance: Patterns of Father-Daughter Incest, 1880–1930." *Social Problems: Official Journal of the Society for the Study of Social Problems* 33, no. 4 (1986): 253–67.

Gotendorf, James [formerly James Nathan]. "Prefatory Note." In *Love Letters of Margaret Fuller, 1845–1846.* New York: AMS Press, 1970.

Grebanier, Bernard. *The Uninhibited Byron: An Account of His Sexual Confusion.* New York: Crown, 1970.

Grill, Johnpeter H. "The European Revolutions of 1848." Lecture presented to students in the graduate seminar on the American Romantics and the 1848 European Revolutions, Mississippi State University, Mississippi State, Miss., 4 April 1996.

Grimal, Pierre. *The Dictionary of Classical Mythology.* Translated by A. R. Maxwell-Hyslop. New York: Basil Blackwell, 1986.

Gutwirth, Madelyn. *Madame de Staël, Novelist: The Emergence of the Artist as Woman.* Chicago: University of Illinois Press, 1966.

Hackforth, R. Introduction to *Plato's Phaedrus,* 3–18. Cambridge: Cambridge University Press, 1972.

Hale, William Harlan. *Horace Greeley: Voice of the People.* New York: Harper & Brothers, 1950.

Hamilton, Edith. *Mythology.* New York: Little, Brown, 1942.

Hardman, Keith J. *Charles Grandison Finney, 1792–1875: Revivalist and Reformer.* Syracuse: Syracuse University Press, 1987.

Hardwick, Elizabeth. "The Genius of Margaret Fuller." *New York Review of Books* 33, no. 6 (1986): 14–22.

Harlan, Elizabeth. *George Sand.* New Haven: Yale University Press, 2004.

"Harro Harring." In *The Oxford Companion to German Literature,* edited by Henry Garland and Mary Garland, 338–39. New York: Oxford University Press, 1976.

Hartman, Geoffrey H. "Romanticism and 'Anti-Self-Consciousness.'" In *Romanticism and Consciousness: Essays and Criticism,* edited by Harold Bloom, 46–56. New York: Norton, 1970.

Hartmann, Ernest. *Dreams and Nightmares: The New Theory on the Origin and Meaning of Dreams.* New York: Plenum Trade, 1998.

———. *The Nightmare: The Psychology and Biology of Terrifying Dreams.* New York: Basic, 1984.

Hauser, Stuart T. "Loevinger's Model and Measure of Ego Development: A Critical Review,

II." *Psychological Inquiry: An International Journal of Peer Commentary and Review* 4, no. 1 (1993): 23–30.

Hawthorne, Nathaniel. *The Blithedale Romance.* Edited by Seymour Gross and Rosalie Murphy. Norton Critical Edition. New York: Norton, 1978.

———. "Egostism; or The Bosom-Serpent." In *Mosses from an Old Manse,* edited by William Charvat et al. Columbus: Ohio State University Press, 1974.

———. *The French and Italian Notebooks.* Edited by Thomas Woodson. Columbus: Ohio State University Press, 1980.

———. *Nathaniel Hawthorne's Tales.* Edited by James McIntosh. Norton Critical Edition. New York: Norton, 1987.

———. *The Scarlet Letter.* Edited by Harry Levin. Cambridge: Riverside, 1960.

Hedaya, Robert. "The Womanizer." *Medical Aspects of Human Sexuality* 19, no. 1 (Jan. 1985): 113–14.

Helps, Arthur, and Elizabeth Jane Howard. *Bettina: A Portrait.* New York: Reynal, n.d.

Higginson, Thomas Wentworth. *Margaret Fuller Ossoli.* Boston: Houghton, 1884.

———. *Studies in History and Language.* Boston: Houghton Mifflin, 1900.

Hintzen-Bohlen, Brigitte. *Art and Architecture: Rome and the Vatican City.* With contributions by Jürgen Sorges. Cologne, Germany: Könemann, 2000.

Holland, Norman. *Five Readers Reading.* New Haven: Yale University Press, 1975.

Holy Bible. Revised Standard Version. New York: Thomas Nelson & Sons, 1953.

The Holy Bible: Authorized King James Version. Self-pronouncing edition. Cleveland: World Publishing, n.d.

Hondrich, Ted, ed. *The Oxford Companion to Philosophy.* New York: Oxford University Press, 1995.

Horowitz, Helen Lefkowitz. *Rereading Sex: Battles Over Sexual Knowledge and Suppression in Nineteenth-Century America.* New York: Vintage Books, 2003.

Hudspeth, Robert N. "A Calendar of the Letters of Margaret Fuller." In *Studies in the American Renaissance 1977,* edited by Joel Myerson, 49–143. Boston: Twayne, 1977.

———, ed. *The Letters of Margaret Fuller.* 6 vols. Ithaca: Cornell University Press, 1983–94.

———. Introduction to *The Letters of Margaret Fuller.* Vol. I (1983).

———. Preface to *The Letters of Margaret Fuller.* Vol. IV (1987).

———. Preface to *The Letters of Margaret Fuller.* Vol. V (1988).

Hughes, Ted. "On Ovid's 'Metamorphoses.'" *New York Review of Books,* 17 July 1997, 18.

Humma, John B. "The Interpenetrating Metaphor: Nature and Myth in *Lady Chatterly's Lover.*" *PMLA* 98 (1983): 77–86.

Ignatieff, Michael. "On Isaiah Berlin (1909–1997)." *New York Review of Books,* 18 Dec. 1997, 10–12.

Irigaray, Luce. *Speculum of the Other Woman.* Translated by Gillian C. Gill. Ithaca: Cornell University Press, 1974.

Izenberg, Gerald N. Introduction to *Impossible Individuality: Romanticism, Revolution, and the Origins of Modern Selfhood, 1787–1802.* Princeton: Princeton University Press, 1992.

James, Henry. *Daisy Miller.* In *The Turn of the Screw and Other Short Novels.* Foreword by Willard Thorp. New York: Signet Classic, 1962.

———. *William Wetmore Story and His Friends.* Vol. 1. Boston: Houghton, 1903.

Johnson, Dr. Samuel, et al., eds. *The Works of the English Poets, from Chaucer to Cowper: Including the Series Edited, with Prefaces, Biographical and Critical,* by Dr. Samuel Johnson: and the most approved translations. The additional lives by Alexander Chalmers, F.S.A. Vol. 20. London: J. Johnson, 1810.

Keller, Karl. "The Puritan Perverse." *Texas Studies in Literature and Language* 25, no. 1 (1983): 139–64.

Kellerman, Henry. *Sleep Disorders: Insomnia and Narcolepsy.* New York: Brunner/Mazel, 1981.

Kelley, Mary. Introduction to *The Portable Margaret Fuller.* Edited by Mary Kelley. New York: Penguin Books, 1994.

Kernberg, Otto F. *Borderline Conditions and Pathological Narcissism.* New York: Jason Aronson, 1975.

———. *Object-Relations Theory and Clinical Psychoanalysis.* New York: Jason Aronson, 1976.

Kincaid, James R. *Child-Loving: The Erotic Child and Victorian Culture.* New York: Routledge, 1992.

Kinetz, Erika. "Is Hysteria Real? Brain Images Say Yes." *New York Times,* 26 Sept. 2006, sec. D1.

Klein, Melanie. *Envy and Gratitude and Other Works.* New York: Dell, 1957.

———. *Love, Guilt and Reparation and Other Works, 1921–1945.* New York: Delacorte, 1975.

Knight, G. Wilson. *Lord Byron's Marriage: The Evidence of Asterisks.* New York: MacMillan, 1957.

Kohut, Heinz. *The Analysis of the Self: A Systematic Approach to the Psychoanalytic Treatment of Narcissistic Personality Disorders.* New York: International University Press, 1971.

———. *The Restoration of the Self.* New York: International University Press, 1977.

Kolodny, Annette. "Margaret Fuller: Recovering Our Mother's Garden." In *The Land Before Her: Fantasy and Experience of the American Frontiers, 1630–1860,* 112–30. Chapel Hill: University of North Carolina Press, 1984.

Kopacz, Paula. "The School Journal of Hannah (Anna) Gale." In *Studies in the American Renaissance 1996,* edited by Joel Myerson, 67–113. Charlottesville: University Press of Virginia, 1996.

Lacan, Jacques. *Écrits: A Selection.* Translated by Alan Sheridan. New York: Norton, 1977.

———. *The Four Fundamental Concepts of Psycho-Analysis.* Edited by Jacques-Alain Miller. Translated by Alan Sheridan. New York: Norton, 1978.

———. *The Language of the Self: The Function of Language in Psychoanalysis.* Translated by Anthony Wilden. Baltimore: Johns Hopkins University Press, 1968.

Lange, Victor. Introduction to *Wilhelm Meister's Apprenticeship: Johann Wolfgang von Goethe's Classic Tale of Youth Awakening to Life and Love.* Translated by Thomas Carlyle. New York: Crowell-Collier, 1962.

Langer, William. *Political and Social Upheaval, 1832–1852.* New York: Harper & Row, 1969.

Lasch, Christopher. *The Culture of Narcissism: American Life in an Age of Diminishing Expectations.* New York: Norton, 1978.

———. *Haven in a Heartless World: The Family Besieged.* New York: Basic, 1977.

———. *The Minimal Self: Psychic Survival in Troubled Times.* New York: Norton, 1984.

Lear, Jonathan. *Love and Its Place in Nature: A Philosophical Interpretation of Freudian Psychoanalysis.* New York: Farrar, 1990.

Lewin, Bertram D. *Dreams and the Uses of Regression.* New York: International University Press, 1958.

Locke, John. *The Works of John Locke.* 11th ed. Vol. 5. London: W. Otridge & Son, 1812.

Lovett, Clara M. *The Democratic Movement in Italy, 1830–1876.* Cambridge: Harvard University Press, 1982.

Lowen, Alexander. *Narcissism: Denial of the True Self.* New York: MacMillan, 1983.

Macdonald, D. L. "Childhood Abuse as Romantic Reality: The Case of Byron." *Literature and Psychology* 40, nos. 1–2 (1994): 24–47.

Maclear, James Fulton. "'The Heart of New England Rent': The Mystical Element in Early Puritan History." In *The New England Puritans,* edited by Sydney V. James, 43–65. New York: Harper, 1968.

Mansfield, Edward Deering. *Legal Rights, Liabilities and Duties of Women: With an Introductory History of Their Legal Condition in the Hebrew, Roman and Feudal Civil Systems.* Salem, Mass.: J. P. Jewett, 1845.

Martin, Jane Roland. "The Contradiction of the Educated Woman." *Forum for Honors* 17, no. 3 (1987): 4–9.

Martin, Sylwia Kohot. "Ralph Waldo Emerson and Adam Mickiewicz: Two Visions of Salvation." Master's thesis. Mississippi State University, Mississippi State, Miss., 1999.

Masefield, Muriel. *Peacocks and Primroses: A Survey of Disraeli's Novels.* London: Geoffrey Bles, 1953.

Masson, Georgina. *Fodor's Rome: A Companion Guide.* Rev. ed. New York: David McKay, 1971.

Masson, Jeffrey Moussaieff. *The Assault on Truth: Freud's Suppression of the Seduction Theory.* New York: Farrar, Strauss & Giroux, 1984.

Maurois, André. *Lélia: The Life of George Sand.* Translated by Gerald Hopkins. New York: Harpers, 1953.

Mazzini, Giuseppe. *Selected Writings.* Edited by N. Gangulee. 1945. Reprint, Westport, Conn.: Greenwood, 1974.

McNulty, John Bard. "Emerson's Friends and the Essay on Friendship." *New England Quarterly* 19 (1946): 390–94.

Mermin, Dorothy. *Elizabeth Barrett Browning: The Origins of a New Poetry.* Chicago: University of Chicago Press, 1989.

Mesmer, F. A. *Mesmerism: A Translation of the Original Scientific and Medical Writings of F. A. Mesmer.* Translated and compiled by George Bloch. Los Altos, Calif.: William Kaufmann, 1980.

Michael, John. *Emerson and Skepticism: The Cipher of the World.* Baltimore: Johns Hopkins University Press, 1988.

Miller, Edwin Haviland. *Salem Is My Dwelling Place: A Life of Nathaniel Hawthorne.* Iowa City: University of Iowa Press, 1991.

Miller, Perry, ed. *The American Puritans: Their Prose and Poetry.* New York: Doubleday Anchor, 1956.

———. *Errand into the Wilderness.* Cambridge: Harvard University Press, 1956. Reprint, New York: Harper Torchbooks, 1964.

———. "'I Find No Intellect Comparable to My Own.'" *American Heritage* 8, no. 2 (1957): 22–25, 96–99.

———, ed. *Margaret Fuller: American Romantic: A Selection from Her Writings and Correspondence.* 1963. Reprint, Ithaca: Cornell University Press, 1970.

———, ed. *The Transcendentalists: An Anthology.* Cambridge: Harvard University Press, 1950.

Milton, John. *Paradise Lost: A Poem in Twelve Books.* Edited by Merritt Y. Hughes. New York: Odyssey, 1962.

Mitchell, Catherine C. *Margaret Fuller's New York Journalism: A Biographical Essay and Key Writings.* Knoxville: University of Tennessee Press, 1995.

Mitchell, Thomas R. *Hawthorne's Fuller Mystery.* Amherst: University of Massachusetts Press, 1998.

———. "Julian Hawthorne and the 'Scandal' of Margaret Fuller." *American Literary History* 7 (summer 1995): 210–33.

Moore, Thomas, ed. *The Life, Letters, and Journals of Lord Byron* [1829]. London: John Murray, Albemarle Street, W., 1920. Reprint, St. Clair Shores, Mich.: Scholarly Press, 1972.

———. *The Works of Thomas Moore.* New York: n.p., 1825.

Morson, Gary Saul. "For the Time Being: A Patchwork in Nine Parts with Loopholes." Paper presented at the eighteenth annual Alabama Symposium in English and American Literature, University of Alabama, Tuscaloosa, Ala., 9 Oct. 1992.

Murray, Margaret McGavran. "Beyond Anomaly: The Educated Woman, Past and Present." *Forum for Honors: A Publication of the National Collegiate Honors Council* 17, no. 4 (1987): 37–51.

———. "Margaret Fuller: Her Own Best Biographer and Analyst." Paper presented at the Modern Language Convention, Chicago, Ill., December 1973.

———. "Margaret Fuller: The Death of An Intellectual Heroine." Paper presented at the annual conference on Lacan, Language, and Literature, Kent State University, Kent, Ohio, May 1988.

———. "Margaret Fuller and her Love for Ralph Waldo Emerson." Paper presented to the Group for Applied Psychology, Cornell University, Ithaca, N.Y., May 1970.

———. "Margaret Fuller and the Language of Sexual Politics in Nineteenth-Century New England." Paper presented at the Modern Language Association Convention, New York, N.Y., December 1978.

———. "Margaret Fuller as Emerson's Audience." Paper presented at the annual conference on Lacan, Language, and Literature, Kent State University, Kent, Ohio, May, 1989.

———. "The Role of Domesticity Transcended: Margaret Fuller, Lydia Maria Child, Mary Boykin Chesnut." In *Men, Women and Issues in American History,* edited by Howard Quint and Milton Cantor, 172–91. Homewood, Ill.: Dorsey Press, 1975.

Myerson, Joel, ed. *Critical Essays on Margaret Fuller.* Boston: G. K. Hall, 1980.

———. "'In the Transcendental Emporium': Bronson Alcott's 'Orphic Sayings' in the *Dial.*" *English Literature Notes* 10, no. 1 (Sept. 1972): 31–38.

———. *Margaret Fuller: A Descriptive Bibliography.* Pittsburgh: University of Pittsburgh Press, 1978.

———. "Margaret Fuller: An Exhibition from the Collection of Joel Myerson." *University of South Carolina Bibliographical Series* 8 (1973): 1–22.

———. "Margaret Fuller: The American Years." Paper read before the Thoreau Lyceum, Concord, Mass., 14 May 1975.

———. *The New England Transcendentalists and the "Dial": A History of the Magazine and Its Contributors.* Rutherford, N.J.: Fairleigh Dickinson University Press, 1980.

———. "Supplement to *Margaret Fuller: A Descriptive Bibliography.*" In *Studies in the American Renaissance 1996,* edited by Joel Myerson, 187–240. Charlottesville: University Press of Virginia, 1996.

———, ed. *Transcendentalism: A Reader.* New York: Oxford University Press, 2000.

Nathan, James. See Gotendorf, James.

Noll, Richard. *The Jung Cult: Origins of a Charismatic Movement.* Princeton: Princeton University Press, 1994.

Novak, Barbara. *The Margaret-Ghost: A Novel.* New York: George Braziller, 2003.

Nussbaum, Martha C. "The Chill of Virtue." Review of *Socrates, Ironist and Moral Philosopher*, by Gregory Vlastos. *New Republic*, 16 and 23 Sept. 1991, 34–40.

Oppenheim, David, and Harriet Salatas Waters. "Narrative Processes and Attachment Representations: Issues of Development and Assessment." In Waters, Vaughn, Posada and Kondo-Ikemura. 197–215.

Ordon, Edmund. "Mickiewicz and Emerson." *University of Buffalo Studies* 23 (1956): 31–54.

Ovid. *Heroides and Amores*. Translated by Grant Showerman. Cambridge: Harvard University Press, 1963.

———. *Metamorphoses*. Translated by Frank Justus Miller. 2 vols. Cambridge: Harvard University Press, 1921.

———. *Ovid's Metamorphoses (Translation in Blank Verse)*. Translated by Brookes More. 2 vols. Rev. ed. Francestown, N.H.: M. Jones, 1978.

Owens, Gretchen, Judith A. Crowell, Helen Pan, Dominique Treboux, Elizabeth O'Connor, and Everett Waters. "The Prototype Hypothesis and the Origins of Attachment Working Models: Adult Relationships with Parents and Romantic Partners." In Waters, Vaughn, Posada, and Kondo-Ikemura, 216–33.

Pagels, Elaine. *Adam, Eve and the Serpent*. New York: Vintage, 1988.

Perrot, Philippe. *A History of Clothing in the Nineteenth Century*. Translated by Richard Bienvenu. Princeton: Princeton University Press, 1994.

"Philip James Bailey." *The Oxford Companion to English Literature*. Edited by Sir Paul Harvey. 3rd ed. New York: Oxford University Press 1964.

Philips, Ambrose. *The Poems of Ambrose Philips*. Edited by M. G. Segar. 1937. Reprint, New York: Russell & Russell, 1969.

Plath, Sylvia. *Ariel: Poems by Sylvia Plath*. New York: Harper, 1961.

Plato. *The Dialogues of Plato*. Introduced by Raphael Demos. Translated by B. Jowett. 2 vols. New York: Random, 1937.

———. *Five Great Dialogues*. Edited and introduced by Louise Ropes Loomis. Translated by B. Jowett. New York: D. Van Nostrand, 1942.

———. *Great Dialogues of Plato*. Edited by Eric H. Warmington and Philip G. Rouse. Translated by W. H. D. Rouse. New York: New American Library, 1984.

———. *Plato's Phaedrus*. Translated and introduced by R. Hackforth. Cambridge: Cambridge University Press, 1972.

Plutarch. *Plutarch's Lives*. Vol. 9. Translated by Bernadette Perrin. Cambridge: Harvard University Press, 1959.

———. *Plutarch's Moralia*. Vol. 5. Translated by Frank Cole Babbitt. Cambridge: Harvard University Press, 1969.

———. *Plutarch's Moralia*. Vol. 8. Translated by Paul A. Clement. Cambridge: Harvard University Press, 1969.

———. *Plutarch's Moralia*. Vol. 9. Translated by Edwin L. Minar Jr. [F.H. Sandbach, and W.C. Helmbold] et al. Cambridge: Harvard University Press, 1961.

Poe, Edgar A. "The Literati of New York City—No. IV: Sarah Margaret Fuller." In Margaret Fuller, *Woman in the Nineteenth Century*, edited by Larry J. Reynolds, 223–26. Norton Critical Edition. New York: Norton, 1998.

Pollin, Burton R. "Poe on Margaret Fuller in 1845: An Unknown Caricature and Lampoon." *Women and Literature* 5, no. 1 (1977): 47–50.

Porte, Joel. *In Respect to Egotism: Studies in American Romantic Writing*. New York: Cambridge University Press, 1991.

————. *Representative Man: Ralph Waldo Emerson in His Time.* New York: Oxford University Press, 1979.

Posgate, Helen. *Madame de Staël.* New York: Twayne, 1968.

Price, Michelle. "Incest and the Idealized Self: Adaptations to Childhood Sexual Abuse." *American Journal of Psychoanalysis* 54, no. 1 (1994): 21–39.

Reiss, Hans. *Goethe's Novels.* Coral Gables, Fla.: University of Miami Press, 1969.

Reynolds, Larry J. *European Revolutions and the American Literary Renaissance.* New Haven: Yale University Press, 1988.

————. "From *Dial* Essay to New York Book: The Making of *Woman in the Nineteenth Century.*" In *Periodical Literature in Nineteenth-Century America,* edited by Kenneth M. Price and Susan Belasco Smith, 17–34. Charlottsville: University Press of Virginia, 1995.

————, ed. *Woman in the Nineteenth Century,* by Margaret Fuller. Norton Critical Edition. New York: Norton, 1998.

Reynolds, Larry J., and Susan Belasco Smith. Introduction to *"These Sad But Glorious Days,"* by Margaret Fuller. New Haven: Yale University Press, 1991.

Richards, Laura E., and Maud Howe Elliott. *Julia Ward Howe, 1819–1910.* 2 vols. Dunwoody, Ga.: Norman S. Berg, 1970.

Richardson, Robert D., Jr. *Emerson: The Mind on Fire.* Berkeley: University of California Press, 1995.

Richardson, Samuel. *The History of Sir Charles Grandison.* London: Sharpe & Hailes, 1812.

Robinson, David M. "Margaret Fuller and the Transcendental Ethos: *Woman in the Nineteenth Century.*" *PMLA* 97, no. 1 (1982): 83–98.

Robinson, David M. (David Moore). *Sappho and Her Influence.* New York: Cooper Square, 1963.

Rosen, Jeffrey. *The Unwanted Gaze: The Destruction of Privacy in America.* New York: Random House, 2000.

[Ross, Mrs.]. *Hesitation; or, To Marry, or Not to Marry?* 2 vols. New York: W. B. Gilley, 1819.

Rostenberg, Leona. "Margaret Fuller's Roman Diary." *Journal of Modern History* 12, no. 2 (1940): 209–20.

Rowland, Ingrid. "The Genius of Parma." *New York Review of Books,* 11 June 1998, 4–6, 8–9.

————. "Titian: The Sacred and Profane." Review of *Titian's Women,* by Rona Goffen, and *Tiziano: Amor sacro e amor profano,* by Maria Grazia Bernardini. *New York Review of Books,* 18 March 1999, 14–17.

Russell, Bertrand. *A History of Western Philosophy: And Its Connection with Political and Social Circumstances from the Earliest Times to the Present Day.* New York: Simon & Schuster, 1945.

Rutman, Darrett B. *Winthrop's Boston: Portrait of a Puritan Town, 1630–1649.* Chapel Hill: University of North Carolina Press, 1965.

Sahli, Nancy. "Smashing: Women's Relationships Before the Fall." *Chrysalis* 1, no. 8 (1979): 17–27.

Sams, Henry W., ed. *Autobiography of Brook Farm.* Englewood Cliffs, N.J.: Prentice-Hall, 1958.

Sand, George. *Indiana.* Translated by Eleanor Hochman. New York: Signet Classic, 1993.

————. *Lélia.* Translated by Maria Espinosa. Bloomington: Indiana University Press, 1978.

————. "Preface to the Edition of 1832." *Indiana.* Translated by Eleanor Hochman. New York: Signet Classic, 1993.

Sandys, George. *Ovid's Metamorphosis: Englished, Mythologized, and Represented in Figures.*

Edited by Karl K. Hulley and Stanley T. Vandersall. Lincoln: University of Nebraska Press, 1970.

Sappho. *The Poems of Sappho.* Translated by Suzy Q. Groden. New York: Bobbs-Merrill, 1966.

———. *Sappho, a Garland: The Poems and Fragments of Sappho.* Translated by Jim Powell. New York: Farrar, Strauss & Giroux, 1993.

———. *Sappho: A New Translation.* Translated by Mary Barnard. Foreword by Dudley Fitts. Berkeley: University of California Press, 1958.

———. *The Songs of Sappho in English Translation by Many Poets.* Mount Vernon, New York: Peter Pauper, 1942.

Sartre, Jean-Paul. "The Imaginary Life." *The Psychology of Imagination.* Translated by Bernard Frechtman. New York: Washington Square, 1966.

Scarry, Elaine. *Dreaming by the Book.* Princeton: Princeton University Press, 1999.

Schacter, Daniel L. *Searching for Memory: The Brain, the Mind, and the Past.* New York: Basic, 1996.

———. *The Seven Sins of Memory: How the Mind Forgets and Remembers.* Boston: Houghton Mifflin, 2001.

Schacter, Daniel L., and Elaine Scarry. *Memory, Brain, and Belief.* Cambridge: Harvard University Press, 2000.

Schapiro, Barbara A. *The Romantic Mother: Narcissistic Patterns in Romantic Poetry.* Baltimore: Johns Hopkins University Press, 1983.

Schenk, H. G. *The Mind of the European Romantics: An Essay in Cultural History.* New York: Ungar, 1966.

Schneiderman, Stuart. *Jacques Lacan: The Death of an Intellectual Hero.* Cambridge: Harvard University Press, 1983.

Sealts, Merton M., Jr., and Alfred R. Ferguson, eds. *Emerson's* Nature—*Origin, Growth, Meaning.* New York: Dodd, 1969.

Shealy, Daniel. "Margaret Fuller and Her 'Maiden': Evelina Metcalf's 1838 School Journal." In *Studies in the American Renaissance 1996,* edited by Joel Myerson, 41–65. Charlottesville: University Press of Virginia, 1996.

Shelley, Percy Bysshe. "A Defence of Poetry." In *Shelley's Prose: Or the Trumpet of a Prophecy,* edited by David Lee Clark, 275–97. Albuquerque: University of New Mexico Press, 1954.

———. *Shelley's Poetry and Prose.* Edited by Donald H. Reiman and Sharon B. Powers. Norton Critical Edition. New York: Norton, 1977.

Shengold, Leonard. *Soul Murder: The Effects of Childhood Abuse and Deprivation.* New Haven: Yale University Press, 1989.

Sifford, Darrell. "First-born Children Often Succeed." *Jackson Clarion-Ledger,* 28 Dec. 1989, sec. 1D.

Slater, Joseph, ed. *The Correspondence of Emerson and Carlyle.* New York: Columbia University Press, 1964.

Smith, Denis Mack. *Garibaldi.* London: Hutchinson, 1957.

———. *The Making of Italy, 1796–1870.* New York: Harper & Row, 1968.

———. *Mazzini.* New Haven: Yale University Press, 1994.

Smith-Rosenberg, Carroll. "The Female World of Love and Ritual: Relations Between Women in Nineteenth-Century America." *Signs* 1, no. 1 (1975): 1–29.

Solomon, Barbara Miller. *In the Company of Educated Women: A History of Women and Higher Education in America.* New Haven: Yale University Press, 1985.

Sophocles. *Antigone*. In *The Oedipus Cycle*.

———. *The Oedipus Cycle, An English Version*. Translated by Dudley Fitts and Robert Fitzgerald. New York: Harcourt, 1977.

Staël, Madame de [Anne-Louise-Germaine]. *Corinne: or, Italy*. Translated by Isabel Hill. New York: A. L. Burt, Publishers, n.d.

Stark, Rodney. *The Rise of Christianity: A Sociologist Reconsiders History*. Princeton: Princeton University Press, 1996.

Steele, Jeffrey, ed. *The Essential Margaret Fuller*. New Brunswick, N.J.: Rutgers University Press, 1992.

———. *The Representation of the Self in the American Renaissance*. Chapel Hill: University of North Carolina Press, 1987.

———. *Transfiguring America: Myth, Ideology, and Mourning in Margaret Fuller's Writing*. Columbia: University of Missouri Press, 2001.

Steele, Valerie. *Fashion and Eroticism: Ideals of Feminine Beauty from the Victorian Era to the Jazz Age*. New York: Oxford University Press, 1985.

Stern, Madeleine B. *The Life of Margaret Fuller*. New York: E. P. Dutton, 1942. Reprint, Westport, Conn.: Greenwood Press, 1991.

———. "Margaret Fuller and the Phrenologist-Publishers." In *Studies in the American Renaissance 1980*, edited by Joel Myerson, 229–37. Boston: Twayne, 1980.

Strauch, Carl F. "Hatred's Swift Repulsions: Emerson, Margaret Fuller and Others." *Studies in Romanticism* 7, no. 2 (1968): 65–103.

Strout, Cushing. "Ego Psychology and the Historian." In *The Veracious Imagination: Essays on American History, Literature, and Biography*. Middletown, Conn.: Wesleyan University Press, 1981.

———. *Making American Tradition: Visions and Revisions from Ben Franklin to Alice Walker*. New Brunswick, N.J.: Rutgers University Press, 1990.

Sulloway, Frank J. *Born to Rebel: Birth Order, Family Dynamics, and Creative Lives*. New York: Pantheon, 1996.

Sussex, Ronald. Introduction to *Culture and Nationalism in Nineteenth-Century Eastern Europe*. Edited by Ronald Sussex and J. C. Eade. Columbus, Ohio: Slavica Publishers, 1983.

Tatar, Maria. *Off with Their Heads! Fairy Tales and the Culture of Childhood*. Princeton: Princeton University Press, 1992.

Taylor, Shelley E. *Positive Illusions: Creative Self-Deception and the Healthy Mind*. New York: Basic, 1989.

Taylor, William, and Christopher Lasch. "Two 'Kindred Spirits': Sorority and Family in New England, 1839–1846." *New England Quarterly* 36, no.1 (1963): 23–41.

Terr, Lenore. *Too Scared to Cry: How Trauma Affects Children . . . and Ultimately Us All*. New York: Basic, HarperCollins, 1990.

Teti, Douglas M. "Maternal Depression and Child-Mother Attachment in the First Three Years: A View from the Intermountain West." In *The Organization of Attachment Relationships: Maturation, Culture, and Context*. Cambridge: Cambridge University Press, 2000.

Tomory, Peter. *The Life and Art of Henry Fuseli*. New York: Praeger, 1972.

Trevelyan, George Macaulay. *Garibaldi's Defence of the Roman Republic, 1848–9*. 1907. Reprint, Westport, Conn.: Greenwood Press, 1971.

Tyler, Alice Felt. *Freedom's Ferment: Phases of American Social History from the Colonial Period to the Outbreak of the Civil War*. 1944. Reprint, New York: Harper Torchbook, 1962.

U.S. Congress. *Annals of the Congress of the United States, The Fifteenth Congress—Second Session, November 16, 1818, to March 3, 1819.* Washington, D.C., 1855. Pages 499–502, 981–1006, 1179–1191, and appendix, 1613–1622.

Vachon, David. "Doctor John Snow Blames Water Pollution for Cholera Epidemic." *Old News,* May and June 2005, 8–10.

Vanita, Ruth. *Sappho and the Virgin Mary: Same-Sex Love and the English Literary Imagination.* New York: Columbia University Press, 1996.

Vendler, Helen. "Feminism and Literature." *New York Review of Books* 37, no. 9 (1990): 19–25.

Viotti, Andrea. *Garibaldi: The Revolutionary and His Men.* Poole, Dorset, U.K.: Blandford Press, 1979.

Virgil. *The Aeneid.* Translated by Robert Fitzgerald. New York: Vintage, 1990.

———. *The Aeneid of Virgil: A Verse Translation.* Translated by Allen Mandelbaum. New York: Bantam, 1971.

———. (Vergil). *Vergil's Aeneid: Books I–VI.* Revised ed. with introduction, notes, vocabulary, and grammatical appendix by Clyde Pharr. Lexington, Mass.: D. C. Heath, 1964.

———. *The Works of P. Virgilius Maro, Including the Aeneid, Bucolics, and Georgics, with the original text reduced to the natural order of construction: and an interlinear translation,* by Levi Hart and V. R. Osborn. March 1833. Philadelphia: David McKay, 1882.

Von Matt, Leonard. *Rome: The Eternal City.* New York: Doubleday, 1955.

Von Mehren, Joan. "Establishing the Facts on the Ossoli Family: An Experiment in E-Mail Research." Paper presented at the American Literature Association, Cambridge, Mass., 25 May 2001.

———. "Margaret Fuller, the Marchese Giovanni Ossoli, and the Marriage Question: Considering the Research of Dr. Roberto Colzi. *Resources for American Literary Study* 50 (2005): 104–43.

———. *Minerva and the Muse: A Life of Margaret Fuller.* Amherst: University of Massachusetts Press, 1994.

Wade, Mason. *Margaret Fuller: Whetstone of Genius.* New York: Viking, 1940.

Walicki, Andrzej. "National Messianism and the Historical Controversies in the Polish Thought of 1831–1848." In *Culture and Nationalism in Nineteenth-Century Eastern Europe,* edited by Roland Sussex and J. C. Eade, 128–42. Columbus, Ohio: Slavica Publishers, 1983.

Warfel, Harry R. "Margaret Fuller and Ralph Waldo Emerson." *PMLA* 50 (1935): 576–94.

Waters, Everett, Brian E. Vaughn, German Posada, and Kiyomo Kondo-Ikemura, eds. *Caregiving, Cultural, and Cognitive Perspectives on Secure-Base Behavior and Working Models: New Growing Points of Attachment Theory and Research. Monographs of the Society for Research in Child Development* 60, nos. 2–3 (1995).

Weber, Max. *Max Weber on Charisma and Institution Building.* Edited and introduced by S. N. Eisenstadt. Chicago: University of Chicago Press, 1968.

———. *The Sociology of Religion.* Translated by Ephraim Fischoff. Boston: Beacon, 1963.

Weidensaul, Scott. *The Ghost with Trembling Wings: Science, Wishful Thinking, and the Search for Lost Species.* New York: North Point Press, 2005.

Weintraub, Wiktor. *Literature as Prophecy: Scholarship and Martinist Poetics in Mickiewicz's Parisian Lectures.* 'S-Gravenhage, the Neth.: Mouton, 1959.

———. *The Poetry of Adam Mickiewicz.* 'S-Gravenhage, the Neth.: Mouton, 1954.

Wellisz, Leopold. *The Friendship of Margaret Fuller D'Ossoli and Adam Mickiewicz.* New York: Polish Book Importing, 1947.

Welter, Barbara. "The Cult of True Womanhood: 1820–1860." In *Dimity Convictions: The American Woman in the Nineteenth Century.* Athens: Ohio University Press, 1976.

Wessell, Leonard P., Jr. *Karl Marx, Romantic Irony, and the Proletariat: The Mythopoetic Origins of Marxism.* Baton Rouge: Louisiana State University Press, 1979.

Wharton, Henry Thornton. *Sappho: Memoir, Text, Selected Renderings, and a Literal Translation.* 3rd ed. Chicago: A. C. McClurg, 1895.

Whicher, Stephen E. *Freedom and Fate: An Inner Life of Ralph Waldo Emerson.* Philadelphia: University of Pennsylvania Press, 1953. Reprint, New York: Perpetua, 1961.

———, ed. *Selections from Ralph Waldo Emerson: An Organic Anthology.* Cambridge, Mass.: Riverside, 1957.

White, Elder James. *Sketches of the Christian Life and Public Labors of William Miller.* Battle Creek, Mich.: Steam Press, 1875.

Whitman, Walt. *Leaves of Grass: Facsimile Edition of the 1860 Text.* Introduced by Roy Harvey Pearce. Ithaca: Cornell University Press, 1961.

Wieland, C. M. *Oberon, a Poem, from the German of Wieland.* Translated by William Sotheby. 2 vols. 1798. Introduced by Donald H. Reiman. Reprint (2 vols. in 1), New York: Garland, 1978.

———. *Oberon: A Poetical Romance in Twelve Books.* Edited by A. B. Faust. Translated by John Quincy Adams. New York: F. S. Crofts, 1940.

Wieseltier, Leon. "'When A Sage Dies, All Are His Kin': Isaiah Berlin, 1909–1997." *New Republic,* 1 Dec. 1997, 27–30.

Wilson, Elizabeth. "Not in This House: Incest, Denial, and Doubt in the White Middle Class Family." *Yale Journal of Criticism* 8, no. 1 (1995): 35–58.

Winthrop, John. "Speech to the General Court." In *Life and Letters of John Winthrop,* edited by Robert C. Winthrop. Vol. 2. Boston: Ticknor & Fields, 1867.

Wolin, Richard. "Prometheus Unhinged." Review of *The Aryan Christ: The Secret Life of Carl Jung,* by Richard Noll. *New Republic,* 27 Oct. 1997, 27–34.

Wordsworth, William. *Wordsworth: Poetical Works, With an Introduction and Notes.* Edited by Thomas Hutchinson. Rev. ed. New York: Oxford University Press, 1987.

Wright, Susan. *The Renaissance Masterpieces of Art and Architecture.* New York: Smithmark, 1997.

Young, Philip. *Hawthorne's Secret.* Boston: David R. Godine, 1984.

Zaretsky, Eli. *Secrets of the Soul: Social and Cultural History of Psychoanalysis.* New York, Knopf, 2004.

Zwarg, Christina. *Feminist Conversations: Fuller, Emerson, and the Play of Reading.* Ithaca: Cornell University Press, 1995.

Index

References to Margaret Fuller are abbreviated as MF, Timothy Fuller (MF's father) as TF, and Ralph Waldo Emerson as RWE.

Bussey's wood, 137, 163

Byron, Lord George, 65–66, 71, 79, 94–95, 169; abused as child, 157; early appeal of, to MF, 158; *The Giaour*, 172; homoeroticism in letters and journals of, 157–58; MF critical of, in "Modern British Poets," 94–95, 97, 157–58; MF quotes, 157, 371; Moore biography of, 65–66, 157; praises Sappho, 441n4 (chap. 23); mentioned, 297

Byronic hero, morality of, 258

Calhoun (Powers), 310, 403, 407

Calvin, John, 88, 89, 187; effect of, on RWE, 88–89; on "erect posture," 89, 429n11; on Scripture's law, 429n9; on self-control, 89; on twisted versus straight path, 88–89, 429n10

Cambria, 290, 291

Cambridgeport, 11–12, 290

Capper, Charles, 2; on Arthur Fuller's martyrdom, 267; on dark side's appeal to MF, 109–10; on "erotic content" of father-daughter interaction, 267–68, 274, 456–57n7; on Higginson's interpretation of mother-daughter interaction, 457n9; on Martineau, 83; on MF's illness at farm, 80–81; on MF's mother breastfeeding MF, 13; on MF's mother's absence, 455n16; on RWE's Greene Street Transcendental jeremiad, 106; on TF reincarnated in MF, 81–82; on TF's estate division, 82

Carbonari, 296

Carlyle, Jane, 295, 298

Carlyle, Thomas, 290; as conversationalist, 125; on *Dial*, 124; MF's encounters with, 295, 298; mocks Romantics, 298; Rebecca Spring's encounter with, 298; mentioned, 62

Carracci, 310

Cartesian dualism, 92

Cass, Lewis, Jr., 381, 398; MF confides in, 390; MF meets, 383; on MF's heroics, 388

Cassandra, 191

Catholic rituals, MF critical of, 288, 341, 343, 371

Cattaneo, Carlo, 374

Cavour, Count Camillo, 331

Cenci, Beatrice, 466n12; MF compares, with Oedipus, 338; MF on, in *Woman in the Nineteenth Century*, 280; MF on portrait of, 310; Nathaniel Hawthorne links MF to, 3, 278

Ceres (Demeter), 197, 200, 221, 288; "Hymn to Demeter," 280; MF as, 357. *See also* Persephone

Channing, Ellen Fuller. *See* Fuller, Ellen Kilshaw

Channing, Margaret Fuller (Greta), 206, 233–34, 338, 354, 365

Channing, William Ellery (minister), 64, 123; as spokesman for New England Unitarianism, 101–2

Channing, William Ellery, II (poet), 102, 123, 192

Channing, William Henry, 123, 204, 237, 400; as Associationist and Christian Socialist, 233, 352, 377, 400; on MF's "peculiar power," 163; on MF's possible marriage, 361; recollections of MF by, 126, 136, 163, 166, 239, 241; visits Sing Sing with MF, 241–42; on wreck of *Elizabeth*, 408, 410, 411, 474n11; mentioned, 62, 64, 65, 101

Charcot, Jean-Martin, 195

charisma, 210, 289; Giuseppe Mazzini and Mickiewicz as possessing, 289–90, 326–27; Max Weber on, 448n9; Mickiewicz on, as source of power, 284

Charles Albert (king of Piedmont-Sardinia), 296, 325, 355, 356, 375; constitution granted by, 342–43, 348; defeated at Novara, 379; Giuseppe Mazzini yields to, 374; republicanism loathed by, 350; surrenders to Radetzky, 358

Chevigny, Bell Gale, 4, 341

Cheyfitz, Eric, 132

Child, Lydia Maria Francis, 61, 102, 237, 245; on Greeleys' Turtle Bay house, 231; on *Woman in the Nineteenth Century*, 224–25

child abuse, 272. *See also* Shengold, Leonard

Childhood and Society (Erikson), 428n15, 454n14

Chodzko, Alexander, 317
Chopin, Frédéric, 148, 303, 304, 316, 319, 345
Christ. *See* Jesus
Ciceruacchio, 340, 391
Circle of God, 304, 306
"Circles" (RWE), 63, 64
Civitavecchia (Port of Rome), 374, 382
Clarke, James Freeman, 64–65, 84, 123;
    early positive assessment of MF by, 135;
    as editor of *Western Messenger*, 65, 123;
    on Elizabeth Randall at seashore, 455n15;
    failure of, to convert evangelicals to
    Unitarianism, 75; on Goethe's morals,
    110; marriage of, 163, 178; meets MF as
    child, 26; mentioned, 58, 62, 73, 96, 100,
    104, 106
Clarke, Rebecca Hull, 202
Clarke, Sarah, 124, 126–27, 132, 202–3, 205,
    361, 375
Clarke, William, 202, 205–6, 248
"Classical and Romantic" (MF), 79–80, 265
Coleridge, Samuel Taylor, 62, 65, 125;
    as conversationalist, 125; sustains
    Wordsworth through *Prelude*, 142
Coliseum Club, 113
Collyer, Robert, 190, 194–95, 217–18; *Lights
    and Shadows of American Life*, 195
Combe, Andrew, 292
Commentaries on the Laws of England
    (Blackstone), 24, 223
communism, 350–51, 352
Communist Manifesto (Marx), 349, 351
Comtesse de Pologne: as early role model,
    36, 316; mentioned, 43, 318, 319. See also
    Hesitation
*Concerning the Moral and Civil Primacy of
    the Italians* (Gioberti), 317
Condition of the Working Class (Engels),
    230
Confessions, The (Rousseau), 58
Congress of Vienna (1814–15), 283; Giu-
    seppe Mazzini dreams of overturning,
    296
Contarini Fleming (Disraeli), 347, 361, 362,
    467n5
conversation, 125
Conversations with Children on the Gospels
    (Alcott), 102–3, 106

*Conversations with Goethe in the Last Years
    of His Life* (Eckermann; trans. MF), 105,
    117, 119, 121, 137
Corinne (de Staël), 59–60
Correggio, 337
Cranch, Christopher Pearse, 93, 94, 236,
    313, 331
Cranch, Elizabeth, 331
Crane, Abigail (MF's aunt), 33
Crane, Elizabeth Jones Weiser (MF's
    grandmother), 11, 75, 235; religious piety
    of, 109; waits for son's return, 402
Crane, Peter (MF's grandfather), 11
Crane, Peter (MF's uncle), 201; mentioned,
    202, 264
Crawford, Thomas, 331
Crews, Frederick, 455n3
"Crito" (Plato), 74
Cromwell, Oliver, 377
Cross, Whitney, 139
cult of friendship, 152
"culture of surveillance," 276–77
Cupid, 200, 293
Cybele, 304, 307; as lover of Attis, 307,
    316

daemonical ("daimonische"): defined by
    MF, 159–60, 208–9, 210; MF drawn to,
    160; RWE repelled by, 160
"Daemonical, The" (MF), 208–9
Daisy Miller (James), 465n21
Dall, Caroline, 91, 178
Dana, Francis, 45, 57
Dana, Henry, 107
Dana, Samuel, 72
Dana Hill mansion, 45, 57; described, 57;
    destroyed, 184–85; Fullers move to, 57
Dante, Alighieri, 102, 294
Davis, Charles, 408
Davis, George, 66–67, 109, 178, 179, 184–85,
    248
Death, as comforting lover, 207–8, 293, 294,
    409
Death of Jane McCrea, The (Vanderlyn),
    447n2 (chap. 32)
Declaration of Independence: MF alludes
    to, 326; mentioned, 189, 223, 351
Deiss, Joseph Jay, 325

Fitton, Miss E., 312

Florence, Italy, 325–26, 342, 350, 391, 392, 395, 399; acceptance of MF's husband and son in, 401; conservative reaction in, 379; MF ill in, 328; repressive environment in, 320

Foreign Review, 66, 144

Fourier, Charles, 285, 350; on "aromal state," 208; on marriage, 319; and Mesmer, 448n14; MF critical of, 301, 319; MF influenced by, 218, 351, 361; and MF's possible Fourierist marriage, 361, 469n25; Paris alive with ideas of, 300; on "transition state," 192, 428n16, 456n12; mentioned, 230

Fowler, Lorenzo, 107

Fowler, Orson, 89–90, 106, 107; examines MF's head, 89, 107; MF attends lectures of, 458n11; MF intrigued by, 107

Fragoletta (Latouche), 149

Francis of Assisi, Saint, 320

Freeman, James, 64–65; on MF, 67, 178

French: attack on Rome, 383, 389; duplicity and aggression, 379, 382; MF letter to RWE about, 388; MF on duplicity of, 374, 384, 385, 386; slaughter Italians, 390

"French Novelists of the Day" (MF), 145, 149, 240, 264

French Revolution (1789), 283; Gioberti rejects radicalism of, 317; Michelet on, 301; and Reign of Terror, 352

French Revolution (1848), 352

Freud, Sigmund, 159, 176, 195, 272, 278

Friedrich Wilhelm (king of Prussia), 348

"Friendship" (RWE), 115

Frye, Northrop, 77, 437n9 (chap. 18)

Fuller, Abraham (MF's uncle), 50, 223, 320; death of, 320, 329, 375; denies money for Ellen Fuller's education, 113, 354; handles TF's estate, 82; leaves little money to MF, 329, 354; misogynist behavior of, 179, 223; as "sordid," 279; TF's family moves in with, 71

Fuller, Arthur Buckminster (MF's brother), 38, 68, 76, 264–65, 375; Capper on, 267; eye injury of, 78, 336; life and death of, 267, 417n12; mentioned, 54, 80

Fuller, Edith Davenport (MF's niece), 12, 76

Fuller, Elisha (MF's uncle), 33, 37

Fuller, Elizabeth (MF's aunt), 32–33, 39; spies on children, 49, 50

Fuller, Ellen Kilshaw (MF's sister), 417n12; assumes MF's classes, 117; and birth of daughter Greta, 206, 233–34; breastfeeding problems of, 233–34, 365; marriage of, 192; marriage problems of, 179, 192, 323, 329, 336; MF visits in Concord, 205, 233, 234; as mother's "pet," 27, 38; rooms with MF in Providence, 113; traumatic life of, 267; mentioned, 54, 92, 102, 279, 354

Fuller, Eugene (MF's brother), 15, 37–38, 80, 336, 402, 404, 417n12; battles father, 76; and death of first baby of, 375; traumatic life of, 266–67; mentioned, 54

Fuller, Henry Holton (MF's uncle), 8, 75, 80, 102–3, 335

Fuller, Hiram, 105

Fuller, Julia Adelaide (MF's sister): death of, 3–4, 13–15, 417n12; MF's reaction to death of, 14, 28; mother's reaction to death of, 3–4, 13–14; mentioned, 152

Fuller, Lloyd (MF's brother), 417n12; commitment of, to asylum, 302, 330, 336; life of, 267; lives with Arthur Fuller, 375; mental instability of, 77, 96, 265, 302; personal problems of, and sin of "self-pollution," 276, 330, 431n8; as Sumner's friend, 396

Fuller, Margaret, career of:

—conversationalist: aim of Conversations, 125, 137, 164; description of Conversations, 124; fifth round of Conversations, 204; impact of MF on young women, 126–27, 171, 173; pedagogical method of MF, 126; similarity of Sappho's classes to MF's, 163–64; skill of MF as, 125; theatrical nature of Conversations, 125, 126, 185

—editor of *Dial,* 123, 124; editorship given to RWE, 186; facilitation of friendship with RWE, 128; no income, 124; overtime work, 128; reviewers mock journal, 128

—journalist at *New-York Tribune,* 1, 229, 235–36; MF on writing for newspaper, 238. See also *New-York Daily Tribune*

Fuller, Margaret, career of (*continued*)
—nurse: Belgioioso appoints MF as wartime, 383; named chief assistant, 388; tends to suffering as, 383–84, 387, 388–89, 393; to son, 407
—radical revolutionary, 1, 392, 394, 399–400
—teacher, in Boston: and night class overload, 113; of private classes, 101, 102–3; recorder of conversations as, at Temple School, 102; at Temple School, 100, 102, 103
—teacher, in Providence: Greene Street School, 105, 108–9; MF's view of Greene Street students, 105–6; rigid routine at Greene Street, 108; RWE's Greene Street dedication, 105, 106, 110, 111; students, interaction with, 105, 106, 108; students' views of MF, 105, 108
—war correspondent: on Austrian aggression, 385, 392; on French assault on Rome, 384; on Legionnaires' leave-taking, 390–91; on war's aftermath, 392
Fuller, Margaret, life, traits, and friendships of: animal magnetism, belief in, 106–7, 158, 186, 189, 202 (*see also* animal magnetism); antislavery, 341; childhood, recollection of (1839), 274; companion, search for ideal, 83, 84, 95; death of father, 81–82, 85; friendships, specific (*see* Barker, Anna Hazard; Hicks, Thomas; Mazzini, Giuseppe; Mickiewicz, Adam; Sturgis, Cary); intellectual perfection, adolescent drive for, 55, 56–57, 58, 103, 277–78; Macaria (character), MF on, 191, 200, 210; Mariana (character), MF on, 52, 207–8, 212; motherhood, conflicted feelings regarding, 366; Nathan, love relationship with (*see* Nathan, James); psychological conflict, 2, 3, 4, 70–71, 97, 110, 239; Romantic passion unrequited (*see* Clarke, William; Davis, George; Nathan, James; Ward, Samuel Grey); Romantic vision, 289–90, 324; Romantic writers, MF drawn to, 27, 64; soul possession as ideal end of pilgrim's journey, 290; trance states,

retreat to, 259, 263, 270, 273, 280; Truth, seeker of, 250, 281
—appearance, 34, 48, 55, 232, 242; at Conversations, 126–27; Dall on, 91, 178; Freeman on, 67, 178; Hedge on, 48, 48–49, 346; Oliver Wendell Holmes on, 56; RWE on, 91–92, 98; William Channing on, 144
—characteristics, 38, 48, 55, 232; athleticism, 474n12; children, affection for, 181, 233–34, 243–44, 397; "dark side" ("shadow side"), 110, 156–57, 159, 240, 262, 266, 273; deep need for love, 177; dissembling, 379, 380; divided self, 107, 110, 115, 128–29, 142, 239, 261, 273, 276–77; superficiality, 70, 107, 239, 271, 432n8 (chap. 14)
—confidence: gaining as woman, 170–71; lacking as writer, 128; as writer, 184–85
—death, 408–10; living worst nightmare, 409
—dreams and nightmares, 21–23, 25, 41, 67, 70–71, 160–61, 175–77, 263, 271; death of Cary Sturgis in, 214, 257–58; death of mother in, 23, 25, 257–58; of drowning, 41, 67, 175–77, 257–58, 335, 409; father as cause of, 160–61, 263; and migraines, 160–61; power of, 41; significance of, to MF, 161, 176–77
—education: Cambridge Port Private Grammar School, 33–34, 45, 49, 55; home-schooling by aunts and uncles, 47; Park's Boston Lyceum for Young Ladies, 47, 48; Parks's dancing school, 47–48; Prescott's Young Ladies' Seminary, 52–53; self-education, 45, 55
—erotic: MF aware of, 134, 161–62, 163–65; power of, over women, 127; strong sense of, in MF, 116, 273; threatens RWE, 132–33
—father: conflicted feelings for "dead," 213, 251; failure of, at farm, 264–65; failure of communication with, 78, 80, 81; fixation on, 273, 278; idealization of "dead," 110, 199, 214, 250–51, 260, 265, 275; identification with, 95, 108, 162, 275; imitation of, 21, 108, 126; Jefferson's letters read with, 76; obsessive need to

please, 17, 20–21, 32–33, 49–50, 50–51, 54–55, 95, 270, 278; positive impact of, on MF, 4, 124–25, 213; reaction to death of, 81–83, 280; tension between, and MF, 47, 74–75, 76–77, 78–79
—father figure, 174; betraying, 358; and Milton as voice of father law, 174; need of approval from, 103, 131–33; Oberon as, 174, 176; Pope Pius IX as, 333, 334, 339, 340–42, 358; price for defiance of, 391, 397, 401; RWE as, 96, 97, 101, 105, 110, 114–15, 129, 165, 198, 335; tyrannical, 368, 391; vision of world purged of authoritarian, 399–400
—fictional selves: Mariana, 52, 207–8, 212; Miranda, 188, 191, 198–99, 229
—friendships, erotic nature of, 154, 155–56, 161, 162, 168–69, 183–84; MF exceeds typical expression of, 439n7, 441n13; and redeeming friendship with Cary Sturgis, 165; RWE's recollections of, with women, 154; as typical of time, 439n8
—friendship with RWE, 86, 90–100, 101, 104; disappointment with, 170–71, 175; early interest in, 84, 95–97; idealization of, 114, 129, 142, 159, 165, 169; and MF's appeal to RWE from Rome, 388; and MF's mockery of "Friendship," 175; as mutually empowering, 134; recognition sought from, 131–32, 162; as replay of MF's past, 85, 86, 92, 95–96, 97, 101, 104, 108, 110, 114, 116, 119, 120–21, 123; widening distance of, 234–35, 238. *See also* Emerson, Ralph Waldo
—garden, 14–15; escape to, as child, 26; in "Sensitive Plant," 248–49
—gender: fluid nature of, 116, 122, 132–33, 195–96; MF on, 53, 95, 122; questions regarding MF's, 53, 95, 153, 168–69; and traditional nineteenth-century roles, 152–53
—hypocrisy, MF on: of Catholic priests, 341; in "The Great Lawsuit," 190, 241; and Sand, 241; in *Woman in the Nineteenth Century*, 220, 224, 225, 279
—illness and pain, 71, 103, 106–7, 108–9, 114, 117, 166, 176; in Europe, 328, 329; nature as escape from, 137, 143, 256;

and "painful youth," 264; in relation to Nathan, 246, 251, 254, 259, 260, 272–73. *See also* Fuller, Margaret, life, traits, and friendships of: migraines
—illusion: escape into, 4, 109, 110, 114, 116, 129, 162, 251–52, 255, 256, 260; last, 365; and mysticism, 119–20, 253, 254; need to escape to, 234, 254–55; pattern of, 109, 129, 248–49, 254; and Romantic personality, 251–52; and trance states, 259, 263, 273
—illusions, positive: of redemptive community, 395–96, 472n9 (chap. 64); regarding history of Roman Revolution, 394; regarding son, 393
—imagination: MF on, 251; power of, in MF, 40, 43, 64, 138, 154, 155, 173, 213; and Romantic Imagination, 253–54
—magnetic power, 127, 158–59; RWE on, 119, 122, 127
—marriage, 1, 179; Christian, 218, 222–23; on Fourier's view of, 319; in "The Great Lawsuit," 188, 192–93, 196–97; reservations about institution of, 243, 317, 319, 323, 347, 463–64n14; RWE's views on, versus MF's, 192. *See also* Ossoli, Giovanni Angelo (MF's "husband")
—migraines (headaches), 105, 106, 107, 108–9, 114, 126, 155, 156, 339, 346, 367, 403, 432n6 (chap. 6), 435n14 (chap. 16); after Conversations, 126, 127; mesmerist cannot alleviate, 106–7; nature as possible reliever of, 137, 143–44; and nightmares, 160–61; at sea, 403
—Miranda: as ideal alter ego in "The Great Lawsuit," 188, 191, 198–99; James Russell Lowell on, 229
—money, need for, 100, 105, 113, 137, 143, 179; in Europe, 320, 328–29, 354, 356, 398; and lack of income from *Dial*, 124
—mother: adult daughter friction with, 328–29, 329–30; apocalyptic letter to, 367–70; careless remarks of, 330; flawed early relationship with, 26–27; reconciliation with, 371, 395, 396, 399
—mother figure, 31, 53, 256; ambivalent feelings for, 256, 257–58, 329
—moves: Aborn house, Providence, 112,

Gerusalemme liberata, La (Tasso), 58
Gespräche mit Goethe (Eckermann; *Conversations with Goethe*), 105, 117, 121, 137. *See also* Goethe, Johann Wolfgang von
Gesuita moderno, Il (Gioberti), 331
Giaour, The (Byron), 172
Gioberti, Abbé Vincenzo: admired by Costanza Arconati Visconti, 322; Giuseppe Mazzini differences with, 374; ideas of, 317; influence of, on Pope Pius IX, 317; MF on, to Costanza Arconati Visconti, 354
—works of: *Concerning the Moral and Civil Primacy of the Italians*, 317; *Il Gesuita moderno* (*The Modern Jesuit*), 331
Girl with the Golden Eyes, The (Balzac), 149
Godwin, William, 193–94
"Goethe" (MF), 2, 200
Goethe, Johann Wolfgang von, 71, 73, 96, 102, 121; belief of, in "daimonische," 159; as conversationalist, 125; MF on, in *Dial*, 2; MF's fascination with sex life of, 110; scandalous sex life of, 431n9; mentioned, 62, 65, 71, 142, 213
—works of: *Faust*, 73, 191; *Iphigenia*, 79–80, 265; *Second Residence in Rome*, 75; *Tasso Torquato*, 73, 427n7 (chap. 10); *Die Wahlverwandtschaften* (*Elective Affinities*), 96; *Wilhelm Meister*, 200, 201, 228, 243. See also *Gespräche mit Goethe*
Golden Ass, The (Apuleius), 200. *See also* Psyche
Goldsmith, Oliver, 34; *Deserted Village*, 34, 36
Gordon, Linda, 267–68
Gott, Joseph, 310
Gray, May, 157
greater Romantic lyric, 125
"Great Lawsuit, The" (MF), 186, 187–88, 188–97 passim; MF revises, 214; RWE praises, 197; Sand in, 193–94, 199; Wollstonecraft in, 193–94, 199
Greeley, Arthur Young (Pickie), 233, 330; death of, 396–97; MF's affection for, 244
Greeley, Horace, 204, 213, 231, 232, 236, 329, 356; MF reveals husband and son to, 397; on MF's life in city, 238; MF

works for, 228; progressive views of, 296; recollections of MF by, 229, 231–32, 244; on son's death, 396–97
Greeley, Mary (Molly), 231, 232, 233, 261, 329; encourages MF's romance with Nathan, 245; on MF's love for Arthur Greeley, 330; quarrels with MF, 255–56
Greeley, Mary Inez (baby), 329
Greeley family: MF at the Turtle Bay house of, 229, 231; MF's fans visit, 237
Green, André, 14; on "dead mother complex," 231
Greene Street School, 91, 105–10
Greenwood, Amelia, 61, 65, 75
Gregory XVI (pope), 283, 286, 317
Grill, Johnpeter, 459n2 (chap. 47)
Groton, Mass.: chaos at, 280; effect of move to, on family, 72–73, 280; Fuller farm at, 46, 72; living conditions at, 75–76, 77
Guardia Nobile, 333
Günderode (Brentano), 175; MF translates, 185

Habsburg, Marie-Louise von (archduchess; Napoleon's second empress), 342
Hague, William, 113, 139, 181
Hamlet (character), 40, 109
Hamlet (Shakespeare), 117, 119
Harring, Harro, 230, 451n6; *Dolores*, 231
Harvard Divinity School, 63–64
Hasty, Captain Seth, 406–7
Hasty, Catherine, 406, 408; recollects shipwreck, 407
Hauffe, Friederike. *See* Seeress of Prevorst
Hawthorne, Nathaniel, 2, 124, 399; links MF to Beatrice Cenci, 3, 278; MF as model for Beatrice Rappiccini, 275–76, 278; MF as model for Hester Prynn, 362, 399; MF visits family of, 233; and models for Zenobia, 150, 247, 425n19, 438n17; on Zenobia and her jeweled flower, 453n27
—works of: *Blithedale Romance*, 150, 247, 453n27; "Rappaccini's Daughter," 275–76; *The Scarlet Letter*, 362, 399
Hawthorne, Sophia, 124, 233–34
Hawthorne, Una, 233–34; MF's affection for, 243
Hedge, Henry, 58, 64, 65, 84, 92, 95; as MF's

friend, 48, 103; on MF's looks in youth, 48, 48–49; view of, on *Dial*, 123; visits MF in Rome, 346

Hedge's Club, 112. *See also* Transcendental Club

Herder, Johann Gottfried von, 101; as father of nationalism, 285; Giuseppe Mazzini influenced by, 297

Hesitation (Ross), 32, 88, 316–17; Comtesse de Pologne in, as role model for MF, 36, 316; echo of, in MF's letters, 398, 464n1; effect of, on MF, 35–36, 319; MF's childhood analysis of, 34; mentioned, 43, 409

Hicks, Thomas, 310, 313–14, 316, 331, 404; paints MF's portrait, 354; on Titian influence, 468n5

Higginson, Thomas Wentworth, 8, 9; on evil of TF as MF's tutor, 56–57, 278; on Fuller family pattern, 268; on Margarett Crane Fuller, 15, 425n6; on MF and Sappho, 163–64; on MF's affinity for Sand, 146; on void in MF's heart, 29, 56

"History of Slavery on the Political Revolutions of Rome" (Bancroft), 79

History of the Girondists (Lamartine), 283

"History of the Late Italian Revolution" (MF), 353, 402

History of the United States (Bancroft), 79

Hoar, Elizabeth, 85, 143–44, 303, 322, 326, 374–75, 388, 400; idealized by MF, 157

Hooper, Ellen Sturgis. *See* Sturgis, Ellen

Howe, Julia Ward, 144

Howitt, Mary, 295, 309

Howitt, William, 295, 309

Hudspeth, Robert N., 293; warns of introspection, 3

Hume, David, 88

Huon, 40–43, 310, 334, 335, 362; mentioned, 401, 409. See also *Oberon*

Huonet, 362

"Hymn to Venus, An" (Sappho), 154

Imlay, Gilbert, 9, 193, 347

Indiana (character): enchantment of, with water, 143; MF compared with, 280; MF's admiration for, 146, 432n15

Indiana (Sand), 143, 144, 146

Instruction pratique sur le magnétisme animal (Deleuze), 209

Iphigenia (character): and Agamemnon's hypocrisy, 279; in "Classical and Romantic," 279; MF on, 79–80, 191; in *Woman in the Nineteenth Century,* 279, 362

Iphigenia (Goethe), 79–80, 265

Iphigenia in Aulis (Euripides), 141

Iphis, 168

Irving, Washington, 204

Isis (moon goddess), 132, 200; cult of, 166–67; MF's interest in myth of, 168. See also *Metamorphoses;* Orphic cults; Plutarch

Italia del Popolo, 359

"Italian Martyrs" (G. Mazzini), 299

Italian revolution, 383, 384, 386–87, 390; mentioned, 401

Italy: geographic and political regions in, 296, 325; intellectual women heralded in, 320; marriage of Roman Catholic to non-Catholic in, 347; MF at home in, 326; MF identifies personal hopes with fall of, 391; MF no longer has home in, 398; multidialects in, 326; revolution begins in, 342; successful uprisings in, 348

"Items of Foreign Gossip" (MF), 230, 236

Jacques (Sand), 145, 148

Jacques Lacan (Schneiderman), 98

James, Henry, 2, 3; *Daisy Miller,* 465n21

James, Henry, Sr., 90, 133

Janet, Pierre, 195

Jefferson, Thomas: MF admires, 78–79; MF reads letters of, 76, 78; mentioned, 72

Jesuits: attacked in Genoa, 342; MF criticizes, in *Tribune,* 341; power of, in Italy, 296, 339, 340

Jesus, 138, 143, 182, 183, 187, 198, 341; charisma and ethic of, 327; as Christ, 102, 187, 189, 287, 288, 456n13; as Elizabeth Crane's redeemer, 235; in "The Great Lawsuit," 188–89, 197–98; MF on, 181, 189, 301; precepts of, advocated by MF, 371, 377; RWE on, 93–94, 120; mentioned, 152, 215, 241

"Jesus, My Strength, My Hope" (Wesley), 138
"jeune France, La" (MF), 145, 146, 149

Kant, Immanuel, 62, 65
Keller, Karl, 137
Kerner, Andreas Justinus, 197, 210, 211. *See also* Seeress of Prevorst
Kilshaw, Ellen, 30–32; departure of, and effect on MF, 33, 46, 280, 290
King, Jane Tuckerman. *See under* Tuckerman, Jane
Kittredge, Charles B., 430n14
Kohut, Heinz, 110
Körner, Theodor, 66

Lamartine, Alphonse-Marie-Louis de Prat de, 348; *History of the Girondists*, 283
Lamennais, Félicité-Robert, 284–85, 300; influence of, on Giuseppe Mazzini, 297; MF meets, 302; Mickiewicz's influence on, 304; *Words of a Believer*, 285
Lasch, Christopher, 29, 78; on MF's neediness, 274–75. *See also* narcissism
Latouche, Henri de, 149, 150; *Fragoletta*, 149
Law of the Father, 174; as conscience in MF, 173
Lectures on Revivals of Religion (Finney), 139, 436n4 (chap. 17)
Lee, Mother Anne, 194
Legal Rights, Liabilities and Duties of Women, The (Mansfield), 223
Léger, Théodore, 245, 453n19; *Animal Magnetism*, 453n19
Leghorn (Livorne), 309
Lehringe zu Sais, Die (Novalis), 72
"Leila" (MF), 172
Lélia (Sand), 144–45, 150, 162
Leone Leoni (Sand), 145
Leopold II (grand duke of Tuscany), 320, 325; forms national guard, 326; grants constitution, 342; leaves Tuscany, 376; repressive policies of, 342
Lesseps, Ferdinand-Marie de, 385–86
Lessing, Gotthold Ephraim, 66, 102
Lettres d'un voyageur (Sand), 145

Leverrier, Urbain Kjean Joseph, 301
Life, Letters, and Journals of Lord Byron (Moore), 65–66, 157
"Life of Sir James MacIntosh, The" (MF), 96
Lights and Shadows of American Life (Collyer), 195
"Lines Composed a Few Miles above Tintern Abbey" (Wordsworth), 454n5 (chap. 40)
liquid metaphor: MF's use of, 140, 159, 339, 354, 373; ministers' use of, 139–40. *See also* water
Liverpool: as Ellen Kilshaw's home, 290; MF's steamer docks at, 283, 291; plight of poor in, 286, 291–92
"Lives of the Great Composers" (MF), 124
livre mystique, Le (Balzac), 145
Locke, John, 62, 88, 100, 101–2, 223
London: poverty in, 295; public baths of, 291–92
London Phalanx, 295
Longfellow, Henry Wadsworth, 29
"Lost and Won" (MF), 81
Louis-Napoleon. *See* Bonaparte, Louis-Napoleon
Louis-Philippe (king of France), 283, 300; escapes Paris, 348; MF on, 301
Lowell, James Russell, 229, 378; *Fable for Critics*, 229, 378
Lowell, Maria, 401; MF on death of child of, 410
Lynch, Anne, 237, 240
Lyons, 307–8

Macaria, 191, 200, 210
Macbeth (Shakespeare), 94, 430n28
Mademoiselle de Maupin (Gautier), 149
Maenads. *See* Bacchantes
Manchester (England), 291; unemployment in, 286
mandala, 289
Manning, Richard and Mary: loan MF money, 329; MF's sense of foreboding to, 332
Mansfield, Edward, 223
Manzoni, Alessandro, 323
Margaret-Ghost (Novak), 3

Mariana: based on MF, 52; in *Summer on the Lakes*, 207–8, 212

"Mariana" (MF), 52

Marquise, La (Sand), 150

Martineau, Harriet, 83, 84; MF and Springs visit, at Ambleside, 292; *Society in America*, 292

Marx, Karl, 230, 286; *Communist Manifesto*, 349, 351; Giuseppe Mazzini critical of, 297; MF not Marxist, 351

Mathews, Cornelius, 229

Mauprat (Sand), 145, 146, 193–94

Mazzini, Giuseppe, 284, 285, 286, 287, 288–89; as admirer of MF, 298, 300; and allies in Austria, 325; appearance of, 295; compared with Mickiewicz, 305; compares Pius IX with Louis XVI, 339; influenced by Herder, 297; influenced by Lamennais, 285; influenced by Mickiewicz, 304; invites MF to speak at boys' evening school, 298; letter of, to Pius IX, 325, 343–44; life and ideas of, 296–97; MF compares, with Christ, 376; MF influenced by, 298–99, 324; MF on, 298, 313, 350; MF's meetings with, 297, 298, 391; MF spreads propaganda of, 302, 309; as republican, 344; returns to Italy, 350, 376; and Risorgimento, 284, 327, 412; as Romantic (radical), 295, 297; Rome entered by, 375; as Sand's defender, 299; visits MF, 376; and war, 384; and Young Italy, 296, 297

—works of: "Italian Martyrs," 299; *Memoir of the Bandiera Brothers*, 297; *Scheme of 1844*, 297

Mazzini, Maria, 309

Melville, Herman, 229

Memoir of the Bandiera Brothers (G. Mazzini), 297

Mesmer, Franz Anton, 189, 195; Fourier as follower of, 448n14; on harmony of spheres, 197; and Society of Harmony, 209

mesmerism (mesmerists), 105, 106, 109, 202, 209; MF visits mesmerist, 106–7, 119, 158–59, 210. *See also* animal magnetism

Metamorphoses (Ovid): calming effect of, on MF as child, 22, 39; Cupid and Psyche, 200, 243; Erysichthon and Mestra, 22–23, 25; Iphis, 168; Narcissus, 28–29

Metternich, Prince Klemens von (Austrian chancellor), 325, 326; goes into exile, 348

Mexican War, 328

Michelangelo, 313; *Moses*, 311

Michelet, Jules, 301

Mickiewicz, Adam, 284, 285, 286, 300; admires and encourages MF to fulfill her needs, 307, 311–12, 321; appearance and personality of, 302, 305, 306; charisma of, as source of power, 285, 326–27; compared with Giuseppe Mazzini, 305; compared with RWE, 306; detests MF's Puritanism, 306, 307, 308; friendship of, with MF in Rome, 349; impact of RWE on, 305, 306; influenced by Andrzej Towiański, 288, 304; life and ideas of, 304–5, 306–7; on MF as Virgin yet sinner, 307; MF influenced by, 307, 322; MF meets, 304, 305; mystical vision of, 306; on Poland as new Messiah, 327; similarities of views of, with MF's, 306; as spiritual leader of the Poles, 284; visits MF in Rome, 346

—works of: *The Books of the Polish Nation and of the Polish Pilgrims*, 304; *Pan Tadeusz*, 304

millennial expectations, 186–87

Miller, Edwin Haviland, 459n5 (chap. 46)

Miller, Perry, 2, 97

Miller, William, 186–87; *Signs of the Times*, 188

Milton, John, 73, 248, 249; MF on Puritanism of, 174; *Paradise Lost*, 174, 248

Minerva (Pallas Athena), 12, 191, 192, 200

Miranda, 52, 188, 191, 198–99, 207–8, 212, 229

Miss Prescott's Young Ladies' Seminary, 52

Mitchell, Thomas, 2

"Modern British Poets" (MF), 94, 97

Modern Jesuit, The (Gioberti), 331

Mogliani, Camillo, 362, 366

Moore, Thomas, 65–66, 157

Morals (Plutarch), 119; Osiris in, 132

Moses (Michelangelo), 311

Mozier, Isabella, 328

Mozier, Joseph, 328, 395, 402; gives jobs to
MF and Giovanni Ossoli, 398

Musset, Alfred de, 148

Myerson, Joel: on Alcott, 442n6 (chap. 24);
on Cary Sturgis and Ellery Channing,
438n6 (chap. 21); on MF's unconventional life, 5

mystery cults, 288–89

Napoleon I (French emperor), 283

Napoleon III (French emperor). *See*
Bonaparte, Louis-Napoleon

narcissism, 27–29, 110; Douglas on
MF's, 431n17; of MF, 254–55; and
MF's friendships, 162; of Romantic
personality, 99; of Shelley, 252, 258–59

Narcissus, 28–29. See also *Metamorphoses*

Nathan, James, 230, 238, 251, 291, 292,
299; as abusive toward MF, 262; Aeneas
compared with, 299; appearance and
personality of, 244, 245–46; marriage
plans of, 329; MF idealizes, as godlike,
258, 260, 275; MF replays painful past
with, 249, 251, 255, 260, 261–64, 271,
274–75, 276–77; MF's erotic feelings
for, 247–50, 251, 258; MF's love letters
to, 245–60 passim, 264, 265; MF's
miscommunication with, 248; MF's
obsessive love for, 252, 253, 254–58,
259–61; MF's pain in relation to, 246,
251, 254, 263, 266, 274; MF's rage in
reaction to betrayal of, 299; MF's
reaction to absence of, 258, 261, 263; as
opportunist, 246, 253–54; publishes in
Tribune, 246, 261; rejects MF, 251, 292;
and sexual proposition of MF, 249–50,
265; "Wayside Notes Abroad," 261;
mentioned, 1, 210, 239, 243

Nature (Mother): healing capacity of, 143–
44; MF in harmony with, 172–73; MF on
anger of, 174; MF's ambivalence toward,
175; MF's failure to merge with, 204; MF
to Channing on worship of, 173; retreat
to, not "strange," 173–74

Nature (RWE), 63, 86, 88–89, 92–94, 111,
137, 187

Neal, John, 107, 109, 110; on women's right
to vote, 107–8

Necker, Jacques, 59

"New and Old World Democracy" (MF),
327–28

Newcastle coal mine, 286, 294

New England Galaxy, 81

"New Year's Day" (MF), 340

New York City: and great fire of 19 July,
258; MF in, 228–29; MF's reaction to,
238, 239

New-York Daily Tribune, 1, 204, 213; MF as
literary editor and social commentator
in, 228; MF's reviews and commentaries
in, 1, 229–30, 236–37; review of *Woman
in the Nineteenth Century* in, 224. See
also *Woman in the Nineteenth Century*

—MF's letters from abroad, 282, 291–92,
293, 294, 298, 301, 302, 303, 306, 308, 310,
315, 317–18, 323–24, 327–28, 333, 339; as
increasingly apocalyptic, 353, 364, 367,
371, 399; MF resumes writing, 348; MF's
praises for Mickiewicz's Florence talk
in, 350

—MF's specific columns: "Items of Foreign
Gossip," 230, 236; "New and Old World
Democracy," 327–28; "New Year's Day,"
340; "Social Movement in Europe," 230

New York Orphan Asylum, 236

Niagara Falls, 202; chained eagle at, 205;
MF's experience at, 204

Nicholas I (czar of Russia), 283, 328; as
ruler of Poland, 284

1984 (Orwell), 272, 457n3

North American Review, 79

Norton, Andrews, 120

"Not in This House" (Wilson), 272

Novak, Barbara, 3

Novalis (Friedrich von Hardenberg), 285;
Die Lehringe zu Sais, 72; MF as admirer
of, 73; mentioned, 66

Oberon (Wieland), 5, 40–41, 52, 271, 310,
334, 335, 361, 362; "Argus eyes" in, 276;
drowning scenes in, 176, 335; erotic
passion in, 41, 42; impact of, on MF,
41–42, 43, 52, 174; plot of, 41–43; power
of dreams in, 41; and prodigal son, 201;

Penniman, Almira Cornelia. *See* Barlow, Almira Cornelia Penniman

People's Journal, 292, 299, 309; MF publishes poem in, 331

Perkins, George, 55

Persephone (Proserpina), 121, 167, 196, 200, 221; bears child Zagreus by father Zeus, 167; and Eleusian mysteries, 191, 221; in "Hymn to Demeter," 214; MF identifies with, 166, 171; Orpheus sees, in Underworld, 191; raped by Hades, 121, 191, 214

Perugia route, 326, 392

Petrarch, 102; and MF's visit to Laura's tomb, 309

"Phaedo" (Plato), 74

Phaedrus (Plato), 119, 140–41, 150–51, 153, 164, 169–70, 181, 182, 185

Phi Beta Kappa, RWE address at, 110, 114

"Philosophy of History, The" (RWE), 102

Phrenological Journal, 292

phrenology, 105, 106, 107; Fowler brothers examine MF's head, 107. *See also* animal magnetism; Fowler, Orson; mesmerism

pilgrimage, life as, 290, 291, 365; MF on, 136, 170, 199–201; MF on aim of, 210, 290; Psyche's life as, 200–201, 243; Thomas Fuller on, 7

Pilgrim's Progress (Bunyan), 102, 136, 192–93

Pius IX (pope; Giovanni Maria Mastai-Ferretti): appearance of, 317; as caring father, 339; disavows war, 352; flees Rome, 370; Giuseppe Mazzini breaks with, 339; grants constitution, 342; issues monitory, 373; life and ideas of, 316; MF defends, 340–41; MF on, 317–18, 340, 341–42; republican early praise of, 318; as temporal ruler of Italy, 325, 373; as traitorous, 368–69

Plater, Emily, 216

Plato: Diotima in, 178, 443n1 (part 5); on erotic desire, 153, 154; on forms, 181, 188; on gender, 150–51; impact of, on MF, 150–51, 169–70; on love's progress, 164; MF finds, inadequate, 234–35; MF's affinity for, 74, 178; mystics defined in, 444–45n3; on "One Man," 219; RWE rereads, 236; on "self-mastery," 174; on

soul as "self-mover," 210; mentioned, 28, 137, 138, 140–41, 198. *See also* daemonical; Socrates

—works of: "Apology," 74, 182; "Crito," 74; "Phaedo," 74; *Phaedrus,* 119, 140–41, 150–51, 153, 164, 169–70, 181, 182, 185; *Republic,* 141, 182; *The Symposium* ("The Banquet"), 119, 140–41, 150–51, 178, 181, 182

Plutarch: *Morals,* 119, 132; mentioned, 137, 138

Poe, Edgar Allan, 27, 229, 240; lampoons MF, 237–38; reviews *Woman in the Nineteenth Century,* 237

Porte, Joel, 89; on exotic/erotic, 438n18; on MF as model for Hester Prynn, 469n29; on RWE's love of MF, 99, 431n18; on RWE's view of MF, 86

Potawatomi tribe, 203

Powers, Hiram, 310; *Calhoun,* 310, 403; *Eve,* 403

Poyen, Charles, 195; and animal magnetism, 210

"Pray without Ceasing" (RWE), 89

precocity, dangers of, 15, 418n19

Prelude, The (Wordsworth), 201, 204, 207, 454n5 (chap. 39)

Prescott, Susan, 52, 157; as mother figure, 53, 54

Price, Michelle, 273

prodigal son, 5, 198, 201, 362, 446n6 (chap. 31); Lloyd Fuller as, 201; Mariana as "prodigal," 207, 277, 472n9; MF on power of story of, 235; paradigm of, and MF, 201, 285, 401; Peter Crane as, 201, 290, 402, 472n9; problems with paradigm of, 201; in *Woman in the Nineteenth Century,* 201

Proserpina. *See* Persephone

Prostitution, in England, 286–87

Proudhon, Pierre, 425–26n2

Providence Daily Journal, 106

Psyche, 243, 293; story of, in Apuleius's *The Golden Ass,* 200

Puritan(s): heritage of, impacts MF, 35, 39, 42, 97, 109, 138–39, 149, 163, 165, 168–69, 212, 213, 306, 324; MF's ancestors as, 7, 12, 68, 74, 138, 147, 199, 213; Mickiewicz

Rossetti, Giovanni, 357, 359–60, 365, 468n13; MF's distrust of, 380; mentioned, 366
Rossi, Count Pellegrino (Pope Pius IX's minister), 1, 368
Rotch, Mary, 354, 375
Rousseau, Jean-Jacques: on education, 16–17; on gender, 58; MF touches manuscripts of, 301; on "true" woman, 16–17; mentioned, 297
—works of: *The Confessions*, 58; *Emile*, 16–17

"Saadi" (RWE), 180
Sacred and Profane Love (Titian), 311, 312, 314, 354, 468n5
Saint-Simon, Count Henri de: on Giuseppe Mazzini, 297; ideas of, 299–300; impact of, on Parisians, 300; influence of, on European Romantics, 285; Sand linked to, 299
Sand, George (Aurore Dupin): Balzac on, 148; and Chopin, 148, 303, 304, 316, 319; collaborates with Sandeau, 148; as Cybele, 316; on erotic love of feminine, 162; life of, 146–48; on marriage via MF, 174; MF compared with, 144, 146–48, 316, 318; MF compares, with Belgioioso, 345; MF critical of, 148, 264; MF defends, 303; MF identifies with, 145, 146, 399; MF meets, 303–4; MF's admiration for, 146, 241, 303; Musset on, 148; as source of "lyrical glances," 222, 434n16; mentioned, 216, 218, 295, 322, 334. *See also* Indiana (character)
—works of: *André*, 145, 148; *Indiana*, 143, 144, 146; *Jacques*, 145, 148; *Lélia*, 144–45, 150, 162; *Leone Leoni*, 145; *Lettres d'un voyageur*, 145; *La Marquise*, 150; *Mauprat*, 145, 146, 193–94; *"La Roche Mauprat*," 193–94; *Rose et Blanche* (with Sandeau), 148; *Les sept cordes de la lyre*, 145; *Spiridion*, 145; *Valentine*, 144
Sandeau, Jules, 148
Santo Spirito cemetery, 334
Sappho: alluded to in *Woman in the Nineteenth Century*, 153, 216, 243; compared with MF, 153, 163–64; "An

Hymn to Venus," 154; influence of, on MF, 153; life and characteristics of, 153; MF critical of, 163; as model for MF's Conversations, 163; RWE calls Cary Sturgis, 152; source of MF's knowledge of, 153–54
Saunders, John, 292, 309
Scarlet Letter, The (N. Hawthorne), 362, 399
Schacter, Daniel, 255
Schapiro, Barbara, 253. *See also* Romantic personality
Schelling, Friedrich, 285
Scheme of 1844 (G. Mazzini), 297
Schiller, Friedrich, 66, 102
Schlegel, Friedrich von, 73, 74, 285; on "Primordial I," 285
Schleiermacher, Friedrich, 73
Schneiderman, Stuart, 98
School for Idiots, 302
Scott, Sir Walter, 119, 120, 294
Scottish Common Sense School, 88–89
Second Residence in Rome (Goethe), 75
Seeress of Prevorst (Frederike/Frederica Hauffe), 197; in "The Great Lawsuit," 194; as hysteric, 448n14; MF's life compared with, 211, 212–13; in *Summer on the Lakes*, 207, 210–12; mentioned, 218
"Self-Reliance" (RWE), 180
"Sensitive Plant, The" (Shelley), 248, 252
sept cordes de la lyre, Les (Sand), 145
Shakespeare, William: Hamlet (character), 40, 109; Jones Very's essay on *Hamlet*, 117, 119; *Romeo and Juliet*, 39, 64, 158; RWE's allusion to *Macbeth* in *Nature*, 94, 430n28; mentioned, 198
Shaw, Sarah, 214–15
Shelley, Percy Bysshe, 69, 73, 248–49; death of, 174; MF admires poetry of, 251–52, 254, 258; on soul out of soul, 162, 252–53; mentioned, 142, 230, 297
—works of: *Alastor*, 29, 252–53, 256, 280, 336; "The Sensitive Plant," 248, 252
Shengold, Leonard, 272, 275; on "soul murder," 273; on victim's need for annihilation, 280
Shepard, Thomas, 7
ships: MF on wrecks of, 403. See also *Elizabeth*

221–22; women and "electricity" in, 217; mentioned, 1, 3, 228–29, 238, 338, 405

Words of a Believer (Lamennais), 285

Wordsworth, William, 100, 142; in conversation with Coleridge, 125; on eternal in man, 95; failure of MF to relive past like, 205; faith of, in nature, 143; on memory, power of, 251, 454n5 (chap. 39); MF meets and comments on, 292; MF misquotes, in letter to Nathan, 255, 454n5 (chap. 40); MF reads, 142; and prodigal son paradigm, 201; sustained by Coleridge, 142; mentioned, 62, 63, 65, 297

—works of: "Lines Composed a Few Miles above Tintern Abbey," 454n5 (chap. 40); *The Prelude*, 201, 204, 207, 454n5 (chap. 39)

Xenophon: on Socrates, 142, 181; and story of Panthea, 216, 245, 362

yearning: beyond adolescent, 327, 341; erotic, 116, 169, 170, 174; for freedom, 205; millennial, 339; for mother love, 29, 31, 53, 97, 261; mystical, 73, 364; to pour out soul, 82; Romantic, 157, 175, 207, 365; sensual, 176; sexual, 240; spiritual, 68, 195, 224; unsatisfied and unspecific, 109, 122, 133; for world purged of sin, 351, 370

Young Italy, 297

Young Lady's Friend, The (Farrar), 61

Young Man Luther (Erikson), 425n7

Zaluska, Countess, 309

Zeus, 167. *See also* Persephone

Zwarg, Christina, 2, 85, 90, 134; on "cant," 190; on Fourier and "transition state," 456n12; on MF's "Items of Foreign Gossip," 230, 451n4; on Vanderlyn's *The Death of Jane McCrea,* 447n2 (chap. 32)